Teaching Elementary Science

THROUGH INVESTIGATION AND COLLOQUIUM

BRENDA LANSDOWN   Harvard University

PAUL E. BLACKWOOD   United States Office of Education

PAUL F. BRANDWEIN   President, Center for the Study of Instruction
Adjunct Professor, University of Pittsburgh

HARCOURT BRACE JOVANOVICH, INC.   New York   Chicago   San Francisco   Atlanta

We are indebted to the following teachers for supplying records of science colloquia conducted in their classrooms:

Rochelle Botwin	Patricia Frechtel	Maxine Hymowech Schackman
Florence Briggs	Betsy Welch Hostynek	Myrna Schensul
Bernice Cohen	Charlotte Lazarus	George Tokieda
Leah Coultoff	Bonnie Pomerantz	Arthur Wiener

Page 85: Reproduced by permission of the Elementary Science Study of Education Development Center, Inc.

Page 103: Adapted from "Rats," S.A. Barnett. Copyright © January, 1967 by Scientific American, Inc. All rights reserved.

Page 185: From *Madeline's Rescue*, by Ludwig Bemelmans. Copyright 1951, 1953 by Ludwig Bemelmans. Reprinted by permission of The Viking Press, Inc.

Page 275: Adapted from Bonner-Phillips, *Principles of Physical Science*, 1957, Addison-Wesley, Reading, Massachusetts.

Page 290: Adapted from *Organisms*, Science Curriculum Improvement Study, Berkeley, California.

Page 317: Adapted from *Matter: Its Forms and Changes*, by Paul F. Brandwein *et. al.* Copyright © 1968 by Harcourt Brace Jovanovich, Inc.

Page 334: Adapted from *Nature and Science* (October 28, 1968), 12, 13, 14, Doubleday & Company, Inc. Copyright © 1968 by The American Museum of Natural History.

Drawings by John Johnston

ISBN: 0-15-588013-6

Library of Congress Catalog Card Number: 74-157878

Printed in the United States of America

Henry Schneer

whose life lit fires in hearths and hearts

All children are born alien. Could anyone know less about the family, the society, the nation, or the world than a newborn child?

For as long as can be remembered, teachers have brought children face to face with each other and with their environment; they have literally given children both membership and citizenship in an increasingly complex society. Having done this, and done it reasonably well within the limitations imposed upon them, teachers are now called upon—as they always will be—to take up additional tasks including the particularly important task, teaching modern science.

Einstein once defined science as an "experience in search of meaning." Today's children need to experience the natural phenomena of the world in a manner that will enable them to search for understanding, for meaning. Teachers are therefore the architects who make the school a home of experience, a rich environment where the citizens and scientists of tomorrow may find relationships, construct mental models, develop an understanding of phenomena.

The facts of science are accumulating incredibly rapidly. In addition, new methods of teaching science, new emphases on what to teach, new curricular organizations, and new materials all compete for a teacher's attention, threatening to absorb his spare time and energy even as he is forced to choose his program and then prepare himself to transmit it.

We hope this book has simplified the process by presenting a method found viable over a wide range of programs for many different teaching styles and types of children—the method of investigation plus colloquium—and by relating it to the new curricula, the currently available concrete and audio-visual materials, and the new editions of textbooks. However, the book is not eclectic. There is a philosophy underlying both the science and the pedagogy presented. The philosophy is made explicit and supported by research from many allied disciplines. The practice which carries out the philosophy is illustrated from records kept by student teachers and graduates-in-service who have taken courses with the authors at Brooklyn College (The City University of New York) or at the Harvard Graduate School of Education over the past two decades or who have participated in seminars given at various universities over the country. These records bring life to the theory and will provide, we hope, realistic guidelines for our readers.

The preparation of the book has spanned many years. During the actual writing, the authors received invaluable assistance from librarians, students, teachers, men and women who have been developing materials for commercial firms, and editors. We wish to thank Ellinor Pedersen, who read and commented upon most of the books in the children's bibliography; Jennifer Pirie, who viewed and evaluated most of the films, filmloops, and filmstrips and helped with the proofreading; Jim Reed, for his advice and comments; and Elisabeth H. Belfer, who offered organizational suggestions from which a logical sequence of chapters and sections evolved. If errors remain, they are the responsibility of the authors.

We hope that the teachers who use this book will add to the wisdom which is already theirs as they try the variety of experiences, investigations, and discussions and incorporate them into their teaching styles.

Finally, we hope that the children in today's classrooms will learn ways to explain relationships so that they may live in tomorrow's world with competence and compassion.

BRENDA LANSDOWN
PAUL E. BLACKWOOD
PAUL F. BRANDWEIN

Contents

1
Starting Tomorrow

2

The Architectonics of Meaning

3

The Architectonics of the Curriculum

4

Evaluation

1

Starting Tomorrow!

1

Meaning through use of materials

Which of the subject areas do we, as elementary school teachers, enjoy teaching most? Is it the one we, as school children, enjoyed learning most? For many teachers this is the pattern—and why not? It seems only natural. A little girl who covered her early composition books with sketches and spent much of her free time in high school creating objects from paper and paste, basket canes, mosaic pieces, or wool, as a grade school teacher is likely to relish those moments when her children make mobiles, paint pictures, or construct dioramas. The adolescent bookworm, if she becomes an elementary school teacher, will surely offer rich experiences in children's literature and may easily branch out into creative language

arts: choral speaking, dramatics, poetry. And the young man who read biographies of national heroes as a child, pored over political maps in school, and engaged in social movements during his high school days may well become a social studies specialist if he decides to teach at the elementary level.

What becomes of those young people who enjoyed science classes, who tinkered at home with chemistry sets, who were the first to offer to do a science project, who bred hamsters in the bathtub after taking the classroom pets home for vacation? We as adults find them most often in science-related careers and very, very seldom in the elementary schools.

The corollary of these observations is that because most elementary school teachers have not enjoyed learning science, they do not enjoy teaching it. In fact, many express a dread of the science portion of the year's curriculum.

If we compare the way science is taught when it is not enjoyed with the way language arts, for example, is taught when it is enjoyed, we find significant differences in methodology. In an unsuccessful science lesson, the teacher talks, explains, asks questions, and even performs the "experiment" while the children watch, search for right answers, and occasionally take turns putting an object in water or reading the level of a thermometer. In a successful language arts lesson, the children share reports on books, choose the voice qualities and emphasis for choral speaking, and become emotionally and intellectually involved in the stories they are reading. Although these examples may seem somewhat stereotyped, each can be observed with little variation in many classrooms. They may help to pinpoint for you—a teacher who wants very much to create exciting and successful science experiences for children—some of the major ingredients of joyful as opposed to boring learning.

To make this presentation applicable to you individually, we suggest that you now think back to two types of lessons you experienced as a child—one during which you felt the full flush of the joy of learning and another where you lost interest and were bored. To make your memories concrete and pertinent to these introductory thoughts, you may want to list the elements of both types of lessons in comparative columns. Try this before you go any further!

Fortunately, science may be taught in ways that joyfully tap the sources of learning, and such methods are not too far removed from those employed in any successful learning experience. Although learning takes place throughout our lives, whether we are inside an educational institution or not, it abounds during childhood. Teaching may be viewed as the provision of an atmosphere to foster learning in certain specific situations. Learning takes place inside the learner, and the more deeply he is personally involved—the more motivated he is—the more actively he will cooperate with the process.

Caroline Pratt made this the basis for the founding and development of the City and Country School in New York City half a century ago. Miss Pratt observed that children playing in the streets used whatever materials were available to dramatize their perceptions of the world around them—to experience in play adult roles, the working of machines, the phenomena of nature. She integrated the child's environment and the school by extending the experiences in which a child expresses interest; enriching these with materials, trips, and books; encouraging the child to relive his concrete experiences through serious dramatic play, as well as discussion.

In adults as well as in children, playfulness can be the basis for creative learning. It produces an atmosphere which can motivate pursuit of the less attractive aspects of learning—the hard work, the nitty-gritty chores. Playfulness can involve things, concrete objects (usually so with children) or ideas (usually true in thinkers). But children also think and thinkers also use things; the distinction is only one of degree. Once can play idly, doodling with paper and pencil, for example; one can play more purposefully with carefully chosen materials which can introduce a child to science learning. It is the discovery of what materials do to each other that engenders thought—thought that can then be clarified and enriched when it is shared during the discussion or colloquim.

We will examine the nature of the materials to which children are introduced, watch the discoveries which can be made through both playful and purposeful manipulation of these materials, and listen to the thoughts these children express about their findings. Both the children's learning acts and the theory underlying the role the teacher assumes will be examined. We will find ourselves somewhat in the role of playing midwife to the birth of science learning in children.

The first two chapters of this book present in detail materials which have been found both stimulating to children of widely diverse backgrounds and helpful to teachers with varied personalities and teaching styles. This extended introduction to the discovery-colloquium method of science learning has been chosen because, by presenting these materials to children, teachers can immediately begin to teach science—they can start "tomorrow" once they understand the nature of these materials and the principles of their use.

Of course, there is more to science teaching than just starting with a set of materials; the necessary follow-up occupies the remaining chapters of the book. We hope you will try out our suggestions slowly and growingly, and then evolve your own interpretations. We hope, too, that the principles will be clear to you as you go along so that you may be playful with our suggestions, creative with adaptations. In any case, we feel sure that you, as have hundreds of teachers, will be encouraged by some of our suggestions in these chapters to try an exciting approach to science teaching—*starting tomorrow*!

Experience as central to meaning

"What an experience!"—a colloquialism implying emotional and intellectual involvement in some happening. A person must be part of an event (it must have some residual meaning) for it to be an experience.

Experiences can be chiefly physical, in the sense of zooming up and down on a roller coaster; experiences may be mostly emotional, in the sense of losing a loved one; experiences can be largely intellectual, in the sense of having solved a difficult problem. Experiences can have other dimensions, too, but none of them is distinct; the roller coaster rider lets out emotional screams; a personal loss does something somatically to one's glands; and an intellectual experience can be physically exhausting as well as emotionally satisfying. A useful, although not too rigorous, generalization might be to say that the duration of the happening—the actual living of the experience—provides the physical and emotional concomitants and that the aftermath—the telling about it, the analysis—provides the intellectual concomitant or the portion where the experience attains meaning.

We hold that meaning is an outcome of experience, involvement, participation, and that no meaning can evolve without these prerequisites. However, learning can take place without meaning if there has been no experience, no involvement. (We use the word *learning* here in the very broad sense of evoking

a change in behavior.) Two illustrations of learning (observable change in behavior) may make these points clear.

Standing straight and secure in the serried ranks of his kindergarten class, Geordie faced the Stars and Stripes and sang:

> My Country tizzerly
> Sweelandov liver-tea
> Ovthee I sing![1]

It is clear that Geordie has learned to make verbal sounds in a certain order and to accompany them with a melody; but has he *experienced* anything—is he involved? Although the teacher discussed the importance of our country and the benefits of freedom—or liberty—Geordie did not attach the meaning to the song. He had no doubt listened, but listening did not evoke any meaning.

Perhaps Geordie, with the eager drive of most young children, will try to attach some meaning to the sounds he made to render a conditioned response meaningful. Perhaps he wonders how one makes tea out of liver, that rather difficult stuff Mom occasionally insists he eat. Maybe it tastes better as tea; he must ask her. Or he might wonder if *"tizzerly"* is a form of dizzily. He could be considering whether the liver teakettle sings because it is like the breakfast teakettle. Although Geordie is probably not trying to attach any meaning at all to the strange words, he may be using this automatic song time to dream of where he will ride his tricycle after lunch—school at his age being only an antemeridian obligation.

Geordie has learned a song, but he has not experienced it. He learned it by rote, without meaning. Because he can now participate in morning exercises, his behavior has changed, but in our sense of the term he has not had an *experience*.

A good deal of learning, both in and out of school, is acquired by rote. Some of it is useful. We repeat the order of the alphabet when looking up a word in the dictionary. We respond on many occasions with such social graces as "please," "thank you," or "pardon me" without experiencing any involvement. Language structure and word forms are acquired by rote; they are first learned from repeating

[1] I am indebted to Rose Mukerji for this anecdote.

a model, without meaning for the learner. All this is learning which has its value, but none of it is experiencing. "Rote learning" has become a pejorative term; as a classroom activity it is looked upon with some disfavor by modern educators.

However, a slightly disguised form of rote learning in considerable favor is found in quizzes or questions by the teacher requiring quick responses and one right answer. The learner is expected to give an automatic response, just as he would if he were asked, What letter comes after D in the alphabet? or What word comes after "Sweelandov?" A teacher may require an answer to: "The elements in a molecule of water are_____." "Lions belong to the family of _____." These questions require quick recall of memorized sentences, a sequence of sounds little different from the order of the alphabet. Again, this is a form of learning which indicates no involvement, no emotion, no thinking—in short, no experience. It does, however, tend to produce the correct answer—the one right word, if that is the aim of learning. Contrast this with our next example.

Beryl is interested in things that grow and crawl and fly. One day, as she intently watched the movements of her goldfish in the aquarium, she asked how the goldfish breathed. Her sitter answered glibly that fish breathe by fitting their fin spines to bubbles of air in the water. Beryl was involved in the problem and the explanation had meaning for her; she could picture it happening. Was this an experience?

Let us follow Beryl's learning. On a much later day during summer vacation, Beryl's father took her trolling on a lake. When a pickerel was lifted into the boat, Beryl observed the panting motion of the operculum and glimpsed the blood-red gills.

"It's trying to get air?" she asked her father.

"Yes," he replied, "these are the gills."

"Gills are like lungs?"

When Beryl next leaned over a pond full of carp, she noticed that the fish used their fins like arms and legs for balancing, and she saw that they swallowed water all the time. "Where does all that water go?" she wondered.

Maybe you would like to discuss with a friend the differences between Geordie's and Beryl's methods of learning. Do they in any way parallel the elements of enjoyable and boring lessons you listed from page 4?

Materials evoke experience

How often does an infant hear his mother say, "Don't touch!"—evidence of the child's desire to explore his concrete environment tactilely. Have you ever placed a puzzle or another attractive set of materials before an adult? Doesn't he, too, begin to manipulate the objects? While an infant's manipulation may be entirely random, early school children begin to manifest some plan in their approach to materials. They develop hunches to test: "It's shiny—bet it feels smooth and hard."; "Banging these together may make a noise."; "It will change shape if I press it." These thoughts exist on a preverbal level; they are not verbalized. Soon come questions which may also be unexpressed, but are suggested by the child's actions: "How far can I make it jump?" or "This acts like magnetism. I wonder where the magnets are hidden?"—questions put to nature, the beginning of scientific investigation.

Almost any material whose nature is not entirely familiar to an observer arouses a desire to touch, to explore, to see what it will do. Materials easily evoke expectancy. When expectancies are not fulfilled (and surprise is a cogent stimulus to accelerated investigation), the unexpected phenomena foster questioning, deeper involvement, emotion. The excitement of discovering what happens produces a desire to communicate to one's neighbors (especially if they are similarly engaged), a desire to share discoveries with one's peers. Materials trigger experience.

Materials can be selected to reveal natural phenomena which, in turn, produce knowledge about our universe. Exploration with materials involves scientific procedures which can be refined during a series of learning experiences.

The teacher selects the materials that each child will use. He listens to children tell about their discoveries and help them achieve consensus (*their own consensus*) on a few of the events.

You may feel that such free exploration—putting materials into the children's hands directly—will evoke intolerable disorder. The following lesson begins in the more conventional way—with the teacher in front of the class directing the session (which almost imperceptibly leads into the free discovery approach).

WHAT'S INSIDE?

Marie Stevens closed the fifth brown paper bag with a tightly twisted rubber band. There the five sat, fat and intriguing, bunched on her table. "One more and I'm through," she thought. Something for each row to handle. She tore off a new plastic bag from the roll, eased it open, inserted a roundish potato and a small apple. She let the bag gape, then trapped a bulge of air around the objects and deftly knotted the plastic after gathering the opening together and screwing it into a short ropey twist. Smiling, she rubbed the cut onion on the last brown paper bag and dropped the sliver inside. She sniffed to make sure the odor was detectable. With the plastic bag and its contents inside, she sealed the sixth brown paper bag. The preparations for tomorrow's science lesson were complete.

—Well, nearly. Miss Stevens peeped into a shopping bag and counted out 35 party favors: little whistles, paper trumpets, and those nose ticklers which unroll like a butterfly's tongue when you blow into them. Thirty-five for 30 third graders, in case some break or don't work. Her eight year olds didn't stand frustration very well. Perhaps most children cannot. Then she added two new rolls of plastic bags, two packages of rubber bands, fifteen cardboard tubes saved from rolls of paper towels by her friends, and she was ready. That is, the materials were ready—*but was she?*

Two years from graduation, with an M.A. in sight after a steady sequence of evening and summer courses, Marie Stevens now faced her most challenging hurdle. It seemed innocent enough—a Workshop; most people considered it a breeze. However, because Marie had chosen to take her required Workshop in science, she had had to achieve some proficiency in a new way of teaching science—at least quite a new one to her. In her most honest moments, she admitted to herself that she felt threatened by it. She had done well in her first two years of teaching; at least she had never lost control of the class; she seldom had to shout to gain the children's attention, and the children liked her. That was important to her. She had been a little shocked when a psychology professor explained that children can sometimes work off their hate for a parent by acting as though they hate the teacher. It seemed unreal to her—at least unnecessary, and thank goodness it hadn't happened to her. Maybe that was because she did have good control; she supplied a lot of work for the children and maintained high standards.

Marie prided herself that she was always clear and precise in her directives, but now she was not to give any at all. She felt sure that many, if not most, of the children would act as her co-students had done when this lesson was presented to her Workshop class; the children in the film[2] which had been shown had acted similarly, with a few exceptions. The film showed how to handle those exceptions. But her children? So wide a range of abilities and, therefore, of interests. She had done her student teaching in so-called homogeneous classes (they weren't actually homogeneous, she had realized). But her school, with its conviction of heterogeneous grouping, was so very

[2] *The Matter of Air,* Starting Tomorrow Programs, 720 Fifth Avenue, New York, N.Y. 10019.

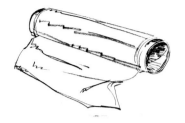

heterogeneous! Why, the first and second graders were grouped together! Obviously, the Principal was trying to wean teachers away from requiring every child to read the same pages in a book. Marie had found that his method hadn't worked well even in science. How could it really? Her children were as mixed in ability, ethnic background, and socioeconomic class as they could be. Well, with materials each child could do his own thing! However, the "thing" for a few might be disastrous. Serina is always different, Leslie never quite catches on, and Ruthanne seems to rub some of the children the wrong way—what would they do? Anyway the Principal, Mr. Pettigrew, was sympathetic when teachers were innovative, and the "Teacher Trainer" had always been helpful and never judgmental with new ideas. What had she to lose? There might even be much to gain. The Workshop professor wouldn't be pushing this new idea so much if it hadn't worked well before; in fact it wasn't so new after all!

Marie fell asleep to some troubled dreams, but in the morning her carefully prepared materials greeted her as though anyone would be happy delving into them.

"What do you think's inside the bag?"
Every eye was focused on the bulging paper bag which Miss Stevens hugged in full view of her expectant eight year olds.
"Candy!"
"Toys!"
"Cookies!"
This wasn't what she had anticipated, but she quickly supplied the hypothesis that it must be wishful thinking!
"How do you know there's anything at all inside?"
"It's fat." Then silence.
"Can you think of some words to describe why you know there must be something inside the bag?" She twirled it at arm's length.
"Bulgy."
"That's an excellent word."
"Thick."
"Big."
"Round."
Miss Stevens made a mental note of these suggestions for " Vocabulary. "
"Well, there's certainly *something* inside. How do you think we could find out what it is?"
"Open it?"
"Oh, but that's too easy. You see, scientists can't open an atom and look inside, but they have some very good ideas about what is inside an atom."
"Feel it!"
"You *could* do that. But scientists cannot reach a star to feel it and yet they have a very good idea about what a star is like inside. Scientists use instruments to help them find out about stars and atoms. Could I be your instrument? Let's pretend I am, and you are using me to do something you

can't do. Could you tell me to do something that could help you decide what might be inside? Carlton, you seem to have an idea."

"Drop it!"

Stretching on her toes and holding the bag high above her desk, Miss Stevens paused. The class held its collective breath. Boom! Hands shot up. As each child responded eagerly when his name was called, the teacher wrote the suggestions on the chalkboard: ball, rock, fruit, brick, paint jar, ...

Which scientific procedures are being encouraged?

"It couldn't be no paint jar."

"Why do you think it couldn't be, Alan?"

" 'Cause the paint jar'd break. I didn't hear no break."

"What do you think of Alan's idea, Violet? The jar was your suggestion."

"I think Alan's right. Maybe it's a rock."

How would you characterize the teacher's role here?

"Shall I cross off paint jar? Would there be anything else you could ask me to do that might help you decide?"

"Shake the bag."

The rattling of the bag and the heavy-sounding objects bumping against the paper brought new hands waving.

"I'm sure it's some kinda fruit, like a napple." Miss Stevens wrote "apple" on the board.

ball
rock
fruit
brick
~~paint jar~~
apple
orange

"Orange."

"I still think it's a ball, maybe two of 'em."

"How many things do you think are in the bag?"

"Four or five."

"No, not that many. Two."

"Or three."

"Children, what senses have you used so far to guess what's in the bag?"

"We've used our eyes."

"And ears."

"And our brains."

"That's not a sense, stoopid!"

"But you did seem to be using your brains. Maybe Ruthanne meant you were using good sense! Well, we've done rather well so far. Now I have a bag for each row." There was excited wriggling in the seats. "And as the bag passes down the row, each of you may feel it and think of what might be inside. Maybe you'll have some new ideas and maybe you'll be more sure of those things we wrote on the board. Monitors, you may start the bags off."

When, if at all, should answers be considered wrong?

The children's desks are in double rows with an aisle between the pairs of desks.

"So far, so good," thought Marie Stevens. "There really is great interest; even those waiting turns seem intrigued and absorbed." Occasionally she urged a child to pass on the bag—to form his idea quickly. Shortly the bags were retrieved by the monitors and returned to the front of the room. Every hand was raised! Miss Stevens called on those who had not yet spoken. "Dean?"

What is the importance of routines? Are there dangers in routines?

What generates this 100% participation?

"I'm sure it's a napple."

"What makes you so sure?"

"There's a little dent on one end where the stalk is."

"Anyone have the same idea as Dean?" Half the class did.

"Serina?"

Any new scientific procedures being used here?

ball
rock
~~fruit~~
~~brick~~
paint jar
apple
orange
animal
onion

A pleasantly dramatic moment for any teacher!

A child can change his assertion in an atmosphere of psychological safety. What were the ingredients of psychological safety for Leslie?

"I'm sure there's a ball inside. When I push it, it comes out again."

"And I think there's a rock, a round one."

"Leslie, you want to tell us something badly."

"There's an animal!"

"Animal?" several children called out in disbelief.

"What makes you think so, Leslie?"

"It feels soft . . . an' warm."

"I felt something soft, too; it was sorta puffy."

"Miss Stevens, Miss Stevens, ..."

"Warren, you are dying to tell us something."

"It's a' onion. I smelled it. And it's hard and round like a' onion."

"That's a new one, along with the animal. Now let's look at our whole list and see if any one of our scientific guesses can be crossed off." Miss Stevens read off each item and the children responded.

"Ball?"

"Yes."

"Rock?"

"No." Violet and Butch thought there was.

"OK, leave it. Fruit?"

"That's apple and orange."

"Brick?"

"No, wrong shape."

"Animal, onion. How many things do you think there are in the bag? We've six ideas here."

"I felt two things."

"There's something else, soft like an animal. I think there are three."

"So now what do we do about the six? Can we decide among them?"

Miss Stevens wondered why Leslie kept insisting on the "animal" inside the bag. Should she tell him it couldn't possibly be, or let the children convince him? "Leslie's always in some other world," she reflected. "I don't really know what goes on with him." She turned to the class cheerfully. "Let's open it now, shall we?"

Very slowly Marie Stevens opened one of the brown paper bags by taking off the rubber band. Then even more slowly she began drawing out the plastic bag. As soon as the knot appeared, a murmur ran through the class. Then as the main part was inching its way into view, little necks began to strain. Silence was complete, almost gasping. The potato showed first.

"Oh, we never thought of that!"

Then, as the apple appeared, cries of, "I was right! I knew it!"

"So how many things were there?"

"Two."

"No, three, with the plastic bag."

"That's what the soft thing was. It made me think of an animal. But it really felt warm."

"What is it, Warren?"

"I know I smelled a' onion."

Miss Stevens handed the brown bag to Warren. "Look inside," she urged.

Warren drew out the onion sliver and held it high. "You fooled us," he said, laughing.

"To think clearly we have to be careful and thorough, don't we? And we have to test our ideas. Scientists test their ideas, too. Warren used another of his senses to find out . . . ."

"His nose," said several.

Tiny Serina was holding a tired right arm stiffly aloft with her left hand. When she caught the teacher's eye, she said firmly, "There's something else inside the bag. There's air!"

"My! How do you know that?"

"There's air inside the bag; it's trapped by the knot."

"Serina thinks she can see air inside the bag, the rest of you think you can see an apple and a potato. How *sure* are you that this is a real apple and a real potato? Are you absolutely certain?"

"They could be fake."

"What other sense would you have to use to make quite sure?"

"We'd have to eat them!" And there was general laughter.

"We may do that yet." Miss Stevens smiled, suddenly thinking that a lesson in fractions would pair very neatly with sharing the apples before recess. She changed her tone sharply.

"Who can answer this one?" She tore off a new plastic bag from the roll and held it so that the thin edge faced the class. "Is there anything inside this bag?"

"No."

"Can you find words to describe how you know that there's nothing inside?"

"Thin."

"Flat."

"Skinny."

"More for 'Vocabulary,' " thought Marie Stevens. Then she put her hand in the opening of the plastic bag, held one edge and swept the bag through the air, closing the mouth quickly. She held the rounded bag before the class. "Now, is there anything in it?"

"Air!" said several.

"I can't see any air! How do you know there's something inside?"

"The shape!"

"Now, each of you is going to have one of these bags." Little jumps of excitement from each seat! "And I want you to see what you can find out about air. But there's one thing you may not do with the bags. What is it?"

"We can't put them on our heads."

"Did everyone hear Simon's remark?" Nods. "These are not space helmets. Why can't they be used as space helmets?"

"You can't breathe in them."

"All right. I'll tear off the bags and the monitors may hand out one apiece."

Some child, even in a first grade, is almost sure to think of air, but the continuation of the lesson when the children investigate air does not depend on this.

Teaching can be a kind of ongoing research.

Arrangement of desks in Miss Stevens' room.

A nondirective way of offering materials. What is the effect on the children?

It took rather a long time to distribute all the bags and some children became restless until they had their own. Miss Stevens made a mental note: next time tie these in bundles of five for each row.

Marie Stevens found it fascinating to watch the individual reactions of the children. Some, slow to start, eyed their neighbors cautiously. Some filled their bags with vigorous sweeps and trapped the air quickly as though it might race away. Leslie was letting the soft bulging surface caress his cheek, and Violet was bumping the hard bag on the desk. Ruthanne evidently had a hole in her bag; she was pushing a stream of air under her chin with a satisfied smile on her face, her eyes shut. Looking at gay, mischievous little Serina she thought, "I bet she's going to burst that bag! Shall I catch her eye and frown her out of it? Stop her?" Bang! All the children laughed. A prickly sense of danger flushed over Miss Stevens.

"Children," she said, in her firmest voice, producing a hush, "Serina's made a wonderful discovery about air, and she'll tell us about it later. The rest of you do not have to experiment with bursting the bags because, although I have a few extras to replace *accidents*, I don't have a second one for everybody."

The class relaxed into various projects. Marie Stevens quickly gave a new bag to Serina, who laughed up at her, and a new one to Ruthanne, saying, "You may need one without a hole."

In this classroom with movable desks arranged in double rows, it was easy to distribute rubber bands and a cardboard tube to each pair of children. As she dropped the new materials lightly before each pair of children, she said quietly, "Maybe you can use these." Some of the children looked at the new pieces and ignored them; some inserted the tubes into the bags and blew through them to inflate the plastic. Warren and Alan joined their bags with one tube held in place with rubber bands and then pushed the air back and forth from one bag to another. They were concentrating and busy.

A few of the children seemed to have run out of ideas and were rather listlessly repeating their previous actions. It seemed the right moment for the final surprise. Beginning with the children whose interest had begun to lag, Miss Stevens gave each child one of the favors, saying quite clearly and slowly to each one, "Try to make this work *without putting it into your mouth*."

There was an immediate lull in the sound. As the gradually increasing buzz suddenly ceased, Marie Stevens realized she had been unaware of the loud chatter with its rising decibels. It wasn't long, however, before there was a short toot. Then another child made his favor squeak, and finally Serina blew out the nose tickler.

"Look, look!" she cried, doing it over and over in rhythmical motion.

The noise level rose again as each child returned more eagerly to his own favor; the room echoed with toots, squeaks, rattling paper, and loud delight. Warren was happily trying to change the tone of his whistle by varying the energy with which he pushed air from his bag. Only Carlton struggled. He couldn't make his trumpet work, and he looked near tears. "I can't make it work," he mumbled.

Miss Stevens went over to him. "Maybe the favor's no good. Here, try this one." She gave him one of the nose ticklers. His expression when the tube first shot out was worth all her fears about the lesson, all the preparations it had entailed—even worth all the noise. She went to the board and wrote the word *Colloquium*[3] on it. One by one the children stopped their investigations and looked at the board, sounding out the strange array of letters. It was easy to gain the class's attention at this point, to have the monitors collect the materials, and to move to the next phase of her first experience-centered science lesson.

With clear directives, she had the children push the desks against the walls and arrange their chairs in a large circle in the middle of the room. Miss Stevens placed her chair on the circumference.

In what circumstances are directives valuable? At what point in this lesson were they avoided?

"When scientists have made discoveries," she began, "they often hold a colloquium." She pronounced it slowly: "kuh · LO · kwee · um." The children glanced at the board. "What do you think it might mean?"

"Another experiment?"

"A kind of discussion?"

"We'll hold one now, and then you'll see what it is. Let's begin at my left. Leslie, what did you discover?"

"When I pushed the bag in, the air pushed back at me. It was soft."

"Violet?"

"I blew up my bag hard. I couldn't bash it in even when I hit it on the desk."

"Leslie found the air was soft; Violet found the air was hard. How can you explain the difference?"

Can you find a principle underlying the teacher's choice of remarks?

"Leslie didn't have as much air in his bag. I blew into my bag and screwed it tight."

"Ruthanne?"

"There was a little hole in my bag. When I squeezed it against my face, I could feel it."

"Carlton?"

"I couldn't make my trumpet work. Something was wrong with it. When Miss Stevens gave me a new favor, I fixed the bag around the mouth end with a rubber band and pushed the bag. Then the nose tickler"—he waved in illustration with his hand—"Zoom!"

"That was fun, wasn't it? Serina, what did you discover about the air in your bag?"

"When I hit my bag of air, it burst with a loud bang and the air came out!"

"Ruthanne and Serina have both told us about the air coming out of their bags. Serina heard her air and Ruthanne felt it. Ruthanne, did you perhaps hear your air, too?"

"There was a little bitty noise, like a whisper."

[3]*Colloquium* has a special meaning in this work. It is a form of discussion, but very different from discussions usually found in the classroom. It will be discussed fully in Chapter 2.

The teacher juxtaposes discrepant events.

The teacher encourages children to describe discoveries she had noticed them make.

"Can anyone explain why Ruthanne heard a whisper and Serina heard a bang?"

"There was more power to Serina's bag. The air came out fast."

"Warren, you and Alan were doing something interesting with your bags before I gave out the favors. Will you tell us about it?"

"Me and Alan joined our bags with the tube. We held them on with rubber bands. Then Alan, he pushed his bag and the air went into mine. Then I pushed it back again."

"Butch?"

"I blew in my bag and it got all cloudy."

"What do you think made it cloudy?"

"I dunno."

"Anyone else have an idea? Violet?"

"Mind was cloudy, too, when I blew into it. Little drops of water. It was wet from my mouth."

After each child had contributed at least one remark and Miss Stevens had juxtaposed contradictory observations to be resolved by the class, she ended the lesson with a final activity.

"That was a fine collection of discoveries about air. After scientists have held a colloquium, they write out their discoveries for other scientists to read. Now, I will be your secretary, and you tell me what to write. Then I will make copies of your Investigators' Log so that each one of you can build a book about our findings in science. What do you think one sentence might be on what we've discovered about air?"

We feel that children *investigate* the materials we give them; they find out what the materials do as they interact. Children do not usually perform real experiments.

The children made their suggestions. For each remark Miss Stevens posed these two questions:

Do you agree with _____ 's statement?
Do you agree with the way he said it?

Children often illustrate their copies of the Log.

The final Log was duplicated for each eight year old. It read this way:

INVESTIGATORS' LOG
When you push air into the trumpet, it gives a toot.
If you push the air harder, it gives a louder toot.
You can feel the air on your face.
Air is hard inside the bag, sometimes soft.
Air can push out a nose tickler.
There must be air inside you. You blow wet air into the bag.

Materials in search of meaning

Let us analyze the lesson.

What meaning do you think the bag, brushed against his cheek, had for Leslie? What evidence indicated that this meaning had changed for him between the time he *felt the brown paper bag* and the time he *talked about* his more extended experience with the *plastic bag*?

What meaning did the burst bag have for Serina? What additional meaning do you think was introduced by the actions, questions, and reactions of Miss

Stevens immediately following the bang and later during the colloquium?

Perhaps one evidence that meaning grows through a child's actions is that he tries new ways to use materials, new ways to see what they will do. The child is, in fact, in a confrontation with a small segment of his environment. In "controlling" this environmental segment he achieves a beginning sense of competence. One might think of the bag, the air, and the child as a *system* of interacting parts.

We can consider the materials, the child, and the teacher as another interacting system—a teaching–learning system. Thus, the word *inter*acting implies that what the child does affects the teacher as much as what the teacher does affects the child.

We can sharpen our vision of what the children in Marie Stevens' third grade were learning by contrasting that lesson with a different presentation of the same topic, a lesson where the teacher demonstrates the use of the materials and then asks the children what they see happening. Since few of the children actually take an active part in such a lesson, it is impossible for an observer to make an even tentative assertion of how much a particular child may have "learned," let alone the meaning this learning had for him. Suppose the experience chart at the end of this type of lesson reads as follows:

We learned that air takes up space.

We learned that air has force.

We learned that air can make sounds.

Wind is moving air.

This is quite a neat summary, probably just what the textbook said should evolve from the lesson. But what does it reveal about the meaning of air for any individual learner? What would a test in which the children recalled these sentences indicate?

If we analyze the activities in Miss Stevens' class, it becomes clear that learning there is taking place on two levels: factual and conceptual or, as we might designate them, data and meaning. Overall, however, there appears to be an emotional concomitant related to each child's personality.[4] Is there any kind of

[4] In this lesson we recorded the actions and words of only a few children; what we learned about them is symptomatic of what would be learned if equal attention were given to the others.

learning which has meaning to the learner if it is devoid of the emotional dimension? Can there be feeling without meaning? Can one derive meaning from an experience without feeling?

Perhaps models[5] might help to establish prototypes of these two particular lessons and provide frames of reference. Of course, they are not the only possible lesson types, but this introductory section will be limited to the contrast of these two.

The yeast model You will recall that yeast is a one-celled plant used to make bread rise and beer foam. A yeast plant absorbs sugar from its warm, wet environment, converts the nutrient into alcohol and carbon dioxide, and uses the energy thus released for growth. Growing occurs by budding or producing daughter cells exactly like the parent except, initially, in size. The froth and foam yeast creates result from bubbles of carbon dioxide which are released as the plant grows and divides. These bubbles, trapped in the protein of flour, provide holes in the dough which result in a "light" cake or loaf when it is baked to a firmness. Alcohol trapped in the beer solution gives zip to that beverage.

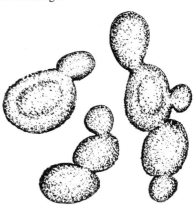

We may consider the original yeast cells as the content of the discipline to be taught—the input, as it were. The teacher then provides the environment—

[5] A new model, recently proposed by J. Richard Suchman, has been labeled Inquiry Training. Chapter II in his book, *Analysis of Learning*, Academic Press, New York, 1966, is titled "A Model for the Analysis of Inquiry." An article describing the procedures involved appeared in *The Science Teacher*, Vol. 27, No. 7 (November, 1960), pp. 42-47. You might like to place the Suchman model somewhere on the spectrum of teaching models in relation to the two described here.

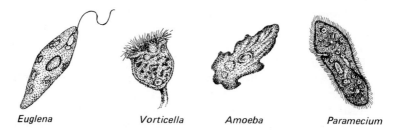

Euglena   *Vorticella*   *Amoeba*   *Paramecium*

sugar, moisture, warmth—by which the data of this discipline multiply and are transmitted without loss of the original knowledge. The output—the knowledge now in the memory of the children—tends to be a replica of the input.

The teacher's style will determine whether the culture (the "solution") is warm and frothy with excitement or cool and slow with measured pace. The learners may be considered test tubes or vessels in which the yeast data are being duplicated. At least for the successful yeast, the end product in each case is an accurate replication of the original knowledge, perhaps with some mutations.

The pond model Several different one-celled organisms of the teacher's choice (for example, *Euglena, Vorticella, Amoeba*, and *Paramecium*) are placed in small ponds. These organisms have been selected because they bear a relationship to one another: they are all one-celled and mobile. Yet each cell has its own structure, different from that of the other species, and each has a characteristic model of locomotion.

As in the yeast model, the teacher controls the light, warmth, and nutrients which permeate the ponds according to his teaching style. Each learner is represented by a different pond, although the materials (the organisms or the content of the discipline) are the same for each. In this model, variety is insured since the ponds have many different residues—mud, organic nutrients, even plants. In this learning situation there are many possible interactions: first, among the various organisms themselves; second, between the environment and the organisms which are capable of changing the whole ecology, resulting in the dominance of some organisms.

Each pond will yield different, although related, data; each child will learn what is meaningful to him. A pond may even yield data which were not part of

the input, although much of the output will overlap between ponds. In addition to the data, there is a rich harvest of process, development, and growth for the whole pond.

We have found the pond model lesson just described accessible to many types of teachers. It allows those who feel most secure as the center of control to ease into a situation where children take the initiative. The lesson begins by arousing great interest in materials, which are initially handled by the teacher. The materials become more meaningful when the children begin working with them directly, each investigating according to his inner drive.

We have found that this lesson is successful with all age levels from the first grade through a graduate seminar. It interests and stimulates thinking in all types of children: those who have never handled materials this way before in the classroom; those who are bright; those who are slow; even those who are disturbed.

The lesson seems meaningful, of course, on a hierarchy of levels. In Miss Stevens' class, the transition from the teacher in command to each child in command seemed to happen so naturally that the classroom atmosphere was not "upset"; the increase in noise was purposeful. Discipline was maintained because the class was absorbed in a learning activity, a meaningful situation.

The meaning of structure in materials

We are using the word *structure* in this book to indicate a pattern of relatedness. When applied to a building, structure refers to the relation of its parts to the stresses and strains on the walls, floors, etc., and to the functions the building is to serve. This pattern of relatedness is made visual in the architect's blueprints and in the engineer's drawings and calculations. Structuring materials in science teaching means that a relationship to some natural phenomenon is revealed when the materials are manipulated. This pattern of relatedness is the concept of the phenomenon. (For an elaboration of the term *concept,* see pages 149-55.)

Magnets and pieces of iron, nickel, and brass, collectively, have a structure. The magnet is related to the iron and nickel because these metals and the magnet interact, but the magnet and the brass do not interact. Therefore, we have a pattern: magnets interact with some metals and not with others. The concept of this phenomenon, discovered when people manipulate the materials, is the nature of magnetism.

Thinking can have structure, too. One set of structures is known as logic. The pattern of *deductive logic* relates statements in the syllogism. The pattern of *inductive logic* was formerly illustrated by *the* method of scientific thinking; scientists are now known to have many methods of thinking, described by Percy Bridgeman as "no holds barred." Finally, in *modern mathematical logic,* known as the axiom-postulate system, the pattern of relatedness is made visual in symbolic logic; for example, $p \supset q$, is the shorthand for the relation "*p* implies *q.*"

The structures described above have *intrinsic* relationships; the patterns belong to the whole. But there are also *extrinsic,* or arbitrarily *imposed* relationships. Imagine that you have been presented with these materials: a leaf, a lipstick, a dime, an awl, a bottle cap, a cracker, a leather strap. The objects do not interact to reveal any natural phenomenon; they do not have a pattern which relates one to the others. You could, however, impose a relationship upon them. Placing some on a shelf *above* the others or arranging them in a long line one after another, the objects have quite an arbitrary spatial relationship. You could impose another arbitrary relationship by classifying them in a number of ways—for example, dividing them into *natural* and *man-made* objects or into the categories animal, vegetable, or mineral, or considering them all to be solid. By classifying objects into such categories and subcategories, we have a taxonomy—a useful arrangement for retrieval, as IBM and other systems prove. When a taxonomy has been established for a set of objects, the result is a pattern

of relationships. Therefore, taxonomy can be considered a form of structure, as we use the term.

Thus, structure may refer to a pattern of relationships which is intrinsic (belonging to the whole), or it may be extrinsic (imposed upon a collection). The concept of the structure of materials used in science teaching is intrinsic—a pattern related to a phenomenon of the natural world.

Structure related to concepts in science

Although structure and concept are sometimes used synonymously, we prefer to differentiate between the meanings of these words. Both refer to relationships; however, the relationships in a concept are always abstract, whereas the relationships in a structure may or may not be. The structure of a building is concrete; one could not apply the word concept to it. But the structure in thinking is abstract, as in the example we gave of logic. (One could refer to the pattern of relationships in any of the systems of logic as a concept; here the words might be used synonymously.) A taxonomy, as we saw, has a structure—a pattern of relatedness—but it is not a concept. Therefore, structure is more inclusive than concept because it can apply to both the concrete and the abstract. A concept is always an abstraction.

Concepts in science have their own hierarchies. The most grandiose abstractions about the nature of the universe may be called *conceptual schemes.* Scholars differ about the manner of formulating these schemes, as well as about their basic number. We find, however, that these conceptual schemes center around three major aspects of the natural universe: the universe at large, mass-energy, and living organisms. These may be stated as:

A. The universe is in constant change.
B. The sum total of mass and energy in the universe remains constant.
C. Living organisms are in constant change.

Each of these schemes includes many concepts. Each concept represents a pattern of abstractions, a relationship among abstractions, that has its place in the hierarchy of concepts. For example, magnetism is included within electromagnetism and this within the electromagnetic spectrum and this, in turn, within the conceptual scheme of mass–energy (B. above). These relationships are conveniently expressed in the words *concept* and *subconcept*; thus we call magnetism a subconcept of the concept electromagnetism and electromagnetism a subconcept of the concept electromagnetic spectrum. These terms, concept and subconcept, are used to designate a relationship within a particular context. They are a convenience, not the designation of any position in a natural hierarchy.

The structure behind the materials used in the *What's Inside?* lesson was that the presence of unseen objects can be manifested to the senses of touch and hearing. The first part of the lesson dealt with familiar objects which could be felt or make sounds through the brown paper bag. The presence and nature of the objects had to be inferred, with only a statistical probability. Similarly, the air in the plastic bag could not be seen, but it could be felt and it could be made to make a noise. In this case, the children began by knowing that the bag contained air, but they inferred that air was a material thing—that it could manifest its presence in the same manner apples and potatoes did.

The last fact was not articulated by the children; it resulted from the pattern of relatedness behind the materials. This structure is related to the subconcept that an invisible gas (air) is made of matter.[6] A more inclusive concept would be that a gas is composed of tiny particles of matter in motion. Under the conceptual scheme concerning mass-energy, this can be stated in its most abstract form as: "The sum total of mass [6] and energy in the universe remains constant."

[6] *matter:* Anything that takes up space and is composed of atoms and molecules.
mass: The amount of matter in an object.

Because the pattern of relatedness in the first part of the lesson was similar to the pattern of relatedness in the second part, the children spoke about air as though it were an object, a material "thing." Without the materials and the kind of experience Marie Stevens offered her third graders, children would not think of air as a substance, matter, on the order of apples and potatoes. The nature of matter is a fundamental concept of science. Experience with the bags brought the grandiose conceptual scheme about mass–energy in small measure to the awareness of the children, a good base for further development later. (We make suggestions for follow-up experiences in Chapter 5.) Structuring the materials revealed the phenomenon that air is matter, that it can do, or be made to do, things that solid matter can do. This, then, is a subconcept of the nature of matter.

Now consider this group of objects: a basin of water, a cork, a small piece of wood, a marble, and a small ball of oil-base clay. What is the structure behind this set of materials? What pattern is revealed when the small objects are placed in the water? Obviously, some float and some do not. Can we refine our perception of the pattern? There are many levels on which to do this; these will be explored in the next two sections. Before reading further, can you formulate the way you would perceive the pattern?

Children may say that heavy things sink, but light things float. That is part of the pattern, part of the way the objects relate to the water. If we add a very tiny piece of clay, lighter than the cork or wood, we will have to think of a new pattern. If we wish to reveal a more inclusive relationship, we might add a ping-pong ball and a ball of clay the same size, some crumpled aluminum foil the size and shape of the marble, and a rock and a piece of sponge cut to the

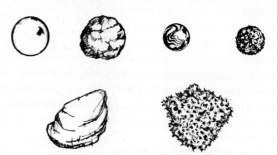

same size and shape. A new phenomenon is then revealed: things heavy for their size sink and things light for their size float. If the children are asked to try to make the clay float, they will eventually mold it into the shape of a boat. In its new form, it still has the same heaviness; older children will seek a new pattern! If we offer children all the above materials at once, many patterns can be discovered; many ways of expressing these discoveries and many thoughtful answers which pose new questions will arise. These materials involve children and have meaning for them on many levels; the materials reveal a cluster of related patterns, yet the problem which challenged Archimedes when he was asked to determine whether or not King Hieron's crown was pure gold is still unsolved. The experience becomes a simulation of scientific endeavor.

Flotation, the concept to which all these patterns are related, might be phrased as a question—Which materials will float in which media?—and answered in a manner which has wide application—Less dense matter floats on more dense media. (Density is understood as weight per unit volume.)

Since this concept relates density of objects to density of media, at some point materials in which the medium is varied must be offered. If we place hard-boiled eggs, a jar of fresh water, and a jar of very salty water before children, the materials will force them to consider the relatedness of the medium to the objects. A collection of small cubes of the same dimensions, but made of various substances (wood, aluminum, plastic, brass, etc.), together with small vials of water, salt water, and oil could also be presented; an arm balance to compare the weights of the unit volumes and some hollow cubes to compare the weights of liquid unit volumes could also be provided.

The concept underlying the way the materials relate to one another guides us in selecting even more sophisticated materials to further the thinking of children. During the course of this book, we follow the process of the child's development in a number of areas as he handles and discusses sequences of structured materials through many conceptual levels.

The concept of flotation, since it is an expression of the nature of matter, comes under the same conceptual scheme as the experience with air. *Sink*

and Float has an additional dimension: Why does anything sink at all? Nothing sinks in an astronaut's capsule while it orbits the earth. We need gravity! From this point of view the flotation concept is subsumed in the conceptual scheme that the universe is in constant change; one of the factors of constant change is the gravitational interaction of matter.

Materials, then, must be structured in relation to concepts. They must also be attractive in order to provide an engaging experience for the child; this, of course, implies that some of the patterns of the phenomena of interaction should be within the child's discovery competence. (The genetic growth of conceptual ability is taken up in both Chapter 3 and Chapter 6.)

One more factor must be considered in selecting materials for children to manipulate if a successful learning situation is to result. As an example, children were offered a balloon in addition to some of the other items used in the *Sink and Float* activity. What did the children do? They leaned on the balloon in the basin of water and made a tidal wave! The tidal wave flooding the floor became a more intriguing experience, psychologically speaking, than the problem which led Archimedes to shout "Eureka!" as he ran naked through the streets of Alexandria. Administratively speaking, we have found it desirable not to include balloons with this activity.

Short lengths of drinking straws might be appropriate for a surface tension experience, especially if soapy water is one of the ingredients. But straws and soapy water suggest blowing bubbles—a form of surface tension, it is true, but one which is much more meaningful at a children's party!

Thus, materials chosen on the basis of their relevance to important concepts in science must be modified in relation to the psychological implications they may have for children.

In selecting materials, how do you discover potentially diverting activities? One way is to look at the materials through a child's eyes, but a pragmatic test is necessary before the final selection. Try the materials out on small groups of children or, if brave enough, on your own class, with the understanding that the aim implied in the structure might not be achieved!

Choosing suitably structured materials requires a

knowledge of science, a sensitive relation to children, and considerable practical experience with this method of teaching. It is time-consuming. Fortunately, new programs being developed over the nation, both by publishing houses and Federally-funded projects, are producing a greater variety of materials. Many of these may be adapted for free investigation by children. Soon, your own experience will suggest variations and improvements, even new developments. You will probably be able to devise new sets of materials which will make a contribution to other teachers.

EUREKA! OR I KNOW WHY IT FLOATS

With some trepidation, Mrs. Diana Ross filled the large transparent plastic basins two-thirds full of water and placed them on a pair of newspaper-covered tables which her first graders had arranged as science stations before going home for lunch. She put a small pile of paper towels at each "station," wondering if they would be sufficient to mop up the mess she anticipated. As she passed the closet, she automatically checked to be sure the wet mop was in its place. She had brought it along out of habit from her days as a kindergarten teacher. But that was eons ago—two high school sons and a junior high school daughter ago. When the school superintendent received a grant to recruit and train a group of ex-teacher mothers in modern methods for his primary grades, Mrs. Ross decided it was time for her to resume her professional life.

Everything had seemed so different in those special university classes. Of course, it was stimulating being with mothers like herself all engaged in updating their ideas about education. But the old security of what had worked before kept coming back. "Worked for whom?" she had conditioned herself to ask, for then she was able to reply, "For me." A quiet classroom of obedient children, well drilled, well organized, and richly stimulated with many ingenious devices, often invented by her. She had had prize bulletin boards, model Parents' Nights, enviable demonstrations for the VIP's the Principal had brought into her kindergarten.

She had even done the *Sink and Float* investigation for her kindergartners toward the end of their year. A large fish tank placed on an upturned carton on her desk, every child could see without needing to rush up for a closer look. She always had assembled a sufficient number of items so each child could have a turn at dropping an object into the tank. And after the first few things were dropped she would ask the class to guess whether the next object would sink or float. Their guesses were universally wild. "I suppose they didn't come under the heading of 'prediction,' " she thought. Prediction, she had learned recently, was a scientific procedure to be emulated by children.

After the objects had been classified and placed under large signs—SINKS or FLOATS—what had been learned? In her reflective moments (and there had been many), Diana Ross suspected that some children became mentally alive only at the moment when they were asked to drop an item into the tank, after climbing the little stepladder—such a neat and useful attraction, she had thought at the time. Their turn over, what was there to hope for? As to questions raised which might motivate the children to go further, to try things on their own, nothing seemed to arise that suggested a follow-up lesson. For some years she had kept a bowl of water and the objects in the science corner, but all the children had ever done was to dump the lot in and fish them out again. Valuable experience? Maybe. But now her whole class of first graders was to have an open invitation to "dump" *en masse.*

Mrs. Ross was now placing plastic bags of "objects" at each station. These materials were a little different from those she used in kindergarten. There was a different principle of selection, she had learned. Of course, you want things that sink and things that float, but the idea was also to choose things that would do both, like pieces of plastic sponge which float at first, then gradually sink. And there were things that could be made to do either. That was it: control the environment. Give the children a sense that they are in command of this little world, this small system of interacting objects. Hence, the plastic bag contained not only bobby pins, pieces of sponge, keys, marbles, ping-pong balls, cork, jacks, and wood chips, but also a ping-pong ball with a large hole in it, a Wiffle ball, and paper jigger cups. Ready to be passed out at the appropriate moment were six-inch squares of aluminum foil and pieces of soap. The soap! Diana Ross was more concerned about the mess it would make than about the splashing she expected from the other materials. She foresaw masses of lather, much hand washing, giggles, and projective play, but nothing investigated about sink and float.

This possibility had been brought up during one science seminar, but the group had reasoned that for children who had not had much chance to play with water, who lived perhaps in an environment where cleanliness was not as much emphasized (some had said overemphasized) as it is in middle-class homes, lathering might be a legitimate activity. But not during a science lesson. Better let them get the lathering out of their systems at a time when messiness did not intrude. Certainly, if the children were stimulated to play "washtubs," they would be diverted from the science involved, from the challenge of why the Ivory soap floats and the other soap sinks. Children might be more attentive to the investigation of flotation if the pieces of soap were quite small and were introduced after their interest in the question of what sinks and what floats had been sufficiently aroused by the other materials. Mrs. Ross chose to safeguard serenity by following both precepts. She did not believe that a desire to create masses of soap bubbles was the property of any one economic class! On her desk she reserved a pile of aluminum foil squares, a paper plate of very small chips of Ivory soap, and a plate of equally small chips of another white soap. Obviously, the soaps that looked so alike but which acted differently were one key to stimulate thinking about the difference between an object that floats and one that sinks.

"And here are my lovely first graders, all ready to be experimenters," she greeted the double row of silent children the sixth-grade monitor had lined up outside her door. "You know your new places and the committees you will work with. See what you can find out about the surprises I have put on your desks." She allowed the children into the room four at a time, calling in each batch the children who were to work together.

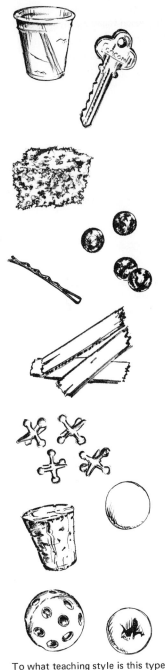

To what teaching style is this type of greeting germane?

If you put all the "directives" in this lesson together, what principle can you find?

Activity began immediately, feverishly. Yes, everything was dumped into the basins, but it was then removed. Each child seemed to select a set of objects to investigate in a variety of ways. Then two or three children would pool their results and start arguing. Quickly Mrs. Ross distributed the aluminum foil to each group with a quiet "Maybe you could use this?" At once the arguing ceased and new directions were taken.

The real excitement for Diana Ross came when the soap chips were placed on the tables and self-direction on the part of the children heightened. Nonchalantly the chips were tossed into the water. Then, wait. Something's wrong. Obviously unstated predictions were present. The two soaps acted differently. All the children concentrated on the soaps using the techniques they had employed with the rest of the materials. Soap was wrapped in aluminum foil, then taken out. Soap was put in the jigger cup with some marbles and after the cup sank it was put afloat again on aluminum rafts. Soap was held in gently curved fingers just below the surface as though a teacher were encouraging a child to swim. Each piece of soap was subjected to sniffing, to discussion, and finally to abandonment.

Why are children separated from the materials during the colloquium?

It was at this point that Diana Ross organized the colloquium. The soap was removed from the basins and placed on paper towels so that it would not cloud the water, the tables were pushed close together into the center of the room, and the children sat in a large circle around the walls away from the materials.

"Let's share our discoveries," began Mrs. Ross. "Each one of you think of one important thing you'd like to share with the rest of us. We'll go around the circle so that each of you has a turn. Let's begin with Dick."

Dick: I didn't discover nuttin'.
Rosa: The marble went straight to the bottom.
Rex: You can pick water up in the Wiffle ball.
Dick: The Wiffle ball sinks.
Bert: No, it floats.
Mrs. R.: What did the rest of you find?

Opinions seemed divided so Mrs. Ross suggested that Dick drop the Wiffle ball into one of the basins so that everyone could watch.

Dick: It floats just like a boat. Part of it sinks and part floats. A regular ball is like that, too. *(Then his voice took on an excited tone.)* So everything else, part, even a small part, must sink or the rest couldn't float. The part of the Wiffle ball that sinks is the part that has water in it.
Charlie: The part of the boat that sinks does it 'cause it's heavy, too.
Gert: Is it because the water makes the Wiffle ball heavy? Does it *not* float because of this?
Mrs. R.: Suppose I cut a piece off the Wiffle ball, a flat piece so that the ball couldn't hold water. Do you think the piece would sink or float?

Again opinion was divided; the teacher cut off a section and dropped it in the water. The children leaned forward to see more clearly. Gert was asked to come up for a closer look and to state what she saw.

Gert: It's floating, but low. So the water doesn't make it sink. But when I
 filled the ping-pong ball with water it sank.
Kathie: Mine didn't.
Mrs. R.: Would you both, Kathie and Gert, show us how your ping-pong balls
 acted in the water?
Gert: Kathie's has a bubble of air in hers. Maybe that's why it floats.
Kathie: My ping-pong ball smelled funny. I think there was soap in it.
Jonathan: The soap floats.
Fran: Only one piece does; the other sinks.
Dick: I know why. It's Ivory. They say on TV that it is ninety-nine and
 forty-four hundredths percent pure and it floats.
David: Nobody said anything about the sponges yet.
Mrs. R.: Suppose you tell us about them.
David: When they are dry, they float, but as soon as they get wet, that's it;
 they sink.
Gert: I wrapped a jack in tin foil and it floated. It sank alone. I did the same
 with soap and it floated, too.
Shelley: I think I know why things float.
Mrs. R.: Please tell us.
Shelley: They float because they have air in them.
Dick: Ivory soap can't have air; it has no holes.
Jo: Air might have been pumped into the middle of it.
Rex: The sponge works that way, too. When it is dry, it has air in it. When it
 is wet, it has water in it instead.
Mrs. R.: What do you think happened to the air when the water came in?
Shelley: The water pushes it out and takes the air's place.
Mrs. R.: Why doesn't the key float?
Danny: It has no air in it.
Mrs. R.: So how could we make it float?
Shelley: If we could make it into a round ball and put air in it, it might be
 able to float.
Dick: It wouldn't be no good then!
Kathie: Who ever heard of a round keyhole!
Mrs. R.: I saw some of you making the marbles float, yet they sank like the
 key did at first.
Danny: I did it. I put the marbles in the little paper cup like they were in a
 boat. Then I put more marbles in and it all sank.
Shelley: That's like the sponge. Water pushed the air out of the sponge and it
 sank. Marbles pushed the air out of the cup and the cup sank.

The Investigators' Log agreed upon by all the children was much simpler
than the thinking and statements which were made individually. It contained
these phrases:
 Things with air in them float.
 Heavy things sink.
 When water pushes the air out of things they sink.

How many instances of the juxtaposition of conflicting facts can you find?

You might like to reread Shelley's remarks to follow the growth of her thinking. What experiences preceded her insight?

Levels of meaning through structure

Take any of the children's discoveries: the Wiffle ball which floated low when water filled the holes, the marbles which sank the jigger cup, the ping-pong ball which sank only when it was completely filled with water, or the imaginary key bent into a circle (probably a sphere!) with air pumped into it. Do you think the experience with materials and the discussion of this experience made the Principle of Archimedes clear to the children? We don't think it did, either! But if we accept that there are *levels* of clarity or concept attainment, all "correct" within their limits, all partial, then we may be able to examine the meanings the children attached to their manipulation of the structured sink and float materials. (Such levels of concept attainment will be discussed in greater detail in Chapters 2, 3, and 6.)

The *Sink and Float* lesson recorded here was the response of a bright first grade from a middle-class community. The children had reached the stage of understanding buoyancy usually found at the second level. At the first level, children are normally satisfied with the discovery that things float because they are light and sink because they are heavy. At the next stage they express their findings, as Diana Ross's children did, in terms of air. Things float if they have air in them. Even where no air spaces can be observed, the children infer the presence of air and use the reverse of the statement: There must be air in the soap because it floats. Note these different levels of concept attainment.

The third stage is illustrated by the following colloquium developed with an advanced third grade.

Bob: My marble sinks in the water. My marble when I wrap it in the aluminum sinks, too, but the aluminum alone floats.
Alice: That's because the marble makes the aluminum heavier, so it sinks.
Rae: Things that are very light float.
Dick: Would my pencil sink, Miss D.?
Miss D.: What do you think, class? [The class can often find an answer, if encouraged to.]
Valerie: I think it would sink.
Miss D.: Let's try and see. Joe, would you do it for us?

Joe: Look, yes it does; the pencil sinks.
Arthur: Maybe a tiny little pencil would float. I have a very tiny one.
Miss D.: Try it, Arthur.
Arthur: Hey, how come it sinks? It's so light.
Howard: But the tissue is much lighter than the pencil. *(The children had dunked tissues in their water.)* That's why. The marble is just the same size as the little piece of soap. The marble sinks and the soap floats.
Joe: That's because the marble is much heavier, I think.
Wade: If things are about the same size, I think the heavier one sinks. Is that true, Miss D.?
Miss D.: Let's see. I have a piece of rubber the same size as this pen. What do you think will happen when I put them both in the water? [A challenge to predict!]
Van: I think the rubber will sink and so will the pen.
Howard: No, Van, we know the pen sinks, but the rubber is lighter than the pen. I think it will float.
Joe: Can we try and see?
Miss D.: Anne, will you try it?
Anne: I see; the pen sinks, but the rubber floats.
Howard: See, Van, if they're about the same size the heavier thing will sink.
Van: Yes, the lighter thing, the rubber, floats.

While these explanations would not have revealed the purity of gold in King Hieron's crown (Archimedes' original problem), they do express the meaning the children derived from handling and thinking about the materials. They handled the materials in many ways—very important in refining concepts; they made many new combinations and observed a variety of interactions. The explanations fitted the observed data; they were meaningful on the level of understanding of these children. That the children are still searching for more meaning in the materials is evidence that they are engaging in genuine concept-seeking activity through procedures remarkably similar to those of the scientist. It is certain that not every child attaches the same meaning Howard did to the materials, but having touched, seen, and heard, they will investigate further in their own time and suddenly the same dawn will break on each brow.

Words are symbols, and what they stand for in the

thinking of the speaker is an important factor. Much later, of course, communication demands that a consensus of understanding be attached to each symbol. Now the Investigators' Log represents the consensus of the assembled group, a kind of common denominator of meaning or concept attainment. That is one reason why the Log statements are so much simpler and more fragmentary than the total wisdom expressed individually during the colloquium.

Sometimes statements made by children may seem utterly incorrect to the adult. Should the adult correct the statement immediately? If so, how? With more words or symbols? After an hour and a half of free investigation followed by a colloquium, one class decided unanimously that things float because they are heavy. Taken aback, the teacher wrote down the statement, but she did ask the children to explain how they saw it this way.

"Ships are made of iron; they are very heavy and they float."

"My ping-pong ball was light when filled with water, but it sank."

It seems to us, the challenge to such statements must come from more investigation, not from a verbal explanation. For the session after the above entry in the Log, the children in the class were grouped in two sections. One group tried to float a sinking variety of soap by flaking it into the water, beating air into it with egg whisks, and then drying the froth on a radiator; the result was similar to dried shaving lather. The other group tried to sink a snowball—a good use of the prevailing blizzard. The children used their gloves to pack the snow harder. They were very disappointed, as well as tired, when they found they could not sink it; the snow always became water before it "sank." The colloquium following this session made no mention of the heavy-so-it-floats theory. The teacher does not have to "correct" a faulty symbolic expression. New materials which supersede the previous ones by introducing new and challenging data motivate more adequate statements. In the same vein, data which support the prior statement re-emphasize earlier concept formulations.

The next stage in formulating the concept of buoyancy will probably attain the level most adults who are not scientists reach.

Now it's your turn You might like to engage in an experience and try to write down the meaning your observations have for you. If so, you will need to prepare some materials—of course! Color the water in an ice cube compartment with a few drops of food coloring. When your colored ice cube has frozen, half-fill a glass with water, add an inch of vegetable oil, and then drop in the colored ice cube. Watch. What happens? Why?

The phenomenon of flotation has very wide applications: gases float on each other and so do liquids; even some solids may be said to float on other solids. Hot air floats on cold air, hot water floats on cold water, and ice floats on some oils. The material which is less dense floats on the material which is more dense. Since the definition of density (weight per unit volume) has two related variables (weight and volume), we can simplify our thinking if we keep one variable constant. Think of one-inch cubes of each material. What would each weigh in relation to the others? If you were to compare the weights of one-inch cubes of the following substances, you might be able to place them in order of density and, therefore, in the order of which would float on which. Try it: wood, cold water, carbon dioxide, aluminum, oil, hot air, hot water, ice, cold air, iron, salt water.

The application of this ordering helps us understand the phenomena of weather, winds, ocean currents, and even the molten condition of the earth's core.

Turning the question to what sinks in what, we must first think of why anything sinks at all. This helps to explain why the expression "hot air rises" has no conceptual base. (It is the cold air sinking which pushes the hot air up!)

The teacher's role in relation to materials

It is evident by now that we place a great deal of importance on materials as the starting point for learning science. Giving a child carefully structured materials to explore freely is one good way to start him along the road to science learning. Of course, it is not the only way, but because our immediate goal is *Starting Tomorrow*, we are emphasizing the guidelines which will allow you to begin child-initiated science exploration, related to concepts, the next time you teach science.

We use the word *teach* here in the sense that it is the atmosphere the teacher creates, as well as the materials he presents, which provide for learning. This atmosphere is due partly to the teacher's personality, partly to the kind of support and encouragement he gives each child, and partly to his awareness of the conceptual goals. As he brings about changes in a child's behavior, he is considered to be teaching, as the child whose behavior changes may be considered to be learning.

We have emphasized that materials must be wisely chosen according to certain concepts, that they are structured to reveal a cluster of related phenomena through their interaction. We have also said that the teacher should allow each child the freedom to explore and investigate in his own way. We have briefly touched upon procedures which help to consolidate learning. If materials are so important, then what is the teacher's role? Certainly not abdication!

To begin with, the teacher selects the materials and prepares them in sets for each group of children. Even when structured materials become more widely available commercially, the teacher will still have to select the items to be used by the children from kits or classroom laboratories. This effort will be less time-consuming than the procedures of Miss Stevens and Mrs. Ross, but no way is known to help elementary school children learn without a great deal of preparation.

The teacher should not be idle while the children work. True, he is not telling, advising, or suggesting, but he is "teaching" in our sense of the word. He is observing, using that perceptive peripheral vision with which all good teachers seem endowed; he is recording dozens of events. And during any lesson the teacher is noting the significant actions of individual children: he is observing progress, change of behavior, and ingenuity; he is mentally noting discoveries which can be brought up during the colloquium; and his other "ear" is listening for children who need support and encouragement, a new piece of equipment, an appreciative smile. The teacher senses the moment when the explorative session should terminate and

the talking and sharing activity of the colloquium should begin. This cannot be determined by clocks or bells, or even by rule of thumb; experience with materials cannot be bound by a certain time period. Termination should come when the teacher, in his artistry, feels that productive activity is about to slip into the type of play which signifies cognitive exhaustion.[7]

The success of the next phase, the colloquium, depends upon what the teacher has observed during the explorative period. In the colloquium he can encourage the shy child he watched doing something of interest to share his discovery with the class, or he can foster expressions of the contradictory or conflicting results he has seen. From observing the way the children used the materials, as well as the way they spoke about their discoveries, he can decide what materials to introduce in follow-up lessons. Indeed, the teacher is busiest while the children are learning, thereby fulfilling his role completely.

Criteria for selecting materials

Until a teacher has had some experience with reliable materials, he will probably find it difficult to select them at random. Since it is never possible to be sure that untried materials will serve well, you might wish to begin with the materials described in one of the lessons in this chapter. They have been successful in a great variety of classes where they have been used by a wide range of teacher personalities. No doubt you will adapt them personally to your style of teaching and to the needs of your children. Teaching will always remain essentially an individual art, but here are some guidelines.

1. The materials should be related to an important concept in science; manipulating the materials should reveal many related phenomena. This is the feature we have called "structure."
2. The materials should be intriguing to the children. Actually a wide range of ages and abilities can be served by any good set of materials. Learners derive

[7]I call this moment "mayhem minus five," meaning five minutes before mayhem breaks loose! This change of tone is well described by Z.P. Dienes, *An Experimental Study of Mathematics Learning*, Hutchinson, London, 1963, Ch. 1, especially pp. 47–48, 54–56.

different levels of meaning from them according to the knowledge they bring to the experience.

3. The materials should interact in many ways; there should be room for many avenues of exploration. Children must be able to present their different discoveries during the colloquium; because most of these discoveries will be related to allied subconcepts, each will contribute to building or enriching a concept. A set of materials that is exhausted after one activity does not provide a very rich basis for learning.

4. There must be enough materials for each child. It is not necessary to have the same number of each item as there are children, but any object that is *essential* in exploring interaction must be available to every child. In the lesson on air arranged by Miss Stevens, each child had to have a favor as well as a plastic bag; there had to be a few spares of each, too. In Mrs. Ross' lesson, however, one basin of water was sufficient for each group because no one user needed a monopoly. In fact, sharing the basin increased interaction among the materials and the children. Moreover, for each group of four children there were at least half a dozen items that sank, half a dozen that floated, and several that presented a challenge. When something—a flashlight or a magnet, for instance—is essential for exploration, there must be one for each child. Sharing in such a case emphasizes peer group status—personal feelings of deprivation or triumph—rather than what the materials can do. Learning energy is diverted to solve an ego problem.

5. The materials should not suggest psychologically extraneous activities (for example, creating a tidal wave with a balloon in water or blowing soap bubbles through a straw).

On digressions—"unrelated discoveries"

Proper use of materials can lead to a concept that does not seem to be directly related to the main one. You cannot control the ingenuity of children—fortunately! Since this can be difficult to handle at first until the larger frame of reference—a more embracing concept than the one anticipated—is seen, we given an illustration.

In an exploration of air with plastic bags, some children close inflated bags with rubber bands and watch them float down to the floor; other children may drop flat bags and report during the colloquium that big things fall more slowly than small things. Well, Galileo refuted an analogous notion some three hundred years ago! So take the main points, size and gravity—for gravity is the diverting concept here—and repeat Galileo's demonstration without the Tower of Pisa.

Take a large object (a board eraser) and a small object (a marble). If you can arrange to elevate yourself by standing on a stool or table without loss of dignity, do so. Otherwise, hold the objects at the same level as high above your head as possible. Ask the children which object will reach the floor first if you let them go at the same moment. You may have to repeat the dropping and ask the class to listen, since not everyone will be able to see or agree on the visual observation. One sound will be heard, or, if there are two qualities of sound, they will be simultaneous.

"But mine didn't land at the same time," a child will object. "Mine wasn't heavier; it was just bigger."

Again, the children's reactions provide the next step: two things the same weight, but different sizes. Hold two sheets of paper aloft, one flat and the other scrunched up, and ask again, "Which will hit the floor first?" Answers vary. The flat piece makes a zigzag course. Why? If this difficulty, which diverts attention from the main concept, could have been forecast, you might have had doll astronauts (with and without parachutes) on hand to offer further thought provocation. However, such diversions rarely occur.

How do children pick up cues to the problem from this demonstration? *Gravity* is usually mentioned as "pulling on" (we prefer "interacting with") *falling bodies*; still there is a third object in the system: what delays the parachute and the sheet of paper? In a *vacuum* all bodies interact similarly with gravity; in air, the larger the body surface, the greater the interaction between the air and the object and the slower the object will fall. At least now we have discovered another fact about air: it can slow the speed of falling bodies. Gravity, which was not a part of the structure of these materials and could have confused the child, has been attended to briefly and the role of air emphasized anew.

Let's take another example. In handling materials

related to the concept of static electricity, children often say that magnetism is at work. Again, simply work with what is said: introduce magnets and ask the children to demonstrate what they mean. They will discover that magnets do not interact with statically electric materials. Then compliment the children for suggesting a similarity between static electricity and magnetism, for finding hidden likenesses is an important part of concept building, as will be seen later. Magnetism and electricity are different aspects of one phenomenon in reality, but magnets do not move electrostatic charges toward them. In the system selected for exploring electricity, magnets do not reveal a structure.

To summarize, materials are important in helping children to make observations about the world around them and to develop concepts about the way the facts they find are related. The road to concept building always begins with experience; structured materials offer one such experience.

Learning always takes place inside the learner. Nervous, muscular, sensual stimulation during manipulation of materials induces a growing awareness of the interactions among objects. Thinking and speaking help the learner to raise his kinesthetic experiences to higher levels of thought. Each child has individual and idiosyncratic ways of learning and building concepts. Allowing him freedom to explore according to his own design does many things to and for him, not the least of which is convincing him of his competence as a learner.

And the teacher? It is the teacher who selects exciting and challenging materials; who encourages children to find meaning in their experiences; who provides the psychological safety to explore, to find dead ends and change direction, to raise questions, to supply answers—in short, to learn.

What can the child discover?

What is discovery?

Discovery has become a GOOD word in education. It is a VERY GOOD word in science education—so much so that we find many science educators eagerly asserting "of course, we use the discovery approach." Having become a good word, discovery—like all much-used symbols—has acquired a variety of meanings.

That research is needed to define and test the various meanings attached to "discovery" is well pointed out by Cronbach. Thus, he cautions:

> In spite of the confident endorsements of teaching through discovery that we read in semi-popular discourses on improving education, there is precious little substantiated knowledge about what advantages it offers, and under what conditions these advantages accrue. We badly need research in which the right questions are asked and trustworthy answers obtained. When the research is in it will tell us, I suspect, that inductive teaching has value in nearly every area of the curriculum, and also that its function is specialized and limited. The task of research is to define that proper place and function.[8]

What does *discovery* mean to you? Why not jot down a sentence which will tether your meaning while you read the following pages?

Very few people disapprove of discovery methods in science education today, but many have reservations about the word; they find it essential to modify its meaning with if's and but's. "Discovery" seems to engender the haunting fear in some that children will be expected to *rediscover* the whole history of science (when it is obvious that they will hardly have caught up with Aristotle in history by the time they reach graduate school!). An exaggeration, perhaps, but one which makes a good point. We might counter with the plea that elementary school children do not have to begin at the beginning. Perhaps they should begin by discovering what Newton discovered; it only took him a lifetime!

There are several popular substitute approaches to science learning which evade the issue of discovery by relegating it to a minor importance or by eliminating it altogether and placing complete emphasis on other learning aspects. One such approach stresses that it is not the amount of knowledge the child acquires in elementary school science education, but the sci-

[8] Lee J. Cronbach, "The Logic of Experiments in Discovery," in Lee S. Shulman and Evan R. Keislar (Eds.), *Learning by Discovery,* © 1966 by Rand McNally and Company, Chicago, p. 76.

entific procedures he learns which are important. Subject matter should illustrate suitable procedures or processes rather than cover particular scientific areas. If these procedures are presented in an orderly progression, the child is expected to learn the way man has organized his knowledge of the world around him. He will have practice in the processes by which phenomena are explained. Emphasis on processes is a substitute for the discovery approach as well as for coverage of the subject matter.

Another substitute approach argues that children will learn more if they study a few subjects in depth, instead of covering so many areas—weather, motion, life, space, etc. *In depth* has become another GOOD phrase! It is more economical to study a lot about a limited area; the facts intertwine and amplify each other meaningfully, building richer concepts. When the exact content of each depth area is specified, however, little leeway remains for free discovery.

A third program allows for discovery, but only after the children have been introduced to a preliminary conceptual ordering. Newer editions of some textbooks add open-ended questions and suggestions for investigation after the facts and theories have been explained and a number of designs for experimental models have been suggested. The child is then left, as it were, "on his own."

If the child is allowed to pursue his own methods of discovery, educators seem afraid that he will learn too little, or too slowly, or fail to grasp important facts which a teacher could introduce. It all adds up to that haunting fear!

The type of discovery we are advocating is mentioned by Gagné as part of his Type 8 variety of learning: problem solving. However, Gagné has not included the effects of colloquia, which help the child clarify and develop the meaning of his discovery after he has made it.

Problem solving as a method of learning requires the learner to *discover* the higher-order principle without specific verbal help. Presumably, he thus constructs the new principle in his own idiosyncratic manner, and may or may not be able to verbalize it once he has done this. . . . the evidence strongly suggests that achieving a higher-order principle by means of problem solving produces a highly effective capability which is well retained over considerable periods of time.[9]

But Gagné cautions us as well, as follows:

Obviously, strategies are important for problem solving, regardless of the content of the problem. The suggestion from some writings is that they are of overriding importance as a goal of education. After all, should not formal instruction in the school have the aim of teaching the student "how to think"? If strategies were deliberately taught, would not this produce people who could then bring to bear superior problem-solving capabilities to any new situation? Although no one would disagree with the aims expressed, it is exceedingly doubtful that they can be brought about by teaching students "strategies" or "styles" of thinking. Even if these could be taught (and it is possible that they could), they would not provide the individual with the basic firmament of thought, which is subject-matter knowledge. Knowing a set of strategies is not all that is required for thinking; it is not even a substantial part of what is needed. *To be an effective problem solver, the individual must somehow have acquired masses of structurally organized knowledge. Such knowledge is made up of content principles, not heuristic ones.*[10]

Discovery, as we have defined it, embedded between structured materials and followed by the colloquium, creates a new environment for learning rather akin to a new medium conveying a new message. In this sense it is an innovation.[11]

We have ample evidence that a child can discover a great many facts and find many important relationships for himself, and can articulate these discoveries in meaningful terms if left free to explore structured materials and encouraged to share his thinking with his peers in a colloquium. In some measure he can repeat the history of science, although his areas of

[9] Robert M. Gagné, *The Conditions of Learning*, Holt, Rinehart & Winston, Inc., New York, 1965, pp. 164-65.
[10] *Ibid.*, p. 170. (Our emphasis.)
[11] Neil Postman and Charles Weingartner elaborate on the meaning of McLuhan's "rearview-mirror" syndrome as a danger to innovation in *Teaching As a Subversive Activity*, Delacorte Press, New York, 1969, pp. 26-28.

rediscovery are limited by the materials offered him. Rediscovery of historically important facts and relationships and attention to and explanation of phenomena give the child a sense of being in the shoes of a scientist. Junior high school children, who have just "discovered" for themselves the nature of the gas oxygen, may express disappointment when they learn that Priestley and Lavoisier made the same discovery one hundred and fifty years before! The special learning environment which we create gives the child a feeling of discovery and competence (and a sense of history, which may come later) by allowing him to do in a half hour what the first discoverer did in many weeks or years.

This kind of discovery, free exploration of a structured environment, is evident in other learning situations that recur regularly. As the individual child grows, he repeats the growth of his race: he crawls; he walks on all fours; he staggers on two feet; he walks upright. All this takes about twelve months but in the evolution of man it took several million years. The potential to stand upright is now carried in the genes of man, but heredity and environment must also interact before this potential can be realized. Reports on feral children indicate that they do not discover how to walk upright; they run like their foster parents, the wolves. Even when reconditioned to a biped form of locomotion after being restored to the human world, feral children revert to all fours whenever they want to move quickly. Their environment was not structured to tap the potential maturation level provided by their genes.

Language learning, too, depends on the environment. The studies of children who never learned to speak are more authenticated than the plight of feral children. The former have usually been the victims of warped adults who kept the children secluded in places where they never heard a voice, never discovered words. Their genetic vocal endowment was used only to make primitive grunts; no structure in their enrivonment met the genetic development: there was no communication through speech. Speech, which can be developed in the span of two years in a child, took man, in his history, many thousands of years to acquire. Potential and opportunity, heredity and environment must interact for optimum development to occur. It is a little like the advertisement of a

smiling Philippine cherub over the subscript: "I can speak Tagalog; why can't you?" We all had the potential, but many of us were not in an environment which gave us the opportunity to develop the language of Tagalog.

This analogy can be very closely extended to science learning. Children have the potential established by their genetic heritage to explore, understand, and explain the phenomena of the world around them. Therefore, they need a structured environment with which to view telescopically the science discoveries of mankind.

Which science discoveries of mankind? What parts of our cultural heritage should we pass on? And can all that we decide to pass on be presented in discovery situations? These are cogent problems.

Throughout much of the history of school education, knowledge has been passed on to the next generation by the repetition of oral or written words. More recently, *experience* has become the central learning activity; a subject that could not be experienced first hand—the ritual for the dead in Ancient Egypt, for example—can be experienced in some measure by the children through dramatics. The current trend in education blends experience with the written word, concrete materials with the facts and thoughts in books.

Books play a large part in sciencing, just as they do in the lives of scientists. Books record what other scientists have achieved, by both thought and experimentation, throughout the ages; books reveal the giants on whose shoulders today's scientist stands; books summarize current knowledge and thought. Journals and recovery systems bring the most recent discoveries to scientists in their particular fields so that research can always move forward and not repeat what is already known. *For scientists, the library usually precedes the laboratory.* Can it be this way with children who are sciencing? What is the relation of reading books to the process of discovery?

Children begin to explore the phenomena of their world long before they can read. For the greater part of the elementary school years, the ability to read the written word lags behind the ability to learn from experience for the majority of young children. During the psychological growth of a child, the concrete precedes the abstract, the ability to speak precedes the ability to read. Reading requires an apperceptive base. Experience with materials and discussion of this experience provide such a base and render reading meaningful. Hasn't each one of us, at times, picked up a book on a subject we knew little about and, moreover, in which we had little interest? If, for some reason, we *had* to read such a book, it was a demanding chore. Without an apperceptive base there can be no inner drive, no meaningful learning. What, on the contrary, is our reaction when we find a book which coincides with and extends our current concerns? We cannot put it down until our apperceptive base is extended and enriched, until new vistas stretch before us. This is also true of children. Both trade and textbooks are read avidly by children who have the kinesthetic, emotional, and intellectual preparation to bring a base *to* the reading. Indeed, reading skills improve rapidly with this kind of motivation. Books offer children many relevant facts not readily available through experience, bringing to their imaginations what it was like to have been a scientist in days gone by and what it is like to be in a scientist's laboratory today.

Perhaps to make the best use of the young child's developing intellectual equipment, it is wise to consider that the laboratory might well precede the library. Of course, in the ongoing process of sciencing, the library is followed by more laboratory and this by more library. For reading to be meaningful to a child, it must be based on knowledge, a roster of facts, possibly unanswered questions—the apperceptive base. A scientist has such a base, a broad one, or he would not be in his profession! Older children, possibly beginning in the sixth grade, whose science learnings have been deep and continuous, can approach a problem through reading, again assuming that these children *have had* the concrete experience necessary to raise the problem as well as to give the written words meaning. For any age, the exploration of new fields requires a concrete introduction. Materials—carefully selected, freely manipulated, and discussed with peers—present an excellent introduction; then books can give wings to further search.

The best moment to introduce a book cannot be forecast; appropriate books should always be available in the classroom. Children are easily encouraged (in fact, they often "find" the books themselves) to

read if the content is pertinent and the apperceptive base has been developed. In Chapter 7, we describe a variety of ways books may be added to discovery-colloquium sciencing—and also introduce the use of films, filmloops, and filmstrips (the latter two to be run by the children themselves). The current generation is not learning by words alone or even by words *and* experience with concrete materials. This is the generation weaned on television and sensory learning —the cool generation which thrives on personal involvement and requires stimulation of the complete sensorium: the touch of materials, the feel of experience, involvement with colored moving pictures, the mental stimulus of thought-provoking words spoken by peers, read in books, and suggested by teachers. Learning means choosing, finding the relevancy, discovering, if you will, *what* there is, *where* it is, and *how* it is from all available sources; to learn is to make a personal synthesis, to discover and build concepts. This was the method the junior high school children cited earlier employed when they regretfully "discovered" that Priestley and Lavoisier had first made oxygen 150 years ago.

The other problem—which portions of our scientific heritage should be passed on to elementary school children—is a delicate question. Which facts of history, whose biographies, whose past contributions shall we offer? In Chapter 6, we present some guidelines for the selection of topics which are most viable today. The works of some scientists must be offered for the children to "discover" them. While many interesting anecdotes and facts about scientists and their contributions are available, a great deal of the history of science provided in books has previously been selected with an unfortunate bias—a bias now being changed. At present, however, no written source of information is available to tell children about a man like William H. Barnes, a black doctor working in Minnesota who found a way to store aortas for as long as five weeks and then tailor them to replace diseased arteries. In 1956, Dr. Barnes summarized his findings in 165 such operations, which resulted in only 17 deaths,[12] more than a decade before Dr. Christian Barnard placed the heart

[12] William H. Barnes *et al.*, "Experiences with 165 aortic homographs," *Surgery, Gynecology and Obstetrics*, Vol. 106 (Jan.-June 1956), 49-55.

of a black man, Mr. Haupt, in the chest of Dr. Blaiberg. Isn't Dr. Barnes a giant who should be acknowledged?

Would it be important for children to learn about the Harlem Hospital doctor, Louis T. Wright, who was the first to use the antibiotic aureomycin on human beings? In 1949 he published an article covering his work in 52 cases of acute peritonitis, often a fatal condition; there were only 4 deaths. [13] Two years later he summarized the results of 235 consecutive cases using aureomycin therapy and found that there had been a 50% reduction in deaths.[14]

There is an interesting record of an eighteenth century slave named Caesar who discovered a cure for rattlesnake bites and other poisons,[15] "For discovering which the Assembly of South Carolina purchased his freedom and gave him an annuity of one hundred pounds."

The history of the discovery of vitamins is often discussed in textbooks, but there is never any mention of the part of Puerto Rican botanist, Conrado F. Asenjo. Through the study of plants on his native and neighboring islands, Dr. Asenjo discovered that the West Indian cherry tree was one of the richest sources of ascorbic acid known.[16] He not only discovered this fact, but extracted the vitamin C (now available in tablets called *Acerola*, the botanical name for the tree which produces it). This doctor's discovery was motivated by his desire to find locally obtainable valuable foods at a low cost for his fellow countrymen. Another vitamin discovery came from the West Indian shark, a nuisance in the nets of fisherman. In 1933, Dr. Asenjo found the oil in the liver of these sharks to be a very rich source of vitamin A.[17]

[13] Louis T. Wright *et al.*, "Treatment of Acute Peritonitis with Aureomycin," *American Journal of Surgery*, Vol. 78 (1949), 15-22.
[14] Louis T. Wright *et al.*, "An Evaluation of Aureomycin Therapy in Peritonitis," *Surgery, Gynecology and Obstetrics*, Vol. 92 (1951), 661-71.
[15] "The Negro Caesar's Cure for Poison," *Massachusetts Magazine*, 4 (Feb. 1792), 103. (Available only on microfilm.)
[16] Conrado F. Asenjo and Ana Rosa Freiri de Guzman, "High Ascorbic Acid Content of the West Indian Cherry," *Science*, Vol. 103, No. 2669 (1946), 219.
[17] Conrado F. Asenjo *et al.*, "Preliminary note on the occurrence of vitamin A in the oil of West Indian Sharks," *Science*, Vol. 78, No. 2030 (Nov. 24, 1933), 479.

In a school situation, children's discoveries are bound by the areas that confront them. If we constantly avoid certain facts or never touch upon some topics, then children will not hear about them or discover their pertinence within those areas. Of course, children learn outside school, too, but here we are speaking of the role of the teacher. Perhaps we need to develop guidelines for selecting from our scientific heritage.

One criterion might be the works of past scientists who have contributed to the topics the children are studying. (For details in selecting topics, see Chapter 4.)

Another criterion could be the lives of men and women who struggled to overcome many roadblocks in their work. It is enormously encouraging for children to learn that famous people sometimes fail and then overcome their failures; there is a link of identification if working hard with poor results occasionally happens to people "who made it" as well as to children.

A third criterion should be representation of all the ethnic groups in America, as well as other nationalities. Elementary school teachers do not have time to search for the scientists whose contributions, although no less great than those of well known men, lie buried and forgotten. Research specialists must make such facts available to children and teachers. Today books are published which give at least the names and note the types of contributions made by forgotten minorities; these can be a starting point. [18]

A final word on the nature of discovery. There is, to be sure, a difference between discovering a fact or relationship, or developing a concept *new to one's personal understanding or experience*, and discovering some relationship which leads to a concept never before discovered, a concept *new to the world*—in a word, original. A child may see a blue mold (*Penicillium*) for the first time, and wonder about it. Alexander Fleming, who discovered the relationship between *Penicillium* and the antibiotic penicillin, also wondered, but in a different way. The joy and wonder of a child and of a scientist may have similar human qualities, but different consequences.

In England just before the American Revolution,

[18] See Teacher's Bibliography under Section IIG for sources of currently available books.

Priestley observed that a mouse under a bell jar became drowsy and soon lapsed into inactivity. If a sprig of mint was placed under the bell jar, however, the mouse soon revived, scurrying about with typical fervor. In this way, Priestley discovered the role of green plants in "purifying" the air: the green plant used the carbon dioxide ("fixed air," in Priestley's terms) and released oxygen. We know now that these reactions occur during photosynthesis. In Priestley's time, however, this relationship was new to him and to the world—it was original.

Children can make similar discoveries today. Mr. Roper had asked his fourth graders in a school in the western United States to collect some pond snails for a classroom aquarium. Don had put his snails in water in a closed plastic bag. When he brought them to school the next morning, he left them on the window sill near the aquarium.

"Those snails are dead ones," his friend, Leonard, told him.

"Gee, they don't seem to move. But I used the pond water to carry them in. Why should they die?"

Roseanne overheard their conversation and suggested, "Maybe the snails are cold or hungry. What do snails eat?" she asked.

Don and Leonard both said "Waterweed." Don dipped his hand into the aquarium, lifted out a sprig of waterplant, and inserted it into the plastic bag with the snails.

Mr. Roper started off the morning's work with a mathematics lesson. Leonard finished his assignment quickly and wandered over to the window sill. The snails were crawling about. He summoned Don excitedly.

"See, they were hungry. They're all right now."

"I don't see any bites out of that weed," remarked Don, to which Leonard had to agree.

"Could it be the warmth of the room and not the weed that woke them up?"

Mr. Roper was more interested in Don's unfinished math, but he quickly observed their intense interest and told them science would be next so that the whole class could share the problem of the snails.

It took several days of investigating and reading, more snails, more bags of water, weeds, cold, and warmth before the class decided that the snails had had a breathing problem in Don's closed bag and that green plants in sunlight provided the oxygen they needed.

It took Priestley many years to come to his discovery, which was then new to the world. Don, Leonard, Roseanne, and the other fourth graders also made a new discovery—new to them, that is. They were aided by materials which posed the problem (a closed ecological system), the sharing of observations and hypotheses among class members, the books which have been written for children on this topic, and the encouragement of the teacher.

It might interest you to reread the *Sink and Float* section and to list the facts the children discovered and the relationships they formulated from their own experiences (we may say that they discovered these relationships, too). No one reached the level of understanding that Archimedes did in any of the lessons quoted. Reputedly, the ancient Greek came upon his concept spontaneously during his ablutions, it was actually an end product of his long effort to test the purity of the King's crown. Discoveries do not have to be completed at once. It is more important for them to be genuine in the child's experience and on the level of his maturity—that they be ongoing and motivated by an inner drive.

Consider the teacher's role in aiding the discovery process. What can the teacher do to foster discovery? What does he not do? The next lesson illustrates two ways in which teachers can affect children's mental operations as they undertake to probe the world about them.

"TENEBRIO MOLITOR"

"Tina!"

But his wife was still in the shower. Fred continued to wrap his lunch, slowly and deliberately, noting that there were still fifteen minutes before he needed to start the car. Time for a quick pipe and a last minute glance through Pound's *Philosophy of Law* for today's quiz. It was good to have time to spare; he arranged his life that way, and Tina was gradually learning to do the same. A very small apartment and only his wife's salary as a substitute teacher to live on at present could so easily add up to tension—even in a new marriage. One more year and his law degree should net him the income a couple could live on with a modicum of dignity. Then Tina could complete her license requirements and gain tenure in the local school system—all before they planned a family. It was good to plan. Good to have time.

By the time Tina's bobby-pinned curls had found their way from the steaming shower to the perking coffee, Fred had assumed a benign judicial air. He waited for the first few swallows to bring her circulation to a state of human receptivity.

"I didn't know you'd taken up fishing."

"Fishing?" Her loosened grip on the cup handle slopped black liquid into the saucer.

"Those worms in our refrigerator . . . I thought they were sweet mixed pickles in the carton. I nearly put some of those squirming brown things on my sandwich!"

"Oh, the *meal*worms!" Her laughter woke her into a happy relaxed state. "What a shame, you had your juices all set for trimmings. I'll buy some pickles today."

"What, pray, are mealworms doing in our refrigerator?"

"They're slowing down their metamorphosis."

Fred bowed slightly as he swallowed between pipe draws. "Does that mean they'll be spending a nice long visit with us?"

Tina left her coffee and went over to the arm of her husband's chair. She cupped his head in her hands and gave him a quick kiss above the bridge of his glasses. Her clean soapy fragrance increased his disposition to accept her life's vectors.

"They're for my fourth graders! You see, the firm that supplies them sent them a week too soon. We haven't finished the ice cube unit yet. They'll just be inert until I take them to school. Besides, they can't escape from the carton if you don't remove the lid."

"Won't mealworms be rather stimulating for some of your more excitable charges? You know, a Freudian reaction and all that."

"They didn't mind the gerbil."

"Oh yes, that hamster with a tail!"

"It's not a hamster. It lives in the desert."

"Well, I thought the whole point of using hamsters with children—and with young female teachers for that matter—was that they didn't have tails."

"I don't think Freud had the key to everything. It's the atmosphere the teacher creates that determines the reaction of the children, in education anyway."

"That's your progressive school background—environment versus the inner urge!"

"Well, it must be something. Since I only had eight credits of summer courses to start me off, you must admit I'm not doing so badly. A creative, accepting atmosphere works just as well with the disadvantaged as it does with suburbia."

"You know, Tina, I sometimes glimpse our future family atmosphere—children crawling midst dogs, cats, and guinea pigs, and being leaped over by a kangaroo rat!" Fred chuckled as he indicated the kangaroo's eight-foot jump with a wave of his pipe.

"And why not? You passed the test already."

"What test? On Dean Pound?"

"No, silly. The test I gave you when we were going steady."

"Say, let me in on it."

"One day you came to the house and I dumped Charlie into your arms; you didn't even wince. So I knew we'd have the same view about living things. That was important to me."

Bran

"Charlie! Yes, I remember him. A rat with a beige-colored hood. So that was a test, was it?" He jumped up, knocked out his pipe, and picked up his attache case. "If I don't scram now, I'll get a zero on today's test."

They hugged for a precious moment. The day, for each, had started on solid footing.

One evening about a week later, the mealworms were paroled from their chilly prison. They had hidden themselves in the folds of the crumpled newspaper which loosely filled their carton. Fred and Tina had finished supper (a substantial casserole with sweet mixed pickles) and were working with assembly-line precision at the kitchen table–desk–dinette—a dropleaf against one wall.

"One, two, three, four into the sandwich bag. Gee, I hope I don't go groping around for the wrong sandwich bag tomorrow!"

"I'm putting all my kaboodle into a shopping bag, so you won't have to worry."

"—a spoonful of bran from the other container, puncture a few breathing holes with a darning needle, staple the top, then into a brown paper bag. Nine. How many of these did you say you needed?"

"Eighteen and a few spares. They brought two new kids into the class today—now there are thirty-six. That's the penalty for having the brightest section on grade. One was a frightened little girl with a high IQ, rejoicing in the name of Angelina."

"I thought your kids didn't have high IQ's."

"There you go again, putting everyone into a stereotype. High for our school anyway," Tina added quietly, her honesty seeming to counteract her convictions.

"How are you going to get all those shoe boxes to school?" Fred indicated the piled obstruction between the sofa bed and the bookshelves.

"I'll manage somehow. A good thing that the children brought most of them. One of the fathers works at Thom McAn's. Let's put the other things in sandwich bags, too; that way it'll be easy to distribute everything."

"Where'd you learn all this efficiency?"

"I don't think I did. It sort of seems obvious to me. Since I haven't yet trained the children to be completely independent in selecting what they

Some school systems group children according to reading levels, some according to IQ's in each grade. The intention is to produce homogenous groups. What evidence is there that ability in science does or does not correlate with IQ or reading level?

Which items will have to be shared? What principle determines which items equal or exceed the number of children?

need—there seem to be so many of them falling over each other in that crowded room—I figure I'd better be able to deliver the equipment in one fell swoop . . . or, you know what?"

"What?" Fred was always delighted to be a sounding board when Tina thought out loud. He loved to watch how the original chaos became order.

"If everything were put into the shoe boxes—enough equipment for each pair of children in a lid or box bottom, then they could be on their own. I know! We'll put enough for *four* children in each box and lid; then they can work in groups."

"Like your own progressive school childhood!" They both laughed.

"I had fun learning. Why shouldn't all children?"

The four shopping bags with their assorted cargo barely survived the subway and bus rides, but by the time the children arrived the shoe boxes were neatly lined up on the window ledge. Each contained two sandwich bags with four mealworms apiece and a small pile of bran, two soda straws cut in half, two small squares of paper for scooping up stray worms, two little flashlights, and four hand lenses. Lights and lenses were supplied by the school storeroom.

It was not the first time the children had found their tables arranged in groups, but it always engendered a springy tiptoeing into place. To these fourth graders, the group arrangement meant something special, an excited sharing, something new to handle. It also meant a serious attempt to keep their voices low, at least not at screaming pitch; once they lost the privilege of working together for a week because their teacher said they couldn't be trusted with freedom. But that was before Mrs. Weiss. She seemed to expect

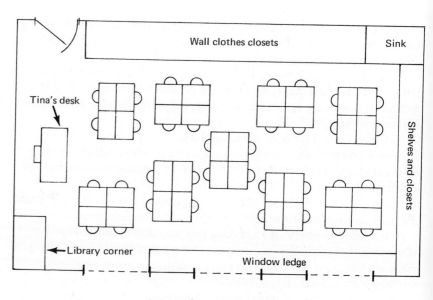

Arrangement of Tina's classroom

them to control themselves, and they tried to live up to her standards. Learning was fun in her class.

Tina waited quietly at her desk, nodding to each child who passed her, greeting each with a look or a hello as the children moved to their appointed seats along the far wall lined with closets.

What relation does seat arrangement have to the quality of learning? To the total atmosphere the teacher creates?

"Nelson's seen the boxes," she thought. The boy was nudging his neighbor and indicating the window ledge.

"Now that I've put some things inside those boxes Nelson brought from home, they are ready for you. You will need to work in pairs. Will you choose your partners at the tables right now?

There should be both freedom and organization in these preliminaries. In what circumstances can teacher organization be omitted?

"You tiptoed so quietly into the room this morning. Do you think you could select one person from each table to go quietly to the window ledge and take one box for the four of you?"

It was the swiftest "quiet" walk Tina had ever seen!

As the lids came off and the box contents were shared, Tina walked around and pushed a lid or a box bottom in front of each set of partners. "You might find it helpful to put the things in here," she said to each couple.

What advantages could this procedure have over prior directives?

Suddenly, from the group near her desk there came a sustained scream. Tina moved quickly toward Angelina, but the child rushed past her and buried herself in the clothes closet, sliding the door shut in front of her.

"And what did you do then?" asked Fred, as they had their tea-time cups of coffee.

Before reading further, try to decide what you would do in such a circumstance.

"Of course I went to the closet, opened the door enough to let my voice reach Angelina, and told her that she needn't go near the mealworms if she didn't want to and that she might like to read in the library corner when she felt like coming out of the closet."

Fred stirred his sugarless coffee as he arranged his thoughts. No, he wouldn't press *his* point. Tina was really upset about something and it certainly wasn't Angelina's reaction. She'd obviously handled that most astutely. But her voice was high pitched and she was sitting almost bolt upright in the butterfly chair.

Emotional overtones often speak louder than words. Why was it helpful to both Angelina and Tina that a "third ear" was there to listen to them?

"What about the other children? How did they react?"

"They looked up for a moment and then went right back to work. There's something so marvelously attractive about living things, especially when you don't have to share them or take turns as they did with the gerbil. Raoul was the one who seemed most apprehensive; you see, he doesn't know how I act yet and maybe he expected I'd be angry or something. Raoul is the new boy who came with Angelina. The other children know we can all accept differences."

"But something else happened?"

By what evidence did Fred know?

"Yes, how did you know?" Tina put her coffee cup on the floor and relaxed into the canvas spread of her chair—that space-consuming butterfly which seemed to fill their small apartment. But it held happy memories for them of the days before they became engaged, so they gave it a place of honor.

What can the child discover?

"Everything was going beautifully. Rutherford—you know how ingenious he is—was trying to get two mealworms to meet in the middle of a straw; Chou Lee was blowing down his straw to push his mealworm out; Patricia was shining the flashlight into one corner of the box—'to see if the light would keep the worms from the corner,' she told us; there was a lot of quiet discussion going on at each table and much scrutinizing through the lenses."

Fred poured himself another cup of coffee and waited.

"And then Mr. Litchfield came in—"

"The new Assistant Principal?"

"Yes, we've grown so much we've got to have two of them—"

"You don't like him?"

"I don't know much about him, except today. Just listen." Tina was sitting stiffly again, holding on to the iron supports of her chair. "First he peered at what the children were doing—and I swear he actually blanched. There was a mealworm crawling along the floor toward his shoe. Janet bent down and scooped it up with a piece of paper . . . so much know-how in such a short time. . . ."

"Litchfield's evidently not a fisherman!"

"Or a biologist! Or . . . well, you'll see. Mr. Litchfield looked as though he were searching for the right word with which to condemn me—and then Angelina emerged from the closet!

"Mr. Litchfield frowned and said in an overloud voice, '*What* is that child doing in the closet?' Of course, Angelina quickly retreated.

" 'She's new to the class, you remember'—Mr. Litchfield himself had deposited her with me—'and she's not ready to work with mealworms yet,' I explained.

" 'I'm sure she'd be quite ready if someone hadn't frightened her.' I saw his eyes turning toward Cyril who was sitting next to Angelina's empty chair. Cyril stared back at him with that insolent expression he uses to counter the threat of authority.

" 'Did *you* frighten Angelina with a mealworm?' he asked in a severe tone. Cyril just held a mealworm by the tail and watched it wriggle. Actually he held it in front of his own face so that he could look at the Assistant Principal at the same time.

"It was Mimi who answered, "No, Mr. Litchfield, we'd only just opened the box when Angelina screamed.'

" 'She screamed?'

" 'Well, she was scared. She maybe hasn't seen them before.'

" 'And have you seen them before?'

" 'No, but we've got the gerbil.' As though that explained everything—perhaps it did. Mimi is so motherly with all living things, be they worms or Assistant Principals."

"Then what?" asked Fred.

"Mr. Litchfield just said, 'Thank you, Mrs. Weiss,' and went out, but I could tell that wasn't the end. At three o'clock there was a note in my box."

Fred read it aloud: " 'Memo to Mrs. Weiss from Mr. Litchfield: Please stop by my office on your way out today.' So you stopped by?"

Imagine possible reasons for Mr. Litchfield's attention focusing on one child as the source of the trouble.

"Well, he said he admired my originality, but wasn't there too much freedom and lack of direction in my lessons? Wouldn't it be better for all the children if they knew what I expected of them—standards of behavior, what to look for in science, et cetera, et cetera,—"

What do you think about these suggestions?

"And you said nothing because there's too big a gap between your ideas and his."

"He didn't even give me a chance to answer. I was afraid he was going to forbid any animals in my room, but, no, he wants me to watch Mr. Rodin teach. Mr. Rodin has agreed to use the mealworms with his class to show me how, if I'll lend him my equipment. The nerve! I do all the work, and he just cashes in."

"You're upset about the interference?"

"No, I think I'm upset because Mr. Litchfield wants to show me how to dominate the children's thinking."

"You don't know he wants to do that."

"Something like it anyway. And I don't want to watch Mr. Rodin dominate his class."

"You think he'll do that?" There was silence while they both searched for the realities of the situation.

What are the realities of the situation?

"Do you think you might learn something useful from Mr. Rodin? After all, he's an old hand at the teaching game. He's chosen to stay with the fourth grade, you once told me, instead of being with a prestigious sixth. Maybe he at least has a wrinkle or two you could pick up."

"But what will my poor children learn with Mr. Litchfield at the helm? He's promised to cover my class while I observe Mr. Rodin."

"They'll survive, no doubt. I wouldn't worry about that!"

"Maybe watching Mr. Rodin will be helpful—for some of his ideas. By the way, Fred . . . and it's not really by the way . . . how did your test go today?"

"Fine! In law you know what you have to look for, you learn it, and the test finds out if you know it. Teaching law must be so much simpler than teaching see-what-you-can-find-out-in-science to kids! And you only need books to do it; there are no briefs in the refrigerator!"

Science is sometimes taught by the law method Fred describes. What kind of learning takes place in such a case?

"Boys and girls!" Every boy and girl responded to the sound of Mr. Rodin's deep voice. "We've the pleasure of a visitor for today's science lesson."

In what way do you call the attention of children to visitors? Or do you?

The heads all turned around to view the visitor.

"Mrs. Weiss has come to see whether you can discover more about mealworms than her fourth grade did!"

"Mealworms?" someone exclaimed.

"Let's remember our hands when we speak. Yes, there are mealworms in those shoe boxes. I want each table to examine the worms to see what they are like, and what they will do. And of course you'll remember that they are living things; they can feel, so you won't do anything to hurt them."

Tina saw one of the taller boys wink and nod to a friend. Mr. Rodin saw it too.

"And no one will use them as a means of scaring anyone else. I'm sure you understand." He stared at the tall boy and then smiled pleasantly.

"As I bring the boxes to your table you can start working." The children set to work much as Mrs. Weiss's children had done. It seemed the directives didn't dampen their ardor. The initial explorations were much the same, too. Mr. Rodin circulated from group to group. He invited his visitor to accompany him.

At the first table a boy said, "See, my worm moves backwards."

"See how many things you can do to it to make it go backwards," suggested Mr. Rodin.

"Can I get some water?" asked the child.

"Certainly. Use one of the small paper cups to carry the water to your desk."

A girl was waving her hand for Mr. Rodin to come over. Tina followed.

"Look, they like to hide under this stuff. What is it?"

"Bran," Mr. Rodin said.

"Like bran flakes?"

"Something like it; what bran flakes are made of. How do you know it likes to hide? Could it be eating?"

"I can't see it when it's underneath."

"Here's something that may help." Mr. Rodin carried an inverted carton with a square hole cut in the top over to the girl's table. A piece of clear plastic was taped over the hole. "How about putting the bran and the mealworms on this plastic and then holding the carton over your head so you can see what's going on?"

"OO—oo, let me, too," from the others at the table.

"Take turns, and then tell each other what you observe."

At the third table, the children were shining the flashlight onto the mealworms and saying, "They don't like the light."

"Did you notice that most of the mealworms are in the box corners?" The children nodded. "How do you think the worms can tell when they are in the corners?"

"They've got things on their heads."

"Antennae."

"They feel with those things. They feel when they're in the corners."

"Can you find out how they sense the light and so know to go away from it?"

"With the antennae?"

"Could you find a way to test that?"

The fourth table seemed to have lost interest. The children were watching the table that had the carton. "Can we have one of those things?" they asked.

"Well, what's your problem? What have you found out? Tell me what you've discovered."

"I want to see if the worms can swim like Bert's doing."

Tina and Mr. Rodin glanced over at Bert's table. He had been asked to find ways to make the worm go backwards, but instead was dropping it into a cup of water and then rescuing it.

What is the value of supplying technical words at this point?

"How about finding out if they drink water?"

"How could I do that?"

"Any ideas?" Since none seemed forthcoming, Mr. Rodin produced several Q-Tips, the kind that have cotton wrapped around one end but not the other. He dipped the cotton ends in water and gave a Q-Tip to each child at the table. "Try these on your mealworms," he suggested.

After twenty minutes had passed, Mr. Rodin made an announcement. "It's time now to make notes on your discoveries. Here are some sheets for you to use. I'd like you to draw one of the mealworms as carefully as you can and then write at the bottom what you've discovered about the animals. Just one or two statements, or a drawing with a label will do. Don't forget to write your name on the paper. I'll give you the next ten minutes to complete the job."

Tina thanked Mr. Rodin for his help and asked if she could borrow some of his Q-Tips and the carton with the plastic panel for her group to use.

"And I'll show you the records when the children have finished. Maybe at lunch?"

Mrs. Weiss decided to let her children have another session with the mealworms that same afternoon. Since there had been no time to share the discoveries the day before, she began with the colloquium.

"Yesterday you made many discoveries about the mealworms. We'd all like to hear what you found out. Chou Lee, let's begin with you."

"Well, I know about mealworms because I go fishing with my father."

"Did you find anything new?"

"Yes, they climb into the straws, and even when I blew into the straw I had a hard time getting them out."

"I used a flashlight to make mine come out. He came out backwards."

"I tried that, but mine wouldn't move. I got another mealworm to crawl into the other end. Then they both stayed there!"

"I found that they went under the brown stuff—"

"It's bran," said Mrs. Weiss.

"—they went under the bran and they stayed in the corners. I don't think they like the light."

"I think they don't like heat. It's the heat not the light they go away from."

"How do you know?" asked several children.

"I put one corner of my shoe box on the radiator and when I put the worms into that corner they all moved away."

"I found they had thirteen sections, two little feelers sticking up at one end, and six legs in front."

There were other observations about the appearance and structure of the worms, about the way they moved, and about their reactions to the bran, to light, to the touch of fingers, to each other. Some of the observations were accurate; others were less so. There were some differences of opinion about what the mealworms did.

"Have any of you an idea of what you'd like to find out about the mealworms today?" Several hands were raised immediately.

In what ways does Mr. Rodin show that he is a more experienced teacher than Mrs. Weiss?

What are the essential differences between Mr. Rodin's and Mrs. Weiss's contact with children? What are the similarities?

Try to rate both teachers using these scales:

	Mr. R.	Mrs. W.
Concerning children:		
Rigid	____	____
Flexible	____	____
Permissive	____	____
Concerning content:		
Rigid	____	____
Flexible	____	____
Permissive	____	____

"I want to find out if it really is the heat or the light they don't like."

"Have you an idea of how to find this out?"

"I think if I had a piece of glass, the light would go through but not the heat."

In what ways does Mrs. Weiss encourage the children to *design* their investigations?

"Would anyone else like to work with Rutherford on his heat-light idea? You would, Raoul. I think you'll find a piece of glass in the science drawer."

"I want to find out if they eat the bran; or maybe there's something else they'll eat."

Mrs. Weiss said, "I have some oatmeal, some bran flakes, and corn flakes. How would you set about finding out what you want to know?"

"I can put a mealworm near each of these things and watch with the magnifying glass. A little of each so they can't get underneath. Can Janet and Patricia help me?"

"I want to know if they drink."

"You might be able to use these to help you." Mrs. Weiss produced the Q-Tips.

"What's that box for?" asked Nelson.

"What do you think you could use it for? Suppose you take it and see if it can help you find out anything."

"Mimi, what idea do you have?"

"I just want to experiment some more."

"Good, you do just that."

And so they all went to work. Tina went from table to table, but did not make any suggestions. She listened and showed appreciation of the comments the children chose to share with her. When she reached Cyril's table, she saw that he had strapped a mealworm to his desk with a piece of plastic tape. The worm was wriggling violently.

"You feel like hurting the worm," she said in a quiet, accepting voice.

"I want to see what it'll do."

"You'd like to see what it will do when it's hurt."

Ways to accept children's feelings are described in Dorothy Baruch, *New Ways in Discipline,* McGraw-Hill, New York, 1949.

A faraway look came into Cyril's eyes and he continued to talk more to himself than to the teacher. "I run away when I'm hurt."

Tina recalled that when Cyril's father had come to school he couldn't tell her how many children were older or younger than Cyril; he thought that there were nine or maybe ten altogether. He said, too, that Cyril gave him more trouble than the others and that beating didn't seem to cure him.

"You run away when you're hurt, but this worm can't run away." Her voice was very quiet, like an echo to his expressed thoughts. Suddenly he looked up into her face.

Perhaps you would like to compare the previous interaction between Mr. Litchfield and Cyril with this interaction. In what way can the two events be related?

"It's nice here," he said.

"Maybe we should make it nice for the worm too?" She peeled the tape and freed the mealworm. Had something else been freed, too?

She turned toward the front tables. Look at that! Mimi was sitting close to Angelina. Mimi had a worm crawling on the back of her hand. Angelina was looking. Slowly Mimi's hand came near Angelina's.

"It won't hurt," Mimi encouraged. The worm crawled from Mimi's brown hand onto Angelina's palm, which looked a little moist to Mrs. Weiss.

Free discovery versus helpful hovering

Free and *discovery* are two separate terms. Of course, their meaning can be related to one another as well as to the meaning of structure in the choice of science materials. We will begin by considering the nature of *discovery* for the children confronted with structured materials in the previous lessons.

The children in both of the mealworm lessons discovered many facts: one child discovered the number of segments and the number of true legs a mealworm has; another discovered that mealworms can walk backward; and several children found that their mealworms chose places that were dark, cornered, or covered, that they moved away from the flashlight, that they wriggled, that they had antennae. No single child discovered all of these facts, but every child discovered several of them. None of them are momentous, but every child's discovery was new, unexpected, and self-selected at the time. The facts each child discovers are of the utmost importance to him—important in the ongoing process of his learning, important to his feeling of competence, important as knowledge that will not soon be forgotten. What has been discovered has been learned through the senses from manipulation of materials; it has been expressed in words and shared without contradiction by peer discoverers. We will probably never know—indeed, it does not matter that we do not know—why each child selected the particular facts he did. It matters only that he has discovered something about a phenomenon of this world and that he has learned it willingly, with inner drive. Expressed facts are most clearly defined, most firmly learned; but there are also peripheral facts—no less valuable, no less important to the learner—which remain at present on the preverbal level: Angelina discovered that she did not have to fear mealworms; Mimi discovered that she could help a friend conquer a fear; Cyril discovered that Mrs. Weiss could accept his feelings about being hurt, although she could not accept his act of hurting. Such things, learned only in a vague and transient manner, are still learnings which can be paralleled and enhanced by similar experiences later. Many facts about the mealworms themselves have also been discovered in this preverbal manner and will be more readily consolidated and clarified with new experiences because of this initial contact. The quality of discovering makes the process learned valuable to the individual.

Facts are only one aspect of discovery. Another is factual relationships. The latter might be considered constructed instead of discovered but we will use the word *discover* here to define the relationships a child expresses as a result of his manipulation and thinking.

The child who discovered that the mealworm moved away from the heat of the radiator expressed a relationship when he said that the heat and not the light of the flashlight made the mealworm back up. Although not yet tested or generalized this was a potential relationship based on the facts available to the discoverer. The question of the reactions of the mealworms to bran and oatmeal expresses another relationship which is being sought.

In the *Sink and Float* lesson, Mrs. Ross's children expressed a relationship between flotation in water and in air when they said that air makes things float. When Miss D.'s third graders said that if things are about the same size the heavier one will sink, they described another relationship. Mr. Roper's fourth graders discovered the relationship between snails, waterweed, and sunlight, and Miss Stevens' third graders found that the harder you push air into a favor, the louder it will toot. These relationships were all based on the facts available to the discoverers. Of course, any statement may be modified after further investigation and the discovery of new facts. The very habit of thinking in relationships is a step beyond collecting data—a step down the road to concept building. This is part of the work of scientists and another aim of our teaching.

The first experiences of discovery in our *Starting Tomorrow* examples are a small beginning and not at all the whole of science learning. Although these initial discoveries seem to be made at random, they were guided partially by the structural possibilities of the materials used and partially by the initiative of the discoverers themselves. However, Mrs. Weiss's second mealworm lesson did reveal that each child had an aim, a need, a desire to find out something rather specific. He had asked a question of his materials; his explorations began to take on the form of a model, a choosing, a beginning concept of certain possibilities.

Some of a child's choices are derived from his own previous experience, but, interestingly enough, some are triggered by what other children have said during the colloquium. Rutherford picked up the suggestion that heat and light are stimuli to mealworms, and Raoul joined him. Some children think up entirely new avenues of search: Nelson's eye went to the plastic-paneled carton: he wanted to find out how it could be used; others thought of investigating whether or not mealworms would drink.

The *freedom to choose* gives the learner a sense of ongoing discovery. Indeed, it reveals some ongoing drive within each child. We cannot tell in what way his work is important to him, but we can see by his concentration and devotion that it has meaning for him. He becomes emotionally and intellectually involved, even as an artist becomes involved in his creations. For, as Bronowski suggested, discovery is nothing less than a creative act.[19]

The structure of the materials not only offers the freedom to make meaningful and significant discoveries; it also sets limits on this freedom. There is freedom within an interactive system—within a small slice of the phenomena of the world. Materials are enticing enough in their relationship to one another and to concepts to be worth the time and energy spent in their investigation. They also limit what may be discovered by centering discoveries around a few related concepts. It is similar to a checker game: the pattern of the board, and number of discs, the rules of the game all form the structure—the limit of *freedom*; within these, however, a player is *free* to devise moves, to design a strategy, to interact with the moves of his opponent.

What happens when a child's freedom is guided, when discovery is subjected to outside suggestions?[20] In his mealworm lesson, Mr. Rodin suggested that Bert find all the ways he could to make the worm go backward. Bert immediately went outside his limitations and asked if he could have water—a good idea in itself. What did Bert do with the water and with the suggestion of making the mealworm back up? To

another child, Mr. Rodin suggested using the plastic-paneled carton to see what the worms were doing underneath the bran. Several children became distracted by the privilege of this offer; they, too, wanted a turn. The turn at the carton became more important than the drive to discover what the mealworms would do. Making suggestions *while the children are in the act of pursuing their own drives* somehow seems to divert their energy; they block their original interest in order to accommodate authority.

You can intuit this feeling somewhat if you imagine yourself pursuing a tactic in a game of checkers. Suppose you are planning a trap for your opponent which will force him to give you a double jump, when a friend whispers that you should try to gain a king instead. Can you empathize with the kind of feeling this would create? A conflict? A choice? A weakening of your drive and your own strategy? One important result of this form of backseat driving is that it blocks the discoverer's own initiative—the specific virtue the materials are designed to cherish.

In a very real sense, the teacher also makes discoveries every time he teaches a lesson. Teaching is an exploration as well as an art. Because of Tina's personality and her experience with an education she enjoyed, she felt free to pass on to her children the kind of learning experience she herself had received. It is true that she lacked the techniques which training in methods courses might have given her, but she approached many new experiences with an attitude of confidence, initiative, flexibility. She felt free to set up new routines with her children—to give them a new kind of learning experience. Although she resented the stringent limits Mr. Litchfield suggested and felt resentful when first asked to watch Mr. Rodin—reputedly a more orthodox teacher—conduct the lesson, she was able to appreciate the foresight and the better preparations of a more experienced teacher and to adopt what she discovered in his class into her own teaching style. Tina's school situation was also structured: her husband, Fred, helped her accept this structure and to move freely within its limits, and she restructured the classroom situation to allow herself a limited freedom. There is always a close relationship between the way a teacher feels about learning and the way his children learn. The

[19] J. Bronowski, *Science and Human Values*, Harper Torchbook 505, New York, 1959, p. 24.

[20] An experimental investigation on this topic is recorded in an article by Brenda Lansdown and Thomas S. Dietz, "Free Versus Guided Experimentation," *Science Education* (April 1965), 210-13.

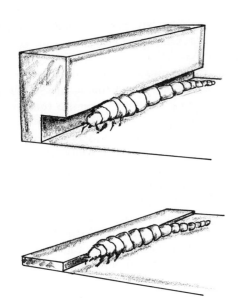

way a teacher feels—the way he perceives the structure, the limits, and the degrees of freedom—forms the base from which he structures his own classroom.

Now It's Your Turn We would like you to have the experience of making discoveries about mealworms without knowing any more than what you have gleaned from this chapter.

You can procure three or four mealworms from many pet and fishing supply stores. If they are not supplied with bran, fine oatmeal will serve as food and shelter. Little mazes which can easily be constructed (see diagram) may suggest other avenues of exploration to you. (See also *The Behavior of Mealworms,* Teacher's Guide, the Elementary Science Study of the Education Development Corp., the Webster Division of McGraw-Hill, Inc., Manchester, Mo. 63011.)

Try keeping a diary of your observations and pursuing your investigations over two or three weeks. You may be in for some fascinating surprises.

What can you discover about these little creatures, whose Latin name is *Tenebrio molitor?*

Discovery as sciencing

Sciencing is for children

What does a scientist *do*? Very few people other than his colleagues have watched a scientist at

work—made a continuous study of his outward and inward acts. However, biographies as well as interviews and records by scientists themselves[21] exist and, through these, we have come to know many of the attributes and actions common to workers on the cutting edge of the scientific plow. We will explore a few of these and try to find what, if any, relationship they have to the little "investigators" in our classrooms.

There are basic similarities and important differences between the two. Both should be kept in mind. We emphasize the similarities when we carefully introduce the child to scientific procedures yet we are aware of the differences even then; the quality of discovering, for example, is quite different. In order to emphasize both the similarities and the differences, we will coin or adapt a word to describe the relationship. When a child races about a room, we do not call him an *athlete*, even though he is running. When he scrawls a sentence or his first essay (a noble paragraph or two), we do not call him a *writer*; yet he is writing. When he paints a picture, he is not called a *painter*, but he is painting. Similarly, when a child engages in some form of discovery, when he constructs a relationship new to him, when he designs a simple investigation, he is not a *scientist*. He is, nevertheless, *"sciencing."*[22] Permit us the license of inventing a word for the present purpose of painting the world of science, if only because we need to rid ourselves of the dilemma which arises when we confuse the child with the adult. True, the child can pretend to be a scientist, just as he pretends to be a merchant when he sells lemonade at his garden gate or a father or a baby when he plays house. It is one of the roles he tries on for size—the reality he may one day become.

Sciencing will mean *engaging in exploration of the material universe for the purpose of seeking orderly explanations of the objects and events observed and testing these explanations.*

An overall similarity between the acts of the

[21] James D. Watson, *The Double Helix,* Atheneum, New York, 1968, is a particularly interesting and readable account of theoretical biologists at work.

[22] Used prior to this writing in Paul F. Brandwein, Fletcher G. Watson, and Paul E. Blackwood, *Teaching High School Science: A Book of Methods,* Harcourt Brace Jovanovich, Inc., 1958.

scientist and those of the child is that they both have freedom within their structural limits. However, the nature of the freedom and the extent of the structure are very different for each.

If you recall that by structure we mean a pattern of relatedness (as previously discussed in terms of the materials the teacher provides for the child and the learning atmosphere which he creates), what patterns of relatedness form the structure within which a scientist operates? A scientist is born into a society, and each society in each historical epoch has its own structure limiting what he may do. The political, cultural, and economic aspects of a society are determined in some measure by the relatedness of the ruler to the ruled. This pattern is repeated whether the society is Babylonian (ruled by priestly kings), medieval (ruled by landowning lords), or democratic and capitalistic (although there are many interpretations of who constitutes the power *élite* in the modern United States, no one denies that one indeed exists).

The scientists of Babylonia were astronomers and astrologers whose work was related well to the needs of trade and agriculture. By observing the planets and stars in those ancient days, astronomers were able to forecast the seasons and provide merchants with compass guidance across the deserts. The astonishing accuracy with which the Babylonians predicted such rare events as eclipses also gave credence to their astrological predictions of personal tragedy or success, blending their reputation for wisdom with a belief in their ability to interpret omens. The pattern of Babylonian society, with its special economic needs and social hierarchy, provided the structure within which the scientists worked; their freedom, no doubt, was to choose the particular heavenly bodies they wished to observe.

Medieval scientists were usually chemists or alchemists. Because of the need for gold and its general scarcity, the lords hired alchemists to search for new sources of this medium of exchange which the merchants had in greater abundance. As we know, the merchants eventually gained dominance since trade as a source of wealth was superior to the transmutation of base metals into noble ones. The alchemists sought gold unsuccessfully within the structure of their medieval society, but many of their individual discoveries later formed the beginning of the knowledge of chemistry.

Today's scientist has hundreds of areas from which to choose. In the United States, however, Federal grants supplying funds for expensive equipment are more readily won in some areas than in others. Opportunities for Government-sponsored research are even available in universities. While private industry pays some attention to basic research which may produce more knowledge than money, it devotes most of its research resources to the search for marketable products. Today, although the choice is wide, it still imposes limits; a structure is present. Within its limits, a scientist can find his own niche—pursue discoveries close to his own interests.

The scientist does not choose his society; he is born into it (he may, of course, escape persecution by moving to friendlier shores). Whatever the society in which he lives, he works within its structure, using its opportunities and accepting its limitations. The child does not choose the structured materials he manipulates; the teacher places them before him. However, the child is then free to do what he wishes with the materials.

The scientist brings knowledge to his work from prior experience and reading, both of which represent a *historical* accumulation of facts and theories. A child brings his *personal* background and prior learning to each science experience; history is represented in a very special way for him. Materials are selected so that the child may discover in a short period of time what is already known to scientists. The original discoveries involved many false leads and tentative theories; concepts were formed as experimentation progressed. The process may have taken months, years, or, viewed as a whole, many lifetimes.

The child, too, begins to form concepts as he works, particularly during the colloquium; the careful selection of materials allows him to repeat historical discoveries and develop appropriate explanations during one or two class periods. He has a mini-experience of what a scientist experiences: he faces the unknown, he freely explores, he follows hunches, he shares his findings and develops explanations cooperatively, he tests tentative theories. The scienist publishes his results; the child dictates or writes his findings which are then reproduced for all to read in the Investigators' Log. In fact, the group authorship of a log is comparable to the many names which are often listed as coauthors of a science article.

The careful structuring of materials does not mean that children will not have to cope with false leads or that they will follow a single path to discovery. To the contrary, children not only observe inaccurately at times, they also pursue paths which are not germane to the major concepts. These many different paths often lead to discrepant events. A discrepant event is often, but not always, the starting point of investigation or research; it is an unexpected happening which does not fit the theory or model we have come to accept.

We all meet such situations in our everyday lives. Billy comes home from school, recounts his successes of the day, and then droops instead of running out to play. For Mother, Billy's quiet lassitude is certainly unexpected; she is confronted by a discrepant event. She takes his temperature to test her hypothesis that "he's coming down with something." She asks him if he has quarreled with Stevie again, or has he lost the precious sweater Grandma knitted for him?

We return from the theater to find the drawers in disorder, the typewriter and television set missing, the front door crowbarred. We ask the police to investigate. And so with the scientist. Suppose he finds a circle in the petri dish where mold did not grow, tracks produced by unexpected masses in a cloud chamber, a solution that looks like a colloid when a precipitate had been expected, or a hurricane that gathers power after apparently expending its energy. The scientist investigates. So does a child: air made a loud bang; air made a little bitty noise like a whisper; "My ping-pong ball sank"; "Mine didn't."

Every investigator, whether a layman, child, or scientist, brings the whole structure of his background to a discrepant event. If we put ourselves into one of the more everyday situations just described, we realize that our thinking would not be exactly logical; it would not follow *the* scientific method. A whole cluster of thoughts and possibilities would probably come crowding in at once. Many lines might be explored. First, we could attempt to assimilate the discrepant event into a pattern we have come to accept: we tell Billy to go out and play, spiriting away the discrepancy. Fleming could have thrown that petri dish away without really focusing his attention on the empty patch; other biologists must have done just that, for this could not have been the first time *Penicillium* had grown in a bacteria culture and inhibited it.

As we have seen, very often children do not notice a discrepant event; the teacher brings it to their attention. Once the discrepant event has been observed and accepted as a challenge, the scientist tends to investigate it using methods very similar to those employed by layman and child. His procedures are many and varied; no one order can be claimed as a guiding rule. We are rather partial to the definition offered by Percy Bridgman, Nobel Laureate in physics: "The scientific method, as far as it is a method, is nothing more than doing one's damnedest with one's mind, no holds barred." [23]

"Doing one's dammedest," of course, includes observing objectively, communicating clearly with other scientists, measuring accurately, forming and testing hypotheses, and following one's hunches, however "unreasonable" they may seem. If a hunch happens to lead somewhere, the "reason" is found later! Two other important techniques are finding hidden likenesses and constructing models (see pages 61-67 and 122, respectively).

Many scientific activities have their counterparts in the life of the child who is sciencing. The opportunity for free discovery within the limits of structured materials seems particularly parallel. The meaning these activities have for a child becomes evident to the teacher during the colloquium. It might be profitable for you to concentrate on a few specific evidences of sciencing as you read the next lesson, making a note when each occurs. In Chapter 2, we elaborate on the evidences of sciencing which can be found in colloquia and place them in a larger framework. A full set of evidences and techniques of recognizing and recording them are found in Chapter 8, where they are used to evaluate the science lessons and the growth of each child.

[23] P. W. Bridgman, "Prospects for Intelligence," *The Yale Review*, Vol. 34 (1945), 450. Copyright Yale Univ. Press.

The next lesson abundantly illustrates the following:
1. Observation stated.
2. Observation clearly expressed.
3. Investigation suggested.
4. Question asked about the topic under investigation.
5. Relationship described or suggested.

HOOK UP A CIRCUIT

"This science unit you proposed for all sections of the sixth grade . . . on electricity, is it going to work with my children?" Aileen Provost toyed with a brownie on her luncheon plate.

"What about your children?" asked the science teacher. "I taught them as fifth graders, but they may strike you, as a newcomer . . . ."

"You didn't teach all of them. Now there are the bussed-in children."

John McIver felt tension gripping his throat. He swallowed too large a gulp of hot cocoa; it burned all the way down. "Count ten," he said to himself while he concentrated on spiriting away the emotional as well as the physical burning sensations. "Tell me about the bussed-in children," he managed to articulate in an unnaturally clipped rhythm.

"Well, it isn't that I don't sympathize with Mr. Rinaldi's idea that children we import to our 'exclusive' area must be integrated within each section as well as within the school . . . ."

"You agree with the *idea*?" John sounded almost empathic now.

". . . but, you see, where I did my student teaching, the children were all grouped by ability—reading ability in each grade. You knew the level you could teach on. But here it's all the way from nearly nonreading to one child who's reading on a high school level. It's an impossible range. And now . . . ."

"And now . . . ," John echoed encouragingly.

"The bussed-in children will probably hold the others back in all courses."

John felt like forcing Aileen to check and see where the new children's reading scores really fell, but instead he said, "You seem to be assuming that reading ability is a measure of other abilities."

"Isn't it?"

"I doubt if science will separate your sheep from the goats."

"Perhaps that isn't the real problem, or not the nub of it." Aileen paused and gazed at her left hand, pushing the engagement ring around with her thumb so that the large stone faced her palm. John waited, finishing his cocoa and keeping half an eye on the ten-minute leeway the cafeteria clock offered.

"I've heard your science classes are a free-for—" she stopped suddenly, embarrassed.

"Free-for-all in what way?" John laughed.

"With materials. They can do anything they like, the children can, and what will happen to my discipline when you leave and I have to pick up the pieces? I'll have to start all over again each time. It's hardly fair. I have to get all the children to learn something, *all* of them." She sighed as though the problem were too much for her.

"I see how you feel. You care very much that all the children learn."

"Of course I do."

"Is it possible that science may even help the children learn?"

"Of course! I don't mean it that way."

"But you're really worried that the new children will take advantage of the freedom I offer and will blow their tops when I leave?"

"Something like that." It sounded too much like the truth for Aileen to admit it freely.

"You're not the first teacher to have reacted this way."

"I'm not?"

"And I always make an offer in such cases. I'll make the same to you. I will stay in your room for the period following my lesson, as your assistant—maybe help a few children individually, or tutor one child—anything that will really help you. All the children are used to my pinch-hitting propensities. Then I can keep an eagle eye on potential trouble. It usually works and eases the transition into the driver's seat!"

"That's really nice of you. Are you sure you can spare the time?"

"I was going to ask you to do something for me."

"Oh?"

"Will you pick one of your children, anyone you'd be interested in watching closely—the one you choose will be of interest to me—and write an anecdotal record of what he does in the science lesson? What he says, too. I'll make a copy so that you can keep it in your files; it will be useful for your reports. For my purpose, this not only helps me learn about the ways an individual interacts with the materials, but it tells me quite a bit about the needs of that individual himself. It's part of the documentation for my M.A. thesis."

"I'd be really glad to do that." Aileen was cheerful for the first time during lunch. The reference to his thesis took away the fear that there was some ulterior motive in John's suggestion.

What benefit might accrue to Aileen from doing this?

"Monday, at ten!" John McIver called out as he dashed off to prepare materials for his afternoon kindergarten classes.

John and Sue McIver were the sparkplugs of the school board committee program to invite children from a nearby city slum area to attend their suburban school. It had taken many meetings and some soul-searching—or had it been some meetings and much soul-searching? This fall the plan had materialized.

No single idea, but a cluster of ideas motivated the plan. Sue had pressed the principle that class should be separate from caste. The city families were black and Puerto Rican, but there were wide differences in income and, therefore, in social and educational expectancies among these people forced by local prejudice and custom to live in ghetto conditions. Sue's plea was that the first children to be invited should come from middle-class families somewhat analogous to homeowners like the McIvers. It was agreed that every effort should be made to have children from the two areas intervisit, first as overnight guests and later for longer periods. Each suburbanite family was to "adopt" a child from the ghetto and the parents were to be brought into contact over common problems. It was hoped that this would be the beginning of genuine social visits. In this way, differences due to social conditioning would be minimal for the adults and almost negligible for the children. Since the families of the invited children were potential home buyers, once the children were established in the school and the families secure in their friendships through intervisitation, the hope was that the new families would be welcomed and feel welcome as property owners.

The Principal, Ignatius Rinaldi, suggested that a minimum of six bussed-in children be placed in one section, even though some classrooms might not have the privilege of getting to know the new children. This would avoid both the token representation and isolation of dark-skinned children.

There were sufficient differences in educational achievement in the school now to warrant the remedial program that had already been instituted. The school also provided programmed instruction in skills and certain high school students were hired to tutor individuals. The whole school benefited from these programs, and they would be extended to any of the bussed-in children who needed them. Mr. Rinaldi did not expect that they all would.

The whole project had become a veritable mission to the McIvers and their friends. John tackled every problem that arose in the school; Sue was a leader among the mothers. Both had participated in summer institutes in the South where children studied and played in a campus school while the adults—black and white, northerner and southerner—learned and tried out new ideas in education. John played his part with a fiery enthusiasm barely controlled by his knowledge of psychology. Sue assumed her role with the naturalness of a mother and of a nurse—the profession she had practiced before her children were born.

The teachers who participated in the planning were dedicated to making the program work, to providing a model for other communities to follow. Newly appointed teachers, however, needed time and help to overcome their unexpressed and frequently hidden or denied prejudices. Aileen Provost was one of these. An English major with an M.A. in teaching, she came from an upwardly mobile lower-middle-class family and had attended a prestigious college. Determined to teach in a "nice" neighborhood, Aileen was quite chagrined when she discovered that her class included many children—black and white—whom she classified as "problems" for one reason or another. Maybe it wasn't reason, but more a feeling. Her fiance, off on military service, was hardly a help.

Sue McIver invited Aileen to tea the Sunday before the first science lesson. John had taken the children on a picnic to see the new fall coloring. The women sat alone on a sunny porch surrounded by indoor window boxes resplendent with bulbous begonias in full flower.

"Tell me about the children in your class," urged Sue. "I know many of the families—of the natives, that is—and their problems. But I've also met the mothers of some of our invited children. I know how it helped when I was doing hospital work, to talk over the cases—at least those I found most trying. Talking often helped me figure out what attitude to take."

"I guess John told you that I was a bit distressed the other day."

"That's no wonder: your first job, a new environment, a need to show what you can do—to yourself, at least. The school board owes you some help, at least a willing ear."

"Well, first of all there's Carl—"

"Yes, he's one of the Calderone family. Every teacher throughout the grades has had trouble with Carl."

"That makes me feel better! He's so jittery and all over the place that it's hard to preserve calm in the room. And he doesn't seem to have any respect for authority unless you clamp down on him like a sergeant major. All the same, there's something appealing about him. He's frail, has quick coordination, makes jokes; he's a jack-in-the-box who shatters the sober moment. I suppose he's one of those underachievers. But how can I quiet him long enough for him to learn? He seeks attention, mine or the children's—a lion's share of it—all the time."

"He doesn't get even the lamb's share at home. The father works nights, so the poor mother has all the feeding, cleaning, disciplining to do, and she has to keep the house quiet while the father sleeps. Carl is the oldest of six children, except for Mary who's in a special school for the retarded."

"Then it begins to add up. But it's still hard to know how to cope with him. Chuck's different: always well dressed—he prefers to be called Chuck although his real name is William. He snatches things from the children and they resent it. And I don't feel I can trust him . . . he's . . . he's one of the bussed-in children. Then there's a very quiet little girl called Nancy. She hardly says a word. I don't really know what she knows."

"Is she Nancy Jones?"

"Yes."

"They live down this street. The father is on the school board."

"Is Nancy a slow learner?"

"I'm not sure what that category means. The Joneses feel that Nancy will develop best if she's not pushed."

"Then there's Luizanne: very much overweight, slow, deliberate, with an accent. I'm always afraid the other children won't wait for her to finish her sentence when she talks."

"Her family is Haitian. Her mother and Monte's parents were most active in helping us make arrangements for the transfer of children and in the selection of parents who might be willing to send their children."

Sue and Aileen discussed a few more of the children and then slipped off into talk about Aileen's fiance and her hopes that he would be home soon.

John spent the first hour of Monday morning in his science office preparing materials for his scheduled lessons of the day. He placed eight paper plates on a trolley for his sixth-grade sections. Each plate contained four flashlight batteries, a dozen lengths of No. 22 cloth-covered bell wire, and four little 1.4-volt light bulbs.

He stuck a row of 4 in. strips of masking tape along the edge of the trolley making it look like a surrey with fringe on top. He placed his reserve materials on the bottom shelf, also on paper plates: a dozen extra batteries, three

How would you expect Carl to react to science materials?

The following lesson did not require bells or buzzers, but these may be useful to offer children whose interest in lights terminates early. (See Matrix 7 on Electrical Interactions, pages 230-36.)

As you note who is sitting with whom, try to think why Miss Provost might have arranged the seating this way. (Carl and Monte share their table with two girls.) In what combinations would you have grouped the children?

dozen extra lengths of wire plus an uncut spool, and the roll of masking tape. Fifteen strippers and fifteen bells or buzzers completed the preparations. (He prepared similar trolleys for other lessons in the lower grades whose schedules called for science that day.)

Aileen arranged her children in groups for the lesson John was to conduct. The 30 children were seated four at a table (made by pushing their desks together), except for Nancy and Luizanne. As Mr. McIver placed a paper plate with its intriguing wares in front of each group, he said, "See if you can make the light light."

Miss Provost's record of Mr. McIver's lesson follows. Her own feelings, when interjected, are italicized. Miss Provost wrote:

Carl goes to work right away. He takes a piece of wire, pushes the cloth down from the end, places the protruding bare tip in his teeth, and strips off the cloth covering with the thumb and index finger of his left hand. He's holding a battery in his free hand. He applies one end of the wire to the top of the battery, holds it in place with a finger, then presses the battery bottom on the other end of the wire against the desk. The bare wire is in an arc from the top to the bottom of the battery.

"Ouch!" Carl calls loudly, jerking his hand away. *(Of course, all the other children look up.)* He skins two more wires, presses one on top of his battery and the other on the bottom, using the thumb and index finger of his right hand. Then, using various fingers of his left hand, he somehow maneuvers the two free ends so they touch various parts of the little bulb. "Damn!" he calls out as the bulb slips away from him. "Here, Monte,"he nudges the boy on his right, "wanna help me?" Monte, having just stripped his wires as he saw Carl doing, is holding two wires together on top of his battery and touching the bottom part of the battery to the little light. Just as Carl nudges him, Monte's light flickers. *(I think one of the wire ends fell somewhere on the lightbulb, but I couldn't really see.)* "Hey, see that," exclaims Monte, "I got mine to light."

"Do it again," urges Carl. "Here, you don't need no two wires on de top; one's gotta be on de bottom."

"But I didn't have any on the bottom and I saw a light."

Carl drops his equipment, replaces Monte's wires, one on the top and one on the bottom of the battery, and holds one wire end to the screw of the bulb. Now both hands and most of his fingers are in use. "Try de udder end somewhere," he tells Monte. Monte probes with the wire and suddenly there's a glitter.

"Yippee! We did it!" yells Carl. Mr. McI. goes over to the table. There is frantic probing, evidently to find the right spot again. Carl, wriggling in his chair, tries to help Monte find the spot. "But we did it," whines Carl.

"Here, you hold this 'ere." He shoves the battery and wires into Monte's hands, takes the two wire ends and the bulb, winds one wire around the screw and touches the bottom of the bulb with the other wire. *(Glory be! And then there was light!)* Carl removes the wire and retouches the bulb, making it blink.

"That's fine," says Mr. McI.

"We're de best scientists." Carl gets up and pats himself on both shoulders. "We're great. Here, Monte, let's me and you put our stuff togedder, de whole lot."

John is gliding around the room now, placing strips of masking tape on each table. As he does so, he says, "Maybe you can use this?" Carl seizes the tape and, putting the two batteries end to end, tapes them together. In the meantime, Monte is winding one piece of wire around one bulb and continuing the same piece of wire around the screw of the other bulb. Carl tapes wires on each end of his battery sequence and touches the unattached ends of his wires to the wires on Monte's bulbs in several places. No light. Next he puts both ends of his battery wires onto his tongue. He jumps up with a "Yow! Dere's juice, all right." He is standing now, and so is Monte. *(Is this where trouble begins? Maybe not; they are both working feverishly.)*

"Look," says Monte, "when it worked last time, we had one wire on the bottom of the bulb." Before he can finish speaking, Carl is touching the bottom of one bulb with the wire. It lights brilliantly.

What knowledge do you think Carl brings to this investigation? What knowledge is new to him?

What is the difference in the two boys' approaches to discovery?

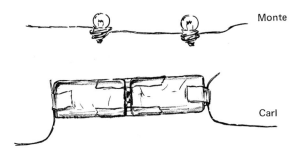

Monte

Carl

"See, I told you," says Monte.

"But only one lit." Carl touches the other bulb. It lights. "We gotta make both work," Carl announces. "Ain't dey bright?" He lights each in turn again. "Dat's 'cos we got both batteries working."

"Let me try." *(Monte is now asserting his rights.)* He holds one wire from the battery so that it runs along the bottoms of both bulbs, touching them both at once. "Now see if there is a spot that will make them both light," he tells Carl. Carl touches the wire Monte is holding with the wire from the batteries. Both lights glow gloriously.

Both boys begin busily taping their construction in place.

"You know what?" observes Monte. "They're both as bright as one alone!" He moves the wire to demonstrate.

"Gee," muses Carl, "dat's queer."

"I wonder why?" asks Monte.

Both boys sit down, replete with success; they contemplate their gleaming circuit with relaxed attention.

A moment later, Carl shoots up like a cricket, leans across the table, and snatches Bud's battery. Bud grabs it back; they tussle and argue. John McIver calls for the colloquium. *(Thank goodness!)*

Can you make each bulb light separately? Can you make them both light at once?

With a large class in a rather small room, the only possible space for a circle of all the chairs is usually around the walls. In what circumstances do equipment and furniture not detract from the interest of discussion? In what circumstances is such an arrangement helpful?

The children push their chairs into a wide circle and the desks into a cluster in the center of the room.

"There was quite a lot of physical illumination going on in this room," John McIver begins. "Let's see how much mental illumination there is. Let's begin here. Vera, what did you find out?"

"Well, I never used any of this electrical stuff before, and I found that you had to touch one wire to the bottom of the battery and wind the end around the bulb, and then take another wire and stick it to the other end of the battery and take the other end of this wire and put it on the bulb, and it lit." She leaned back in her chair and gave a wide grin.

"Ronnie?"

"I was working with Vera."

"Did the two of you find something else?"

"Yes, if the wires aren't held tightly on the battery, it doesn't work."

"Luizanne?"

"I couldn't . . . make . . . the light . . . light . . . until Mr. McIver . . . gave us the tape. Then I . . . put one end . . . of . . . a wire . . . on the bottom . . . of the battery . . . and the other end . . . round the bulb . . . and put the bulb . . . on the battery . . . and it worked."

"You used only one wire?" asked John.

"Only one wire."

"Did anyone else manage to light the bulb using only one wire?" Apparently no one else did.

Why is the word "circuit" introduced at this point?

"I wonder if you'd show us your circuit? I think everyone would like to see it."

Luizanne got up slowly and deliberately from her chair, went to her table, and held up her circuit. The light was off, but she pressed the tape and the bulb glowed. Albert's hand was raised.

"You've got to have a round circuit to make the juice flow."

"Tell us what you mean by round."

What type of child needs to be pressed to explain further? What type is best left with his first statement? What does this elaboration reveal about the meaning the materials have for Albert?

"Well, the electricity comes out of the negative end of the battery and goes along the wire and back to the positive end of the battery. It can go through the light or anything else, but it's got to have a round circuit."

"Monte?"

"I had two wires at one end and my light lit."

"You must have had a round circuit," said Albert.

"Could you show us?" asked Mr. McIver.

"It only happened once, I didn't have time to find out about it, because Carl and I began working together."

"Would you like to find out about those two wires at one end, next time?" Monte nodded. "So what did you and Carl discover?"

"We put two batteries together and two lights and got them both to work."

Carl was off his chair and back to his table. He held up the circuit proudly. "See, they're real bright."

"That's 'cause you've got twice as much juice—two batteries," said Albert.

"But one light or two lights, they both shine the same," countered Monte.

"Here," said Carl, shoving the circuit toward Monte. "You hold de batteries." He did. Then Carl showed how the loose ends could touch different places and light one or both lights. "De're both as bright as one," he affirmed.

"Any idea why?" asked Mr. McIver.

"Nope," said Carl, but several children looked thoughtful.

"Chuck, I saw you and Rodriguez doing some interesting things. You were with Albert and Bud."

"Rodriguez and I worked together. We made the wires hot—so hot they burned us."

Carl shrugged his shoulders with a look of who-doesn't-know-that? John McIver intervened. "It's interesting, isn't it, that several of you can make the same discoveries at about the same time? I noticed many independent discoveries of the same thing. Scientists have this experience, too. But you had something else you wanted to tell us, Chuck?"

"Yes, we used the covered wire to do the same thing, but it didn't get hot."

"That's because it's heavy," said Ronnie, "the electricity can't get through when it's heavy."

"Heavy" and "light" have many meanings for children. What other uses of these words do you recall?

"How do you know that?" asked Mr. McIver.

"I tried the same thing Chuck did, and I could feel it wasn't hot." Bud was waving his hand.

"Bud?"

"I did that, too, but I thought it could have been hot but I couldn't feel it because of the asbestos."

"Asbestos?"

"The covering."

"How do you know it's asbestos?"

"Asbestos keeps the heat away; Miss Orestes told us last year in Fire Prevention Week."

"Chuck, Rodriguez, Ronnie, and Bud all investigated hot wires."

"I did, too," broke in Carl.

"And Carl. When you held a bare wire across the battery from top to bottom, the wire got hot. On that you all agree. You seem to disagree about whether the covered wire got hot or not. Some of you have reasons about why it did or didn't. What shall we do about this?"

There was a kind of confused murmuring. John tried another tack: "Why did you skin the wires in the first place?"

Toward what concept is Mr. McIver now structuring his question?

"To let the electricity through," said Carl.

John McIver asked the children what they wanted him to record in their Investigators' Log, which would then be duplicated and given to each child.

Why did Mr. McIver let the question rest at this point?

The children agreed on the following statements:

We discovered that we have to have a round circuit to make the light light.
We put two wires on a battery, one at one end around the top and the

Discovery as sciencing   55

Statements beginning with "we" represent consensus. Individual discoveries have the child's name appended.

other on the bottom. We taped the wires on. We took the free end of one wire and wrapped it around the bulb screw, and touched the free end of the other wire to the bottom of the bulb, and the bulb lit up.

Luizanne lit the bulb using only one wire.

Carl and Monte used two batteries and two bulbs and both lights were bright, but one light was just as bright.

Chuck found that a wire got hot if he put one end on the top of the battery and the other end on the bottom. Ronnie found that the covered wire did not get hot—she thinks it didn't.

"Does anyone have an idea of what he might like to do on Wednesday when I will be here again?"

Delighted smiles and a few shaking shoulders greeted this remark.

Monte went back to the problem of how he had managed to make his light flick on with two wires on one end of his battery. Carl wanted to see how many bulbs he could light with two batteries. Albert planned to find out why two lights shone with the same brightness as one light in Carl and Monte's circuit. Luizanne wanted to find a way to turn her light on and off with some kind of switch. Chuck asked to use a big battery—the kind with terminals on top; he said the bulb would be brighter with a big battery. Rodriguez decided to work with covered and uncovered wires to find out if both got hot in a circuit without a bulb. Vera and Ronnie asked to have one of the two bells they had seen on the trolley; they wanted to try to make it ring. Nancy said she would just like to experiment some more with the materials; she was the only child in the whole class who did not make her bulb light.[24]

[24] A film for teachers on the way a lesson such as this one works with fourth graders is supplied by Starting Tomorrow Programs, 720 Fifth Avenue, New York, N.Y. 10019. "A Lesson Doesn't End" in their *Starting Tomorrow* series includes materials so that viewers can try to set up circuits themselves.

The meaning of errors in discovery

If you examine Aileen Provost's description of Carl and Monte's activities and conversation, you should find all of the six aspects of sciencing previously defined. Several recorded acts and statements by the other children also illustrate their sciencing activities. Actually the whole class participated in these scientific procedures, although we will concentrate on only one-third of these children in this section.

Perhaps you are concerned that some of the statements seem incorrect and some of the remarks irrelevant. In Chapter 2, "Meaning Through Use of Language," we will focus on the aspects of speech in this and subsequent lessons. For the present, we will analyze some seemingly false trails of thought, as well as the fact that Mr. McIver neither gave the children answers nor corrected their statements.

Monte's two-wires-from-one-end problem which gave him a momentary glimmer of light was an unsure or fleeting observation that he didn't have time to pursue. He decided to investigate the problem during the next lesson. Can you explain what might have happened? A planned investigation resulted from Monte's free exploration. He accepts the challenge: did the bulb light or not? It is a kind of discrepant event since everyone else, even Monte himself in his joint investigation with Carl, seemed to need *one* wire from each end of their battery to complete a circuit. (The fact that Luizanne needed only one wire altogether seems to have escaped Monte.)

Albert's statement that Carl's lights were bright because there were two batteries in the circuit ("you've got twice as much juice") seems obvious, doesn't it? Actually it is only a partial statement. We might say that based on the evidence available to the children at that time, the statement was correct. However, there are two possible ways of hooking up flashlight batteries and each method will have a different effect on the lights. When do you think John McIver's children will be ready for that discovery?

The problem of a wire not getting hot in a short circuit because it is covered evokes reasons from the children ("because it's heavy" and "the electricity can't get through") which raise additional questions that require explanations. Bud asserts that the wire might have become hot, but the asbestos prevented one from feeling it—a statement given him by another teacher and a transfer from last year's Fire Prevention Week. What link makes Bud put these two observations together? Relating perceptions is certainly one of the activities of scientists—but which perceptions?

How you associate appropriate rather than inappropriate facts.

The attempt to associate facts—to relate observations—is certainly a step along the road to sciencing; it may even *be* sciencing. Testing the association or relationship after predicting the results would be the necessary follow-up. When John McIver juxtaposed all of the facts and relationships suggested by the children and left the resulting confusion in their laps, their doubts increased. Their need to explore further was indicated by the willingness of several children to take up one or another of the problems during the next lesson. The responsibility of demonstration and the obligation to clarify the thinking involved lies with the children, with the people who are sciencing; that is where it belongs. The children are in the process of discovering, of checking and formulating concepts. Like any other aspect of education, science is not a finished product; like all learning, sciencing is an ongoing activity. The activities and responsibilities of child, teacher, and scientist are once more congruent.

The range of unclear concepts and incorrect observations resulting from the science lesson worried Miss Provost. She felt the outcome was chaotic and told Mr. McIver so! However, Aileen did admit that materials were a salvation for Carl; when she focused on his activities during the writing of her record, he seemed transformed, a different person from the Carl she knew.

"This is a first lesson, not the end product," John assured her when they discussed it during a common free period. "How much learning do you expect to take place in one lesson?"

"It's not that; plenty was learned, but some of it was plain incorrect."

"If someone tells you a correct answer after you've stated something incorrectly, do you remember it forever?"

"No—o, because otherwise I would have achieved 100% on recall exams." She laughed.

"You don't necessarily recall incorrect ones either. This is a process of finding out, checking, testing, repeating, which the children will undergo just as real scientists do. Many of the facts the children discovered were correct, and their joy made a deep impression on them. But did you notice how there was unsureness about the partial statements or the dubious ones?"

"You helped that by asking how sure the children were."

"Did I do that only for the doubtful answers?"

"I think you did."

"That's bad. I want them to rely entirely on their own evidence. I didn't mean to give clues that way. I'll have to watch myself. See how valuable it is to have someone taking notes?" They both smiled at the thought.

"How will children ever find out they are wrong if you don't give them even a clue?"

"By the materials I bring in next time. You see, scientists also relate facts to make generalizations which do not always pan out. And how do they realize this? They observe facts which don't fit—discrepant events. So I will structure the next lesson to make the inadequacy of some of the children's statements obvious to them. The situation will spawn discrepant events."

"What sort of materials?"

"Well let's take all this business about hot wires. I hadn't expected the lesson to go in this direction."

"You hadn't?"

"Well, it's all part of the structure, but usually classes don't do that first. I think it was the cloth-covered wire that facilitated that avenue of exploration. Or maybe the need of children like Carl for excitement spread to the other children. He obviously knew about short circuiting. I'll bring in plastic-covered wires for the next lesson. They can't be skinned with the teeth!"

"And what about the asbestos covering? Is that true?"

"Take a look." John handed her a new wire. It had an outer coat of tough blue plastic and an inner black layer.

"Doesn't look like asbestos to me."

"And how do you think the children will use these wires?" John asked.

"They can't get at the metal ends very well."

"Then I'll give them these," and he held up a pair of strippers. "It's quite hard to get the covering off these even with the strippers. My guess is that the children will strip the wires only for a short length at the ends."

"What will that tell them?"

Try the short circuit yourself to see what happens.

"What do you think? Try the short circuit yourself with this wire." Aileen did.

"What about Luizanne's problem? Will you bring in switches for her?"

"I think I'll present structures of switches, things that will conduct electricity and some that won't: short strips of various metals, paper clips, nails, lengths of different wires, pencil stubs, strips of aluminum foil, bits of wool, cotton, plastic."

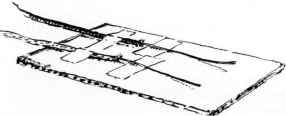

"Why not some asbestos?"

"That's a good idea. I hadn't thought of it."

"Won't aluminum foil melt?"

"It may, and then Luizanne will discover fuses! I usually show the children how to make a safe gap to test materials across: strap the ends of the wires onto an asbestos mat and the strips can be slipped under the ends."

"And you'll bring in the big type of battery for Chuck?"

John nodded. "Then I think I'll make a record of his acts next time."

"I wish you would."

And John felt a rewarding glow flush through him.

Follow-up possibilities for this lesson are described in Chapter 5. There you will be able to follow the growth of ideas and the clarification of observations which subsequent periods of sciencing can engender.

The teacher's role in fostering discovery

Structured materials freely explored certainly foster discovery; such discovery is of the "each to his own" nature, as well as part of a common conceptual scheme which may be discussed and clarified in a colloquium. While the children are essentially left alone during the investigation period, we have seen that, in reality, the teacher is still very occupied. He is an essential part of the structured situation—a necessary cog in the wheels of discovery.

The materials the teacher presents to the children at the beginning of a lesson must be carefully adjusted to the total situation: simple enough to offer avenues of investigative interest to every child, and rich enough to allow the children to explore a variety of learning paths. Items added at judicious moments are intended to stimulate further activity, to deepen thinking, or to facilitate operations; they are offered with a nondirective statement such as, "Maybe you could use this?" Two types of soaps were offered after the children were well into the *Sink and Float* problem, although both soaps may be included with the initial materials in some classes; the aluminum foil was not introduced until the children were trying to sink some objects and make others float. In the air investigation, further exploration with the plastic bags was stimulated by distributing party favors; new facts about what air will do then came to light and, with them, new joys of discovery. Masking tape is provided when children need something to hold the battery, wires, and bulbs in place; strippers are presented when they struggle to rip off the plastic covering from the electrical wires.

None of these suggested procedures is an absolute rule. We cite them to illustrate how some teachers furthered the discovery drive and to emphasize that the moment of presentation is not arbitrary, but a result of the teacher's judgment in relation to the children's needs and to their stage of interaction with the materials.

However, the "hands off" policy is a basic rule. If discovery is to be valuable to a child, he must experience it as a part of his sciencing; discovery must come from him, from his self-initiated interaction with the materials. The child is not discovering if the teacher encourages him to seek certain results, suggests that he do specific things, or tells him how to go about his work. In a discovery situation the teacher does not demonstrate, suggest, tell, or hover!

Naturally, the teacher stands ready to help in an emotional crisis; the psychological safety in which a child explores must not be blocked. "Will I get electrocuted if I touch the batteries?" is a frequent question. The teacher offers support to the fearful child: "Of course not," is his immediate reassurance; he may illustrate by touching the terminals to show that he does not drop dead! A vital matter is not open to investigation.

"Will my turtle die if we try to find out what he'll eat?" Emotional support can be readily given. The teacher may suggest (or ask, if it is reasonable to expect that the children will know) the kind of food which is essential—in this case, protein; some protein can then be included in each offering to the turtle. Children are not being conditioned to discover that adults abdicate this central role; instead they are being assured that the teacher provides a steady centralizing presence.

Facts and relationships from the nature of the interaction of materials are to be discovered by the children. This is an essential part of sciencing. Sometimes children are blocked in their manipulation of materials; they try certain arrangements and do not seem to succeed. This is not an emotional crisis, but a part of the frustration of discovery—a part of sciencing. However, such frustration must remain within the individual's tolerance level.

The teacher is a wise judge of each child's emotional limitations. Luizanne tried to hold the wires on her battery to light the bulb: they wouldn't hold. At that moment, Mr. McIver circulated around the room offering strips of masking tape. The children did not have to be shown what to do with the tape; they responded eagerly to the remark "Maybe you can use this?" With the bulbs and batteries deftly secured in place, the hands were free to manipulate the wires. Carl had already solved this problem by using Monte's fingers! He, too, welcomed the tape.

Nancy was the only child in Miss Provost's class who failed to make the bulb light. Do you think she learned anything at all about a circuit? What would you do to assure her of greater success next time?

As we have indicated, discovery is an ongoing process. It is not concluded at the end of each lesson. In fact, in this respect, sciencing for children is very close to the work of scientists. Each period of investigation raises more questions than it answers. Each child usually has an idea of what he would like to investigate during the next period. Sometimes children state specific needs: Ronnie and Vera wanted to make a bell ring; Chuck wanted to use a large battery; Luizanne wanted to work with switches. Then the teacher knows what materials to supply at the next lesson.

When problems such as "errors" in fact or relationships face a class, new materials may have to be selected on the basis of the teacher's analysis. To explore the hot wire problem, various types of covered wire as well as a variety of bare wires will have to be available so that the relationship of the metal path in a circuit can be separated from the function of the plastic or cotton wire covering. The concept of electrical conductors is part of this problem; it might be furthered by Luizanne's switch

investigation if she is given asbestos, plastic, and cotton along with the metals. In the colloquium the children might find that both air and various types of wire covering are nonconductors of electricity which will break a circuit.

A teacher facilitates discovery by introducing more complex materials after a child has discovered the essential relationships. (In discussing the *Eureka!* investigation, we suggested a more sophisticated lesson in which the children are presented with salt water and fresh water, thereby varying the medium of flotation, while using constant floating bodies—eggs. Another approach would involve objects having the same volume (size and shape), but different densities, that could be tested in water. Since the sixth-grade children have already discovered, at least kinesthetically, the essential elements of a circuit (close contact of metal to metal, the use of both terminals, the complete path), Mr. McIver will bring in sockets and screw drivers next time to facilitate circuit stability (or bulb holders to which wires may be easily attached in slots). The children's attention can then be directed toward discovering other aspects of circuitry.

Discovery is enormously stimulated during a colloquium. The details of this will be fully examined in Chapter 2, but we have already seen many features which foster the ongoing discovery process as children share their observed facts and tentative relationships.

Discrepant facts come to light during the colloquium. When the teacher juxtaposes seemingly contradictory statements made by the children, his manner is nondirective. He is conveying that both observations and/or suggestions are equally worthy because they come from the assembled investigators: "Can you find a way in which both these statements are correct? Can you account for them? Or do we need to look more carefully? Did short-circuited wires get hot when they were covered, or didn't they?" Two discrepant facts. "They didn't get hot because they were heavy. They didn't get hot because they were covered. They might have been hot, but we couldn't feel them through the covering." Three discrepant explanations. Since the teacher is not judging these statements—not choosing among them —the children accept the challenge to think, to do, to discover further. The teacher makes continued discovery possible as much by not putting a value judgment on any results as by bringing in suitable materials.

In the air investigation, Leslie said that air was soft in his bag while Violet said that it was hard in hers. Discrepant facts. Violet explained that the bags had a different amount of air in them, providing a way for all the children to include these discrepant facts in their schema of knowledge. In the *Sink and Float* lesson, however, the discrepant fact that one soap sinks and the other floats, although both look and feel alike, cannot be included in the one schema of thought all the children had accepted: lightness and heaviness determine flotation. They then discovered a new relationship, actually a model of a relationship since it was not based on an observation, but on a mental construct: one soap was Ivory and had air in it. Another group discovered a different model: things had to be light for their size to float; Ivory must be lighter for its size than the other soap.

A model resolves discrepant events. This resolution suggests predictions which can then be tested. The value of an explanation or model can be discovered through further activity. A teacher notices discrepant events and brings them, with total approval, before the gathered assembly.

To teachers who like each lesson to be a finished product—to be neatly summarized, to arrive at a definite stage of knowledge or a certain page in the text—discovery lessons may seem chaotic or, at least, disquieting. Discovery lessons are not for those afflicted with *lysiphobia*, the fear of loose ends! Nothing is tied in bundles during a discovery lesson, except perhaps a little happiness in each child as well as some tension upon which the next lesson draws. A carefully wrapped and tied parcel can be put away for Christmas and forgotten; a piece of knitting demands attention until it is finished. Discovery is unfinished business, and unfinished business keeps gnawing at us. We think about it and thinking gives birth to wonder, to energy, to drive, to an urge to discover further. The unfinished business of discovery lives inside the discoverer and needs only opportunity to be released. The type of lesson we have been describing brings release—and more tension!

Discovery resides with the *lysiphile*!

Finding likenesses, external and hidden

Whether people perceive likenesses more readily than differences or vice versa seems to depend as much on the extent of the differences as on the familiarity of whatever is observed.

Those of us who meet a new ethnic group for the first time usually have two reactions: we cannot tell one individual from another *within* the group, and we immediately notice the major external differences that distinguish *between* groups. Yet individuals stand out strongly *within a familiar group*, while the human characteristics *between familiar groups* blend as one.

An infant whose family pet is a Dachshund does not immediately recognize a German Shepherd as another "doggie." All he sees is the obvious *difference between unfamiliar groups*. Considerable education is necessary before a person perceives that the skeleton of a frog is structured along the same pattern as his own—again, the *differences between groups*. On the other hand, before a person pays a naturalist's close attention to the swarm of small creatures that buzz and crawl in a summer garden, he fails to distinguish between the flies, gnats, spiders, and beetles which may compose a summer evening's annoyance. Upon gross inspection, these all appear to be very much alike; they're "bugs." Individuals *within an unfamiliar group* appear uniform.

A baby will respond with the word "Dada" to each male entering his house—at least for an embarrassing period. However, the external differences between "Mama" 's and "Dada" 's seem gross enough for him to perceive them as separate groups. Indeed, it is a long time before he thinks of "Mama" 's and "Dada" 's as *parents*, thereby finding similarity *between groups*.

Via attributes and analogy

A large part of a child's education consists of helping him to see likenesses which are not obvious. In the long run, it is an economy of effort to be able to process many data into a category, to recognize many dissimilar objects as a group.

Objects can be grouped in many ways. We will investigate only two principles here: grouping by

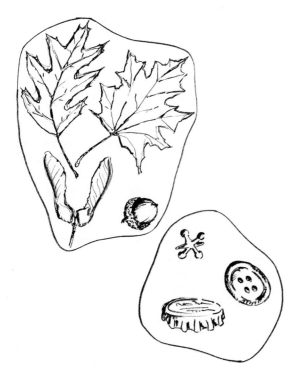

envelope or a small plastic bag containing assorted objects or pictures and then ask him to put some of them into groups—or "sets," if he knows that word. Suppose the bag contains a red oak leaf, an acorn, a green maple leaf, a maple fruit, a red soda bottle cap, a red jack, and a green button. Into what groups would you place these objects? Since you do not have the concrete things in front of you, use your imagination to try a few ways. This activity provides a lot of opportunity for initiative, doesn't it? Choosing all the colored or pointed and rounded objects would be grouping by external likenesses. Suppose the items are grouped as the illustration at the side of this page instead. Can you describe these sets? Can you find the principle of selection? If you wanted to add a package of dried yeast (those granules which come wrapped in a foil envelope) to the illustration, where would you put it? Why? That's a hard one. Do you see any resemblance between the yeast and the red marble problems? What about a mushroom? Would that be more difficult to place?

Ten to twenty buttons, no two the same, in an envelope for each child offer another good challenge to thinking and originality. The buttons can differ in size, color, material, shape, number and position of holes, and texture. As kindergarten, first- and second-grade children group and rearrange such objects, many likenesses become apparent to them. Each child needs a chance to find words for his classification, to communicate his basis for selection. Each child needs a chance to figure out the theory behind a partner's grouping and to try to fit new objects into the sets as they are perceived and described.

Such activities—individually, with partners, or in small groups—intrigue children, stimulate their thinking, give them a valuable opportunity to notice likenesses and to classify objects into their own selection of categories.

Many suggestions and a variety of materials are now available for teachers to use in helping children develop the ability to group things by likenesses. A very productive set of materials, the *Attribute Blocks* developed by William Hull,[25] consists of wooden triangles, squares, circles, and diamonds in two sizes

[25] *Attribute Games and Problems*, the Webster Division of McGraw-Hill, Inc., Manchester, Mo. 63011.

obvious external likenesses and grouping by internal or hidden likenesses.

In many schools now, very young children are given opportunities to group objects in various ways, each group representing one or more likenesses. As a mathematics project, such grouping is thought of as placing the objects in "sets," but this activity might just as easily be labeled "sciencing." Scientists group, and categorize, and classify phenomena and facts according to a variety of likenesses.

There is a basket of small toys in the center of a kindergarten table. One child selects a truck, a ball, and a wooden triangle. He may say, "I have a set of red things." Another child takes out a tiny doll and a jack; "I have a set of small things," she says. A third kindergartner takes a teddy bear and smilingly remarks, "I have a set of one teddy bear." All of these selections were based on external likenesses. To challenge the children's thinking, the teacher takes out a red marble. "Could this be a member of any of the sets you've described?" she asks. Two of the children are likely to claim the marble. How do you think the disposition of the marble is settled by the children?

Another approach can be to give each child an

(large and small); each shape and size comes in red, yellow, green, and blue. Very simple to highly complex games and exercises are suggested in accompanying printed materials. An analogous set of blocks has been designed by Z.P. Dienes, [26] which has both thick and thin pieces as well.

A very important prelude to structuring exercises with *Attribute Blocks* is to allow each child a period to play freely with them. The blocks will fascinate him and he will immediately begin to build or make flat designs with them. Of course, the free discovery of what the blocks can do will help to familiarize him with their attributes—their likenesses—as he experiences the satisfaction of self-motivated exploration. During these free discovery periods, a child may make several of the arrangements suggested in the lesson guides and he can be asked to describe these. When the free discovery phase is exhausted, the child is ready for more structured suggestions. Such a suggestion (not included in the guide) is to give each pair of children (because they enjoy working this way) an open manila folder on which two wide streets crossing each other at right angles have been ruled. One street may be labeled "Triangle Street" and the other "Green Road" (or any other combination of the blocks' attributes).

> "This is a map. Pretend that the blocks are houses and place them where they belong on the map," the teacher suggests. "Put all the houses that do not belong on the streets in the Parking Lot. Can you find a way to name the blocks in the Parking Lot? Try it."

Can *you* categorize the blocks in the Parking Lot?

There are many other types of suggestions which stimulate thought and activity in children. For example, they can be given loose labels to place as street names according to their choosing. A principle evolves from this activity: sometimes houses will be at the intersection and sometimes they will not; in the latter case, we say that the intersection is an empty set. This principle is related to whether the labels of the intersecting streets indicate similar or different attributes. For instance, what occurs when the streets are labeled "Red" and "Green"? What

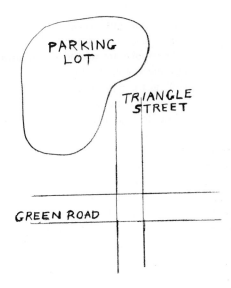

happens when the labels are "Red" and "Triangle"? [27]

When you try these games with children, you will probably discover not only that it is essential to allow free play with the blocks prior to more structured work, but also that the children will begin to play with the materials again as they become tired after a period of avid concentration on suggested problems. This is often projective play in which the blocks become objects or people interacting in the child's imagination or environment. [28]

The science lessons recorded thus far offer many examples of the children themselves relating observed data by external likenesses. Work with structured materials followed by a colloquium seems to engender this. After Miss Stevens dropped the bag, during the *What's Inside?* lesson, Alan said "It couldn't be no paint jar . . . 'cause the paint jar'd break. I didn't hear no break." This in reality is a negative likeness, a

[26] Available from Herder and Herder, 232 Madison Avenue, New York, N.Y. 10016

[27] A television program (part of a series of teacher training programs) available in kinescope (16 mm sound film), shows third-grade children from a low socioeconomic area making this discovery. Ask for TV-213, "Attributes at the Crossroads. The Logic of Intersection," from the T.V. Center, Brooklyn College, City University of New York, Brooklyn, N.Y. 11210. Mark envelope: "Attn: Creative Interaction TV Programs."

[28] This phase has been well described in Z. P. Dienes, *An Experimental Study of Mathematics Learning*, Hutchinson, London, 1963, Ch. 2.5 and pp. 47-48. Distributed by Herder and Herder, 232 Madison Ave., New York, N. Y. 10016.

not-likeness, which seems just as easy for children to cope with as a direct relationship. Paint jars breaking and the noise they make are related to the dropped bag and no breaking noise: the two noises were not alike. After handling the bag, Dean said "I'm sure it's a napple. . . . There's a little dent on one end where the stalk is." The feel of the object and a visual memory of an apple present external likenesses. Referring to the Wiffle ball in the *Eureka!* lesson, Dick said: "It floats just like a boat. Part of it sinks and part floats. A regular ball is like that, too." Wiffle ball, regular ball, and boat have an external likeness in the manner in which they float. In the investigation of circuits, Monte remarked: "You know what? They're both as bright as one alone," when two bulbs were hooked up in the circuit he and Carl had invented.

You might like to find other examples. In teaching discovery-colloquium lessons, you will observe that children very readily express external likenesses as a result of their science experiences.

Although *hidden* likenesses are less easily perceived by their very nature, children as early as the first grade (and even some mature kindergartners) talk about hidden likenesses.

Hidden likenesses take the form of constructs, hypotheses, or models; they are mental leaps. They represent concepts which may underlie data, phenomena, or events. Relating data through hidden likenesses represents a higher level of thought than grouping according to external likenesses; it offers, too, a greater opportunity for originality, even creativity.

Finding hidden likenesses can provide a common denominator or a single way of viewing two or more discrepancies. Another way to cope with discrepant events is to retest or look at the data again to see whether the events were accurately perceived, whether they were really discrepant. In the electricity lesson, finding that wires did and did not get hot when they were covered in a short circuit, while bare wires always became hot did require more accurate data. During the lesson on air, however, when Ruthanne heard a whisper come out of the hole in her bag while Serina heard a loud bang, one child found a common explanation through the use of the word "power." The level of noise made by the power

of the air constituted a hidden likeness which resolved a discrepant event.

Diana Ross's children in the *Eureka!* lesson found a hidden likeness between the boat and the Wiffle ball. Dick remarked, "The part of the Wiffle ball that sinks is the part that has water in it." Charlie then found a hidden likeness between the Wiffle ball and the boat: "The part of the boat that sinks does it 'cause it's heavy, too." Heavy becomes Charlie's construct or hypothesis linking the phenomena of the way a boat floats and the way a Wiffle ball floats. This hidden likeness starts Gert thinking; she asks: "Is it because the water makes the Wiffle ball heavy? Does it *not* float because of this?"

Finding hidden likenesses is not only an elegant level of sciencing; it often motivates the asking of questions. Today many people consider asking questions, rather than solving problems, the essence of a scientist's activity; we must, therefore, revere questions in sciencing.

Are you wondering what Mrs. Ross's children meant by "heavy"? The term was certainly undefined, yet three of them immediately used the word in a similar context. To each of them it represented a hidden likeness, a meaningful concept linking the phenomena together. (You will find many different uses of the word "heavy" when children talk together in colloquia. When used, it always seems fruitful in that other children pick up the word and further their thinking with it. As adults we can only listen, and marvel.)

A little later in the *Eureka!* lesson, Shelley discovered a more sophisticated hidden likeness (or do we think it is more sophisticated because it seems more meaningful to us as adults?): "Water pushed the air out of the sponge and it sank. Marbles pushed the air out of the cup and the cup sank." The discovery of the role of air in flotation often propels children whirling on to the next level of the principle of Archimedes.

There is an age or maturity level at which children become capable of grouping objects according to hidden likenesses. At every age, we all continue to find external likeness between things and events, but the *spontaneous* switch from external to hidden likenesses comes at about five and a half years. This was pin-pointed by an experiment conducted in

China.[29] Children of various ages were given pictures to put into groups. They were then asked about their groupings. At five and a half children would place pictures of a chair, a stool, a table, and a bookcase together and call them "furniture," a bicycle, an auto, and a truck were termed "transportation" or "for people to travel in." Several types of groupings were also revealed between the stage of not being able to group at all (four years) and that of grouping according to a generalization.

If untutored development is the same for American as it is for Chinese children, we can expect the ability to group via hidden likenesses to prevail throughout elementary school. Indeed, this level can reach considerably abstract heights by the end of the elementary grades. Consider the following "invention" by Carol, a sixth grader in a suburban Midwestern school.[30]

Carol and her classmates had been investigating simple machines: pulleys, inclined planes, wedges, and the like. The children had a wide range of abilities; that all-enveloping, often useless term "heterogeneous" could be used to identify the group. At the end of three weeks' work, much of it "laboratory work," the children had grasped the nature of a simple machine. Some had begun calculations of mechanical advantage, others of the efficiency of machines; some merely understood machines on a descriptive level. Nevertheless, the class in general had a fairly good understanding of the way simple machines saved effort and increased the speed of work. They had had experiences in search of a specific meaning; they apparently "understood" the statement: "Energy gotten out of a machine does not exceed the energy put into it."

At the end of one lesson, the teacher asked the children to bring in one simple machine they used at home and to explain it to the class. Carol brought in "a very simple machine" which she had "invented." In any event, she told the class she could not find any mention of the machine "which came from my

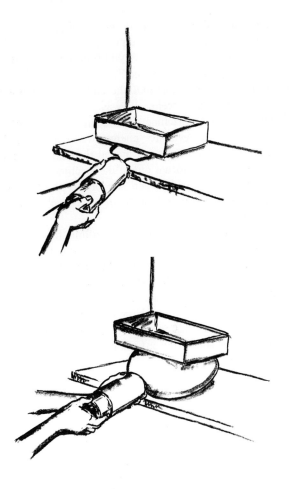

brain" in any library reference. She was willing to concede that it might have been done before, but since this could not be proven, she was ready to explain her invention before the class.

As you can see, the "invention" is elegant in its simplicity. A load of some sort (Carol used a small box) is placed on a balloon. As the balloon is blown up, the box is pushed up. A weight [the box], Carol explained, has been moved through a distance. Therefore, work has been done.

Her explanations, aided by her diagrams, were clear. Her balloon machine did work. She had applied the hidden likeness of known machines to a new situation. Soon, however, she was in trouble. The children wanted to find out which type of machine Carol's invention was specifically. One of the boys

[29] Wang Hsien-Tien *et al.,* "An Investigation into the Development of Concepts in Children 4–9 Years," in *Xinli Xuebao–Acta Psychologica Sinica*, No. 4, (1964) 352–360. We are grateful to Tuan Ho for orally translating the article.

[30] Observed by Paul F. Brandwein. Study to be reported when further data is secured.

asked her which machine it was: a lever, an inclined plane, a screw, a wedge, a pulley, a wheel-and-axle? "It is none of these," Carol said triumphantly. "It's a new kind of simple machine."

The teacher recognized the children's viewpoints as a discrepant event. It was clear that Carol's invention was a machine; the hidden likeness to other machines was evident: energy went into Carol's machine and a weight was moved through a distance —so energy was gotten out of the machine. Was there a hidden likeness between any one type of known machine and Carol's though, or was Carol's really a new type?

In order to help the children think this through —and resolution of this discrepant event did not come at once; it took a day or two—the teacher asked them to apply the terms they knew (*effort, resistance,* and *fulcrum*) to Carol's machine, and then to figure out the relationship of these basic elements. In this way, the children could compare Carol's machine with the usual types and ferret out it's hidden likeness, if one existed.

If you are familiar with standard simple machines, try to find a hidden likeness between one or more of them and Carol's "invention."

The ability to perceive hidden likenesses can extend in complexity throughout a child's elementary school life. It is applicable to areas other than science, of course; in the hands of a wise teacher it can often help children to overcome blocks in their thinking. It is helpful to adults in the same way. During the mealworm lesson, Mr. Litchfield (page 38) was actually condemning Angelina for screaming when she saw the worms. Mimi told him, ". . . but we've got the gerbil." She saw a hidden likeness in being afraid of strange new animals: since she had evidently conquered her first fear by having the gerbil in the classroom, she implied that Angelina could also overcome her fear of the mealworms through famil- iarity. Mimi later demonstrated this hidden likeness when she encouraged Angelina to let the worm crawl over her hand.

Mrs. Weiss used the principle of hidden likeness to help Cyril with his attitude toward living organisms (page 42). You can probably find the hidden likeness in that incident.

As we have seen, finding hidden likenesses is one way to solve discrepant events. However, since they occur during most science investigations, discrepant events can be solved in many other ways: checking observations, repeating investigation, adapting the previously held theory. A more radical approach may be required—a new model may have to be constructed to explain all of the events.

Discrepant events may lead to even more elegant results in the sense that new avenues can emerge as part of the solution. A scientist may begin by investigating one phenomenon only to find himself discovering a fact or investigating a phenomenon in a different area. He may begin with one purpose and end up with another.

Alexander Fleming's discovery is a case in point. While investigating bacteria growing on a nutrient in a petri dish, Fleming noticed a patch where the bacteria had disappeared—an unexpected, discrepant event. An investigation of this patch led to the discovery of penicillin, the active agent in a mold. Starting out with one objective and ending up with another is often referred to as *serendipity*, a delightful word with an ancient and rather amusing history. The legend, first appearing in printed form in the six- teenth century, had several versions in various Asian countries.[31]

Three Princes of Serendip (one name for Ceylon) were setting out on their travels. A typical tale of their adventures records that they noticed the grass at the border of their route had been cropped short along the left-hand side, while the grass on the right border of their route was luscious. Putting two and two together and coming up with five, the royal youths asserted that a mule blind in the right eye had passed this way ahead of them.

Although neither the main purpose of the youths nor their unexpected discovery can be considered momentous in today's terms, the word *serendipity* originated from this legend. The elements in the modern sense of the word are present in this story, however: the solution of the problem of the cropped grass (the discrepancy that it was cropped only on one side) required the finding of a hidden likeness (the visual image of grass eaten by a mule); a model then had to be constructed (the mule was blind in

[31] *Serendipity*, ed., Theodore S. Remer, University of Okla- homa Press, 1965.

one eye). An original search, the adventure, resulted in a new and unexpected finding.

Of course, serendipity, as applied to science today, has a deeper significance, a more meaningful content. It also requires a prepared mind, as the saying [32] goes. As previously mentioned, biologists before Alexander Fleming must have had bare patches in their bacteria cultures, but Fleming's prepared mind made the observation serendipitous. Serendipity in its modern sense often includes playfulness; a scientist may investigate something which seems to have no particular connection with his primary investigation. Clinton Davisson, a physicist who worked in the Bell Telephone Laboratory at Murray Hill, New Jersey during the first third of this century, exhibited both the playfulness and the prepared mind which often lead to serendipity. He was eventually awarded the Nobel Prize for his experiments and theory.

Davisson had been asked to conduct experiments to solve a lawsuit controversy concerning the early development of the vacuum tube (the precursor of neon lights and television tubes) through which electrons flowed. Having produced the data required by the lawyers, Davisson switched the electric terminals of the tube so that the electrons flowed in the reverse direction. [33] The results surprised him: the electrons hit a metal target and were bounced back in a scatter pattern unlike any of the patterns he had seen under other conditions. This event was the beginning of a long series of experiments in which

[32] "Serendipity comes to the prepared mind."
[33] Personal communication to one of the authors from Lester Germer, who worked with Davisson on his later experiments.

Davisson bombarded many kinds of metal targets with streams of electrons of various energies. Then one day a bottle of liquid air exploded. Released so suddenly, the liquid air hit the metal target in the apparatus and changed the nature of its crystal structure. Large crystals had been formed from several smaller ones. Again the scatter pattern of the bombarding electrons changed. Davisson's prepared mind recognized a significant problem, certainly a series of discrepancies, in this unexpected direction of investigations. After several years of thought, study, and more experiments, he came to the conclusion that electrons could act like waves as well as like particles, just as light does. He found a hidden likeness between electrons and light, and for this he received the highest award given to scientists.

When sciencing, children not infrequently enjoy the experience of serendipity—on their own level, of course. It may occur if they extend themselves beyond the interactive system under investigation; they may bring in new materials which they find spontaneously, or they may do things with materials that most of the class will not do. As a rule, children do not have prepared minds to interpret their findings, to pursue implications to a conclusion; this is where the teacher's role in the colloquium helps. In the following lesson record, you will find a number of discoveries of external likenesses, a few of hidden likenesses, and at least one delightful example of serendipity—where a child uses material outside the system playfully and the teacher uses this fact to help the children achieve a model based on a new hidden likeness.

SERENDIPITY FROM WATER PLAY

Marybelle Bradford felt like running up the long flights of subway steps—she even contemplated jogging along the three crosstown blocks to her home, but she kept her joyous feelings inside instead. She was not afraid of the neighbors' stares. It was just that her unusual behavior might arouse the curiosity of the police—yes, the police. They always seemed to be around when they weren't needed. "Shush!" she told herself, "don't go hiking those prejudices. This is Tuesday night. Tuesday. Tuesday, the good evening of the week."

On Tuesday nights the dim tenements she passed faded in her imagination into what they might become. Might? On Tuesday nights she used the word *could*. The brownstone houses of her home block shouted "would!". She recalled her own school days when she and Christina had picked their way around uncollected garbage, used the empty beer cans in the front yard for playthings, and hopscotched over the legs of drunks in the hallway. She did run a few yards after crossing the last avenue, as though the sudden turning of the lights gave her an excuse to continue with all deliberate speed. Funny, how that phrase cropped up tonight. The run brought her into full view of the balcony atop a two-story bowfront. Even in the poor street lighting, the azaleas she and her sister had given their mother for Easter seemed bright, and last year's hyacinths were in full flower. The two long window boxes were filled with frilly petunias; each morning their colors greeted Marybelle with increased brilliance—or so it seemed to her. True, the Japanese maple in the redwood tub wasn't doing so well. Maybe the soot.

Each house on the block was evidence of *might* becoming *could*; each house—no, it wasn't the house, but the tenants and the Block Committee—showed what taking hold can do, even when landlords are not too eager to do their part. Bulbs grew in neat beds, the stoops were freshly painted, the railings mended, rose bushes here and there skillfully pruned. Even the hallways smelled different—no longer that sickly insecticide odor which had greeted her return from school. The tenants had gotten together and replaced carpets on the stairs—carpeted stairs which seemed to say, "Now we are back to the pride of our younger days when carriage-owning folk lived here." Yet it wasn't quite that. It was a *new* pride.

Mrs. Bradford was bending near the oven, a tray of hot muffins in her potholder-protected hands—those hands grown rough and gnarled before their time. Christina's voice came from the large front room reading a favorite bedtime story to her two youngsters. Even when their grandma put them to bed, the children would not go to sleep until their mother returned from her meeting and completed their daily routine.

"How was the Workshop?" Mrs. Bradford asked, returning her daughter's greeting while she poured two cups of steaming cocoa.

"Those professors at State U. don't know a thing about the little ones I teach."

"But I thought, like, you enjoyed Tuesday evenings?"

Marybelle pushed her coat into the closet and slipped her feet into soft scuffs. "Sure, there're lots of good ideas and one day they'll be useful. Say, Chris, tell us about the meeting."

Chris washed down a mouthful of warm muffin with a soda she'd taken from the refrigerator. "It looks like, y'know, we'll be able to start the school—"

"You mean, next September? And they'll take Alfredo and Leatrice?"

"Well, y'know, last Tuesday Mrs. Jones thought she could get Tyler College to help—giving materials, y'know, and maybe working with the mothers who'd work in the classrooms and things like that. And Tyler said they would."

"They'd pay you to work there, dear?" Mrs. Bradford pushed the plate of muffins toward her younger daughter.

"Right on! Like I'd work there in the classrooms, y'know, and get me an education at the same time."

It all seemed too good to Marybelle: her sister on the way to a real job, her nephew and niece getting a real education in a school run by black mothers working together to provide the kind of education their children merited. I'd sure like to teach in the Free School, Marybelle retreated to her most treasured thoughts. They wouldn't pay much, but just think—a chance to do all I've read about, to try things which really make children learn and grow. And if Chris is working . . . well I could take a cut. But then she reflected the children in her classroom in the public school might have a teacher who didn't care; didn't she owe them a break?

"Wake up, gal! Tell us what you learned tonight. Anything we can use in the Free School?" Marybelle was startled by her sister's voice.

"So children are supposed to learn about change, like the seasons. We take them on a spring walk and they see what's happened since they took the walk in the fall." By the tone of Marybelle's voice, her mother and sister knew this was not the point of the Workshop.

"Of course, my children don't remember that long. They don't make the connection. But the children where I student-taught, and where most of the workshop teachers now teach, live hopped-up lives. Why, someone said two of her children flew to South America for Thanksgiving! Those children see the change of season in a few hours. Seven year olds don't have long memories anyhow, and the homes my particular children come from, well."

"Welfare check to welfare check," added Christina.

"The dusty trees aren't very pretty anyway."

"How about a nice trip to Foley Park?" suggested Mrs. Bradford.

"You know what happens on a long trip? The kids get so excited about the trip itself, just going away from school to a strange place an' all, they forget all about my reason for the trip!"

"We plan to take the children on lots of trips when the Free School starts. I think it will work."

"Yes, but you'll do it often, not just when someone thinks of ordering a bus."

"That's all you did today?"

"No, this was the lead-in. Motivation, no doubt. The profs have even heard something about short memories, so Dr. Steinway said chemistry provides observation of a quick change,"—Marybelle was mimicking his voice.

"So you did chemistry?"

"Sure! They had a whole stack of white powders and some liquids like vinegar, water, iodine, litmus. And then, of course, 'See what you can find out!' "

Her mother nodded. She'd heard that last remark each week. She rocked herself gently in her chair. It was peaceful in spite of Marybelle's take-off—her two daughters both looking forward to better things because of their Tuesday meetings.

"So if we'd had chemistry, we dropped a little of each liquid into the bits of powders, one at a time, and knew what was there. Those who hadn't had

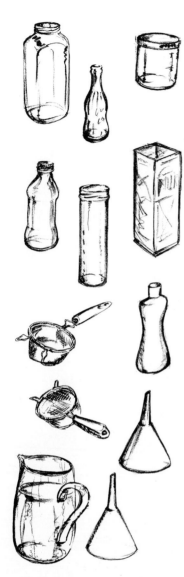

Playfulness?

chem, they made muffins!" She laughed as she took another bite into the juicy raisins buried in the fragrant bran. "*White* muffins!" Her mother smiled, emphasizing her agreement with increased rocking.

"What do they expect my children will do? They've never heard of sodium bicarbonate—one of the powders; they've never handled bits of powders; they don't know about tests."

"But you'll find a way; you always do."

Confidence seeped through the kitchen, as it did every Tuesday evening. It seeped into Marybelle's second-grade classroom two days later.

Class 2-7 of the Carver School was housed in a brand new building in the slum section of a northern city. The room was equipped with water, a sink, and movable tables in the convenient shapes of trapezoids. In spite of the air of enlightenment from the building itself, most of the rooms carried over that aura of discipline and fear, that feeling of *never learn* which so many slum children endure. It was different in Marybelle's room. Polaroid color portraits of each of the children decorated the walls, labeled with the child's given and family name. The portrait faces were smiling, as were those in the room. Children moved independently, not as a block, and there was noise—talking, laughter, a buzz of conversation.

Six groups of four children were to work around the tables. On each table were seven or eight containers of various shapes, two plastic funnels, two strainers, and a pitcher of water. Marybelle Bradford felt that the children would enjoy concentrating their attention and activities on water, finding some of its properties, and then making statements about water's shape, texture, and state.

In one particular group, Warren filled several of the containers with water. Roland took the funnel and put it in a bottle; then he poured a little water into the funnel and watched it drip down inside.

"Hey man, lookit this!" he shouted. He continued to pour water through the funnel, a little at a time and then in larger doses. "Oh boy," he shouted gleefully. He seemed to be enjoying himself thoroughly.

Sue placed the strainer over a glass vase. Then she poured some water into the strainer; it splashed on her table. "Aw, gee. You made it all wet," Denise said. "Get some paper towels and clean up the mess."

"Yeah, I gonna do that," Sue replied.

Warren and Roland, the boys at their table, were busy pouring water from one container into another while the girls wiped up the spilled water. When the table was clean, Denise took one of the paper towels and poured water through it. Roland seemed to like the idea and proceeded to do the same thing. "Hey, man. That's cool," he said.

The children at the other tables were similarly engaged; after another ten minutes, Miss Bradford collected the materials at the side of the sink and arranged the children in a semicircle for the colloquium.

Miss B.: Our workers looked very busy today. Would anyone like to tell us what he did?

Silvester: I put water in one bottle and then put the thing [strainer] in the other bottle, and when I poured the water it went through the thing in the bottle.

Paul: When I used the funnel no water was spilled, but when I didn't use it then the water got all over.

Rae: What's a funnel?

Miss B.: Can anyone help Rae?

Betty: The funnel is the thing that look like a hat upside down that you put water in and it come out the bottom.

Miss B.: Go to the sink and see if you can find a funnel to show Rae. *(Betty finds one and holds it up to the class.)*

Denise: I put the paper towel over this thing and the water go through.

Ellen: It go through the strainer, too.

Kirk: It go through anything that got holes in it.

Bob: Yeah. You gotta have something with no hole if you wanna put water in it 'cos water stay like in the bottle, but it don't stay in the funnel 'cos it got a hole.

Miss B.: What about the paper towel? Why does water go through that?

Bob: I dunno. Can I see one?

Miss B.: Yes, you may. *(He holds it up to the window and looks through it.)*

Bob: It got holes, too. See, you can see the holes when you look like this.

Silvester: Let me see. Oh yes!

They pass the towel around and each child looks through it.

Miss B.: Did anyone discover anything about how the water feels?

Sue: It's wet.

Willis: Water can be cold.

Leroy: It could be hot like when I wash sometime—boy, it's hot. *(He laughs.)*

Miss B.: Did anyone discover anything else about water?

Silvester: When you spill water into something but it don't go in, it makes a splash and you get wet.

Miss B.: How does water pour? Up, down, sideways, or all of them?

Silvester: It goes down.

Miss B.: What does that make you think about water's shape?

Bob: It ain't no circles or something like that. It not like that.

Miss B.: Bob gave a very good answer. Now let's think very hard, like all investigators do, and see if we can think about water's shape. Is it round, square-shaped, like a bottle?

There was silence for a moment.

Rae: Water can be like drops and then it look like round things.

Bob: Water can't have no shape 'cos it go into bottles and things and always fit inside. It can't have no shape.

Miss B.: Does water always take the shape of the container it's in?

Jo: Yeah. Water always fit into what you put it in.

The colloquium continued in this vein for several more minutes. Then the Investigators' Log was dictated and discussed. Miss Bradford wrote just what the children said. When she duplicated the Log, she gave it in two forms. Each child received a copy of both, used them for reading, and then drew illustrations.

Here the word for the "thing" might have been supplied.

At what point are generalizations voiced?

Why is this redirective question appropriate here?

Why did this question lead nowhere?

Bob may be associating the water with geometric shapes learned in a recent lesson. Is he trying to please Miss B. by using his new vocabulary here?

This question phrases something the children have not said. What do you think about this?

INVESTIGATORS' LOG

We pour water in a funnel and it come out.
We pour water in a strainer and it come out.
We pour water in a paper towel and it come out.
Water go through things that have holes in them.
We pour water in a bottle and it stay there.
We pour water in a can and it stay there.
Water stay in things that don't have no holes.
Water is wet. Water can be hot or cold.
Water don't have no shape. It fit in all shapes of containers.

What are the educational advantages to this recording procedure?

THE SCIENTISTS' WAY OF WRITING

We poured water into a funnel and it came out.
We poured water into a strainer and it came out.
We poured water into a paper towel and it came out.
Water goes through things that have holes in them.
We poured water into a bottle and it stayed there.
We poured water into a can and it stayed there.
Water stays in things that have no holes.
Water is wet. Water can be hot or cold.
Water has no shape. It fits into all shapes of containers.

There can be many ways of following up the kind of lesson just recorded. We will discuss several of these in Chapter 5.

Marybelle Bradford had decided to try some form of the suggestions she had gleaned from the Workshop at the State University. She felt sure that the apparent backwardness of some of her children was due more to their past experiences in school than to their lack of intelligence. Because the children had had limited experience with the tools and products found in most middle-class homes seemed no reason to suppose that they could not cope with strange new materials. It meant only that a new way, perhaps a new order of presentation, was indicated. She was quite thrilled with the results of the water and jar investigation. All the facts her textbook listed as part of the knowledge to be acquired had been suggested by the children. And there were discoveries the book had not included: the paper towel investigation pleased her very much somehow.

What should she do about those powders? Offer a few choices at first, maybe? Even so, she had some misgivings. She took the opportunity to test her version of the lesson when half the class was out of the room. She felt she could learn more about the way children worked if she could intently watch a small group of seven year olds rather than the whole class. One hour a week some of her children went to speech therapy and a few were called to practice in the school's budding orchestra. Twelve children remained in the room; Miss Bradford arranged them in four groups, three at each trapezoid table.

Three small paper cups labeled A, B, C, were on each table; each cup contained a small quantity of a white powder. On each table she placed six

Sugar

Salt

Flour

spare cups, three plastic spoons, and a small pitcher of water. As a contribution to the Workshop she was attending, Marybelle Bradford made a record of the activities of Bob, Anne, and Betty as well as of the colloquium with the entire group of twelve investigators.

More paper cups were available on Miss Bradford's desk.

At first the children did not touch the powders. Then Bob poured some water into one of the cups. Betty did the same. Anne looked into the three cups marked A, B, C and raised her hand.

"Can we use what's in these?"

"Sure, use anything on the table you need."

What concept motivated the selection of salt, sugar and flour? The other powders used in the Workshop were plaster of Paris, sodium bicarbonate, and boric acid.

Anne took a heaping teaspoon of powder C and put it in an empty cup. Then she put her finger in the cup to feel the powder. Bob put a teaspoon of powder A in his cup of water and stirred. Betty followed suit with a teaspoon of powder B. Then Anne added water to her cup of powder C.

"Hey, lookit," she called the teacher's attention. There was a clump in the bottom of her cup. She began to break it up and mix it with more water. Bob added more powder to his cup. He looked at it carefully for a moment. No powder was visible. He struck his finger in it and tasted it.

In what way does working in a small group hasten discovery?

"It's sugar," Bob announced. Betty then tasted hers.

"Mines is salt."

"Lem'me see," said Bob. He tasted Betty's liquid and nodded.

Betty tasted Bob's liquid. "Boy, this is sweet!"

What do you think Bob was looking for?

Anne was still busy mixing and had gotten a milky looking fluid.

"Hey, look, I got milk!"

"Oh, yeah! Lookit that," said Bob. He tasted it and made a face. "That ain't no milk."

Anne laughed and added more powder C.

Betty was watching her closely. I think it look like what my mother make when she bake a cake."

Anne added more powder C. "Look how it float to the top," she said.

Bob then made this observation: "I think the sugar dissolve in the water, 'cos look . . . you can hardly see it any more."

Betty remarked, "You can't see mines either. I guess it done the same thing."

Is this an external or a hidden likeness?

Bob then poured a little of his mixture into another cup and added more water. He tasted it and said, "Yep, that's sugar all right."

Anne was still adding more of powder C to what had become a gooey, sticky mixture. "Hey, don't this look like paste?"

"Lem'me see," said Bob. He examined and returned it.

Betty put four or five teaspoons of powder B into her cup, tasted it, and made a face. Then she put water and powder A in another cup. She tasted it and said, "Hey, Bob, I got the sugar one, too." Then she added a teaspoon of powder C to the same cup and tasted it again.

"I think it still sweet. You do it."

Bob tasted and agreed it was still sweet.

The children then started to mix all three powders together; Miss Bradford, sensing the end of profitable discovery, collected the materials, had the children clean up the tables, and arranged the chairs in a semicircle for the colloquium.

Miss B.: As I walked around the room, I saw some very interesting things going on. Would you like to tell us about them?

Jo: When I put sugar, salt, and the other powder in water it all turn white.

Neil: When I got water, I put salt and flour in it.

Miss B.: How do you know what you put in the water?

Neil: I tasted it.

Jo: Yeah. Me, too.

Miss B.: Did anyone do something else?

Paul: I put a powder in the water and it turn white.

Miss B.: Do you remember which powder?

Paul: It was in the cup with C on it.

George: I think the powder look like milk.

Rae: I think the sugar and the powder in the water are white.

Miss B.: Does anyone know what made the water turn white?

Ellen: I think it was the flour 'cos it turn white in the water, but the sugar didn't turn so white.

Tom: The sugar didn't turn so white because the sugar was light.

Ellen: He mean the flour was heavier.

Bob: I know what he mean. The sugar was light—light like a feather, so it didn't turn so white.

Miss B.: Does anyone else think the flour was heavier? (*Several hands go up.*) Nita, why do you think the flour was heavier?

Nita: Mine was all sticky; it stuck to my hands.

Paul: Mine didn't do that. Mine look like milk.

Jo: Nita wrong.

Miss B.: What do you think we could do to find out about this?

Jo: You could do it.

Ellen: You could do it now and we could see?

Miss Bradford then put a little flour in a cup of water and showed it to the children. A few children called out, "Nita wrong!" *Then she put a lot of flour in another cup of water and showed it to the children.*

Miss B.: What have we found out?

Ellen: It's paste; you gotta put in a lotta powder.

Betty: When I pour out the one with salt, I saw some at the bottom was left.

Miss B.: Did anyone else see this? (*No hands are raised.*)

Bob: Anne and me are scientists. We found out when you mix sugar and water it dissolve and make it sweet.

Paul: What that mean?

Neil: Sugar was still there, but you couldn't see it.

Jo: We knows it there 'cos we can taste it.

Paul: Oh! It look like it invisible, but the sugar still there.

Bob: Salt do the same thing sugar do.

After a few more minutes of colloquium, the Investigators' Log was composed. The corrected form follows.

Miss Bradford recalled that she was supposed to warn children about tasting unknown chemicals. But her children tasted everything. It seemed better to give them only safe powders at this point, and forget the warning.

Have you noticed the way "heavy" has been used in discussing flotation, electricity, and now solutions? Has such a varied use of this term occurred in your teaching? Why does Miss Bradford use the children's phraseology?

Here is a point where teacher demonstration is the best procedure. Why is it appropriate?

Betty insisted on having her discovery in the Log.

INVESTIGATORS' LOG (SCIENTISTS' WAY OF WRITING)

We put a little salt in a lot of water and it dissolved.
If you have a lot of water, more salt will dissolve than if you
have a little water.
When Betty put a lot of salt in a little water, some of it was in
the water and some fell to the bottom.

It is interesting to note that all the discoveries about sugar and flour were
omitted. It may be that Betty's discovery presented an unsolved problem
which captured the children's attention. When Miss Bradford asked the
children if the salt in Betty's cup was dissolved or not, some said yes and
some said no. Bob said, "One will go easy away, but the rest don't." On this   Could he have meant *one spoonful?*
point most of the children remained confused. Lysiphiles?

What materials would you offer the children for their follow-up lesson? On
what basis would you make your choice?

Keys and chaos

Data assail us. Through the senses of smell, sight, hearing, touch, and taste, stimuli bombard us all day long, all life long. In order to survive the onslaught of stimuli, sentient beings process these data in a combination of conscious and unconscious ways.

We could not possibly survive if we gave the same attention to every stimulus. Some data are blocked out: we may not notice the odor of polluted urban air; we may fail to perceive a sparrow hawk diving after a field mouse; we may not pay any attention to a whiskey advertisement or the dust on a shelf.

Children, too, block out many of the stimuli offered them in school—much to the teacher's chagrin. There is avid competition for reception of stimuli (the stock in trade of Madison Avenue) and many devices are employed. (The opaque projector is excellent for centering children's attention on a little bright spot on the ceiling; the TV screen is, of course, the supreme attention riveter.) We have seen that structured science materials which employ the eyes and hands, involve thought, and are followed by speech, focus the learner's attention on data which can then be processed in a form accessible to him.

Data can be forced upon us through repetition, assimilated in rote form, memorized mechanically rather than processed consciously. Or we can make a conscious effort to remember the data we learn by rote; the names of United States Presidents are often retained in this way. Another meaningful method of

conscious rather than rote processing is to organize the data: by placing them in categories, groups, and subgroups according to their external likenesses; by relating them to conceptual schemes, where the first step is to find hidden likenesses; and, of course, by using the imagination, as a poet does.

Let us illustrate through an example. A row of carefully chosen trees line a campus walk. Students have traversed the walk for four consecutive years, passing by these trees twice each day. Therefore, the trees act as a daily double stimulus to the students' eyes (as well as to their noses in the flowering season). Some students remain virtually unaware that the trees are there. Except for the welcome shade provided during a summer semester, others may not be aware that the trees have any particular characteristics; the stimuli are blocked or forgotten as soon as they are perceived. A few students read and memorize the labels: "ginkgo, linden, maple, spruce"; going home it is "spruce, maple, linden, ginkgo." They have processed the data through the conscious effort of rote. Some students place the trees into meaningful categories: deciduous and evergreen; smelly orange fruit, *pince-nez* fruit, sailing fruit, cones; stiff horizontal branches, rounded outlines, triangles. These are groupings from external attributes. More data can be processed by categorizing stimuli according to their external likenesses than by memorizing them by rote. A few students group the trees according to hidden likenesses: as simple to complex in the evolutionary scale, judging by the leaves or the fruit; by photosynthesis efficiency in relation to structure; or by raising a question, "Why did the ginkgo survive when other species of that evolutionary era became extinct?" These rather sophisticated hidden likenesses (and hidden differences within hidden likenesses) approach the structure of conceptual schemes through which the most data is categorized and processed. Imaginatively, folklore and poems about these trees may be written in endless number, each selecting data suitable to the mood or emotion.

If we, as science educators, restrict ourselves to the data of science instead of all stimuli, we must still decide which data to process and which to block out in our elementary school curriculum. Even if we concentrate on science data alone, so many facts compete urgently for inclusion that we have an insoluble problem. We still must choose. However, we choose an *organization* rather than a set of facts or a block of knowledge. We have already chosen in this book: we emphasize conceptual schemes; we select clusters of related facts which can lead children toward a few basic concepts; we choose procedures which encourage children to relate facts according to hidden likenesses. We believe this organization helps children process maximum data in a meaningful manner. We will describe how the practice of finding hidden likenesses can build into conceptual schemes in Chapters 3 and 4.

As previously stated, we view finding *hidden* likenesses as the *beginning* of a process which eventually builds concepts; there is much more to come after this *Starting Tomorrow* level. The process of finding *external* likenesses also reaches a higher level, the building of keys or systematic branched classifications similar to a family tree. Scientists engage in the extension of both hidden and external likenesses. Children sciencing in the upper elementary grades can extend the procedures of finding hidden and external likenesses by building keys and concepts.

In "Finding Likenesses, External and Hidden" (page 61), we described ways in which children may practice finding external likenesses, relating the activity to the mathematics of sets. We emphasized that children should choose their own methods of grouping objects and give verbal descriptions of the principles underlying their selections. Trying to discern the principle underlying someone else's selection was also found to be an excellent activity. In other words, the process of categorizing has constructive and analytic phases. Analysis can often be fostered as a game most easily won by the person or side who discovers the strategy for winning first. The strategy is actually an empirical analysis of the scheme of organization.

The game *Info*, devised by the Minnemast Project,[34] is one such activity. The shapes on the cards represented at the bottom of this page are in two colors: the solid lines are red; the dotted lines are blue. The heavy outlines represent frames. They are arranged on the chalkboard ledge in a classroom. The children in this class are separated into two teams. A piece of chalk is hidden behind one of the cards, without the children's knowledge. Each team, in turn, must ask questions answerable by yes or no in order to locate the chalk. The side which asks the final question and finds the chalk wins. There is a strategy for winning! Mature first graders soon develop a strategy which results in certainty in four questions. More colors and/or shapes can be used for older children.

Now what questions would *you* ask? Maybe you

[34] Minnemast: *Minne*sota *M*ath *A*nd *S*cience *T*eaching Project under the leadership of Paul C. Rosenbloom, now at Teachers College, Columbia University.

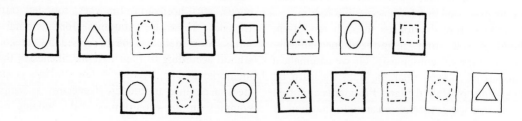

would like to work with a partner who pretends to have hidden the chalk behind one of the cards. (He will have to say something to himself like "Behind the blue triangle with a frame.") How many questions will you need to determine where the chalk is? How many questions are needed to solve the problem in four colors? Four shapes, framed, and not framed?

Are you willing to figure out these problems before you turn the page? Can you bear the loose ends? Are you a lysiphile?

The cards are shown again on the next page, grouped according to their attributes. The strategy is to reduce the uncertainty of where the chalk is hidden by one half of the possibilities with each question. You might begin by asking, "Is it behind a framed card?" A negative response omits all eight of the framed cards. Now can you go on?

The strategy for this game is similar to that used by panels on such TV programs as "I've Got a Secret" or in the familiar "Animal, Vegetable, or Mineral?" game. (Choosing among three categories, of course,

means that only one-third of the possibilities can be eliminated with a single question.)

The principle behind the game of *Info* is a binary system of classification: each group or subgroup either does or does not have the attribute named. The system of classification is diagrammed below.

As you can see, the key begins with one category and breaks into double the number of categories at each level. After four questions, each of the 16 possible cards can be defined. For instance, the chalk might be behind the framed card with the noncircle shape which has no angles and is not red—in other words, behind the framed blue ellipse. Seven-year-old children do not analyze their strategy through such keys; they approach the problem pragmatically. By the third or fourth grade, however, children can diagram their procedure.

It is not necessary to build a key that subdivides into two categories each time, but binary classification is advantageous because it can be easily fed into a computer whose circuits end in little electric lights

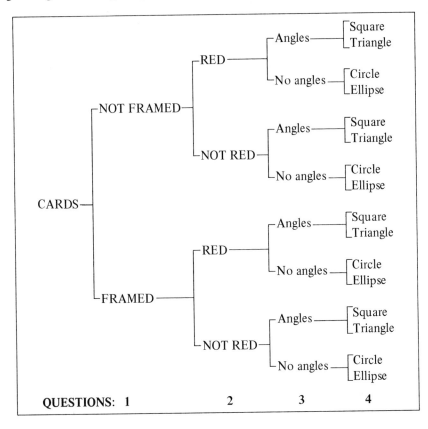

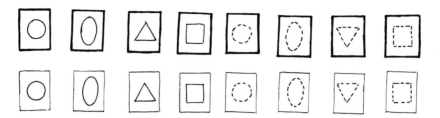

which have one of two states: on or off. The binary system is the most efficient type of key because it reduces uncertainty by half with each question, but we allow the children to discover this themselves. They will construct many other types of keys before they arrive at binary classification. As an example, let us see how children might build a key to discover what object in the aquarium the teacher has in mind.

This might be begun by saying "I'm thinking of something in the aquarium." The children will play this game many times—sometimes in teams, sometimes in pairs. At first their questions will be random ones: "Is it the frog?"; "Is it the *Elodea*?" They will gradually become expert in reducing the number of their questions (the announced purpose of the game).

One boy diagrammed his questions with this key:

AQUARIUM
- ANIMAL
  - Goldfish
  - Frog
  - Snail
- VEGETABLE
  - Long leaves
    - *Vallisneria*
    - *Sagittaria*
  - Short leaves *(Elodea)*
- NONLIVING
  - Rock
  - Gravel
  - Sand
  - Water
  - Air

Think of an object yourself and then figure out the number of questions required. Or play the game with a partner using the above key.

Now suppose the key were in the format shown at the top of page 79. Using this key, one can be sure of finding the "thing in mind" in three or four questions, depending upon which column categorizes the object.

Constructing keys is an organized way of rendering data retrievable. Children in the upper elementary grades enjoy constructing the most efficient key for any set of data.

Constructing keys is a very tidy activity that puts everything in an appointed place. At least in the binary system, there are no loose ends. Since the basis

for categorizing is the presence or absence of an attribute (an eternal likeness), each item does or does not belong. It is an excellent game for the lysiphobe!

Extending this activity to finding *hidden* likenesses is not nearly as clear-cut. At this stage, the scientist sits in mental contemplation before a sea of data. His aim is to find or construct an order from factual chaos. All facts are seldom included. Invariably there are loose ends which raise questions and provide discrepant events. Even the order raises questions: Is it a good fit? Will it predict? Will it suggest further investigation and experimentation?

Scientific theories and conceptual schemes are vast orderings of what may seem to be unrelated facts. Darwin related hundreds of observations in his theory

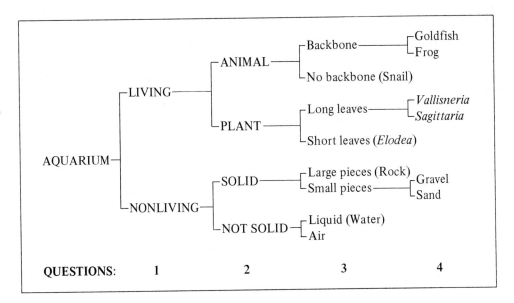

				┌Goldfish
			┌Backbone────	└Frog
		┌ANIMAL──		
			└No backbone (Snail)	
	┌LIVING────			
				┌*Vallisneria*
			┌Long leaves───	└*Sagittaria*
		└PLANT──		
AQUARIUM─			└Short leaves (*Elodea*)	
			┌Large pieces (Rock)	┌Gravel
		┌SOLID───	└Small pieces───	└Sand
	└NONLIVING─			
			┌Liquid (Water)	
		└NOT SOLID─	└Air	

QUESTIONS: 1   2   3   4

of evolution, but he did not use *all* his data; if he had, the theory would not have needed modification so soon. The various models of the atom that physicists have constructed using much of the data known to them and the constant change of the model throughout history comprise another case in point.

In a smaller way, children who have found a hidden likeness between two data are facing a chaos of possibilities. When Betty said, "The funnel is the thing that look like a hat upside down that you put water in and it come out the bottom," she was choosing her analogy from many possible alternatives. When Bob said, "The sugar was light—light like a feather, so it didn't turn so white," he was con-

structing a model of what might have happened to the sugar and flour; many other models or factual organizations were possible. When Carol constructed her simple machine, she faced a sea of facts about levers, pulleys, wedges, screws, wheels and axles, and inclined planes; she produced an analogous contraption whose specific likeness remained hidden even from her, although she explicitly found its general organization familiar. As we pursue follow-up sessions of the beginning lessons recorded thus far, we will see a greater ability to organize data into conceptlike wholes and to find hidden likenesses among many data developing in the children.

Children tolerate uncertainty easily. They are

Vallisneria

Elodea

Sagittaria

Finding likenesses, external and hidden   **79**

continually faced with an ocean of unorganized data and are only at the threshold of their goal of finding meaning in groups of stimuli. They are content to make slight headway, to find a limited order among some of the facts. Nine-year-old Patrick watched his father dig a compost pit for their first residence outside the city limits. "The leaves and other garden matter go into the pit," his father explained. "It all rots and makes a rich kind of earth which I'll put in the flower beds next year. And the flowers and trees will feed on it." An ocean of facts! A moment or two of contemplation. "You mean it goes round and round?" Patrick asked. "Something like that," replied his father. "Is that what they mean by 'conservation'?" Another datum from somewhere has slipped into place.

You may remember specific children who always ask for the right answer; children who insist on knowing exactly what you mean; children who want statements about all, every, and forever. Do they tolerate uncertainty? Do they enjoy making order out of chaos, a limited order with enticing loose ends? We can only ask what made these children this way. We can only answer that, while they may never become creative scientists, the world also needs excellent librarians!

Here we ask the teacher to encourage a child in finding hidden likenesses; to look through the child's eyes when he orders data *his* way—when he says flour is heavy so it turns white in water; to wait for a child to refine *his* model of what is happening so that he may progress from thinking that "water makes things heavy so they sink," to "air being pushed out and the object then sinks," to "heavy for its size." These are all organizations of data through hidden likenesses, calisthenics on the road to concept building.

Teachers need to plan for this kind of sciencing. It is not essential that the teacher enjoy finding order in chaos, but children in the act of growing surely require this privilege. Can you end a lesson with loose ends flying?

The Investigators' Log is only a tiny summary of the learning that takes place during a lesson; it represents a limited consensus. A Log is immensely valuable in helping a group to clarify what individuals have discovered, to communicate their findings.

Sometimes, however, even the Investigators' Log is not entirely agreed upon.

In Marybelle Bradford's class, Betty had to insist before her unique observation "... some of it (the salt) was in the water and some fell to the bottom" was included. She clearly saw a hidden likeness between this phenomenon and the sticky flour mixture, a likeness which motivated investigation by the whole class. Mr. McIver's lesson resulted in a variety of loose ends: asbestos, wires that did and did not get hot, lights that looked equally bright when one or two were in the circuit, a circuit made from one wire, and another made from two, and so on. More questions were missed than answered. The *Eureka!* investigation will obviously not be finished until the children are much more mature.

All of this unfinished business means that the child does not consider his own way of finding order—in a chaos of facts, in his individual discoveries and in those shared in the colloquium—completely satisfactory. In each session, however, children find some order among the facts by relating them through hidden likenesses. The child who is allowed to find hidden likenesses in his own ingenious way and who is encouraged to formulate his own order from a chaos of facts is engaging in a form of sciencing. He is doing just what a creative scientist does.

Very rich data from scholarly investigations during the past few years substantiate that the creative scientist tolerates ambiguity, enjoys a chaos of data, and finds his satisfaction in constructing an order among some of the facts involved.

Investigating the personality factors related to creativity in young scientists, Dorothy Garwood used tests to separate those of high creativity from those of low creativity. [35] She concluded that "The highly creative individual obtains satisfaction from the integration of initially disordered and complex phenomena. He thus tends to admit into consciousness disordered, irrational, nonconscious material which is ordinarily repressed, in order to achieve the satisfaction of integrating it creatively in a complex personal synthesis."

[35] Dorothy Simeon Garwood, "Personality Factors Related to Creativity in Young Scientists," *Journal of Abnormal and Social Psychology*, Vol. 68 (January-June 1964), 413-19.

Very often children introduce seemingly irrelevant data which may eventually be integrated into a new relationship. The untrained person considers a fact irrelevant if it is not included in the particular rationale he has in mind. However, a child does not recall and use an odd fact unless he feels it relates to the lesson in some way. A teacher may never know in what interesting ways his children use odd facts unless he encourages them to explain their conclusions. During the electricity lesson, the children introduced asbestos and the heaviness of wires into the colloquium. These facts had meaning for the sixth graders, and using these apparent irrelevancies helped them to understand the nature and purpose of the covering of electric wires. It seems that "irrelevancies" are a form of hidden likenesses. They are a form, too, of the unexpected which may lead to a serendipitous discovery.

In another study, Gerald Mendelsohn and Barbara Griswold found that the highly creative person used more peripheral cues in solving problems than the less creative person, and suggested that highly creative persons "may deploy their attention more widely and receive more cues." [36] They block out fewer data!

If this is true, then allowing children greater freedom to look, manipulate, and listen permits peripheral as well as clearly perceived cues to act as stimuli. The use of peripheral cues and "irrelevant" data is good practice for the young creative scientist. The more material available to him, the richer his synthesis of the facts may be—providing, of course, that he can tolerate the intervening chaos!

A minute number of people in the United States today are creative scientists. Is it worth our effort to base elementary science education on the kind of science activity in which these few engage? We might put the question another way: Why are there so few creative scientists? Has early education been responsible for limiting their number? There is evidence that the more creative person is less successful in high school than his potential warrants and often does not reach college. High grades are a major criterion in the scramble for admission to college; the more creative person is less apt to concentrate on obtaining the highest grades because these are given to children who do most accurately what the teacher demands. Creative persons feel free to ignore both authority and accepted patterns. Tracing the successful scientist back to what first interested him in his particular field, we find that the highly creative scientist developed a love of his subject very early in life—much earlier than the less creative scientist. [37] Is elementary school too early? That is where the interest of a creative scientist begins. Surely we have the responsibility of making science alluring in the first place.

In addition to fostering an interest in a subject for the personal satisfaction of the individual, there is a cogent social reason for fostering and developing creative joy in a subject. More and more, routine problems are being solved by computers. The new man of science provides data for computers. Finding the questions is now the key issue, since the answers can be computed very quickly. Norman Mackworth, in giving the eleventh Walter Van Dyke Bingham Lecture, pictured the future scientist with a computer keyboard in his office to find answers to every problem he thinks up, but according to Mackworth this may throw the young scientist into "a state of fascinated anguish. All this potential problem-solving power will be at their fingertips. For the first time they will have absolute freedom to think. . . . Nothing to do but think may be a mixed blessing when creative ideas do not come fast enough. . . ." [38]

These thoughts have been poignantly illustrated in the education of two brilliant young men, John Stewart Mill and Norbert Wiener, both of whom showed early signs of their prodigious wisdom. Mill was encouraged by his father to talk about his readings, to explain and synthesize the ideas in his own words, in his own way. Norbert's father insisted that his son always have a precisely correct answer to the question under consideration. Is it entirely an accident of history that Wiener developed the science of cybernetics—the science of computers—while Mill

[36] Gerald A. Mendelsohn and Barbara B. Griswold, "Differential Use of Incidental Stimuli in Problem Solving as a Function of Creativity," *Journal of Abnormal and Social Psychology*, Vol. 68 (January-June 1964), 431-36.

[37] Garwood, *op. cit.*

[38] Norman H. Mackworth, "Originality," *The American Psychologist*, Vol. 20 (1965), 51-66.

created a new logic, putting an ocean of facts together in a new way?

We have never tried to determine what potential for scientific creativity exists in any of our elementary school classrooms. We can observe that young children usually exhibit very easily the aspects of sciencing just described. Not only the "gifted." Not only the middle class. Not only the educationally advantaged. We have found evidence of creative sciencing among all types and ages of children who have been given the opportunity to make their own discoveries and to share their ideas in colloquia. You will find many of these examples in the lessons recorded in this book. Surely the elementary classroom is a place where children should be encouraged in their attempts to make order out of chaos.

The meaning of patterns

Everyone tries to organize the data in his environment in order to process or reduce the abundance of stimuli. Words expressing generalizations are examples of one such form of organization in our language. Think of the variety of items and the few essential likenesses each of these words conveys: suburbia, starchy foods, Chinese. Finding external and hidden likenesses organizes data by a few similarities, by some of their common attributes. Part of each datum is considered alike.

Types of patterns

What are the likenesses?

If the whole datum is repeated so that each part is exactly like the other, and this repetition is linked by a common structure or relationship, we have an organization by pattern. In finding likenesses, the nature of the similar parts is essential; here the pattern of organization, the structure linking the data, becomes important. Patterns may be concrete or abstract, just as likenesses may be external or hidden.

A scientist devotes much of his time and effort to finding patterns—regularities in the universe. Once the relationship among a few data has been uncovered and its regularity established, other data may be predicted and located.

What is the pattern of relationship? Predict where more daisies could be expected.

Acids fizz with a carbonate. The structure is the pattern of the relationship between hydrogen ions [39] in the acid and the carbonate radical in the carbonate. (Together they form carbonic acid, which breaks up into carbon dioxide and water; the carbon dioxide bubbles off, fizzes.) The pattern of this relationship, the structure between the parts, enables us to predict: when a carbonate fizzes, an acid could be present; when an acid makes a substance fizz, a carbonate may be present. The discovery of a pattern for the apparent motion of the stars across the sky enabled ancients to predict the coming of each season; this pattern has both a temporal and a spatial relationship—a concrete structure which can be perceived by the senses. In what way would you characterize the acid–carbonate structure?

Concrete or abstract?

A wallpaper pattern is based on a two-dimensional spatial relationship which enables a decorator to match strips of it in a total continuous pattern.

[39] An ion is an atom or group of atoms which has gained or lost one or more of the electrons in its outer shell.

The footprints of a bird hopping or running over a snowy surface show the positions of each foot in a regular linear relationship. The melody theme in a musical composition is another type of repetition—a temporal pattern. In what way would you characterize these relationships?

The repetition of actions by a person with a compulsion neurosis is an abstract pattern, one it took a Freud to discern. The red shift in the light spectrum of stars moving rapidly away from us is another abstract pattern. Both the compulsion and the red shift patterns contain an observable element which suggests repetition, but the link or structure relating each repetition in a pattern is an abstraction, a mental construct.

Mathematics has many patterns, most of them built on abstract structures. What is the link between numbers in a series 2, 4, 8, 16, . . .? (One is obvious, but mathematicians can construct many others.) Since 2, 4, 8, and 16 are not the same, we could argue that this series does not fit our definition of "pattern" which states that the datum must be repeated. This is because the stimulus here is visual. In mathematical terms, we could say that the *number* is *doubled* at each step. *The number* then becomes a datum if we think of it as *the result of the last doubling*. In the final analysis, the whole area of mathematics is abstract.

Two-dimensional symmetries The relationship one datum of a pattern bears to the remaining data (or the relationship of pattern units to their neighbors) is determined by structure. Pairs of items are related by the structure of symmetries. In spatial patterns symmetry is achieved by moving an item in a certain prescribed way. *Motion along a line* is called *translation symmetry*; it can be seen in borders—around a skirt, along a ceiling, at the edge of a flowerbed, in the decoration of Grecian vases. *The motion of rotation around a line* (an axis) produces *bilaterial* or *mirror symmetry*. (Children often think of this motion as a flip. If a triangle were lying on the table with a wire along one of its sides, and you flipped the triangle around the wire, where would each corner lie? The first and second positions together form a bilateral symmetry.) We are all familiar with bilateral or mirror symmetry; it can be seen approximately in our own bodies and in those of most animals, in many leaves, a pair of tongs, a sweet-pea flower. *The motion of rotation around a point* is known as *rotational symmetry*; a snowflake, a daisy, a starfish, and a wheel are examples of this.

A fourth type of symmetry exists which does not seem to fit into the category properly. Actually *glide symmetry* can be thought of in two very fitting ways. A child hopping with both feet parallel on wet sand leaves a bilateral symmetry of left and right footprints, a flip around an axis running between the feet. If the child walks instead of hopping, one half of the symmetry *moves along a straight line parallel to the axis*; it undergoes a glide. Two of these motions achieve glide symmetry. We could look at the repetition in another way. Take any pair of left and right footprints made in sequence and call this a unit, a datum; and moving this datum along a vector which represents the distance and direction of one step, we locate the next pair of footprints—simple translation symmetry.

Concrete or abstract?

Translation symmetry

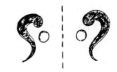

Bilateral symmetry

Rotational symmetry

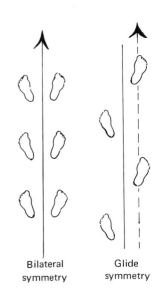

| Bilateral symmetry | Glide symmetry |

Glide symmetry seen as translation symmetry.

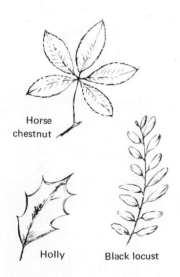

Horse chestnut

Holly   Black locust

Children can name the types of symmetry and find the axes.

Try to fit the shapes to the section. How many axes of symmetry does each have?

Being part of patterns, symmetries can have abstract as well as concrete structures. Perhaps the study of symmetries belongs more to mathematics or logic than to science. However, mathematics makes scientific descriptions more precise; it provides a way to codify patterns. Codifying patterns according to structures of symmetry is a form of classification, an economy of thinking; it generalizes, offers a pattern of search for prediction. For example, once the structure of the binomial expansion has been found, one can write any binomial expansion in its algebraic form:

$$(x + y)^3 = x^3 + 3x^2y + 3xy^2 + y^3$$

The expansion has a bilateral symmetry. This is obvious from studying the coefficients or powers. One might say that the x's and y's are not "reflected." On one hand, the variables x and y are interchangeable ($(y + x)^3$ yields the same essential pattern); it is preferable however, to think of the x and y variables as data just as we thought of the numbers as datum in the series 2, 4, 8, 16,. . . .

Sometimes an abstract symmetry can be translated into a visually symmetrical form. We could see the bilateral symmetry of the binomial theorem when we expressed its expansion algebraically. Some symmetries become visual if they are translated geometrically. For example, the equation $x^2 + y^2 = r^2$ does not look symmetrical. Its essential symmetry becomes evident if we draw the graph of this expression, it is a circle—rotational symmetry. In fact, all conic sections have symmetries, but the algebraic expressions which relate to them do not appear symmetrical. The paths of planets, moons, comets, and space capsules describe conic sections. Finding the dimensions of these paths enables scientists to predict where heavenly bodies and astronauts will be at certain times; codifying the symmetries in algebraic expressions helps the prediction.

Children can be encouraged to find symmetries in natural phenomena, to recognize and know the names of the various symmetries and to locate the point or line around which each symmetry is built. Activities should not only embrace mathematics, but art: designs with potato prints, leaf blueprints, exhibits of leaves; both the form of the individual leaf and the pattern of arrangement can then be analyzed and appropriately named.

Dr. Z.P. Dienes, the mathematician who developed multibase blocks as concrete materials for children, has described some absorbing games which

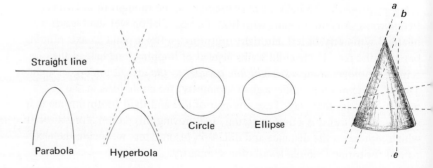

Straight line

Parabola   Hyperbola   Circle   Ellipse

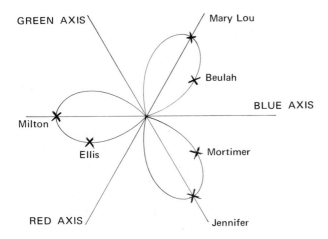

Where would each child land from a green flip? What movements of this trefoil would put Mortimer in Ellis' place?

can induce children to think in terms of flipping patterns around axes of symmetry.[40]

Easy to very stimulating exercises in bilateral symmetry are also provided by the Mirror Cards.[41] By placing a small mirror in certain positions, sets of pictures are made to look like the sample *mirror cards*. The position of the mirror, of course, is the axis of symmetry. The problems range from simple to very complex and include some which are impossible; the cards appeal to children beginning in the third grade.

If children are given two mirrors and small colorful patches of cloth or paper, they will discover (by making patterns of rotational symmetry) that the smaller the angle between the mirrors, the greater the number of

Where would you place the mirror on the two mirror cards above to obtain each of the patterns at left? Try to predict which of the patterns at left will be impossible.

[40] Z.P. Dienes and E.W. Golding, *Exploration of Space and Practical Measurement*, Herder and Herder, New York (1966), pp. 48-57.

[41] Mirror Cards (18418) and Teachers' Guide, developed by Marion I. Walter, are sold by the Webster Division of McGraw-Hill, Inc., Manchester, Mo., 63011.

repetitions. (Two mirrors at an angle is the principle upon which kaleido-scopes are built.)

One-egg twins sometimes provide evidence of mirror symmetry. If there are such twins in your school, ask the children to find the "reflections." (An example would be cowlicks in hair growth which sweep in opposite directions.)

Three-dimensional symmetries Only symmetries or patterns based on two-dimensional structures have been discussed thus far. Of course, there are also three-dimensional patterns. A honeycomb is built by stacking hexagonal solids in a three-dimensional pattern. The regularity or repetition of stacking gives the honeycomb its characteristic appearance. Crystal forms are another example of three-dimensional patterns. Suppose we think of a cube. It has two different planes of symmetry; it can be cut in half parallel to a face or diagonally through opposite edges. Young children should be given small blocks to handle, to find what they can do with them. If these blocks include solid shapes (such as halves or other fractions of cubes, prisms, tetrahedra, etc.), the children can learn kinesthetically about symmetries; names for solids can be given during the experience.

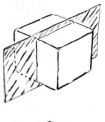

When children build with these blocks, they are really "stacking" them. If they stack them in a pattern, they may be making models of crystal growth. Molecules in a crystal are stacked according to a structure; an ordering of molecules builds the shape of the visible crystal. A salt crystal, for example, has a cubic form: each sodium or chloride ion is surrounded by six of the other ions; it is as if each ion were at the center of one of the planes of a cube surrounding a central ion.

There are three different *rotational* symmetries to a cube: an axis running through the centers of opposite faces forms one line of rotation; an axis through opposite corners provides another; an axis joining the midpoints of opposite edges is the third. How many similar views of the crystal can be seen if you turn a cube through each of these rotations?

A two-dimensional pattern can be made, or visualized, as a result of several dynamic factors operating in three dimensions. To illustrate, fill a hollow cone (a paper cup or the corner of an envelope) with fine sand or salt and attach it to a frame with a long string; it will act as a pendulum. Then cut a hole at the apex of the cone large enough to allow the sand or salt to flow

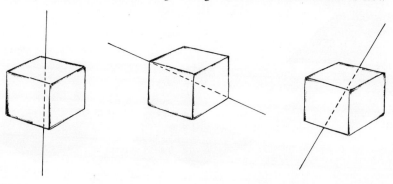

slowly through. When the pendulum is swung over a base of dark construction paper, a pattern will be traced on the paper (shown above). This visual two-dimensional symmetry results from a three-dimensional structure acting in time; it is both a spatial and temporal pattern. The rhythmic swing of the pendulum also has its own symmetry due to the abstract relationship between the length of the string and the pull of gravity. The pattern traced can be a straight line, an ellipse, or a circle. If the cone of sand is attached by two strings to a bar, more complicated patterns may be traced.

It is technically difficult to obtain clear pictures with such home-made equipment. Suggestions for obtaining clearer patterns are described in *A Teachers' Guide to Pendulums*, developed by the Elementary Science Study of Newton, Mass. [42] Filmloops illustrating different types of pendulum arrangements and obtainable patterns are available from both McGraw-Hill and the Ealing Corporation, 2225 Massachusetts Ave., Cambridge, Mass. 02140.

Other dynamic spatial and temporal patterns operating in three dimensions are illustrated by the muscular motions of the wings of a bird in flight, the legs of a crawling centipede, the body of a fish as it swims, and certain movements of a dancer or athlete. The patterns of the *latter two* can be made visual in two dimensions by using a stereoscopic camera.

The movements of the bodies in the solar system are also three-dimensional patterns in time. Our observation of these patterns, however, seems two-dimensional: the path of the sun across the sky from day to day and season to season; the path of the moon in days and months; the nightly and yearly paths of the planets. To test a child's understanding of these patterns which form data in every elementary school science series, we can ask him what he thinks he would observe if the angle of the earth's axis were perpendicular to the plane of the ecliptic. (Both daily and seasonal observations would be affected. See page 88.)

Abstract patterns Abstract patterns are mental constructs. There is probably no limit to the number of abstract patterns the human mind can construct.

The earth's axis makes an angle of 23½° with the plane of the ecliptic. (The ecliptic is the imaginary circle where the plane of the earth's orbit meets the celestial sphere.)

[42] Now the Education Development Center, 55 Chapel Street, Newton, Mass. 02160. The publications were marketed by the Webster Division of McGraw-Hill, Inc., Manchester, Mo., 63011.

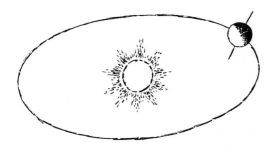

Our earth bears this relation to the plane of the ecliptic and the sun.

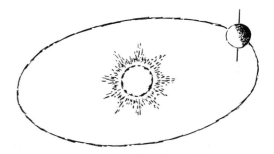

What kind of seasons would there be on earth if this were the relation?

We have already mentioned one that Freud described: the pattern of a compulsion neurosis; something in the human emotional dynamics of a person makes him perform the same acts again and again regardless of their appropriateness to the situation. Without a neurosis, people may transfer a pattern of behavior; Mrs. Weiss discerned that Cyril was repeating a pattern of behavior toward the mealworm which paralleled his father's behavior toward him.

About a century ago, Ernst Haeckel discovered that a mammal embryo repeats part of the development of the animals in simpler phyla. "Ontogeny recapitulates phylogeny" became the expression of this extended pattern.

An abstract relationship may be perceived between the structure of a society and the structure of thinking of the people who live in that society. In the rigid structure or division of classes in feudal society, lords and serfs had completely separate identities; feudal thinkers tended to place Right and Wrong, Beauty and Good into absolute and unchanging categories. A merchant society is much more fluid. A merchant can be rich or poor (or both) during his lifetime; he can be ruler or ruled. His category is not fixed. He can evolve, change. Feudal thinkers emphasized groups or wholes, rather than individuals or items; thinkers in a merchant society tend to apply evolutionary concepts to values and mores, to emphasize the role of the individual. Extended through the range of history, this becomes a pattern—a pattern of thinking about thinking! (Systematized patterns of thinking are logics.)

Individuals within any society have patterns of thinking. For the most part, these patterns do not differ radically from prevailing patterns, but there will be individual idiosyncrasies which belong to a particular person and his pattern of living. In this way, we can distinguish a work by Monet from one by Degas, or a musical composition by Beethoven from one by Mozart.

Children have patterns of thinking, too. By following the remarks of one child during a series of colloquia, we can often see that he is pursuing one special thought, one special way of looking at his experiences. We will now examine three children's individual patterns of thought.

A DOUGHNUT IS A SQUISHED ROD

Zach Gottfried had attended a summer institute concerned with the new ideas and materials being developed for elementary science education. His next year as a fifth-grade private school teacher proved so rich in developing drive and interest in science among his boys that the school appointed him science coordinator for the following semesters. Zach's job, a new one to the school, was to help regular grade teachers enliven their science programs by offering materials, making procedural suggestions, and at times, even taking over the teaching. The school ran from kindergarten through the eighth grade and most of the grades had two sections. Since Zach ardently believed that every child must have materials to manipulate during his investigations, he devoted an enormous amount of time to finding and assembling suitable "things." Zach was an ingenious inventor, excellent at constructing accurate equipment from household wares, but fourteen classes and a range of nine years provided him with an enjoyable challenge. He was not taxed with the responsibilities of a family; his time was willingly and fully spent.

Zach's materials proved alluring to the children. They went to work with a will and showed all the delighted ingenuity he expected. However, the science period was limited; how else could the visiting Mr. Gottfried get around to help everyone? The schedule allowed forty minutes—a little long for the scattered interests of kindergarteners, their teachers predicted, and perhaps a little short for the intellectual interests of busy eighth graders. For the upper classes, however, good grades in the "important" subjects were essential so the boys could win placements in prestigious high schools. No more time for science could be spared.

On each grade level, forty minutes proved to be inadequate for the experiences the new science coordinator offered. Zach had an additional problem: he believed children ought to discuss their findings before switching to another subject or lesson. "When they put their discoveries into words, they know what they have learned," he explained. "By listening to them, I know how far their thinking's gone and what to bring in next time."

So the forty-minute investigation was further reduced, and then the week's wait before a follow-up lesson often necessitated a short discussion-reminder before the materials were presented in their new form. In the upper grades, Zach was able to arrange a double period occasionally, even at the expense of waiting two weeks for the follow-up lesson.

"Something solid seems to happen if the doing and thinking and talking are rounded out. The kids can wait to pick up where they left off." Then, too, the teachers of the older children seemed to find time to introduce scientifically-allied concepts while other subjects were being studied. The molds some fourth graders were growing led them to books, and "the reading period might just as well be on fungi as on a fourth-grade reader," the classroom teacher said. In another fourth grade, the colors and shapes of molds inspired art work, and some children wrote imaginative stories about how it would feel to be a mold spore!

In the third grade, Zach Gottfried decided to record the colloquia, the subtly guided discussions of discoveries which clarify thinking and develop and test explanations (see Chapter 2).

That semester the third grade was working with magnets. Each child was given two doughnut ceramic magnets, an alnico rod magnet, and a rather

Textbook publishers are including more and more "hardware" with printed materials. In a program with which we are familiar, experimental materials are supplied in sufficient quantity for use by a whole class.

Later we describe a "free choice" classroom where the teacher is only called upon when needed.

Where schools have more liberal time allotments, science teaching becomes easier. However, it can occur within a restrictive time period (see Chapter 7).

weak steel horseshoe magnet. [43] Over the spring semester (from February to June), Zach wrote down the boys' conversations, especially their remarks during the colloquia. Time did not permit a colloquium to be held during each session, so there are fewer recordings than there are weeks. And of course there were the usual vacations, time off for achievement tests, and an occasional cold which kept the teacher at home.

From the total colloquia, we choose to follow the remarks of three particular boys. Sometimes a child made only one remark during a colloquium, sometimes several; each boy did not speak every time. However, since each child was exploring the materials, might be conversing with a neighbor during the exploration, and was certainly listening to others during the colloquium, we must assume that he was learning many things, engaging in germinal thinking even when he was not contributing orally to the group. He did express what he most wanted to say; he verbalized what was most important to him. As will be seen, each child chose to ply a theme; each had a pattern to his flow of language, a pattern evidently reflecting his flow of thought. Maybe the pattern fit his personality; maybe it was related to a current absorbing interest. We cannot know. But from the bare remarks which follow, we can perceive a hidden pattern behind each boy's total remarks.

Leonard

Maybe you would like to underline the phrases related to the concepts of "power" as you read.

First we will follow Leonard. He is concerned with whether force, strength, and power appear or disappear as he investigates the magnets.

Early February

"Doughnuts stick to any part of the horseshoe. I'm surprised, because I can make the doughnuts push apart. Horseshoe magnet is not as strong, if it is a magnet."

Late February

"I read in a book that one place in the core of the earth is magnetic."

"When you put a magnet to metal, the metal becomes a magnet. See!" [He held a magnet to three paper clips in series.]

"On both sides of the wood they push each other."

Early April

"All magnets have power."

[Another boy pointed out that a magnet attached to a paper clip or some other iron object becomes a magnet itself, and another clip will stick to *it*.]

"They won't stick forever."

[Back to the concept that the earth has lodestone in it; the children thought this made the earth magnetic. One child said he had read that there is lodestone at the south pole as well as at the north pole.]

How would you correct statements which seem to reflect erroneous concepts?

"Impossible! Because a compass has a special metal on its ends that only point north."

"The rods aren't as strong as the doughnuts." [Mr. Gottfried asked, "Why?"] "Because they are stretched out."

[43] Magnets produced by The Learning Center, Princeton, N.J. 08540.

Mid-April

[After using iron filings with the magnets.] "Look! The filings stand up. When the magnet is taken away, it falls down. The force must go up."

[At the beginning of the colloquium, Mr. Gottfried had posed the question, "How is a rod magnet like a doughnut magnet?" Children had given various external likenesses. Then:] "A doughnut is a squished rod."

Late April

"I know! Magnetic forces are like muscles. The magnetism pushes or pulls things, like muscles in your arm."

[Interpreting a picture one boy had drawn of iron filings on a paper placed over two doughnut magnets (reproduced at right):] "The magnets are pulling each other."

Ethan

Leonard extended his observations to contribute points about relative strengths and the coming and going of power; in contrast, Ethan's pattern of interest centered on what the poles of the magnets were doing.

Late February

[A group of boys had piled the magnets on a dowel so that they rested as shown at the side of the page. Someone said, "One side sucks; the other side pushes."]

"Not true. Might be true in one case, but one side sticks and if you turn it around, it pushes."

Early March

"You can make a chain of paper clips stick together with a magnet at one end, and a piece of metal will stick to the end of the chain."

Early April

"Magnets can make iron or steel into magnets."

"Oh, I remember; they will only be magnets for a while. Part of the magnetic power is sent to the other paper clip."

"I can't make the rods stick to the sides of the doughnuts; they always roll off and stick to the ends. The ends seem stronger."

"The doughnuts are stronger. They have bigger ends."

[Mr. Gottfried asked, "How can you make the rod like the doughnut?"]

"Bend it into a circle."

[" Will the bend be magnetic like the side of the doughnut?" Mr. Gottfried continued.]

"Hmmmmm."

[Later during the lesson:] "I think if you cut the rod in two pieces it will still be magnets. A way to make a rod stronger would be to cut it into little pieces smaller than the middle and put them side by side in a circle, and you would have a stronger magnet."

["Why?"]

"Because the magnet is stronger than in the middle when its ends are bigger. It works because each little piece becomes a magnet with ends bigger than the middle."

Each child must say it in his own way!

Sent via the ends, no doubt.

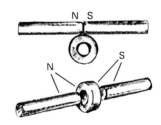

Try to figure out the relationships of the poles in these two systems.

It is up to the teacher to figure out what a child means when his phrasing is strange.

Other children made these discoveries during March.

Other boys drew these diagrams:

(1)

Ethan probably thinks of the "force" in this way, meaning the distance between the flat surfaces which serve as poles is shorter in a doughnut than in a rod

(2)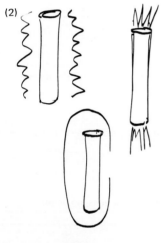

(3)

Mid-April

["How is a rod magnet like a doughnut?" Mr. Gottfried asked.]

"They both have two ends."

"The force is at either end. So in a doughnut the force is stronger because it can come around." [See Ethan's diagram (1) below.]

[Reacting to drawings of iron filing orientations made by three other boys (see diagrams in (2) below):] "These guys haven't done any experiments!"

End of April

[Looking at diagram (3), another boy asked Ethan, "What is pulling?"]

"The ends; the bottom of the magnet is trying to pull the filings, but they won't go around because of the cardboard."

"The ends are pulling the filings across."

June

[Mr. Gottfried asked what would happen if the magnetized paper clip he had in his hand were cut into two pieces.]

"It will become two magnets, each with two poles."

Ethan's pattern of thinking led him to concentrate on the magnetic poles or ends, helping him to imagine them as potential ends joining each other within the length of a rod magnet; if the rod were cut into as many ends as possible and arranged in a circle, a flat doughnut magnet with a stronger push and pull would result.

Ethan's concept is analogous to Leonard's "squished rod." However, Leonard sought the strongest power (even squishing a rod is a powerful motion!); Ethan arranged the ends where the pull seemed concentrated so they added up to the greatest possible pull.

Do these thought trends reflect personality characteristics?

Dudley

Dudley seemed more intrigued with what went on around the magnet: its field of interaction, the space between magnets.

Early February

"One side of the doughnut is a magnet; the other side is not a magnet."

"It has like a force field which pushes them apart."

Late February

"The force around. There is a force on all sides of the magnet. A north side and a south side; the book said so."

"Turn both over; both will push away. If you want them to stick, you have to turn one over."

Early March

"The magnets will stick through my tongue, see!" [His tongue occupied the *space between* the magnets.]

Mid-March

"At home I took two bar magnets and placed them flat and I could make one turn around using the other without touching it."

Early April
    ["Magnets interact with _____ ?"]
    "Iron and steel."
    "The force goes into the paper clip."
Mid-April
    [Dudley draws his diagram of the way iron filings react with the magnets.]
Late April
    [Someone said that force leads to motion.]
    "Here is an example: lift a book and let it fall." [He does just that!]
    "The magnet pulls itself to the radiator."

These examples show individual patterns of response—idiosyncratic ways of coping with materials, of thinking about interactions. Each child is consistent in his approach, his central theme, although each varies his pattern of thought. The growth in thought revealed by the children's words indicates that they are learning. Free discovery permits each to find his own way, to use his natural responses to build his thoughts into a learning pattern, to consolidate fleeting responses into a structure of thought—learning in its deepest sense.

All of these individual freedoms are bound by the set structure of the materials involved. Children reach similar conclusions because there is a concept which binds and relates the materials through their interactions. Children will achieve similar meanings via different routes, led by their own thinking patterns.

Leonard, Ethan, and Dudley were limited by the structure of their materials: three of the objects were magnets—similar in nature, but different in shape. This structure relates the materials by their analogous functions and forms; there is a similarity in their differences. Such built-in analogies (hidden likenesses) helped the children to discover a broader view of magnetism than they could have from using only one magnet or identical magnets.

The magnets show a pattern of behavior. There is a pattern to their parts; there are broad, flat poles in the doughnut and small poles in the rod. The strengths of the various magnets and their parts form another kind of pattern, a *series* of comparative strengths. The middle of both the rod and the horseshoe magnets shows no strength of pulling or pushing. The ends of the horseshoe are weak; the ends of the rods are stronger; the ends of the doughnut are strongest. The ends of the magnets are enlargements of the orientation pattern of their atomic dipoles; each atom is a tiny magnet with north and south poles.

Ethan inferred a hidden likeness from this: the ends pulling on each other are repeated within the magnet. He had formed this mental pattern before Zach asked him what cutting the magnetized paper clip into pieces would do. Ethan extended his pattern of thought about magnetic ends to the unseen by talking about his ideas and discoveries in the colloquium. He predicted that the pattern would be repeated inside of the rod; he saw a strength in exposed ends, and thought of arranging bits of the rod in a circle so that it was all ends like the doughnut.

Leonard discovered the structure of the series of comparative strengths, and used his imaginary strength to think of "squishing" one type of magnet into another type.

Dudley noticed that magnetism manifests itself in the space around a magnet. The dowel helped to reveal this fact to him; so did the feeling he had when he held two magnets near one another. Some of the boys measured how many inches away the magnet could still interact with the clip; Dudley felt the magnet draw itself to the radiator.

There are patterns in the structure of materials, in the way children learn, and in the way people build concepts. We will now discuss how a teacher can look for and recognize these patterns.

Perceiving emerging patterns in thought and behavior

Patterns exist in the way people think, in the way they behave, and in the way they organize curricula. One of the roles of education is to change children's thought and behavioral patterns by means of their curriculum, a process sometimes considered as fostering growth. In the type of education we advocate, we do not envisage one pattern of behavior, or even one pattern of thinking; although we lean heavily upon the conceptual pattern of science curriculum, it is not the only one possible.

Children should be free to choose and develop their own patterns of behavior and thought; these will then be related to the group with which each child identifies. At the beginning of this century, the aim of a son of poor immigrant parents was often to become middle class; education at that time helped him substantially. Upper class children, in turn, went to private schools where entirely different patterns of behavior and thought were developed.

Many of today's children, especially in urban centers, feel more closely associated with some of the minority drives than with the American dreams of bygone days. A classroom can create an atmosphere where growth in several directions is possible—where each child, given a choice within some structure, develops his own patterns of behavior and thought. Thus the teacher must be able to perceive and foster the emerging patterns in each child's personality.

Most children fit into the created classroom atmosphere; either family and school project the same values or the child has learned to adjust to the fact that they do not. Children in such classrooms make very few choices; various means are employed to ensure a great measure of conformity. Those who fail to conform in spite of overt and covert pressures are considered misfits or problems; yet a "misfit" child has his own patterns of thought and behavior which are meaningful to him. Descriptions follow of two such children and the ways in which their teachers perceived the children's individual patterns and offered them opportunities to grow, to change.

Kristina—the "disrupter" Each teacher who knew she was to have Kristina in her class next September girded herself. Kristina's reputation was like a dark shadow falling before her—to everyone except Barbara Milton. Miss Milton had decided that there was always a bright light behind an object which cast a shadow. Certainly if noise, activity, interaction, and excitement represented brightness, Kristina produced it. The trouble was that Kristina's activities in most classrooms spelled disruption—disruption of peace, quiet, busy deskwork, and attentiveness.

In Barbara's sixth-grade class, however, the atmosphere was different: work was organized around activities; the children spoke together about what they were doing, often in a crescendo; each child could freely choose the area in which he wished to work. Since self-motivated study was not initiated until the sixth grade in this school, the first month always seemed chaotic to the principal. However, as the year progressed, the work produced by Miss Milton's class and the general bearing of her children were both so encouraging that the faculty were interested in having free-choice classrooms in the lower grades as well. After all, isn't that what kindergarten is like? If it works at both ends, why not in the middle? It might be worth trying with mixed age groups!

On the Monday morning before Thanksgiving, Kristina zoomed into Miss Milton's classroom—as usual, after work had started. She breezed past a table where three children were working with clay, flattening a ball one child had just rolled. "Oh you; you're an ol' meanie," shouted a boy much smaller than Kristina as he re-rolled his clay.

Kristina stopped momentarily by a group of children who were busy with multibase blocks.[44] "You've got a base five flat in the wrong box," she remarked.

"So put it back in the right place," countered Clayton, and went on arranging his blocks for a problem in base six. Kristina stood for a moment absorbed in Clayton's work. Then she wrote the subtraction problem Clayton's blocks illustrated[45] on the blackboard with the tip of the chalk; this made piercing screeches. Two children put their hands over their ears; Barbara gritted her teeth. The screech technique had been Kristina's *tour de force* against each of her previous teachers.

Miss Milton went over to Clayton's desk, looked at his blocks and then at Kristina's subtraction on the board. "Can you convince Clayton that your record is correct for his problem, Kristina?" Kristina gave a delighted smile; she and Clayton talked quietly for a while.

A few moments later, Barbara saw (and heard!) William chasing Kristina around the room. When they reached the lockers, William hit Kristina on the shoulder with a book he had in his hand. Kristina turned around, made a face and poked out her tongue. William returned to the library corner where, no doubt, he had been disturbed by a punch from Kristina in the first place. After quietly hanging up

[44] Developed by Z.P. Dienes and marketed by Herder & Herder, New York.
[45] In these books a *flat* is a square of units. It represents the base squared.

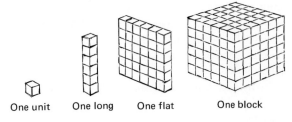

One unit   One long   One flat   One block

her coat and scarf, Kristina surveyed the room. Her eyes came to rest on the science table where Angel, a recent arrival from Puerto Rico, was busy swinging two metal washers. The washers were suspended by strings from tongue depressors taped to the edge of the table. Kristina sauntered over to Angel, with whom she now seemed to be making friends after her earlier teasings about why hell could be found in an angel. (The name is pronounced Ahn-hell.)

For a few minutes the two children sat on the floor swinging the pendulum and trying to make them hit one another. Then Kristina noticed a ball of clay on the table. She molded this around her washer and said, "Race you; bet mine goes faster. Let's start them together." The pendulums were the same length; both children held their bobs to one side. "One, two, three, go!" Quiet attention. The swings of the two pendulums were almost identical; as they slowed down, they became slightly out of phase. "Wait a minute." Kristina moved quickly and gracefully across the room to the clay crock, took out a

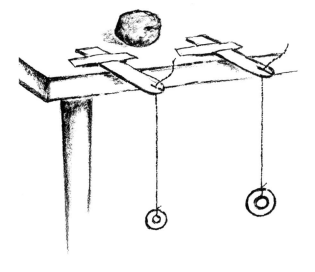

lump and fixed it over the other clay bob. "Ain't that nice an' big? Bet it goes faster now." The children started the pendulums swinging again. Same result. "Gosh!"—and Kristina went over to tell Miss Milton about her discovery.

"Why does it happen?" she asked.

"Why do you think it happens?" replied the teacher.

"I dunno," but Kristina looked thoughtful. "Do we hafta write up what we did?"

"Why don't you and Angel make one record; if you help him with his English, maybe he'll do the illustrations. Here's a piece of carbon paper. Then each of you can keep a copy."

After lunch, Kristina and Angel were back at the pendulums. Another pair of children joined them at the far side of the table. They were all shortening and lengthening their strings, watching the way the light and heavy bobs swung. "Don't make no difference the size of the weight," announced Kristina, but the others were intent on their own work and did not seem to hear her.

Barbara Milton went over to the group and placed a stop watch and card on the table near Kristina. The card read, "Can you make your pendulum swing twice as fast as Angel's?"

For a while, Kristina and Angel were absorbed in working the stop watch. Then Kristina read the card to Angel and said "S'eezy." She pulled her string until it was half the length of Angel's, gave him the stop watch, and said, "Time half a minute; I'll count swings." Then, "That's not twice, not nearly."

"Huh?" Angel said.

They worked feverishly for the next 20 minutes including the other two children in their problem. Each child began making a record of the length of string and the number of swings his bob made in 30 seconds.

They finally found a length which swung twice as fast as another length. "It's much, much less than half," Kristina announced.

Miss Milton found time to hold a colloquium with the group; she proposed that they record their results on a joint graph which would be hung on the wall. She also suggested having the string length in inches along one axis and the number of "round trip swings" along the other axis.

A week later, after other children had worked at the science table, all concerned held a joint colloquium and discussed the shape of the graph. (It is a parabola.)

How do you perceive Kristina's patterns of behavior and thought. In what way did Miss Milton use the curriculum to foster growth, to change patterns?

Rick—who "played house" Rick was nine and very small for his age. [46] (All of his teachers had found him immature; they reported that he "played house" instead of attending to his studies.) The second time Rick came to science class, he rushed in ahead of everyone else to read the Investigators' Log he and his co-workers had dictated during the first free discovery lesson.

Rick concentrated on the Log. He was not a facile reader, so it took him some time. He smiled when he reached the last sentence—the one he had contributed. By this time, the other children had arrived; the materials were placed on the table: strong alnico magnets, tin cans, glass jars, paper cups, Canadian nickels, and six-inch squares of paper, aluminum foil, leather, cardboard, and plastic.

Rick put a nickel inside a tin can and placed his magnet on the outside. He found that the nickel stuck to the inside of the can. Then, using the tin can as a telephone, he carried on an imaginary conversation with no one in particular. No one participated in this "house play" with Rick.

The other children were investigating the interaction of the magnet and the nickel through layer upon layer of various materials. Copying this activity, Rick found that the magnet and the nickel interacted through layers of leather, paper, foil, and more leather. At this point the array evidently looked like a sandwich to Rick, because he pretended to eat it!

Finally he returned to his tin-can assembly. After making the nickel stick to the inside of the can again, he carefully removed the magnet and discovered that the nickel still stuck. He and a neighbor borrowed the teacher's watch to find our how long the nickel stayed there—three minutes and 59 seconds.

[46] Adapted from B. Lansdown, "Each Child Has His Tempo," *Nature and Science*, Teacher's Edition, Vol. 4, No. 9 (Jan. 30, 1967), T1, T4, copyright © 1966 by The American Museum of Natural History, Doubleday & Company, Inc.

If "playing house" is Rick's present *modus vivendi* to learning, why shouldn't he be allowed to use it as a bridge in his learning pattern?

Rick did not present the same exhausting challenge that Kristina did. He was quiet and unobtrusive; he was immature, to be sure. But suggestions from the other children helped to get him started, and he did contribute his own ideas later. Rick's activities did add up to learning. He even introduced measurement when he timed the magnetization of the tin can, giving a touch of scientific precision!

Previous teachers regarded Rick's "houseplay" as an excuse to avoid lessons. His teacher here recognized this behavior pattern as a pause or interlude between constructive activities, activities which must largely be suggested by other children.

A teacher can find Rick's type of emerging learning pattern by watching and sometimes by listening. Teachers are accustomed to observing characteristics of individual children's behavior, but they may not always consider such atypical behavior to be a genuine learning pattern. Observations are more often made with the idea of helping the child become more conventional in his behavior. It takes time, thought, and an open attitude toward new possibilities to find the thread of learning in what seems to be difficult behavior. It takes even more time and thought to find ways in which to weave these patterns into a particular classroom situation. This can be most easily achieved if teachers set aside a period to discuss various learning behaviors with other teachers;[47] such behaviors can then take on new meanings and be given the leeway they need to blossom fully.

Whole classes as well as individual children may display at least partially unorthodox patterns of learning. Every teacher has found that one year's fifth grade, for instance, acts very differently from his fifth grade the year before. The same lesson is also learned very differently by children of different ages. Of course, there are age patterns, too.

The age pattern variant was illustrated by Zach Gottfried, whose lessons were recorded in the previous section, when he tried his magnets in the kindergarten one day. For the first session, the

[47] Administrators can be helpful in providing for this.

children were given rod magnets and iron filings encased in plastic; for the second, two rod magnets apiece; for the third, both rod and doughnut magnets. At the end of the three sessions, Zach compared the pattern of learning of the kindergartners with that of the third graders.

With kindergartners, the success of the magnets seems to show that manipulative materials are the *only* way to interest and motivate them. (I had previously tried a lesson where I directed activities from the front of the room.) The kids were clamoring for more magnet lessons, and actually cheered when they saw me arrive with a box of materials.

They feel free and investigate with no inhibitions. They are noisy, but with a definite purpose. They are the most fun to teach when they actually have the materials and can discover things for themselves.

After three sessions they actually begin to articulate their discoveries. Simple description of facts: magnets push and pull; they work through certain materials, such as paper; the rod and the doughnut look different, but do the same things. The third grade did not come to a verbal level of understanding until after about six to eight weeks of discovery and colloquium. [We have compared the growth of sophistication from first to third grade colloquia. See *Eureka!* lesson, pages 20-25.]

The kindergartners always seemed to be at a play level, although I could see that they were honestly investigating the magnets and making discoveries without expressing them. The more talkative children were content to remain at play, while the quiet ones came up with the surprising remarks. (Had they been bored before?) The most antisocial seemed the brightest.

Some patterns can be sensed quickly; others have to be sought. Before patterns can be usefully perceived in either case, they need to be studied. A teacher can study patterns through careful watching and sensitive listening, but he usually has to take notes so that the emerging patterns can be separated from apparently irrelevant data. Before a pattern is fully realized, before the repeated unit is isolated, he hardly knows what to observe. Patterns finally emerge after reading, rereading, and thinking about the recorded facts. Kristina's rushing about disturbing other children is obvious, but are there some deeper patterns to her activities?

Let us group together, juxtapose, some of Kristina's relevant behavior. All her interactions were with boys; she gained their attention through attack or horseplay. Well, Kristina was large for her age, physiologically mature, perhaps approaching an early adolescence. Her interactions were constructive or cooperative when an intellectual concomitant was present: she was quickly able to record the base six subtraction Clayton was puzzling over; she worked cooperatively with Angel exhibiting leadership; she easily perceived the problems the pendulum materials and Miss Milton's added suggestions posed. In other words, Kristina is physically and intellectually more mature than most of the other children in her class.

The freedom and flexibility of Miss Milton's classroom—its atmosphere of structured, but open, opportunities—allowed Kristina to reveal her behavior pattern. If she had been seated all the time, perhaps engaged in hitting her neighbor, it would not have been obvious that the *boys* were her objective; it might have seemed that hitting was. Kristina freely chose to work a math problem in an algorism when this was not her area of study at the moment. The challenge of the pendulums (never an easy problem for elementary school children) was worth her attention and also led to graphical recording—another mathematical challenge. Of course, Miss Milton's praise of an acceptable act, even when it was overshadowed by the noisy chalk screech, helped to bring Kristina's positive feelings to the surface as well.

With all the teacher's responsibilities—and one must marvel at his range of abilities—he cannot be expected to keep a running commentary on everything that occurs in his classroom. Wherever he finds a problem, however, it is advisable for him to make a few anecdotal records of the lesson or session involved. This can be delegated to a student teacher; it provides excellent training for an aide. Recording problem situations in the classroom might be a fine activity for upper level children who are studying human behavior as well.

Notes cannot be kept on every child in a class at once, of course; those whose patterns of behavior seem atypical, puzzling or troublesome to other children or to the teacher should be given the closest attention. Over the course of the year, every child can be observed. (Ways to organize these observations are given in Chapter 8.)

Patterns emerge when records are thoughtfully studied. However, a possible pattern may be sensed during the actual recording. Recognizing a pattern of physical behavior or of cognitive learning is the beginning of understanding the way in which an individual responds to his environment (in this case, the classroom atmosphere). The way most children respond tells us something about the atmosphere itself! Beginning to understand an individual's patterns provides a guide for choosing materials which might be used in his curriculum to foster growth—to lure the Kristina's toward constructive leadership, to allow the Rick's the needed pauses in the day's occupations.

Patterns shown by an entire class indicate the direction a class unit might follow.

The teacher's role in using patterns

A curriculum is planned in relation to concepts and subconcepts, but several possible subconcepts may be introduced in beginning and developing a unit. The direction a follow-up lesson will take is influenced by what the children did with the initial materials (their pattern of behavior) and what they said during the colloquium (their pattern of thinking). Of course, allowances can and should be made for individual children to be given special directions on the basis of their needs.

One of the major interests during the sixth-grade *Hook Up a Circuit* lesson conducted by Mr. McIver was in wires that got hot when short circuited from both ends of a battery. This was a pattern repeated by several children. Mr. McIver decided to let the class choose what to explore at the next lesson; there were various suggestions, trends which could be related—developed into patterns—later. But let us suppose (as happened with a later class) that he had wished to extend this pattern of interest in hot wires into a larger pattern of learning. The pattern of interest does point along its own conceptual arrow:

hot wires → resistance; hot wires used for heating irons, for electric heaters, for stoves; hot wires—so hot that they glow—used for electric lights; hot wires—so hot that they melt easily—used for fuses. These are all practical extensions of the idea, avenues which suggest materials for exploration. The concept of the hot wires is a subset of the energy scheme: electrical energy is converted to heat energy and light energy.

After perceiving this conceptual pattern—the children's pattern of interest—how does the teacher carry out its implications? First the children can be supplied with the words "electrical energy" when needed during the colloquium. At a later date, the ideas that heat energy can be converted to light energy and that electrical energy can be converted to heat energy will be verbally expressed, first by the children in their own way and then by the teacher in scientific terms.

As for the materials, the bridge designed to help Luizanne explore the nature of switches (page 58) can be used equally well in investigating fuses. Or various materials can be tested across a single pole, single throw knife switch. The gap in the knife switch becomes part of a circuit when bridged by an electrical conductor. Various wires and widths of aluminum foil strips can be placed across the gap; the effect of nonconductors of electricity can also be studied in this manner. Some materials get hot, some glow, some burn out, some will not conduct the current so that nothing obvious occurs (a bulb put in the circuit will not light).

The colloquia could then explore a whole range of phenomena from heat to light to melting—in fact, the entire range of the electromagnetic spectrum. All this is an extension of the pattern of interest in wires getting hot!

Sooner or later during an investigation of mealworms children will discover a "white thing" among the worms. Of course, there will be much speculation about the nature of this white thing. The children may have to be assured that nothing has been added to the box of mealworms since they last handled it; the white thing, therefore, came from inside the box—"from the mealworms," the children assert. Their first idea is usually that the object is a cluster of eggs, applying the pattern that lowly creatures do lay

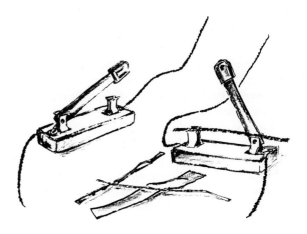

eggs. But a closer observation reveals an interesting structure to this white thing. Children begin to observe the structure of a mealworm's body inside the object: it has "lines" (segments), a "head end," places where six legs might be, a "rear end." And the thing "wriggles" when touched; eggs do not.

To help the children develop a pattern of thought about the larva-pupa stages in the insect life cycle, the teacher might pose the question: "Have you ever seen anything like this before—other wormlike creatures that crawl and eat and then have a nonmoving stage?" Invariably someone will suggest that a butterfly goes through these stages: a caterpillar, a cocoon, a butterfly. Once this pattern has been articulated, the children predict that the mealworm will turn into something that flies. Watching and waiting are the obvious procedures, but other aspects of the habits of the not-yet-metamorphosed mealworms can be pursued in books. The pattern of the insect life cycle shown in books will lead to further thought when compared with the mealworm investigations; such thought, in turn, suggests further investigation, and investigation leads to larger patterns. These extended patterns will eventually develop into the conceptual scheme that living organisms are in constant change, that the change is characteristic of the species, and that part of the insect life cycle can be the pupa.

Many other patterns can emerge from mealworm investigations. Most of Tina Weiss's children (page 33) were interested in the life functions of the mealworms. The second lesson explored whether or not mealworms ate, drank, were sensitive to light and/or heat. How did they find their way around: antennae? eyes? touch? How did they "know" when they were in the corner of the box, since they seemed to spend more time there than anywhere else? How can we be sure that they spent more time in the corners than in the open? Timing the number of seconds they spent in each place would be one way of finding out.

From such voiced interests, the teacher perceives the major patterns of class thinking and relates them to various conceptual schemes. One pattern might be essential life functions: eating, drinking, eliminating, growing. Another might be sensitivity to and interaction with the environment. A more sophisticated class might see a pattern of "getting too big for one's skin." Insects molt. What happens to the skin when human beings grow? Or turtles? Is there one pattern or are there several patterns here?

One of the patterns emerging from Marybelle Bradford's class was the disappearance of salt and sugar in water: "Salt do the same thing sugar do." "It [the sugar] look like it invisible, but the sugar still there." The conceptual scheme embracing these and other subconcepts is that matter can neither be created nor destroyed. Tasting revealed the presence of the sugar. To what other developments can this pattern lead?

Invisibility can be overcome by giving the children crystals of copper sulfate, potassium permanganate,

or even a small tablet of food coloring to drop into a glass of water (carefully so that they can see the motion which disperses the particles of colored matter—the natural motion of water unaided by stirring or other outside disturbances). The appearance of the color in the glass can be watched and sketched every few minutes: it will move, disperse, and eventually color the whole glass.[48] The idea of very small particles of matter or molecules in constant motion can be easily developed in a colloquium with older children.[49]

Not only do the crystals disperse in solution; they can be retrieved through evaporation as well. Every part of the universe is in constant change, constant motion. Matter can neither be created nor destroyed. Simple patterns into larger patterns. Larger patterns into conceptual schemes. The thinking and learning patterns revealed by the children; the structural patterns behind the study units; the patterns in the structure of each set of materials—all grow, blend, coalesce into grandiose schemes through a teacher's perception.

[48] For details of this investigation, see *Science in Your Life: 4* by Herman and Nina Schneider, D.C. Heath, Lexington, Mass., 1965, pp. 64-65.

[49] Clear presentations of the molecule model appear in *Concepts in Science* by Paul F. Brandwein *et al.*, Harcourt Brace Jovanovich, Inc., 1966; grade 2, pp. 1-24; grade 4, unit 4.

2

Meaning through use of language

Can a dolphin think?

Sounds, symbols, and meanings

The dolphin has been a voluntary friend of man since before the Christian era. Indeed, man has found that he can project his own emotions and abilities onto this highly developed, social mammal. This early anthropomorphic statement comes from Plutarch: "The dolphin is the only creature who loves man for his own sake. . . . The dolphin . . . has no need of any man, yet is a genial friend to all and has helped many."

An example of the dolphin's love of "man for his own sake" is commemorated on an early Greek coin which shows a boy riding a dolphin. Such phenomena occur frequently. Nearing shore, a dolphin engages in antics interpreted by man as an "invitation to play." A person (usually a child) joins in the antics, caressing and stroking the mammal. The dolphin often dives under the person, lifting him onto his back. Rider and dolphin move out to sea, returning shorewards later.

In what ways is this sequence of events similar to, and yet different from, a nursery school child who draws a companion into the doll corner and engages in the role-playing of mommy, daddy, and/or baby? Does either behavior require thought?

Without defining thought at this particular time, we can, no doubt, agree that each behavior requires intelligence and has been learned partly as a result of social experience. The dolphin behavior which

Plutarch interpreted as "helping many" is an outgrowth of the mutual aid these mammals display during their regular group life. When a calf is born, another female helps the mother both during delivery and after birth (by swimming in the vicinity of the baby). Thus two females, mother and "aunt," share the responsibility of caring for the infant. The fact that a dolphin's first experience is one of cooperative endeavor may imprint[1] this group-action response in its behavior pattern. In any case, the dolphin will engage in mutual aid throughout its life whenever other dolphins are in danger. An injured dolphin is regularly buoyed aloft by some group members (so that its breathing hole is above the surface of the water), while others keep the sharks at bay. Buoying humans in play has also been transferred to humans in need.

A child who role-plays his family life reflects the particular social experiences of his home, yet there may be cogent differences between these acts of dolphin and child. Because children talk while they play, we do know that they have mental images of the details of family life. We do not know whether dolphins have images of aiding, breathing, or survival while they engage in socially helpful behavior. A recent experiment did indicate, however, that a dolphin can take the initiative in teaching a human. Margaret Howe spent two and a half months "living in" with a dolphin, Peter, who conditioned her not to be afraid of its nibbling along her limbs.[2]

Does the presence of images make the difference between thought-full and thought-less behavior?

There is some evidence that animals might, at times, be able to conjure up images of what is not immediately present. We can infer from observations that animals dream; we can see saliva drip and muscles twitch and hear growls from a cat stretched out in sleep. Something like images or sounds or smells seems to be present in the brain of the sleeping feline. Humans can be awakened and asked what they have experienced. Lacking speech, animals cannot

inform us. Electrodes placed in certain parts of a human's brain can evoke *déjà vu* experiences. Humans can describe what they seem to be experiencing while their brain is being electrically stimulated. Animals, including dolphins, react as though in pain or pleasure when certain areas of their brains are stimulated through electrodes. We do not know, however, whether such sensations are purely physiological or whether they are accompanied by images.

Can dolphins "think of" something not present? Images (let the word include recall of smells, sounds, tastes, and tactile sensations as well as sight) do seem to be a necessary assumption when an organism acts as though something not physically present is motivating his behavior. For example, dog owners are often eager to tell of incidents when their pets have associated certain clothes with an impending walk or even when a master has been led to the scene of someone in distress. The first could be conditioned response, but does the second require images and/or thought? In what ways is it similar to, or different from, an incident in which a child hurts himself on the playground and a friend runs to find an adult?

All are examples of intelligent behavior, but does any of it require thinking? If images can be regarded as signs or symbols, then an early definition of thinking by Sir Frederic Bartlett might include the behavior cited:

> Thinking may be regarded as a high-level form of skilled behavior, requiring signs and symbols for its expression, yet still possessing many of the characteristics of the earlier established bodily skills.[3]

Some scholars believe that thinking may be inferred whenever cognitive behavior is manifested. In the category of cognitive behavior they include the use of tools to solve problems whether such behavior is exhibited by a baboon who uses a leaf as a spoon, by Köhler's ape who raked a banana into his cage by joining two bamboo sticks, or by a child who adapts a tool to a particular job. Such thinking without the use of words is often referred to as *preverbal*.

Two other examples of preverbal cognitive be-

---

[1] *Imprinting* is the term applied to newborn ducks, chickens, etc. who follow whatever moving object they encounter first. Of course, this is usually the mother bird, but it can be a human (the experimenting psychologist!). Thereafter, the birds will follow the same object.

[2] John Cunningham Lilly, M.D., *The Mind of the Dolphin*, Avon (Doubleday), N.Y. 1967.

[3] Sir Frederic Bartlett, *Thinking: an Experimental and Social Study*, George Allen and Unwin, London, 1958, and Basic Books, Inc., Publishers, New York, 1958. p. 198.

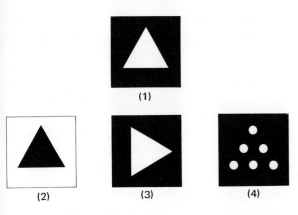

(1)

(2)   (3)   (4)

havior are the ability to generalize and the ability to extract principles. Work is in progress plumbing the depths of the dolphin's abilities. Perhaps we can consider that the dolphin generalizes when it applies to humans the behavior it normally displays to its own species: buoying aloft, playing with swimmers, gently running its teeth along the limbs of a companion. Chimpanzees seem to be able to generalize visual stimuli. Look at the patterns shown here.[4] A rat trained to respond to the upright white triangle (1) makes only random responses when presented with any of the other triangles. A similarly trained chimpanzee, however, recognizes both solid triangles (2) and (3) as well as triangle (1). A two-year-old child will recognize all four triangles.

Generalizing is certainly a form of cognitive behavior. Does it require thought?

The higher primates can generalize. The dolphin's brain is even larger than man's and well convoluted; how widely can it generalize? We can assume experiments will establish that dolphin abilities surpass those of primates. Will dolphins be found to surpass man's ability in this cognitive realm as they can now be said to in the "ethics" of their social life.[5]

Generalizing through perceived external likenesses may be nothing more than recognition of the Gestalt, the whole which Gestaltists have long believed to be a

[4] S.A. Barnett, "Rats," *Scientific American*, Vol. 216, No. 1 (January 1967), 78-85.

[5] Described in *The Mind of the Dolphin, op. cit.*

function of the visual cortex of the brain. Our cortex completes (4) so that it appears visually as a triangle of small circles, just as we perceive the figure shown below left to be a circle.

The ability of the cortex to perceive discrete stimuli on the retina as wholes has recently been found to be a property of the neural linkages in the visual cortex.[6] A stimulus on the retina passes from the eye to the cortex via electrical impulses along a series of cells (neurons) connected by synapses. When a stimulus falls on certain regions of each cell, the impulse is triggered; it is inhibited on the other parts. Moreover, the synapses constitute a kind of "wiring" so that some cells "wired" together will be triggered fully only if all are stimulated. This pattern of "wiring" constitutes the Gestalt: edges, lines in certain positions, and motions in certain directions may trigger a group of cells. The "wiring" arrangement seems to have evolved in relation to objects which help a species survive. Chickens, for example, are able to peck grains on hatching. They must therefore perceive grains as Gestalten.

For a chimpanzee, but not for a rat, edges which form a triangle in various positions must be so "wired" to trigger them as a group; a series of small circles must be "wired" for the two-year-old child to perceive a line. The ability to perceive these as Gestalten may be part of the organism's neural equipment, but the training required to generalize the different forms as triangles may well be classified as cognitive behavior.

Can simple generalizing be classified as thinking?

Cognitive behavior which results from abstracting principles appears to rely on other factors than those provided by purely perceptual stimuli and the neural organization of the visual cortex. A monkey can be trained to respond to "the odd one" of two similar and one dissimilar drawings or objects. The sets of objects may be varied, but the monkey will continue to choose the one which is different from the other two.

Does abstracting principles require thought?

Thus far in our brief inquiry into when thinking is or is not present in intelligent behavior, we have considered the following points:

[6] David Hubel, "The Visual Cortex of the Brain," *Scientific American*, Vol. 209, No. 5 (November 1963), 54–62

1. Does the presence of images (visual, auditory, olfactory, tactile) imply thought? Images do imply residues of some experience distant in time and place and, therefore, going beyond the present. Tapping these residues would seem to require thought.
2. Does cognitive behavior, with or without the presence of images, imply thought? Some seemingly intelligent behavior can be partly accounted for by the body's neural structure and social conditioning. Cognitive behavior manifested by animals who invent and use tools, rearranging objects in their environment to suit their personal needs, may be regarded as preverbal thought when the actions are not random or trial and error. A third form of cognitive behavior previously considered, the ability to abstract principles, was exemplified in the response of a monkey to the principle of "the odd one." It is possible to argue that all of this behavior be included in thinking.
3. The behavior of both animals and children discussed thus far has been of the preverbal type, but in each case where the child was involved his level of achievement showed some superiority. There can be quite complicated preverbal behavior requiring a high-level cognitive ability which only humans can master. Such a situation is presented by the Mirror Cards (discussed earlier in *Two-dimensional Symmetries*, p. 84). A master pattern (labeled "Mirror Card") and two test patterns are reproduced here. In what positions would you

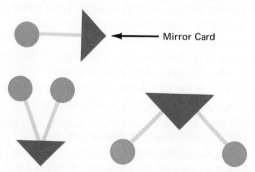

Mirror Card

place a mirror on the "Mirror Card" to match the pattern on each test card? *Try to describe in words how you can tell.* Most adults and all

of the children we have seen work with these Mirror Cards failed to express in clear communicative statements how they knew where to place the mirror and how they knew whether it was or was not possible to complete the test pattern. A high level of cognitive behavior is required by some of the more difficult sets, yet a verbal description of the mental process involved in even the simpler sets is unbelievably challenging. There seems to be a kind of nonverbal cognitive behavior which requires much thought.

4. Language is a way in which humans can communicate thought. No animal is yet known to possess this ability.

We now turn to the role of communication as an indicator of thought. Animals communicate through sounds and gestures. Generally, however, these have been found to be responses to physiological states: hunger, pain, pleasure, fear, sexual arousal. Recent work with dolphins suggests that they do have a language which goes beyond this emotive stage. Not only are scientists trying to learn this language—a long roster of different sounds (to us)—so that they can communicate with dolphins under water, but dolphins are now being taught to make humanoid sounds above water which have attached meanings. In spite of these encouraging achievements, there is grave doubt that the subtle linguistic structure of human communication can be achieved.[7] Our language seems to be a unique evolutionary development (at least on this planet) that is essential for high-level conceptual thought. Bartlett makes this clear in the final definition of human thought in his book:

> The skills of the body are attached to the world of the moment, but thinking can meet those far away in any direction and even those which have no time or place.[8]

Whether we define thought in terms of an organism's use of images, tools, signs, symbols, or words, or whether we include intelligence in our definition, in

[7] See Noam Chomsky, *Aspects of Theory of Syntax*, M.I.T. Press, Cambridge, Mass., 1965 and Carol Chomsky, "Language Development After Age Six," *Harvard Graduate School of Education Bulletin*, Vol. xiv, No. 3 (Spring 1970), 14–16.
[8] Bartlett, *op. cit.*, p. 200.

terms of communication or cognition it would seem that only those who possess a linguistically structured language can generate thinking at its highest potential level: mathematics, logic, philosophy, science theory, or other advanced conceptual areas. Interestingly enough, it would seem that only those who *possess* language can rearrange nonverbal symbols into new creative forms. We speak of painters who think in images, musicians who think in sounds, choreographers who think in movement, a Marcel Marceau who thinks in gestures. *Possession of a language seems the* sine qua non *for creative as well as conceptual thought.*

The aim of science learning, as we envisage it, is to foster conceptual growth. The use of language in relation to the development of concepts appears crucial, therefore. We shall accordingly follow the relationship between thought and language which has been intriguingly explored by a Russian psychologist, the late Lev Semenovitch Vygotsky.[9]

One of Vygotsky's theses is that language and thought stem from different roots. There can be language without thought; little Geordie's rendering of "My Country tizzerly" and the meaningless repetition of scientific definitions in order to pass multiple choice quizzes are two examples. Also, Vygotsky asserts that there can be thought without language. He cites as one example the type of thinking involved when both animals and humans use tools in personally meaningful ways. Vygotsky calls this *preverbal thought.* The evidence that preverbal thought occurs at all is that the motions employed are not random, but purposeful: a mechanic may make a number of adjustments before he repairs a machine just as a child does when he first tries to nail two pieces of wood together. Vygotsky sees this as qualitatively similar to Köhler's ape piling up blocks to reach a suspended banana in his cage.

A human who has learned to speak has a more complicated way of using tools than a baby or a primate but all three are considered to be experiencing preverbal thought. In all of them there is a seemingly sudden moment of achievement, an insightful phase which indicates that there was a goal in mind, and a recognition that this goal has been reached. This type of cognitive behavior in adult apes may indicate their peak of ability; in humans it is first reached before they are one year old. K. Büehler, who worked with babies in experiments similar to Köhler's, writes:

(The babies' reactions) were exactly like those of the chimpanzees, so that this phase of the child's life could rather aptly be called the *chimpanzoid* age; in our subject it corresponded to the 10th, 11th, and 12th months. At the chimpanzoid age occur the child's first inventions—very primitive ones to be sure, but extremely important for his mental development.[10]

Preverbal thought by chimpanzees and babies cannot be put into words, but similar activities by people possessing language usually can be verbalized. The colloquium fosters this transition from the preverbal thought, which occurs during the discovery period of a science lesson, to concept growth.

Vygotsky explores another level of non-articulate thought which he calls *inner speech.* Inner speech is possible, of course, only for those who have developed a linguistic ability. In inner speech, thinking is not substantiated by silently formed phrases, but by very abbreviated word forms (mostly predicates) which are rapidly shifted in thought as a problem is explored and perhaps mentally solved. This is thinking in pure meanings, using semantics rather than phonetics. Vygotsky holds that inner speech is used when anyone thinks to himself. It is possible that the nonverbal creative processes of painters, musicians, and dancers include inner speech.

Vygotsky supports his thesis that thought and language stem from different roots by demonstrating that there can be words without thought and thought without words. A purpose of education, therefore, is to coalesce these two independent genetic strains of thought and language. For a child, such coalescence first becomes possible at about two years (the same age when the child surpasses the chimpanzee in his ability to generalize the category of "triangle" by including the little circles in triangular form).

[9] L.S. Vygotsky, *Thought and Language*, ed. and trans. by Eugenia Hanfmann and Gertrude Vakar, M.I.T. Press, Cambridge, Mass., 1962. The work was originally written in 1934, four years before Vygotsky's untimely death at the age of 38.

[10] K. Büehler, *Die Geistigen Entwicklung des Kindes*, Quelle & Meyer, Leipzig, 1928, p. 7. Quoted in Vygotsky, *op. cit.*, p. 42.

This crucial instant, when speech begins to serve the intellect and thoughts begin to be spoken, is indicated by two unmistakable objective symptoms: (1) the child's sudden, active curiosity about words, his question about every new thing, "What is that?" and (2) the resulting rapid, saccadic increases in his vocabulary.[11]

The earliest stages of speech in a child are emotive expressions somewhat like the "vocabulary" we can distinguish in animals, particularly the higher primates. In some animals, we can differentiate a whole roster of grunts, clicks, squeaks, and rattles which, although communicative, convey feelings rather than abstractions; they are not symbols to the animal. (The full meaning of a dolphin's vocabulary is not yet known.) But when a child makes the momentous discovery that everything has a name, he begins to use each name as a symbol for the object itself. At this stage, thought becomes verbal and speech becomes rational. At present, it seems improbable that any animal could achieve this level of understanding.

Distinct from training, education plays the role of helping thought and language to coalesce, to become mutually illuminating. While children manipulate the materials in science programs, much is happening on the preverbal level. Thought without language is taking place. Only during the colloquium, or occasionally during a short verbal interchange among members of a small group working together on the same materials, does language bring its riches to learning. The obverse can be seen in the methods formerly employed to teach science by (1) only reading or (2) repetition of what the teacher said; in either case, there has little coalescence because there was scanty previous thought.

The coalescence of language and thought is not merely a juxtaposition or addition of two human abilities; an entirely new product is formed by this interaction. "Thought," writes Vygotsky, "is not merely expressed in words; it comes into existence through them."[12] This process is abundantly illustrated in our colloquia: experience evokes language; language produces thought; thought may require new language; and so on.

[11] Vygotsky, *op. cit.*, p. 43.

[12] Vygotsky, *op. cit.*, p. 125.

As part of the *What's Inside?* lesson, Marie Stevens challenged her third graders by asking them to express how they knew there was anything at all inside the brown bag. The children offered several synonyms in describing the bag's three dimensionality. When the transparent plastic bag filled with air was shown and the children asserted that it contained air, Miss Stevens again challenged them, saying that she could see nothing inside. The children assured their teacher (and, moreover, themselves) that they knew because of "the shape." *Shape* was the generalization chosen to represent all the previous synonyms. In classes where words which represent the three dimensionality of matter have not been elicited, young children often cannot establish why they think air is in the expanded plastic bag.

The first part of Marie Stevens' lesson was a group session until teacher-initiative had slipped into child-initative. We learned what a few of the children thought—those who spoke. In the *Eureka!* colloquium, however, we can follow the thought growth through the language of individual children. Let's start with Dick:

Dick: I didn't discover nuttin'.

Then he combines Rosa's idea of the marble going straight to the bottom with Rex's mention of the Wiffle ball.

Dick: The Wiffle ball sinks.

But Bert disagrees, and Dick is asked to try the Wiffle ball in water. This experience evokes a new thought and his words take wings, finding a hidden likeness; his voice becomes excited. Thought and language continue to interact.

Dick: It floats just like a boat. Part of it sinks and part floats. A regular ball is like that, too. So everything else, part, even a small part, must sink or the rest couldn't float. The part of the Wiffle ball that sinks is the part that has water in it.

Quite a long way from "nuttin'," which was probably an accurate expression of his preverbal thought at the time!

The aspect of mutual aid is essential in a colloquium. Not only was Dick motivated by the verbal expression of two other children's ideas, but Dick's remarks—especially the phrase "part of it [the boat]"—in turn motivate Charlie.

Charlie: The part of the boat that sinks does it 'cause it's heavy, too.

The word "heavy" makes Gert think about her preverbal experiences.

Gert: Is it because the water makes the Wiffle ball heavy? Does it *not* float because of this?

Gert had not spoken before, but the language of the other children must have evoked thoughts in her. She asked a question of nature—a real scientist! Mrs. Ross helped Gert find an answer to her question. But then she came upon a discrepant event. Seen or expressed discrepant events generally evoke thought. First, however, the discrepancy must be visually scrutinized to make sure the observation was accurate; then a new statement is made:

Gert: . . . when I filled the ping-pong ball with water it sank.
Kathie: Mine didn't. *(They try again.)*
Gert: Kathie's has a bubble of air in hers. Maybe that's why it floats.

Fruitful as the thought of air might have been, it lay fallow. Kathie said that her ping-pong ball smelled of soap and the group began to explore the discrepancies between Ivory and the other soap. Then Shelley, who had not spoken until then, showed that Gert's words had influenced her thoughts. Shelley's language, in turn, stimulated several other children's reactions:

Shelley: I think I know why things float.
Mrs. Ross: Please tell us.
Shelley: They float because they have air in them.
Dick: Ivory soap can't have air; it has no holes.
Jo: Air might have been pumped into the middle of it.
Rex: The sponge works that way, too. When it is dry, it has air in it. When it is wet, it has water in it instead.

The "water in it instead" remark engendered new thought until Shelley summarized the colloquium with a piece of wisdom any eight year old would have been proud to discover.

Shelley: That's like the sponge. Water pushed the air out of the sponge and it sank. Marbles pushed the air out of the cup and the cup sank.

We can be fairly certain of two things here:
1. Without the colloquium, these thoughts would probably not have resulted.
2. If there had been no experience and the words had been spoken by the teacher, the children would, at best, have had words without thought.

A view of education

Our view of *education* extends beyond having the learner do what is asked of him. For us, learning is essentially active and should be motivated by the learner himself. This active learning role is in contrast to the type of thinking engendered by *training*, where each new stimulus is chosen by an outside agent and thinking is dependent upon suggestions from some authority with a foreknowledge of predetermined goals. We believe that self-initiated learning together with its expression in the learner's own words, organizes learning into a whole interactive system, into meaning for the learner.

In both education and training, however, *word and actions are cogent interactive factors*. Each trainee is expected to achieve at least a limited number of the same physical and/or intellectual skills (the yeast model). In our view of education, of course, there are overall goals and more limited subgoals (the pond model), but the expectancy is not that all individuals will arrive at exactly the same outcome. Dick, Shelley, and Charlie all learned different things, although their total learnings were related to the concept of flotation. Each child took an active part, a self-catalyzing part, in using the materials; each found a different set of facts; each must have had a different experience on the preverbal level; and each expressed his own thoughts in individual statements which revealed different viewpoints. [13]

[13] An experiment, conducted on kittens, showed that an animal's own movements change what it sees and hears. *Passive experience* fails to evoke normal development. (*Passive learning* may produce an analogous result in children.) Richard Held, "Plasticity in Sensory-Motor Systems," *Scientific American*, Vol. 213 (November 1965), 74–94.

A major point in this view of education is that the range of possibilities is *offered*, suggested by the teacher's activity, not *given* by authority. Most of the learning is due to the child's activity, to his way of integrating the new experience into his previous background. Each stage of learning is not a lone, individual experience. The richness of the thinking a lesson produces is due as much to mutual aid during the colloquium as to individual free experience with the materials.

It is probably not accidental that high-level social activities are found in animals whose group life is interdependent. The social organization observed by Washburn and DeVore among the baboons of Kenya is a fascinating example: the mothers educate their offspring to use a stick to dig for ants and a cup of leaves to scoop up water; in travel, the stronger males assume protective positions.[14] And after all his studies of individual children, Jean Piaget now insists that group interchange is essential for intellectual development:

> Experience is always necessary for intellectual development.... But I fear that we may fall into the illusion that being submitted to an experience (a demonstration) is sufficient for a subject to disengage the structure involved. But more than this is required. The subject must be active, must transform things, and find the structure of his own actions on the objects.
>
> When I say 'active,' I mean it in two senses. One is acting on material things. But the other means doing things in social collaboration, in a group effort. This leads to a critical frame of mind, where children must communicate with each other. This is an essential factor in intellectual development. Cooperation is indeed co-operation.[15]

Miss Provost's anecdotal record of two of her sixth graders, Carl and Monte (page 53), illustrates a social stimulus pulling preverbal thought toward a higher level of thought-filled activity.

[14] S.L. Washburn and Irven DeVore, "Social Life of Baboons," *Scientific American,* Vol. 206 (June 1961), 239–240.
[15] Eleanor Duckworth, "Piaget Rediscovered," Elementary Science Study *Newsletter*, Education Development Center, Inc., June 1964, 2–4.

Carl uses the masking tape Mr. McIver left on the table to attach his two batteries, end to end. (This is certainly a preverbal insightful action; it happens immediately, without trials.) Monte winds bare wire around the screw threads of his two bulbs. Carl now tapes wires onto his batteries and touches Monte's lights with the free ends. (Here Carl engages in trial-and-error movements but with a purpose: to make the lights light.) When they do not, another gesture (not expressed in words, but obviously related to symbolic data previously learned) is evident when he touches the two wire ends to his tongue and says, "Yow! Dere's juice, all right." (Now Monte puts his own thoughts into words...) "Look, when it worked last time, we had one wire on the bottom of the bulb," which leads to successful action this time. The bulbs light, one at a time. Monte's thoughts are reflected in words: "But only one lit." Carl has a new thought: "We gotta make both work." The next action is Monte's. He replicates the arrangement in which he joined two bulbs by winding one wire around both of their screw parts: he runs one of Carl's wires so that it joins the bottom parts of both bulbs. (His own previously expressed thought "wire on the bottom of the bulb" has merged with the visual arrangement of a wire joining both screws. (Then he invites Carl to a trial and error activity...) "Now see if there is a spot that will make them both light." Soon "both lights glow gloriously," as Aileen Provost writes.

As the boys busily tape their construction in place, Monte continues to think: "You know what? They're both as bright as one alone!" (Serendipity in the making! Carl seeks the sagacity to explain this...) "Dat's queer. I wonder why?" The problem gnaws, gestates, and is expressed in the colloquium. When John McIver asks the children if they have any ideas they would like to pursue during the follow-up lesson, Carl expresses his: he wants to see how many bulbs he can light with two batteries. (A mental picture of "both as bright as one" gleams in his eye.)

Later, the boys construct large, complicated circuits. After several investigation periods and colloquia, these sixth graders arrive at a satisfactory explanation of the effects of parallel and series circuits.

It is never hard to follow aspects of growing

thought in a recorded colloquium; they are an integral part of its structure and procedure. Would you like to try? The next section contains a record of two second-grade colloquia, each following a lesson on "Sound." We suggest that you:

1. For each child, write "E" beside his first remark if it seems to be emotional rather than factual.
2. Circle a word introduced by one child which encourages other children to contribute a series of thoughts. Underline this word when others use it.
3. Make a a statement or statements about the role(s) of the teacher which foster(s) the expression of hidden likenesses.
4. State the concepts of sound to which each set of materials is related. Find some evidence that some children have begun to think before their first remark. Name these children and describe your evidence.

SOUND STATEMENTS BY SEVEN YEAR OLDS

The morning was crisp and the sun not yet risen as the car pool of young teachers sped along the parkway.

"Do you think you can hold those milk bottles steady in the back seat?"

"You mean in case they turn into orbiting satellites when you take the cloverleaf on two wheels!"

"That's not fair; you know I'm an expert driver."

"What's in the bottles anyway?" from a girl next to the driver.

The car decelerated, stopping at the red light with only a slight skid on the unsanded ice.

"Whoops!" Joan Henderson leaned forward in the back seat and put her arm across the lurching package of bottles. "There goes Newton's inertia!"

"You know too much," Myrtle laughed, taking her foot off the brake. The car moved onto the snowplowed thruway with remarkable pickup, ". . . ever since you took that Frontiers of Science course."

"Newton's not frontiers," Joan shot back, "that's the old hat I learned in high school. I really should have named the elements in our interactive system and said your bottles are moving forward in the relative motion of the car. Our frame of reference being–"

"By that time my bottles would have been on the floor with all bells ringing."

"So you see, it's a good thing my classical reflexes show in emergencies."

Nancy Vesipian, Myrtle's student teacher, tried her question again: "What have you got in those milk bottles, Mrs. Schur?"

"Bells," replied Myrtle.

"Large and small, like the last time?"

"Same size." Myrtle Schur was passing a car on the road. She re-entered her right lane just before the double solid line began.

"Is the lesson to be on 'Sound' again?" Nancy persisted, adjusting the top part of her body so it was in line with the seat belt once more.

"Sure! And will you take down the colloquium for me again?"

"I'd be glad to. But I can hardly keep up; your children were so talkative last time."

"Myrtle's children talkative?" This from the fourth member of the car

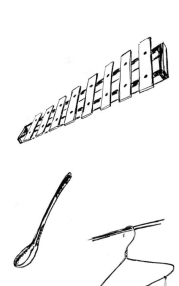

pool. The low voice continued, "When I taught them last year they were as quiet as mice."

"Well, it's the materials," Miss Richards. "Why, when I helped Mrs. Schur set them up—a xylophone, large and small jars, bells, oh, and the flowerpot chimes . . . they were delightful . . . and, and various sticks, and some rubber bands around cigar boxes—I could hardly keep from trying them out myself."

My fourth graders are great doers," said Joan, "but I'm blessed if I'm going to hold a DIScussion after every little footling experiment. They don't know what they've found out until several days of tinkering have gone by."

"Trouble with you," jested Myrtle, "is that you give the children too much verbal competition. And, by the way, have you managed *not* to give those clear explicit directives on how to do the experiment at the start of the lesson?"

"Certainly not! The kids would probably use the materials as weapons if I didn't orient them with a what-do-you-think-is-going-to-happen? demonstration."

"I guess we attended different workshops!" Having left the better-kept neighboring district, the car was now crunching through the encrusted snow, of the slum streets. Small children, some in threadbare coats and without galoshes, were picking their way over heaps of dirty snow while a mother in a neat traffic guard uniform and earmuffs held up the teachers' car. A snowball hit the side window. "One of my derring-do fourth graders," announced Joan. Her quip relieved the tension.

Nancy still persevered with her student teaching experiences. "I didn't believe any of this 'til I saw it happen. I didn't believe the children would do anything constructive with the materials either."

"But you said they intrigued you," Miss Richards remarked.

"Yes, but I'm not in the second grade, and I've got considerably more background."

"Which probably inhibits you!"

"I think you are right, Miss Henderson, I don't believe I would have been half as ingenious as the children turned out to be. But it's the colloquium which astounded me the most. When I typed it up last night, I couldn't believe what I'd written."

"Maybe you shouldn't!"

"Now, Joan, quit being so bright. Nancy's my good right hand."

"She's a lefty, I noticed!"

"All right, my good left hand. And I hope I'm passing on to her how to keep 'hands off' when the children investigate the materials and how to listen instead of talk during the colloquium. I learned the hard way."

" 'Teacher listen, children speak.' Where did I hear that?" mused Miss Richards.

"Sounds like Jimmy Hymes." Myrtle was backing neatly into a clear parking space near the school. "But now we have the rubric, 'He who does the talking, does the learning.' "

"That's why I must know so much," laughed Joan.

"Could be!" Myrtle Schur stuck the official *Board of Education, P.S. 341* sign on her windshield. The group climbed out onto the snow-banked sidewalk; each made her way to her respective classroom laden with parcels.

Mrs. Schur's children had been selected on the basis of their *putative* intellectual potential. They were mostly from middle class homes or had upwardly mobile, lower socio-economic backgrounds. Here is a record of Mrs. Schur's first lesson after the children had worked with the materials on page 110.

What is your opinion of "homogeneous" grouping?

Mrs. S.: Who would like to tell us what he has discovered after working with these objects?

Don: The things made different noises.

Daisy: Some noises were nice and some weren't.

Mrs. S.: Could you explain that a little better?

Diasy: The xylophone was pretty to hear, but the bottles just made sound.

Chris: The flowerpots were fun. They were kind of like xylophones.

Note the number of different children who make a contribution. There were 24 in class that day. How many analogies can you find?

Daisy: They didn't sound like the xylophone; the xylophone makes music.

Chris: The flowerpots reminded me of the xylophone 'cause they went from little to big, just like the bars on the xylophone.

Sophie: The pots look like the musical bells my little sister has at home.

Albee: I hit the flowerpots with a stick and some of them sounded nice.

Matthew: But they didn't sound the same. The little ones sounded sweet and the bigger ones sounded like . . . deeper.

Ellen: You could hear the deep sound better on the drum. That's why they use them in a band. The little drum sounded prettier.

Mrs. S.: When you tapped the flowerpots and the bars on the xylophone, did you hear anything different?

Patricia: Some sounded high and some sounded low.

Marguerita: We have a piano and the same thing happens.

Mrs. S.: Could you explain that a little better?

Marguerita: On one end of the piano the sound is high, and on the other end the music is low.

Daisy: I heard that on the xylophone, too.

Albee: The pots sounded high and low, too, on different ends.

Renée: I heard different noises, but I couldn't tell they were high and low.

Does this remark of Renée's suggest a hypothesis about her to you? Does her next remark (page 114) sustain your hypothesis about her sense perceptions

Marguerita: See, the little pots make high sounds and the big pots make low sounds.

Mrs. S.: Did anyone hear high and low sounds on anything else?

Rose: The two bells made different sounds.

Virian: The big bell sounded high and the little bell sounded low.

Sarah: No, that's not right. You got mixed up. The big bell sounded low and the little bell sounded high.

Phil: The jars did that, too.

Matthew: These things are like people. Big people voices sound lower than little children voices.

Mrs. S.: Can anyone put what we have said into a good sentence so that our recorder can write on the board?

Phil: Big things make low sounds and little things make higher sounds. Is that right? (*The class agrees and it is written on the blackboard.*)

Mrs. S.: Does anyone have an idea why this happens?

Matthew: Could it be 'cause the bigger things have more space to make more noise? Like the big flowerpot has more air inside, so the sound has to go through more air.

Chris: The xylophone doesn't have any air in the bars. I don't think that's the reason.

Mrs. S.: Maybe the rubber bands could help us. No one has mentioned them yet.

Rod: I didn't hear any difference and they didn't even sound nice.

Rita: Some of the rubber bands were thin and some were thick.

Zina: Oh, they were supposed to be like the xylophone!

Mrs. S.: What do you mean?

Zina: They were put on in a special way. The skinny one was first, then fatter and fatter.

Chris: Yeah, they went from skinny to fat, like the pots from little to big.

Gray: And they made different sounds.

Mrs. S.: Could you describe the difference in sounds?

This might have been better phrased: "Try describing the difference in sounds," for instance.

Gray: The skinny one was high and the fat one was low, just like we said about the other things.

Perry: Gray took out the pencil and then the rubber band just snapped.

Gray: I put it back and when I put the pencil under different parts we heard different sounds. The shorter the rubber band got, the higher the sound got.

Mrs. S.: Did anyone notice how the rubber band moved?

Perry: The thin rubber band moved a lot.

Mrs. S.: And what did that sound like?

Perry: High.

Daisy: The big things don't move as much as the little things when you tap them. Is that right?

Rice Krispies (or Puffed Rice) on a drum shows this well.

Mrs. S.: Why don't we try.

Daisy: (*tapping the drum*) The top of the little drum looks like it moves more than the big one.

Sophie: I can't see them move at all.

Marguerita: Let's see the little bar on the xylophone. You can't see it move so good. But I know little things move fast 'cause they have less to move.

Gray: The top of the drum has to move more 'cause it's so big, and it makes a deep sound. Like a big drum in a parade—that really makes a deep sound.

Mrs. S.: Who can say that very clearly for us? Remember what moving has to do with it.

Matthew: Things that have to move a lot make low sounds.

Ellen: And things that don't have to move so much make high sounds.

Marguerita: On my piano all the keys are the same, so I don't understand why some are high and some are low.

Perry: The piano has wires inside it. Some must be long and some must be short. The short move faster than the long ones. Isn't that right?

After Myrtle Schur and Nancy Vesipian distributed the bottles and the other materials that were prepared for the follow-up lesson, each table (accommodating four or five children) had the following items:

1. One milk bottle with some air removed, tightly corked. A wire with a bell attached suspended from the cork into the bottle. [16]
2. A second bottle, as above, with no air removed.
3. A long piece of garden hose.
4. A paper cup and string telephone (two cups connected by a long piece of string).

The colloquium following the investigation of these materials was recorded:

Mrs. S.: Now that you've handled the equipment for a while, who can tell us something he has discovered?
Perry: The two milk bottles are the same.
Phil: Yeah, they look alike to me.
Matthew: They both have corks in them.
Ellen: They both had bells in them, too.
Mrs. S.: Then do we all agree that the bottles were exactly the same?
Rod: Well, I'm not so sure. They look the same, but they didn't do the same things.
Sophie: Mine didn't do the same thing either. 'Cause when I shook one bottle I heared the bell ring, but the bell in the other bottle didn't ring.
Rod: Yeah, that's what I mean. One bell rang. The other bell you couldn't hear.
Hannah: Maybe the bell is broken.
Sophie: No, I looked. I held the bottle up and looked under. I could see the nail in the bell go to the side, but I couldn't hear it.
Mrs. S.: Sophie, would you demonstrate this for us? (*Sophie does.*)
Sophie: See, you don't hear.
Mrs. S.: Does anyone have an idea why this bell won't work?
Gray: I tried both bottles and I could hear the bells. One was very quiet, though.
Daisy: No, I couldn't hear the bell in one of the bottles when I tried. But I saw black burned stuff in one of the bottles—ashes.
Rod: I didn't see that.
Hannah: Sure, look! There's black stuff in the bottle we had, too.
Chris: Mrs. Schur, is that why we can't hear the bell?
Mrs. S.: Maybe someone can help us find out.
Ellen: Which bottle had the black stuff in it?
Perry: That's a good idea. Can I try the bottles, Mrs. Schur?
Mrs. S.: Yes.

[16] Muriel Mandell, *Science for Children*, Sterling Publishing Co., New York, 1959, p. 66.

How's that for a prediction?

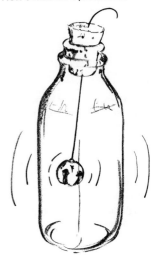

What is the difference between the preliminary remarks at the last colloquium and this one?

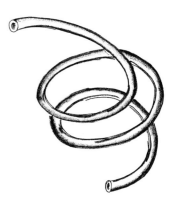

Why doesn't the bell work?

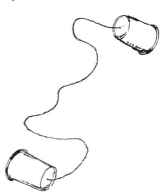

"What makes you think something was burned in this bottle?" might be a better question.

Perry: The bell in the bottle without the ashes rings. The other with the ashes don't ring.

Sarah: I'll try my bottles. Yeah, the same thing happens.

Ulrick.: I don't see what that means. The ashes aren't stopping the bell.

Mrs. S.: Are you sure they are ashes?

Renée: They look like ashes. I could even see a piece of a match.

Chris: Something must have been burned in this bottle and not in the other.

Mrs. S.: Why do you think something was burned in this bottle?

Don: To put ashes in the bottle.

Mrs. S.: Who remembers what happened to the candle when we put the top of the pumpkin back on?

Daisy: The candle went out.

Chris: Yes, because there was no air left to let it burn.

Ellen: The candle went out, too, when we put a glass over it.

Although the children are finding hidden likenesses, there is a factual error here. Can you find it? (*Hint*: Where would the carbon dioxide be? Why is there less air in the bottle with the ashes?)

Mrs. S.: Can anyone tell us how those experiments can help us now?

Matthew: The burning stuff used up the air. There's no air in the bottle. That's why the cork's on so tight—to keep the air out.

Perry: There's a cork in both bottles, so there's no air in both of them.

Matthew: But there's only ashes in one bottle, and that's the bell that doesn't ring.

Daisy: The bell won't ring 'cause there's no air. The fire used up the air and now you can't hear the bell.

Mrs. S.: How could we prove what Daisy says is true?

Scientific procedures—prediction, testing, control—suggested by a second grader. What structure in the materials led to this?

Marguerita: We could pull out the cork and let the air in. Then we could burn something and put the cork in.

Mrs. S.: All right, let's do this. (*She uncorks and recorks the bottle.*)

Zina: Now you can hear the bell.

Mrs. S.: I'll put some papers in the bottle and light them. Now I'll replace the cork.

Sarah: I hear the bell just a little now.

Gray: Yeah, you need air to hear the bell good. If there's no air, you can't hear. Right!?

This record was made several years before conditions on the moon became nursery school conversation!

Mrs. S.: What did you learn about the other materials?

Rose: I talked to Rita with the telephone.

Frank: It looks like a telephone. If you talk in one cup, you can hear from the other. I got one of those at home.

Rita: I even went in the closet and I could hear Rose.

Phil: My real telephone doesn't have cups and strings. But it's got a ear place and a mouth place.

Albee: It's got wire, not string.

Matthew: This is like a telephone. The string is like the wire. It's not as good as a telephone.

Mrs. S.: You must have to yell very loud to hear with this telephone.

Phil: No. You could talk very quiet and still hear.

Chris: If the string's not pulled good you can't hear.

Daisy: That's what happened to us. Hannah wasn't pulling the string and I couldn't hear what she said.

Mrs. S.: Are you saying that tightening and loosening the string makes a difference?

Matthew: It must. They couldn't hear when the string was loose.

Rita: I felt something funny on my head when Rose talked.

Mrs. S.: What do you mean, something funny?

Rita: It felt like a buzz.

Ulrick: I didn't feel that.

Rita: I'll try with you. *(She does.)* Do you feel it?

Ulrick: Yeah. It's like. . . . I don't know.

Mrs. S.: That's called vibration. That's how we hear sounds, by vibrations. Perhaps we could do some experiments next time with sound vibrations.

Rod: I didn't talk with the telephone, but I talked with Lionel through the hose. That worked swell.

Lionel: I heard it from over there. *(Indicates opposite corner.)*

Simone: I could hear through it, too, when Sophie talked to me.

Sophie: But Gray kept stepping on it on purpose.

Simone: Then I couldn't hear what she said.

Mrs. S.: Why not?

Simone: It stopped her voice from getting out.

Matthew: I know! It's like the bottle with no air. He stopped the air in the hose, and you can't hear without air.

Ulrick: There's no air in the string and you could hear through it.

Matthew: There is air in the string and air all around it.

Mrs. S.: Of all the materials we worked with today, which do you think helped sound become loudest?

Gray: Not the bottle. You could hear, but not good.

Chris: The string worked pretty good, but the hose was the best.

Perry: I think so, too.

Mrs. S.: Why do you think that is true?

Perry: I don't know.

Frank: 'Cause everything you say goes right in the hose and out the other side. It don't get mixed up in the air outside.

Don: I saw a picture about a boat, and the captain whistled in the hose to call somebody in the bottom of the boat.

This is the first time the teacher has rephrased a child's statement. What do you think about this?

What is the effect of the teacher's supplying the right word at this time?

The meanings language nourishes

He who does the talking, does the learning. For example, seven-year-old Frank:

"Cause everything you say goes right in the hose and out the other side. It don't get mixed up in the air outside."

Or Matthew:

"It's like the bottle with no air. He [Gray] stopped the air in the hose, and you can't hear without air."

Or Gray:

"Yeah, you need air to hear the bell good. If there's no air, you can't hear. Right!?"

Or Daisy:

"The bell won't ring 'cause there's no air."

In what ways are these statements different from rote repetition? When children in a class are asked to repeat after the teacher in unison, everyone is talking. Everyone is using language and, presumably, making impeccably correct statements. Frank's, Matthew's,

Gray's, and Daisy's statements are self-catalyzing, phrased to suit their own meanings, to reflect their individual thoughts.

In colloquia, a child occasionally repeats more or less what another child expressed a few speeches earlier—a phenomenon which also occurs when adults engage in this kind of colloquia. The face of the speaker repeating the remark shows that, for him, it is the breaking of a new dawn, his first realization of the relationship involved, his own initial expression of wisdom. It is unique to him. He is completely unaware that anyone presented this wisdom before! If the teacher calls attention to this with something like "Jimmy just said that," the child always looks hurt as though he is being reprimanded.

However, the fact that the child is repeating should not be discounted. It may actually benefit the colloquium. Although peripheral perception and subliminal stimuli exist, a person has not turned his potential learning into thought which is communicable to himself or to others until he verbalizes his thinking. Although a speaker may repeat what someone else has just said word for word, the repetition of a phrase or word in a slightly different context occurs more frequently. The phrase or word then becomes the nucleus around which the thoughts of several people crystallize.

Matthew: . . . he stopped the *air in the hose.* . . .
Ulrick: There's no *air in the string.* . . .
Matthew: There is *air in the string* and air all around it.

When verbalized, the crystallized thoughts sometimes take on strange meanings. Matthew's statement "There's air in the string" did not sound quite right; the mental picture or "symbolization" did not reflect the observed reality. But everyone had so avidly pursued the relationship between air and sound that Matthew was eager to apply this thought to the string telephone. Hearing his own words engendered new thoughts. With only an "and," Matthew offered a substitute statement in his second clause: "and air all around it."

The "air inside" has now been superseded by a more acceptable observation based on reality. However, the substitute statement is not related to the phenomenon. It is a loose end which Mrs. Schur will take up during the next lesson. How? With new materials which will focus the children's attention on vibrations. She will have coat hangers hooked onto chair backs. Each hanger will have a row of Puffed Rice suspended individually on fine threads close together. A heavy rubber band will be placed nearby. [17] There will be a triangle with a tapper, Puffed Rice on top of a drum and a light drumstick, a single rubber band over a cigar box, and a tuning fork. At some point, a suggestion for the children to put their fingers on their vocal cords while they speak will be introduced. The colloquium will develop the analogy of vibrations through solids and gases.

A colloquium produces meaning in each child who expresses his thoughts in his own words, encourages the growth of meaning by providing words or phrases around which the thoughts of several people can crystallize, and helps a person who hears what he has said and realizes that the words have not conveyed his meaning by giving him a chance to correct or clarify his statement. To the teacher, a colloquium indicates the areas which need further clarification.

Sometimes a child will make a statement which other children then correct. An example of this occurred during Mrs. Schur's first lesson on sound:

Marguerita: See, the little pots make high sounds and the big pots make low sounds.
Virian: The big bell sounded high and the little bell sounded low.

Evidently Virian meant to agree with Marguerita, but he could not have meant what he actually said. Paying close attention to what was going on, Sarah jumped in with: "No, that's not right. You got mixed up. The big bell sounded low and the little bell sounded high."

Matthew: These things are like people. Big people voices sound lower than little children voices.

When the teacher requests a generalized statement Phil shows uncertainty. Specifics are nearer to the children's thoughts, but the colloquium can lead them to higher levels.

Phil: Big things make low sounds and little things make higher sounds. Is that right?

[17] Mandell, *op. cit.*, p. 65

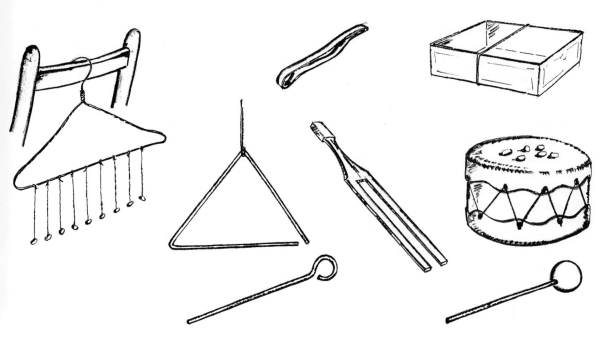

The class listens and considers Phil's statement: each child weighs it with his thought, his experience, his previous verbal expression. The children agree. The generalized statement, made by a child and approved by the other children, is then recorded on the blackboard; later each child will copy it in his Investigators' Log. The act of writing is a higher level of symbolization than a spontaneous reaction from any individual child. It helps codify, if you will, a new learning, a new stage in thinking.

One reason why the cooperative aspect of colloquia nourishes meaning is that hidden likenesses are frequently expressed. The tendency to find hidden likenesses seems to be a natural ability for children of elementary school age. It is an important step toward an even higher level of thought—that of analogy. We have seen that analogies are not unknown even to second graders. Bells and flowerpots are like people! ("Big people voices sound lower than little children voices.") While children find hidden likenesses naturally, the colloquium fosters their further development. As soon as one child begins saying "it is like," many others follow suit:

Chris: The flowerpots reminded me of the xylophone 'cause they went from little to big, just like the bars on the xylophone.

Sophie: The pots look like the musical bells my little sister has at home.

And in the next sequence in discussing the sounds of the flowerpots and the xylophone:

Patricia: Some sounded high and some sounded low.
Marguerita: On one end of the piano the sound is high, and on the other end the music is low.
Daisy: I heard that on the xylophone, too.
Marguerita: See, the little pots make high sounds and the big pots make low sounds.
Sarah: The big bell sounded low and the little bell sounded high.

From this pooled interchange—the expressed experiences and thoughts of a number of children—comes the alliance of "large" and "small" with "low" and "high" and, later, with the varying degrees of movement "big" and "little" things undergo as they produce sound. Here is the experiential background as well as the verbalized thought which will establish later a relationship between pitch, frequency, and energy in the children's learning. Naturally, it is not within the scope of a second grader's ability to encompass all of these related ideas individually. Interchange during the colloquium educes such relationships from the whole group. Each child benefits.

Does everyone learn?

There are many, many different meanings which language nourishes. We will explore several in Chapter 3, but only one aspect will be discussed here. Of the 24 children in Mrs. Schur's class, 19 spoke during the first lesson; 22 spoke during the second, including five who did not contribute before. After both lessons, some children had spoken only once. How much is each child learning when the whole class engages in a colloquium?

Certainly the thoughts of those children who speak often and express themselves clearly can be most easily followed since they are in sequence. But what about those children who speak less frequently or who do not speak at all?

The first colloquium began with emotive comments; the speakers discussed sounds that they did or did not like, find pretty, etc. The second colloquium began with concrete factual observations—already a higher level of thought has been attained. Since both of these colloquia exhibited splendid relationship thinking, we may assume that, after an experience with materials, a considerable amount of untapped preverbal learning resides in each child—a potential which can be verbalized. We can therefore suppose that each child's awareness of what he has learned is initially near the emotive or purely factual level of thought. When a child does not make a remark until late in the discussion and then says something like Rita's "Some of the rubber bands were thin and some were thick" or Zina's (immediately following) "Oh, they were supposed to be like the xylophone," he must have been doing a considerable amount of thinking as he listened to and identified with the comments of his peers. What kind of thinking is this?

It is very different from the preverbal thinking we associate with a person or animal using tools or rearranging objects in his immediate environment in order to achieve a goal. The thinking children engage in while listening to a colloquium is similar to that employed by adults when wrestling with a problem silently. Vygotsky calls it "inner speech." The syntax and logic of inner speech are quite different from the spoken cognate. This is why one sometimes has so much difficulty in expressing one's thoughts. The dynamics of inner speech are fluid; words, mostly predicates, are used as scant symbols, and there is a constant oscillation between partial statements and visual images. It is at this stage, too, that many experiences, not only those just acquired, are brought to bear on a situation. Experiences with little meaning, which have been retained, residues of physical experience, stimuli which have produced action but whose meanings have not been plumbed can all be conjured to semi-awareness during inner speech. It is a period during which the chaos of data is faced. Marguerita's sudden recollection that the piano played high sounds at one end and low sounds at the other (when size and pitch although not named as such, were under consideration) forced her to say "On my piano all the keys are the same, so I don't understand why some are high and some are low." A question put to nature from a discrepant event found by juxtaposing a prior experience with the relationships currently articulated by the group. Marguerita must have been engaging in inner speech which she was then able to translate into language.

Elegant thinking goes on during a colloquium. We perceive the external elegance; the internal is inferred.

Learnings derived from a discovery-colloquium approach to science have many meanings. They form a hierarchy, actually a pyramid. On the base level of *experience* there is an enormous number of stimuli, kinesthetic learnings, vague potentials—all on the order of the dolphin's or chimpanzee's preverbal thoughts. Language is first used to express concrete factual data—the most obvious discoveries. Children can usually list many more of these data than one colloquium produces, but probably not all of the peripherally received experiences which reside only in the muscles and nerves. Talking about discoveries and accumulating pooled learnings (usually centered on one or two areas), stimulate inner speech. Although usually focused on one part of a specific problem, inner speech draws heavily on experiences which have not really been thought about, but which exist as preverbal learnings on the experiential level. Hidden likenesses and analogies develop on this level. Clear summary statements in the Investigators' Log—even more limited, but much more precise—comprise the final stage of thought, the apex of the pyramid.

What a beautiful growth from the sociable dolphin to the sociable seven year old!

The colloquium as sciencing

The dynamics of the colloquium

The colloquium is an essential part of sciencing; scientists themselves find colloquia necessary. A significant example follows.

Before the battle for Britain during World War II, Cambridge University in England was the .hub of scientific research on the nature of the atom. Ever since the establishment of the Cavendish Laboratory during the mid-nineteenth century at that previously strictly humanities-oriented center of learning, physical scientists from all over the world had gathered in Cambridge to pursue their research—first under the leadership of James Clerk Maxwell, then J.J. Thomson, and later Ernest Rutherford.

In the Cavendish Laboratory, Thomson discovered the electron, Geiger built his counter, Wilson developed the first cloud chamber, and Rutherford studied the radioactivity produced by the alpha and beta particles which some atoms emit. When Lawrence Bragg, the crystallographer, was elected Cavendish Professor in 1938, a new laboratory was begun. Although not completed in 1939, the government took over the building for war purposes; most of the scientists there moved to the safety of the United States, pooling their researches with scientists from various nations and working on the atom bomb projects.

Nine years later, the Cavendish Laboratory, now with its own cyclotron, was back in the hands of the physicists. However, the building was still incomplete, only two of the rooms bore their permanent labels in wooden letters affixed to the doors. One room was labeled "Colloquium." In such a room in an earlier building, in 1895, X-rays were demonstrated and discussed a few weeks after Wilhelm Konrad Roentgen's discovery. Scientists in all research laboratories regularly present their discoveries to co-workers through colloquia. Such a presentation is followed by an interchange of thoughts on the problems raised—a kind of thrashing out of the viewpoints of many interested scientists. From this new thinking, new hypotheses to be tested, and new tentative explanations will emerge. The colloquium takes place wherever research scientists work.

The other permanent label read "Tea Room!" This room did not exist solely in deference to British custom nor because scientists often worked through their lunch hours, forgetting that hunger recurs approximately four hours after breakfast. The Tea Room at the Cavendish Laboratory had served a more defined function which might also be considered sciencing. Since the turn of the century, it had provided a period of relaxation during which, by mutual consent, work problems were not discussed. But there might be heated discussions about the potential of cricket players in the Australian–English Test Matches, or who would win the annual Oxford and Cambridge Boat Race, bantering between English and American scientists about their national institutions, exchanges of personal anecdotes, jokes, or witticisms. The Tea Room provided a precious time when professors and fellows could engage in friendly emotional releases before returning to their research —research which would be continued by a future colloquium. Isn't this similar to a child's need to engage in projective play after a period of strained mental challenge? Colloquium and relaxation, intellectual sharing and banter or play, are indeed science and sciencing cognates.

The children's colloquium

The colloquium in a school situation is definitely not what Joan Henderson meant by DIScussion—that is, a teacher asking questions and children trying to find the right answers. The outcome of a colloquium cannot be preordained; each child is not expected to discover the same set of facts nor to see the same hidden likenesses. It may be useful to recall that the word *colloquium* comes from the Latin *col* (for *con* or *cum*), meaning "together," and *loqui*, "speak." It is, therefore, *speaking together*—among peers. The colloquium caters to the intellectual needs of people who have participated in common experiences. Individual reactions to these common experiences are never completely similar, resulting in the richness of speaking thoughts together, engendering thoughts by the verbal expression of various observations.

In order to pool different reactions to experiences, colloquium participants must discover a number of interactions among their materials. Therefore, materials must do a variety of things to one another in order to stimulate thinking along a network of interlacing paths. Not only must the materials be chosen for their rich interaction potential, but the interactions must then be initiated by the children themselves, so that each one is stimulated to think freely from his own viewpoint and is not trying to fit an answer into a preordained framework. Of course, unknown to the children, a general large framework exists because the materials have been selected to lead toward relevant concepts via their interactions.

The first part of the children's colloquium is a pooling of observations, getting a collection of facts into the arena, so to speak, to make individuals aware of common data seen from different viewpoints. This is the beginning of speaking together. The children speak to one another. A circular arrangement of chairs is an obvious aid here. Instead of focusing on the backs of their colleagues' necks and the teacher's authoritative face at the front of the room, the children look into each other's faces when they talk. The teacher's face is one of the many in the circle, and he is not the center of attention since he speaks infrequently.

You may have noticed that the teacher begins each colloquium by asking that the young investigators tell "us" what they have discovered. Once the first child speaks, a nod from the teacher keeps the contributions moving from one to another around the circle, until one of several possibilities occurs. As we have seen, one of these, the discrepant event or contradiction, may be noticed by the children ("My ping-pong ball sank" and "Mine didn't") or by the teacher. The latter may have to extract the contradiction from seemingly unrelated observations or remarks, perhaps separated by several other contributions. ("Ruthanne and Serina have both told us about the air coming out of their bags. Serina hears her air and Ruthanne felt it. Ruthanne, did you perhaps hear your air, too?") The tone with which the contradiction is expressed blesses both children with ultimate truth! The intent illustrated here is to honor each observation as an honest remark made by a careful, unbiased investigator. It is then the responsibility of the colloquium members to examine the discrepant events and to interpret them in a way which is acceptable to all participants—to provide an explanation or a solution.

Another possibility which may interrupt the pooling of discoveries occurs if one child begins to make analogies; this is often followed by a generalization: "It floats just like a boat. Part of it sinks and part floats. A regular ball is like that, too." *Then his voice took on an excited tone.* "So everything else, part, even a small part, must sink or the rest couldn't float."

A third possibility is that a child may offer an explanation of the phenomena just described in the colloquium. We recall that "sciencing will mean engaging in exploration of the material universe *for the purpose of seeking orderly explanations of the objects and events observed* and testing these explanations." Such explanations are, therefore, the crux of the colloquium.

During the mealworm colloquium, one of Mrs. Weiss's children said "I think they don't like heat. *It's the heat not the light they go away from.*" And one child offered an explanation of the Ruthanne–Serina discrepant event with, "*There was more power to Serina's bag.*" These explanations are certainly not world-shaking theories; we do not expect them to be. We do expect children to attempt explanations while sciencing. These explanations will not be judged right or wrong, but at some point, they should be tested . . . for the purpose of seeking orderly explanations of the objects and events observed and *testing these explanations.*

Just as offering explanations seems to be a natural activity in the course of a colloquium, so does offering either a way to test these explanations or some facts to support them. The mealworm explanation above was followed by "How do you know?" The investigator, who had already applied a test, answered: "I put one corner of my shoebox on the radiator and when I put the worms into that corner they all moved away." Not a thoroughly controlled investigation, but a good beginning. The "power" in Serina's bag was supported by the statement: "The air came out fast."

Colloquia reveal conceptual arrows

In Chapter 1 (page 17 *ff.*), we emphasized the importance of considering concepts and conceptual schemes as bases in choosing science materials. By these, we mean adult-level concepts, guides for curriculum designers and teachers. When children use structured materials as a basis for discovery-colloquium sciencing, they begin to develop their own concepts. The psychological stages of such individual conceptual development are very different from the full-blown concepts which form the structure of the curriculum or lesson, but they are related.

Psychologists have worked out schemes which pinpoint the various stages in conceptual growth. Those of Vygotsky and Piaget are presented in Chapters 3 and 6. The statements children make during colloquia represent steps in the concept-building process; to the attuned listener, they reveal the thinking processes—the growth from concrete to abstract thinking in each child. We have named these vectors of mental growth *conceptual arrows*.

The discovery-colloquium strategy of science education is structured to foster growth along conceptual arrows. This growth may be described as moving from (1) concrete, personal involvement with structured materials and the preverbal thought this involvement engenders, to (2) interaction of thoughts and words as observed data are presented at the beginning of the colloquium, to (3) interaction with the words and thoughts of co-workers, to (4) the formulation of explanations and, finally, to (5) testing the explanations. This process is partially represented in the following chart. (The complete chart appears in Chapter 8.)

Concept-seeking skills encompass those activities during the colloquium which place verbal data accurately and clearly before the assembled body. These data form the basis for making more general statements and, finally, for offering explanations. Each step in concept attainment includes levels of thought which may range from finding external or hidden likenesses to constructing a model. Models may be anything from a child's very simple explanation of a phenomenon to a theory established by scientists.

The analysis of colloquia in terms of the sciencing evidenced is an important aspect of the full evaluation of science lessons and, therefore, the growth of each child along his individual conceptual arrows. Such an analysis is begun by scoring the colloquium record, using the code described below.

Concept-seeking skills

Communicating

Observations (*obs*): Whenever a child makes a remark describing what he has done or discovered ("My bulb lit"; "The ping-pong ball floated") or applies data from some prior experience ("My piano makes high and low sounds like the xylophone"), it is marked *obs*. (No score is given for such expressions as "I dunno" or "Me, too.")

Stated clearly (*cl*): A clear statement refers to objects by name, instead of using "thing" or "they"; it describes an event in terms that others can understand. The *obs* examples above would also be scored *cl*.

EXPERIENCES	CONCEPT-SEEKING SKILLS		LEVELS OF CONCEPT ATTAINMENT	
	(Conceptual Arrow)			
	COMMUNICATING	THINKING	FINDING LIKENESSES	
			EXTERNAL	HIDDEN
Free discovery with concrete materials	Observations: Stated clearly Accurately perceived Relevant to the concept	Noticed discrepant event Said "I think" or "Is it right?" Asked when, why, how, where question	Generalized Compared Classified	Generalized Made an analogy Suggested a model

Accurately perceived (*ac*): As we have seen, children's statements often reflect a too hurried look. In contrast to the above examples, the statements "The Wiffle ball sank" and "Mine didn't" suggest that both children need to check their observations again to see what really happened. Faulty perceptions or inaccurate observations are sometimes marked ✗ (or ✗ if headed columns are used). Some remarks (those used to construct a model, for example) may not involve perception. This is also true of emotive remarks.

Relevant to the concept (*re*): This term refers to the concepts related to the materials. It attempts to distinguish between emotional reaction ("That was fun") and the pooling of data or attempted explanation ("The wires got hot"; "The shadow moves when the sun moves").

Thinking

Noticed discrepant event (*d.e.*): This code applies not only to contradictory data, but also to facts which seem to contradict original expectations or intentions. ("You know what?" observes Monte. "They're both as bright as one alone!" "Gee," muses Carl, "dat's queer.") Both boys' remarks would be marked *d.e.*

Said "I think" or "Is it right?" (*th*): We want to encourage children to risk statements—to try them on for size, as it were. To be unsure, to suggest, to question correctness are all attributes of sciencing.

Asked a when, why, how, or where question *(?)*: Monte's remark immediately following the discrepant event above ("I wonder why?") would be scored *?.*

Steps in concept attainment

Finding external likenesses

Generalized (*gen, gen ex* or *gen hid*): Since generalizations can be based on external or hidden likenesses, these items may be scored with an additional *ex* or *hid* if desired. "Objects lighter for their size than water float" is *gen hid* but cannot be scored *ac* because the amount of water needed for comparison is not stated. "All men have five fingers" would be scored *gen ex*. It could also be scored *ac* if the child is likely to know of no exceptions.

Compared (*com*): Comparisons are based on external likenesses; they compare items which are accessible to the senses. ("The flowerpots went from little to big"; "The bean is much taller today.") Using the word *like* in a comparison usually means *the same as*. ("The book is red like the curtain.")

Classified (*clas*): A classification relates an object to a more inclusive category. "Is this a flower?", asked about a weed without a flower, would be scored *clas* because the child is thinking of a possible relationship.

Finding hidden likenesses

Generalized (*gen hid*): (See under "*Finding external likenesses*")

Made an analogy (*ana*): An analogy is a comparison on an abstract level. It also may include the word *like*, but here the likeness is in the mind of the speaker. ("A funnel is like an upside down hat" or "Gee, I can feel it; it's like the wind" [of two strong alnico magnets held near one another].

Suggested a model (*mod*): A model made by a scientist is an elegantly constructed explanation of some natural phenomenon. It goes beyond fact by providing a mental or symbolic image which explains a whole cluster of relationships. Mathematicians construct models in highly abstract symbols and then find new relationships by operating on these symbols. Scientists also do this when, for example, they write equations to account for energy transfers as electrons change their positions relative both to one another and to nuclear particles. Darwin constructed a model through his evolutionary theory when he offered an explanation of how man might have appeared on earth.

Children who offer explanations of facts and events they have observed are engaging in model making, but on their own level. The level of an explanation, therefore, not its rightness or wrongness, interests us as we analyze colloquia, for even scientific models are open to constant modification or major change. With this in mind, we feel we can consider all children's explanations to be *models*. Like explanations, models need testing; first, however, they must be invented and stated.

Analyzing colloquia

Of course, every colloquium is unique since it evolves from the nature of the materials used and relies on the children's degree of intellectual sophistication as well as on their previous experience, if any, with discovery-colloquium sciencing. Dynamically, a colloquium is usually a rather zigzag movement from the beginning data to the suggested models. Coding the children's statements along the margin of a recorded colloquium renders these dynamics visible. A sequence of such coded records indicates the dynamics from one period to another. Following the coded remarks of a particular child during one or several colloquia enables us to recognize the dynamics of that child's growth along his own personal conceptual arrows.

In scoring the two colloquia which follow, the concept attainment codes are underlined or encircled so that they stand out from the concept-seeking skills.

Analysis of Mrs. Ross's first grade colloquium

Dick: I didn't discover nuttin'.

Rosa: The marble went straight to the bottom. obs,cl,ac,re

Rex: You can pick water up in the Wiffle ball. obs,cl,ac

Dick: The Wiffle ball sinks. obs,cl,re

Bert: No, it floats. obs,cl,ac,re,d.e.

.
.
.

Dick: It floats just like a boat. Part of it sinks and part floats. A regular ball is like that, too. So everything else, part, even a small part, must sink or the rest couldn't float. The part of the Wiffle ball that sinks is the part that has water in it. obs,cl,ac,re, (ana) ,gen ex

Charlie: The part of the boat that sinks does it 'cause it's heavy, too. obs,cl,re, (mod)

Gert: Is it because the water makes the Wiffle ball heavy? Does it *not* float because of this? obs,cl,re,?, (mod)

Gert has really asked a why question and answered it with a model.

.
.
.

Gert: It's floating, but low. So the water doesn't make it sink. But when I filled the ping-pong ball with water it sank. obs,cl,ac,re,d.e.

Kathie: Mine didn't. obs,ac,re,d.e.

.
.
.

Gert: Kathie's has a bubble of air in hers. Maybe that's why it floats. obs,cl,ac,re,th, (mod)

Kathie: My ping-pong ball smelled funny. I think there was soap in it. obs,cl,ac,re,th

Jonathan: The soap floats. obs,cl,re

Fran: Only one piece does; the other sinks. obs,cl,ac,re,d.e.

Dick: I know why. It's Ivory. They say on TV that it is ninety-nine and forty-four hundredths percent pure and it floats. obs,cl,re, (mod)

David: Nobody said anything about the sponges yet. obs,cl,re obs,cl,ac,re, (mod)

David: When they are dry, they float, but as soon as they get wet, that's it; they sink.

obs,cl,ac,re,com

Gert: I wrapped a jack in tin foil and it floated. It sank alone. I did the same with soap, and it floated, too.

obs,cl,re,th

Shelley: I think I know why things float.

.
.

obs,cl,ac,re, (mod)
obs,cl,ac,re,d.e.
obs,cl,re, (mod)
obs,cl,ac,re,com

Shelley: They float because they have air in them.

Dick: Ivory soap can't have air; it has no holes.

Jo: Air might have been pumped into the middle of it.

Rex: The sponge works that way, too. When it is dry, it has air in it. When it is wet, it has water in it instead.

.
.
.

obs,cl,re, (mod)

Shelley: The water pushes it out and takes the air's place.

Mrs. R.: Why doesn't the key float?

obs,cl,ac,re, (mod)

Danny: It has no air in it.

.
.

obs,cl,re, (mod)

Shelley: If we could make it into a round ball and put air in it, it might be able to float.

obs,cl,re

Dick: It wouldn't be no good then!

obs,cl

Kathie: Who ever heard of a round keyhole!

Mrs. R.: I saw some of you making the marbles float. . . .

obs,cl,ac,re, com
An obvious similarity.

Danny: I did it. I put the marbles in the little paper cup like they were in a boat. Then I put more marbles in and it all sank.

obs,cl,ac,re, (ana) , (mod)

Beginning of (gen hid.)

Shelley: That's like the sponge. Water pushed the air out of the sponge and it sank. Marbles pushed the air out of the cup and the cup sank.

A glance at the preceding analysis shows that this colloquium moves dynamically from pooling to explaining data. The change in quality of the models from earlier to later comments is of particular interest. Gert thinks the bubble of air is the reason for flotation. Half jokingly, Dick recalls the advertised purity of Ivory soap. David suggests that wetness makes things sink. Shelley, Jo, and Danny pursue the air theme; Shelley elaborates until she produces the beginning of a generalization—a larger reason why things float in water.

From the scoring, we also note that near the end Kathie and Dick relax into playfulness (the Tea Room stage!).

Dick's conceptual arrow is interesting. In three close stages, his remarks develop from "nuttin' " to a simple (although inaccurate) statement, "The Wiffle ball sinks," to rather elegant analogies and generalizations. After this, his contributions are more infrequent and playful.

Another sink and float colloquium

Our second colloquium has somewhat different dynamics. This was also a sink and float lesson—a follow-up of one with the same kind of materials Mrs.

Ross's children used. (However, Mrs. Child's first graders were inner-city children.) Presented with hard-boiled eggs and small basins of plain and very salty water, Mrs. Childs's children investigated eagerly, dunking eggs in both waters and expressing much surprise. The colloquium began with statements of a few observed facts (not recorded here); there was soon a flurry of explanations and testing.

Elma: This one (*pointing to the salt water basin*) has more water; that's why it floats.

obs,cl,ac,re, <u>com</u>, (mod)

Mrs. C.: What could you do to find out?

Elma: Put more water in this one. *(Brings the plain water level up to that of the salt water.)*

obs,cl,re

Pat: It still sinks. I think it sinks because the water is cold.

obs,cl,ac,re,th,d.e., (mod)

Juan: No, because the egg is heavier.

obs,cl,re,<u>com</u>,(mod)

Pat: But we tried all the eggs in both waters. *(Demonstrates.)* See, they all float in this water and sink in that.

obs,cl,ac,re,d.e.,<u>gen ex</u>

Durham: The egg sank in this water, but floated in the other.

obs,cl,ac,re,d.e.

Pat: This one has something in it; that's why it floats. *(Lifts out some of the salt that has settled to the bottom)*

obs,ac,re, (mod)

Durham: It's soap powder.

obs,cl,re

Juan: No, it's sugar.

obs,cl,re

Si: It's like sea water.

obs,cl,re, (ana)

Mrs. C.: What makes you think so?

Si: I dunno!

Pat: The eggs floated because there was soap in the water.

obs,cl,re, (mod)

Elma: It's not soap; there were no bubbles. It's sugar.

obs,cl,ac,re,d.e.

Mrs. C.: Durham thinks it's soapsuds. Elma thinks it's sugar and Juan thinks so, too. Si thinks it's like sea water. What could we do to find out?

The children were cautious about tasting the water, so Mrs. Childs suggested taking only a tiny sip and demonstrated herself to give assurance. "It's salt!" was the consensus.

Mrs. C.: Why do eggs float in salty and not in plain water?

Durham: Because the salt keeps them up.

obs,cl,re, (mod)

Juan: The salt makes the water heavy.

obs,cl,re, (mod)

Mrs. C.: Juan thinks the salt makes the water heavy, and Si says the water is like sea water. What do you think about this?

Si: The water is like sea water because it has salt in it.

obs,cl,re, <u>com</u>

Pat: Salt water makes you float.

obs,cl,re, <u>gen ex</u>

Elma: It makes you stay on top of the water.

obs,cl,re, (mod)

Mrs. C.: How?

Pat: Salt water is stronger than plain water.

obs,cl,re, <u>com</u>

Elma: What would happen if we took off the shells?

obs,cl,re,?

Mrs. C.: There's only one way to find out. . . .

This colloquium followed an experience where a discrepant event was patently present in the interaction between the children and their materials. Two seemingly similar eggs and two seemingly similar liquids produce different reactions. Even though resolution of this contradiction dominated the colloquium, early statements show a rich pooling of facts as well as models; later, concept attainment predominates. Discrepant events keep challenging the flotation models as their emphasis changes from the quantity of water, to its coldness, to one egg being heavier, to the soap, sugar, or salt in the water. The final models, completely adequate for the six-year-old levels of development, are based on salt keeping the eggs up because the salt makes the water heavy. Note that here, as in several other colloquiua, "heavy" has a special meaning for the speaker.

The conceptual arrows of individuals are particularly interesting in this colloquium. You might like to compare the sequence of statements made by Elma, Durham (whose first remark was a repetition of what was said just before), Si, and Pat. The thought progression is impressive. Could we want more from any group of six year olds? Does this colloquium show you anything about advantaged vs. disadvantaged education?

Now it's your turn As children become older and "brighter," they also become more verbal. In fact, very often they produce more verbalization than thought! One purpose of the colloquium is to encourage children to speak meaningfully—to chisel meanings into productive thought. A teacher may frequently have to ask speakers to clarify their statements—to offer supportive reasoning.

Here is a colloquium on which you can practice scoring:

Four girls in a sixth-grade class worked with materials similar to those given to both of the first grades just examined. Mrs. Adler had provided the girls with these materials:

1. A toothpick and a needle.
2. A walnut, a rock, and a sponge—all about the same size.
3. A rubber ball and a rubber ball with a hole.
4. Pieces of Lifebuoy and Ivory soap.
5. A cellulose sponge and some aluminum foil.
6. Two hard-boiled eggs.
7. A small container of fresh water and another of saturated salt water.
8. A large bowl of water.

Toward what concepts of flotation are these materials structured?

Mrs. A.: Tell us about the soap.
Belle: Ivory floats; Lifebuoy sinks.
Mrs. A.: Why do you think this is?

Shades of our first graders!

Laurie: Ivory is lighter and Lifebuoy is heavier, so Ivory floats.
Enid: They were about the same size, so it wasn't the size that made the difference.
Yvette: When I wrapped the Lifebuoy loosely in foil, it floated, but when I wrapped it very tightly, it sank.

Words come easily, thoughts slowly, for these children.

Mrs. A.: Why do you think this happens?
The girls all looked puzzled.

Mrs. A.: What might you have pushed out when you wrapped the soap so tightly?

Yvette: It must have been air.

Belle: Air must make things lighter.

Enid: That must be why the sponge always floats. It's full of air.

Laurie: That's right. The rubber ball with the hole floats because of the air in it. When the water gets in, it sinks. I wonder if the rubber in the ball floats?

Mrs. A.: We can try and see. *(She cuts off a piece of the rubber and drops it in the basin.)*

Enid: See, it sinks. It must have been that the air kept it floating and nothing else.

Mrs. A.: Could that explain why the Ivory floats?

Yvette: Perhaps it has extra air in it.

Enid: Maybe like whipped cream. Maybe they mix it with an electric mixer.

Belle: If they do that, do you get as much soap as in the other soap that's about the same size? [Belle is using the term "same size" in relation to money's worth.]

Laurie: I don't think so. It seems that you pay for the soap and the extra air that they put in it to make it float.

Mrs. A.: Why did the loose foil float and the tightly pressed ball of foil sink?

Laurie: I know. When the air was pressed out, it became heavier and it sank.

Mrs. A.: What about the walnut and the stone?

Enid: Although they were about the same size, the stone sank and the walnut floated.

Mrs. A.: What about the needle and the toothpick?

Enid: I don't think anyone pumped air into the toothpick! It must be something else. The volume was about the same, but the weights were different. *(Aside to Laurie.)* I heard about volume on a television program last year. I think that's what all this is about.

At this point, Mrs. Adler asked whether a pound of lead would float as a pound of sponge would. She was not able to record the discussion because it became long and confused. Noting that her redirection was not a good one, she took another tack.

Mrs. A.: What are all things made of?

Laurie: Molecules.

Belle: If the molecules are closer together, the thing is heavier.

Enid: That's what makes different volume.

Belle: What's volume?

Enid: Amount it contains of a substance. Look . . . a jar of air and the same size jar full of lead—the volume is the same, but the two things don't weigh the same . . . *I think.*

Mrs. A.: What about the eggs?

Belle: I think the water in the jar where the eggs sank was boiled and that made them sink, for some reason. Yvette and I couldn't figure it out.

Enid: You should have had Laurie for a partner. She tastes everything. There was salt in the water where the eggs floated.

Did the younger children's teachers give such a leading directive? Was this essential here?

A redirective question: Belle and Laurie have introduced a discrepant event—consumer values—which will not lead toward a scientific concept. You can probably think of other good redirective questions.

Mrs. Adler is using the structure of the materials to start the girls thinking about hidden likenesses. What is the structure and what are the likenesses here?

Enid notices a controlled variable.

TV offers vicarious experience and vicarious language. When does thought enter in?

Why do you think the girls did not perceive the hidden likenesses in the materials Mrs. Adler named?

Preverbal thought? (Air boiled out makes things heavier?)

Yvette: Salt water must be heavier than regular water so it must hold the thing up better.

Enid: So the weight of the water must make a difference in whether the the things sink or float.

Laurie: Sure, the water must push up on things the way air pushes on things.

In spite of this beautiful seeking out of a hidden likeness—an elegant model to be sure—Mrs. Adler felt that she must supply an explanation. She noted in her record: "At this point, I tried to explain about density with pictures and imagery, using the words *weight and volume*. When I used *unit volume* in my vocabulary, the children became so bewildered that I dropped the idea and let them summarize more or less on their own."

Belle: I know, but I don't know how to say it.

Yvette: All things lighter than water for the same size float on water. The other things sink.

Laurie: Things that push down on the water less than the water pushes up will float. If they push harder, they will sink.

Yvette: For instance, if you had a cube of water like a baby's block, it might weigh two ounces. A cube of sponge that is the same size might weigh half an ounce. The sponge would float because four cubes of sponge weigh the same as one cube of water.

Enid: Water can hold up anything that weighs less for each volume. Anything that weighs more for each volume will sink in water. *(Enid then made a drawing.)*

Mrs. A.: Why do some things seem to hang in water? They don't sink or float?

Enid: They must weigh the same for each volume as water.

Belle: Things that are heavier than water for each piece of volume will sink. Things that weigh the same for each volume don't sink or float.

Yvette: Stuff that is lighter for each volume than water will float.

Inner speech not yet translated into language.

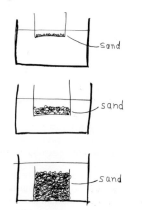

Why has Belle found a way to say it now?

As you read the next lesson, *They Learn as They Speak Together*, continue to exercise your skill at scoring and analyzing a colloquium. As this becomes a fairly easy procedure, you may also be able to begin thinking about the role the teacher plays in the colloquium. Reviewing the teacher's remarks during the last three colloquia will provide additional facts for you to consider.

As a general rule, we have said that teachers should not give facts during a colloquium (and, more particularly, during the preceding discovery period). However, in this next lesson you will find that Mrs. Eliot occasionally gives facts to her fifth graders. As you analyze her lesson, decide what do you think about this.

The materials Mrs. Eliot provided are those often used for following up the *What's Inside?* lesson (pages 7-14). After reading about Mrs. Eliot's class, decide what structure links her materials with those Miss Stevens used in *What's Inside?*

THEY LEARN AS THEY SPEAK TOGETHER

"When you enter this room, you probably won't notice that the teacher is present." The Principal made this synoptic comment as he and his out-of-town visitor approached the glass-paneled door marked 103.

The visitor had received a variety of warnings before entering other rooms:

"All the children will rise and you will be formally introduced."

"We made a special class of all the most troubled children in the third and fourth grades and gave them to Miss Rosenthal. She's very accepting and wise. The children seem to relax and grow with her."

"You may think Mr. Frederick is overly strict, but the children love him. He has a sense of humor, but is never sarcastic—and his class makes excellent progress. He has high standards and his fifth and sixth graders meet them."

And now: "You probably won't notice the teacher."

"Well, Mr. Peatman's school certainly isn't lock step," thought the visitor. "I wonder if he has any basic philosophy, or is it all catch-as-catch-can?"

The visitor didn't even notice the teacher's desk at first; children occupied the front of the room. They were grouped around a circular table discussing something eagerly, with more or less controlled, but distinctly audible, voices. Along the window ledge, four or five boys and girls were working individually, each with a . . .

"What are those children looking at?" the visitor asked his guide.

"They're using little microscopes. I'll show you one in my office." The visitor had expected the Principal to ask one child to demonstrate his microscope and tell what he was doing with it. But no, not in this classroom. No one, not even the teacher, had looked up when the two men entered. Not even the teacher? Where was he or she?

In the far corner near the sink, sheltered by a nook of standing shelves, a woman in her forties was listening to an animated recitation by two boys. Each had a book resting on his knees and referred to pages from time to time.

"They are probably discussing two works by the same author," whispered Mr. Peatman. "That's one of Mrs. Eliot's favorite activities. I think I recall from her lesson plan that the author is Krumgold and the books are *Onion John* and *And Now Miguel*."

"A good way to get the children to think, I would imagine."

"Mrs. Eliot's long suit. She has all manner of stimulating devices which absorb the children—even at home, the parents tell me proudly!"

The Principal elaborated on the way back to his office. While he reveled in his own unorthodoxy, he always felt it was necessary for visitors to understand the firm principles behind his apparent laxity.

"Mrs. Eliot is preparing for the Assistant Principal's Exam . . ."

"I thought a recent requirement for that was to teach in one of the slum schools?"

"All of Mrs. Eliot's experience has been with the economically disadvantaged. She felt the need to have a spin with a middle-class group in a more prestigious neighborhood."

"And you find she knows enough to extend your brighter children?"

The Principal sensed a subtle touch of prejudice, but decided to counter it obliquely with quietly stated facts. "The fascinating thing about Rosa Eliot is that she was known as an *excellent* teacher in the disadvantaged neighborhood. You know, I sometimes wonder whether excellence in education shouldn't be forged in the slum areas, where children's motivation for academic success must be fostered and fed by their own successful experiences in school. Most of the children in my school, on the other hand, will learn with whatever teacher they have—or their parents will want to know why!"

The out-of-towner then plunged into the main interest of his visit—the selection and utilization of the school's staff. "Is Mrs. Eliot your only black teacher?"

"Actually Mrs. Eliot's background is Puerto Rican, although her husband is black. I do have an Afro-American teacher in one of the kindergartens, though."

"Did the Board of Education assign these people to you?"

"No such luck! They both came to me under special circumstances. Mrs. Wright in the kindergarten was a Head Start teacher. Because of the problem of continuing pre-school growth which a good Head Start program provides, Mrs. Wright suggested a plan . . ."

"I've heard the Head Start program doesn't always offer permanent benefits."

"Let's say that sometimes experiences in the early grades push Head Start children back on a level with those who have not had their opportunities. Personally, I think it has to do with the kind of teaching in those grades. Again, excellence in teaching benefits everyone! Mrs. Wright thought that she might help bridge the gap if she continued with the same group of children she had taught for the previous two years. Maybe she wanted to prove that the slip back is unnecessary—that it is the school's responsibility to provide and maintain educational opportunities. Anyway, she persuaded the Head Start parents to sign transfers and the Board of Education to start a new kindergarten in a spare room in my school; then she arranged for the busing. You see, she's quite a dynamo! For the first week, she accompanied the children on the buses each morning. Now two paraprofessionals, parents actually, ride on the buses and help with the classwork."

"Did all the parents agree?"

"Only two refused."

"How did Mrs. Eliot manage her transfer? Moving a teacher out of a slum school is not easy to justify."

"Well, as I said before, Mrs. Eliot wanted another kind of experience before submitting to the Assistant Principal's exam. One of our local colleges, which places student teachers both in this school and in the one where Mrs. Eliot was teaching, brought her need to my attention. I requested her. Her two children come to this school, too, so that's an added advantage—for her and for us. She drives them over with her each morning. Both she and her husband have advanced degrees. He's a dentist in fact, so there are high expectations for the children."

"I notice that you seem to sponsor, or condone, a great many different— shall we say—teaching styles." The visitor's mind refused to formulate his real question properly.

"I judge teaching largely by what happens to the children, and partly by the initiative and adaptability of the teacher. A teacher who is willing to try new approaches and yet can maintain successful and eager learning on the part of the children is tops in my account. But there are, of course, many, many teaching styles which can achieve this."

"Your parents don't object to the experimental use of their children?"

"I don't think of innovations this way, and I doubt that parents do either. The parents are usually in on our discussions about new plans. They seem to judge the school largely by whether or not the children hate to be absent!"

But the visitor was not listening. He was still wrestling with his question. Suddenly, he shot out—"Do Mrs. Eliot's children really learn anything? Facts, I mean. It all seemed as though the children were pooling their ignorance!"

Mr. Peatman laughed. The two men were comfortably seated in the Principal's office near a tank of tropical fish. "You might be interested to read this." He pulled out a file. "It's a record I made of what Mrs. Eliot's children said during one of my supervisory visits to her classroom. I come, of course, to help, not to judge."

The visitor suppressed a gulp.

"You see, my evidence of a teacher's skill is what the children do and say, of their growth in doing and saying over the year. It seems to me to be our joint responsibility. But since the teacher actually does the work, it's my job to suggest the next steps . . . after observation."

"What's your major criterion of a teacher's ability?"

"I think ability grows in the kind of environment I try to keep in this school. I judge the success we are achieving together—well, sometimes by a glint in the children's eyes, by their enthusiasm in tackling a new problem or by how long they continue to work on a project. And you know something else? Because a teacher's reputation runs before him, I sometimes judge our progress by the enthusiasm with which a new class responds to each teacher it will have in the new year."

Mr. Peatman felt he was goading the visitor a bit. "But you must excuse me, please. You have the notes to read and I promised Mr. Fredericks I would drop in on his class about ten this morning. They're analyzing some graphs they made on pendulum lengths.

The visitor settled back to read the document. The quiet gliding of the angelfish and the darting of the neon-flashing tetras in the warmly lit tank seemed to reflect his own conflicting emotions.

Fifth Grade   Mrs. Rosa Eliot   Date: 3-15-68   Hour: 10:30 a.m.
The children were grouped in fours around tables made by pushing two desks together. Each group had four magnets and two plastic containers—sandwich

boxes. Sharing the boxes seemed to produce no problems for the children. In each box were:

1. A piece of aluminum foil.
2. A cork.
3. Something that resembled a cork wrapped in aluminum foil.
4. Another cork with something like a tack inserted in some part of it, also wrapped.
5. A United States nickel.
6. A Canadian nickel.

The visitor read the description of what the children did, some of their random comments, and then moved to the section labeled "Colloquium."

José: There was a Canadian nickel in the box.

Sam: I made it stick to the side of the container.

Gerrit: There is something in the tinfoil.

A *Wally*: The magnet only attracts the Canadian nickel, not the U. S nickel.

Kate: It only attracts one of the corks.

Wally: No, that's because the Canadian nickel was near the cork. The Canadian nickel is the only thing to attract.

Dorothy: Oh, no! One cork moved.

Pamela: If you rub the magnet to the container, you can magnetize through the container.

Wally: Yeah, I still say there is only one part of the cork that moves toward the magnet.

Brian: There must be a piece of metal in the cork.

Dorothy: Yes, the points won't move, but the sides will.

Wally: Only *one* side of the cork moved.

Francis: Try it on the other side of the container. *(They do.)*

Ian: I discovered it! There must be a thumbtack in one part of the cork.

Anthony: When I put the magnet on one certain part of the tinfoil, it moved.

Ian: I saw a little round thing there, and it moves. So it is a thumbtack.

Mrs. E.: What else did you have here?

Ian: A Canadian nickel.

B *Vyelle*: An American nickel.

Mary: I saw a plain cork, but nothing else happened.

Kate: There was something else that looked like a cork with aluminum foil.

One irrelevancy is followed by several others.

Art: Why is this cover taped down on the container?

Lynn: So we couldn't open it.

Rick: So the objects couldn't get out, but the magnet could get through.

Jessica: It was plastic we could see through.

April: If we dropped the container, it wouldn't break.

Why does the teacher redirect at this point?

Mrs. E.: Well, what did your group discover?

April: We found that almost everything moved except the cork that wasn't wrapped in foil.

Mrs. E.: Did all of you make this observation?

Anthony: Yes.

Mrs. E.: Did everyone else in the class find this to be true?

Stacy: Yes.

Lee: Out of the two nickels, *only* the Canadian nickel moved.

Mrs. E.: You all agree?

Everyone: Yes.

Mrs. E.: Why do you think this is so?

Pamela: Because the two nickels are made of two different materials. I think the Canadian nickel is made of metal and the magnet will pick it up. The American nickel is made of something not metal.

Francis: I read a book that says the American nickel is one quarter nickel and three quarters copper. So, this magnet won't pick it up.

Mrs. E.: (writing at the board)

"<u>a</u>luminum
<u>ni</u>ckel
<u>co</u>balt"

Did you know that you were using alnico magnets? *(The children nodded and smiled as they read what was on the board.)* I think you need to know that nickel is a magnetic substance. Does this tell you anything about the Canadian coin?

C

Art: I think the Canadian coin is of pure nickel.

Denise: I think it must be made of more nickel than the American nickel.

Todd: If it's not nickel, then maybe it is a combination of nickel and another metal—but it has more nickel than the other metal.

Timothy: Well, I think it's pure nickel.

Mrs. E.: There has to be more than 27% nickel in a mixture of metals for the mixture to interact with a magnet. Did you know that we import our nickel from Canada? Did you make any other observations?

D

Brian: Anything that has metal in it or on it was moved by a magnet.

Gerrit: That's wrong! 'Cause our nickel is made of something metal and the magnet didn't attract it.

Mark: The tinfoil contains metal and was not attracted to the magnet.

Doris: Well, I know there was metal at one end of my cork because I was able to make the cork stand up on one end.

Mrs. E.: Did everyone have a cork with a piece of metal at one end?

Ronald: Well, we don't really know this was a thumbtack—but whatever it is, it's in the middle of one side.

Beth: Well, mine was near a corner on the side.

E

Karl: Oh, shucks! I bet you put them in different places.

Chorus: Oh—h—h!

Mrs. E.: Do you have anything more to say?

Rahmi: Yes, I like this way of science because we can discover for ourselves.

Mrs. E.: What did you do in order to discover for yourselves?

Ian: Observation.

Ronald: Experiment.

Considering that these children are fifth graders, it is strange that some of them still think that magnets interact with *metal*!

F *Mrs. E.*: Did you reach any conclusion as a class?

Lynn: Yes, some things can be attracted and some can't.

Rick: I think we all learned something new about the Canadian nickel.

Vyelle: We discovered that magnets will attract some metals even through plastic.

General comment: This was fun.

"An unusual lesson," the visitor thought. "I wonder what Mr. Peatman does with the notes he takes? Maybe the capital letters designate criticisms. No, he said he wasn't judging. I'd find it hard to evaluate this lesson—it's too unusual."

Mr. Peatman returned, followed by two small boys. "Take a good look at the angelfish and the tetras if you want to. I hope they'll help you with your problem."

The boys glued their noses to the fish tank, talking quietly and making notes. They seemed to be no more aware of the visitor than the children in Mrs. Eliot's class were.

"Soooooo." (Mr. Peatman hoped his visitor would leave soon. He had a conference scheduled with some parents and two teachers of a second-third-fourth-grade class who wanted to start a neighborhood study project using Polaroid cameras and tape recorders.)

"Very unusual," the visitor said, referring to the report.

"Oh, yes, yes. . . ." The Principal sounded vague.

"What do you do with these notes?"

"Oh, they form the basis for a conference with Mrs. Eliot to discuss the next steps. I also make notes to remind me of the points I want to bring up. Would you like to see them?"

"Thank you, I would."

"Then I must ask you to excuse me. Here are the notes." With a slight bow he was gone. The boys were still busy.

The visitor read:

Notes for our conference: Rosa Eliot

Congratulate her that only three children did not talk in the colloquium. (I must watch for these three next time: Nellie, Alice, and Hank.) Two children were absent.

After she has read the record and had her say, focus on the marked points:

A How can we help the children think of the *interaction* between magnet and iron or nickel, instead of the anthropomorphic "attraction"? Maybe a lesson or two directed to this point?

B Do the children realize that Canada is a part of *America*?

C Since the children had no way of knowing this fact and needed it for their thinking, it was a well-chosen moment to give information. Note to our science specialist: obtain some pieces of nickel so that children can experience the interaction of magnets with nickel as well as with iron and steel much earlier in the grades.

D The 27% fact was appropriately given. What should it have led to? Maybe all that was necessary after this was to juxtapose Denise's and Todd's insights. Can Mrs. E. discover the effect of her giving information?

E Congratulate her on placing thumbtacks in different positions in the corks.

F What happened at the end?

To watch for later in the year:

Do children improve in accuracy and extent of observation?

"Unusual," murmured the visitor, "very unusual."

A secretary came to show him out. He looked around at the fish tank as he left. The boys were no longer there.

The power of the colloquium

Rex's first remark after he and the other first graders had investigated the sink and float materials (page 22) was:

Rex: You can pick water up in the Wiffle ball.

And his last contribution stated:

Rex: The sponge works that way, too. When it is dry, it has air in it. When it is wet, it has water in it instead.

In the same class, Shelley did not speak for a long time. When she did, she said:

Shelley: I think I know why things float. . . .because they have air in them.

And after some intervening remarks, she summed up the thinking of the group this way:

Shelley: That's like the sponge. Water pushed the air out of the sponge and it sank. Marbles pushed the air out of the cup and the cup sank.

What classroom experiences led these children from "here" to "there"? To what may we attribute their growth in thinking?

Recall Rae, an immature second grader from Miss Bradford's inner city class. Let us review Rae's remarks after her "water play." She entered the colloquium (page 71) by asking:

Rae: What's a funnel?

A little later, she offered the following hidden likeness:

Rae: Water can be like drops and then it look like round things.

After Miss Bradford's follow-up lesson with the white powders and water, Paul made this statement at the beginning of the colloquium:

Paul: I put a powder in the water and it turn white.

At the end of the discussion, he, too, had found a hidden likeness:

Paul: Oh! It look like it invisible, but the sugar still there.

How do early remarks which are purely personal or factual become, less than half an hour later, statements of hidden likenesses with original juxtapositions of phenomena? What happens in between?

When faced with the bells in the corked bottles, Matthew, a second grader, first remarked:

Matthew: They both have corks in them.

An external attribute that was easily perceptible. Later, he linked the hose to the bottles with:

Matthew: I know! It's like the bottle with no air. He [Gray] stopped the air in the hose, and you can't hear without air.

If six- and seven-year-old children from various economic strata can progress from stating the personal and obvious to finding rather surprising and elegant hidden likenesses during 15-30 minutes of colloquium what may be expected from mature eleven year olds? Consider the following remarks of the four girls working with Mrs. Adler (page 126).

Girl	First remarks	Last remarks
Belle:	Ivory floats; Lifebuoy sinks.	Things that are heavier than water for each piece of volume will sink. Things that weigh the same for each volume don't sink or float.
Laurie:	Ivory is lighter and Lifebuoy is heavier, so Ivory floats.	Things that push down on the water less than the water pushes up will float. If they push harder, they will sink.
Enid:	They are about the same size, so it wasn't the size that made the difference.	They must weigh the same for each volume as water. (In response to, "Why do some things seem to hang in water?," after she had drawn diagrams to illustrate the three possibilities.)
Yvette:	When I wrapped the Lifebuoy loosely in foil, it floated, but when I wrapped it very tightly, it sank.	Stuff that is lighter for each volume than water will float. (Following her analogy of the unit baby's block of water and the four unit sponge.)

The first remarks are very similar to those made by the third graders who worked with sink and float materials. However, these older children quickly move from finding simple hidden likenesses ("Things float when they have air in them.") to constructing elegant models which approach adult concepts.

Since nothing except the colloquium occurred to bridge the gap between the concrete "here" and the more abstract "there," we must assume that the power of the colloquium propels investigators along the learning road.

Although, thus far, we have examined the development of individual children who spoke both at the beginning and at the end of the colloquium, we may also assume that such progress is characteristic for all children. If we compare the set of statements made at the beginning of any colloquium with the set of statements made at the end, the individual progress of every child is illustrated.

Initial discussion elicits an awareness fostered by experience with the materials: personal reactions ("Some noises were nice and some weren't.") or observations of external attributes ("There's a little dent on one end where the stalk is."). At the end of the colloquium, more abstract levels of thinking exist—hidden likenesses, analogies, models—and questions are raised for further study. Even children who do not speak at first show evidence of having engaged in inner speech when they finally verbalize their thoughts; their statements are more developed than the earlier remarks of other children. Of course, we have no reason to suppose that the quieter children would have offered more developed analyses than their peers had they, too, spoken earlier.

If the goal of the period of investigation with *materials* is the achievement of discovery—rich in *potential*, rich in sensory and psychomotor experience, the goal of the *colloquium* is *expressed thought* —thought analyzed and synthesized. The time devoted to a colloquium could well be the most precious in a school day, since it provides for the most concentrated development of the learning for which *human beings* are uniquely adapted.

The overall, or gross, result of the colloquium is

the summing up of several preconscious, subliminal, or casual activities. Whether perceived or unperceived by the teacher, all of these activities are actually experiences *in search of meaning*. These activities, probes, or searchings are essential steps along the road to concept building; they are stages along the conceptual arrow.

Perception is also sharpened during the colloquium. Without accurate perception, models would never survive further investigation; they could not lead the child to an understanding of his world. We have to encourage accurate perception related to the phenomena which are revealed to a child during his manipulation of materials. We are not speaking of primary perception here—the registering of figure and ground, seeing wholes instead of the mosaic of dots which our retinas register. The primary part of perception seems to be without thought; Kubie [18] calls it "preconscious," and the Gestalt psychologists tell us it is innate—an achievement of the visual cortex, whose physiology we are now beginning to understand. By perception, we mean a child's observance of the facts which he chooses to notice and which he will turn into language later during the colloquium—a *conscious* probing.

During Mrs. Eliot's lesson when alnico magnets were used to discover hidden likenesses (and hidden differences!) inside the plastic boxes, ten-year-old April observed:

April: We found that almost everything moved except the cork that wasn't wrapped in foil.

Mary, on the other hand, only saw:

Mary: . . . a plain cork, but nothing else happened.

Both of these observations are inaccurate as stated.

Everyone brings prior comprehension and expectancies to an experience. It is probable that the richer the expectancies, the greater the experience (and, in turn, the richer the previous experience, the greater the expectancies). A doctor looking at a patient perceives many slight cues, forms a quick interpretation of what the problem might be, and then asks a few particular questions to test his model.

An experienced teacher with excellent peripheral vision will note one child's clouded brow when, for example, a certain word is spoken. It may be a *key* word in the Ashton-Warner sense. [19] The perception is then considered and related to that particular child's behavior. (A beginning teacher might not even notice a clouded brow; other more central and immediate problems would probably demand her attention.)

As children gain practice in manipulating structured sets of objects, they bring more experience and greater expectancies to their science investigations; their perception is sharpened. The colloquium pinpoints the need for accuracy as it builds expectancies.

In the section *Can a Dolphin Think?* the ways in which language and thought coalesce during the colloquium were explored rather thoroughly. New thought is created from this coalescence. Perhaps we should give one more example. Thoughts about the two nickels were expressed by several children (page 133). First:

Lee: Out of the two nickels, *only* the Canadian nickel moved.

This is a discrepant event because the word *nickel* implies one object to the children. Everyone agrees. Mrs. Eliot asks the children why they think this is so. Their verbalized consensus creates new thought and Pamela comes out with a surprising model:

Pamela: Because the two nickels are made of two different materials, I think the Canadian nickel is made of metal and the magnet will pick it up. The American nickel is made of something not metal.

Pamela is thinking that there must be some difference in the composition of the two nickels although they both look alike; she is suggesting a metal-nonmetal dichotomy. From his stored information, Francis then recalls the proportions of nickel and copper in a United States nickel and Mrs. Eliot volunteers that

---

[18] Lawrence S. Kubie speaks of the Preconscious System in his book, *Neurotic Distortion of the Creative Process*, University of Kansas Press, Lawrence, Kansas, 1958.

[19] *Spinster*, the story of a teacher who ran an infant school in New Zealand and taught beginning reading to Maori children by writing meaningful and emotionally laden *key* words on cards. Sylvia Ashton-Warner, *Spinster* Bantam, New York, 1959.

nickel is a magnetic metal. Verbally expressed, these facts engender new thought:

Art: I think the Canadian coin is of pure nickel.
Denise: I think it must be made of more nickel than the American nickel.
Todd: If it's not nickel, then maybe it is a combination of nickel and another metal—but it has more nickel than the other metal.

These children have discovered the metallic composition of two nickels from (1) experience with the materials, (2) sharpened perception from observations shared in group interchange, (3) thinking together about the phenomena, and (4) the interjection of two necessary facts. They have used (1) tools (magnets) to extend their senses, (2) group interchange to extend their thinking, and (3) language to share their thoughts; they have formed a model of the unseen— *What's Inside?* the two amalgams—by employing procedures very similar to the ones scientists used to "find" what's inside the atom.

Another contribution of the colloquium is that it often exposes discrepant events. (Scientifically, discrepant events recur frequently during a series of experiments by one or a group of scientists and through comparisons of present results with published experiments in the same field.) A research scientist's new observation is therefore related to the works of many others in the field. Children's sciencing is temporally and spatially telescoped; the colloquium concentrates prior observations revealing discrepant events through the social nature of speaking together.

Just as structured materials presented to a child telescope scientific discoveries made over decades or even centuries, so discrepant events—revealed through the pooling of many observations—telescope the history of concept building or model making. Similar phenomena perceived from a variety of viewpoints and juxtaposed through the remarks of several young investigators are concentrated into data and explanations which mature scientists on their level would have to derive from scattered journals and conferences.

Thus, the social aspect of the colloquium also fosters the perception of hidden likenesses which although apparently a natural ability in children can be stimulated by verbal interchange as well. Once one child starts "It is like . . . ," several others will begin to draw on their past experiences, juxtaposing similarities from various fields of activity. During colloquia following manipulation of nickel and cork materials similar to those used by Mrs. Eliot's class, some children will say that something is hidden in both the aluminum-wrapped cork and the Canadian nickel which interacts with the magnet.

The colloquium also stimulates questions and suggests avenues for further investigation. At the end of Mr. McIver's sixth grade lesson on electricity, many children expressed unsolved problems they intended to pursue during the next lesson. Here, too, the social nature of the colloquium makes a contribution: a child is sometimes hesitant to investigate a problem he raised earlier but may show an interest in a pertinent question someone else offers during the discussion. For example, Albert became intrigued when one light shone as brightly as two in Carl and Monte's circuit.

To summarize, during a colloquium:

1. Perception is sharpened.
2. Discrepant events result from the children's collective observations, expressed in their own language.
3. Hidden likenesses are found and stated.
4. Models are constructed.
5. New questions are raised which stimulate further investigation.
6. Potential learning is actualized. Preverbal and preconscious experience are consciously probed into awareness.
7. Learning moves dynamically from the concrete toward the abstract.
8. Thinking and language coalesce to enrich thought.

The power of the colloquium resides in the interaction between language and thought. It moves children from the learning stage of "here" (after work with materials) to the "there" of their own verbal, orderly explanations of the phenomena. First, the colloquium probes into meaning from many directions. Then random probes are discarded and those rich in expectancy are retained and pursued. *At this point the colloquium becomes a probe into experience in search of meaning, in search of structure. It moves the learner along conceptual arrows.*

The teacher's role in relation to colloquia

During the total science experience which occurs in what we think of as a lesson, a preponderance of thought and action over speech can be expected. Much *thought* by many children on various levels—preverbal, "inner speech," interactive—and action with materials occur among members of a group. The *talk* eventually fostered by a colloquium is sparse but precious; it is the essence of the thinking. In the end, very few statements compare with many unexpressed thoughts within each child.

For the teacher, too, there must be a preponderance of thought over talk, even during the colloquium. His actions are many: looking, listening, and perceiving. His *talk*, too, represents an essence: his analysis of what is taking place within each child—of the relationship of the children's thinking to the conceptual scheme by which the lesson is bound.

Not only during colloquia, but during every lesson, the basic role of the teacher is to create a situation where learning can take place. A warm accepting atmosphere where the act of learning is the major freedom is partly a result of the art of teaching and partly a result of the personality of the teacher. Classroom atmosphere emanates from the way a teacher feels about children and the way he feels about the process of learning. When a creative atmosphere exists, many manifestations on the children's part will indicate that they recognize and are responding to its presence. In such a climate, children can make "errors" without shame or blame. They can voice seeming irrelevancies, feeling rather than knowing that the teacher's role is to decipher their meanings. If a child is ridiculed, the teacher supplies a frame of reference to take away the sting. Indeed, "freedom to fail" is an important aspect of a creative learning atmosphere. Psychological safety—the freedom to form hypotheses and models, and to err—in doing so—is, in Maslow's sense, an essence of teaching. [20]

In the circuit lesson, Carl reacted with a "who-didn't-know-that" shrug when Chuck remarked that wires got hot enough to burn.

Mr. McIver responded with "It's interesting, isn't it, that several of you can make the same discoveries at the same time? I noticed many independent discoveries of the same thing. Scientists have this experience, too."

Marie Stevens protected the feelings of eight-year-old Ruthanne when another child said she was "stoopid" for calling brains one of the senses they had just used.

Miss Stevens turned a *bon mot* by saying "Maybe Ruthanne meant you were using *good sense!*"

Whether or not the children understood her double meaning is inconsequential; they certainly perceived the implication in their teacher's tone.

When there is a feeling of psychological safety, thinking is likely to soar. Evidence of a safe creative atmosphere can be seen on the faces of the children, in expressions of relaxed contemplation, more smiles than frowns, intent concentration on a speaker even when he is slow or hesitant, and the gradual dawn of understanding during a pregnant silence.

Apart from creating an atmosphere of psychological safety, a teacher can overtly contribute to the success of the colloquium as well. For example, the teacher decides when to call for the colloquium. He must choose the precise moment before interest in the materials has abated, but after a certain satisfaction of discovery is evident. If the colloquium is called before the children are ready, the children will probably not "hear" the teacher and he will know that the appropriate moment has not arrived.

In a colloquium, the seats are arranged so that the speakers can see each other's faces (a circle is preferable). The seats are removed from the materials which might still fascinate the children and detract from the thought-into-language process which requires considerable effort. (Although, at times, we have seen that individual children need to go back to the materials to demonstrate or even to test a statement.) The teacher chooses the first speaker, either by asking who will "tell us" of his discoveries or by naming a certain child. The practice is to continue around the circle in order after the first speaker. Hence the teacher's initial choice requires a certain wisdom. He may be a child who has not yet

[20] A theme that runs through the writings of Abraham H. Maslow is that an atmosphere of psychological safety (where a child feels safe enough to dare) provides an environment for self-actualization. Advocates of the new science of bio-cybernetics claim that they are able to measure nonverbal communication.

contributed to a colloquium, but whose discovery that day evoked bubbling enthusiasm. Or the first speaker may be chosen so that the most verbal children, who can be relied upon to jump into the fray anyway, will not be reached for a while. Children who worked as a group and are now sitting together may be called upon for a joint report. The teacher makes the choice. The teacher tries to see each remark through the particular child's eyes. If the remark does not seem to be clear to anyone, the teacher may ask the child to clarify it. Frequently, though, the children will understand each other better than the teacher. (We saw this in the various uses of the word "heavy " See pp. 22-24, 55, and 74). This phenomenon often occurs when children use a low socioeconomic dialect that the teacher's thinking has not yet encoded. Asking for clarification in this type of situation only stems the tide of interest.

The teacher, on the contrary, may feel that the remark is not clear to the child who made it, that he has not fully put into words the thoughts he is generating. When Pat and Elma developed their ideas about the role of salt water in flotation, Mrs. Childs asked them to elaborate (page 125).

Pat: Salt water makes you float.
Elma: It makes you stay on top of the water.
Mrs. C.: How?
Pat: Salt water is stronger than plain water.

Or the teacher may feel the whole class would benefit from clarification if a word used by the speaker could engender inappropriate thought. When Albert used the expression "round circuit," Mr. McIver needed to know whether he was thinking of its shape or a continuous electrical path. If the other children thought that Albert meant the shape, then they would build mental images around this word. The verbal interchange (page 54) went like this:

Albert: You've got to have a round circuit to make the juice flow.
Mr. McI.: Tell us what you mean. . . .

Albert gave a lengthy explanation which indicated that he had the continuous path or complete circuit idea in mind. But Mr. McIver recalled the potential danger of the word "round" and helped Albert use a more adequate phrase in a later lesson (not recorded in this book). He asked Albert if the circuit could be square as well as round; Albert smiled and replied that round was just a manner of speaking. At that point Mr. McIver introduced the alternative phrase "complete circuit," which the class then adopted.

The right word at the right time! But when is the right time? How does one know?

One doesn't always! Mrs. Schur introduced the word "vibration" at the wrong time (page 115). None of the children picked it up, so it could not have had any meaning for them at that particular moment. But when Mr. Rodin and Mrs. Weiss offered the word "bran" (page 41) for the "brown stuff" with which the mealworms were interacting, one child made the word meaningful by asking "Like bran flakes?"

The right word at the right time can not only facilitate reference to an object, but also correct a misconception. In one of the later electricity lessons conducted by Mr. McIver, the children were still using the word "juice" for the flow of electricity. The word conjured up the image of a liquid. The inappropriate language produced inappropriate thought (page 115). Albert had used the word "juice" in the first lesson. ("You've got to have a round circuit to make the juice flow.") Nancy, (who couldn't make her light light during the first lesson) was trying to explain the functioning of a circuit in a later lesson. When a circuit was suspended on the bulletin board, she said that the juice flowed down more easily than it flowed up. Mr. McIver suggested that she use the words "electrical energy" instead of juice, saying that that was a way scientists might say it, and he turned the circuit upside down. The new words were not completely meaningful to Nancy at the time, but their use, coupled with the reorientation of the circuit, shifted her thinking to seek an explanation not connected with gravity. Later on, when all the children were using the words "electrical energy," it was easy to help the class think of the conversion of electrical energy into heat energy in order to explain the hot wires in a short circuit and the glowing wires in electric bulbs and heaters. The right word at the right time facilitates thinking; it can even give wings to thought.

There have been many examples of the teacher juxtaposing statements to point out discrepant events

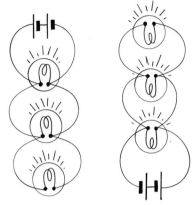

and then throwing the responsibility for the solution back to the colloquium: "What do *you* think about this?" On the one hand, we have seen that children can be helped to check facts: "Did everyone notice this?" (or "get this result?"). (We suggest that the teacher ask this whether the observations are accurate or not; otherwise the children will depend on authority to supply cues to the error instead of making the judgment by themselves.) On the other hand, the children may find hidden likenesses to encompass the discrepancies.

Sometimes a statement of hidden likenesses spells danger to the teacher. How does one tell an outrageous comparison from a genuinely creative one? Maybe it is not important to make this nice distinction. If a child finds a hidden likeness, it is probably relevant to him in some important way. Who, at first blush, would think that a row of flowerpots suspended on ropes resembles adults and children? But remember Matthew (page 111).

Matthew: These things [bells, bottles, pots, xylophone] are like people. *(Fortunately he could explain.)* Big people voices sound lower than little children voices.

Bartlett calls comparisons of this kind—hidden likenesses drawn from a field of experience totally different from the one under consideration—"adventurous thinking." [21] Hobbes called it "train of thoughts unguided" and "wild ranging of the mind" [22] compared with regulated thought. Graham

Wallas refers to it under "illumination," [23] and Bruner calls it a "creative analogical leap." [24]

Adventurous thinking involves the willingness to take a risk, to move beyond the evidence, to choose one path among many possible paths. A funnel to little Betty (page 71) "is the thing that look like a hat upside down that you put water in and it come out the bottom." Of all the possible hidden likenesses, she chose a much modified hat!

As adventurous thinking goes beyond the evidence, it may suggest models. Sometimes these models ignore the known facts and have to be superseded; the metal–nonmetal dichotomy Pamela set up to explain the difference between the Canadian and United States nickels is an example (page 133). Sometimes the basis for adventurous thinking is not clear to anyone, just as hidden likenesses may seem irrelevant at first. In the sixth-grade girls' sink and float investigation, Belle suggested that boiled water would make an egg sink (page 127). (Hadn't she ever boiled eggs from cold water?) However, Belle's reasoning was even obscure to herself and to her partner, Yvette. Some reflection was necessary before Mrs. Adler realized that the role of air was the hidden likeness from which Belle had constructed her model. She had probably observed air bubbles coming out of water that is beginning to heat. The role of air in flotation had been under consideration; removal of air *had* produced sinking in *other* circumstances!) Even though adventurous thinking may not seem to make sense at the time, respect for the thinker demands that we consider it. In some cases, the children themselves will gasp at a colleague's remark as though *they* think it is out of context. Further thought may reveal its significance. Thinkers need this psychological safety as they speak together.

Children may also ignore a quiet, tentative statement by a child whose status in the group is relatively inferior. Here the teacher needs to verbalize the standards which provide psychological safety. When a teacher remarks, "Would you, Charles, make your statement again? I think everyone would like to hear

[21] Sir Frederic Bartlett, *Thinking: An Experimental and Social Study*, George, Allen and Unwin, London, 1958, Chs. 6–8.
[22] Thomas Hobbes, *Leviathan*, London, printed for Andrew Crooke, 1651, Ch.3.

[23] Graham Wallas (sic), *The Art of Thought*, Harcourt Brace Jovanovich, New York, 1929, pp. 79–107.
[24] Jerome S. Bruner, "Going Beyond the Information," *Cognition: The Colorado Symposium*, Harvard University Press, Cambridge, Mass., 1950, pp. 41–69.

your splendid idea," many good things happen! Perhaps this is the moment to point out that since the burden of thinking lies with the group, so does the burden of communication. During a colloquium, just as in any other classroom event, a teacher refrains (if possible!) from repeating or rephrasing a child's remark. If encouraged to do so, the *child* can make himself heard in the colloquium. If necessary, *he* will then be able to rephrase or elaborate his idea to an eager and attentive audience.

Probably the most difficult part of the teacher's role in a colloquium is to redirect the thinking at points of *impasse* or when the children run off the track—the track being some relationship to the cluster of concepts under consideration. When Mrs. Eliot's children started offering reasons for the teacher's choice of materials (page 132):

Lynn: [the box is taped] So we couldn't open it.
Rick: So the objects couldn't get out, but the magnet could get through.

etc.

Rosa Eliot allowed the children to liquidate their interest in her choice, and then said to April, who had just made a remark (her first during the colloquium):

Mrs. E.: Well, what did your group discover?

After the sixth-grade girls became interested in the low value of air-filled soap to the customer, Mrs. Adler asked a new question that, however, was still related to the role of air—the topic which had set the girls off on the wrong track:

Mrs. A.: Why did the loose foil float and the tightly pressed ball of foil sink?

Children may lose interest in one aspect of the materials after they have considered it for a while. The teacher then redirects the attention of the colloquium to another subset of the materials: "Nobody mentioned the sponge" or "What did you find out about those corks?" or "What were your mealworms *doing*?" after the children have been concentrating on description and number of parts.

A colloquium rarely needs redirecting; it usually generates its own dynamics, following the interest and thinking of the children. If it *seems* to be going nowhere, but the children are still eagerly presenting their observations and thoughts, the thinking is probably engaging in what Bartlett calls the "wandering search." Scientists know this phenomenon only too well. How else can they make order out of chaos? When the journey's end is not known, how can the path be straight? While the teacher is aware of the possible concepts to be approached, the situation is completely open ended for the children. They must never feel that there is *one* right way or *one* right answer. The teacher's structuring of the materials and of the colloquium is designed only to reduce frustration to the tolerance level of the children, to provide a balance between success and challenge. The *children* can then feel success, experience a sense of competence, enter the network of interlacing paths, and construct an orderly map from them.

Does the teacher's role in the colloquium include giving facts or offering "correct" explanations? We asserted earlier that suggestions should never be offered or information be given during the periods of free discovery with materials. As a general principle, we also embargo giving information and offering explanations during the colloquium.

Is this shocking? Or a relief? Shouldn't the wisdom already formulated in the world be made available to the children? Recall that this entire section is under the overall title *Starting Tomorrow*. At the start—*tomorrow*—you withhold facts and information. We are discussing the first steps to introduce what may be a new way to teach and a new way for children to learn. Later we will discuss the role of books and references; they come *after* the kind of experiences we are now presenting. We might even say that the teacher who feels it necessary to give explanations does not belong with the discovery-colloquium type of lesson—the offering of facts being such a rare phenomenon in this experience. Children find more pertinent facts in books if they are used at a later stage when readers can bring their own experiences and thoughts to the printed word. (This aspect will be explored in Chapters 5 and 7.)

On one or two occasions thus far, the teachers in our illustrations have given facts—the right word at the right time can be valuable. We have also seen that the right word at the wrong time is not absorbed by the children and, therefore, is not harmful. *Names* of objects and phenomena are arbitrary; since they cannot be discovered they must be supplied by some authority. *Facts* which can be readily discovered by the children need not and should not be told. Discovery is the main motivation for learning. The confidence this process builds is one of the attitudes we wish to engender in children; it is a part of their experience of sciencing.

But occasionally a fact, an essential cog in the group's wheels of thought, is needed. In the full flush of converting thought into speech, searching in an encyclopedia may only serve as a millstone! Mrs. Eliot supplied the fact about what percentage of nickel is required in an amalgam for nickel to exert its magnetic properties (page 133). With this in mind, the children were able to construct a model (several models in fact) to explain the discrepant events posed by the two nickels. Mr. Peatman, the Principal, thought that the magnetic properties could have been discovered by the children at an earlier stage, when they first investigated magnets, and made a note to himself to ask the school's science specialist if pieces of nickel could be made available. This is one way of letting children have information at their disposal when they need it. Planning for discovery is a part of curriculum building.

Since we advise teachers to allow children to discover most facts for themselves, we reduce the chances of giving incorrect information—something many elementary school teachers fear. In fact, one reason science has been a stepchild of the elementary school curriculum is the teachers often feel insecure in the face of the rapidly expanding field and its many branches. Elementary school teachers, on whom so many varied demands are made, have traditionally been afraid of not being able to explain scientific phenomena adequately. Fortunately the discovery-colloquium way of organizing science learning almost always avoids this pitfall.

There *are* moments when a teacher may recall what seems to be an appropriate parallel to a topic under consideration. At such times, the choice of a really similar concept is dependent upon the teacher's understanding of the subject in question. Mrs. Schur

had this problem with her second graders when she recalled their previous experiences with a candle burning in a pumpkin and related them to the removal of some air from the closed space around the bell after paper and been burned in the bottle (page 114). There was a confusion in her thinking between the candle consuming oxygen and producing heat. It was not the consumption of oxygen which produced the reduction of gas, but it *was* the consumption of oxygen which made the candle go out. [25]

When a candle burns, its carbon joins with the oxygen in the air to form carbon dioxide. Actually as many carbon dioxide molecules are formed as oxygen molecules are consumed. And, molecule for molecule, every gas occupies the same space. There is one proviso, however: *the temperature (and pressure) must remain constant.* The heat of the burning paper in the bottle with the bell, *not* the consumption of oxygen as the paper oxidized, reduces the gas in the space. The heated air expands and some of it pushes out of the bottle; pushing the cork into the neck of the bottle, traps the hot expanded air in the same space which the cool air had filled. The partial vacuum reduces the sound of the bell.

Interestingly, this error ("The burning stuff [candle] used up the air. There's no air in the bottle.") did not sidetrack Mrs. Schur's children. They repeated the erroneous phrase, but continued to relate their thinking to real observations (page 114).

Chris: Yes, [the candle went out] because there was no air left to let it burn.

Matthew: The burning stuff used up the air. There's no air in the bottle. That's why the cork's on so tight—to keep the air out.

Daisy: The bell won't ring 'cause there's no air. The fire used up the air and now you can't hear the bell.

The children have a way of substantiating their statements. They predicted that if the cork were pulled out the air would come in and the bell would

[25] Interestingly enough, not all the oxygen is consumed when the candle goes out! There is a delightful filmloop showing this: *The Mouse and the Candle,* Ealing 80-83 (produced by Educational Services Inc.), available from the Ealing Corp., 2225 Massachusetts Avenue, Cambridge, Mass. 02140. (A mouse still breathes after the candle is extinguished.)

ring. That is just what happened! Reverse the process—burn the paper, snap on the cork, keeping the air out, and:

Sarah: I hear the bell just a little now.

Gray: Yeah, you need air to hear the bell good. If there's no air, you can't hear. Right?

It seems that when children are deeply engaged in their own thinking, deeply motivated by group interchange about *their* experiences with material, they remain very slightly authority-oriented. It seems less harmful for an adult to make an error under these circumstances than when adults attempt to dictate all that has to be said or "thought." How fortunate! We do not condone errors on the part of the teacher, but we do not lay heavy blame on a slight lapse from perfection either. We are all human. Not all of us are science virtuosos! In this incident, Mrs. Schur was drawing from a teacher demonstration she had used before she was introduced to the discovery-colloquium way of educing scientific learnings from children. And look what she did contribute! She created an atmosphere in her class where learning was an adventure. She conducted a colloquium during which exciting thinking took place. And, through her own research, she incidentally devised the choice of materials which were so significantly structured. She created a situation in which the children could uncover structure, through which they could grow.

The teacher has one final responsibility in relation to the colloquium: the Investigators' Log. The Log represents a summary in the children's own words, a consensus of the main features of their day's learning. With younger children, the teacher introduces the advent of the Log in a manner such as this:

"When scientists have made discoveries and talked them over with other scientists, they record them in print. Now I would like to be your secretary (this removes the pen-pushing threat!) and I will record the statements you make and agree upon. Then your Log will be duplicated and you each will have a copy. All your Logs together will form a book—a record of your discoveries." Then the teacher asks for an initial statement. Whatever the first child says, the teacher asks, "Do you all agree with the statement?" Then, if they do: "Do you all agree with the way it is said?" And the matter rests there, even if the teacher thinks

the statement agreed upon is incorrect. Could *you* bear this? Isn't this real sciencing? Don't scientists continuously revise their statements with time and further experimentation? If all the children agree on a "false" statement, that is what they have learned! Should we let it rest? For that Log, yes. But it does give us the cue for the next lesson: to bring in *materials* which challenge the incorrect statement.

After one "sink and float" experience, some third graders wanted the following statement in their log: "Things float because they are heavy and sink because they are light." They were all sure of it: a very heavy ocean liner floats, but the ping-pong ball with the hole in it was light and sank. So the statement went into the Log, but the next lesson included objects of the same size and different densities, introducing another dimension to the group's thinking. "Light for their size" became a statement in the Log. What do you think happens when children read over their Logs for a whole unit? Right! They are surprised at their own sophisticated growth.

As we mentioned before, the Log contains only a few of the facts and simple models which have been stated or thought. It represents a kind of essence of the whole group's experiences.

With older children, or those able to write without undue labor, the secretary of the class might record the Log on the board for each child to copy. Or, with really competent writers, each child could record his own summary and perhaps a science lesson could be devoted to reading and discussing those individual Logs which the teacher feels will challenge the group. After all, discussing the meaning and effect of one's written communications is not only a first-rate sciencing experience; it is first-rate education in any area!

A teacher may evaluate some features of the colloquium he is conducting in a simple and interesting manner. This requires an observer—excellent practice for a student teacher!

The observer is given a seating plan. (In the illustration here,[26] we have made a compromise between a circle and rows of desks.) The observer

[26] Adapted from Brenda Lansdown, "Do You Grow Chrysanthemums?" *Nature and Science*, Vol. 4, No. 2 (October 3, 1966), Sec. I.

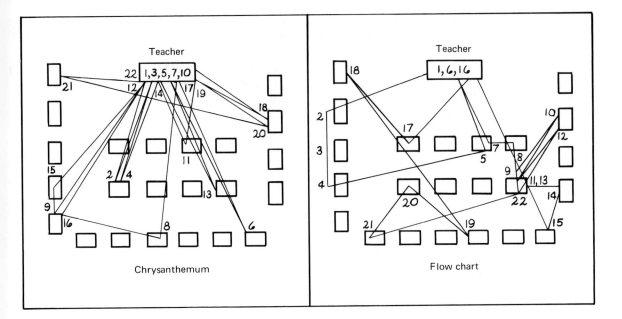

Teacher

22 | 1,3,5,7,10

Chrysanthemum

Teacher

1,6,16

Flow chart

writes numerals in sequence beside the position of each speaker. Usually the teacher speaks first; if so, a (1) is written beside the teacher's place. A (2) is written next to the seat of the child who answers, a (3) next to the third speaker, and so on. After about fifteen minutes of colloquium, lines are drawn to connect the numerals sequentially.

From an inspection of the pattern this diagram produces, the teacher can learn quite a lot: Who never spoke at all? Which children tend to argue back and forth? Which children jump right in and which hold back? Which children respond most readily to the teacher's remarks? We have named the two example patterns in this figure, the *chrysanthemum* and the *flow chart*. Which one represents the colloquium we have outlined? And what is the ratio of the number of times a teacher spoke to the number of times all the children made remarks? Is it a better colloquium when this speaking ratio of teacher to children is 1:1 or 1:7?

To summarize, the role of a teacher in a colloquium is to:

1. Select the proper moment to launch the colloquium.
2. Select the first speaker.
3. Provide psychological safety so the efforts of each child will be protected.

4. Help children perceive accurately.
5. Encourage clarity of expression.
6. Juxtapose discrepant events.
7. Supply the right word at the right time.
8. Redirect thoughts at moments of impasse.
9. Arrange for the recording of an Investigators' Log which represents the children's consensus in their own language.
10. Note features which can be incorporated to motivate the follow-up session.

By reading some colloquia records, you can decide what type of speech the teacher uses to assume each of these roles.

A note to the reader

Shouldn't we pause now to take stock?

We have reached the end of our suggestions for *Starting Tomorrow.* Our intent was to help those of you who have never tried the discovery–colloquium type of science lesson before and, indeed, to introduce it to teachers who have never taught science at all. To do this, we selected materials which have had wide success with children and teachers of many types; we gave illustrations which we hope will forecast the successes and difficulties you may encounter; and we analyzed the activities of both children and teachers to provide a guide for thinking about the lessons you will give during your initial teaching experiences.

We hope that you will feel the same way that hundreds of teachers have felt who first tried to teach science the way we suggest: amazement at the virtuosity of children. We hope that your first attempts will generate the enthusiasm necessary to join us as we consider how to continue to foster this process of learning we have named *sciencing*.

We turn now to an analysis of the deeper meaning of concepts and the way in which they develop in people, and to the development of conceptual schemes as a basis for our choice of materials and lessons in science.

2

The
Architectonics
of
Meaning

3

Steps in concept building

Concept is a word found very frequently in all forms of educational literature; the prestigious mental image it conjures up suggests a high level of thinking. It can easily be differentiated from rote memory or from recall or from recognition of the right answer. The word itself implies a type of conceiving, a creative effort which categorizes abstractions. However, we also find the word used in more humble situations. It may be the aim of a kindergarten lesson; "the children develop a concept of triangle" is, indeed, a simple level of abstraction, the recognition of an attribute. However, a first-grade program which wants children to develop the "concept" that the sun warms the earth cannot be deemed an abstraction,

not even a generalization. It is a *fact* that the sun warms the earth.

In our view, *children are not able to experience full conceptual thinking or to have real concepts until they reach adolescence*, and we impute a comparable meaning to the word.

Developmental psychologists such as Vygotsky and Piaget also take the view that preschool and elementary schoolwork must all be on a preconceptual level and that only as adolescence approaches (perhaps beginning with mature sixth graders) can abstract conceptual thinking even begin.

Many writers do use the word "concept" in describing the thinking of very young children, and they have every right to do so. After all, the word is in the public domain and, because of such long and wide usage, *concept* now signifies a wide range of thoughts. So that we may agree on one meaning, we ask your indulgence in following us in both theory and illustration as we describe our way of looking at the development of conceptual thinking in children, and as we choose words to name the various stages involved.

The Vygotsky schema
of conceptual development

The path toward a concept—what we call the conceptual arrow—has its source in the need to make some order out of the chaos of data which assail us. Concepts embrace the more elegant, the more abstract, and the more comprehensive schemas. But where does it all begin? It begins with perception.

Syncretic thinking

We *perceive* two or more objects together and we link them in our thinking. There may be neither a logical nor a functional relationship between them, but there is a perceptual relationship.

From the back seat, a child sees the car windshield wiper moving. His father is holding the steering wheel. Steering wheel—windshield wiper. What makes the wiper move?—father holding the steering wheel. Then the wiper stops moving, and father still has his hands on the wheel. He must not be holding the wheel right, so the wiper is moving.

A child is looking at a certain picture book when a clap of thunder shakes the room. So he won't look at the book again—it makes the thunder come.

Linking random events through a common perception is called *syncretic thinking*. It is the first level of thinking, found very frequently in nursery-school-aged children. It is their chief mode of the kind of reflective thought that attempts to explain the world around them.

A four year old was gazing at a gray rabbit in a cage in a children's museum. "Where do rabbits come from?" he asked. "Where do you think they come from?" replied the adult with the child. The boy gazed around the room. It held several cages with assorted animals. His eye rested for a while on a furry skunk, then roamed around until he saw a pigeon,—a gray pigeon. "You know what?" he said quietly, as if to himself, "The skunk eats a pigeon and there's the rabbit."

Even during the nursery-school years, a higher level of thinking is beginning. This little boy's probable recognition of the common attributes of gray and furriness cannot be considered syncretic, but the process by which the rabbit came into being is purely syncretic. Older children, even adults, may exhibit syncretic thinking at times. If they are approaching an area or concept quite new to them, they sometimes begin at the syncretic level:

A fourth-grade class, new to the discovery-colloquium type of science lesson, had been exploring with these materials: soda bottles with balloons secured over the necks by rubber bands, basins of very hot water, and basins filled with ice. (Can *you* anticipate what would happen with these materials?) The nature of air came up during the colloquium and the children said it contained oxygen and nitrogen. (Actually they said "hydrogen," but the teacher substituted the word *nitrogen* without explanation, since the nature of either gas seemed unknown to the children.)

The teacher then asked, "Any other gases in the air?"

"Charcoal," said Raoul firmly.

"How do you know?"

"I saw it on TV." [The glories of the lecture approach!]

"What did you see on TV?"

"When men go into space there is no air, so they take charcoal granules in the capsule with them."

Charcoal, space, and air appeared together on TV. Raoul formed a syncretic heap with them; they belonged together—they were linked.

Graduate students in a science workshop sometimes struggle to build concepts which have somehow escaped them during their college training. The students' colloquium after a period of discovery with materials can reveal syncretic thinking:

During a first period, some students worked with the materials just described above. In the colloquium, the idea of molecules increasing in energy (they said *"moving faster"*) due to heat was introduced. So the *molecules were pushed* into the balloon.

When the same group studied airplane lift in another period, the students established that air *molecules were crowded* under the wings ("pushed tightly together") and that this produced a greater pressure under the wings than on top of them, lifting the plane.

Then, in a third period, the students were asked to decide what would happen if a lighted electric bulb were placed under one of two milk cartons, both open at the bottom and balanced from the two ends of a beam. One student wrote: "The heat directly under the carton might push the air molecules more tightly together and make them go faster."

Here the perception of crowded molecules is associated with the image of pushing and this, in turn, merges with the image of heat making molecules move faster! Rather than consider this utter confusion, it can be regarded as syncretic thinking in which the perceptions appeared over a span of time instead of synchronously. Previously, the images—not the meaning of the phenomena—were symbolized in words which linked the images together. (There are several examples of syncretic thinking during the colloquium with Mr. McIver's sixth graders. Maybe you would like to try to locate them!)

Complex thinking

After the happenstance of syncretic thinking, *complex thinking*[1] occurs. Complex thinking also is based on perception, but perception of *external*

[1] Syncretic and complex thinking are described in L. S. Vygotsky, *Thought and Language*, M.I.T. Press, Cambridge, Mass., 1962.

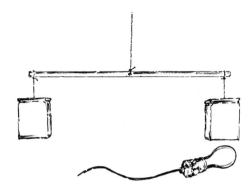

likenesses. Things are linked together because they are the same size, color, or shape. They may be grouped by one or several of their common attributes. In another form of complex thinking, objects are grouped together because they have a similar function: a knife, a fork, and a spoon; a bike, a car, a bus, and a train.

Complex thinking is *fluid thinking*. Sometimes the linking attribute changes with each object that is added to the collection: a shirt and a sock are grouped together because they are blue; then a shoe is added because it goes on the foot as a sock does; then a purse is added because, like the shoe, it is made of leather; and so on. This is called *chain complex thinking*.

Complex thinking frequently occurs when elementary school children make their first stab at explaining a new phenomenon.

A group of fourth graders from a low socio-economic district was watching a desert terrarium in which an iguana (a kind of lizard) buried itself under the sand.

"How does it breathe under there?" asked Dorothea.

"I know!" said Edward, and he leaned heavily on his elbows placing his cheeks between his hands. His words came slowly, with many hesitations. "You need oxygen to breathe ... water is H-two-Oh, so it has oxygen. ... Fish have gills to breathe oxygen in water. Rocks must have oxygen. ... so lizards must have sort of gills to breathe oxygen from rocks."

This is seemingly a strange kind of reasoning, and we might tend to dismiss it as something a normal adult couldn't cope with until we realize the meaning behind this kind of thoughtful explanation. . . . Edward was putting things together through common attributes or likenesses, but he did this in sequence, changing the attribute with each addition.

Breathing is linked to oxygen, oxygen to water. Water and its oxygen (no separation of the ideas that oxygen is part of the molecule of water and can also be dissolved in the liquid) are linked to breathing by gills. Gills are used for breathing oxygen from strange places, so rocks must have oxygen and lizards must have gills to breathe it.[2]

Here it is easy to note the relationship between thought and word—the way words engendered new thoughts as Edward heard his own speech.

There have been many forms of complex thinking in the colloquia quoted this far. We naturally expect a rich explosion of complex thinking in the early elementary grades. For example, let us review some of the statements by Miss Bradford's second graders after they poured water through funnels and strainers (page 71):

Denise: I put the paper towel over this thing and the water go through.
Ellen: It go through the strainer, too.
Kirk: It go through anything that got holes in it.
Bob: Yeah, you gotta have something with no hole if you wanna put water in it, 'cos water stay like in the bottle but it don't stay in the funnel 'cos it got a hole.
Miss B.: What about the paper towel? Why does water go through that?
Bob: I dunno. Can I see one?
Miss B.: Yes, you may. (*He holds it up to the window and looks through it*).
Bob: It got holes, too. See, you can see the holes when you look like this.

Here the first link in the children's thinking is functional: "water go through." Then water going

[2] Brenda Lansdown, "They Mean What They Say—But Don't Say What They Mean," *Nature and Science*, Vol. 4, No. 4 (October 31, 1966), sec. 1, copyright © 1966 by The American Museum of Natural History, Doubleday & Company, Inc.

through is associated with having "holes in it." Bob's negative addition—"the bottle"—is another form of complex thinking. Adding the opposite or negative of an attribute, a *not-likeness*. (A bottle has *no* hole in the bottom is a complex thought.) Miss Bradford redirects thinking to the first problem: why the water went through the apparently solid towel. Bob evidently thinks "it gotta have a hole" and tests his idea by holding the towel against the light. It has holes and, therefore, fits in the category of what water will "go through."

Grouping things by common attribute is reflected in our language. The *legs* of a table are perceived as attaching the table to the ground just as human legs form similar underpinnings. A *head waiter* suggests the top of something. Even opposites can be named by a common word occasionally. Think of the verb *to cleave*. A child cleaves to its mother. An ax cleaves a log in two. Two opposites joined together by complex thinking and, therefore, designated by a single word! You may be able to find other words which stem from complex thinking. They exist in many languages—maybe all—but, of course, more richly in those of historic vintage.

Just as older children, even adults, still employ earlier or more primitive types of thinking on the road to concept attainment, we find that younger children can also experience more advanced thinking. Oscillation back and forth from one type of thinking to another usually occurs:

A four-year-old boy was on a trip with a Head Start Program, when the group encountered an elderly man with a very long beard.

"That's God!" said the little boy, delightedly.

"No," explained his teacher, "that's not God. That's a man."

"It *is* God," the child insisted. He was not to be convinced by his teacher's words. The principal attribute of God to this very young lad, for whom the world was just expanding, was evidently long beardedness.[3]

Thus, the first two stages along a conceptual arrow are based on the perception of *externals*.

In *syncretic thinking*, objects which have no

[3] We are grateful to Aileen Grubin for this anecdote.

intrinsic relationship are lumped together because they are perceived together.

In *complex thinking*, an external or real concrete likeness is perceived. The objects can be linked or related through one or more attributes, through a common function, through opposites, through a shifting chain of associations where the linking attribute may change with the addition of each new object, and even through a diffuse association (grouping triangles with trapezoids because the corners remind the child of the same thing, for example).

Preconceptual and conceptual thinking

The following two stages of thought complete the road to concept building. Both are based on finding *hidden* likenesses.

It might be easier to describe the third stage if the fourth, or most generalized, level of *conceptual thought* (found with the maturity of adolescence) is discussed first. Since you, the reader, have reached the level of conceptual thought, you can delve into your own thinking to establish its nature.

In what kind of mental operations do you engage when you think about:

The conversion of electromagnetic
    waves into particles?
Democracy?
Operators in mathematics?
Beauty?

Obviously, your thoughts on any of the above topics are not concrete. The words or phrases do not conjure up concrete images; you do not dwell on common attributes, such as red or edible. You must think of these concepts as abstractions related to abstractions. As you think about them, you do several things, probably simultaneously. There is a *fluid shifting* from one aspect to another of a concept.

For example, you may relate democracy to people in general, to special groups of people, to the power of ruling, to the right to voice opposition and freedom of choice, to restraints, or to a thousand other abstract parts of subconcepts. Then, for a moment or two, there may be an image: people casting ballots, a town meeting, a picket line, or you may put some fleeting thoughts into word symbols:

Demos is a Greek word meaning *people*. Who are the people? In Greece, the *demos* meant the free men, not the slaves. There are people in the United States, the *demos*, who are deprived of votes at times. If democracy means rule by the people, the people are very different in different periods of history and in different countries. The *demos* must therefore represent some sort of abstraction; it cannot be concrete. Words do not suffice in conveying the full meaning. The remainder of the word *democracy* refers to *rule*. This, too, is an abstraction. When we can put together these two abstractions, *rule* and the *demos*, the relation is a concept—an abstraction related to an abstraction without reference to the concrete.

If we let our thinking roam to the most general meanings possible, each of the other items on the list can also be analyzed in these terms of abstraction related to abstraction without reference to the concrete.

Now we are ready to consider the third stage of mental development, of progress along conceptual arrows—the bridge joining complex thought to real concept. Vygotsky's *preconcept* is characterized by growth into abstract thought, but always retains some nexus with the concrete. When a child begins to use abstract instead of purely concrete, sense-perceived terms, he has entered this preconceptual phase.

Children pick up abstract terms in the same way that they first learn a language, by interaction with people in their environment who use such words. Children hear the abstract terms in context, then gradually abstract the principles and begin to use the words as language universals.[4] Feedback from the environment dynamic interaction with people and situations necessitate continued refinement and new applications. We can see how important it is for the school to supply opportunities where concrete experience requires the use of abstract terms and where adults supply the words in correct context.

Of course, as the *child* begins to use the abstract words, new thoughts come to him, enriching his language. In general, this is the conceptual arrow along which a child passes from complex to full

[4]"[Language] universal is the generality that words stand for relations instead of being unique names for one object." Eric H. Lenneberg, "On Explaining Language," *Science*, Vol. 164, No. 3880 (May 9, 1969), 640.

conceptual thought. Toward the end of the preconcept stage, the child is using appropriate words and phrases in an adult manner, but without an abstract understanding of the concept they convey. He will usually include some concrete reference in his statement. Then, gradually and without realizing the change, he completes the transition to full abstract thinking.[5]

We can recognize both the concrete and the abstract in the following preconcept statements:

In photosynthesis, green plants make sugar.

The water cycle is the same water going round and round between rain and rivers and plants and air.

It's the molecules moving very fast that create the pressure in the balloon.

Children sometimes learn to use conceptual language long before they have developed the designated concept. This is illustrated in the following exchange with one of the authors:

"How is it," asked Paul Brandwein of a six year old, "that a chicken and not a cat always hatches from a hen's egg?"

"Because the hen lays it," answered the child.

"But why doesn't a puppy or a kitten hatch from a hen's egg?"

The boy looked incredulous. "Surely," he offered patiently, "surely you know about DNA?"

Here is an example of children at the appropriate age and level of maturity vacillating between preconcept and concept thinking.[6]

Gifted sixth graders had been studying a unit on space. Their materials at this particular session were: deflated balloons, strips of paper (to be blown upon), two ping-pong balls hanging close together (to be blown apart). Below is a part of the colloquium which followed:

Nancy: When you let the balloon fly, air comes out and it flies. So maybe when a jet goes, something

is stored inside it and it comes out and makes it fly.

Pam: That's why a jet doesn't have propellers; the gas that is stored up inside pushes the jet forward.

Tom: Air rushes into the jet, goes to the generator, and comes out with such force it pushes the jet forward.

Ruth: But a rocket goes where there's no air. It goes in space.

Nancy took a concrete observation and invented a probable analogy—really a model—of what might happen in a jet to make it fly. Pam found a negative likeness (a not-likeness) between airplanes and jets (jets do not have propellers) and she amplified Nancy's "something" by saying that there was a gas inside the jet. Tom identified the gas as air and told how it gets in and out of the jet; he used adult language correctly, but did not show that he knew why the gas rushing out at the back pushed the jet forward. Ruth took his thinking—no longer in the realm of the tangible, but in the realm of abstract thought—and related one abstraction to another abstraction by posing a problem (a discrepant event): "A rocket goes where there's no air. It goes in space."

This is an example of Bartlett's "adventurous thinking."[7] The children are seeking a broader frame of reference that includes jets and rockets—a hidden likeness on this abstract level. In this particular case, the unit was being taught by a student teacher who did not have sufficient experience to offer the children the next step: to ask a question like "Where are the gases that are doing the pushing?" This might have made the children think of the unequal pressure (lack of equilibrium) between the gases inside a jet or rocket. One way to illustrate this is to think of where the air is pushing inside a sealed balloon and to compare this with a balloon "let fly." In the first, there is equilibrium; in the second, there is more molecular energy pushing toward the front of the balloon. This is the principle Tom missed. The transfer of this principle to rockets would then reveal that rockets carry their own fuel inside them and that the tremendous energy a rocket produces is due to

[5] This transition from the preconcept stage is described in L.S. Vygotsky, *Thought and Language*, M.I.T. Press, Cambridge, Mass., 1962, pb. Chapter 5, secs. XVI and XVII, pp. 77-81.

[6] Adapted from Brenda Lansdown, "How Good Was My Science Lesson," *The Packet*, Vol. 16, No. 1 (Spring 1961), 22, D.C. Heath and Company, copyright 1961.

[7] Sir Frederic Bartlett, *Thinking: An Experimental and Social Study*, George, Allen and Unwin, London, 1958, and Basic Books, Inc., Publishers, New York, 1958. pp. 138-63.

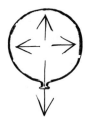

the sudden combustion (and, therefore, expansion) of fuel to hot gases—heat energy once again!

The role of language

We will now take one word—mother—and follow the development of its meaning from the concrete to a full abstraction. At first, the word is entirely concrete and ego-centered: *my* mother. Then the child realizes that other children have mothers—persons who are related to them in the way *my* mother is related to *me*. This relationship is a partial abstraction. However, the abstraction is still concretely based for the child; he does not view it as an adult does. Some psychologists have suggested that, at this stage, the word conjures up an image in which the faces of various mothers and the things mothers do are superimposed so that the common characteristics stand out and the differences recede. In actuality, the child probably finds common attributes among various human mothers. Then the surprising discovery may come that kittens have mothers called cats or that guppies have mothers who are fish like themselves. The blending picture no longer suffices; the link becomes: mothers have children who resemble themselves. Now there is an attribute of likeness, admittedly generalized. Thus far, movement along the conceptual arrow is still at the complex level of thinking. Once a child can verbalize that "plants and animals reproduce their own kind," he is beginning to voice abstractions—he has reached the preconcept stage. A further development within this stage would incorporate the motherhood of an ameba or a virus and other rather abstract generalities. Finally, when a child thinks of the molecule DNA reproducing itself, he has reached conceptual thought. But those tall spirals of colored plastic steps in museums which represent DNA molecules do not,

in themselves, produce a concept in the beholder, although they may help. What does build a concept?

One factor in concept building is the opportunity to broaden the referents which are brought together under one term, under a language universal.

A cross-cultural study by Jerome S. Bruner and some of his graduate students[8] points up the role of elementary schools in guiding children along the road toward conceptual thought. Children in Senegal, West Africa, in Mexico, and in Alaska were given tests which differentiated the early stages along the conceptual arrows. The children were presented with cards which had pictures of familiar objects (peach, banana, then potato, then meat, then milk, then water, air, germs, stones) that were adapted to represent known things in each country. The children were then asked to find a name which would include all the objects. The cards were presented in sequence so that each additional card required a more abstract or more generalized label for the group than the previous card.

In categorizing ability, Senegalese bush children were found to be much more similar to Mexican peasants and unschooled Eskimos than to their (Senegalese) blood cousins who attended school. Similarly, schooled children in all three countries resembled one another in their levels of abstract thought (defined by the task) much more than the schooled resembled the unschooled in the same country—even though some of the schools were authoritarian, emphasizing rote and memorization more than originality and independent thought.

The conclusion drawn was that simple peasant life provides a limited range of stimuli which can be accommodated with very little processing or encoding. When school is attended, however, a plethora of new data is presented which the stimulated person must relegate to categories. Peripherally, an interesting finding was that as the peasant, bush farmer, or natural Eskimo matured unschooled, he developed a much finer perception for detail than the adult who had attended school, as though the importance of small signs or cues for survival had become more meaningful.

Finding labels for categories is a very early stage

[8] Jerome S. Bruner, *et al. Studies in Cognitive Growth*, Wiley, New York, 1966.

along the conceptual arrows. Even so, within it, there is a rise in the level of abstraction; labeling a peach and a banana "fruit," for example, is much more specific than finding a description like "necessary for life" to encompass a larger grouping which includes air. Sometimes the children separated "stones" from the other objects, labeling them "nonliving" and the remainder of the group "living." (An abstract category including every item would be *matter*.)

As you can see, the categorizing is by external likenesses except for the final label. The test probed into substages of complex thought, emphasizing growth along the complex conceptual arrows. A major characteristic of all stages of conceptual thought is growth—growth during the child's education (in its widest sense), growth within a new area of study for a person of any age, and growth or expansion of existing concepts for any thoughtful, studious person who has acquired the ability to think in concepts during adolescence. Since growth is a major characteristic, we must admit that stages or levels of growth are not precise, static points. This is why we describe the process of thought development as movement along conceptual arrows.

Thinking takes place inside a person. One person cannot know what another thinks or at what level he is thinking unless there is some communication between them. Some psychologists believe that various forms of nonverbal behavior do reveal a child's place along conceptual arrows, but we feel that the spoken word can give a much more accurate indication. The general level of a person's conceptual growth is revealed by what he says, particularly when he uses words to construct models of phenomena. Now, it will probably be easy for you to assign each of the following statements to one of the four levels of thought we have discussed—syncretic, complex, preconcept, concept:

It's raining because I am sad.

The high percent of water vapor in the air makes its saturation such that the perspiration on my skin cannot evaporate.

There are black clouds in the sky, so that's why it's raining.

When water vapor condenses around particles in the air, it comes down as rain.

By design, schools can provide many opportunities to help children move along conceptual arrows, and we believe that language is one of the major tools which can implement this motion. Mention has already been made of the role of adults in supplying the right word at the right time. When a child needs a word to describe a process, he chooses whatever he deems appropriate or he asks "what-do-you-call-it?" But the word he chooses may conjure up an inappropriate image.

We found this when Mr. McIver's children were using the word *juice* for the flow of electricity. In relation to gravity, the word suggested "flowing" to Nancy, who used "juice" to explain the effects of a circuit in terms of it being "easier" for electricity to go down than up. When the words *electrical energy* were substituted and the physical circuit was turned 180° so that Nancy's *down* was *up*, another explanation—a better model—had to be found. As we saw, *electrical energy* had the advantage of being conceptually based: electromagnetic waves are one form of energy. Since energy can be changed from one form to another, the same words enabled the children (in a later lesson not recorded here) to offer an explanation of why wires in an electric heater got hot (the electrical energy was changed into heat energy) and why the thin wire in an electric light bulb glowed (the electrical energy was changed into light energy).

We saw, too, that the right word at the wrong time is not helpful to concept building. Mrs. Schur's children were not ready for the word *vibrations*.

The question is often raised: Should we introduce children to words which they cannot fully understand and for which they have little or no experiential background? American education is moving from the belief that children should learn correct forms and memorize definitions on the say-so of authority (to make sure that their statements are impeccably correct) to the belief that children should learn about only things with which they have had first-hand experience. Both of these beliefs are still with us to some extent and, while educators may weave theories about the better way or even posit a third alternative, the choice may not reside in their hands.

We might agree that children of elementary school age can have had little or no experience with atoms or molecules. The number of children who have the chance to look through an electron microscope at huge organic molecules is miniscule, even if the visual experience would be meaningful. So some science programs, most reasonably, do not offer these non-experiential abstractions to young children. Educators and science programs may so propose—but television disposes! Children hear about atoms and molecules; some learn that there is such a thing as DNA even before they can read! After children can read, they have access to many books written in very simple language which explain the unseen world. The chances are that their first contacts with these new and fascinating words—whether through television, in simple books, or by overhearing adult conversations —will evoke quite inappropriate meanings in the child. It is essential that the school cope with these realities. Now let us follow a few examples of the development of conceptual arrows from the time a child first hears the word *atom* (probably, unhappily, as an adjective with *bomb*) to the time when he may have the equipment to cope with the concept.

An example: toward a concept of the molecule

Although the word *atom* may be more familiar to a child, the word *molecule* is easier to present in experiential terms. In the beginning, *atom* may be relegated to "molecules are made up of atoms."

There are many games which children can play to sharpen their sense of smell. Cakes of perfumed soap can be hidden for the children to find. Berry baskets can be covered with double cheesecloth to obscure various odoriferous objects inside from vision: banana, apple, soap, cocoa, lemon, cinnamon. Children try to figure out what is in each basket without removing the cloth. Or liquid substances can be dabbed on folded cheesecloth squares.

A cut onion can be left in the room. Someone will make a remark about its smell; a little later some other child will notice the odor, and, later, another. What is the general directional sequence of the children detecting the onion odor? (There are individual differences in olfactory sensitivity, but a total classroom order of perception can usually be established.) Or an excellent challenge to thought could

be, "In what direction would you look for the onion?" Discussion of this point by third or fourth graders usually leads to the suggestion that some *thing* must have traveled from the onion to their various noses. Calling the "something" *tiny particles* is appropriate, although some child is likely to suggest *atoms* as the word. It can then be corroborated that atoms are indeed tiny particles, but that scientists call the *things* which come from the onion molecules. As the teacher uses this word, so do the children. In all these cases, after several game-like experiences, the children may be asked how they can smell something which does not seem to *touch* their noses. Again, the idea of something small—tiny bits of a substance— moving through the air is suggested, giving the children a second opportunity to relate the tiny particle or bit of substance to the word *molecule*. After subsequent experiences, when the word *molecule* is being used freely by the children, they can be asked to tell in their own words what *they* mean by it. The children will have various ways of expressing the different meanings they have attached to the word. Listening to each mode of expression, the teacher gleans the level of thinking of each child.

In even the most primary grades today, children make discoveries about water evaporating (becoming a gas) and freezing (becoming a solid). They also explore the disappearance of salt and sugar in water. ("Oh! It look like it invisible, but the sugar still there.") The term tiny *particle* or *molecule* may be supplied to explain something in the water which can be tasted but not seen. And the water that disappeared (as vapor), only to reappear from the air upon condensation, was also composed of tiny particles or molecules, too small to be seen.

From a wide roster of experiences[9] and from

[9] A number of activities and explanations may be found in: Elizabeth B. Hone, *et al., A Sourcebook for Elementary Science,* 2nd ed., Harcourt Brace Jovanovich, Inc., New York, 1971. (See index for page references on *atoms* and *molecules*.) Paul F. Brandwein *et al., Concepts in Science,* Harcourt Brace Jovanovich, Inc., New York, 1966: grade 2, pp. 1-24; grade 4, units 3 and 4; grade 5, unit 2; grade 6, unit 5. Herman and Nina Schneider, *Science in Your Life:* 4, 3rd ed., D.C. Heath, Lexington, Mass., 1965, unit 3. Herman and Nina Schneider, *Science for Today and Tomorrow:* 6, 3rd ed., D.C. Heath, 1965, unit 1. Herman and Nina Schneider, *Science in Our World:* 5, 3rd ed., D.C. Heath, 1965, unit 3. Abraham S. Fischler, *et al., Science, a Modern Approach:* 6, Holt, Rinehart & Winston, New York, 1966, unit 1.

many opportunities to talk about these experiences together, the children will learn to use the word molecule to represent the experience of "some*thing*" which is too tiny to be seen but which can be recognized as a specific entity.

Thus far, the word molecule has represented something which can travel or move, but there has been little concentration on its intrinsic energy of motion. For fourth graders or for some mature third graders, another experience brings the heat energy of molecules into focus. The following materials are set before each group of four children: four soda bottles with balloons secured over their mouths by rubber bands, a basin of ice, and a basin of very hot water. The children move the bottles from one basin to the other. When a bottle is left in the hot water for some time, the balloon expands above the bottle mouth. When a bottle is left in the ice, the deflated balloon is actually pushed inside the neck of the bottle. (For a more detailed account of this experiment, see Matrix 2, page 200.)

During the colloquium, children think on various levels. The less mature child will think syncretically ("Air from the room goes through the bottle and into the balloon."). At the complex level, a child might say, "The hot air molecules go into the balloon." There is usually some point of impasse when the teacher or a child asks "Why?" about the last model. At such a moment, the teacher might suggest, "Would it help you to know that molecules move very, very fast all the time, and that they move faster when they have more energy or when they are heated?" Sometimes an analogy may channel the children's thinking in a new direction: "If you were all standing rather still in the middle of the room, would you take up more or less space than if you were dancing the hully-gully?" (or whatever the current vigorous teenage dance may be).

Because an explanation of the phenomenon witnessed in this exploration relies on the comprehension of unseen activities—even more unseen than hidden likenesses, the children need further experience to enhance meanings of the models which were probably appreciated by only a few children at first. This experience can be an analogous situation which touches another dimension of learning—the kinesthetic—thereby helping children along the conceptual arrow. Here is one such experience which has proved successful:

The teacher shakes some marachas (or beans enclosed in a coffee can) and asks the children if they can tell when the beans are moving with little energy and when they are moving with more energy. He shakes slowly and then fast; the children can tell easily. And don't be surprised when some little thinker says, "Like the molecules." So, "If these beans were molecules, can you tell when they are moving with lots of heat energy and when they are moving with little heat energy?"

Now the teacher asks some of the children to pretend that *they* are molecules of air and to stand crowded together while the rest of the children form a "balloon" by holding hands in a circle around the "molecules." The "balloon" starts to close in on the "air molecules." The "air molecules" are asked to respond to the heat energy accompaniment (fast or slow motion) of the bean marachas and the balloon children are asked to react like the "balloon." Children often assert that they are really *balloon molecules*. Indeed they are! it makes a charming dance for all the children in the room as the balloon bulges to allow room for the vigorous, hully-gullying air molecules and then contracts when the molecules become slow, quiet, and cool. The "balloons" can then change places with the "air molecules."

This is a kinesthetic experience of the hot and cold air in the balloons and soda bottles. But the link between the dance and the balloons is tenuous; it does not become an integral part of the children's thinking until they have a later chance to draw on the hidden likenesses of the molecule dance and the air molecules. Here is a record—not really a colloquium—of a teacher trying to find out what his children thought after their molecule dance experience. The children (third graders from low-socio-economic families) were same ones who, before the dance, had thought that charcoal granules were "a gas" and that air went through the bottle to blow up the balloon. (This record, for the most part, did not specify which child spoke. However, many different children did participate.)

Ans: Before when somebody said about air, I thought air was made of molecules and oxygen and nitrogen.

Teacher: It is made of two gases. What are their names?

Ans: Oxygen and nitrogen.

Teacher: What do they do?

Ans: Move.

Ans: I thought it was heated air you put in, but later you told me about the gases. *(The teacher had said: "Most of the air is a gas called nitrogen and the rest is oxygen. The gases are made of small particles called molecules.")* I knew the heat from the bottle was getting them so that the balloon blew up.

Teacher: What is air made of? [This similar question is asked to see if the explanation that air is composed of two gases had meaning for the children or if they still think air is "made of molecules and oxygen and nitrogen."]

Teacher: What is air made of?

Ans: Oxygen and nitrogen.

Teacher: Liquid? Solid? Gas?

Ans: Gases.

Teacher: What are those tiny particles?

Ans: Atoms and molecules.

Teacher: What do the molecules do? [Note he omits the less appropriate word "atoms."]

Ans: They move fast and slow.

Teacher: When do they move fast?

Ans: When they are hot.

Teacher: Does everyone agree?

Ans: They move slow when they are cold. Cold feels better than hot; I touched it.

Teacher: Why does the balloon get big when the bottle is hot?

Ans: The heat brings it up.

Teacher: What happens to the molecules?

Ans: They get so hot they try to get away.

Ans: They move around real fast.

Teacher: Why don't they get out of the bottle?

Ans: They can't.

Ans: They go into the balloon.

Ans: The ballon gets bigger.

Ans: The balloon blows up. In ours, the bottom of the balloon almost burst it was so fat.

Why isn't this discussion classified as a colloquium?

This teacher had been experimenting with several new sets of science materials. No particular class unit had been developed. After about six weeks of a variety of experiences, the children were asked to write what they remembered from the science lessons. Although the lesson just recorded was the first in the series, most of the class remembered something about "molecules"—either that they were tiny particles, or, more frequently, that they moved fast or slow according to the heat.

We cannot claim that the children at this juncture have anything like a concept of the molecule, but they can use the word in a correct, although limited, way in exchanging ideas and phrases with each other or with an adult. Of course, they are still thinking in the concrete—they may picture molecules as beans or children, even though they call them "tiny particles" —their experience and their language have been enriched. Throughout the next few grades, they need other experiences in which molecular motion can by used to explain many observed phenomena. For example, one opportunity can be offered when the children are studying the water cycle in relation to weather. Here, they can begin to explain evaporation and condensation as the heat energy given to and taken from the water molecules.

Or, when children are exploring with thermometers, they can be challenged to explain the expansion of alcohol or mercury. Again, they will be able to use the idea of heat energy making the molecules move faster, making the molecules take up more room as they move.

As a gifted sixth-grade girl explained: "It's like in summertime; the doorknob is hard to turn because the heat expands it."

And another child said: "Also, cement on the street cracks because heat expands it."

When asked to explain further, one child added: "The molecules become more active. The stuff is less dense; it takes up more room."

Eventually these children may be encouraged to apply the word *energy* to its various forms: heat energy, light energy, and electrical energy.

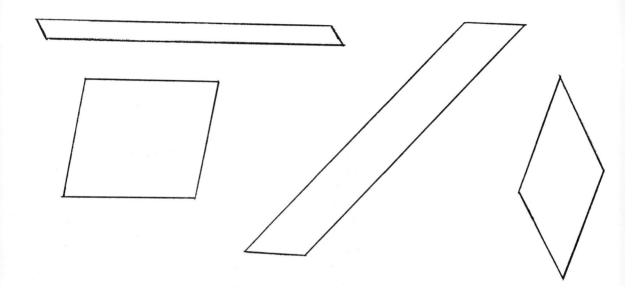

At some stage, the statement (passed over rather cavalierly at first) that molecules are composed of smaller particles—the atoms—will need further development. This can be accomplished quite naturally in chemistry. Sugar is burned; the end product is carbon. "The carbon *atoms* came from the sugar molecule." When carbon is burned, it produces the detectable gas *carbon dioxide*. Its name reveals the nature of the atoms in the gas molecule. "Atoms are the smallest particles which act as individual elements. Atoms joined together form molecules." Further elaboration of the relation of atoms to molecules is provided by a study of photosynthesis: the absorption by green plants of water through the roots and of carbon dioxide from the air, which then join to form the carbohydrate molecule via the energy of the sun.

Many angles of perception result from such investigations: much extension of the frames of reference, followed by thinking and speaking together, helped by the teacher supplying the right word at the right time. The importance of perceptual variability can be illustrated by asking, "What does he know of a parallelogram who only one parallelogram knows?" One would probably be drawn with the long sides parallel to the bottom of the page; others could be a very skinny one, one which is almost a square, one placed with the narrow sides parallel to the bottom of the page, one standing on a corner. Do these drawings enlarge your previous concept of a parallelogram? Now try to describe the various parallelograms in words which include all the shapes, proportions, sizes, and positions drawn. In the end, the word *parallelogram* conjures up not only the examples experienced, but a kind of interaction between one's perception and one's fluid thinking about them—in short, a concept.

Now it's your turn Now you are probably ready to try to analyze children's levels of concept development. Two separate seventh-grade colloquia follow. We suggest you score the applicable remarks with these codes:

> syn: syncretic
> compx: complex
> prec: preconcept
> conc: concept

Of course, there are no absolute answers, but if you were to analyze these colloquia with others and then discuss your opinions, you might agree on the evidences. In any case, the exercise and the discussion will, naturally, clarify your concepts of conceptual development! Both classes used wet and dry steel wool in enclosed spaces with stretchable covers. Although the principle was the same, formats differed.

The first seventh grade   The first class had jars with pieces of balloon stretched tightly over the mouths and secured with rubber bands. Dry steel wool had been placed in some of the jars; pieces of steel wool soaked in vinegar for an hour (to dissolve the "rust-arrester") and then rinsed in water were placed in the other jars. All of the jars had been prepared the night before the lesson. In those with wet steel wool, the rubber coverings were deeply depressed.

Dry steel wool

Bea: There could have been less air pressure in the jar so that it [the balloon] fell down instead of being flat.

Hank: The rusting process caused the diaphragm to be depressed.

Jock: The water caused the rust and the diaphragm to be depressed.

Marlo: Rust occurred in jars where the diaphragm was depressed because the oxygen which the rust took in caused the diaphragm to be depressed.

Anne: The diaphragm was depressed because there was more air pressure outside the jar than inside. Rust was formed when the steel wool and the oxygen joined.

Susanna: The jar with the rust has a depressed top since, at first, there was an equal pressure and it was level. After a while, the steel wool absorbed the air so there was more pressure on top and the air pressure pushed the top in.

Wet steel wool

Nathaniel: I thought of why the one with the depressed diaphragm has rust in it and the other didn't. I think that the rust needed oxygen to form so it took oxygen from the air in the bottle, leaving the bottle with less air, and so the air from the outside pushed the diaphragm in.

Burt: In order to rust, oxidation, steel wool needs air and water.

Madeline: Oxygen combined with the iron in the steel wool and caused rust.

Penelope: When the oxygen from the air combined with the iron from the steel wool and water, it oxidized and there was a chemical change. A new molecule different from oxygen was formed. It was a rust molecule.

The second seventh grade   For the second seventh grade, the teacher used test tubes instead of jars; a small balloon was fitted over the end of each tube. Both backgrounds of these children and their thinking about the materials were different from those in the first class. In case you feel that the children in this discovery-colloquium lesson (their first) exhibit too low a level of thought, we are including some comments by their teacher which indicate how far above the children's usual performance their remarks are.

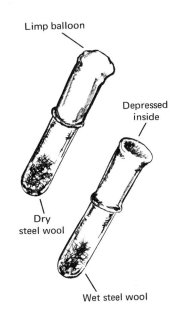

Limp balloon

Depressed inside

Dry steel wool

Wet steel wool

This is a seventh-grade class in a special service school. Many of the children are from underprivileged homes. They have low IQ's and emotional problems. If only you could see them now, broken into groups discussing what they see. How excited they all are. I don't have to yell, "Stop talking because you are interrupting the lesson" or, "You are not paying attention." I have also learned more about the children in one group by observing them for a few minutes than in the two months I have had them. How good one feels watching these children with many discipline problems working together in harmony, discovering things for themselves, observing, discussing, sharing. . . . Just look how these children can reason. I could never see this fully in my regular lessons. By giving the children freedom in reasoning and discovering things for themselves, their "true being arose."

While one group was experimenting, the teacher recorded part of the interchange which was taking place freely.

Joseph: I think this experiment is on how steel wool rusts. But what are the balloons on top for?

Prudence: I think if you put the test tubes on the flame of an alcohol lamp the balloons will expand. They will get bigger and bigger. Don't you think so?

Group: Yes.

Ross: Could be that the water turned the steel wool to rust.

Martha: No. When you just wet steel wool it doesn't change color. Look, if you put water into the tube that is dry, the steel wool will not change colors. My mother uses steel wool at home and when she finishes with it the color is the same.

Ross: You might be right. What do you think, Joseph?

Joseph: I don't know. Wait . . . *(He is very excited.)* . . . I've got it! Steel wool wouldn't rust if you just put water on it. What must have happened is that Mr. Wilbur left the water on the steel wool for some time, maybe a day or a week. Martha, your mother throws the steel wool out right after she is finished with it. That is why it doesn't rust. It takes time for steel wool to rust.

Martha: *(takes off the balloons and smells)* Here, everyone, smell this. It doesn't smell. I told you before it was water.

Joseph: You see, water doesn't smell. Yes, Martha was right at the beginning; it was water not chemicals. *(Martha had thought she smelled "chemicals." She actually smelled vinegar in which some of the steel wool had been soaked.)*

Group: Yes. *(All agreed.)*

Joseph: I still don't know what the purpose of the balloons were.

Then, during the colloquium, this group of children pooled their observations and thoughts with those of the rest of the class.

Mr. W.: What did you observe?

Charlotte: I saw two test tubes, each containing steel wool. In one test tube, the steel wool was dry; in the other, it was wet.

Joseph: We agree that this is an experiment on how water can change steel wool. If water is placed on steel wool and left for some time, the steel wool will begin to rust—that is, change to yellow.

Mr. W.: How did your group come to this conclusion?

Joseph: First we thought that chemicals were placed into the test tube that was wet and those chemicals caused the steel wool to turn yellow, but then, after smelling the wettest tube, we decided it was water because it didn't smell and chemicals have a smell. What I didn't understand is the purpose of the balloons.

Ward: I didn't understand that either.

The group remained in a thoughtful silence.

Rosita: The balloons have something to do with air pressure.

Mr. W.: How do you know that?

Rosita: Because one balloon was pushed in and the other wasn't. Something happened to the tube that was wet which caused the balloon to be pushed in.

Joseph: Look at that! Our group didn't even notice that!

Ross: How come there was some black materials on top of the steel wool in the wet test tube?

Alan: Mr. Wilbur must have heated that test tube.

Joseph: No. If Mr. Wilbur heated the test tube, the whole steel wool would have turned black. The reason why it is black is that it is starting to rust.

Martha: My mother uses steel wool and when she throws it away after it is wet, the steel wool becomes darker. Mr. Wilbur left the steel wool in water for some time.

Jack: Now I understand. The steel wool was left for some time in water and it began to rust.

Then the bell rang. Some children who wanted to speak yelled, "Ah-oh. . . ." As they left the room for their next period, I could hear them discussing what they had seen and asking their friends questions about things that happened that they didn't understand.

The next day some of the children told me that they had tried the experiment at home. How wonderful!

What would *you* plan for the next session?

4

Conceptual schemes in science

We live in a world of increasingly accelerated change. By the year 2000, children in today's classrooms will be citizens of an earth (and undoubtedly other planets, too) which those of us who feel moderately comfortable now will probably not even recognize. Then how can we even suggest the appropriate educational content of classes—in science, particularly—in the strange and new world of the year 2000? It is said that roughly 90% of all known science has been discovered in the last 90 years and that approximately 90% of all the scientists who have ever made contributions to the world of fact and thought were alive at the middle of this century.

Explanations and facts are changing at an accelerated rate, not only in the field we call science, but also in other areas of life that affect our values, our ways of thinking, and, therefore, plans for education.

A very long time ago, almost anyone who did any thinking at all *knew* that there was an Absolute Truth, an Absolute Beauty, and an Absolute Good. Even though everyone could not find these Absolutes, the certainty of their existence became a beacon lighting the way through the storms of personal vicissitudes. Later scientists and other thinkers became secure in the knowledge that every event had a cause and every cause was followed by a predictable event. These absolutes have now been replaced by the science of probability.

Realization of accelerated change has its impact on teachers from time to time. Those of us born around the turn of the century, even in industrial areas, have lived in homes lighted by gas and gone to town in horse-drawn buses or streetcars when the airplane, radio, and television were still unknown. Today a teacher who tells a student, "When I was a little girl, there was no TV," is regarded as a contemporary of Noah! Now even a high school student can say to a kindergartner, "When I was a little boy, no one thought seriously of riding in a space capsule. It was science fiction!" and the preschooler will surely think the young man must have conversed with dinosaurs.

All over the nation, we are being shaken up by the new approaches and new content being tested in education, to say nothing of the new technology. Whereas a century ago it was quite safe to teach children that 2 plus 2 always makes 4 and that the three angles of a triangle add up to 180°, it is now commonly accepted that they do so only if certain axioms and postulates are acknowledged. Science textbooks a generation ago told children that "animals prepare for winter" and that the electron "wants" to jump to an orbit or shell of lowest energy. Today it is no longer considered fair to the child to impute volitional attributes to animals or atomic particles.

We indeed have become a "shook-up" generation. How much more shaken will the next generation—or pupils—be?

The value of conceptual schemes in a changing world

Fortunately, in teaching the would-be leaders of the twenty-first century, the realm of science provides some fairly persistent, long-range features when compared with a man's lifespan. *These are the conceptual schemes.*

Of course, conceptual schemes, like concepts, are inventions of man. They are formed by relating many concepts to a larger whole. Obviously, a conceptual scheme processes or encodes far more data than does any one concept.

Perhaps the most overall and *unchanging* conceptual scheme is that everything in the universe is in constant change! We might consider this statement from several angles:

Energy is constantly being transformed from one form to another—from electromagnetic to light to mechanical to thermal and back again.

Matter is constantly being transformed through the rearrangement of atoms and molecules.

Mass[1] and energy can be transformed into one another through nuclear reactions. In fact mass-energy is a single concept in modern science.

Living organisms are in constant change, absorbing matter and energy from the environment, reproducing themselves, and finally becoming part of the environment at death.

However, this overall conceptual scheme that everything is in constant change has an obverse: The total amount of mass-energy in the universe is conserved.

In relation to the universe, *matter, energy*, and *life* are far-reaching concepts around which conceptual schemes can be built. To construct these conceptual schemes, curricula must be organized—first into divisible subconcepts which can be studied by children of various maturities. These conceptual schemes cut across the organization into subject areas (such as weather, plants, space, machines) which we commonly find as the warp and weft of science curricula, but they embrace and emphasize the procedures of scientists by placing these areas in a larger framework. Although the schemes are interlocking, we can adopt a favorite scientific procedure and extract an area or phase from a system of interacting objects[2] and concepts to study at any particular time. One fruitful way of grouping concepts and subconcepts and providing for the various levels of growth by elementary school children is shown on page 166.

The conceptual schemes embrace concepts and subconcepts which represent various aspects of *matter, energy*, and *life*. Notice that the concepts and subconcepts are not placed in *grades*, but in *levels* which parallel Vygotsky's stages in conceptual growth. Each concept level forms, if you will, part of

[1] The difference between *mass* and *matter* is important at the conceptual level of thinking. *Mass* is the amount of matter in an object. *Matter* is anything that takes up space. The concept of *mass* is essential in thinking about cosmic, nuclear, and some other reactions. For most of the work in elementary school, however, the concept of *matter* is more relevant to the experiences and intellectual levels of the children.
[2] In *Science Curriculum Improvement Study*, Robert Karplus introduced the words *system, interaction*, and *object* and the ways to relate them to elementary science.

CHART OF CONCEPTUAL SCHEMES

	CONCEPTUAL SCHEME A The universe is in constant change.	CONCEPTUAL SCHEME B The sum total of mass and energy in the universe remains constant. In nuclear reactions, a loss of matter is a gain in energy.		CONCEPTUAL SCHEME C Living organisms are in constant change. A living organism is the product of its heredity (genetic code) and its environment. Living organisms have changed over the ages; some have become extinct.	
		EMPHASIS ON ENERGY	EMPHASIS ON MATTER	EMPHASIS ON HEREDITY	EMPHASIS ON ENVIRONMENT
CONCEPT	Nuclear reactions produce the radiant energy of the stars and consequent changes. Universal gravitational interaction governs the relations of celestial bodies in space—time.	Energy manifests itself along an electromagnetic spectrum. When energy changes from one form to another, the total amount of energy remains constant.	When matter changes from one form to another, the total amount of matter remains constant.	Changes in the genetic code produce changes in living organisms.	Living organisms are interdependent with one another and with their environment.
PRECONCEPT	Bodies in space (as well as their matter and energy) are in constant change. The matter of which the earth is composed is in constant change. The motion and paths of the celestial bodies are predictable within specific frames of reference (relativity). There are daily, seasonal, and annual changes within the solar system.	A loss or gain in energy affects molecular motion. Energy gotten out of a machine does not exceed the energy put into it. The sun is the chief source of radiant energy in our solar system. A change in the state or manifestation of matter is accompanied by a change in molecular energy. Energy can change from one form to another.	In chemical and physical changes, the total amount of matter remains constant. In chemical change, atoms interact to produce changes in molecules. Matter consists of atoms and molecules in constant motion. A change in the state or manifestation of matter is accompanied by a change in molecular motion. Matter consists of elements and compounds.	The cell is the unit of structure and function. A living organism develops from a single cell.	The capture of radiant energy from the sun is basic to the growth and maintenance of living organisms. Living organisms interchange matter and energy with their environment. There are characteristic environments, each with its characteristic life.
COMPLEX	There are regular movements of the earth and moon. There are daily changes on earth.	Energy (push, pull, fire, etc.) must be used either to set an object in motion or to stop it. There are many forms of energy.	Matter commonly exists in solid, liquid, and gaseous forms. Matter has properties which can be detected by the senses.	Living organisms which have a common structure are related. All living organisms go through a birth, growth, death, decay cycle. Related living organisms reproduce in similar ways. There are different forms of living organisms.	Living organisms live and grow in different environments.

a *conceptual arrow*. It is not assumed that a child fully grasps the concepts of matter, energy, and life, for each child's conceptual thinking develops at his own rate.

Conceptual thinking is a later development in the adolescent years. The elementary years give the child experiences in syncretic and complex thinking and in searching for the concept, at the preconcept level. The conceptual scheme with its concepts and subconcepts at different levels forms the matrix for the concept-seeking and concept-forming activities which follow the conceptual arrows of the curriculum.

The manner in which children may be exposed to the various levels of each conceptual scheme is illustrated throughout this book. In Chapter 5, there are suggested activities which are appropriate to the various cells of the chart.

Building a conceptual scheme

Exposure to various activities is a necessary but not a sufficient condition for the building of concepts. The same is true of colloquia, they alone will not build concepts. It is possible for a child to be exposed to all the appropriate *contents* and not build any of the suggested subconcepts into this thinking. This seems to happen not only in the elementary school but also at higher levels of education. We have met a young man who, having majored in physics even to the doctoral level, admits that although he can work most accurately all the problems he has encountered in the study of quantum or relativity, he is quite unable to *think about* their concepts. He did not develop an understanding of the conceptual schemes involved; he acquired the technical skills but

did not pursue the interaction of the abstractions which build concepts.

The same difficulty troubles some elementary school teachers. We feel that they are not to blame, and we hope that this book will help them progress along their various conceptual arrows and allow them to encompass some important parts of all the conceptual schemes.

If teachers do not have a conceptual framework, there is little chance that the children in their classrooms will find the threads of science's conceptual schemes to guide them in building concepts themselves. The children will continue to wander among data without finding a conceptual arrow.

We seem to be posing the question, "Who doctors the doctor?" Fortunately, there is a close parallel between the dictum "Physician, heal thyself!" and the acquisition of conceptual schemes in science. We mentioned before that no one can teach a concept to anyone else, that one can only create a situation in which the "learner" can be helped to build a concept himself—*inside* himself. Just as the doctor who heals himself still needs a hygienic environment, the tender care of nurses, and even the latest medical journal— the child needs a sensitive and wise teacher.

We have not said much about the role of books in the field of science. Books are experiences as well; they are probes into a field where something has already been discovered by the child—an extension of the facts and concepts learned from materials and colloquia. Books are significant, indeed, although we prefer them in somewhat different sequence from their usual presentation (see Chapter 7).

Nevertheless, how does one proceed to acquire a concept? For the purpose of illustration, we introduce Mr. Robert Fotheringay.

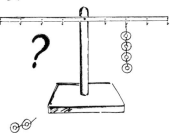

Where would these two washers have to be placed to balance the other four?

BOB FOTHERINGAY'S CONCEPT

Bob Fotheringay was a dynamic and well-liked teacher of a fifth grade in a suburban school. He had always been able to lead his children to find mathematical relationships between the weights hung on the arms of a balance in equilbrium and the distance of the weight from the fulcrum.[3] He

[3]For an article on how children may *discover* the relationship of weight to distance: Brenda Lansdown, "Turning Discovery into Thought," *Nature and Science* (Teacher's Ed.), Vol. 3, No. 15 (April 18, 1966), T 1 and T 4.

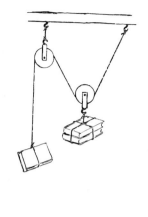

Where do you think they would fit in?

had let his children work with pulleys hung from the ceiling beams; he had given the class various crowbar arrangements[4] and encouraged them to predict the effort they would use to lift an enormous rock.

He had found that the children regularly discovered (with his assistance) that the length of a pendulum (not the weight of the bob) determined the time of its round trip; and he had an interesting way of leading children to find out that the length of the pendulum is measured from the point of attachment to the center of gravity of the system. He provided a pair of pendula: one with a small spherical bob and the other with a yardstick as the bob. The problem was to make the two swing together in the same rhythm. Evaluating his units, he was satisfied that a majority of his children could calculate the mechanical advantage of machines correctly and, if given adequate data, could find the length of a pendulum whose round trip time would be double that of the original. Then one year Mr. Fotheringay noticed that the new science textbooks being issued talked of the need to relate all science teaching to concepts or conceptual schemes. Well, if others could do it, so could he. Looking at a chart similar to the one on page 166, he asked himself, "Where in this grid are my pendulums and machines?" Where, indeed?

He found some cells in the chart which seemed vaguely related to his teaching. Then he began to wonder what a conceptual scheme really was. Was his own thinking conceptual? Did he teach facts and correct answers or develop concepts?

Alas, the answer was all too clear. His children "knew" a great deal, but to what picture of the universe was all this knowledge related? Bob Fotheringay decided that he needed to grasp the appropriate conceptual schemes first and then he could apply himself to their transmission. It turned out to be a much more arduous task than he had anticipated; it took him several days—in fact, nearly two weeks.

Since adults are capable of thinking conceptually and those who have been through college have had some experience, at least from time to time, in this exercise, they are able to build concepts comparatively quickly, although not always without effort. The stages in their concept building are very similar to those in children. Adults, too, can grow from syncretic to complex thinking, along conceptual arrows to full conceptual thought, and, finally, to a grasp of conceptual schemes. The rate at which adults achieve this depends on many variables, as does the amount of help they need. Mr. Robert Fotheringay's experience illustrates one way and one rate. But the pattern of achievement—the road he took along the conceptual arrows—is fairly widespread.

So after school one snowy day, when there was no point in clearing the driveway (it would be buried again in the next hour), Bob sat down in his

[4] Helpful books and ideas for classroom materials on pulleys, levers, and other machines: Hone *et al.*, *A Sourcebook for Elementary Science*, Harcourt Brace Jovanovich, Inc., New York, 1971, Chapter 22; Brandwein *et al.*, *Concepts in Science* (Teacher's Ed.), Harcourt Brace Jovanovich, Inc., New York, 1966, Vol. 6, Unit 4; Schneider, *Science in Your Life* (Teacher's Ed.), D.C. Heath, Lexington, Mass., 1965, Unit 7.

study and began to look at what he knew about simple machines. He wrote down a few trusted statements:

Work is pull or push times distance.
Input of work in foot-pounds equals output of work in foot-pounds.
    He added, "Almost."
Effort overcomes resistance of an object.
Machines are devices that perform work in response to work done on them.
Energy is capacity to do work.

Suddenly he seemed to have no energy! Words, words, words kept shooting through his head, tumbling against one another too quickly for him to repeat his well-known definitions: input, load, resistance, output, work, energy, fulcrum, foot-pound, effort, distance, motion, energy, resistance, energy, resistance, energy, resist. . . . These last words started throbbing. Bob decided that a cup of coffee would clear his head, and then maybe he'd play with his youngest, Jamie.

Jamie was three. He was sitting disconsolately on his teeter-totter in the basement romper room when his father entered. Obviously, a game of seesaw was indicated. Bob sat on the free end of the teeter-totter and jerked the laughing infant up high. Thoughts intruded upon the joyful scene. "I'm six times Jamie's weight, so I'm sitting one-sixth his distance from the fulcrum. Weight times distance equals weight times distance." Remembering his older brother he thought, "Fat boys don't have much fun at school." Jamie was set for a piggyback ride, so his father, in response to Mother's call, piggybacked him right up to the evening's ablutions. And the fulcrum was fortunately forgotten . . . for a while.

At supper the three older Fotheringay children were full of chatter about their day's events. Mother was giving an attentive ear, so Bob slipped off into his dreamworld—the world of machines with lots of clear facts and no clear links. "What does link them all together?" he asked himself.

"Anything the matter, dear?"

He blinked, shook his troubles out of his head, and offered to help his nine-year-old daughter with her history project after dinner. Later, the sleepiness brought on by good food having been dispersed through discussing the project of the Eskimo's diet with Laura, Bob accepted his wife's announcement that she was pooped and was off to bed; then he settled down once more to consider the problem of the concepts behind machines.

This time he began by working some problems. They gave him a feeling of ease, of success, of taking hold. Then he decided to read some of the teachers' guides at his disposal; they were always full of good suggestions. He read also in several other books, two written especially for children, and then turned to his college physics text. He seemed to know it all. He *did* know it. So what was the problem? The concepts? He was chasing concepts in a field that was as clear as daylight in each of its separate parts. Somehow the concepts had not meshed with their corresponding operations. He yawned and decided to call it a day.

For the rest of that week the exigencies of living occupied his energies and kept his thoughts on mundane affairs, or maybe he occupied himself just to have some respite from the gnawing problem of finding the conceptual schemes behind his familiar levers. It was not until Saturday that the gnawing intruded again.

He was accompanying his two middle children to the science museum while the eldest boy was off on a scout hike and Jamie was entertaining one of his nursery school friends in romper room block play. The three Fotheringays had paused in front of an elegant diorama of an Eskimo fishing for seal near an airhole. Laura was pouring out questions and her younger brother was hoping a seal would emerge and be speared. The children soon realized that Papa was off in another world, so they began recounting their observations to each other, sometimes simultaneously. Suddenly Laura saw a notice that headphones which gave a talk about each exhibit could be rented. Bob was easily persuaded to allow his children to become absorbed in a dollar's worth of lectures.

His own thinking had been triggered by a simulated "trip to the moon" and the children's weights on the various scales geared to the masses of planets. "I know what ties all these machines together. It's gravity! All the lifting is effort *against* gravity; the pulley works *with* gravity; the free fall ram of the pile driver drops *because of* gravity; and I'm sure there's something in that conceptual chart about universal gravitation." He smiled with relief and allowed his children to pull him to the next diorama for a new recorded lecture. There was a stuffed squirrel on a tree. Bob said aloud, "Nutcracker!" His children looked up, wonderingly. "The nutcracker is not connected with gravity. It's just a little old second class lever! And gears are not related to gravity, nor need a wheel and axle be."

On the way to the bus, Laura slid on a strip of ice and fell with a bump. Bob found comforting her a great solace.

For the most part, Sunday was occupied with preparing for the week's lessons and correcting papers. Fortunately, the science lessons were to be on the temperature of snow slush and whether an ice cube weighs the same when it melts. "Is there a conceptual scheme behind these activities?" he wondered briefly. "Forget it!" he told himself promptly.

The following Thursday, the Fotheringays were invited to supper with their friends, the Archeks. Ivan Archek was Assistant Principal at the school where Bob taught. Ivan had majored in mathematics and minored in philosophy for his master's. Ivan and Bob had been friends for a long time; the parents and children frequently intervisited.

As soon as dinner was over and the wives had withdrawn to attend to the bedtime rites of the younger Archek children, Bob drew his friend into the problem absorbing him. It was briefly outlined. Ivan was immediately interested; finding wide generalities was his stock in trade—not only in his own thinking, but as an aid to his administrative responsibilities.

"Can you give a specific illustration of the problem, Bob?"

"Take that neat experience which the children always enjoy: lifting or dragging a roller skate hooked onto a spring balance up different slopes. First the children lift it. Say, it weighs four pounds. Then they drag it up a slope where the ratio of horizontal to height is 2:1. The kids are surprised that the pull registers only two pounds. So I show them that if they multiply pull by distance, the work remains the same: four foot-pounds. The children counter that it's less work to pull the skate up the slope than it is to lift it in air. So I clarify for them the difference between *work* for a scientist and the children's view of work."

Do you have any reaction to these teaching procedures?

"Maybe you should cue me in on that one. I'm not sure I know."

"Work is defined as the pull or push or effort needed to move an object a certain distance. I ask a child to push against the wall as hard as he can. I choose one of my vigorous boys who, of course, obliges until the veins stand out on his neck. Is he working? Some of the children think he is. The boy does himself. But he is not, not to a scientist. Then I ask a delicate girl to turn the page of a book. Is she working? . . . Well, you get the point."

"Good experiences. . . ."

"Well, now let me take you further into *my* problem. Let's lower that slope some more. Each time the distance gets greater, the pull gets less."

"So when it's horizontal, there's no pull at all and the skate goes on forever!"

"You philosophers are always too logical! In an ideal situation, you would be right. But there's friction. The greater the friction, the less far the skate goes and the greater the pull registered on the scale."

How would one drag a skate to show *most* friction?

"Then there must have been friction before, and your readings on the scale couldn't have multiplied so neatly."

"Not exactly, but near enough."

"Near enough for what?"

"To prove that the input of work equals the output: it's always height times distance in foot-pounds."

"Wouldn't it be more correct to say that the energy gotten out *cannot be greater* than the energy put into?"

"Know what?" Bob jumped in his seat. "That sounds something like one of those conceptual schemes! But you see, *I'm* still thinking concretely. Let me go further with this friction idea. On a trip one day my little Laura slipped on an icy stretch and fell. It occurred to me that her feet were moving forward very fast with only a little push and, of course, if she hadn't lost her balance—say her feet were all alone, like the skates—they'd have gone a very long distance. If someone had measured the push or pull on her—say with a spring balance—it would have registered nearly zero."

You might be interested to note Bob's sequence of hidden likenesses.

In what way is Bob's train of thought influenced by Ivan's remarks?

"Don't your children worry about the apparent loss of weight when they pull the skate along different slopes?"

"Sure they do. That's when I explain the difference between weight and mass."

"You *explain* it? Do the children get the idea?"

What major interest(s) motivate(s) Ivan's series of questions?

Bob paused a moment. "Y'know, they don't seem to. It's a hard concept to get across. But neither Laura nor Peter seemed to worry when they 'lost weight' on the moon scales in the museum. Well, that's an exotic experience—not real, like pulling the skates. . . . But listen, I'm thinking of something."

"Go ahead."

"In space, in orbit, a capsule does go on forever. Or it could; there is no friction. There you have the perfect mathematical relationship: push approaches zero while distance approaches infinity. Newton's inertia!"

"Neat! Now you're leaving the concrete. Go on."

Bob was really excited. He held his pipe in the bowl of his hand and moved to the edge of his arm chair. "When the astronaut space-walks, he floats along at five or so miles a second, not feeling motion. But when he gives a slight tug or pull on the umbilical cord, he zooms into the capsule. First he is in a state of equilibrium; it is as though he isn't moving at all. The tug at the cord is a pull, and the work he does is shown as the pull times the distance he moves with regard to his previous state—his distance moved toward the capsule. Since there is no friction and no weight, all his effort goes into motion, into his change in position. He zooms fast—like Laura's feet as she fell on the ice." Bob relaxed back into his chair and resumed his pipe smoking.

"You know what?" he said, after a moment. "The astronaut's weight-lessness would be a good way to show children the difference between weight and mass. There's obviously a good mass of astronaut up there!"

"The children might be able to figure that one out themselves if you posed the problem."

"You mean like I did!"

"Why not?"

There was a sound of quiet voices outside the door as the two wives returned to the living room.

"I still don't quite have it," said Bob, with conflicting emotions of irritation and relief.

The next day, Bob and Ivan found themselves at the same cafeteria table for lunch.

"May I talk some more about my conceptual schemes problem, or are you bored," asked Bob?

"No, go right ahead. I'm interested."

Why wasn't Bob able to pick up the idea of energy when Ivan first mentioned it?

"I'm beginning to think that the key concept is energy. As you reminded me, and the conceptual schemes chart stated, energy gotten out of a machine cannot exceed the energy put into it. Energy is the capacity to do work, but, if we think of it doing the work, then the energy put into a machine equals the useful plus the not-useful energy gotten out of it. That not-useful energy accounts for the slight loss due to the heat of friction or other energy resulting from moving an object. But what I can't tie together are all those different kinds of motion. The work is the push or pull times the distance, and the distance can be immense, like the space-walking astronaut; the motion can be *stopping* action, like catching a baseball in a mitt; it can be increasing speed or changing direction. these are all concrete events. I can't tie them together."

"There's one thing I wondered about. In my physics courses, we used the word 'force,' and you use 'push' or 'pull.' Why? Easier for the children to understand?"

"Oh no, it's not that. Force is a Newtonian word and I'm trying to help the children think in modern physics terms—to apply the new terms to the older concepts. That's why I'm bothering about the conceptual scheme behind machines for myself."

"But surely physicists use the word 'force' themselves?"

"Colloquially, modern physicists can afford to use any term they choose because their thinking or interpretation is modern. They don't usually write about force in reporting their researches. But the children don't have the concept, and the everyday use of the word 'force' does not *suggest* the modern concept. So I prefer to avoid the word as much as I can. The words 'push' and 'pull' do fairly all right."

"No force of gravitation then?"

"Don't need it. I use the idea of interaction of a system. Here, it's not a whim of mine. You philosophers ought to understand the importance of the meaning of terms! Read this." Bob pulled a piece of folded paper from his notebook. The following quotation[5] was typed on it:

Newton's law of gravitation refers to "force" and implies that the acceleration of a falling body is due to that force. But what *is* force? How do we picture it? Do we imagine that some sort of invisible demon is engaged in a perennial tugging contest? If we try to think out the idea carefully, we are bound to confess that there is no justification for conferring upon some mysterious agency the same sort of pulling effort that we can exert with our own muscles.

When Ivan tried to hand back the paper, Bob didn't even notice it. His eyes were fixed somewhere in space while his thinking darted over the conceptual matrix avidly seeking an arrow. He began to think out loud.

"There's something about change of direction, like rockets and jets—retroactive rockets and that stuff. I'll always remember an assembly program put on by Mrs. Andersen. . . . She was teaching a third grade then, and the kids had been talking about rockets to the moon. . . . It was the time of the first Gemini flight, I recall. . . . Yes, Grissom and Young. . . . Well, Mrs. Andersen played some delightful music of the spheres—from Holst's *Planets*—I think and those children rushed about the stage being jets. Whenever they wished to change direction or speed they held their hands against their bodies and pointed their fingers in the directions jets would be angled. They of course moved in the opposite direction, giving out a loud 'p-sh-sh-sh.' It was delightful. I remember particularly one boy on a retro-rocket re-entry. He came zooming across the stage backwards, his hands spread out from his back trouser pockets like the tail feathers of a bird, slowing himself with bursts of 'p-sh-sh' from both retro-rockets."

"Yes, I recall that program, too. Jennie Andersen's quite an all-round girl

[5] F.W. Westaway, *The Endless Quest*, Blackie and Son, London, 1934, p. 552.

who integrates her whole curriculum. She's working on an ecology project now with her second grade."

"It has something to do with change of direction, or velocity. . . . Jeepers—it's vectors! Vectors and energy. That's the conceptual scheme behind all machines!"

Suddenly it all seemed so clear to both men. They didn't have to discuss it any further.

The adult conceptual arrow

The road along the conceptual arrow toward concepts, and thus toward conceptual schemes, is individual. Each of us finds his own way. A characteristic common to every concept builder is the search for meaning within a forest of facts, for a general scheme to encompass all of the possible specifics of a problem. One must therefore be acquainted with as large an assortment of facts as possible, for it is the misfit (like the nutcracker) that allows one to identify and eliminate the inadequate scheme. Bob Fotheringay's knowledge of many types of machines shifted him from his initial idea that gravity was their binding concept. Another common characteristic of concept building is long periods of floating chaos when the thinker tries one path or another in a matrix of conceptual arrows. At this point it is a question of finding a way of relating concepts so that they will *lead to* a conceptual scheme. However, frequent descents to the concrete result, provide other starting points from which to search. Then there must be periods of gestation, times when other activities fully occupy the person's overt attention. And there must be articulation, either in a colloquium or with a good listening friend or by trying to put the ideas into writing. And there seem to be periods where oceans of irrelevancies come to the fore—but are they really irrelevant? Then, suddenly, comes the insight, perhaps indicated by a single word, a symbol, "Vectors!" After that, release. At leisure, later, the newly found conceptual scheme in its many applications and ramifications of meaning can be developed more fully.

That is the concept-building process. As to its meaning, again we say that it is individual. In case the insight which Bob Fotheringay achieved does not coincide with your own ideas, we will now elaborate slightly on the way he arrived at this meaning.

Bob began with plenty of concrete experiences with the various forms of levers, pulleys, screws, and wedges that form the content of most textbook chapters on simple machines. He also had an ability to work mathematical problems which depict relationships among the variables. He had, too, an apt definition of each term. As a teacher, Bob was fully equipped to pass on to today's children the ideas about simple machines which Isaac Newton developed in the seventeenth century. He had even gone a bit further; he had accepted the notion that concepts change and that a change in language accompanies this change of concepts. He saw that interaction had replaced cause and effect, and he had read and accepted that force was an ancient notion for which the invention of "interaction of a system" provided a better framework. When he realized that concepts were to be emphasized as the new trend in teaching science, he wished to incorporate this aim into his own teaching program. He undertook to investigate the relation of his favorite science unit to a larger conceptual scheme, and in doing so, realized that he had been leaving his children with a lot of data and no concepts, similar to his own involvement.

Early in his search, Bob came to the conclusion that "energy" was the real source of push and pull and that the books had often called this "effort" or "force." From his steady use of formulas he knew that the energy put into a machine is never more than that gotten out of it. Although his formulas emphasized the equality of input and output, in the real situation the energy output is usually less if one measures only the useful energy (the effect one is looking for, like how high the crowbar will raise the rock), and does not measure the energy converted into heat through friction or lost due to the resistance of the air through which the object is moving.

Later on, when he was considering this energy component of his conceptual scheme, he realized that he could ask the children to think about the various types of energy involved. There is muscle energy in using the lever, which is changed into mechanical energy or energy of motion—the lift. There is the mechanical energy due to gravity added to the muscle energy of the man who pulls down on the pulley in order to lift the hayload up against the pull of gravity. (The pulley helps the man use his muscles as if they were stronger.) And, of course, there is the basic idea that energy is conserved. Bob had always asked his children to consider the relationship between the long pull on the compound pulley rope that resulted in a short movement of the hayload and the total equivalence of the energy expended and used. The next time he taught the unit on photosynthesis, he planned to bring in the role of the sun's energy in the formation by green plants of starch which is eaten by the man working on the pulley, converted to his muscle energy, and then to the mechanical lifting of the hay.

When he came upon the gravity link halfway through his concept seeking and concept forming, he was bothered because gravity *seemed* to act like a form of energy. But he had read somewhere that the nature of gravity and its relation to the whole spectrum of energy was still an unsolved problem of science. Einstein had worked on this for a number of years and never succeeded in finding a relationship. Hundreds of physicists since Einstein have been working on the electromagnetic phenomenon of energy and, even now, very few are concentrating their investigations on gravity. It would be good to tell the children about this unsolved science problem.

The aspect which gave Bob Fotheringay the most difficulty was relating the different kinds of motion manifested through the application of pull or push, relating the kinds of evidences of work done. Work can be manifested in the strict scientific sense if a body is set in motion after being at rest, if a body moving slowly is speeded up or a fast-moving body is slowed down, if a body moving in one direction is set off in another direction. He was thinking about all of these types of motion when the visual memory of children being jets produced the sudden insight, the click which jelled the floating concepts and data. For Bob, "change in direction" had a hidden likeness to "vectors."

An example: the concept of vectors

What are vectors? Vectors are quantities which have two components: They involve both magnitude and direction.

"A man walks at the rate of four miles an hour." (A nonvector statement; only magnitude is mentioned.)

"A man walks at the rate of four miles an hour toward the house." (A vector statement; it has both magnitude and direction.)

"The child moved a fifteen pound package." (Nonvector)

"The child lifted the package up." (Nonvector)

"The child lifted the fifteen pound package up." (Vector)

A vector is a useful concept when one wants to consider change of direction or change of motion in the same direction. For instance, a billiard ball shot with a certain velocity (which is a vector) hits another billiard ball either at rest or in motion; they hit at a certain angle to the tangent at their point of contact. In which directions and with what speeds will the two balls move after impact? Or, we could say, along which vectors will the two balls move after impact? Children intuitively experience these factors when they play marbles. Control of input energy to produce a certain output energy is experienced kinesthetically. So are the vectors.

Bob Fotheringay gained his sudden insight that the concept of vectors was the hidden likeness among all kinds of machines while thinking about relative motion in space, not while thinking about machines. He came upon the space frame of reference because he was trying to think of a situation where input energy would be equal to output energy; in other words, he was seeking a situation where friction took only a very slight toll on the useful energy. And the space thought led him to Jennie Andersen's assembly.

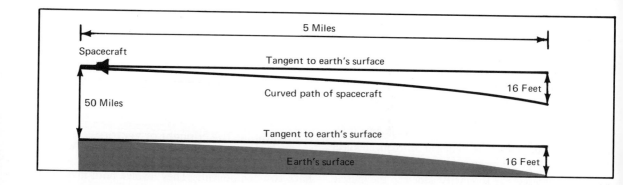

5 Miles

Spacecraft

Tangent to earth's surface

Curved path of spacecraft

16 Feet

50 Miles

Tangent to earth's surface

Earth's surface

16 Feet

An orbiting space capsule provides an interesting application of the vector concept. Let us say that the space capsule is in orbit 50 miles above the earth's surface. This path is the result of two motions which have direction and speed and are therefore vectors. A push from the launching rocket is sufficient to make the space capsule travel five miles every second in a line parallel to a tangent to the earth's surface (one vector). The interaction with gravity is sufficient to make the space capsule drop toward the earth 16 feet every second. These two vectors result in a circular orbit. As long as there is no change in motion, the vectors remain in equilibrium. This equilibrium is communicated to astronauts inside the capsule as weightlessness. If the space capsule fires its rockets away from the direction of motion, this will increase the speed—increase the vector parallel to the earth's tangent. A new equilibrium between this new vector and the one representing interaction with the earth will result in an elliptical orbit.

The hidden likeness of vectors in space and vectors in machines relates a concept to another concept and approaches a conceptual scheme. In machines, a push *down* on Bob's side of the teeter-totter became a push *up* for Jamie. Each vector was associated with a certain distance from the fulcrum and the distances moved by Bob and Jamie. Input work balanced output work. Turning the vertical rotary handle of an egg beater or a hand drill becomes a horizontal rotary of the beater blades or drill bit—a change in vectors. The nutcracker handle moves a long distance to make a short movement which cracks the nut—again, a change in vectors. The hammer of a ram starts a stationary pile moving a little way into the ground.

The two concepts behind machines relate to energy and vectors. We can now see that the energy aspect belongs squarely under Conceptual Scheme B on the chart. The preconcept statement:

Energy gotten out of a machine does not exceed the energy put into it.

is perhaps the most obvious. But this is part of a more inclusive concept:

When energy changes from one form to another, the total amount of energy remains constant.

Muscle energy becomes mechanical energy; the combustion energy of fuel becomes the energy of motion. On the complex level where a child would think of energy in terms of push and pull or fire or a falling body, the concept would be:

Energy must be used either to set an object in motion or to stop it.

Change in motion implies the vector concept, especially if the motion is related to *work* (defined as push or pull times distance which is magnitude plus direction).

Some interlocking concepts may cross over to another conceptual scheme. In Conceptual Scheme C:

Living organisms interchange matter and energy with their environment.

In our example, the environment used the muscle of man, and, of course, man's muscle energy is derived from the energy of the sun in the first place. Another relevant preconcept statement is present in Conceptual Scheme C:

The capture of radiant energy from the sun [by green plants] is basic to the growth and maintenance of all living organisms.

There are hidden likenesses between the energy and vectors related to machines and the energy and vectors of man in space.

Vectors can develop into very complicated mathematics (quaternions), but in their simpler forms they can become part of the thinking of second-grade children. Examples of building concepts of vectors with children are given in Appendix II, pages 397-98.

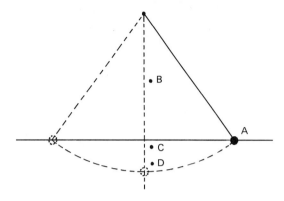

Now it's your turn A way to test whether or not you can build a concept which includes energy and vectors is to try to supply a scheme which will include all of the phenomena of the following pendulum investigation. Watch the behavior of the pendulum and then try to apply concepts of vectors and energy to what you see happening. Hang at least a yard-long pendulum, preferably from a peg-board.

Start the swing at A (see figure). How far does the weight rise on the other side? Put a peg at B so that the string catches against it as it passes. Again, start the swing at A. How far does the weight rise now? Take the peg out of B, insert it in C, and repeat the procedure. Try again with the peg at D. What happens? Try to construct a model which will explain the phenomena in terms of vectors and energy.

JENNIE ANDERSEN'S CONCEPT

A different process for acquiring a conceptual scheme was experienced by Jennie Andersen.

Prior to the weekly staff meeting at school, Mr. Archek arranged for the teachers to have a brief period of relaxation over tea and cookies. On the Monday afternoon after Bob Fotheringay's insight into his conceptual scheme problem, he sought out Mrs. Andersen to thank her for the inspiration her assembly program had given his science problem. He explained what had happened.

"I know what you went through," she replied, to his surprise. "I had a similar experience last summer."

"You did?"

"You remember I attended an institute on the new programs in science teaching?"

"Yes, you gave us a report."

"During one lecture it dawned on me that I had been giving my children a very limited experience in the field of biology, when it would have been entirely possible to enrich their thinking much more with the same amount of time and energy spent."

"I always thought bio was your *forte*. Why, I've tumbled over guinea pigs as I walked into your room, chased ducks down the corridor for you, and I recall what a splendid time Laura had in your class last year when she was allowed to take home the butterfly cage and watch the Monarch emerge from its pupa."

"With all these experiences, I realized during the institute that, although I had been exposing the children to lots of experiences, they'd gained a lot of facts. . . ."

"And danced them, written poems about them, painted them. . . ."

"Granted . . . but . . . little or no thinking!"

"Huh?"

"Everything was in isolation, except emotionally, and therefore it did bubble over into the rest of the curriculum."

"That's a whole lot already."

"Yes, but I still had a kind of anthropomorphic approach—a little sentimental, I'm afraid. I actually believed that instinct drove nesting birds to care for their eggs, that baby geese had an innate fear of hawks, and that hibernating animals knew they should stock up for winter."

"Wait a minute. Birds have no nesting instinct?"

"It seems that the more animals are studied, the more important the environment becomes in understanding their full development."

"Like children."

Why do you think Mrs. Andersen was able to build her conceptual scheme much more easily than Mr. Fotheringay built his?

"That was just it. I had this well-rounded concept about the role that the school could play in providing an environment where children could flourish emotionally, physically, and mentally . . . but somehow or other I had never transferred the concept to animals or plants, although now it seems so obvious to me."

"What's obvious?" Bob couldn't help feeling a little low that the "obvious" in his field had escaped him so long.

"You could say that I had a minor concept—if there is such a thing—about animals and plants reproducing their own kind, and another about the environment which surrounds living things making some difference in the way they grow. But what dawned on me during the summer was that any organism, because of its heredity, affects the environment as much as vice versa."

"You mean the ducks changed your children?"

"Well, that! I suppose so. But my new concept was larger than that. I suddenly realized that all living things take food and air from the environment . . . and that changes the environment . . . and then they give it back in the form of wastes . . . change again . . . and when living things die they become part of the environment. A beaver colony changes the trees and water flow in making a dam, grass holds the soil covering together, microorganisms change the food in the intestines—just about everything is an interlocking of heredity and environment. It's a great big all-embracing idea!" Jennie waved her cup of tea to demonstrate the vastness; a brown wave slopped into the saucer.

"Whoops!" said Bob, thinking, however, that the tea illustrated a vector. He said out loud, "How will your new concept affect what you are doing with your seven year olds? You won't cut out the creativity, I hope!"

"Oh, no! Instead of having the children just take experiences as they come, I can enrich observation and thinking by providing a framework of looking for differences—differences in things which through heredity are alike. For instance, instead of just collecting things on a nature walk, I thought we could look for similar plants which had differences when found under different conditions: plants which need light to grow, grow taller in the shade than they do in the full sun. Then we could notice dying or dead plants and learn that they form part of the humus for new growth. The longer a pebble's been tossing around in a stream, the smoother it is. That's not life, of course, but you find them on nature walks. And look what they do when they get caught in an eddy!"

"You mean the pothole business?"

"Sure. And then there's the whole role of earthworms. . . . It's fascinating."

"Tell me about that egg and nesting business. No instinct, huh?"

"It was Dr. Daniel Lehrman[6] and some co-workers who made the particular investigation we heard about. They mated doves and let them raise a brood. To make sure they could do it, I suppose. Then they held them three to five weeks in isolation. After that they presented the females with a nest and some eggs in it, but the birds would not sit. Even stranger, the birds did not ovulate. But when a mated male and female were presented with eggs in a nest, both birds sat on the eggs and the female ovulated. But even more strange was that if nesting materials were present in the cages before the introduction of the nest and eggs, a greater number of birds sat on the eggs when they were introduced and there was more ovulation.

"Through dissections and testing they discovered that the presence of the male actually stimulates the production of a hormone in the female, and this seems to start the whole operation."

"Fascinating! It seems that the interaction idea which we apply to physical science is also useful in bio. What about the geese?"

There were stirrings among the faculty and a general movement toward chairs. Jennie said, "I'll find the reference and give it to you." Bob and Jennie took their seats for the meeting.

When it was over, Bob had another question for Jennie. "If you are going to emphasize the interaction between environment and heredity, won't you have to do something about introducing your children to heredity? How'd you do that on a second-grade level?"

"Oh, I learned of an absolutely fascinating approach to the meaning of heredity at the workshop; it even implied the role of genes."

"Really?"

"The lesson was devised by Dr. George Tulloch, the well-known entomologist and bio professor, when he was working with Minnemast. I kept a record of the lesson, partly taped and partly noted directly after. Before I tried it, I couldn't believe it would work. I'll lend you a copy."

The next weekend, Bob had the pleasure of spending some of his time thinking about the following record, which illustrates the lesson Dr. Tulloch devised.

[6] Daniel L. Lehrman, Philip N. Brody, and Rochelle P. Wortis, "The Presence of the Mate and of Nesting as Stimulus for the Development of Incubation Behavior and for Gonadotropin Secretion in the Ring Dove (*Streptopelia risoria*)," *Readings in Animal Behavior*, Thomas E. McGill (ed.), Holt, Rinehart and Winston, New York, 1965, 206–212. Reprinted from *Endocrinology*, 1961, Vol. 68, 507–516.

LESSON ON HEREDITY[7]

Materials collected in advance:

Envelope containing poker chips; one for each child.

Envelope containing pennies with the same mint date from Denver (a D under the date); one for each child.

Box of four more pennies with assorted dates; one for each child.

Box with a Tootsie Roll for each child. I opened each roll and inserted one or more pieces of aluminum foil cut into simple geometric shapes, between the candy and the wrapper.

Two sets of rexographed sheets: one set with the outline of a Lincoln head on it (page 181) and one for recording the dates and mint of the pennies (page 182).

A stopwatch.

Courage!

Eight children.

I gave each child a blue poker chip. No instructions. The children looked at them, turned them over, dropped them, and ran their fingers over the surface.

After a few minutes, I told the children to put the chips on the right side of their desks. I asked, "What did you find out?"

George: Well, first of all, it's a chip.

Henry: It's round and blue. Poker chips come in red and white, too. My daddy uses them, and each chip is like a different piece of money.

Bertha: It twirls.

George: Both sides are exactly the same. The middle is smooth, but there are rough lines on the outside of the chip.

Henry: I've been looking at all the other chips and they're all the same.

I gave one penny to each child.

Bertha raised her hand and said, "This is interesting."

George was excited and added that this was the greatest science experiment ever.

I let them look at their pennies and then asked, "What can you tell me about the pennies I gave you?"

Heather: It's a 1961 penny.

Hindy: So is mine.

Ralph: Mine, too.

Henry: Does anyone have a penny with a different year? [*No!*] Then how come we all have the same year penny? You [*to me*] must have given them to us on purpose. It's too much of a chance that we would all get the same pennies.

I admitted that I had done this and added that it could possibly happen by chance, but that it would be very rare. I asked Stevie what he had found out.

Why is Stevie called on here?

[7] Adapted from Brenda Lansdown, " 'Family Tree' Grows in Brooklyn from Observing Coins and Candy," *Minnemath Reports*, Vol. 2, No. 3 (Summer, 1964), 6, 7, 11. And, with some additions from the original record, the article also contains a record of this same lesson taught to fourth graders.

Stevie: It has a picture of Abe Lincoln. The color is gold if it is clean and copper if it is not. The back looks like a choo-choo.

George: It's not a train; it's a train station. I knew it was a penny because it sounded like one when you dropped it while it was still in the envelope.

Ralph: It's not made of gold. All pennies are copper. The thing on the back is not a train or a station. I went to Washington and saw it. It's the Lincoln Memorial.

Claire: What does the letter under the 1961 mean?

Stevie: I have a "D" there, too.

George: We all do. It may be the name of the company that makes the pennies.

I asked if they knew who makes the coins. No one did. I explained that the United States Government made the coins, and told them about counterfeiters. George said that on TV they put the counterfeiters in jail. I told them that the "D" stood for Denver where there is a Government mint, and that there was one other mint in Philadelphia.

What is your opinion of volunteering this information?

Gary: How do you know if the "P" is for Pittsburgh, Peekskill, or Philadelphia?

Me: The only other city that has a mint is Philadelphia, but it puts no letter on the pennies.

Heather: What is that word that is spelled L-I-B-E-R-T-Y?

I told her.

Hindy: Mine has that too, and four words on the top.

Henry: They're all exactly the same; the penny is just like the chips.

Note the hidden likenesses the children find and which children find them.

I gave out the first set of rexographed sheets and asked the children to fill in the blanks. While they worked, they interchanged ideas on Lincoln.

Henry: By the way, I know where Lincoln was shot. He was at his favorite theater. He picked a good and a bad place. Do you want to hear why? [*Yes*] It was good because there were lots of people there and bad cause it was dark.

Ralph: When I was in Washington, I went to the wax museum and saw a model of the building where he was assassinated and the man, Booth, who did it.

Henry: The presidents after Lincoln were Johnson, not this one now [*1964*], and U.S. Grant. I learned that from the milk cartons.

I asked the children to stand and then had them touch the floor without bending their knees, pull their thumbs back to touch their wrists, put their right arms in front of their necks then around behind them to touch their right ears, and then spread their fingers.

Stevie: Some things I can't do and the others can, and some I can and they can't.

I asked the children to put their heads down on their desks and try to estimate when a minute had passed while I timed them with a stopwatch. The estimations ranged all the way from 25 to 130 seconds! I told each one how long his head had been down and they wanted to repeat the game again and again. I tried it myself and couldn't estimate correctly either.

George: I guess someone can, but not us.

Your name _____

Today's date _____

Rare pennies are:
1909 . . . $45
1900 . . . $10
and others.

Your name _____

Today's date _____

Penny dates

Date	Mint
1. ____	____
2. ____	____
3. ____	____
4. ____	____

Bertha: I saw a program last week where a woman always knew the exact time without a watch. That was until she fell in love, that is.

I gave four pennies to each of the children. They began to ask each other what year and mint they had. Again I asked them what they had found out.

Henry: They're all the same, except for the year and the mint letter.

I gave out the second set of rexographed sheets. The children wrote the year and mint (if any) of their pennies on the sheets. They read the years to the rest of the class. Scott said no one had the same dates.

Ralph: It would be difficult for us to get the same because there are so many different coins and so few of us.

I asked if anyone had a 1930 penny; if so, I'd give them two pennies. No one did. I said if anyone had a 1898 penny, I would give them 200 pennies. I also made offers for some other dates.

Henry: It's like my stamp collection. Rare stamps are harder to find and are worth more than common stamps are.

I gave out the Tootsie Rolls and told them they were not to eat them until we had finished with them.

Henry: They all have three segments like insects. They are roundish and long and good to eat.

Hindy: They all have different shaped foil in them. They all looked the same from the outside, but they had hidden differences inside to surprise us.

George: Please, can we eat them now?

They ate them.

Ralph: We're sort of like Tootsie Rolls. [*Laughter*] I don't mean we're candy. We're all alike and yet different, too.

Bertha: Yes, we're all about the same age.

George: We all have different color hair. My mother one day came home with black hair instead of brown, and her hair suddenly became curly.

Heather: People are born with a certain color hair.

I asked how many children had curly hair, blue eyes, etc., and wrote on the board:

Hair:	curly	1	straight	7
Eyes:	blue	2	brown	6

Stevie: My whole family has curly hair and blue eyes.

George: My father has brown hair—straight, and brown eyes. I'm like him.

Ralph: We have some things the same as our parents and sometimes we look more like our grandparents.

The next day we made genealogical trees of eye color and hair for each child's family.

Now it's your turn If you were teaching this lesson to children in any specific grade, through what activities could you build it into an even deeper understanding in follow-up sessions? Think of heredity and environment and the interaction between the two.

3

The
Architectonics
of
the
Curriculum

5

The matrix of a unit

Designing the next steps

The tidy way to plan a unit is to have a beginning and an end and a series of well-measured steps in between.

The beginning stems from our acquaintance with the children: the knowledge we have already given them, their abilities, their rates of assimilating new experiences. The end is found in our intended goals: the as yet unattained knowledge, attitudes, and skills with which we expect to endow the children (or most of them, allowing, of course, for individual differences) by the end of the unit. The series of well-measured steps is the lessons: the plans we make for each new day, the motivation, procedures, materials, and evaluations which each lesson encompasses.

We make these tidy plans in methods courses and present them to our principals in plan books, but when we face the children—well, things never seem to happen exactly as planned!

Is it good or bad that planned study units often fail to go according to Hoyle? What should be changed? The way we plan? The way we prepare the children? Our expectancies? Should we change our steps or our goals, or scrap the planned ideas altogether? This last is the most appealing, if only because it would save endless paper work! But would it save anything else?

It might be good to backtrack for a moment here, to ask why we organize science into units at all. Why not teach any good lesson that strikes our fancy or that is suggested by available materials, an intriguing article in a journal, or even by our own fertile imaginations?

We return to the principle to which this book is partisan—concept building. To build a concept, anyone must have many confrontations and experiences with related subconcepts; he must be able to perceive phenomena from a variety of perspectives; he must have a chance to talk about his observations in his own words and, preferably, interchange his viewpoints with those of his peers.

It is for the purpose of concept building that we present science ideas in units instead of in isolated one-shot lessons, however intriguing those might be. Each unit is organized around a concept and cluster of subconcepts underlying one of the major conceptual schemes. Because concepts are built by each individual according to his own idiosyncratic ways, progress along a conceptual arrow cannot be planned in a series of logical steps—in a way each child will surely follow.

The near bank, the far bank, and stepping stones

The analogy of crossing a river is useful. One bank is the known—the starting place. Each child knows where he is; the teacher, in general, knows where the class stands. The far bank is the concept, known to the teacher, but as yet *terra incognito* to the children. Between the near and far banks is the flowing, ever-changing river which must be crossed. The easiest way to reach the far bank is to walk over a bridge: the teacher plans; the children follow. Such a method is epitomized in the *Madeline*[1] books by the "Twelve little girls in two straight lines" who not only promenade together, but brush their teeth and go to bed in unison by the clock. Everyone starts together, moves together, ends together and the teacher, Miss Clavel, is always in command. The teacher plans, the children follow mechanically, without initiative—all except Madeline, of whom we will see more later! The children have changed position, adapted their behavior to a routine. But has anything else changed?

Can we grant for the moment that one purpose of education is to change children for the better?

Leaving "better" undefined, but sensed, can we say that progress in "two straight lines" has changed Madeline's companions for the better? The children are probably not even aware that they have crossed the bridge, any more than they were aware of the other rigid routines in their day. Miss Clavel's way of having these children cross the Seine is very tidy: it is planned; it achieves its goal; it proceeds according to Hoyle. (You are probably naming this rote learning. We agree!) And something *has* happened to the children; they have adapted their behavior to the teacher's leadership. How well is this adaptation sustained?

Adaptive behavior.

↓

Sustained adaptation?

The book tells us.[2] As soon as the twelve little girls are out of their teacher's sight (which is only when everyone is in bed), anarchy breaks loose. The disorderly break in the plan disturbs Miss Clavel's sleep. The teacher acts with efficiency, dispatch, and, surprisingly for such an authoritarian figure, with great kindness. Order, the *status quo*, is restored. The plan triumphs.

There are other "planned" ways to cross the river of learning—to bridge the gap from the known to the unknown bank—but ways which are planned conceptually. This river has stepping stones, a few large ones and many little ones; the small stones form wandering, branching patterns that eventually converge on the bigger stones. The children hop from one small stone to another, each child following his own pattern—absorbed, purposeful, and spontaneous. The teacher stands on the next large stone and from time to time gathers the children around him. Then they hop away again along their chosen routes to the next big stone. And when they finally reach the opposite bank, they have viewed it from many different angles, perceived it from several vantage points. They have moved toward the far bank along conceptual arrows —they have chosen their paths meaningfully—and something has changed inside each child—for the "better." Learning has taken place.

Through an interpretation of this analogy, we can

---

[1] Ludwig Bemelmans, *Madeline* (1939), *Madeline's Rescue* (1953), *Madeline and the Bad Hat* (1957), *Madeline and the Gypsies* (1959), *Madeline in London* (1961), The Viking Press, New York.

[2] Ludwig Bemelmans, *Madeline's Rescue,* The Viking Press, New York, 1953.

answer questions about the plans which seemingly went astray.

The unit does have a beginning; it is where we stand on the near bank with our current knowledge, our *terra firma* from past crossings. The unit does have an end; it is a concept or, rather, some new point along a conceptual arrow for each child. And there are some large stepping stones in between: the subconcepts, the chosen activities, the topics, and the sets of possible materials whose manipulation may lead children toward the concept. But the stones are not in an ordered series; rather, they form a matrix: there are many possible ways to cross them. These large stones may be the points made in a textbook unit, the concepts and activities within a conceptual scheme. Or they may be the possible concepts and activities suggested in program booklets for the teacher with no written material for the children. Or they may be activities and aims listed in curriculum guides. They are indeed landing points on the way across the river. These large stones can be selected in advance—in the sense of statistical probability. One or another set of stones may evoke the children's interest; these sets, may be related in concept, but wander in different eddies. In between each stone there is that chaos—the lesson itself! Since chaos has an unpredictable course—the way children use the materials, the data and explanations they bring up during the colloquium, the surprises of interest—no teacher can write a detailed plan in advance.

We recall, too, that concepts are built from a sea of chaos. But the chaos is not absolute; it is composed of many related facts and phenomena from which a pattern, or a trend, or a new relationship can be woven. Each individual does his own weaving, as he thinks and speaks about his experience, as he shares his thoughts and listens to the statements of others, and as the teacher throws problems back to the children for further thought and investigation.

So we plan. We choose the concept; we select the matrix of possible subconcepts; we find the materials which are structured to evoke the related phenomena. We survey the *likely* choices of large stepping stones, but we leave unselected the little ones which evoke and sustain the interest of the learners.

Adaptive behavior → Sustained adaptation The children first evidence learning by manifesting adaptive behavior: they relate to the materials with interest. The interest is sustained since the children continue to explore the materials without direct leadership from the teacher or, rather, without authoritative domination. Their learning is self-initiated within the structure or framework of crossing from one large stepping stone to the next. The chaos of the lesson—the unexpected events, the acts of each individual—is patterned; the total chaos has a statistical average of motion. It is very much as though the lesson itself were movements of gas molecules in a jar—individually chaotic, but collectively limited, predictable, planned.

One more type of event may occur as a class of

children crosses the river via either the bridge or the stepping stones: the act of the nonconformist. Probably the best explanation of why the Madeline books are never resting on library shelves is that Madeline arouses in each reader the desire to initiate behavior, the drive to act as one feels, the courage to flout the rules of authority. Madeline is the youngest, the nonconformist, the one who breaks the routine:

> And nobody knew so well
> How to frighten Miss Clavel.[3]

She gets lost, nearly drowns, has an appendectomy. She crosses the Seine by walking along the parapet of the bridge! This is indeed self-initiated behavior, found in even the most routinized classrooms.

Adaptive behavior → Sustained adaptation → Initiating behavior Self-initiated behavior is also found on the stepping stones. A child may hop beyond the large stone where the teacher waits; a child may go back to the original bank or even further down the river to another set of stones, that is, into another matrix. Of course the teacher can call the child back; he can say, "We don't do it this way." or "Please stay on the topic." or "That's for another lesson." Divergent behavior, original thinking, the awkward question, the strange remark, the unorthodox way of doing things can be labeled *creativity* or *sabotage* or both. Of course, we enjoy and cherish the atypical act, encouraging it to realize its fullest potential without allowing it to disrupt the classroom. Later we will discuss how one of the evaluative points of a lesson can be the number of children who manifest initiating behavior, who feel free to go beyond sustained adaptation and, of course, far beyond their first adaptive behavior.

Matrices for some *Starting Tomorrow* lessons

As we have seen, the matrix of a unit is related to a conceptual scheme which embraces concepts, subconcepts, and topics; it is also related to children who have specific ranges of intellectual background. Units, therefore, may be presented at different conceptual levels: they can lead toward an understanding of subconcepts on complex or preconceptual thinking

levels; for older children, they can lead more directly to full concepts. We have said that whether a statement represents a concept or a subconcept is an arbitrary designation, a relative arrangement; however, all levels of a concept may be subsumed under one of the more grandiose conceptual schemes (see chart on page 166).

Freely and individually manipulated materials are the vehicles which lead children toward one subconcept or another; the colloquium is the vehicle which reveals the interests, the problems, and directions of the investigations and then converts preverbal learning into clarified thought.

For both the children and the teacher, completely free investigation of concrete materials is the starting point. If children have had very little teacher-directed learning, they will respond quickly to a science lesson which offers structured materials. But the longer a child has been accustomed to having an adult tailor his life and/or his schoolwork, the more extended his free experience with the materials must be before he has the courage to move from adaptive behavior to sustained adaptation, and it will be longer still before he dares some initiating behavior—unless he is a Madeline! A teacher who has never allowed children to manipulate structured materials freely may also need several such experiences himself before this kind of lesson becomes a convinced habit. Hence, our *Starting Tomorrow* lessons earlier were fully free investigations with materials which advocated a strictly "hands off" and, above all, "voice off" policy for the teacher.

After one or more colloquia, however, we find that children usually begin to furnish their own suggestions about what they wish to do with the materials "next time." We saw how Mr. McIver's children planned their work for a follow-up lesson (page 56). More and more, colloquia channel the thinking of individuals and promote patterns of behavior, unique drives, or vectors of investigation. Such drives or patterns were revealed through the colloquia following Zach Gottfried's lessons on magnets (pages 88-94). We can say then that a personal suggestion for investigation becomes part of the structure—part of the interactive system of child and objects. Psychologists view this bringing of knowledge, desire, and awareness to a situation as an

[3]*Ibid.*

apperceptive base, a necessary condition for cognitive learning.

Going a step further, we might say that a child, after becoming profoundly interested in some materials and/or in a colloquium, borrows a library book and reads of an investigation pertinent to the unit which he would like to try. The chances are that the book gives not only the how-to-do, step-by-step procedure, but also the what-to-expect—the outcome. This is usually true of most television programs for children which suggest home "experiments." Much as we may deplore this "cookbook" guide to science learning, it is with us even when we are not *with it!* We have found, however, that when a child asks to do an "experiment" from a book or from a TV presentation in the context of the discovery-colloquium science structure, he usually considers the directives of such an "experiment" flexible and open-ended. After all, he freely chose the book and selected the "experiment"; he found the freedom in class to follow his inclination. Moreover, he probably forgot the book's or the program's outcome and adapted its procedures to his own desires! Such choice can well be considered sciencing—repeating and adapting the investigations of a colleague!

As will be seen later in Chapter 7, we consider books and other learning aids to be essential to science learning, *but the explanations and suggestions must follow experiences with materials, at least until a reservoir of experiences has been acquired.* Words have meaning when they are brought to an apperceptive base. They enrich when they extend existing knowledge. Words written in books chosen by the child are likely to have meaning to him just as words spoken in a colloquium have meaning—because they also are brought to an apperceptive base. We are saying that suggestions, guides, parallel investigations, *when selected by the child as an outgrowth of his own experiences and thoughts*, are not harmful; indeed, at times, they serve as essential roadsigns along the various conceptual arrows. If there is freedom of choice to do or not to do, then the suggestions, guides, and an investigator's own drives may be considered *part of the structure.*

In a similar vein, a teacher may make "suggestions." Does this seem to negate our principle of free discovery? Not if considered in the proper context.

Let us suppose that a small child, seeing a lion or a puma at the zoo, says, "Kitty!" "Why does he remind you of Kitty?" would be a proper, thought-provoking question. And when that has been answered in whatever way the child chooses, a follow-up question could well be, "In what way is he different from your Kitty?" It is almost as though these were redirective questions during a colloquium. Again the child has the apperceptive base; he found the hidden likeness (or maybe he only perceived the external likenesses). He is free to answer or not answer the questions. And his answers are accepted as stated.

A voiced suggestion is more imperative than a written one. In general we favor suggestions, where appropriate, written on cards and left with the materials. Just as a child is free to use some of the materials and not others, he is free to use or not use the **Suggestion Card**. Again, it must be emphasized that suggestions are part of the *follow-up* procedure, after the children are in the habit of freely investigating, choosing what they wish to contribute to colloquia themselves, and making their own models.

When you find a suggestion card with a set of materials, you might like to analyze the nature of the suggestion: Is it fully open-ended, with many possible answers? Does it prepare the child for some scientific procedures? In what way does it make an essential contribution to the structure of the materials?

Thus, the whole matrix from which specific units may be chosen or developed consists of sets of materials which are structured around some major concept; these sets of materials may or may not include suggestion cards. No concept, however, stands alone; it is interrelated with a number of other concepts. No class of children stays strictly within one narrow investigative range, much less within the limits of one concept. We will find that, although the sets of materials chosen may *center* around a major concept, implications that other concepts may be brought in—indeed, may be germane—will be present. At times, a teacher may wish to search for sets of materials within an allied matrix to expand the directions his children's thoughts are taking. He may find that booklets or textbooks will offer suggestions for follow-up activities once the development has taken place in the initial lesson. So we regard these matrices as guides, suggestions—*a few choices* to be changed, extended, developed as colloquia suggest. Many teachers substitute more easily obtainable materials for some of those we list; other teachers combine these science units with study in another subject area.

With these provisos in mind, we will now describe some follow-up matrices for a few of the *Starting Tomorrow* lessons and give a few examples of how units have been built from each matrix (see also chart on page 191).

Matrices 1-5 and 7 extend the physical science lessons described in the section *Starting Tomorrow*. They have the following organization:

a. **Vygotsky level of thought** appropriate for the follow-up matrix.

b. **The near bank**—*prior understandings* which are assumed or should be listened for in the children's oral expressions.

c. **The far bank**—*points along the conceptual arrows* which children might be expected to approach as a result of engaging in the unit.

d. **Stepping stones:**

Sets of *materials* from which the teacher may choose.

Expected child activity in relation to the materials offered.

The next sections differ for the matrices on physical and biological sciences. The rationale for the differences is explained on pages 236-37. For matrices on the physical sciences:

e. **Models for the teacher**—ways the teacher may think and talk about the *phenomena* encountered in the matrix as a whole. This section gives the science background of the matrix related to the concepts involved. Portions of the Chart of Conceptual Schemes (page 166) which apply are excerpted. Acceptable scientific terminology is introduced.

f. **Potential models for the children**—direction of conceptual arrows given for each set of materials. The objects in the system which the children may select or refer to are listed here for quick reference. The phenomena to be perceived are followed by the ways in which children might be expected to express models

and the ways the teacher may help to advance the children's conceptual growth.

Matrix 6 (*Physical Interactions*) suggests that the reader try to construct a matrix on the phenomena of the phases of matter.

Matrix 8 (the biology of *Mealworms*) attempts to help the teacher think about the relevant concepts from a different angle and to guide the children's conceptual development along comparable lines. The matrix emphasizes that, in the biological sciences, first data is sought and then patterns are found, whereas the patterns in the physical sciences are more apparent and are followed by model making which explains them. (Again, see rationale on pages 236-37.) Hence the next sections for the biological sciences emphasize data collecting and pattern finding. For Matrix 8 on mealworms the sections are a-d as in matrices 1-5 and the following:

e. **Models and patterns for the teacher**—ways to think and talk about the *data* encountered in the matrix as a whole. The data which might be expected from observation of the materials are given and the patterns which relate these data are outlined. The models suggest some of the modern thinking about the patterns.

f. **Potential patterns and problems for the children**—direction of conceptual arrows. For each set of materials, the observable data are given and the patterns which the children might become aware of as they find relationships among the data during the colloquium are suggested. The patterns usually raise problems which need further investigation; hence this last section is devoted to problems which suggest follow-up activities.

Most of the matrices end with a section on sample ways teachers have used or could use each matrix to teach specific units.

Although the matrices in this chapter center on the materials used for discovery and the conceptual arrows that can develop during the colloquia, it is assumed that books and audio-visual aids will also be made available for the children to use freely. A list of books and other learning aids suitable for each matrix can be found in the Children's Bibliography.

CHART OF CONTENT AND ORGANIZATION OF MATRICES FOR *STARTING TOMORROW* FOLLOW-UPS

MATRIX TITLE	SUBSECTIONS	TEACHING METHOD EMPHASIZED	SAMPLE UNIT(S) DERIVED FROM MATRIX
1. Air (Gas) Is Matter	a. Vygotsky level of thought. b. Near bank—prior understandings. c. Far bank—points along conceptual arrows. d. Stepping stones: Materials and expected child activity. e. Models for the teacher with excerpts from Chart of Conceptual Schemes (page 166). f. Potential models for the children.	FREE DISCOVERY (with occasional Suggestion Cards) and COLLOQUIUM. Bibliography offers opportunities to extend learning through books and audio-visual aids.	Miss T. and first graders; Mr. F. and third graders.
2. Gases and Heat Energy			Mrs. K. and sixth graders.
3. Gases and Mechanical Energy			Brief suggestions.
4. Liquid-Solid Interactions			Mrs. de V. and third graders.
5. Chemical Interactions			Brief suggestions.
6. Physical Interactions	Reader Activity: Construct a matrix on the phases of matter.		
7. Electrical Interactions	As for matrices 1–5.	As for matrices 1–5.	No suggestions because the children's interests can be followed quite simply from the matrix.
8. Mealworms	a–d as for matrices 1–5. e. Models and patterns for the teacher. f. Potential patterns and problems for the children.	As for matrices 1–5.	Miss Y. and fourth graders.

Units in physical science

Matrices to follow *What's Inside?*

The *What's Inside?* lesson (page 7) had two parts: one showed that air is a real substance, a part of matter; the other emphasized ways in which a scientist can find out about phenomena which he cannot contact directly—by making the matter do something that reveals its existence to the senses. The Black Box Investigations by M.E. Batoff (see Teacher's Bibliography, Section II E.) are splendid extensions. We will concentrate on the *air is matter* aspect here and develop three matrices for which *What's Inside?* could be the first lesson.

MATRIX I: AIR (GAS) IS MATTER

For children at the complex level of thinking.

The near bank—prior understandings.

Children should have had some practice in naming objects (things made of matter—actually composed of molecules—in contrast to things that are not: a button vs. happiness, snow vs. a smile, water vapor vs. an idea). It would be helpful if the children had been previously introduced to the practice of naming objects in a system, such as the elements in a set, "the materials I used," "the objects in our aquarium."

If children hear the teacher use the word *interaction* and are encouraged to use it themselves to describe that objects in a system have changed, it furthers the thinking which takes place during the colloquium.[4]

If the words *object, system,* and *interaction* are

[4] The ways of looking at and describing phenomena through the use of the terms "object," "system," and "interaction" have been well illustrated in six books developed by Robert Karplus, initiator of the SCIS (Science Curriculum Improvement Study) program and published by the University of California at Berkeley, 94720. Pertinent here are *Material Objects, Interaction and Systems,* and *Subsystems and Variables.* All have teacher and student editions as well as materials kits. Rand McNally in Chicago is the distributor of the new editions and titles.

understood beforehand, it greatly facilitates the progress of this unit, but, if necessary, they can be learned as the unit progresses. Although the children may not be able to distinguish the word *object* from abstract nouns like love or happiness, it is assumed that they have had experience in examining the properties of objects and even in naming them.[5] The nub of this unit is that air—a gas—is matter (made of molecules); it is an object which can be perceived by the senses and, therefore, is similar to the concrete objects the children have handled, seen, described, named.

The far bank—points along conceptual arrows toward an understanding that:

1. Matter has properties which can be detected by the senses.
2. Gases are a form of matter (objects).
3. There are different kinds of gases.
4. Air is an object (matter).
5. In a closed system, the total amount of matter remains unchanged.
6. Matter is made of tiny particles in constant motion.

[5] Suggestions for such activities are described on pages 270-71.

Stepping stones:

INTRODUCTION: Same as *What's Inside?* lesson. (Order of use of the following sets of materials is arbitrary.)

MATERIALS	EXPECTED CHILD ACTIVITY
A Perfume on a small piece of cheese cloth. A banana and an onion, each wrapped in cheese cloth. Each item is hidden in a separate berry basket and each basket is wrapped in double layers of cheese cloth. (These objects can also be	Sniff, discuss, identify.

MATERIALS	EXPECTED CHILD ACTIVITY

placed in small paper lunch bags; seal each bag with a rubber band and punch large needle holes in it to let the odor escape.) An open bottle of ammonia in the room, screened from view.

If the children are likely to recognize the odors of vanilla, cocoa, and/or cinnamon, these items can be placed in other berry baskets (or paper bags).

If three different odors are involved, children can be grouped in threes and each given a different odor to smell; this arrangement suggests exchanging. If there are six odors, then six children may be grouped together.

B Children sit four at a table. There are four pinwheels and soda straws, a tube from a roll of paper towels and one from a toilet roll, and two plastic funnels on the table.

Children blow through straws, funnels, and tubes to try to make the pinwheels whirl. Some swoop pinwheels through the air.

C Aquarium tank or clear plastic basin. Three or four children around each, according to size of vessel. Plastic tumbler, soda bottle, straws, sponge around each vessel.

Children blow through straws into water; see bubbles. They hold bottles under water so that air bubbles escape. Plastic tumblers may be lowered into water to trap air. Sponge is squeezed under water.

Suggestion Card:
"Try to make air visible."

D Three balloons, filled until six inches in diameter: one with helium, one with air, and one with Freon-12.

Children toss balloons and note differences in "feel" and reactions.

Teacher preparation

Helium balloons are sold at circuses, zoos, and similar places. It is difficult for most teachers to find access to a helium tank. Freon-12 comes in a pressurized can, with an adaptor for balloon filling.[6] Care must be taken in filling a balloon with Freon-12 not to let the liquid touch the hands. (It is like coming in contact with an ice cube tray taken from the freezer.) One inserts the adaptor into the neck of a balloon which has been stretched with a pump and presses the nozzle sideways. It is recommended that one keep the can upright, but in practice it is often easier to tip it downward; this, however, may let some liquid into the balloon. Freon-12 quickly becomes a gas at room temperature so wait for any liquid accidentally poured into the balloon to become gas before giving the balloon to a child. All of the balloons should be filled only until they are each about six inches in diameter.

Six balloons, two with each gas, may be optimum in any classroom. Children take turns playing with the balloons until everyone has had a chance.

E For each group of four children, a quart plastic "turkey" bag is sealed with a cork and a zinc thimble. Each bag contains ½ ounce (15 cc) of Freon-11.[7] Air is squeezed out of the bags. Bags are "served" on aluminum plates covered with ice cubes.

Children handle the bags. As they warm, they fill with gas. Children return them to the ice to watch them contract.

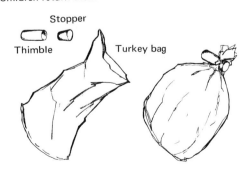

Stopper

Thimble   Turkey bag

[6] Freon-12 with adaptor may be obtained from American Science and Engineering, Inc., 20 Overland Street, Boston, Mass. 02215 (617-262-6500).

[7] Turkey bags, thimble, cork, and Freon-11 are all obtainable from American Science and Engineering, Inc. Materials are also supplied with the kit and booklets for the unit on *Subsystems and Variables*, Science Curriculum Improvement Study (SCIS), Rand McNally, P.O. Box 7600, Chicago, Ill. 60680.

Freon-11 gives the same cold, "burning" feeling that Freon-12 does and should not be allowed to touch the skin. Thus, we use the strong, safe plastic "turkey" bags provided commercially. Freon-11 is also poured from a pressurized can by pressing the nozzle sideways; pour into a graduated medicine cup until it is half full. Then quickly tip this liquid into the turkey bag, squeeze the air out, and seal the bag by gathering the neck end in a loose twist and then pushing the twisted neck of the bag firmly into the thimble with the cork.

MATERIALS

F While the children are working with the materials in **E**, place on each table a small basin of hot water and a flexible 100 ml graduated cylinder on a firm base[8] with 20 cc of Freon-11 and 20 cc of colored water in it. Have the room well ventilated.

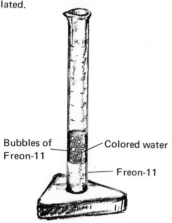

Bubbles of Freon-11 — Colored water

— Freon-11

EXPECTED CHILD ACTIVITY

Children watch liquids in cylinder separate into colored water on top and "another liquid like water" on bottom. Slowly, the "bottom" liquid (Freon-11) bubbles through the colored water on top.

Warming the cylinder with the hands speeds the bubbles. Warm water speeds the inflation of the "turkey" bags from **E**, as children dip their corners into the water.

G Four children at a table. Each child has a paper plate covered with a thin plastic like Saran Wrap. Each plate has a small amount of the following on it: onion, ammonia, water, cinnamon.

Suggestion Card:
"Which ones can you smell? Which ones disappear?"

Children discuss, compare, and name the items they have. They watch to see which ones disappear. Sniff.

---

[8] From American Science and Engineering, Inc. Only a small volume of Freon-11 should be allowed to evaporate. A firm base prevents tipping.

Models for the teacher—ways to think and talk about the phenomena encountered in this matrix:

Under Conceptual Scheme B on the chart of Conceptual Schemes (page 166): **The sum total of mass and energy in the universe remains constant**, one column emphasizes the concept of energy and another emphasizes the concept of matter. This matrix falls mostly in the latter column. We choose the relevant subconcepts shown at the right.

EMPHASIS ON MATTER

COMPLEX PRECONCEPT	
In chemical and physical changes, the total amount of matter remains constant.	
A change in the state or manifestation of matter is accompanied by a change in molecular motion.	
Matter commonly exists in solid, liquid, and gaseous forms.	
Matter has properties which can be detected by the senses.	

The relative energy and motion of molecules determine whether a substance appears as a solid, a liquid, or a gas. A solid has molecules with the least energy and the most restricted motion; a gas has molecules with the most energy and the least restricted motion. A liquid, of course, is in between the two. The free motion of molecules in a gas allows them to travel easily. When two or more gases are adjacent, diffusion or mixture occurs at the points where the two surfaces join (at the interface). In time, the gases can become thoroughly mixed: oxygen and nitrogen are mixed in the air; the molecules emanating from the substances in the berry baskets diffuse through the air to reach people's noses.

The freons are a group of substances which have recently been made available to elementary schools for use in science teaching. Freon is a synthetic. The several substances bearing this generic name are distinguished by numbers: 11, 12, 113, 122, etc. Commercially, freons are used in refrigerators and to propel paint, cosmetics, and insecticides from pressurized cans. They are nontoxic, but, to prevent *accumulation*[9] in a classroom, they should be used only with good ventilation and children should sniff cautiously.

Freon-11 is a liquid which becomes a gas at $78°$ Farenheit. Since this is below body temperature, the warmth of a hand or a warm room can make the liquid boil. A very small amount of liquid becomes a very large amount of gas, illustrating that molecules of a gas occupy a much greater volume than the same molecules do in liquid form. Freon-11 looks very much like water, but has a strong odor and is much denser. It does not form a solution with water, but a layer under it. If this lower layer is warmed, bubbles of Freon-11 gas will pass through the water on top.

Freon-12 boils at $-22°$ F and therefore is a gas at ordinary temperatures. It is much heavier than air and balloons filled with Freon-12 feel "heavy" and fall to the ground.

Just as water boils or evaporates when its molecules absorb heat energy, so the freons turn from liquids to gases when their molecules absorb heat energy. (Heat energy absorbed from the skin produces the "burning sensation.")

[9] Freons are nontoxic, but heavier than air. Too great a concentration would displace the air in the lungs.

When molecules are crowded together or given a push, they acquire mechanical energy. The increased energy of the molecules in a stream of gas may be felt on the skin or the mechanical energy may be manifested, pushing an object like a pinwheel (see **B**). It is the mechanical energy of crowded molecules which stretches a balloon filled with any gas. Large numbers of gas molecules which have absorbed mechanical or heat energy become visible as bubbles when moving through a liquid. The bubbles are seen because the gas and the liquid reflect light differently.

There are many, many different kinds of gases; air is one mixture of gases with which we are familiar. Oxygen, nitrogen, and carbon dioxide are the chief gases in air (there is a much smaller quantity of the latter than the others). Each of these gases has its own properties which can be detected by our senses or through interactions with other substances (objects). Oxygen, for instance, will make a glowing splinter burst into flame; it interacts with iron (if water is present) to form rust. Carbon dioxide (a weak acid) turns a weak solution of bromthymol (or bromothymol) blue to a greenish yellow. It also makes limewater milky: small particles of chalk (calcium carbonate) are formed from the combination of carbon dioxide and lime (calcium oxide). Not all of the above is directly pertinent to this matrix. The extended knowledge, however, may help the teacher, in turn, to extend his activities and thinking and thus build up reserves of flexibility.

Gases, as we have said, are composed of molecules which are comparatively far apart and in rapid motion. At a given temperature and pressure, the same unit volume of gases all contain the same number of molecules. Thus, if a molecule of one gas is heavier than the molecule of another gas at the same temperature and pressure, a given volume of gas composed of the heavier molecules will weigh more than the same volume of gas composed of the lighter molecules.

Assuming that the pressure under which helium, air, and Freon-12 exist in the three balloons in **D** is approximately the same, the helium balloon will feel light, the Freon-12 balloon will feel heavy, the air balloon will be in between. The helium molecule is very light, the Freon-12 molecule is about 30 times as heavy, and the average weight of the molecules composing air is in between. In relation to the air in a room, the crowded molecules in the helium balloon plus the weight of the balloon itself are still lighter than the same volume of the surrounding air. Hence, the balloon floats to the ceiling. (It is actually pushed up by the heavier air molecules.) The Freon-12 balloon not only contains much heavier molecules than the average molecules of air, but the molecules have also been *compressed* into the balloon by a pressurized can. Thus, the Freon-12 balloon sinks in air. Molecules are crowded into the air-filled balloon. Therefore, it contains more molecules per unit volume than the same volume of air does. This added to the weight of the balloon itself makes the air-filled balloon sink also, but less "heavily" than the balloon filled with Freon-12 does.

One of the plastic bags filled with half an ounce of Freon-11 in **E** forms a closed system. Nothing can enter or leave—except energy. When heat energy is transferred from a child's hand, warm water, or air to liquid Freon-11, the molecules acquire enough energy to move rapidly apart and appear to increase in volume inside the bag. All the liquid soon disappears; all the Freon-11 molecules have enough heat energy to act as a gas. The plastic bag fills out until it looks and acts like the plastic bags of air the children used in *What's Inside?*, except that it *feels* a little heavier. When one applies ice cubes to the bag of Freon-11 gas, the whole system shrinks, heat energy is transferred to the ice, and the gas become a liquid again. Matter within the system is conserved throughout these interactions.

Some substances like the onion and cinnamon in **A** lose only one kind of molecule due to heat energy; the other molecules in the substance are not released into the air.

We favor the use of the concept of interaction between or among objects in a system as a way of thinking about phenomena. Phenomena are what we see, feel, hear happening—the nature of their interaction is explained through a model. A model cannot be seen; it is an invention or creation by the thinker. Models can be constructed on many levels: a young child's model is much less sophisticated than the model a scientist makes. A model may lead to the formulation of hypotheses about "what would happen if . . ." which should then be tested in

practice. There might be a prediction before the testing. Observing and describing the phenomena, forming models, formulating hypotheses, predicting, and testing are, of course, all procedures in which scientists engage. On the child's level, these procedures constitute sciencing.

Now let us describe the phenomena expected from the interactions of the objects listed under MATERIALS, and see how we may put into words the models we can expect children to make to account for these interactions.

Potential models for the children—direction of conceptual arrows:

A *Objects in the system*: Perfume, onion, banana (cinnamon, cocoa, vanilla), ammonia, child's nose, and the air between the basket and his nose.

Phenomenon: Nose smells hidden object.

Model to describe the interaction: Small particles move from the hidden object through the air to the nose. Since we know that air is made of matter (from the plastic bag experience in *What's Inside?*), air matter must also be in small spaced particles to allow the particles of perfume, etc. to pass through it. The particles must have a motion of their own. If the children name the particles "atoms," as they frequently do, we give them the word *molecules*.

B *Objects in the system*: (1) Straw, breath, pinwheel; (2) funnel or tube, breath, pinwheel; (3) arm, air, pinwheel.

Phenomena: Pinwheel turns freely or with difficulty according to the way the air stream is delivered.

Models to describe the interaction: (1) The stream of air from the straw has more energy than the air in the rest of the room; it pushes the pinwheels. (2) When the mouth is held close to the tube or funnel, air blown through the opening fails to turn the pinwheel or turns it intermittently because the air stream is bounced around and off the tube or funnel walls. The energy is dissipated, not directed in a coherent stream. If the mouth is held some distance from the tube or funnel opening, the air stream which does enter goes straight through the tube or funnel and turns the pinwheel. It is very difficult to turn the pinwheel by blowing through the funnel. (3) The interaction of the air and the pinwheel is the same, whether the air is moving against the pinwheel or the pinwheel is moving against the air. If the children say that the air has "force," we give them the word *energy*.

C *Objects in the system*: Source of air, water, straws, chest muscles.

Phenomenon: Large and small bubbles or pockets of air appear in the water and rise.

Model to describe the interaction: A source of energy pushes the air under the water. The water pushes the air up. The air becomes visible because it reflects light differently from the way water does.

D *Objects in the system*: Balloons filled with helium, air, and Freon-12; the air in the room.

Phenomena: One balloon floats up; another falls heavily; the third stays down.

Models to explain the interaction: There is a different gas in each balloon. One gas is lighter than the same volume of air and one is much heavier. The third is slightly heavier than air. Particles of gas are crowded into the balloon and stretch it.

E *Objects in the system*: Closed system of Freon-11 in plastic bag, source of heat energy.

Phenomenon: Liquid Freon-11 changes to gas. The gas fills the bag.

Model to describe the interaction: Heat energy is transferred from the air or a warm hand to the particles of liquid Freon-11. The particles move faster, become a gas, and take up more room. There is the same amount of matter (same number of particles of Freon-11) in the system both before and after the interaction.

F *Objects in the system*: Colored water floating on Freon-11, source of heat energy.

Phenomena: Freon-11 slowly bubbles up through the water and escapes into the air. If the heat energy is increased, the bubbles appear faster.

Models to describe the interactions: At 78° Fahrenheit, the Freon-11 particles have absorbed enough energy to become a gas. Heavier than water as a liquid, freon sinks. Water is heavier per unit volume than the freon gas, so it pushes the gas bubbles up.

G *Objects in the system:* Onion, ammonia, water, cinnamon, air, and nose.

Phenomena: Ammonia disappears with a strong odor. Water eventually disappears, leaving no odor. Cinnamon and onion are detectable by their odor, but they do not disappear.

Models to describe the interactions: Sometimes all the particles of an object absorb enough heat energy to become a gas. In other objects, there must be more than one kind of particle: some can escape into the air and others cannot—at least, not with the energy normally available in the air.

Sample ways to use the matrix

1. Miss T. tried the *What's Inside?* lesson with her first graders. During the colloquium, the children seemed particularly interested in the feel of air: air against the face, the hard push back due to the air inside the plastic bag, the stream of air from a hole, the wet air from a bag which has been breathed into at length and is then squeezed suddenly against a neighbor's cheek. Miss T. asked the children if air could be seen. The children said you could see wind. "Do you see the wind or the interaction of the air with objects?" asked the teacher. The first graders were not sure. At one point in the colloquium, the children said they were sure that air was an object because you could feel it so strongly there must be something there! Miss T. then asked them if objects could be seen. Again, doubt.

Miss T. used the materials in stepping stone **C** in the next lesson. Clear plastic basins, straws, bottles, sponges, and plastic tumblers were available. Miss T. said, "Maybe today you can manage to see air by using the objects in front of you." Apart from the expected activities engaged in by most of the children, there were individual discoveries. One child used the straw as a dipper (he has tropical fish at home) and said that he could see air trapped in the top of the transparent straw when the water was in the lower half. "If there were no air, the water would come all the way up." Another child blew bubbles from a straw and caught them by holding a bottle full of water in the basin (initiating behavior). The bubbles displaced the water in the bottle. Now the children were sure they could see air . . . if it was in water.

Interest in the current science unit was still high. Miss T. chose her next set of materials from stepping stone **D**. She managed to have a balloon for each child, so that one-third of the children had balloons filled with helium (she gave all of these to girls), one-third had balloons filled wtih Freon-12 (all boys), and one-third had air-filled balloons (both boys and girls). She introduced the balloons at the end of a rhythms lesson when the children were free to move barefoot over the music room floor. Of course, surprise at the way the balloons acted prevented them from dancing to the music. But soon the boys with the Freon-12 balloons were playing a kind of football, most of the girls were dancing like fairies as they tried to hold onto or catch their helium balloons, and the girls and boys with the air balloons were trying to catch the more unusual ones that belonged to other children! The science lesson followed with some quieter investigation in groups of three.

During the colloquium, the children dismissed the helium balloon by naming it. It seemed most of them had been to the circus! They were puzzled by the heavy balloon. "It's got something different in it." "A heavy air." "Helium's a light, very light air." Miss T. gave the children the word *gas* for different kinds of air. "What is the gas in the heavy balloon?" the children wanted to know. She told them about Freon-12.

To give the children a chance to investigate a new kind of air more closely so that they could extend their understanding (there is more than one kind of heavy "air"), Miss T. started off the next science lesson with materials from stepping stone **E**. The children were excited and puzzled by the phenomena the bags of Freon-11 exhibited. Miss T. gave them a basin of hot water. They made the bags puff up and discovered that they could return them to their "empty" state again by placing them on the ice.

Of course the children were delighted when their bags puffed up with gas; they were eager to talk about why and how it happened. During the colloquium, Miss T. reminded them of the word *system* they had learned before. She asked the children to name the objects in this system. Since they named the liquid "freon" (Miss T. said, "Freon-11" and asked how it differed from Freon-12), the gas, and the plastic bag as the objects, Miss T. rephrased her question to separate the objects "before the interaction" from those "after the interaction." They were able to do this, but they were not aware that the liquid matter was the same as the gas matter. The children thought the hot water was part of their system (as indeed it was) and, when they were asked if anything had been added to the "closed system of the bag and liquid," they said "Yes, heat." Miss T. gave them the words *heat energy* which they used, but she felt they were probably thinking of heat energy as another object! The concepts behind the interaction were obviously too advanced for her six year olds. The Investigators' Log maintained throughout the unit contained these statements:

There are different kinds of air; they are gases.
Some gases are light; some are heavy. Helium is light and freon is very heavy.
Gases are objects. You can see and feel them.

Why didn't the children make any reference to heat energy?

2. Mr. F. was teaching a third grade. Toward the end of the year, he gave the *What's Inside?* lesson as an introduction to a series of experiences he hoped would grow into a study of weather. It seemed essential to him that an understanding of the nature of gases and the relative densities of warm and cold air should precede an air mass-cold front study.

The colloquium revealed to Mr. F. that his children considered air as a kind of light fluid, a homogeneous substance which could flow and push very much like a stream of water. Therefore, he decided that an emphasis on the particulate nature of matter would be appropriate and, for this, he chose the materials in stepping stone **A**.

He gave each group of four children a berry basket containing a banana, some cinnamon, perfume, and peanut butter. Then he opened a bottle of ammonia and left it in one corner of the room. The ammonia attracted most of the attention and started the colloquium. The children were able to establish the order in which groups of children noticed the odor. It was a straight line from the corner of the room. Silence! Then one child said, "Something must be coming from the ammonia bottle to us." "Bits of ammonia," said another. "What about the berry baskets?" was Mr. F.'s redirective question. "Bits must be coming from them, too." There were a number of elaborations of this theme. "If the bits move, how do they get through the air?" The children said, "*You* can get through air, so why can't tiny bits?" "Air gets out of your way when you move; it's like water when you swim, only easier." (Still the analogy with a liquid!)

"The bits you are talking about are *molecules*," said Mr. F. "Will you try to use this word and describe a model of what you think happens?"

The Investigators' Log contained these statements agreed upon by everyone:

Molecules came off the ammonia and moved through the room.
Molecules came off the banana, cinnamon, peanut butter, and perfume. We could smell these objects across the room. Molecules must have moved through the air.

Just as Mr. F. was writing down the last sentence, one quiet child came up with, "But what I want to know is why the molecules move in the first place?"

A combination of stepping stones **E** and **F** seemed indicated for the next lesson. The children had used the words *heat energy* in a previous unit, so they were able to apply it both to the phenomenon of the liquid freon becoming a gas in the turkey bag and to the gas bubbling off faster when the cylinder was heated. Of course, they had to know about the mysterious heavy liquid. The children thought the liquid in the bag behaved like "puddles and rain." They began to talk about the molecules of freon gas and freon liquid, molecules of water, and molecules of air. It seemed that substituting the word *molecules* for *bits* and verbalizing the experiences of the liquid-to-gas changes during the colloquia had emphasized the particulate nature of these forms of matter. There were no more references to gas which implied it was a continuous fluid. Mr. F. wondered if the children could extend their molecular model of gases and liquids to solids. Maybe they could with solids containing more than one kind of molecule. That was it! A variation of stepping stone **G** seemed to be the solution.

A drop of ammonia, a drop of salt solution, and a tiny piece of peanut butter were placed on each child's plate. A Suggestion Card at each table of three or four children read: "What can you do to make the objects on your plates disappear fast?" The children blew on them, put their plates in the sun, waved a note book back and forth over them.

The colloquium produced statements that some objects did not disappear at all, but you could still smell them so they must have more than one kind of molecule in them! That was true of the water drop—it was salty. Salt was left after the water had gone.

It seemed time to draw some threads together and to present them to the class. "Some of you have described a model of a solid—peanut butter—as being made of molecules; some of you said that molecules escape from a liquid like Freon-11 or ammonia; some of you said the molecules were in the air. You also said that heat energy made the molecules move faster and that then some escaped from the solids or escaped from the liquids. Can you describe a model which would account for the different ways molecules behave, say, in ice, water, and steam?"

There were some suggestions along the conceptual arrows of molecular motion and energy, but only from a few children. Mr. F. said that they might enjoy reading about the way scientists think of molecules. He told them they would find some good descriptions in Unit 4 on "The form of things" in *Concepts in Science 3,* [10] and in Chapter 3, "Molecules of Matter," in *Science in Your Life 4,* [11] and in a few library books on the classroom shelves. The children eagerly read parts of the books and it seemed that everyone wanted to try out some of the suggested investigations. Avid investigations were soon underway in pairs and small groups, even individually. By the end of a month the colloquia, having pooled the results of the many separate investigations, showed considerable clarity on the molecular nature of matter.

What happened to the weather unit? The year was over. Maybe in the fourth grade? Anyway these children now had good backgrounds to use in coping with air densities and cold fronts!

[10] Brandwein *et al.,* Harcourt Brace Jovanovich, Inc., New York, 1966.
[11] Herman and Nina Schneider, D. C. Heath, Lexington, Mass., 1965.

MATRIX 2: GASES AND HEAT ENERGY

For children at the preconceptual level of thinking.

The near bank—prior understandings.

Children need to know that matter is made of tiny particles (molecules) which are in constant motion and that matter can appear in a solid, liquid, or gaseous state. If the children do not use the terms *system* and *interaction*, they can be introduced to them during the unit.

The far bank—points along conceptual arrows toward an understanding that:

1. When gas absorbs heat energy, it takes up more space.

2. When a gas gives up heat energy (transfers it to another system), the gas contracts.

3. When a liquid absorbs heat energy (when energy is transferred to it from another system), it changes to a gas and takes up much more space.

4. Cold air is heavier than hot air. Cold air sinks and pushes hot air up.

5. Heat energy can be changed to mechanical energy. Some children will be able to describe expansion and contraction of gases in terms of the relative motion of molecules. Certainly, the more mature children can be expected to use the molecule model.

Stepping stones:

INTRODUCTION: Same as *What's Inside?* lesson in order to establish that air is an object and that moving air interacting with a solid object moves the object.

MATERIALS

A For every four or five children, a basin of very hot water and a basin of ice cubes. For each child, a soda bottle with a small balloon stretched over its mouth. The balloons have been stretched by inflating them with a pump. A few spare balloons and sources for more hot water and ice should be available.

EXPECTED CHILD ACTIVITY

Children place bottles alternately in hot water and ice. They observe that the balloons stand up stretched when the bottles are in hot water and that they are pushed into the necks of the bottles when they are on ice.

B For every three children, three soda bottles of different sizes: small, medium, and large. Bottles have been kept in the refrigerator. A small balloon is stretched over the mouth of each bottle immediately after it is taken from the refrigerator (or an insulated bag).

Children notice that the bottles are cold. They hold their hands around them. The balloons begin to inflate. Sometimes the children hasten the warming process by placing the bottles on a radiator or in the sun. Children notice that some balloons inflate more than others.

MATERIALS

C For groups of four or five children, a soda bottle for each child. Some bottles were taken from the refrigerator before being capped with balloons, some were taken from the radiator before being capped, and some were capped at room temperature. A basin of very hot water and a basin of ice cubes for each group.

D For each child: a large plastic tube open at both ends[12] with a balloon stretched over one end of the tube; a one-inch piece of birthday candle stuck in some oil-base clay. One matchbox per table is distributed after appropriate warnings to tie back braids and ties and to strike the matches away from one's body.

EXPECTED CHILD ACTIVITY

Children place bottles alternately in the ice and hot water and show great surprise at the varying results. They take off and replace balloons and still find no consistent results.

Children light the candles and place the tubes over them, pushing the tubes down into the clay. They watch the balloons bulge. They remove the tube, repeat the activity and watch the balloon inflate *less*.

E For each child: a plastic tube,[12] a one-inch piece of birthday candle in oil-base clay. A flexible rubber square.[13] One matchbox per table after warning as in **D**.

Children light their candles, and hold rubber squares over the mouths of the tubes. They watch the rubber become depressed. They repeat the activity, pressing their hands over the tube mouths. They watch the clay bulge into the tubes and feel the skin of their hands pushed into the tubes.

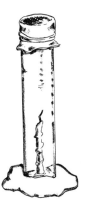

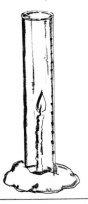

---

[12] The plastic tubes are 6 in. long and 1 ⅛ in. in diameter, obtainable from the Webster Division of McGraw-Hill. Order code: ES0213. Tube investigations are from the booklet *Gases and Airs* prepared by the Education Development Center, Newton, Mass. and published by the Webster Division of McGraw-Hill.

[13] From the Webster Division of McGraw-Hill. Order code: ES0223.

MATERIALS

F For every four children, a sealed quart turkey bag with half an ounce of Freon-11. (See Materials in stepping stone **E** in Matrix 1, page 193.) An aluminum plate of ice cubes and a small basin of warm water.

G Each child makes an air-current detector.

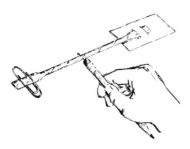

H A metal spinner[14] placed on the bare light bulb of a reading lamp. (One of these in the room.)

[14] *Classroom Laboratory 2*, Hy Ruchlis, Harcourt Brace Jovanovich, Inc., New York, 1966, 57.

EXPECTED CHILD ACTIVITY

Children take the bag off the ice; it inflates, faster when they dip a corner in warm water. They place the bag back on the ice. The activity is repeated several times.

Use it near warm or cold regions in the room (see diagram at left). Flap rises in warm regions; sinks in cold regions.

Children take turns turning on the electric switch and watching the spinner. When light is turned off, spinner slows to a stop.

Models for the teacher—ways to think and talk about the phenomena encountered in this matrix:

Again, gases and heat energy fall under Conceptual Scheme B on the chart (page 166), but this time, for the most part, in the column which emphasizes energy. We have seen, however, that units derived from one matrix may move into allied areas and require a consideration of other concepts. Where appropriate, we will discuss these. The most relevant concepts for this matrix are:

CONCEPTUAL SCHEME B

The sum total of mass and energy in the universe remains constant.

EMPHASIS ON ENERGY

PRECONCEPT

A loss or gain in energy affects molecular motion.

A change in the state or manifestation of matter is accompanied by a change in molecular energy.

Energy can change from one form to another.

The models for the teacher described in Matrix 1, *Air (Gas) is Matter*, also apply to Matrix 2. Please reread pages 194-96 if you feel in need of the background. In addition, here we will re-emphasize certain features which apply particularly to this matrix.

When molecules absorb heat energy they not only move faster, but they also take up more space. We say that a gas expands when heated. An experience which helps children grow along this conceptual arrow is the molecule dance to maracha accompaniment described in the lesson given by Mrs. Jennie Andersen (page 158). As a gas expands, its molecules move faster and farther away from each other: the gas becomes less dense; it weighs less per unit volume than it did in its cooler state. These concepts form the basis for models which explain winds, clouds, and other weather phenomena. The same principles apply to liquids and solids, and suggest models which help to explain such phenomena as ocean currents and why pouring hot water on the metal cap of a glass jar loosens it.

When matter is free to move, its interaction with gravity is such that the denser materials settle below the less dense materials. All matter is subjected to a gravitational interaction with all other matter, but the strength of the interaction of small masses of matter with the comparatively huge mass of the earth results in the small pieces of matter moving toward the center of the earth. No matter, then, has an inter-action with the earth *per se* which pushes the object away from the earth. In a system consisting of the earth and some matter, there is a movement toward, never a rising away from. So why does a helium-filled balloon fly up? There is another object in this system: the air. The air, being the denser, settles below the helium; it interacts more strongly with the gravity of the earth than the helium does. Since the air is settling nearer the earth, *it pushes the helium up*. Similarly, hot air does not rise; cold air sinks and pushes hot air up! Cold water sinks and pushes hot water up. Water sinks and pushes bubbles of air up. Warm air being pushed up by gravitational energy can come in contact with a solid which is free to move and push it (the metal spinner in stepping stone **H**). There can be interaction among various types of

energy: gravitational energy can be changed to mechanical energy; gravitational energy interacts with the various densities of gases produced by heat energy.

Perhaps a good way to think about the exchange of energy is to consider molecules of one system contiguous with (interfacing with) the molecules of another system which is transferring or sharing the energy. All energy in a system or in various sub-systems must be accounted for. The total amount of energy in a system remains constant, just as the total amount of matter in a system remains constant. In this concept we exclude the change of matter into energy and vice versa which takes place in nuclear reactions.

Potential models for the children—direction of conceptual arrows:

A *Objects in the system*: A closed subsystem of the bottle, air, and a small balloon capping the bottle opening, another subsystem of hot water, and a third subsystem of ice. Children's energy to transfer one subsystem to another.

Phenomena: Balloon inflates when bottle is in hot water, or is pushed inside the neck of the bottle when bottle is in ice water.

Models to describe the interaction: Heat energy from the water is transferred to the glass and thence to the air inside the bottle. The molecules of air inside the bottle move faster, take up more space, and push into the balloon. This model suggests the *hypothesis* that the system is *expanding, not* that the hot air is *rising* into the balloon. A prediction would be that if the bottle and inflated balloon are turned upside down, the balloon would remain inflated. *Test:* Turn the bottle upside down.

When the subsystem of bottle, air, and balloon are placed in the ice cubes, energy from the warmer bottle subsystem is transferred to the ice which then melts (its molecules move fast enough to be in a liquid instead of a solid state). The air molecules within the bottle slow down, take up less space. The free warmer molecules of the air outside the balloon push into the neck of the bottle. The balloon marks the interface between the warm and cold air.

B *Objects in the system*: Three closed subsystems: small, medium, and large bottles of similar shape capped with small balloons; cold air inside bottles. A subsystem of warm room air.

Phenomena: Balloon on small bottle inflates slightly; balloon on medium bottle inflates more; balloon on large bottle inflates most.

Model to describe the interaction: There are more molecules in the large bottle than in the small one. If each molecule in each subsystem absorbs the same amount of energy, the greater number of molecules will require more space to accommodate the increased motion. If all the *balloons* are the same size, the balloon on the larger bottle will inflate more than the balloons on the two smaller bottles.

C *Objects in the system*: Three subsystems consisting of soda bottles capped with small balloons; each subsystem has air at a different temperature in the bottle. Subsystems of ice and hot water. Children's energy transferring bottle subsystems to hot and cold subsystems.

Phenomena: Balloons on the bottles taken from the refrigerator inflate a lot in hot water; those on bottles taken from the radiator sink more into the bottle neck when on ice; balloons capped at room temperature have reactions in between. Children at first do not take into consideration the varied temperatures of the bottles of air. If they remove and replace the balloons and then repeat the activities, the differences in results become less marked.

Model to describe the interaction: When there are two contiguous systems with different temperatures, heat energy transfers from the hotter to the colder system until the two systems are of the same temperature. The greater the difference in temperatures (other things being equal) the greater the amount of energy transferred. Children will not state this so concisely, but they will move along a conceptual arrow toward the model. This set of materials highlights the importance of controls. There are as many variables here as there are different temperatures.[15] Children may have to be asked

whether they noted the differences in the temperatures of the bottles. It is possible that the activities will need to be repeated with each child controlling the conditions of the bottles from the beginning.

D *Objects in the system*: A closed system of a small lighted candle in oil-base clay and a plastic tube sealed with a balloon at one end and pressed into the clay at the other end.

Phenomena: Balloon inflates and candle goes out.

Models to describe the interaction: The air in the system absorbs heat energy from the candle and expands; it pushes into the balloon.

A problem sometimes arises in the colloquium: children may say the candle went out because it used up the oxygen and that, therefore, the balloon should have been depressed into the tube! When a candle burns, its carbon joins with the oxygen in the air to form carbon dioxide. Molecule for molecule, there are the same number of carbon dioxide molecules as there were oxygen molecules. At a given temperature and pressure, all gas molecules take up the same space. In this investigation, only the expansion due to the absorption of heat energy is relevant to the model. Again, children who repeat this activity when the air in the tube has been warmed may think their results are inconsistent. A discussion of the initial air temperature may help clarify the puzzling results.

E *Objects in the system*: At first, the objects are an open tube over a burning candle; both are stuck in oil-base clay. Later, the open end of the tube is closed with a flexible rubber square or with the hand.

Phenomena: Rubber square is depressed into (or skin of hand is pushed into) the tube. Clay bulges into tube.

Model to describe the interaction: The heat energy is transferred to the air in the system before the top of the tube is closed. All the expansion takes place while the system is open. Once the system is closed, heat energy is transferred from the tube and into the air in the room through the plastic tube wall. The molecules have less energy and therefore move closer together; they take up less space, so the molecules of the air in the room push in against the rubber. The skin of a hand is less elastic than rubber, but it is pushed in enough so that raising the hand pulls both the tube and the clay with it. The room air then

---

[15] A number of experiences with heat and temperature leading to a model of *thermal equilibrium* are found in the booklet *Temperature* by the Science Curriculum Improvement Study, University of California at Berkeley, 1966. Revised editions published by Rand McNally, Chicago.

nteracts with the clay and tube air, pushing the clay nto the tube.

F *Objects in the system*: A closed subsystem of a sealed quart plastic bag containing half an ounce of Freon-11. Other subsystems of warm water and ice cubes.

Phenomena: When Freon-11 is warmed, the whole bag inflates. When it is placed on the ice cubes, the subsystem returns to its original contracted condition.

Models to describe the interaction: The total amount of matter in the bag subsystem remains constant. Absorption of heat energy changes the liquid to a gas, increasing the motion of the molecules and the space they take up. Ice absorbs heat energy from the Freon-11 gas, slowing down the molecules of Freon-11 and liquefying or condensing the gas.

G *Objects in the system*: Air current detector; hot and cold air in the room. Child's energy transferring detector subsystem to hot and cold subsystems.

Phenomena: Flap of detector rises, falls, or remains horizontal.

Model to describe the interaction: Cold air is heavier (denser) than hot air; it falls and pushes the hot air up. When the flap of the detector is in a region where the hot air is being pushed up, the air molecules below the flap have more mechanical energy than those above it and the flap is pushed up. When the flap is in a region where cold air is falling, the air molecules above the flap have more mechanical energy than those below it and the flap is pushed down.

H *Objects in the system*: A metal spinner, electric light bulb (source of heat energy), air.

Phenomena: When light is turned on, the spinner begins to move—slowly at first, then fast. When the light is turned off, the spinner gradually slows to a stop.

Model to describe the interaction: When the light is on, the air around the light bulb absorbs a great amount of heat energy. It is pushed up as the surrounding colder air less affected by the bulb falls. The warm air molecules are pushed up against the vanes of the spinner. The spinner moves in the only way it can, turning on its pivot. When the bulb is turned off, the hot air is no longer pushed up and interaction which moves the vanes ceases.

A sample way to use the matrix

Mrs. K. introduced herself to the sixth grade at the beginning of the year with the *What's Inside?* lesson. As a new science specialist, she needed to find out something about the children's levels of thinking. This particular group seemed eager and knowledgeable, and they did think of air as a substance made of molecules, but they used expressions like "force," "gravity pulls," and "air sucked into a vacuum." At the end of the lesson Mrs. K. selected a shelf in the room and labeled it the *Mystery Shelf*. She promised that the next day a system of objects would appear on the shelf to justify its name.

The children arriving early the next morning were a little disappointed when the mystery objects turned out to be three almost flat plastic bags, sealed in a secure but unusual way and resting on aluminum dishes of ice cubes. A few children handled the bags and, to their surprise, found that each bag puffed up like a balloon. They also discovered that cooling a bag on the ice produced a little liquid inside instead of a lot of gas. Naturally the children began talking about the phenomena. (This was in stepping stone F.)

When Mrs. K. returned for her next lesson, she began with a colloquium. She helped the children to use the terms *interaction, heat energy*, and *system*. By the end of the period, they had formulated that no matter had entered or left the system, but that heat energy had interacted with it and produced obvious changes.

For the next lesson, the tables were arranged so that children sat together in groups of fours. On half the tables Mrs. K. placed the materials from stepping stone A (soda bottles capped with balloons, a basin of hot water, a basin of ice) and on the other tables she placed the materials from stepping stone D (plastic tubes and balloons, candles in oil-base clay). The children went to their own tables and started to work with the materials.

During the colloquium, they said that hot air expanded and went up into the balloon. Mrs. K. turned one of the soda bottles with an inflated balloon on it upside down. She reminded them that they had used the expressions *heat energy* and *interaction* the last time and that perhaps these words would help them think of a *model* to explain what happened to the molecules inside the bottles and tubes. From this lesson the children again developed the model that they were dealing with closed systems and that no matter had entered or left them. The interaction with heat energy had brought about a change in volume, a respacing of the molecules.

Before the next lesson, three bottles appeared on the *Mystery Shelf* (stepping stone **C**). The bottles were the same size and all of them were capped with balloons, but one of the balloons was inflated, one drooped, and one was pushed inside the bottle neck. A **Suggestion Card** by some balloons and a half dozen empty bottles read: "How did this happen? Can you use these bottles and these balloons to make it happen again?"

During the next few days, the children solved the "mystery" and set up other bottles with balloons in various positions.

During the next lesson, Mrs. K. had the children make air current detectors (see diagram in stepping stone **G**, page 202) without telling them what they were. She asked them to test the balanced straw in different parts of the room and then in different parts of different rooms at home. "Maybe by the open refrigerator door," she suggested.

The next science session again began with a colloquium. Some children had charted the flow of air in their rooms and described a model in which the cool air entered the window, fell to the floor, was pushed across the room by more incoming air, then absorbed heat energy from the radiator, and was pushed up and across the ceiling and out at the top of the open window. Most of the children could now refer to *dense* and *less dense* air, as well as hot and cool air, and the interaction of all of these with gravity.

Before going on to the next unit, Mrs. K. left a reading lamp and a spinner (stepping stone **H**) on the *Mystery Shelf* with a **Suggestion Card** which said, "If you can describe in your own words a model that explains this 'mystery,' I can learn how much *you have learned* so far this semester."

MATRIX 3: GAS AND MECHANICAL ENERGY

For children at the preconceptual level of thinking.

The near bank—prior understandings.

Children must know that gases are matter composed of molecules.

The far bank—points along conceptual arrows toward an understanding that:

1. Gas molecules can be crowded together by mechanical means.
2. Two regions of gas, with one region containing molecules which have been more crowded together than in the other region, will exert unequal pressure on an object separating the regions. The object will be pushed toward the region of less pressure.
3. A moving stream of gas molecules exerts more pressure in its vector of motion and less pressure at right angles to its vector of motion.
4. Molecular pressure and consequent mechanical energy can be greatly increased by a combination of heat and crowding.

Stepping stones:

INTRODUCTION: Same as *What's Inside?* lesson to establish that gases are matter. If the children do not know that matter is composed of molecules, stepping stones A and G of Matrix 1 might follow.

MATERIALS	EXPECTED CHILD ACTIVITY
A^1, A^2, and A^3 are on each table for three children.	
A^1 A notebook paper laid across two books.	Children blow below and above the paper!

| MATERIALS | EXPECTED CHILD ACTIVITY |

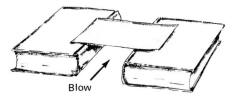

Blow

Suggestion Card:
"Blow under the paper."

A²   A 3 × 5 or 6 in. strip of paper projects from a book.   Children blow in different directions.

Blow

Suggestion Card:
"Blow from the book across the top of the paper."

A³   A 3 × 5 in. card is tacked at both ends so that it curves   Children blow in different directions.
to a ruler which is balanced over a pencil. A straw.

Blow

Suggestion Card:
"Blow through straw above curved card."

B¹, B², and **B³** are on each table for three children. (Children
stand or crouch, so remove chairs.)

B¹   Two ping-pong balls, hanging 1 in. apart, are taped from   Children blow.
the side edge of a table.

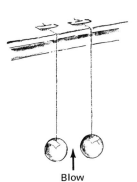

Blow

Suggestion Card:
"Blow between the ping-pong balls."

MATERIALS	EXPECTED CHILD ACTIVITY

B² Two apples hang on the other side of the same table 1 in. apart.

Children blow.

Blow

Suggestion Card:
"Blow between the apples."

B³ A hollow wedge made from a manila folder is at the end of the table. Thread is tied to the edges and joined about 1 ft away (see figure at left).

Children jerk the wedge off the table edge.

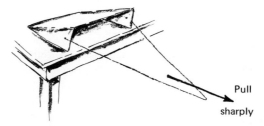

Pull

sharply

Suggestion Card:
"Pull sharply."

A card at the center of the table reads: "After you have investigated the materials, try to agree on some models to describe their interactions."

C¹ and **C²** are on each table for four children.

C¹ Two blown-up balloons closed with spring clothespins.

Children let balloons go, they blow them up and let them go again.

C² Two Jettos (from Woolworth's) with deflated balloons attached.

Children blow up balloons and attach them to the Jettos. The Jettos roll.

MATERIALS

D A sausage balloon with a straw attached to it with plastic tape. Nylon (fishing) thread is slipped through the straw; the ends are pulled very taut and attached to two objects which are placed as far apart as possible and slope up. The balloon is blown up and held closed with a spring clothespin. Spare balloons, straws, plastic tape. (One or two prepared balloons are sufficient for the whole room.)

EXPECTED CHILD ACTIVITY

Children open clothespin and watch the balloon soar up the nylon thread slope. They try many times to make balloon go farther and faster.

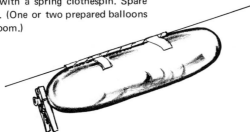

Models for the teacher—ways to think and talk about the phenomena encountered in this matrix:

Like Matrix 2, this matrix falls under Conceptual Scheme B in the column which emphasizes energy.

CONCEPTUAL SCHEME B

The sum total of mass and energy in the universe remains constant.

EMPHASIS ON ENERGY

PRECONCEPT	CONCEPT
	When energy changes from one form to another, the total amount of energy remains constant.
	A loss or gain in energy affects molecular motion. A change in the state or manifestation of matter is accompanied by a change in molecular energy.

Molecules which have been crowded or compressed into a space have absorbed mechanical energy. Their energy is greater than that of the molecules in the rest of the system. The compressed part of the system exerts a push on the remainder of the system; it can move objects which separate the two parts of the system.

Many books explain these phenomena using the Newtonian concept of "action and reaction."

Newton's models served very well in the seventeenth and eighteenth centuries. The twentieth century employs other models—other ways of looking at the universe—and these newer methods must be offered to our children who will do the thinking of the twenty-first century!

Children understand the principle of disturbed equilibrium very easily through a hoop demonstration. Four children hang onto a wooden or a metal hoop; they pull. There is equilibrium: no change. If child **D** lets go, what happens to the other children? **A** and **C** represent opposite vectors which balance one another. But now **B** has no opposite vector. Child **B** moves in the direction of the arrow (see figure below).

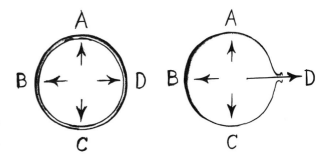

This analogy may be applied to a blown-up balloon which is released. When the opening is closed, the crowded molecules press in all directions. When **D** is opened, the balloon flies in the direction of the unbalanced vector **B**.

We can apply the principle of unequal molecular energies to each of the systems represented by the matrix materials.

Potential models for the children—direction of conceptual arrows:

A¹ *Objects in the system*: Air above and below, supported paper, source of moving air.

Phenomenon: Paper moves down when air is blown below it.

Model to describe the interaction: At first the molecular energy above and below the paper is in equilibrium. When the air molecules are blown from below the paper, those above the paper have more energy. The air molecules above and the paper interact with the region of less energy; they move toward it.

A² *Objects in the system*: Air above and below a strip of paper secured at one end, source of moving air.

Phenomenon: Paper strip vibrates and rises when air is blown above it.

Model to describe the interaction: At first the molecular energy above and below the paper is in equilibrium. When the air molecules are blown from above the paper, those below the paper have more energy. The air molecules below and the paper interact with the region of less energy; they move toward it.

A³ *Objects in the system*: A balanced ruler with a curved card on one arm, surrounding air, a stream of air blown through a straw parallel to the ruler and above the card.

Phenomenon: The ruler acts like a seesaw, rising on the side with the curved card.

Model to describe the interaction: The air molecules above the card are blown away in the manner of the preceding systems, but here there is an additional factor: the curved surface. When the stream of air molecules blown through the straw hits the curved surface, not only are the molecules above the card blown away, but some of the air molecules in the stream bound off the curve; this reduces still further the total number and therefore the total energy of the air molecules above the card. The

curved upper surface of an airplane wing employs this principle. Two-thirds of the lift on an airplane wing is due to this phenomenon.

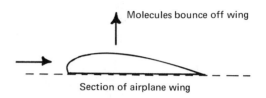

Section of airplane wing

B¹ *Objects in the system*: Two suspended ping-pong balls, the air around them, a source of moving air (blowing).

Phenomenon: The ping-pong balls move together when air is blown between them.

Model to describe the interaction: Before the investigation, the energy of the air molecules is the same in all directions: the system is in equilibrium. Blowing between the ping-pong balls pushes away the air molecules that are between them. The push of the blown-in air molecules is in the same direction—straight ahead, not sideways—so that the pressure between the balls is reduced. The molecules on the other sides of the balls push them together—to the region of reduced pressure. (These molecules and the ping-pong balls interact with the region of less energy; the balls move together.)

B² *Objects in the system*: Same as in **B¹** except that two apples replace the ping-pong balls.

Phenomenon: These heavier objects also move together when air is blown between them.

Model to describe the interaction: Same as for **B¹**.

B³ *Objects in the system*: Large card bent to form a hollow wedge; thread with which to move card; hand and arm to pull on thread supplying energy; surrounding air.

Phenomenon: When sharply tugged, the card rises.

Model to describe the interaction: Moving the wedge forward crowds the air molecules under it, increasing their mechanical energy. They interact with the card and with the molecules of less energy above the card, pushing the card up. In the same manner, the angle of an airplane wing traps the air from the propeller under the wing. One-third of the lift of a propeller-driven airplane is due to this phenomenon.

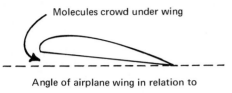

Molecules crowd under wing

Angle of airplane wing in relation to
plane through the airplane's body

C¹ *Objects in the system*: Balloon inflated until
molecules are crowded, a clothespin closing this
subsystem, the surrounding air, hand to remove the
clothespin.

Phenomenon: As the balloon contracts, air flows
from its opening. The balloon zooms a zigzag course
in roughly the opposite direction.

Model to describe the interaction: Mechanical
energy has increased the activity of the crowded
molecules inside the balloon. The molecules composing the balloon material, although stretched, still
cohere. Equilibrium is reached when the balloon
molecules and the crowded air molecules inside the
balloon balance the pressure of the air molecules
surrounding the balloon. When the balloon is released, air rushes out of the opening, reducing the
pressure in that direction. The balloon interacts with
the surrounding air by moving in the opposite
direction. The uneven contraction of the balloon
molecules changes the direction of maximum pressure
inside the balloon, accounting for the zigzag course it
assumes.

C² *Objects in the system*: Jetto, air molecules
crowded into balloon, surrounding air, table (or
floor).

Phenomenon: As the balloon contracts, air flows
from the Jetto spout and the Jetto rolls in the
opposite direction.

Model to describe the interaction: Same as for **C¹**
except that there is no zigzag course.

D *Objects in the system*: Inflated balloon attached
to a straw; taut, sloping string through straw, clothespin closing balloon, hand to remove pin; surrounding
air.

Phenomenon: When clothespin is removed, balloon zooms part way up the string.

Model to describe the interaction: Same as for **C²**.

A sample way to use the matrix

Experiences in **A** and **B** provide the foundation for
reading about how airplanes fly; experiences in **C** and
D precede studies about jets and rockets.

Matrices to follow
Serendipity from Water Play

Marybelle Bradford introduced the white powders
investigation on a level suitable for children who
presumably had had very little experience with
common household utensils. It was significant that
the use of funnels, sieves, and variously shaped
bottles for pouring water intrigued her second graders
and that the colloquium revealed considerable learning. The set of materials Miss Braford used was, for
her class, an appropriate introduction to the white
powders—the real beginning for matrices on chemistry. When these matrices are developed for children
at the upper complex, preconceptual, or early conceptual levels, the introductory investigation of white
powders need not be confined to using only water as
a mixing agent. For sophisticated children, water and
several other liquids such as vinegar, an iodine
solution, and a litmus solution might well be presented in the initial lesson.

There are many ways to "serve" solids and liquids
to children. Teachers often show great ingenuity in
finding appropriate vessels locally. We have seen paint
palettes with slight depressions and plastic ice cube
trays used to hold powders for mixing, waxed paper
attached to pieces of cardboard with paper clips for
very small quantities of powders, and, for stirrers,
toothpicks, plastic spoons, tongue depressors, and
straws. Liquids can be served by medicine droppers
from babyfood jars. Souffle papers can be used as
individual mixing cups, but they tend to become
soggy and sometimes the paper interacts with the
liquid reagents by changing color.

One of the important problems that occurs while
discovering the properties of liquids and solids as they
interact is how to keep the substances "pure,"
uncontaminated by the other materials in use. The
children discover ways to keep the substances separate as they work. Establishing procedural rules is
part of the learning process. We have found that a
child tends to stir a mixture with the server he used

Drinking straw scoop

1 oz. paper
jigger cup

1 oz. graduated
medicine cup

Paper plate

to deliver the second substance. If the medicine dropper is used to put the liquid into the solid, it will probably be used as the stirrer, very often clogging the dropper. With plaster of Paris, the dropper frequently becomes clogged beyond repair! Faster learning and more rapid success occur if the solid is added to the liquid. For this purpose, scoops can be made from drinking straws by cutting them diagonally into short lengths. Any number can be provided at negligible cost.

The powders can be placed in one-ounce paper jigger cups (which may be purchased in lots of 100 at paper goods counters) or in small cupcake papers and easily labeled with identifying letters. The powders in their cups and a dozen drinking straw scoops are placed on a paper plate in the center of the group of children using them. (The paper plates with curved sides hold more materials than those with flat edges.)

For liquids, we recommend the use of one-ounce clear plastic polyethylene medicine cups; these enable the children to see color changes clearly. The flexible polyethylene cups can be rinsed out very easily, leaving no trace of the reagents which were in them. If there is a choice, we prefer graduated medicine cups to unmarked ones.[16] Some children engage in serendipitous discoveries by comparing the volume marks of ounces, tablespoons, milliliters, and cubic centimeters. Children and teacher can use these terms in referring to the volume of liquid in each cup.

[16] One-ounce polyethylene medicine cups, graduated or plain, are available in lots of 100 from Selective Educational Equipment, Inc. (S.E.E.), 3 Bridge Street, Newton, Mass. 02195.

MATRIX 4: LIQUID-SOLID INTERACTIONS

For children at the upper level of complex thinking.

The near bank—prior understanding.

Children need to know that some substances can "disappear" in water but "still be there" and that some substances do not dissolve. For the purposes of this matrix, it is assumed that the children have had experience with liquids and know some of their essential properties, and that their contact with various solids has included granular substances with different sized grains: sand, gravel, salt, flour, etc.

The far bank—points along conceptual arrows toward an understanding that:

1. A solid dissolved in water can be recovered by evaporation.
2. Some substances which look alike superficially can be distinguished by their interaction with certain other substances.
3. Reactions established under (2) distinguish a substance even when it is part of another substance or in a mixture.

Stepping stones:

INTRODUCTION: There are many appropriate ways to start this unit and a great variety of good combinations of materials. A teacher would need to appraise the previous experiences of his children and balance these against how much "messing around" [17] he can endure! *Serendipity from Water Play* indicated a good approach for young and inexperienced children. Some children progress well when started with several solids and several liquids; others do better with one liquid and two or three solids; some progress faster with a single solid and several liquid reagents. Labeling the paper cups containing solids by letter helps children refer to them accurately during the colloquium.

MATERIALS	EXPECTED CHILD ACTIVITY
A Children work in pairs, preferably seated opposite one another at a table. A paper plate between them holds three small cupcake papers one-quarter full of cooking soda, salt, and plaster of Paris, respectively. A dozen straw scoops are on the tray. One child has 5 cc of water in each of the three plastic medicine cups in front of him; the other has 5 cc of white vinegar in each of his three medicine cups. A central supply of the powders in pint ice cream containers, spare straw scoops, spare cupcake papers, plastic spoons, water and vinegar in babyfood jars with two medicine droppers in each.	Children scoop up powders and stir them in each of the liquids. They add more powders, use the same scoops over again, and eventually make "soup" of all the things in front of them. Children may ask for "seconds" of materials. They should throw away their cupcake papers, rinse the medicine cups thoroughly, and then help themselves from the central supply. Sometimes it is a good idea to tell children to replace their used scoops; some teachers prefer to let children decide this for themselves.
B Water and vinegar as in **A**. Garden limestone, sugar, and flour in cupcake papers, labeled A, B, and C. Straw scoops.	Very much as in **A**. If this is the children's second or third experience, there will be less mess and more "purposeful" activity.
C Every child has three medicine cups with 1 cc of water in each. For each pair of children, three other cupcake papers contain: a crushed Alka Seltzer tablet, cooking soda, and, side by side in the third, some Tang or lemonade crystals and some cooking soda. Straw scoops. A central supply of extra powders, water, and straws.	Children mix the powders with the water and show surprise at the two which fizz. Then they try various combinations with their "seconds."
D For every two children, one has a dilute solution of bromthymol blue in his three medicine cups and the other has a dilute litmus solution or pink and blue litmus papers in water in his three cups. Boric acid, cooking soda, and citric acid in cupcake papers labeled A, B, and C.	Children put powders into liquids and note color changes. They usually mix some of the powders and obtain the reverse color reactions.

Teacher preparation

A few drops of bromthymol blue concentrate in half a pint of water should produce a deep sky blue solution. The litmus solution should be between a pale blue and a pale pink (mauve).

E For every two children, one has a dilute bromthymol blue solution in his three medicine cups and the other has a dilute litmus solution or blue and pink litmus papers in water in his three cups. Three cupcake papers labeled A, B, and C contain ¼ teaspoon of instant tea with lemon, plain instant tea, and Tang or powdered lemonade.	Children put powders in liquid and compare the color changes in their own liquids. Then they compare their color changes with those in their partner's liquids and with previous experiences, if any.
F For each pair of children, a plastic bag containing a tablespoon of cooking soda and two ounces of white vinegar in a three-ounce paper cup with enough bromthymol blue in it to turn it yellow (a dozen drops). The air is squeezed out of the bag before it is sealed securely with a tie. A central supply of plastic bags, bromthymol blue, cups, vinegar, soda, ties.	Children tip the vinegar into the soda and enjoy the various interactions which occur. They may want to repeat the investigation. They can have access to the central supply to test their ideas.

---

[17] See David Hawkins, "Messing About in Science," *Science and Children*, Vol. 2, No. 5 (February 1965).

MATERIALS,

G (For this investigation, the liquid is dropped onto the solids.) Each child has a paper plate on which the letters A, B, C, D, and E have been written; these correspond to the letters on five medicine cups. The plates are covered with thin plastic. A small scoop of powder A is near A on the plate; placed near B, a small scoop of powder B, etc. The medicine cups contain: flour, salt, cornstarch, cooking soda, and sugar; a straw scoop is in each. Four children can work at a table with four plates. In the center of the table are a large babyfood jar one-quarter full of a dilute iodine solution and four medicine droppers, or short lengths of drinking straws with large diameters.

EXPECTED CHILD ACTIVITY

Children drop the iodine solution on the powders on their plates. They add samples of the other powders, not always matching the letters on the plate, and drop iodine on them. They discuss which powders interact and which do not; then realize they have not been careful to keep a record. Extra plastic is available so that children may remove what they have used and start over.

Teacher preparation

The iodine solution is made from Lugol's iodine solution; add a few drops in water until the color is similar to strong tea.

H For every four children: four plates covered with thin plastic; a central plate containing small piles of starchy foods like peas, beans, corn (fresh, unfrozen, or soaked), small pieces of banana, cereal, and nonstarchy foods like hard-boiled egg whites, lettuce, cheese; toothpicks for carrying pieces of food to plates; a large babyfood jar one-quarter full of dilute Lugol's iodine solution; four medicine droppers or short lengths of straws.

Children take samples of each food and drop iodine on them.

I For every four children: four cupcake papers containing a tablespoon of sand, iron filings, salt, and Tang, respectively; a straw scoop in each cup; a dozen one-ounce medicine cups with 5 cc of water in each; paper towels.

Children put the solids in water. They pour some mixtures through paper towels and ask for a magnet. They show considerable ingenuity, such as waiting for the Tang to dry on the towel.

Suggestion Card

"Mix each of these with water. Then plan together ways to separate the substances from the water again."

J Each child has a 6 to 8 power magnifying glass [18] and a glass microscope slide. In the center of every four children are hot concentrated solutions of salt, epsom salts, boric acid, and Tang with one medicine dropper or short length of straw in each babyfood jar. A basin of water (for rinsing slides), paper towels, and tissues are also available. A piece of thin plastic may be used over paper plates instead of slides and rinse water. [19]

Children drop solutions on slides and watch the crystals form.

[18] American Science and Engineering, Inc. (20 Overland St., Boston, Mass. 02215) has a triple-hand lens with 2X, 6X, and 8X magnification.

[19] Some additional activities which could be incorporated in this matrix are found in *Mystery Powders*, the Webster Division of McGraw-Hill, Manchester, Mo. 63011, 1967. Produced by the Elementary Science Study (E.S.S.) of the Education Development Center, Inc.

Models for the teacher—ways to think and talk about the phenomena encountered in this matrix:

CONCEPTUAL SCHEME B

The sum total of mass and energy in the universe remains constant.

EMPHASIS ON MATTER

PRECONCEPT	In chemical and physical changes, the total amount of matter remains constant. A change in the state or manifestation of matter is accompanied by a change in molecular motion.
COMPLEX	Matter commonly exists in solid, liquid, and gaseous forms.

The central concept in all of the above investigations is that matter has properties which can be detected by the senses. More sophisticated activities than simply looking, touching, and smelling are involved. Because the children are doing things to produce interactions, various scientific procedures are discovered and emphasized: keeping records, using small quantities for testing, keeping substances unmixed when purity is essential. Children at the upper level of complex thinking can begin to appreciate the consistency of a reaction. They cannot do this at first. For instance, when iodine turns dark blue or black with starches, children at the lower level do not think of iodine as a test for starch. This matrix helps them along the conceptual arrow that substances have consistency in their interactions.

This matrix leans toward the preconcept that "in chemical and physical changes, the total amount of matter remains constant." Children at the upper complex level will not realize this whole statement, but they can begin to appreciate that the solid that has been put into a solution can be extracted again. They begin to learn about reversible reactions such as the color reverses in acid–alkali indicators.

We have introduced the children to two acid–alkali indicators: bromthymol blue is blue with alkalis and yellow with acids; litmus is blue with alkalis and pink with acid. Another name for alkali is base. The latter is used more frequently by chemists and perhaps is the better term. However, if the children are also being introduced to the word *base* in mathematics as they study multibase arithmetic, it is better to use the word *alkali* in science.

An acid and a base have a special relationship; they neutralize each other. That is, when an acid and a base are mixed, a point is reached where the mixture is neither acidic nor basic. If the solution is evaporated at this point a new solid appears called a *salt,* which is often crystalline. To go slightly deeper into the interaction, we can consider that an acid is what is formed when a soluble oxide of a nonmetal is dissolved in water. Carbon is a nonmetal. Its oxide is carbon dioxide and carbon dioxide dissolved in water forms *carbonic acid*—a weak acid, but an acid nonetheless. This solution turns blue litmus pink and bromthymol blue to yellow. On the contrary, a base is formed when a soluble oxide of a metal is dissolved in water. Calcium is a metal. Calcium oxide (lime) is its oxide and lime in water (slaked lime or limewater) is a base. This solution turns pink litmus blue and yellow bromthymol to blue. When a calcium oxide solution interacts with carbonic acid, a new solid calcium carbonate (chalk), is formed. To give another example, we can dissolve sodium[20] (a metal) in water, thus forming the base *sodium hydroxide* (caustic soda). Sulfur dioxide dissolved in water forms sulfurous acid. Caustic soda and sulfurous acid neutralized interact to form sodium sulfite.

Carbonates are unstable compounds. When mixed with acids, carbonates break up and give off carbon dioxide. One way to test for a carbonate is to see if it gives off carbon dioxide when it interacts with an acid.

The acid–base relation of a solution is calibrated on a pH scale.[21] The scale ranges from zero, which is

[20] This is a theoretical example. In practice, one puts a tiny piece of sodium metal in water to form sodium hydroxide. Hydrogen is given off—a potentially dangerous operation!

[21] The origin and meaning of the letters pH are rather complicated. If the reader is interested, he may refer to a high school chemistry text such as: Gregory R. Choppin and Bernard Jaffe, *Chemistry*, Silver Burdett, Morristown, N. J., 1965, Chapter 17.

most acidic, to 14 which is most basic. A pH of 7 indicates a neutral solution. Different indicators change color for different ranges of pH.

The learnings children develop from units derived from this matrix are partly conceptual, of course. In large part, however, this matrix offers a rich opportunity for children to discover and develop certain procedures which sciencing requires. We will emphasize these in addition to the potential models we describe.

Potential models for the children—direction of conceptual arrows and potential learnings of science procedures:

A *Objects in the system*: (1) Cooking soda and water, (2) cooking soda and vinegar, (3) salt and water, (4) salt and vinegar, (5) plaster of Paris and water, (6) plaster of Paris and vinegar.

Phenomena: (1) Soda disappears in water, (2) soda fizzes and gives off carbon dioxide, (3) and (4) disappear without fizzing, (5) and (6) both harden into rocklike substances.

Models to describe the interactions: Vinegar interacts the way water does, except with cooking soda whose chemical name is *sodium bicarbonate*. In this interaction there is a fizz, a gas given off. Salt dissolves. Plaster of Paris hardens.

Potential procedural learnings: Because of the mixing of substances due to the use of the same straw in more than one mixture or intentional mixing "to see what happens," there will be abundant discrepant events during the colloquium. To the question, "Why do you think you have so many different results?" the children will easily see that the powders and liquids became contaminated. They will devise ways to keep the substances pure. Their first suggestions may not all pan out, but after another colloquium the class will probably have some excellent rules. Children will want to try both vinegar and water, and they may come to the conclusion that there is water in vinegar. For follow-up sessions children can arrange procedures to serve themselves from a central supply.

Even when the substances are kept separate, children often forget which powders they have used. A grand chance for keeping records! According to the ability of the children, they can make their own record charts or the teacher can supply rexographed forms with such headings as: *Name of substance, Mixed with, Interaction*. Children always try to name the substances they use. Often the correct names come from someone in the class. A not-quite-correct name may, too. The teacher can supply the name at this point. Changing the name of cooking soda to sodium bicarbonate helps children to recognize it as a carbonate in its classic reaction with an acid.

B *Objects in the system:* (1) Limestone and water, (2) limestone and vinegar, (3) sugar and water, (4) sugar and vinegar, (5) flour and water, (6) flour and vinegar.

Phenomena: Limestone remains a powder in water, but fizzes gently in vinegar. Sugar, of course, disappears in vinegar and in water. Flour makes a sticky paste with both liquids.

Models to describe the interactions: Limestone is calcium carbonate and, therefore, gives off carbon dioxide with an acid. With vinegar, the gas comes off slowly. Children may suggest that the fizz is like the soda they drink. If they do not know the name of the gas, it can be given to them. The children may then think that there is vinegar in a soda drink which gives off the gas. At this point, the children do not know about acids in general. However, the reason sodas give off carbon dioxide is that the gas is put in the bottle under pressure; it is *pushed into* the liquid. Children often figure this out for themselves if the teacher poses a question of this type: "Why doesn't the soda drink fizz when the cap is on?"

Potential procedural learnings: Same as for **A**.

C *Objects in the system:* (1) Alka Seltzer powder and water, (2) sodium bicarbonate and water, (3) sodium bicarbonate and citric acid (can be read from the label on fruit drink crystals) and water.

Phenomena: Alka Seltzer powder fizzes in water. Sodium bicarbonate and citric acid fizz in water. Sodium bicarbonate alone in water does not fizz.

Models to describe the interactions: Two substances in water fizz; substances alone do not. (Children may want to try out the fruit drink crystals alone with water if they have had no experience mixing these drinks.)

Children should be encouraged to read the labels on the Alka Seltzer bottle and on the Tang package. They may identify the acid and carbonate as the common substance. Children very easily hear the common sounds between carbonate and carbon dioxide, and they suggest where the carbon dioxide gas comes from. That it is released only when an acid is present may or may not be established by the children at this point.

One fact they may be helped to consider is that there is no fizz if there is no water, even when both a carbonate and an acid are present.

Potential procedural learnings: If children formulate some model which suggests that a carbonate and an acid in water give off carbon dioxide, they can then *predict* what might happen with other acids and carbonates. Cooking soda is the most dramatic carbonate to use, so the variable can come from other acids: vinegar, lemon, grapefruit, sour milk. (Sour is the taste of acid!)

Formulating a hypothesis (generalization, in this case), making a specific prediction: "Cooking soda and lemon will fizz," and then testing the prediction are the procedures which might come from the set of materials in **C**.

D *Objects in the system*: (1) Bromthymol blue (BTB) and boric acid, (2) litmus and boric acid, (3) BTB and sodium bicarbonate, (4) litmus and sodium bicarbonate, (5) BTB and citric acid, (6) litmus and citric acid.

Phenomena: Bromthymol blue turns yellow with boric and citric acids. Litmus turns pink with acids and blue with sodium bicarbonate.

Models to describe the interactions: Bromthymol blue and litmus both change color with acids; they are acid indicators. BTB remains blue or turns from green to blue and litmus turns blue with an alkali. If the children had mixed excess sodium bicarbonate with the acids, they might have discovered that the BTB turned back to blue and that litmus changed from pink to blue. Litmus indicates an in-between or neutral stage when it is mauve. BTB turns greenish as it passes from acid to alkali, or vice versa.

Potential procedural learnings: Children may formulate a hypothesis that BTB and litmus will show the same phenomena as above with other acids and alkalis. Tests could be made on lemon, rhubarb, ammonia, soap, detergents, etc.

E *Objects in the system*: (1) BTB and tea with lemon, (2) litmus and tea with lemon, (3) BTB and plain tea, (4) litmus and plain tea, (5) BTB and Tang (or lemonade), (6) litmus and Tang (or lemonade).

Phenomena: BTB and litmus change color with lemon and Tang. The tea and Tang colors modify the yellow and pink.

Models to describe the interactions: Children will not know by looking at the powders that one tea has lemon in it and the other does not. They should be able to construct the model that an acid is present. They might guess that it is lemon. The acid in fruit drinks is citric acid. The children might associate the name, when it is given to them, with citrus fruits.

Potential procedural learnings: Children might make the hypothesis that citric acid is in all citrus fruits. The children cannot test for *citrus* acid, but they can test various citrus fruits for acid reactions.

F *Objects in the system*: A closed system of a plastic bag, vinegar, BTB, sodium bicarbonate, and no air.

Phenomena: When acid is tipped into the carbonate, there is great fizzing activity and the yellow BTB turns blue in the region of the powder. The gas from the fizz eventually inflates the bag.

Models to describe the interactions: Acid and carbonate produce carbon dioxide, which takes up more room than the powder and liquid. Sodium bicarbonate is an alkali.

A further model might be constructed by some more mature children that the same amount of materials are present before and after the interactions. Nothing has been added to or taken from the closed system.

G *Objects in the systems*: Iodine and each of the following: flour, salt, cornstarch, sodium bicarbonate, sugar.

Phenomena: Both the cornstarch and flour turn a deep blue-black. Some children perceive the interaction of iodine with sugar as turning yellow or with sodium bicarbonate as being orange. In any case, these changes are slight. Salt does not interact with iodine.

Model to describe the interactions: Iodine turns blue-black in the presence of starch.

H *Objects in the system*: Iodine and each of the following: peas, beans, corn, banana, cereal, hard-boiled egg white, lettuce, cheese.

Phenomenon: Iodine turns black with each of the first five substances.

Model to describe the interaction: There is some starch in peas, beans, corn, banana, and cereal.

I *Objects in the systems*: Water and each of the following: sand, iron filings, salt, Tang.

Phenomena: Both the sand and the iron filings sink to the bottom of the water; salt disappears completely; Tang crystals dissolve, but color the water.

Models to describe the interactions: Sand and iron filings do not interact with water (except to become wet); salt dissolves, but you can taste it; Tang dissolves but you can taste it and see the coloring. Salt and Tang reappear when water is evaporated; iron filings can be retrieved from the water with a magnet; sand can be retrieved through filtering.

J *Objects in the system*: Hot concentrated solutions of salt, epsom salts, boric acid, Tang; air.

Phenomena: Drops of solutions dry up and crystals appear.

Models to describe the interaction: Heat energy in the solutions evaporates the water into the air. As the solution loses water, it cannot hold as much solid in solution. The solids reappear as crystals. Crystals of substances have characteristic shapes: salt is cubic; epsom salts elongated; boric acid is a powder; Tang has flat crystals.

Sample ways to use the matrix

1. Mrs. de V. had given her third graders considerable experience in free discovery–colloquium science. She thought they were ready to start with a problem and then analyze it. She opened the unit with the materials in **F** (vinegar, BTB, and sodium bicarbonate in a sealed plastic bag), but did not make the source of her materials available to the children. She wanted them to discover what the materials might be through various interactions. The colloquium pinpointed these questions by the children:

1. What is the yellow stuff?
2. What makes the fizz?
3. Where does all that gas come from?

To lead the children toward finding out about the yellow "stuff," Mrs. de V. gave materials adapted from the set in **D**. She did not have any citric acid so she substituted vinegar. She did not want to complicate the findings by having the fizz, so she used ammonia instead of the carbonate. Among four children she set up three babyfood jars containing the liquids BTB, vinegar, and ammonia; each jar had a medicine dropper in it. The powdered boric acid was in a souffle cup. There were plenty of straw scoops available and each child had several souffle cups for mixing. **A Suggestion Card** read: "Find ways to make the yellow stuff."

A lot of mixing occurred, and the yellow stuff appeared and then disappeared. Excitement was high, but the colloquium showed confusion as to what had produced what. Ground rules for mixing were set. Mrs. de V. gave the children the names of bromthymol blue and boric acid when they asked for them.

After the next session with the same materials, the children associated the appearance of yellow with BTB and the acids. The children said vinegar had an acid taste; they were told it contained acetic acid. To extend these findings, the next group of materials was from **E**: tea and lemon, plain tea, and fruit drink crystals with BTB.

To answer the fizz question, a variation of the materials in set **B** were also given: lime, sodium bicarbonate, sugar, salt, and vinegar. The children asked for the "real names" for the lime and cooking soda, and realized that the word *carbonate* appeared in both. A discussion of the gas and its relation to fizzy drinks ensued.

The question of why there was so much gas was partly answered by observing the slow liberation of carbon dioxide from lime in contrast to its abundant liberation from sodium bicarbonate.

The next set of materials were from **C**, again adapted: Alka Seltzer, sodium bicarbonate, sodium bicarbonate and boric acid, and water. The evolution of gas from boric acid and soda is slow; of course, from Alka Seltzer it is rapid. The children were now ready to try their hand at setting up the experience of their first session. Could they make the blue stuff turn yellow, while producing the gas that filled the bag? Various combinations of acids and carbonates were tried. The best results came from Alka Seltzer and a cup of BTB. Some of the children were sure they had duplicated the first experience until someone remembered opening his bag and smelling vinegar. The children tried again and concluded that there was more than one way to produce the effect, but that you had to have an acid, bromthymol blue, and a carbonate that fizzed easily.

2. Miss Bradford followed her two sessions with the aim of letting her second graders extend their experience with the properties of materials. She wanted, too, to introduce them to the procedures of naming the objects in their system and of thinking in terms of interactions.

Her third session adapted the materials in set **A** (cooking soda, salt, and plaster of Paris). She let them use only water.

During the colloquium, the children began to express their observations in terms of the way the objects interacted with water. They developed a vocabulary for describing the properties of the materials before and after the interactions.

The next set was from **B**. Sodium bicarbonate was used instead of lime, along with sugar and flour. The interacting liquid was vinegar. So far there had been evidence of interactions with all the solid–liquid combinations. Materials from **G** showed that iodine reacted in a startling way with some powders and showed very little or no change with others. The children decided that since the salt, sugar, and soda were made wet and were colored yellow, there had been a change and, therefore, there was an interaction.

Materials from **I** suggested no change with sand and water or with iron filings and water. The wetness could be dried off so there really was no change. Could one dry off the water from the salt and the Tang? The solutions were left on the radiator overnight! Whether there had been an interaction or change produced a lively colloquium. The unit ended with materials from **J** and descriptions of the crystals.

MATRIX 5: CHEMICAL INTERACTIONS

For children at the preconcept level of thinking.

The near bank—prior understandings:

1. Gases, liquids, and solids are composed of molecules in constant motion.
2. Molecules can absorb or give up energy. This affects their motion.

The far bank—points along conceptual arrows toward an understanding that:

1. In chemical and physical changes, the total amount of matter remains constant.

2. In chemical change, atoms interact to produce changes in molecules.

3. A change in the state or manifestation of matter is accompanied by a change in molecular motion.

4. Matter consists of elements and compounds.

Stepping stones:

MATERIALS	EXPECTED CHILD ACTIVITY
A For every four children: four babyfood jars, each covered with a drumhead of stretched balloon held on by a rubber band. The jars contain: rustable steel wool, wet steel wool, dry steel wool, only air. Spare dry steel wool.	Children observe the one depressed drumhead; pull off the drumheads and examine the steel wool; replace the drumheads after trying various combinations of dry and wet steel wool and try to get the drumhead to depress again.

A steel wool pad is unrolled and cut into about 20 pieces, each of which is fluffed into a loose ball. The number of rustable steel wool balls needed for the class are soaked overnight in a vinegar solution (white vinegar diluted with three or four times its volume of water). This solution removes the rust-arrester. The vinegar is rinsed off in fresh water before the steel wool is placed in the jar. The babyfood jars are set up about three hours before the class begins.

Depression

Rustable steel wool   Wet steel wool   Dry steel wool

MATERIALS

B For every four children: four soda bottles with same fillings as for set **A**. Bottles have stretched balloons over their mouths. Extra soda bottles are in reserve.

EXPECTED CHILD ACTIVITY

Same as for **A**, except that it is difficult to remove the steel wools so children are likely to only add wool. They may ask for extra soda bottles.

Teacher preparation

Stretch the balloons by inflating them with a pump (from the dime store). Allow them to deflate before fitting them over the mouths of the bottles. This makes it easier for the balloons to inflate again during the interaction.

C For every three children: three plastic tubes ($6 \times 1\frac{1}{8}$ in. in diameter),[22] each with a yellow stopper in one end. The tubes are inverted over a basin of water. (Tubes may be held in a wooden stand by a rubber band.)[23] One tube contains two pieces of rustable steel wool; one contains one piece; the third contains only air.

Children observe the risen water. They change the set-up in many ways and discuss their observations.

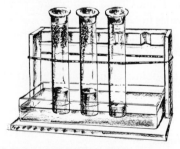

Starting setup

---

[22] A booklet entitled *Gases and Airs* by the Elementary Science Study (E.S.S.) of the Education Development Center, Inc., gives many extensions of the experiences described here. The booklet and other materials are distributed by the Webster Division of McGraw-Hill, Manchester, Mo. 63011, 1967.

[23] Tubes, stoppers, wooden stand, and syringe used in stepping stones **C** and **D** may be purchased from Selective Educational Equipment, Inc. (S.E.E.), 3 Bridge Street, Newton, Mass. 02195, or from the Webster Division of McGraw-Hill, Manchester, Mo. 63011, 1967 if you have difficulty obtaining any of the materials.

Teacher preparation

Allow 48 hours for the interaction after the materials have been set up, or let children observe beginning state of tubes and return two days later. First place the open tubes in water; then position the steel wool near the top and insert the yellow stopper.

MATERIALS

D For every three children, set-up as in **C** except tubes are filled with nitrogen, air, and oxygen. The water level in the oxygen-filled tube has risen more than one-quarter up the tube. Rustable steel wool in each tube.

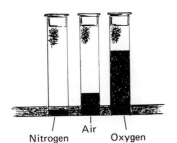

Nitrogen   Air   Oxygen

EXPECTED CHILD ACTIVITY

Children observe and discuss.

Suggestion Card

"Predict what will happen in the next 24 hours. Support your prediction with a model and a hypothesis."

Teacher preparation

To fill a tube with gas, place a stopper in one end of the tube, fill the tube with water, and invert it over water. The gas to be delivered is in a syringe with a flexible plastic tube attached. Insert the open end of the plastic tube of the syringe under the water-filled, stoppered tube and press the syringe to force out the gas. [23] The gas replaces the water in the tube.

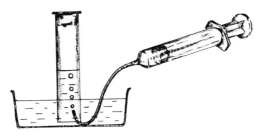

Nitrogen is obtained by drawing the gas from two tubes where the steel wool has used up the oxygen. The nitrogen is drawn into a syringe. Lifair [24] is oxygen in a pressurized can. One inserts the nozzle of the Lifair can into a flexible plastic tube. The other end of the tube is inserted under an inverted stoppered tube filled with water. By pressing the nozzle, oxygen is forced in and replaces the water in the tube.

E For every four children: two babyfood jars of bromthymol blue solution and two babyfood jars of limewater. Straws.

Children blow through straws into liquids. They may mix liquids.

[24] Lifair may be obtained from Pharmasol Laboratories, Inc., Buffalo, N. Y.

Units in physical science   **221**

MATERIALS

F For every four children: two wide-mouthed glass jars (half-pint peanut butter jars). Both jars have birthday candles fixed in oil-base clay on the bottom. Inverted lids close jars. Just before class, a thin layer of limewater is poured into one jar and a thin layer of bromthymol blue into the other. Matches are distributed with suitable warning as to method of use and advice not to screw on the jar lids.

EXPECTED CHILD ACTIVITY

Children light candles, place lids over jar mouths (in reverse) and watch. They shake liquids and/or relight candles and repeat.

Teacher preparation

Bromthymol blue (BTB) should be bright green in the concentrated solution. A few drops in six ounces of water make a usable solution. Sometimes the tap water is slightly acidic or basic, and this may turn the solution greener or bluer.

G Materials **F** from Matrix 4. (Sodium bicarbonate, vinegar, and BTB in a closed plastic bag.)

Children tip the vinegar into the soda and enjoy the various interactions which occur. They may want to repeat the investigation. They can have access to the central supply to test their ideas.

H For general class observation at free intervals: four wide-mouthed jars (peanut-butter type). In each is a thin layer of BTB. Into one is placed a medicine cup containing germinating seeds; into another, a wedge of paper towel containing a few mealworms with bran or fine oatmeal; the third contains a medicine cup with yeast, water, and sugar; the fourth is the control jar. All jars have their caps screwed on.

Children observe and discuss.

Teacher preparation

Quick germinating seeds such as mung beans, radish, or wheat are soaked for five or six hours, rinsed well, and then left on a damp paper towel in a covered dish for 48 hours.

I For every four children: two birthday candles stuck in oil-base clay in the bottom of a basin; water in the basin comes one-third of the way up the candles; a pint and a quart mason jar; matches.

Children light candles and place jars over them. They watch and discuss. Wait. Repeat.

Suggestion Card:
"Collect as many observations as you can about the lighted candles under the jars."

J[1] For every four children; four medicine cups, each containing one-half teaspoon of one of these substances: anhydrous sodium carbonate,[25] sodium phosphate (chemical name is disodium hydrogen phosphate), copper chloride, and

Children look, examine, discuss.

[25]Some crystals have molecules of water combined with them. When the water of crystalization is driven off, the substance is reduced to a powdered, anhydrous form. Sodium carbonate will be crystalline when it is first evaporated from the solution. If left in the air, it will crumble to a powder as it loses the water molecules from its crystals. Using the anhydrous form of sodium carbonate helps to distinguish it from the white, crystalline sodium phosphate.

MATERIALS

cobalt chloride.[26] Plastic spoons, a magnifying lens, and a small paper plate for each child.

Suggestion Card:
"How much can you learn by looking?"

J[2]   The substances in J[1], straw scoops, and a small jar of water. For each child: a paper plate covered with thin plastic, a medicine dropper, a lens, toothpicks for stirrers.

Suggestion Card:
"What happens when you add water? (Take a small scoop of each substance onto the plate. Drop water on them and use the toothpicks for stirrers.) Now try to get the original crystals back."

J[3]   Children work in pairs, two pairs to a table. One of each pair has a half-teaspoon of one of the colored substances in J[1]; the other has one of the white substances. (Souffle cups are convenient holders). In the whole room, all possible combinations of colored–white pairs are included. Each pair of children has two seven-ounce plastic glasses,[27] each one-quarter full of water.

---

[26] These chemicals and the allied activities are suggested by the Science Curriculum Improvement Study (S.C.I.S.), University of California at Berkeley. The Teacher's Guide describing these and other investigations is *Systems and Subsystems,* a S.C.I.S. unit from Rand McNally, P.O. Box 7600, Chicago, Ill. 60680, 1968, pp. 76-83.

[27] Clear seven-ounce polyethylene glasses are sold in lots of 20 or 25 in most supermarkets.

EXPECTED CHILD ACTIVITY

Children take a few crystals or grains of powder onto their plates; they add a few and then more drops of water. There will probably be mixing of solutions. Some children may want to start over again in response to the **Suggestion Card.** They can rip off the thin plastic and replace it with a fresh cover.

Children make solutions and mix them. They may ask for plastic-covered plates on which to evaporate drops of the mixtures or for towels to filter off solids; a colloquium may raise these questions.

Models for the teacher—ways to think and talk about the phenomena encountered in this matrix:

The model which runs through this matrix and binds the various experiences together is that atoms can be rearranged to form parts of different molecules. That molecules have a natural energy of motion and that they dissociate into *ions* (see page 225) when in solution are basic facts which allow different combinations to result from various interactions.

Children who are eight to eleven years old (the variation is great) can come upon the concept of rearranged atoms as they begin to use the words the teacher introduces to describe their models which explain the interactions. During such a series of experiences as those offered in this matrix, children

CONCEPTUAL SCHEME B

The sum total of mass and energy in the universe remains constant.

EMPHASIS ON MATTER

PRECONCEPT

> In chemical and physical changes the total amount of matter remains constant.
>
> In chemical change, atoms interact to produce changes in molecules.
>
> Matter consists of atoms and molecules in constant motion.
>
> A change in the state or manifestation of matter is accompanied by a change in molecular motion.
>
> Matter consists of elements and compounds.

speak in the conceptual language of adults while maintaining the concrete base for their descriptions.

When steel wool rusts in an enclosed system and the water rises in the tube or the flexible rubber drumhead becomes depressed, children figure out that something has gone out of the air. If no child suggests that it is oxygen which has been used (although children usually do state this fact as a model), the teacher can name the gas. "If the *molecules of oxygen* are no longer in the air, where are they?" is a good lead question. However, such a question or its answer (as a model) is often offered by the children during a colloquium. Madeline, a seventh grader, said "Oxygen combined with the iron in the steel wool and caused rust (page 161)." Madeline came upon this model during the first colloquium. Fifth and sixth graders need several experiences and several colloquia to build such models.

Essential for the growth in thinking is that children begin to use the chemical names for the substances in their systems. Chemical names are indicators of relationships, just as family names of people or generic names of plants and animals indicate relationships. It is surprising how often children can supply either the correct name or one close to it if they are given the chance. "What would you call rusty iron if you knew its molecules were composed of iron and oxygen atoms?" From the variety of suggestions given by the children, the teacher confirms or supplies the scientific term *iron oxide*.

One extension of this piece of knowledge is that children could supply the chemical names for the molecules composed of calcium and oxygen, copper and oxygen, and carbon and oxygen. The latter has two proportions of combination: a teacher can ask what the children think the difference is between carbon *mon*oxide and carbon *di*oxide? Apart from giving the chemical difference, some child often knows that carbon monoxide is poisonous (it is in the fumes from automobiles) and that carbon dioxide is "what you breath out" or "is the gas in soda pop."

The other extension is that the children may have noticed the teacher using the word *atom*. Here is the time to clarify the difference between the meanings of atom and molecule. Since these are imposed terms,

agreed upon internationally by scientists, there is little point in trying to *discover* such a convention. An atom is the smallest part of an element. A molecule is the smallest part of an element or a compound. And a compound? Molecules composed of two or more elements form a compound. But a molecule is also the smallest part of an element which can exist alone. Free oxygen is diatomic; free nitrogen is diatomic. Ozone is composed of three atoms of oxygen bound together. Helium, however, is monatomic; its molecule has only one atom of helium in it.

Naturally the children do not need to receive all this information at once. It is information given as needed to clarify thinking, very much as Mrs. Rosa Eliot supplied her children with the composition of alnico magnets (page 133) and the fact that "There has to be more than 27 percent of nickel in a mixture of metals for the mixture to interact with a magnet" (page 133). The children needed these facts to aid their thinking; the facts could not be discovered. When children who have been given new words begin to explore their usage, many of them may be glad to read further on the subject. [28]

Children always enjoy deciphering codes, and that is just what chemical names are—codes. We give the following facts for the teacher so that he may think in these terms, use them when appropriate, and offer them only when they will further the thinking during a colloquium. In chemical nomenclature, the metal name is said first: *iron* oxide, *calcium* carbonate. A name which ends in *ate* represents a molecule containing oxygen. What are the elements in the compound calcium carbonate? In sodium phosphate? The *bi* in sodium *bi*carbonate refers to the presence of hydrogen. This is not important except when children want to know the chemical difference between sodium carbonate (washing soda) and sodium bicarbonate (cooking soda).

Additional codes which may be useful for the teacher to know are: A metal or its oxide dissolved in water is a base or alkali. Sodium in water forms

---

[28] Background reading on many of the topics in this matrix, for teachers who would enjoy it and for children, is found in several of the units in Brandwein *et al.*, *Matter: Its Forms and Changes,* Harcourt Brace Jovanovich, Inc., New York, 1968.

sodium hydroxide or caustic soda. Calcium oxide in water forms calcium hydroxide or limewater. Note the code *hydr* in hydroxide? Conversely, a nonmetal oxide dissolved in water forms an acid. Carbon dioxide in water forms carbonic acid (in this case, a very weak acid). Sulfur *di*oxide in water forms sulfur*ous* acid; sulfur *tri*oxide in water, sulfur*ic* acid. Phosphorous pentoxide in water forms phosphoric acid. When an acid and an alkali (a base) meet in a solution, they interact to neutralize each other and the result is a salt which, when evaporated, is often crystalline. If the neutral substance formed by the interaction of an acid and a base is not soluble in water, it shows as a precipitate—a granular substance rather than a clear solution—which can be filtered off.

When an acid and a base neutralize each other, all the atoms in the system can be accounted for; there is, of course, conservation of matter. A few examples using chemical formulas may help clarify this for a teacher who did not take a course in chemistry.

(1) $Ca(OH)_2 + H_2CO_3 \rightarrow CaCO_3 + 2H_2O$
     Limewater   Carbonic   Chalk   Water
                acid

(2) $NaOH + HCl \rightarrow NaCl + H_2O$
     Caustic   Hydrochloric   Table   Water
     soda   acid   salt

Notice that water is always formed in addition to the salt.

Conservation of matter can be established by counting the number of atoms of each element on one side of the equation and comparing these with the number of atoms of the same element on the other side of the equation. A further exercise in the conservation of matter can be applied to the equations which express in chemical code the interaction of an acid with a carbonate:

(3) $NaHCO_3 + CH_3COOH \rightarrow CH_3COONa + H_2O + CO_2$
     Sodium   Acetic acid   Sodium   Water   Carbon
     bicarbonate   (vinegar)   acetate   dioxide

(4) $CaCO_3 + 2HCl \rightarrow CaCl_2 + H_2O + CO_2$
     Calcium   Hydrochloric   Calcium   Water   Carbon
     carbonate   acid   chloride   dioxide

Although it is seldom wise to require elementary school children to write symbolic equations, they can engage in two preliminary experiences. If they and you are so inclined, children can practice decoding chemical symbols by trying the exercises in Unit 1 in *Now Try This 6.*[29] For instance, children cannot only find the elements in the names of chemicals, but they can write the equations using the chemical names. For example:

1. Calcium hydroxide and hydrogen carbonate becomes calcium carbonate and water.
2. Sodium hydroxide and hydrogen chloride becomes sodium chloride and water (hydrogen hydroxide!).

For the experiences labeled **J** in this matrix, the teacher may think about solutions in the following manner. When a salt dissolves, it separates into two electrically charged subsystems. The metal part or ion is positively charged; the nonmetal ion is negatively charged.[30]

You will recall that atoms are composed of negative elctrons moving rapidly in shells around a positive nucleus composed of protons and neutrons. Atoms become bonded into molecules when they share one or more electrons in their outer shells. In solutions, the metal subsystem forms an ion which lends an electron and the nonmetal subsystem becomes an ion which has borrowed an electron (or two or more electrons). Some of these ions have characteristic colors; these ions color solutions. For example, the ions of copper are blue or blue-green. The ions of cobalt are red or purplish. Ions of carbonate, phosphate, or chloride are colorless. It should now be possible to predict the colors of the crystals, solutions, and mixtures which are produced by the activities under **J**.

Potential models for the children—direction of conceptual arrows:

[29] Herman and Nina Schneider and Brenda Lansdown, *Now Try This 6*, D.C. Heath, Lexington, Mass., 1966, Unit 1. A workbook to accompany reading and experiences in Herman and Nina Schneider's *Science for Today and Tomorrow*, D.C. Heath, Lexington, Mass., 1968.

[30] For a clear and detailed description of a model of ionic bonding between atoms in solids and ionic dissociation in solutions see Brandwein, *op cit.*, pp. 52-55, 202-203, and 353-61.

A *Objects in the systems*: Four closed subsystems separated from the air by flexible rubber drumheads. Each subsystem contains room air and, in addition, three of the four contain either rustable steel wool, wet steel wool, or dry steel wool.

Phenomenon: The subsystem with the rustable steel wool has a depression in the drumhead and the steel wool has rusted.

Model to describe the interaction: Something (oxygen) has been removed from the air and has joined with the steel wool (making iron oxide). The oxygen molecules removed from the air have reduced the space occupied by the molecules in the jar and upset the equilibrium of the gases on the inner and outer sides of the drumhead. The more energetic molecules of room air have pushed the balloon into the space left by the oxygen molecules. There is now only nitrogen in the jar. Water is necessary for rusting to take place. The rust-arrester must be removed from the steel wool before the oxygen will interact with the iron.

B *Objects in the systems*: Four closed subsystems and air surrounding them, separated by small balloons. Bottles contain rustable steel wool, wet steel wool, dry steel wool, and just air.

Phenomenon: In the bottle with the rustable steel wool, the balloon is pushed inside. (The larger the bottle and the smaller the balloon, the more the balloon is pushed inside the bottle.)

Model to describe the interaction: Same as in **A**.

C *Objects in the systems*: Three closed subsystems, water, and air. One subsystem has two pieces of rustable steel rool; the second has one piece; the third is only air.

Phenomena: Water rises in the two tubes containing the rustable steel wool, but does not in the third tube. However long one waits, the water never rises more than a fifth of the way up the two tubes.

Model to describe the interactions: The gas removed from the air composes one-fifth of the air's volume. (Oxygen is one-fifth of the composition of air; the remaining four-fifths is nitrogen.) The surrounding air interacts with the water and the reduced gas pressure in the tubes. The air in the room exerts greater pressure on the water and pushes it into the tubes.

D *Objects in the systems*: Three closed subsystems over water: one containing nitrogen, one air, one oxygen. Rustable steel wool in each. Surrounding air.

Phenomena: Given time, water rises to top of oxygen-filled tube; one-fifth of the way up in air-filled tube; does not rise at all in the nitrogen-filled tube.

Model to describe the interactions: All the oxygen molecules in the oxygen-filled tube combine with the iron to form iron oxide. Water is pushed in by the interaction of the surrounding air with the water and the reduced pressure in the tube as the oxygen molecules are removed. One-fifth of the air in the air-filled tube interacts with the iron to form iron oxide. Nitrogen does not interact with iron.

E *Objects in the system*: (1) Bromthymol blue and the carbon dioxide in children's breath and (2) limewater and carbon dioxide in breath.

Phenomena: Bromthymol blue turns greenish-yellow, then yellow. Limewater turns milky. Yellow BTB left in the air for an hour or two turns back to a greenish color. If blown into long enough, the limewater clears again.

Models to describe the interactions: Carbon dioxide becomes an acid in water and turns BTB yellow. (Children will have had to investigate the interaction of BTB with acids and bases prior to this.) The BTB turns back to its original color because the carbon dioxide eventually escapes into the air. Carbon dioxide forms a compound with limewater. The milkiness is small grains of solid which can be filtered off. Calcium hydroxide (limewater) and carbon dioxide in water forms calcium carbonate. The final clearing of the water is due to the calcium carbonate dissolving in the weak, excess carbonic acid (carbon dioxide and water).

F *Objects in the system*: (1) A closed system of a burning candle, air, and BTB. (2) a closed system of burning candle, air, and limewater.

Phenomena: After the candle has been lighted several times and the gas in the jar swirled around, the BTB turns a yellowish-green. Left in the room the BTB turns back to its original blue-green color. The limewater turns milky after the candle has been lighted once.

Models to describe the interactions: Carbon

dioxide was formed. The candle must have contained carbon. (Sometimes a small black patch of soot appears on the cold metal lid.)

G (As for **F** in Matrix 4.)

H *Objects in the systems*: Four closed subsystems, each containing BTB, air, and one of the following: germinating seeds, growing yeast, live mealworms, just air.

Phenomena: After a few hours, the BTB in the mealworm and seed systems changes to greenish-yellow. The yeast system turns the BTB bright yellow in about an hour.

Models to describe the interactions: The growing organisms produce a substance which turns BTB a yellowish color, indicating an acid. Children may compare it with their breath. If all the plants and organisms are breathing, they must be taking oxygen from the air. (This suggests a closed-space hypothesis and test.) Carbon must come from them as it does from the candle.

I *Objects in the system*: Burning candle in closed system, water, and surrounding air.

Phenomena: What children usually observe is that the water in the jar goes down at first and then rises as the jar cools after the candle has gone out. The water usually rises much less than one-fifth of the way up the jar. The candle under the larger jar burns longer than the candle under the smaller jar. What is usually not observed until a repeat of the investigation is that bubbles of air issue from the bottom of both jars as the candles burn.

Models to describe the interactions: When the candle burns, the heat energy is transferred to the molecules of air in the jar. These take up more room and push the water out of the jar. (The bubbles can be seen escaping.) When the candle goes out, the air in the jar begins to cool. The less energetic molecules take up less space and the surrounding air interacts with the water which pushes up into the jar.

The larger jar supports the burning of the candle longer than the smaller jar does because of the relative amounts of oxygen in the two jars.

What about the carbon dioxide formed? The carbon from the candle joins with the oxygen of the air to form carbon dioxide. But carbon dioxide is a gas and, molecule for molecule, the space occupied by the carbon dioxide is the same as the space occupied by the oxygen! Hence, if there had been no change in temperature to push the gas out of the jars, there would have been no change at all in the first and final volumes! A small change, perhaps, because a little of the carbon dioxide might have dissolved in the water. The models described here were not known to Myrtle Schur when she asked her second graders how the candle experiment could help them think about their sound investigations (page 114). There is one more elusive point in the candle burning demonstration: The candle goes out before all the oxygen is used up! A dramatic illustration of this is shown in the filmloop *The Mouse and the Candle*[31] mentioned earlier. In this filmloop, a couple of mice gambol cheerfully after the candle has gone out. A few minutes later, the mice seem a bit drowsy, but act as chipper as ever when they are taken out of the closed jar. A less dramatic illustration, but one from which the children can make this discovery themselves, is to burn one candle in a closed tube over water and another candle under a similar tube with a ball of rustable steel wool in it. If the starting level of the water and the level after the jars have cooled are carefully marked and the whole apparatus is left overnight, the water level of the steel wool tube will have increased, indicating that the wool was able to rust in the remaining oxygen after the candle had used what oxygen it did before going out.[32]

J¹, J² *Objects in the system*: Anhydrous sodium carbonate; crystals of sodium phosophate, copper chloride, and cobalt chloride[33]; water.

Phenomena: Anhydrous sodium carbonate looks powdery, not crystalline. Sodium phosphate has needle-shaped crystals which lose water at room

[31] Produced by the E.S.S. of the Education Development Center, Inc., Newton, Mass. 02160 and marketed by The Ealing Corporation (No. 80-083).

[32] This and similar investigations are described in the booklet *Gases and Airs,* written by the E.S.S. of the Education Development Center, Inc., Newton, Mass. 02160 and marketed by the Webster Division of McGraw-Hill, Manchester, Mo. 63011, 1967.

[33] These substances may be obtained from American Science and Engineering, Inc. The Teacher's Guide describing these and other investigations is *Systems and Subsystems,* a S.C.I.S. unit from Rand McNally, P.O. Box 7600, Chicago, Ill. 60680, 1968, pp. 76-83.

temperature and become dusty looking. Copper chloride forms a mass of blue-green, needle-like crystals. In water, the sodium salts are colorless, the copper salt is a blue-green, and the cobalt salt is a pinkish-purple. Evaporating the water by placing a drop of solution on plastic or on the indentation of an upturned medicine glass will return the crystals to their original form. Sodium carbonate first forms needle-shaped crystals.

Models to describe the interactions: In water, the salts separate into metal and nonmetal ions. These ions give the characteristic color to the solutions.

J³ *Objects in the systems*: Solutions of (1) sodium carbonate and sodium phosphate,[34] (2) sodium carbonate and copper chloride, (3) sodium carbonate and cobalt chloride, (4) sodium phosphate and copper chloride, (5) sodium phosphate and cobalt chloride, (6) copper chloride and cobalt chloride.

Phenomena: (1) results in a colorless solution, in (2) a blue-green powder appears, in (3) a red-purple powder appears, in (4) a blue-green powder appears, in (5) a purple powder appears, and (6) results in a greyish-purple solution.

Models to describe the interactions: To have a basis for building models on these interactions, it is really necessary to find their end products. After all, the total amount of matter is conserved, but the combination of atoms in the molecules may have changed. If the mixture of solutions remains clear, then evaporating the mixture by placing a drop on plastic or on the upturned bottom of a medicine cup or a seven-ounce plastic glass will reveal a combination of the original crystals. But when a powder appears, it should be filtered off, either through a paper towel folded in the neck of a jar or through filter paper and a funnel. The solution coming through the filter paper (the filtrate) should then be evaporated and the crystals examined.

The children will find that when the mixture is of two substances with a common metal or nonmetal ion, the original crystals reappear. Hence, (1) and (6), after evaporation, will reveal a mixture of white needle-shaped crystals in (1) and of blue-green and pinkish-purple needle-like and squarish crystals in (6).

[34] We did not plan for solution (1), but some children might try it.

Where insoluble powders form, there will be two new substances produced by a switching of ions; very likely some of the original crystals will also be present, those which have not interacted either because they were in excess or because the mixture was not stirred. The chemical names help us decode what has taken place:

(2) Sodium carbonate and copper chloride becomes sodium chloride and copper carbonate. Children should be able to recognize the cubic, colorless crystals of sodium chloride (common salt) in the evaporated filtrate. They will then be able to offer a model of what occurred:

(3) Sodium carbonate and cobalt chloride becomes sodium chloride and cobalt chloride. Salt again! Children will be able to hypothesize about the color of the ions. Cobalt salts result in the pinkish-purple tinge; copper, the bluish-green. The names offer a cue for decoding.

(4) and (5) are easy to decode from the above examples.

Sample ways to use the matrix

The principle of selecting the order of sets of materials might be that one needs to help the children realize that chemical names give clues to the elements in compounds. If the teacher uses the words *elements* and *compounds* appropriately, the children will pick up the nomenclature and probably want to discuss the words briefly. Similarly, the word *atom* can now be used by the teacher and its relation to the word *molecule* made explicit. The children need these words to discuss the interactions observed. They will use them in correct conceptual reference as they apply them to concrete situations. Use and under-standing of chemical nomenclature can be established through the rustable steel wool series of investigations (**A** through **D**) and/or the carbon dioxide series (**E** through **H**). Each set of materials may need to be used several times with different purposes in mind, purposes evolving from the colloquia. How many times each set needs to be used and adapted and how many sets need be tried, are up to the teacher and the results of the colloquia.

The most exciting sets of materials are the **J** series. They make the children feel they are "doing real chemistry." Being able to explain what occurs through the detective approach of using the codes to make models to describe the interactions gives the children a sense of power, of competence. Fifth and sixth graders can achieve this sense of power and competence with the materials in this matrix.

The units derived from this matrix are for competent young people. Not only is there much abstract thinking involved (the upper level of preconcept thought), but children have to be able to manage matches safely and to understand that chemicals are not to be eaten!

MATRIX 6: PHYSICAL INTERACTIONS

As a follow-up of the white powder and solution investigations, a more advanced concept is possible for children at the upper level of preconcept thought and, even more richly, for those entering the conceptual level: the concept of *phase*. This has only recently been introduced into elementary school work. The possibility was explored by the Science Curriculum Improvement Study and published in a teacher's guide and workbook entitled *Phases of Matter.*[35]

The word *phase* is applied to the uniform, homogeneous appearance of matter. When tea dissolves from a tea bag into water, one sees the brown seeping through the colorless liquid. There are two phases: the tea and the water. When tea is uniformly mixed in water, there is only one phase because the appearance is uniform. Oil on water is two phases; homogenized milk, one phase. Often when solids are dissolving in a liquid, a wavy pattern appears, indicating a lack of uniformity. The same wavy patterns can be seen at times when hot air rises from a sunbaked surface such as a tarred road. These wavy patterns are called *schlieren.*

Phase and schlieren represent fundamental concepts in physical interactions. Explanations and materials for investigations have been made available to teachers through the SCIS booklets. We suggest that readers might like to consult these books and construct a matrix of materials from them for discovery-colloquium lessons. The pattern of teaching described in the books is much more directed than we have been advising. The materials could easily be adapted to the pattern of learning we have called discovery-colloquium. It would be a valuable exercise to use these booklets to construct such a matrix.

Matrix to follow *Hook Up a Circuit*

At the end of the free discovery lesson which John McIver conducted with a fifth grade, we saw that the children had suggestions about what they wished to investigate during the next lesson (page 56). These individual or small group projects do not militate against having a matrix of choices because the chances are that the children are hopping on some small stepping stones within or near the subconcepts the matrix offers. It is possible, at times, to hold colloquia with a group of children whose investigations relate closely to one another, instead of with the whole class at once. A teacher may decide after glancing over a matrix that one child or group of children needs a certain set of materials and that another group could best be presented with a different set. Since no matrix pretends to be exhaustive of possibilities, a teacher may find additional materials by searching in text or trade books on the subject under study.

[35] *Phases of Matter: Teacher's Guide* and *Student Manual,* S.C.I.S., University of California at Berkeley, 1968. Some introductory activities may be found in the S.C.I.S. booklet *Subsystems and Variables,* obtainable from Rand McNally, P.O. Box 7600, Chicago, Ill. 60680.

MATRIX 7: ELECTRICAL INTERACTIONS

For children at the preconcept and concept levels of thinking.

The near bank—prior understandings.

Children should have a general notion of energy: that it can take several forms and that energy must be used to set an object in motion or to stop it.

It is conceivable that children who have had little opportunity to engage in colloquia have the above understandings more or less in a preverbal form. Units based on the following matrix will serve to bring these understandings to awareness.

The far bank—points along conceptual arrows toward an understanding that:

1. Energy can change from one form to another.
2. Electricity in motion is accompanied by magnetism.
3. Magnetism in motion can generate electricity.

Stepping stones:

INTRODUCTION: As for lesson described in *Hook up a Circuit* **(pages 48-56).**

MATERIALS	EXPECTED CHILD ACTIVITY
A For every four children: 4 sockets, 4 light bulbs, 4 switches, 4 size-D dry cells, 2 bells or buzzers, 2 screwdrivers, 1 stripper, 20 short lengths of insulated bell wire, masking tape. For sets of material, in **B** through **F**, the children work in pairs.	Free discovery. Children often work in pairs making complicated circuits by pooling materials. To some, the teacher might suggest: "Can you make the light light and the bell ring in the same circuit?"
B Simple circuit with battery, light, and switch. Materials to place across switch opening: pencil "lead" (carbon), strips of aluminum foil (different widths), iron paper clip, brass paper clip, strips of plastic, heavy string, wood strip (pencil). Or, materials can be placed across bare wire ends taped to the table.	Children try the materials across the open switch and note which allow the light to go on. To some, the teacher might suggest: "Which of these materials will serve as switches?"
C Basic circuit materials and circuit blueprints (see pages 231-36).	Each pair of children sets up one of the circuits. When all are ready, the room lights are dimmed and all the switches "thrown." Children compare the brightness of the various circuits.
D A battery and two switches (one for use as switch; one as a bridge for materials) or a switch and bridge. Strips of aluminum foil of various widths, fine wire from a multistrand electrical cord, iron wire, thick copper wire.	Children try various materials across the bridge and close the circuit. Some materials heat up and melt.
E A cell, a switch, a coil of insulated copper wire, a tenpenny nail or bolt, steel paper clips, a small compass. Instead of paper clips, iron filings in a clear plastic envelope can be used. Spare dry cells.	With and without the nail inserted through the coil, children attach coil to cell and discover it interacts with compass, iron filings, and steel clips. They increase the number of coils; use two cells to increase strength of magnetism.
F Coil of insulated copper wire turned many times around a compass. A similar coil of wire attached to the first coil. A bar or rod magnet.	Children do many things with the magnet in relation to the coils of wire. They hold the coils in many relationships to the compass.

Suggestion Card:
"Push the magnet rapidly in and out of the second coil."

With the above experiential background plus the understandings evolved from the colloquia, children explore individually or in small groups many suggestions for further electrical phenomena to be found in text and trade books. They try out some of the suggested investigations, but frequently invent their own circuits. [36]

[36] Many suggestions are to be found in *Batteries and Bulbs II: An Electrical Gadget Suggestion Book,* Education Development Center, Inc., Newton, Mass. 02160. (Later published by the Webster Division of McGraw-Hill, Inc., Manchester, Mo. 63011.)

Models for the teacher—ways to think and talk about the phenomena encountered in this matrix:

CONCEPTUAL SCHEME B

The sum total of mass and energy in the universe remains constant.

EMPHASIS ON ENERGY

CONCEPT	Energy manifests itself along an electromagnetic spectrum.
	When energy changes from one form to another, the total amount of energy remains constant.
PRECONCEPT	The sun is the chief source of radiant energy in our solar system.
	A change in the state or manifestation of matter is accompanied by a change in molecular energy.
	Energy can change from one form to another.

For this matrix, we have included models for the teacher with the potential models for the children. Each of the sets of materials provides an opportunity to explore many models underlying the observed phenomena. How many of these models the children can develop will vary greatly, depending on the background of the individual child who may be ten or more years old. We think that by offering the teacher a rather full and detailed description of current models, he will be equipped to recognize and develop the conceptual arrows along which his children seem to move.

Models for the teacher/Potential models for the children—direction of conceptual arrows:

A *Objects in the system*: Complete circuits of various complexities, some incomplete circuits.

Phenomena: In some circuits, the lights are brighter than in others. In circuits with one cell, a light, and a bell or buzzer, sometimes the bell sounds feebly but the light does not seem to glow. In other circuits with several cells in series, one or two bulbs may blow out. The bell or buzzer sounds when the circuit is complete and sufficient electrical energy is flowing through it.

Model to describe the interactions: A dry cell is not really dry at all, but a damp paste which functions as a solution would. In a solution, soluble compounds separate into two parts called ions. A negative ion has more electrons than protons and a positive ion has fewer electrons than protons. In a compound in the solid state (before it goes into solution), the ions share the electrons. It is this sharing which bonds the ions together as a compound and leaves it electrically neutral. We may say, therefore, that the ions in solution are those that have "borrowed" an electron, the negative ion, and those that have "lent" an electron, the positive ion.

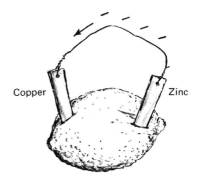

Copper   Zinc

A solution of an acid, base, or salt into which are placed two dissimilar metals such as zinc and copper joined by a copper wire will move electrons in an electric current. A weak current is obtained through the use of a lemon (see the diagram above). The zinc strip collects electrons and the copper strip receives them after they have traveled through the wire. A dry cell works on the same principle, but there are other parts and other chemicals designed to make the battery more convenient and longer-lived. Instead of zinc and copper strips, the case is made of zinc and a central carbon rod replaces the copper. The paste is made of water, carbon, manganese dioxide, and ammonium chloride.

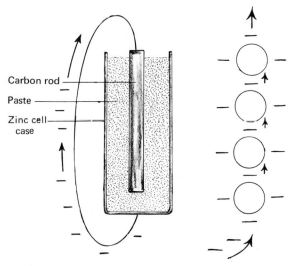

Carbon rod
Paste
Zinc cell case

However, the electrons do not flow through the wire as water would in a tube. After all, the copper wire is solid, not a hollow tube. An extra electron reaching one side of a copper molecule upsets the electrical equilibrium and pushes another electron from the other side of the molecule; this is repeated all along the wire. It is more like the movement of a row of dominoes standing on their edge; when one is pushed, they all fall down. The "push" or energy moves along the row. The dominoes do not change places. Another example is the wave motion through a Slinky.

We must keep in mind the size of the objects in this model. They are incredibly small! We might approximate that ten million atoms, side by side, would span an inch. It would take 1800 or so electrons to weigh as much as a proton from the nucleus of an atom. And many billion electrons pass one point of a wire during one second when a current is flowing.

There's another aspect of this model which we must keep in mind as we view the phenomenon of electricity. Electricity and magnetism are thought of as one phenomenon; they operate as electromagnetic waves. Whenever an electron is in motion (and it always is!), electromagnetic waves radiate out from it. When an electron in the form of electrical energy moves through a wire, electromagnetic waves ripple out from the wire at right angles to the direction of the current. These are the electromagnetic waves which carry television and radio impulses from the station antennae to the set antennae. Light, X-rays, and radiant heat are all forms of electromagnetic waves, waves which are distinguished from each other only by their frequency—the number of wave crests crossing one point per second.

Keeping in mind the conceptual scheme that energy can be neither created nor destroyed, we can apply the model of electromagnetic waves to describe the interactions under *Phenomena* for this stepping stone.

Electrical energy generated by electrons is traveling through the wires of a circuit. A certain number of electrons[37] are moving, representing a fixed total of energy. When the electrons move through the bell part of the circuit, the electrical energy is transformed into *mechanical* energy: the hammer of the bell vibrates and the bell rings, reducing the amount of *electrical* energy in the wire. This reduced amount of energy is flowing through the tungsten wire of the light bulb. Usually a circuit is arranged so that the electrical energy is sufficient to heat the tungsten wire to the glowing point: it lights! Well, this circuit is complete or the bell would not be ringing. Electrical energy must be passing through the bulb, but not enough energy to make it glow. (If the room were dark, we might notice a tiny glow.)

By thinking of the current as electrical energy and by thinking of a certain total of electrical energy in the circuit at one time, we can explain the phenomena in various circuits by figuring out where the electrical energy is transformed into other kinds of energy, thereby reducing the available energy in its electrical form.

The hot wires investigated by Carl in the *Hook Up a Circuit* lesson (page 52) had all the available

[37] The word electron is used here with the understanding that its motion is in the form described on this page.

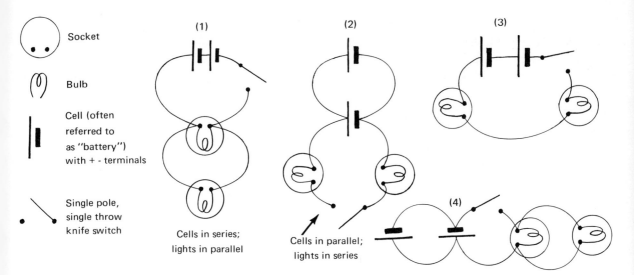

Socket

Bulb

Cell (often referred to as "battery") with + - terminals

Single pole, single throw knife switch

(1) Cells in series; lights in parallel

(2) Cells in parallel; lights in series

(3)

(4)

electrical energy flowing in the copper wire; no energy was used to light a light or ring a bell, it heated the wire instead; much of the electrical energy turned into heat energy all along the wire.

B *Objects in the system*: Open circuit with cell, light, and switch; various materials placed across the switch or across two bare wire ends taped to the table.

Phenomena: Metals and carbon complete the circuit so that the light lights. Nonmetals do not allow the light to light.

Model to describe the interaction: Most atoms have "places" for eight electrons in their outer shells. Of course the total number of electrons in all the shells of an electrically neutral atom equals the number of protons in the nucleus. It is the number of electrons in the outermost shell of an atom which gives it its chemical characteristics—we might say electrochemical characteristics because these are closely related. Of the possible eight electron spaces in the outer shell, metals have less than four filled, nonmetals more than four. You can guess how the atoms with a few electrons in the outer shell will act! So the atom of a metal is in the position of "he who hath not, even that which he hath shall be taken away from him." The atoms of metals part with an outer electron easily. When atoms of metals are aligned in a wire of, say, copper, an electron arriving at one end of the wire pushes the electron off sequentially to the other end of the wire (pages 231-32).

In this investigation, the metals will carry the electrical energy and the nonmetals will not. However, there is also a difference in the ease with which the electrical energy passes through the metals. Copper is one of the best carriers. A thicker wire, of course, allows more electrical energy through than a thin wire, or allows it to pass more easily.

C *Objects in the system*: The objects are presented by the International Electric Symbols (see illustration above). Children can easily guess the object each symbol represents; a good way to present the symbols is to hold up a card showing each one and to ask the children to select the object they think is pictured from an array of electrical equipment. Or they may each pair cards (symbols) with objects on their tables.

There are two basic ways to assemble cells and lights: in series and in parallel. The children can pair hook-ups to physical representations. This leads to the four possible combinations of series and parallel lights and dry cells (see diagrams (1)-(4) above). With one such diagram or blueprint in front of each pair of children, we have never found a child who could not interpret it straight away!

Phenomena: Series cells and parallel lights give the brightest display. Parallel cells and series lights give the weakest. The other two circuits are in between in brightness.

Model to describe the interaction: In circuit (1) above, the electrons at the zinc or negative terminal of one cell push to the positive terminal of the next cell when the circuit is closed. The second cell already has electrons at its negative terminal, so twice the electrical energy is available when dry cells are hooked in series.

In circuit (2), electrons are again at both zinc terminals, but when this circuit is complete only the electrons from the cell nearer the lights move. The electrons in the other cell are not pushed to a positive terminal. They remain, as it were, in reserve. When the near cell begins to lose its electrical energy (only so much can be generated from the chemical reactions in the paste), the second cell takes over. Hence cells in parallel do not produce brighter lights than one cell does, but their supply of electrical energy lasts longer.

When lights are hooked in parallel as in (1) or (4), the electrical energy meets double wire paths—the tungsten wire and the copper wire to the other light—at the sockets. When electrical energy is moving through a thick wire, there are more atoms with electrons to be moved, so more electrical energy can go through the wire with the same amount of initial push from the cell. Of course, parallel wiring of lights draws more electrical energy from the cells; they are used up faster. In series lights like (2) and (3), all the available electrical energy goes through both lights, but each one turns the available electrical energy into heat and light energy, leaving less electrical energy for the wires.

Possible problem for investigation and thought: What happens when one light is unscrewed in circuit (1)? In circuit (2)? Apply the circuits to types of Christmas tree lights and maintenance costs.

D *Objects in the system*: A source of electrons (at the negative terminal of a dry cell), copper wire in circuit interrupted by other strips of metal.

Phenomena: Some of the strips get hot; others glow or melt.

Model to describe the interactions: We have spoken of electrical energy pushing electrons along copper wire with ease. Or to state this in another way, there is little resistance to electrical energy in copper wire. But exactly what meaning can we attach to the word *resistance*?

An analogy comes to mind. A person walking down an empty corridor can progress with ease. If the corridor is crowded with people, he meets considerable resistance to his progress. If he tries to push his way through at a greater rate, he will become hot (and bothered!) in the process. His mechanical energy of walking will be converted to heat energy. But this is only a partial analogy; other factors must also be considered in circuits.

Each dry cell delivers a certain quantity of electrons at its negative (zinc) terminal. Electrons, being of like charge, push against each other. They act like a row of boys sequentially pushing each other off a diving board. The push is steady or constant. In electrical terminology, a size-D cell has an electrical push of 1½ volts. Where each electron can push another electron off the far side of a copper atom, there is little resistance. But if many electrons are pushing electrons off only a few copper atoms, there will be a backward push of electron against electron. This backward push constitutes the resistance. We can easily understand that this is what happens when a thick copper bell wire (such as #22) is attached to a thin wire such as the fine tungsten filament in a light bulb. It happens, too, when a rush of easily moving electrons encounters an atom whose outer shell electrons do not move as easily. Such metals offer more resistance to electrical energy than copper does. This resistance converts the electric energy into heat energy. It is a kind of electrical friction. The heat can become so great that the motion of the wire molecules is increased to the point that the metal becomes liquid: it melts. Or if liquefying is not a property of that metal, the molecular motion will radiate heat and then, as the frequency of the motion increases, the radiation will take the form of light— energy manifesting itself along the electromagnetic spectrum!

E *Objects in the system*: Source of electrons, a coil of copper wire, an iron bolt or large nail, steel paper clips, compass.

Phenomena: When the circuit is complete, the coil of wire and iron filings interact. The iron bolt inside the coil increases the amount of iron interacting with the wire. The coil of wire acts like a compass or

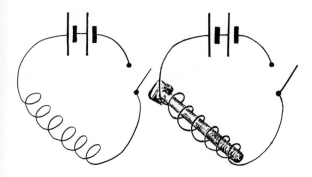

magnet; this can be seen when one pole of the compass moves away from one end of the coil and the other compass end moves toward it. More coils and/or more cells (in series) increase the magnetic effects.

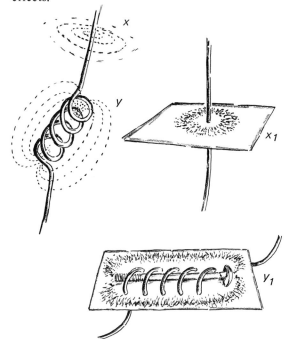

Model to describe the interaction: When an electron moves, electromagnetic waves radiate out from it at right angles to its direction of motion (see point x in figure above). If the wire through which the electrons are flowing is coiled, these planes of electromagnetic waves combine. Their effect is concentrated; it is just as though the coil of wire were a magnet (see point y in figure). If a soft iron core like

a bolt is pushed through the coil, it seems to concentrate the magnetic effect: the iron core becomes a magnet, a temporary one. More coils or more electrons flowing (cells in series) increase the strength of the magnet. If the wire and the coil are run through pieces of cardboard via slits as in x_1 and y_1 (below left) and iron filings are sprinkled on the cardboard surfaces, completing the circuits and gently tapping the cards (to reduce the friction of the filings against the cardboard) will reveal the patterns shown.

F *Objects in the system*: Two coils of copper wire making a complete path. A compass inside one coil. A bar or rod magnet and the space around it as it is pushed in and out of the other coil. Muscle energy.

Phenomena: As the magnet is pushed rapidly in and out of the second coil, the compass needle in the first coil oscillates. Actually, the jerk of the bar through the coil moves the needle in one direction; withdrawal of the bar moves the needle in the other direction.

Models to describe the interaction: The magnetic field around an electromagnet differs from the field around a permanent magnet. In the permanent magnet, the field is comparatively static; the lines which the iron filings follow represent directions of stored energy, energy which does work when another magnet or iron is moved into its vicinity. The field surrounding the electromagnet, generated by the moving electrons, is in constant motion. The electromagnetic waves move out in sequence from the wire, much as waves of water disperse from a pebble thrown in a pond. The "pebble" in this case is the moving electron.

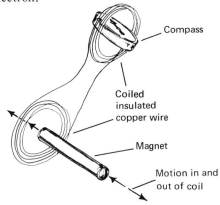

Compass

Coiled insulated copper wire

Magnet

Motion in and out of coil

When the bar magnet is pushed vigorously through the coil of wire or when the wire is moved rapidly over and around the magnet, the magnetic field around the magnet is disturbed by the electromagnetic field around the electrons of the copper atoms. (Recall that these electrons are readily detached.) The magnetic field and the electrons in the outer shells of the copper atoms are moving in relation to each other. This interaction of the magnetic field with the electrons moves the electrons along the wire. It is the converse of moving electrons generating the magnet field (in the form of waves). The movement of electrons in the coil of wire makes, of course, a small electric current. It is registered because, as it flows around the other coil, the electromagnetic waves it generates flow out from the coil and interact with the compass needle. As the magnet moves in one direction through the coil, electrons are pushed one way along the wire and the compass is deflected East or West. When the magnet moves in the other direction (when it is withdrawn through the coil), the electrons are pushed in the opposite direction. This flow of electrons pushes the compass needle in the opposite way, West or East. Because of the friction on the pivot of the compass, there is a slight lag in reaction, but timing the jerking of the magnet in and out of the coil and speeding up the action build the current and hence increase the deflection of the compass needle. This is, of course, an alternating current.

Since energy can be neither created nor destroyed, we can seek the source of the electrical energy here in the alternating current. Our muscle energy is transformed into mechanical energy which moves the magnet in and out of the coil. This action is converted into electrical energy which becomes mechanical energy when it moves the compass needle! This investigation is a simple replica of the way electricity is generated in a powerhouse. A source of energy from steam or falling water turns a turbine which turns a coil in a strong magnetic field and this generates the electricity we use in houses. But behind the steam is coal or gas whose energy has been stored from plants that originally absorbed it from the sun. The waterfall comes from on high because the sun evaporates the water on the ground and deposits it up on a mountain. Our muscle energy comes from the food we eat which also came, in the first place, from plants that absorbed energy from the sun.

The conceptual scheme of a unit on electricity can thus be all embracing.

Units in biological science

The nature of investigation for the physical sciences differs from that for the biological sciences. The difference stems, it would seem, from the different manner in which physical and biological phenomena impinge upon man's senses. The physical universe manifests patterns of regularities which have been observed throughout the centuries: the rhythm of the seasons, the alternation of day and night, gravitational interactions between bodies which are observed (at least) as free falling bodies. These patterns have appeared very similar and fairly constant over the ages because the constant change in the universe is slow when compared with man's life span. What has changed remarkably is the way man looks at the phenomena, the way he explains them, the form into which he puts the observations. He has evolved from believing that day and night were due to a mythical chariot to asserting that the universe was geocentric, to finding that the heavenly bodies were obeying eternal Laws of Nature, to our current view: one can select certain objects in a system, observe their interaction, and formulate models to describe them.

The physical universe shouts its regularities—its patterns—to us; we find the forms for these regularities. In biology, the patterns tend to be hidden; they do not impinge upon the senses in the flagrant fashion of seasons or gravity. It took a Darwin a lifetime to discover a pattern of evolution, and even then the man in the street, as well as many scientists, refused to believe this pattern existed. Even in life histories, the patterns of the life cycles of animals became common knowledge very slowly and much data collecting in this field is still going on today. Biologists first collect data and then look for regularities. Physicists see the regularities and then collect data to make a model of the interactions. Stephen

Toulmin, who has elaborated very interestingly on this theme, puts it this way:

> Natural historians, then, look for regularities of given forms; but physicists seek the form of given regularities. [38]

These differences become apparent as one tries to construct matrices in the two areas. Seeking materials which interact in ways the child can manipulate becomes one of the guiding principles in a physical sciences matrix. Children cannot manipulate a guppy in its aquarium or an opening flower in this manner. There must be a lot more data collecting in the biological units before a pattern can be perceived; more time has to elapse before a pattern of growth becomes evident. Patterns become apparent more easily through graphical or statistical representation; hence, there can be a greater emphasis on recording procedures in the biological sciences, even in the early grades. Looking, careful observing, detailed comparing, and model making based on these procedures in biology often precede controlling a factor in the environment—the activity akin to manipulating materials in the physical sciences. Just as we select with great care the materials we put before children in the physical sciences so that each child can experience a telescoped period of discovery, in the same manner we have to telescope the time of observation in the biological sciences by providing directions of thought via Suggestion Cards. Thus, there tend to be more of these in the biological matrices than we found necessary in the previous ones.

Another change in the biological unit is in the analysis of the children's use of the materials. Instead of *phenomena*, we will now have a section on *data*. Most of the preliminary activity with the biological materials is observing, collecting data—even when the children do things to the organisms, such as shining a flashlight on them, they are gathering data. The colloquia, therefore, center first of all on organizing the data and finding patterns among them. What seems to happen when the mealworms interact with a flashlight? Not all the same things happen all the time

with every mealworm. Is there a pattern here? We may have to collect more data and pool the observations of everyone in the class to discover the pattern or trend that mealworms tend to some degree to move away from the light. Much of biological study in the elementary grades centers on collecting data and establishing patterns through various means. Only later is it feasible to construct models to account for these patterns. Darwin collected an immense amount of data. He found the pattern of evolution: development from simplest to more complex. Later he constructed a model to account for this pattern: struggle for existence and survival of the fittest.

Finding patterns among data is very tentative at first and frequently raises problems or suggests ways to consolidate the data through graphs or records which then lead to a clearer pattern. Models are in order on the teacher's level, for the models guide him in selecting questions (the Suggestion Cards and queries raised during colloquia) and help him recognize the patterns the children seek.

Conceptual schemes and their supporting concepts still form the guide lines for selecting materials. The overall conceptual scheme in biology is that living organisms are in constant change and, more particularly, that this change is due to the interaction of environment and heredity. Both environment and heredity are present in all biological changes, just as matter and energy were inseparable in the physical sciences. But again, as we found that either matter or energy can be emphasized in the physical sciences, so either heredity or environment can be emphasized in biology.

A study of mealworms is an example of the use of a matrix in biology. The first lesson was described in Chapter 1, page 33. It was a general exploration of the larva stage of an insect in relation to light, heat, food, etc. The concept of heredity interacting with the environment and the concept of life functions interacting with heredity may be separated logically. But psychologically and with the materials at the children's disposal, their interaction is likely to underlie each exploration. We shall offer, then, one matrix, although conceivably any one group of children will probably provide data which emphasizes one aspect or the other during the colloquium.

[38] Stephen Toulmin, *The Philosophy of Science*, Hutchinson University Library, London, 1953, p. 53.

MATRIX 8: MEALWORMS

For children at the preconcept level of thought.

The near bank—prior understandings.

Children need to know that living organisms reproduce and go through the birth, growth, death, decay cycle. They need to realize, or be reminded, that animal organisms can feel, that they react positively or negatively to stimuli.

The far bank—points along conceptual arrows toward an understanding that:

1. A mealworm is the larva stage of an insect; it changes into an inactive pupa and later into a beetle.
2. A mealworm has many of the organs humans possess, but in different forms.
3. Mealworms live and grow in a special environment of almost dry grain and in the dark.
4. Beetles mate and lay eggs which grow into larvae.
5. Larvae molt as they grow bigger.
6. A mealworm's life processes include eating, excreting, breathing, responding to stimuli.
7. There is variability in a mealworm's reactions.

Stepping stones:

For each pair of children, there is a basic set of materials to which different objects are added. The basic set is: mealworms, a container, a square of paper for lifting worms, bran, and (usually) a magnifying glass.

MATERIALS	EXPECTED CHILD ACTIVITY
Introduction: Basic set + flashlight, short straws.	As in lessons described in *Tenebrio molitor* (pages 33-42).
A Basic set + molted skins, pupae, straws.	Children test skins and pupae the same way they tested the larvae.
B Basic set + pupa, beetle, Q-tip dipped in water at one end, a piece of apple or potato, cut up bits of banana skin, small dry paint brush.	Children examine the three stages (larva, pupa, beetle) in relation to previously tried stimuli and in relation to the water and the apple. They use the paint brush to lift the beetle (it clings to the bristles).
C Basic set + fine oatmeal, another cereal, sawdust.	Children set up situations to find out which materials the mealworms will eat and how they find their way to the food.
D Basic set + (pupa, beetle optional), ice in a small plastic vial half covered with a cloth, hot water in a similar vial also partly covered.	Children find out whether larva and/or beetle will stay over ice or warm water and what the pupa does on each cloth.
E Basic set + materials for constructing mazes. [39]	Children construct mazes and try putting the larvae in them.

[39] Information on using corrugated cardboard for constructing mazes can be found in *Teacher's Guide: Behavior of Mealworms,* E.S.S. of the Education Development Center, Inc., published by the Webster Division of McGraw-Hill, Manchester, Mo. 63011, 1966, pp. 14-15. Other suggestions for studying mealworms in this booklet may also be of interest.

F Basic set + beetles, source of light (such as a gooseneck lamp) shared by four to six children, black construction paper.

A group of children around one lamp will design and carry out various investigations.

Suggestion Card:
"Try to find out whether beetles and larvae prefer the light or the dark."

Models and patterns for the teacher—ways to think and talk about the data encountered in this matrix:

CONCEPTUAL SCHEME C

Living organisms are in constant change.
A living organism is the product of its heredity (genetic code) and its environment.

	EMPHASIS ON HEREDITY	EMPHASIS ON ENVIRONMENT
PRECONCEPT		Living organisms interchange matter and energy with the environment. There are characteristic environments, each with its characteristic life.
COMPLEX	All living organisms go through a birth, growth, death, decay cycle. Related living organisms reproduce in similar ways.	Living organisms live and grow in different environments.

The four-stage pattern of life cycle—egg, larva, pupa, adult—is common to many insects. The caterpillars which invade our summer gardens are the larvae of butterflies and moths. Larvae are supported and protected by tough skins. When they eat, they grow too big for their skins and molting occurs. The skin usually splits down the back near the head end and a soft larva emerges. At this stage, the skin stretches before it hardens. Caterpillars, with only a moderately tough skin, molt about five times before becoming a pupa, but the hard-skinned mealworms undergo nine to twenty molts during their growth.

The mealworm eggs take a week to hatch under favorable conditions, the larval condition lasts several months, and the pupa stage takes one to three weeks, according to conditions. Adult beetles live only a few months; the female lays several hundred eggs.

The four-stage cycle, in which the young are very different in form from the adult, is called *metamorphosis*. Some insects, such as the cricket, do not have a larval stage; from eggs, they hatch into *nymphs*, resembling small adults. As they molt, they simply become bigger, keeping their same general form. Crickets, therefore, have a pattern of three stages in their life cycle: egg, nymph, adult.

The order in which the stages of an insect's life cycle occur is determined by its heredity; the rate at which the stages change is affected by the environment—a glorious example of the interaction of heredity and environment! As we saw in the *Tenebrio molitor* lesson, Mrs. Weiss kept her mealworms in the refrigerator to slow their metamorphosis.

It is very important to help children avoid using any terminology which suggests purpose, wish, or human foreknowledge on the part of animals. Hence, there should be an objective behavioral description of the molting process as a phenomenon if it is observed. But why does the larva molt? Not *so that* anything else may happen! The molt is a reaction to certain states within the body of the larva interacting with the surrounding environment. Larvae slow down before they molt and this may account for some of their variations in behavior when presented with other stimuli. It is one of the reasons children have to find trends or statistical patterns among their data, rather than discover phenomena from observations.

That a great many changes must be going on inside an insect's body to bring about the dramatic developmental changes may be inferred by the children if they consider the insect's metamorphosis from pupa to adult. At first, the children think the pupa is "eggs," but closer observation reveals that the organism responds to touch, particularly at its tail end, and then children discover parts analogous to the mealworm larvae. The pupa does seem static and unchanging. But when we consider the adult which emerges and realize that the pupa is not taking energy from its environment, we realize that it must be using stored energy to make a fundamental rearrangement of its parts. It is really the most active stage in the life cycle. How erroneous (or short-sighted) to call it a "resting stage"!

Children can make a model to show how much must be happening inside the pupa. Biologists lay these changes to biochemical reactions of enzymes and hormones. In the current science sections of newspapers we read descriptions of insect control through the administration of hormones or radiation which prevents fertility or metamorphosis. Models were constructed before these hypotheses were formulated which led to the practical tests. [40]

[40] Recent thinking on the interaction of the environment with the heredity of the mealworm is recorded in the Education Development Center's booklet *Teaching Guide: Behavior of Mealworms, ibid.* Activities which children can conduct in a similar vein are described in *Science: A Process Approach,* Part Six, A.S.S.S., 1966, pp. 221-32, where Brine Shrimp and Daphnia are the organisms used.

Potential patterns and problems for the children—direction of conceptual arrows:

A *Objects in the system*: Mealworm larvae, molted skins, pupae, straws.

Data: The skin does not respond to stimuli, although it has hollowed parts analogous to the larva. The pupa (at first children call it the "white thing" or the "egg") does wiggle if touched. Nothing has been added or subtracted from the closed system where the mealworms were kept.

Patterns suggested through the colloquium: After a preliminary pooling of data, the children usually become interested in what the "white thing" is. The teacher can ask, "Do you know of any other animals which look a little like a mealworm larva and then have a stage in which they do not move about?" Children usually think of cocoons and then see the pattern that the "white thing" might become a butterfly.

Problems which suggest follow-up activities: Does the pupa (word given by the teacher) become a butterfly? Take one home and watch it carefully.

How does the larva shed its skin? Again, take one home and watch it.

How long between molts? Watch and record.

How long does the mealworm stay as a pupa? Here it might be well to have each child isolate a pupa and keep a record of his observations. But we need to time the beginning, so the pupa must come from the last molt of a larva which has been watched. Because of the time element, it might be good to have the children think of controls and variables, without first discovering that they are essential!

If the children have done some of the activities with light and heat (**D** and **F**), they will know that environmental conditions affect the mealworm. What conditions must be kept constant? Or better still, which should vary? Children will find that not every result is the same. Here is a chance to plot the range of results (number of days to pupate) and find the pattern. The children may then make models to account for the variations. [41]

B *Objects in the system*: Mealworm larvae, pupa, beetle, moisture, bran, banana skin, apple.

[41] Science procedures emphasized: making accurate observations, keeping records, and using controls and variables.

Data: Larvae eat the bran and hide under it; beetles eat the banana skin and apple. Both go to the wet Q-tips at times. Sometimes larvae go to the apple.

Patterns suggested through the colloquium: Beetles seem to spend more time near the moist things than the larvae do. But do they really?

Problems which suggest follow-up activities: The whole class can collect data on the preference of larvae and beetles for dry or moist environments. A Q-tip, moist at one end and dry at the other, or a damp paper towel at one end of the box and a dry towel at the other end could be the test material. A larva is placed between the dry and moist areas. Each child clocks the minutes his larva spends at each end. The experiment is repeated with the beetle. Results can be tabulated to find the pattern: the ratio of total times spent in each area for beetles and larvae.

Similar investigations can be done to see whether the beetles prefer the banana, apple, or moist Q-tip. Because food is involved, do not allow the beetles to eat for a couple of hours beforehand.

Does the pupa react to being on a damp towel or on a dry towel?

C *Objects in the system*: Mealworm larvae, bran, fine oatmeal, cereal, sawdust.

Data: The children will have various and not very precise observations about where the larva spent most of its time and whether or not it ate.

Patterns suggested through the colloquium: Mealworms hide under anything that provides darkness. They wander without seeming to have any direct drive toward food; they end up in the sawdust as often as they do in the food.

Problems which suggest follow-up activities: Do hungry mealworm larvae go to sawdust as often as they do to food? After letting the larvae go two hours without food, place them between a pile of sawdust and a pile of bran. Each child can collect his own data. How many larvae end up in the sawdust; how many in the bran? The same type of investigation can be held to determine if the larvae prefer bran to the other cereal. Provide various types of hiding materials: paper, wool, excelsior, sawdust. Where do they spend most of their time?

Do mealworms sense food? Place hungry larvae six inches from a pile of food. Both mealworm and food are on a piece of white paper. Trace the motion of each mealworm or the paper with a pen. Do this several times on the same piece of paper from the same starting place. Is there a pattern to indicate the mealworms sensed where they were going? If so, at what point did they begin to direct themselves toward the food? To decide whether the mealworms go to the food to eat or to hide, put a few flakes of bran or cereal and a mealworm in a small, closed box and see if the food is eaten (disappears!).

D *Objects in the system*: Beetles, larvae, ice cold area, hot area.

Data: Organisms definitely move away from the cold area and away from the hot area if the heat is extreme.

Patterns suggested through the colloquium: Extremes of heat and cold are not preferred by mealworm larvae or beetles.

Problems which suggest follow-up activities: Is there a preferred temperature for larvae and beetles? Children can be helped to design an investigation. Have babyfood jars with water of temperatures varying from very hot to ice cold in a circle. *Thermometers* will be needed in each jar. Place several larvae in the circle. (Repeat later with beetles.) For each radius of the circle, children could construct a graph with the number of organisms on one axis and the varying temperatures on the other.

E *Objects in the system*: Mealworm larvae, mazes.

Data: Each child will tell which path his larva took. If the maze path is wide, the larva will remain close to the walls.

Patterns suggested through the colloquium: Larvae seem to follow the walls of the maze, but make random choices when they reach the corners.

Problems which suggest follow-up activities: A choice point or corner in a maze is a new situation. What does a mealworm do in a new situation? At first, the worm turns left and right a great deal. Then its activity slows down. It begins to turn in the direction its head is moving, sometimes one way, sometimes another. This leads the larva into a small circular area. Since normally a mealworm does not move rapidly, it seldom moves very far from its preferred area and can thus find its way back by chance. When we place the larva in an entirely new situation, it acts in a manner that habitually brings it back to its nearby old and preferred location. If the new environment is not altered, after a while, the worm adjusts—moves less rapidly. Children can make a model to show why this pattern is an advantage to the organism's survival.

F *Objects in the system*: Beetles, larvae, source of light, source of shadows.

Data: This depends on what the children design. They will report that the beetles cluster most often in some light intensity. Larvae have their range of preferred light intensity, too.

Patterns suggested through the colloquium: There are optimum intensities of light for beetles.

Sample ways to use this matrix

Sets of materials **A** through **D** could really be offered in any order. Since each set offers a number of problem investigations (and we have given only a few of the possibilities for each here), interest may center for a number of lessons around each set. There is a limit to the interest span in dealing with mealworms, evinced by any grade of children. Waning interest should be honored by a change in matrix. Several stepping stones can be straddled at one time. Many of the problems extend through time, so several activities may be going on concurrently: waiting for a pupa to become a beetle or a larva to molt and, in the meantime, holding whole group activities on compiling data for statistical analysis. Hence, one set of materials may be started before another set has been finished.

Sometimes the children wish to follow the insect life cycle from the egg stage. For this, a few beetles can be kept in a quart jar half-filled with bran. Place a paper towel over the bran and keep a fresh potato and/or pieces of banana skin above the paper. Leave the top of the jar open so that the bran will not become moldy. Since only adult beetles were placed in the jar, the appearance of larvae means that eggs were laid and hatched.

TO THE EDGE OF DISCOVERIES: THE PLANNING AND DEVELOPMENT OF A UNIT IN BIOLOGY

During the last full month of the school year, Miss Yonika decided to introduce her bright fourth graders to microscopes. The school was the only elementary one in a country town situated some 20 miles from a New England city. Her class, one of two fourth grades, was composed of the better readers. (By the end of this year, their reading ability would range from seventh grade through high-school levels on the standardized tests.)

Before launching into the actual preparations of the unit, Miss Yonika set out to find microscopes for her 28 children. It seemed essential to her that each child should have one. Some of the children owned their own or could borrow one; there were four in the school and five could be borrowed from the Junior High. Her grand total was 14, in assorted sizes, powers, and conditions.

Since Miss Yonika felt that there should be a one-to-one correspondence of children to microscopes, she decided to conduct the investigative sessions in two shifts. This would require an extended period if a colloquium were to follow the double-discovery period. The reading and language arts period, usually scheduled from 1:30–3:00 each afternoon, was just the double period she needed. The children were doing well in their reading and it was the end of the year, so time could be taken from the language arts *per se* for work with a microscope. She arranged the program so that half the class would work with the microscopes during the first 30 minutes, and the other half would have their turn during the second 30 minutes. Each group of children would read while their peers used the microscopes. The last half hour would be a combined clean-up and colloquium.

These arrangements took care of only the mechanisms of the unit: the periphery. The core would be the subconcepts and the appropriately related materials in conjunction with which the microscopes would be used. The overall concept under which this unit fell was "A living organism is the product of its heredity (genetic code) and environment." (See the chart on page 166). However, the concept level Miss Yonika chose for her class was that "That cell is the unit of structure and function [of a living organism]."

In order to choose potential stepping stones, Miss Yonika browsed through the unit on *Small Things* [42] and the last chapter in her fourth grade text. [43] In these books she marked experiences with materials that she thought would be interesting to the children. She jotted down the concepts, or rather the subconcepts toward which she thought the unit should point, and she listed the necessary understandings she believed her children had. Then, by eliminating a few parts and adding a few others as she paired the subconcepts with the materials, she prepared the following matrix. She realized that there were some basic materials appropriate to each lesson so it was necessary only to add those specific to each lesson.

The near bank—prior understandings.

She assumed that the children had a general understanding that living organisms were composed of cells, but that they would not know what cells looked like or did, nor would they be aware of the varied shapes and sizes of cells.

Miss Yonika had her own way of writing these memos. We record them in the format we have used before.

The children had had a unit on photosynthesis during the year, so they should know that the sun is the ultimate source of energy for our planet. They had done some work with white powders and had extended this to be basic chemistry of starch and sugar.

The far bank—points along conceptual arrows toward an understanding that:

1. Living organisms interchange matter and energy with the environment.
2. The cell is the unit of structure and function; a living organism develops from a single cell.

[42] *Teacher's Guide: Small Things,* E.S.S. of the Education Development Center, Inc., published by the Webster Division of McGraw-Hill, Manchester, Mo. 63011, 1965.

[43] Paul F. Brandwein *et al., Concepts in Science 4*, Harcourt Brace Jovanovich, Inc., New York, 1966, pp. 285-99.

Stepping stones:

For each child, there is a basic set of materials: microscope, slide, cover slip. For every seven children: several light sources, a jar of water, three eyedroppers, paper towels, facial tissues.

MATERIALS	EXPECTED CHILD ACTIVITY
A Basic set + a hair.	Children learn to prepare a slide of a hair and focus the microscope.
B Basic set + onion skin, tweezers.	Children make a slide of one layer of skin and examine it under microscope.
C Basic set + onion skin, tweezers, stains (either eosin Y or methylene blue).	Children make a slide of onion skin using stain instead of water.
D Basic set + blood cells.	Children make a slide, look at it under microscope; they may ask for stains.
E Basic set + a toothpick, squamous tissue from inside cheek, stains used in **C**.	Children make a slide with stain; they examine it under microscope and compare it with the other cells seen previously.
F Basic set + pond creatures.	Children make a slide, examine it, ask for stains.
G Basic set + yeast in warm sugar water.	Children make a slide and examine it.

Suggestion Card:
"Use your highest power."

H Basic set + salt, sugar, Epsom salts crystals.	Children make slides of each, examine them, and compare them with cells.

Suggestion Card:
"Look at these without using water or cover slip."

Conceptual arrows expected from the colloquia:

A No concepts, just technical skills.

B A cell is a unit with different parts in it.

C An onion skin cell has a definite shape, a wall, and a nucleus.

D There are different kinds of cells. A red blood cell has no wall and no nucleus.

E Here is another kind of cell. Cells have different shapes, sizes, and parts.

F One cell can be a whole living creature.

G One cell that is a living plant can take food from the environment, grow big, and divide into two cells.

H Crystals are not alive. Children might say this is because they do not move or grow. If so, give them drops of hot concentrated solutions so that they can watch the crystals forming! Discussion would have to bring out that crystals do not exchange energy and matter with the environment.
Suggestion: Will an onion skin cell dissolve in water? Will one crystal divide and become two?

Here is the record of what happened during this unit:

The First Lesson

The first science period was devoted to helping a few children at a time learn to use the microscope. The children made slides of their hairs and learned to focus the lens, adjust the mirror, and prepare a slide with as few air bubbles in it as possible. Most of the children were able to look at a hair and make some remarks about the way it appeared to them. They also took a good look at the bubbles in the water on their slides!

There was no reason to hold a colloquium since this was practice in techniques.

Each child had a microscope, a slide, a cover slip, and an eyedropper. A jar of water, paper towels, and facial tissues were on each table.

Free discovery with expensive materials is not in order!

The Second Lesson

This took place the following day. The first half of the class was divided in two groups of seven. Each group of seven gathered near one of the two electric outlets. The outlets had adapters in them to which lamp cords were attached. Seven of the children gathered around each of the two tables and learned to share the light from the available lamps. Each child had his own microscope, slide, and cover slip. In the center of each group were pieces of onion, tweezers, a jar of water, and four eyedroppers. Miss Yonika showed each group how to peel a thin onion skin from between the layers of onion and suggested that the children use very small pieces for their slides. She then divided her time between circulating among the children who were reading and answering calls for assistance at the microscopes.

*A quick demonstration of how to peel the onion seemed more efficient than a **Suggestion Card.***

The children worked hard and with much concentration. They looked down each other's microscopes, but in general saw only dark splotches since all of the pieces of onion were too large and too thick. However, the children gained ability in adjusting the microscopes and in making slides. There was no colloquium. The children were still concentrating on techniques.

It began to dawn on Miss Yonika that this was going to be a slightly different kind of unit from her usual discovery–colloquium type. Much of the launching went into technical skills, which the children, however, seemed to enjoy. The emphasis was on looking and would then be on judging or interpreting what was seen. Since seeing clearly was the prerequisite for interpreting and thinking about the observations and certainly for finding patterns, the next lesson should concentrate on more successful viewing.

Adaptive behavior
↓
Sustained adaptation

The Third Lesson

Miss Yonika began this lesson by reminding the children that their pieces of onion skin were too thick for clear viewing last time; again she demonstrated how to skin one layer off the onion. After the membrane-like layer had been peeled off, she told them that only a tiny area of it was necessary for a successful slide. "You have something else on your tables which will help you see more clearly," she added.

The children literally dove into their work, proceeding with feverish haste. By this time everyone had realized that half an hour with the microscope was insufficient for complete success; eagerness was far from exhausted after half an hour.

*Materials **C**. One table had eosin Y; the other methylene blue. Each stain was in one section of an aluminum TV dinner tray; the onion was in another section; toothpicks and eyedroppers were in the third.*

This day, the Friday of the first week, the children had trouble with the lights. One tensor lamp had burned out and sharing the remaining ones became a problem. The children did not even wait to clean their slides when they needed to make a new one. Every moment seemed to go toward the culminating act of seeing what was under the lens. Interestingly enough, all of the children used the stains instead of the water before dropping on the cover slip. There were many calls for help: to "find" the object, to adjust the lamp. Miss Yonika was kept busy with the sciencing children. The readers seemed to manage very well on their own.

One boy, apparently discouraged with his efforts with the onion skin, wandered over to the window sill where there were several aquaria. He sucked up some pond water with an eyedropper and looked at it under his microscope. Most of the other children had adequate views of onion skin cells.

The colloquium was quite revealing to Miss Yonika.

As soon as the colloquium circle had assembled, Ivan called out, "The dye tastes terrible!"

Miss Y.: You had troubles today, but also successes. Name one of either.
Ivan: The onion skin with red dye on it looked like a honeycomb.
Mary: Mine looked like brown bricks.
Thelma: I had cells.
Jennie: Mine was more like barbed wire.
Miss Y.: You've seen something that looks like honeycomb, barbed wire, bricks, and cells.
Dottie: I put blue and red dye on mine. Half looked different. I saw cells and wrinkles.
Stanley: I saw things sort of diamond shaped. *(Indicates triangles and lines with his hands.)*
Wendy: My bubbles were blue and the stone wall was red.
Shaughan: I had a bad day. I saw nothing.
Miss Y.: When I looked down your microscope and there was no slide under it at all, I saw—well—everything! Any idea why?
Shaughan: (very enthusiastically) It was the dirty lens.
Faith: I saw dim black lines and scratches. Clean ones on the bottom.
Natalie: I saw tiny brown polka dots.
Miss Y.: Where were they?
Natalie: On what you saw with your eye.
Mannie: I saw some pond water; I saw a thing swim across. *(Describes with hand movements how it swam.)*

Miss Y.: That is called a *Paramecium. (She had looked down his microscope.)*
Sheila: Your eyelashes can get on the lens and you can't see.
Keith: I had a gouge on my slide.
Alice: I saw cells. There were two lines, each a different color.
Pierre: There were cracks on my slide. Looked like lightning.
Miss Y.: You had the good slide.

No mention had been made of how to use the stains.

Adaptive behavior
↓
Sustained behavior
↓
Initiating behavior

Ivan was the child everyone noticed on entering the room. He would call out loudly from time to time, disturbing the quiet atmosphere. He would become discouraged easily and then seek some nonacademic employment!

What is the effect of Miss Yonika articulating to the children that troubles are acceptable?

Initiating behavior. The red and blue dyes were on different tables, clear across the room from one another.

The periphery of water bubbles often appears blue.

So that's why he had a bad day!

Later Natalie explained that she could see the piece of onion skin without the microscope, but the nuclei showed up only under magnification.

Mannie contributes from his initiating behavior.

Pierre's "cracks" are his way of describing "lines" (cell walls). Miss Yonika is trying to encourage him to say more because his slide was well made and his focus was very clear.

Charles: Mine looked like brick walls or cells.

Ronnie: I know we weren't looking for the bubbles today, but I did. I looked at a bubble just for fun; it was rainbow colored.

Why did he feel free to do this and to report it?

Miss Y.: You saw a great many colors?

Ronnie: I saw the onion through the rainbow colors.

Result of having his initiating behavior accepted?

Jud: I had too much dye so I didn't see much.

Larry: The second time I looked I saw lines like messed up hair—lots of colors.

Larry, too, had both dyes.

Ivan: I had blue cells like bricks.

Keith: I put dye on my hair. It looked like beads—lots of colors.

Penny: I tried it at home with iodine. Iodine makes the nuclei show.

Until now, all the contributions had been of the data type. Miss Yonika now introduces some thinking about the data.

Miss Y.: What are nuclei?

Penny: Nuclei are found in all cells except there are none in blood cells.

Verbal or experiential information?

Miss Y.: But what are they?

Penny shrugged her shoulders.

Adelaide: I did that at home, too. They looked like bricks. They looked the same dyed or undyed.

Miss Y.: All the words you've been using describe one thing.

Jud: All parts of the onion.

Miss Y.: Do you know what the parts are?

Jud: Cells.

Penny: Creatures. Different live plants or creatures put together to make a larger thing.

Miss Yonika certainly didn't expect this after Penny's first contribution.

The children laughed.

Miss Y.: Penny is trying to explain something. Penny see if you can make it clearer. *(She declined. It probably did not sound right now that her thoughts were put into words. Doris helped out.)*

Words are beginning to generate new thoughts.

Doris: All things put together make the onion skin.

Faith: All the things make the onion skin.

A new idea for *Faith.*

Ronnie: Maybe it's different layers you're seeing. *(He indicated with his hands that he thought layer upon layer of cells might make up the onion.)* *The school bell rang for the children to get ready for the buses.*

Adventurous thinking. Remember his first contribution?

Miss Y.: I think you've all realized the importance of having just a single layer of cells and the importance of having clean slides. Maybe next week you can all take a good look to see whether you can find the cells and nuclei using the stain.

Her use of language emphasizes Ronnie's contribution.

"Nuclei" name perceived objects for the children. As yet, the word has only a slender meaning for them.

In thinking over the day's work, Miss Yonika took note of all the surprises. The children evidently did not have much of an idea of what a cell was; they certainly did not realize that it was a unit of life. They did not seem to know the relationship of one cell to the whole multicellular organism. But until clear perception could be achieved, the children must base their ideas on insufficient evidence. Perhaps the item of first importance then would be to provide them with a jar of detergent water and a jar of clean water and plenty of tissues. The children needed to be encouraged to make sure that there was nothing extraneous on their slides or cover slips before they placed the onion and the stain there.

Materials **C** plus detergent and clear water. Both stains were available to all.

Last time he saw only the cell walls.

Last time Ronnie concentrated on bubbles but then made the remark about cells being in several layers.

Even though some children are still referring to "bricks," "bubbles," and "dots," Miss Yonika tries not to interrupt or correct them. Here they are communicating with one another.

An analogy, but not a hidden likeness.

Children had plastic cover slips which scratch easily.

Miss Yonika wanted the children to establish the idea of cells before considering the nucleus. What effect did her redirection have?

It was Penny who first introduced the word *nuclei*. At one point Miss Yonika had written on the board: "One nucleus. Many nuclei."

Miss Yonika begins by giving information. Why? Then she continues really to think out loud. The children nodded in response or looked as though they were considering the questions.

The Fourth Lesson

The next lesson began with a brief statement about the provisions for cleanliness. Again the children went to work with a will. The colloquium showed progress in thinking for many of the children.

Charles: I saw blue bubbles—like dots inside one layer.

Ronnie: I tried to get one layer and put the slightest bit of blue and red dye on it. There was only one layer and it looked like a fence. I could see the nuclei.

Miss Y.: What Charles calls bubbles, you call nuclei.

Ole: I thought I saw a hair, but it was the side of the slide.

Pierre: There are veins in the cell—not a nucleus. It's veins, like in a body.

Stanley: Mine was like Ronnie's, but darker.

Miss Y.: Do you know why it was darker?

Stanley: I used more dye.

Thelma: I had red-orange cells with stringly bluish bubbles.

Sheila: Mine was like a cave with writing on the wall.

Alice: I used red and blue; it made many different . . . [The next word was undecipherable.]

Miss Y.: Could you see whether the blue and red stained different parts?

Alice: No.

Larry: It branches. Red, blue, green—like in a wrist.

Ronnie: Those were scratches.

Wendy: Nothing interesting today.

Shaughan: Mr. George [a visitor] got a good one for me. I saw bricks and nuclei. It [the nucleus] wasn't black, but red.

Miss Y.: Let's hold that a moment.

Keith: I saw veins and nuclei. Saw the same as Pierre.

Mary: I had blue—blue dots; the lines were red. It made the slide yellow-red round the bricks in many of them.

Doris: (aside to Mary) Your slide wasn't clean.

Charles: The dyes made it stand out.

Miss Y.: Now you know why scientists use stains. By the way, what stood out?

Penny: The nucleus.

Shaughan: My lens was wet.

Pierre: I wanted to get a bright field with the plane side [of the mirror]. Then I saw bubbles; maybe they were molecules.

Miss Y.: Molecules are too small to see under the microscope. Is the whole onion made of cells? Do you think all the cells have the same shape?
Tomorrow we might try to look at scallion leaves and roots.

Shaughan: Roots don't have cells . . . maybe not on the outside anyway.

The bell rang. Some children had to leave promptly. The others cleaned up.
From this day's work the children seemed to have a clearer idea that cells were bricklike structures with dots inside. "Cell" and "nucleus" still remained

undefined terms, but the children were using the words in the preconcept sense, as adults use them. In order to build a concept of "cell," the children needed to have experience with other cells of different shapes. Some of the children had not found the nucleus. Miss Yonika thought the differential (which the book on *Small Things* had suggested would be brought out by the eosin and methylene blue stains) was not clear. She tried some Lugol's iodine solution on an onion skin herself after school and found that the nucleus stood out clearly. She had never tried, however, to make a single-layer cell slide from parts of a scallion, but it did seem like a good idea!

Because the children really had no concept of what a cell was, Miss Yonika thought another kind of cell from a similar plant would help. But because the assumption that the children started with some idea about cells turned out to be largely erroneous, the class had hardly left the near bank!

Apart from the new material offered by the scallion, Miss Yonika thought it might be interesting to go back to the first experience the children had had, that of making slides of their hairs, and to use the hairs as a measure of the cells. This would help them to compare the cells of the onion skin with those in the scallion. It would also add to building the concept of the cell as a very small thing.

A suggestion she had read, but not included in the matrix.

The Fifth Lesson

It turned out to be "one of those days." There was a feeling of irritation in the class; minor squabbles broke out over the use of the lamps and over whose place was here or there. This day more slides were broken than the sum of those broken during all the previous periods.

With all this, the colloquium turned out to be one of the most profitable. Miss Yonika decided to convey to the children that she understood it was "one of those days."

What could Miss Yonika have learned about the children's thinking if there had been only exploration of materials and no colloquium? What evidence can you find of *new* learning taking place during the colloquium?

What influence on the course of the colloquium might this recognition of feelings have had?

Miss Yonika directs the thinking today, rather than calling for individual reactions. What might the latter have produced?

Most children had not taken up the hair-as-measure suggestion.

Miss Y.: Today everyone seems to hate everyone else!
Chorus: Y-e-s!
Miss Y.: In what ways are all the cells you've seen alike or in what ways are they different?
Jacqueline: Some are long and thin; others fat and chubby.
Charles: The onion has larger cells; the scallion smaller ones. I measured the length of a cell with my hair. It was six or seven hairwidths.
Miss Y.: Did everyone understand?
Chorus: No!
Charles repeated his observations with more description.
Miss. Y.: *(further illustrating by marking the width of a book by moving her finger across it)* The hair made a good measure of Charles' cell. From what part of the scallion was it?
Charles: The stem—the white part.
Penny: I had a thin scrawny cell. *(She went to the blackboard and drew it; see art at right.)*

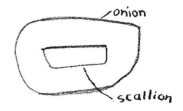

Why didn't Miss Yonika correct this arithmetic operation?

The hairwidth comparison would be independent of the powers, but the children do not see this.

First use of word *stain* by a child.

Ivan is responding to Miss Yonika's constant directives (which tend to interfere with the children's own thoughts) by being "original." In what way did Miss Yonika's response affect Ivan?

Miss Yonika realizes that her questioning is getting nowhere.

Do you recognize the "complex" type of thinking?

Only through a colloquium could this meaning have been revealed and clarified.

Why does Fred feel free to walk over to a friend during the colloquium?

Following Fred's lead toward materials **F**.

(Penny had gone for pond water the day before, too. During her reading period she had gone to the library and borrowed a book on pond life. She found a paramecium picture. Miss Yonika pronounced the name for her.)

Miss Y.: Did you use the same microscope both days?

Penny: Yes.

Miss Y.: Why did I ask that?

Keith: Different microscopes have different powers. You see more details with some.

Shaughan: If one microscope was 60 power and the other something else, you could---subtract to compare sizes?

Ronnie: If you use two microscopes, you should check to see if the powers are the same.

Miss Y.: How could you *measure* them?

Charles: A hairwidth is a good measure.

Miss Y.: Your hairwidths can be your rulers—your microscope measures. You've explained that cells are different sizes. In what way are their shapes different?

Larry: Onion roots are different from the leaf. *(He showed with his hands; see diagram in margin.)*

Miss Y.: How many saw the nucleus today? *(About two-thirds of the children raised their hands.)* What did it look like?

Stanley: Brown and round.

Miss Y.: By nature?

Stanley: No, stained.

Miss Y.: How did you know it was a nucleus?

Ivan: It had a sign on it!

Miss Y: (laughing) For those who didn't have a sign, how did you recognize the nucleus?

Charles: Brown and round.

Miss Y.: Have any of you changed your minds about whether the whole of the onion is made up of cells or not?

Ivan: Cells are not everywhere. There's space between—like you've got veins. Our bodies have spaces.

There was a lot of cross discussion as the class tried to understand where the spaces to which Ivan referred were. Some children tried to explain what he meant to others. Ivan insisted that he didn't mean "anything like that." He then went to the board and drew a cell. It turned out that he thought the wall was the cell and its content was all space.

Several children: The whole thing's the cell.

Miss Y.: Cell wall is the name for the outside of the "brick." The whole thing is the cell, including the nucleus.

Fred: (walking over to Ronnie) What do you call that thing I saw under my microscope?

Ronnie: Paramecium.

Fred: I had a paramecium. It swam across.

Miss Y.: Was it one cell?

Fred: Yes.

Miss Y.: Did your paramecium have a nucleus?

Fred: Yes.

Penny: No!

Miss Y.: Could it have had one although you didn't see it?

Penny: Yes.

Miss Y.: How could you find out?

Penny: Follow it; look harder.

Miss Y.: What did you do to make the onion nucleus stand out?

?: Focus.

?: Squish it.

Miss Y.: What were you using when you first saw the onion cell nucleus clearly?

Jacqueline: Stain.

?: That would kill it.

Miss Y.: Why might it be a help if it were dead?

?: It would be still.

Miss Y.: Do you think there are the same number of cells in an onion seed as there are in the grown onion?

Vague opinions about layers growing, cells being larger but not increasing in same number, or there being more cells.

Miss Y.: How would you like to see one cell become two?

Chorus: Yippee!

Miss Y.: That'll be our next lesson!

Shaughan: All you have to do is cut it in two!

The bell rang.

Keith: We all began as two cells.

Penny had said that all cells except blood have nuclei.

(Question marks occur when answers were so quick that it was impossible to record the speaker's name as well.)

The second time *stain* is used instead of *dye*.

She had materials **G** in mind.

Quiet wisdom heard by only a few.

Toward the end of each colloquium, Miss Yonika was able to sense the next lesson from her familiarity with the matrix possibilities. This is not always possible during the colloquium, of course, but when the next lesson can be suggested, the children are able to look forward to it. This forms an appropriate stimulus which carries over even a week of waiting. Usually the Investigators' Log serves as a stimulus to solve unanswered questions and problems; because of the time-bind, this class never reached the Log activity. The "carrot" Miss Yonika was able to offer each time left the children in a happy state of expectancy, even on off-days when a lack of technical success or a feeling that there never had been enough time for work with the microscopes had produced unrest.

For the sixth lesson, Miss Yonika had in mind that the children should watch budding yeast. That was what was behind her question about one cell becoming two. She was aware that it required a high magnification to see budding, so after school she warmed some yeast in sugar water and made a slide for viewing under the children's microscopes. Only the higher powered instruments showed the budding in any way. However, the small cells were quite visible, even under the lowest powers. It seemed that this might be another period of frustration!

The yeast activity could be paired with another set of materials. Which one might make a suitable partner for the next lesson? Well, yeast is a plant, but the children could hardly be expected to know this. However, the difference between plant and animal cells came to her mind as a suitable co-topic. The

This differs from Mr. McIver's lesson where the children suggested what to do the next time. Try to account for this difference.

children with the lower-powered microscopes could scrape squamous tissue from the insides of their cheeks for viewing, and the colloquium could feature the plant–animal dichotomy as well as the budding of yeast. She made a slide of her own squamous tissue and stained it with methylene blue. The nucleus was clear, and the wrinkled flat cell without a cell wall showed up well.

The Sixth Lesson

During her lunch hour the next day, Miss Yonika emptied a package of yeast and an envelope of sugar from the cafeteria into a jar of warm water and left it in a warm spot in her classroom. She placed a small glass dish of yeast on each of the two microscope work tables (just before the lesson), and put clean toothpicks, eyedroppers, and methylene blue in the sections of the aluminum TV dinner trays.

Why didn't she name the yeast?

Her directions take the place of **Suggestion Cards**. Is any leeway left to the children? Read on and see!

Her instructions to the children were to use the "grey stuff" if they had high powers and to scrape the cells gently off the insides of their cheeks with toothpicks and stain their slides with methylene blue if they had low powers. (She demonstrated the gentle stroking method necessary to obtain the squamous tissue. When each group had a good slide, they could switch places.

All the children immediately attacked the yeast, high power or no! Keith exclaimed, "I can't see anything," and then discovered he did not have a cover slip on his slide. His yeast was too thick until he squashed it out. Mannie looked at his slide and burst out with, "Oh boy!" Keith then dove back to his own microscope.

Miss Yonika began the colloquium by passing around the original and now frothing jar of yeast. She didn't say a word.

Larry: It's like the fresh milk straight from the cow.
Jennie: Like before you let the dough set.
Thelma: She means yeast.

A hidden likeness between molds?

Ivan: When you let something happen to peaches, it smells.
Faith: My grandfather has a doughnut shop. Yeast is put into it to make the doughnuts expand.
Shaughan: It's iodine mixed with milk.

Identification of the material is subtly acknowledged by the teacher. What is the difference in effect between Miss Yonika's way and just saying "Right"?

Miss Y.: What name did several of you give it?
Chorus: Yeast.
Miss Y.: What does yeast do?
Thelma: It makes the bread rise—expand.

Miss Yonika did not know what Fred was referring to. She offered a redirecting question.

Fred: When you have trouble with the septic tank, you flush it down.
Miss Y.: Why does it make the bread rise?
Ronnie: I don't like the smell.
Don [a new child in the group]: The little round things go up?
Fred: It expands.
Penny: It's multiplying; it tries to fill up space.
Miss Y.: What does multiplying mean?
Sheila: Multiplying means making more things.
Ivan: Bumping up and down.

A better question!

Miss Y.: So what does a cell multiplying mean?

Natalie: It's like they're cut up into two. Makes more, but there's less [material].

Keith: If you cut up paper, the population of the paper is larger but not the size. In cells, both get larger.

Miss Y.: That's a terrific idea. Will you say it again so that everyone can see what you mean? *(He does.)*

Miss Y.: What do you think a living organism needs to multiply?

All: Food.

Dottie: Energy. . . . The sun gives energy. *(She looks embarrassed, then giggles.)*

Miss Y.: You are saying interesting things. You giggle because you don't feel sure. But let's all listen.

Dottie said nothing, but looked relieved.

Miss Y.: What is yeast's food?

Dottie: Energy—from hot water.

Charles: Starch made it. . . . Starch made . . .

Miss Y.: You've got a hunch.

Jacqueline: Dough has starch in it. The cells of yeast get energy from starch.

Don: More starch, more energy.

Thelma: Sugar is made in plants and plants get energy from the sun. Then it expands?

Shaughan: Does sugar have starch in it?

Miss Y.: Sugar and starch are both carbohydrates. *(Emphasizes the parts of the word.)* What kinds of atoms do you think are in both starch and sugar?

Charles: Carbon dioxide and hydrogen.

Ivan: Plants make sugar when they're growing. When it [the new yeast cell] gets away from the plant, it still needs the same kind of food.

Wendy: Like a baby?

Ivan: When the sugar gets into them, they have the same formula.

Miss Y.: What happens to yeast when it eats sugar?

Ole: The atom explodes.

Miss Y.: Yeast is a one-celled plant.

?: It multiplies.

?: Expands.

?: Makes another one.

Miss Y.: Did anyone see a big one and a small one together?

Faith: Each one turns into two; each of these two to two more. They divide.

Charles: Like two water drops run together.

Penny: Just the opposite.

Charles: No, sugar gets into the yeast and it gets bigger.

Penny: Then it divides.

Miss Y.: Next time I am going to try to bring in a film of yeast budding. It is doing what you thought you saw, but the photography is speeded up—just the opposite of slow motion. Speeded up photography is called time lapse. *(She writes this term on the board.)*

Thought generated by Natalie's words are expressed in new words by Keith.

There had been a previous unit on photosynthesis; but this is adventurous thinking.

Here we learn why her adventurous thinking had an uncertain ring. Charles offers more adventurous thinking.

Dottie's hunch and Charles' words produce thought in Jacqueline. Further interaction affects Don, Thelma, and Shaughan.

Why does Miss Yonika answer this question instead of throwing it back to the class?

An original way of thinking of carbon, oxygen, and hydrogen.

Why is this information needed here?

(Again, question marks appear when quick answers made recording the speakers' names impossible.)

Each is right from his own standpoint.

The Seventh Lesson

The following lesson was the last one of the year which could be devoted to science due to end-of-semester activities and other obligations. Miss Yonika was eager to land the children on some stepping stone, and cell division seemed to be closest to the general interest. She had an excellent filmloop of yeast budding in mind. [44] But there were other interesting loops on allied subjects, too. She decided to make a day of films. She brought in one of frogs' eggs dividing until the tadpoles emerged, and she kept one of paramecium and other pond creatures in reserve.

The children watched the filmloop on yeast with great interest. After it was finished, Miss Yonika asked them to tell what they saw.

Ivan: It multiplied more than twice.

Fred: Inside the nucleus it was moving around—like a person blowing on coal and something comes out.

Miss Y.: Are the cells alive?

Penny: We're made up of cells and we're alive. Why shouldn't they be?

Miss Y.: Can you describe the nucleus?

Doris: Black with white beads.

Pierre: It squeezes out—like a baby born from its mother.

Sheila: Little bugs . . . walking around.

Miss Y.: Did you notice anything in the cell itself besides the nucleus?
    Nods. . .

Miss Y.: I'll give you its name; it's protoplasm.

Doris: Like jelly?

Miss Y.: Yes. What happened to the new cell after it was born?

Penny: It formed a scar where it broke off.

Shaughan: Another one formed beside it, and another . . . a whole bunch. One cell makes one cell and keeps on going.

Miss Y.: How many cells are in *a* yeast?

Shaughan: One. Then it forms two.

Ivan: Keeps on multiplying.

Miss Y.: What do you think happens in an onion?

Charles: It stays together and when there's enough for a layer, then it makes more layers.

Miss Y.: How many cells in an onion?

Ivan: Billions. It's not one-celled.

Miss Y.: Now you might like to see another time-lapse filmloop of the way a frog's egg, which is one large cell, divides to become a tadpole. [45]

During the viewing, the children's perception selected the phenomena of photography rather than the meaning of the film. They were excited by the

Margin notes

Filmloops last a few minutes.

A beautiful analogy.

A hidden likeness.

Doris is bringing meaning to some previous reading. She is given assurance because there is no way to find out experientially.

An unforeseen problem comes into view: the difference between a cell dividing to make two and dividing to create a multicellular organism.

---

[44] Produced by the E.S.S. of the Education Development Center, Inc. and available from the Webster Division of McGraw-Hill, Manchester, Mo. 63011. (For 8 mm: Code 19379; for super 8 mm: Code 7479.)

[45] Produced by the E.S.S. of the Education Development Center, Inc. and available from the Webster Division of McGraw-Hill, Manchester, Mo. 63011. (Ask for Frog Egg I, II, and III in 8 mm and in super 8 mm.)

speeded up wriggles of the emerging tadpole, surprised into giggles at changes of focus. Toward the end, the filmloop stuck and the picture dissolved into a sea of moving shadows. Miss Yonika explained that the machine was stuck and said, "Maybe you'd like to see it all again. This time try to figure out what is being formed as the cells divide." The children were quietly attentive and the machine behaved well! A colloquium followed.

The children had kept tadpoles and frogs the previous year.

Miss Y.: What did you see?
Doris: Were the cells making up the frog? Was the frog coming out of the egg?
Miss Y.: Maybe you'd like to explain to Miss Tremont (*another teacher who had come to view the film*) what you saw.
Thelma: First there's one egg.
Chorus: No! A cell.
Thelma: Ok, cell. Two-four-eight, then so many!
Doris: First it makes a backbone, then legs, then stomach, then eyes, then head.
Charles: Correction. How can there be eyes without a head?
Doris: Ok. Head first, then eyes.
Jacqueline: The tadpole is all the cells together. Then it separates from the jelly.

Since only a few children contributed to the colloquium, the class was asked if they would like to view the film again. They wanted to. The descriptions a few children had given served as guidelines to sharpen the perception of the others.

There was no discussion after this second complete showing. Miss Yonika announced that she had one more filmloop and that it would show a clear view of *Paramecium* and some other pond animals. [46]

If it had not been the last chance to tie up the science unit, Miss Yonika would not have shown a third film at this time. However, the outcome was unexpectedly interesting. The children watched the movements of the paramecium with concentration. They realized too that this was not time-lapse photography.

After the film was over, Miss Yonika suggested that since the paramecium was alive it had to eat, digest, and get rid of wastes. She explained the vacuole explosions in order to differentiate the vacuole from the nucleus. Shaughan said that there were hairs that helped the paramecium move. "Hairs are like feelers; the hairs tell the brain."

Miss Y.: Does a paramecium have a brain?
Penny: Maybe the nucleus is the brain.
Charles: The nucleus is the nerve system?
Thelma: Is the nucleus an egg?
Charles: The heart?

[46] "Comparative Sizes of Microscopic Animals" produced by the E.S.S. of the Education Development Center, Inc., and available from the Webster Division of McGraw-Hill, Manchester, Mo. 63011. (For 8 mm: Code 19386; for super 8 mm: Code 17486.)

The children were obviously tired and the session was nearing its end. They evidently felt this, too, for when Miss Yonika said, "You're just about ready to read books on the nucleus . . ." there were cries of "No . . . no-oo. Tell us!" What better moment could there be for offering information? At this point, it probably would be meaningful to many of the children. She said, very simply, "When a cell divides, the nucleus divides first."

"Is that *all*?" was the disappointed cry, as though after all this labor the swan had laid an ant's egg.

Miss Yonika elaborated, "When frog cells divide, they don't become yeast. And when yeast divides it doesn't produce a tadpole. Why?"

Shaughan said, "The nucleus determines the kind of animal it is."

Thinking that her children would surely have heard the label DNA, Miss Yonika asked who had heard of the letters. No one! Teaching is so full of the unexpected! Briefly she told them that DNA was an abbreviated name for the molecule in the nucleus which determines the kind of cell the division produces.

Then from somewhere out of the awed group came the words: "DNA—Determines Nuclear Activity!"

During a spare half-hour among the end-of-year activities, Miss Yonika asked the children to write what they had learned from the microscope unit. She phrased it: "Many people believe that children do not learn anything when they work on their own initiative, when they are not told just what to do. I would like to have some evidence that a good deal is learned this way. If you feel you've learned some facts or had some new thoughts, will you write these down?"

These papers are analyzed in Chapter 8 and quoted in Appendix I on evaluation. One girl wrote a letter to the teacher on behalf of the class after school was over. It read:

Your ideas and answers have brought us all to the edge of discoveries in the wonderful microscopic world of science. Our gratitude to your help is greater than our thanks.

In some ways this was an atypical unit, but then every unit has its measure of unorthodoxy. As is often true in biology, the materials did not interact to suggest phenomena; the emphasis was on the children's interpretations of what they saw under their microscopes. Much of the learning process was one of developing a background for perceiving plant life—for recognizing parts. Seeing and thinking went hand in hand as the children learned to know this section of the unseen world.

The colloquia followed the usual pattern of moving from factual observations: "I saw dim black lines and scratches" to finding hidden likenesses: "If you cut up paper, the population of the paper is larger but not the size. In cells, both get larger." However, much of the momentum of the colloquia came from the teacher's questions rather than from juxtaposed data, discrepant events, or children's interchanges about their observations. At times, the teacher found it difficult to choose the kind of questions which would evoke new thoughts. At points of impasse she sought to redirect the thinking toward one or another of the subconcepts of the unit, and the children's reactions indicated clearly whether each choice was an appropriate one or not. When she tried to establish a clearer view of what the cell was by diverting the children's attention from the nucleus ("Let's hold that a moment"), the children continued to talk about the nucleus! The result was almost the same when she emphasized that the hairwidth was a good microscopic unit; the only follower was the boy who had already tried it. However, she had success with her suggestions for new materials. "How would you like to see one cell become two?" evoked a response of "Yippee!" The suggestion, "Tomorrow we might try to look at scallion leaves and roots" raised a challenge: "Roots don't have cells . . . maybe not on the outside anyway." In each case these new materials, providing new but allied experiences, brought the thinking in the colloquia to a higher level. Each choice directed the explorations toward a stepping stone somewhere on the matrix of subconcepts. The presence of pond water in the room lured some children toward initiating behavior and introduced *Paramecium* as another kind of cell.

But see evaluation of papers in Chapter 8, pages 374-77.

Many technical problems were tackled and overcome. Microscope work is solidly based in technical skills. It was amazing to watch the proficiency with which, after the first lesson, these nine year olds prepared slides and focused them under their lenses.

Growth in perception was noticeable. At first the scratches, bubbles, and rainbow colors from refraction claimed as much attention and interest as the cells themselves. Then "dots" became nuclei, cell walls took on specific shapes rather being like barbed wire or writing on the walls of a cave. Although not specifically expressed, the cell was now perceived as a unit since it was referred to and talked about: larger cells, scrawny cells, hexagonal cells, and rectangular ones (these were indicated rather than named); the cell that can swim; the cell that divides.

With low powers and instruments in questionable condition, much can still be seen, perceived, and thought about. But there are limitations. The film-loops served as an adventure into higher-powered microscopy—without the necessary technical skill and the frustration of a time limit. The children were ready; the filmloops were precisely appropriate to the data the children had tackled. They now had eyes to see and knowledge to guide their perception. The filmloop experience was a fitting culmination.

6

Choosing the next units

The architectonics of the curriculum are, for us, the intermeshing of three cogwheels:

1. The conceptual schemes of science.
2. The genetic development of concepts in the child.
3. The sociological background of the child.

Cogwheel 1: Conceptual schemes of science

We recall that the three major conceptual schemes are:

A. The universe is in constant change.
B. The sum total of mass and energy in the universe remains constant.
C. Living organisms are in constant change.

Many subconcepts of hierarchical difficulty fall under each of these schemes. Selecting the appropriate subconcept level and pairing it with the genetic development of the child's conceptual arrow is a major concern of the person designing a curriculum. Although one can see that the three major conceptual schemes overlap and interact (is a child swinging freely on a suspended rope-seat a study of the body as the matter of a pendulum, a study of gravity in relation to the universe, or a study of an organism's sensations?), units of study based mainly in any one of them may readily be devised.

A reasonable suggestion at once comes to mind: each year any group of children should be exposed to units in all three of the areas so that, over the elementary school years, the major concepts will grow in extent and in depth for every child.

This seems obvious and reasonable, yet a case to

mandate it could hardly be constructed. One of us (Lansdown in The Dalton Schools, 1942–1945) designed and taught a curriculum in which there was only one unit a year for each of grades five, six, and seven.

The fifth graders (mostly gifted children) studied theories of evolution through observing the ecological interaction between various animals and their environments in a living museum which they kept. This museum contained pond creatures of various complexities, as well as praying mantises, fish, salamanders, toads, chameleons, snakes, hamsters, and rats. They bred many of the animals and observed variations in the progeny.

The sixth graders had a year of chemistry beginning with the problems and possible experiments of the alchemists (because in history they are studying the Middle Ages) and proceeding to a study of the interaction of atoms and molecules in various mixtures of elements and compounds. This study developed a beginning concept of the atomic nature of matter and the fact that in a chemical reaction matter is conserved.

The seventh graders studied electricity. Since this was during World War II and there was a shortage of home services, the class ran an electrical repair shop for the parents and faculty. The children paid close attention to fire and insurance laws, while their theoretical studies led to a consideration of the electrical nature of matter and the conversion of matter into energy in radioactive phenomena. After a reading of the Smyth report,[1] the children, then in the eighth grade, asked what all the "secrecy" was about in relation to the atomic explosion of 1945, since even they knew that some elements converted their matter into energy in the ratio of $E/m = c^2$! The universe at large received little attention during this sequence, chiefly because it interested the teacher less!

Year-long units have much to recommend them, but three or more units a year, with at least one drawn from each of the three conceptual schemes, are likely to be more appealing. We do not feel that the

[1] See Henry de Wolf Smyth, *Atomic Energy for Military Purposes: The Official Report on the Development of the Atomic Bomb under the Auspices of the United States Government, 1940–1945,* Princeton University Press, Princeton, N.J., 1945.

difference is vital. What is vital is that each unit can be placed along a conceptual arrow pointing to one of the major conceptual schemes.

Cogwheel 2: Genetic development of concepts in the child

The concepts toward which the units are directed may be thought of as one cogwheel. This wheel must mesh with another set of cogs on the wheel of the genetic development of concepts in the child. We have discussed (Chapter 3) the development of conceptual thought according to the Vygotsky schema and described how carefully structured experiences foster development from syncretic to preconceptual thinking during the elementary school years. We indicated, too, that mature sixth graders might approach true conceptual thought. Growth from one Vygotsky level to another depends partly on maturation, but even an adult may think syncretically at first when confronted with a new concept. However, progress toward conceptual thought is much more rapid in the adult, since he is more adept at conceptual thought in general.

In this chapter, we will follow the growth of genetic conceptual achievement as schematized by Jean Piaget. Piaget's system, allied to gradual physiological maturation, concentrates first on concrete, tangible experiences and then moves toward verbal expression. Vygotsky's system centers more on speech as it relates to thought, although he too emphasizes concrete beginnings. The two psychologists are not in opposition; each knew and revered the work of the other. Their differences narrowed as Piaget's work grew and proliferated. Vygotsky died in his thirties in 1934, but Piaget, now in his seventies, has continued to offer new data, refined theories, and new experimental designs. All of his later work emphasizes not only the effect of intellectual *effort* on the part of the child in the process of concept building, but also the value of social *interchange* among peers during the learning process.

Both Vygotsky and Piaget consider that thinking begins during the preschool years. Vygotsky expects syncretic thinking at this stage, while Piaget labels preschool thought egocentric. The terms are not cognates. Only the genetic timing is similar. Both scholars state that a full flowering of conceptual thought is possible during adolescence, but not before. While Vygotsky names this simply the period of "conceptual thought," Piaget calls it the period of "formal operations." Here there is a close similarity in the phenomena described; they are practically cognates. The processes named by both have an order—a sequence, but they differ in quality. The age at which each step appears or is possible seems to vary, within limits. Each appearance relies partly on the child's maturation and partly on his experience and educational exposure.

Piaget lived through the change from a largely agricultural Swiss economy to the age of TV technology; during this time he saw a drop in the age levels at which his stages of thought became possible. He now asserts that there is much that education can do to hasten conceptual growth. However, there is much that education does at present to truncate it. The kind of educational procedures advocated in this book are similar to those Piaget described as speeding up the conceptual development of children:

> The teacher must provide the instruments which the children can use to decide things for themselves. Children themselves must verify, experimentally in physics, deductively in mathematics. A *ready-made* truth is only half truth. . . .

> Words are probably not a short-cut to a better understanding . . . the level of understanding seems to modify the language that is used, rather than vice versa. . . . Mainly, language serves to translate what is already understood; or else language may even present a danger if it is used to *introduce* an idea which is not yet accessible.[2]

Is Piaget talking about language *given* to the child by an adult (explanations) or language *used* by the child to express his ideas in his own way?

The major distinction between the theories of the two psychologists is that Piaget emphasizes genetic stages of development—the stages of maturation when

[2] Eleanor Duckworth, *ESS Newsletter,* "Piaget Rediscovered," Education Development Center, Inc., Newton, Mass. (June 1964), 4. (Our emphasis.)

certain types of thinking become possible, when they are likely to appear—whereas Vygotsky emphasizes education. Piaget's method is to probe into the existing stages of thought. Once each Piaget level is achieved, the ability to think at that level is part of the person's permanent intellectual ability. He achieves an equilibrium when each stage becomes settled in his mental equipment. He no longer uses his earlier, less mature ways of thinking. Vygotsky also states that a maturation process is at work during childhood, but he believes syncretic thought may reappear at any time during adult life when a particularly difficult new concept is approached. Vygotsky researched more on the development of thinking through education than he did on discovering the existence of thought. Vygotsky sees the learner's own words as generating new thought.

The cogs which represent the subconcepts of the major conceptual schemes of science must mesh with the cogs which represent the genetic level of the child if understanding is to take place and learning is to be meaningful. It becomes essential, therefore, for the teacher to expect and to recognize evidence of when a child can or cannot grasp the subconcept offered.

Egocentric level

The earliest level of reflective thought, according to Piaget, is *egocentric*. At this stage the child has not fully differentiated himself from the outside world. He may feel that an external event is happening to him personally, even because of him. A three- or four-year-old child may think the moon follows him as he walks—that he can even make it move! Early nursery school abounds with illustrations of this kind of thinking. Here we can sense that expecting a child of three to grapple with a ball's interaction with gravity would not be a profitable expectation. The event requires a model for explanation. He grapples with gravitation physically when he zooms down a slide, but this is kinesthetic, not mental. It is valuable concrete experience not yet endowed with reflective thought.

Another aspect of the egocentric stage is that the child assumes that his view of the object is absolute. If his perception changes, this is either because the object has changed or because it is another object. His home looks different if he enters by the front door from the way it looks if he enters through the back porch because the house has changed! It may even be another house! It is not another view of a static house!

Since concepts are built through synthesis from multiphase contacts with and perceptions of the same phenomenon, we can see that concept growth, as such, cannot be expected in the nursery school. A child needs many, many sense experiences with the same object, but we have to wait until he realizes that it is the same object—until he is aware that his perceptual vantage point has shifted and that the object has not changed. Obviously, opportunities for many and varied experiences with objects the child can handle—can relate to physically—are not only enjoyable and worthwhile activities in themselves for the three- and four-year-old child, but an essential stretch of road along the conceptual arrow. Games and activities during the late nursery years or kindergarten which help a child to discover through touch, sight, and words the various attributes of things—blocks, for instance, lead toward the concept that shape, color, and permanence of form all may belong to *an object*. The inside, outside, color, taste, smell, seeds, and pie "form" of a pumpkin provide experiences which later allow it to be categorized as "fruit." At this egocentric level, the child concentrates on only one aspect at a time. The pumpkin cannot be a pumpkin and a fruit simultaneously. He himself cannot be both an American and a New Yorker at the same time. Certainly it comes as a tremendous revelation to a child when he discovers that his Mommy was once a child with a Mommy of her own. At this stage, double relationships cannot be encompassed at one time. So, of course, a child of nursery school age cannot conceive that the earth "turning" and the sun "rising" produce the same appearance.

Nursery school teachers all know how personal time is for the child at this age. It is "time for a snack," not 10:00 A.M.; "time to clean up," not 11:30 A.M. Two days from now is thought of as "going home, going to bed, coming to school, going home and to bed and coming to school again." Experienced time is personal: fast when one enjoys oneself; slow during painful or unhappy periods. But children can *feel* the beat of time in musical and bodily rhythmic experiences and *recall* a short sequence of regular activities. Such sense experiences form the basis for discovering that time is not personal, but that it is related to objective phenomena.

The cogs in a science curriculum which mesh with a child's level of conceptual development during the nursery school years are these:

1. Rich multisensory experiences with the same phenomenon or object.
2. A chance to witness real change—to see that it takes time to experience: to watch eggs hatch and plants grow, to roll balls down slopes, to swing; to be told about sequences in personal terms ("the day after tomorrow you will be five").
3. Physically experiencing space: running, walking, leaping across a playground or a large room.
4. The opportunity to compare weights (buckets full of sand or water) and heights (children back-to-back).
5. Experiences with the unseen interactions of a magnet and iron and of pulleys and gravity.

All of these cogs provide vital activities of interest to the child. All of them form concrete bases for various conceptual arrows.

Egocentric experience at the egocentric stage supplies the sensory knowledge which later allows the child to learn that objects have a real, independent existence outside *him*, that matter has its own properties or attributes, and that space and time are relationships which are independent of him.

There are aspects of growth during the egocentric stage which education can hasten. Nursery school and Head Start programs where children share experiences with their peers and talk freely to an accepting teacher who provides vocabulary and sentence structure as a model rather than as correction, create an environment in which a child can begin to learn that there are viewpoints, observations, and opinions other than his own. His viewpoint begins to shift around the same phenomenon, and he takes on an objective rather than a purely subjective view of the world. The fact that other children relate to the objects he may want, and had previously considered a part of himself, impresses the fact upon a child that he and the objects are not one, that he cannot magically make them obey his will. The "ego" becomes less a "center" of his viewpoint.

Socialization is an essential part of growth in thinking. Appropriate socialization encourages a child to make comparisons of height and width, more than and less than, heavy and light, fast and slow. Socialization sharpens vision, emphasizes the importance of listening, and affords many opportunities for verbal communication.

A child who is given many opportunities to follow his urges to learn through all his senses, and who feels the support of adults in the process, builds a sense of competence in himself—a knowledge that he can control some part of his environment, that he can cope with phenomena. He develops confidence. The process of learning what he can control—how he can control certain objects—forms a bridge from the omniscient viewpoint of the younger child (his egocentric domination of his environment) to a sense of the real interaction of an individual with the environment. We see these features beginning during the nursery years; we see them continue, in good school environments, in the kindergartens and first grades.

Intuitive level

Piaget's next stage is the *intuitive*, found from about the age of five to about the age of seven. It has some of the characteristics of the egocentric level, stemming from the fact that the child still concentrates on only one feature or variable at a time. It departs from the egocentric level in that the intuitive is related to perceptual clues rather than to personal sensing. Examples will help to bring the difference into focus. Show a child a group of objects (say, six) placed close together in a row. If the same objects are spread further apart, the child will say that there are more of them. If two similar jars are both filled to the same height with colored liquid, a child will say that each has the same amount—that the liquids are equal. If the liquid from one jar is then poured into a low wide jar and the child is asked which jar of "lemonade" he would prefer, he may choose either the tall jar ("because there is more in it") or the low jar ("because there is more in it; it is wider"). He is

unable to think of the height and the width of the jar simultaneously. If a ball of clay is rolled into a long thin sausage, the child may say there is less clay in the sausage "because it is thinner" or he may say there is

more clay in the sausage "because it is longer."

At the intuitive level, the child has no understanding that number, matter, and volume are conserved during transformations. He has no sense of reversibility. He focuses on one attribute at a time. One way of explaining the child's thought at this level is to say that he cannot cope with two variables at once. Another is to say that he does not have a concept of the conservation of matter or the conservation of volume. Even if the child performs the operations himself (if he pours the liquid back into the original bottle after marking the expected height or if he rolls the clay back into a ball), he will not think that the volume of matter necessarily remains constant during the process. Closely allied with the concept of conservation is the concept of reversibility. That reversing a process can demonstrate the conservation is not apparent to the child who has not gone beyond the intuitive level of thought.

The intuitive stage is also characterized by a reduction in the egocentric point of view. Toward the upper level, the child begins to understand that a toy placed near his left hand is also near the right hand of a friend opposite him. He sees the other fellow's viewpoint.

The "whole and its part" problem: Another aspect of the intuitive level is the "whole and its part" problem. When a child is shown pictures of, say, three horses and one cow and asked, "Show me the animals," he will point to all the pictures. If this is followed by, "Show me the horses," he will do this correctly, too. But when asked, "Are there more horses or more animals?" the child asserts, "There are more horses." "Why?" "Because there is only one cow." Once specific attention has been focused on the horses, the child removes them mentally from the group of animals. What is left is the other group which has been mentioned—the animals. To the child, there is only one "animal" left.

There is a stage in each child's history when he seems spontaneously to resolve all of these problems completely. A slightly different timing may be involved in the solution of each type of problem, but it seems that a certain maturity has to be reached before a child's intuitive viewpoint changes and he achieves the next level of thought—the stage of conservation or reversibility. A striking example of how this can happen was provided by one of our experiences. We were working with teachers in a low socioeconomic district. The area under study was, as it happened, mathematics. The second graders had been studying sets. (This was during tryouts of the Minnemast Project.) The teacher was trying to get the children to select subsets from whole sets. The selection was easy. But, when the children were asked to express their choices in terms such as "The tulips are a subset of the set of flowers," they always tripped up on the sentence and said, "The tulips are a subset of all the *other* flowers." They were responding exactly in the Piaget manner to the question "Which are there more of—the tulips or the flowers?" When these problems were discussed later at a teachers' conference, a third-grade teacher was also present. Since third graders, then eight years old, are supposedly past the intuitive stage, we asked her to try out the problem in her classroom. Now these third graders had had no training at all in the wisdom of set mathematics, whereas the second graders were in their third year of such a study. Nevertheless, at the first trial, all of the third graders were able to express the subset as a part of the whole set!

It is intriguing to speculate on the possibility of educating children to reach higher levels of thought at earlier than average ages. Of course, psychologists have attempted this. A number of factors appear to be involved. First, the child himself must be allowed to manipulate the materials—physically to change the positions of the before and after configurations of beads, liquids, clay, etc. He needs to have words to describe the facts he perceives: taller, wider, more, less, bigger, smaller, etc. In order to describe the conservation, he must be able to juxtapose comparative terms: "one is higher, but the other is wider";

"these are farther apart but the others are closer together, so there's the same number."

A recent, very careful study[3] found that children could perform the operations when directives were given in language which paralleled conservation principles such as comparatives of pairs of variables, even when the children themselves did not show evidence of having an understanding of conservation. It was found that children could be trained to apply conservation language to one particular situation, but that they could not transfer this language spontaneously to a new situation. Use of the probing method of inquiry, so well developed by Piaget, revealed that such children did not have an understanding of conservation. This may be an example of language "used to introduce an idea which is not yet accessible."[4] There was slight evidence that children who gave partial conservation answers on a pretest could be helped to the next level of thinking through training and the use of conservation language. The conclusion drawn from this series of experiments strengthens Piaget's original statements that there must be integration of concrete experience, language, *and* maturity to bring about a new level of thinking.

A view of cognitive development held by some psychologists is that if a child can predict operationally what will happen in a test of conservation, he must have an understanding of conservation. Let us examine an investigation done by one of the authors and consider what may be inferred from the results.

Each of 62 six year olds was presented with two containers (see diagrams 1 and 2) and asked to pour the water from container 1 into container 2. Before doing this, it was suggested that he mark the top of the level in 1 with a marking pencil and that, after pouring the liquid into container 2, he mark the level there. Then the child was shown another container identical to number 1 (we will call this container 3), and was asked to determine what level the water would reach *before* he poured it from 2 to 3. Of the 62 children, 59 marked as shown in A (see page 264).

[3] Recorded in a "Comment" (by Barbel Inhelder, *et al.*, from the Geneva group headed by Piaget) on the article, "On Cognitive Development" by Jerome Bruner and the Harvard group, *The American Psychologist,* Vol. 21, No. 2 (February 1966), 160–64.

[4] Duckworth, *op. cit.*

Most of these children had placed the two similar containers together and carefully juxtaposed the mark. When asked where they thought the water would reach if it were poured from container 3 into container 4 (one exactly like number 2), they marked as shown in B (see diagram). When asked if there was "more" or "less" liquid in container 1 than in 2 or 4, 59 said "no difference," "the same," "the mark is at the same place," or shook their heads as they said "not more."

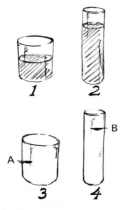

This investigation seems to support the hypothesis that a child manipulating the materials can show evidence of understanding conservation before the age at which Piaget deemed possible. Whether the evidence really points to an understanding of the conservation of volume or not depends on what criterion is acceptable. If one accepts the operational as evidence, this investigation supports the hypothesis. But if the criterion is language, then we cannot be sure from this evidence what meaning the operation had for the children. Prediction in acts often precedes expression in language. They did respond to an investigator's question. But knowing, as we do, that a six year old cannot hold three variables in mind at once, what meaning could the query "Is there more or less liquid in *container 1* than in *2 or 4*?" have for the child? He might quite possibly have been thinking of only 2 and 4 when he said they were "the same." After all he had marked 4 by comparing it with 2. He might still have *thought* that the volume of liquid changed as it was poured from 1 into 2 or from 3 to 4. We do not have enough evidence to decide.

Keeping in mind the likely stages of thought

development in first and second graders, what appropriate science experiences would lead them along conceptual arrows? —Observations of changes in the phenomenal world described in terms of the already experienced interactions of certain objects? This would strengthen the trend away from egocentricity and toward the acceptance of the material objects in the world as separate entities from the child's own existence. Especially if records are kept, such observations can be seen in daily and monthly weather changes, in the growth of plants and animals, in the interactions of magnets with objects and of objects with water. At the intuitive level of thought, children can talk about their observations in accurate terms and can give descriptions which communicate them to others, but they can deal with only one variable at a time: "today is colder than yesterday" rather than "today is colder than yesterday, but less windy." Much experience with a variety of objects of various shapes, colors, textures, and sizes accompanied by appropriate names for the attributes, practice in matching and comparing according to one attribute at a time, and placing objects in sets and describing the criterion all illustrate activities which build upon the potentials of children at the intuitive level of thought. It is difficult for children at this stage to arrange objects in a long series. They can do this only by comparing each item with another; placing objects "in between" others in a series is often too much of a challenge. But children can record the changes they observe by means of charts or simple graphs; they can describe what they see and listen to what their peers have seen. They do need help in noticing and accounting for discrepancies, for this requires holding several factors in mind at once.

While we have described thinking at the intuitive level mostly in terms of deficiencies of abilities which are expected to develop later, there are, of course, many positive features of this age. There is avid collecting of data, as experience with and names of objects are sought. Children enjoy grouping things in many ways. The nature of an arrangement gives a clue to the thinking involved. There is usually a common attribute to the collection; "red things," "What I want to play with," "*my* things," "long things." We recognize this as an expression of complex thought in the Vygotsky sense. There is a need to ingest experiences kinesthetically, orally, and visually. While these activities were at first a part of the egocentricity of the child, they now become objectified and can be represented symbolically in words and by diagrams.

Level of concrete operations

The eight to ten year old achieves complete decentralization; he becomes able to envisage reversibility in concrete operations and to construct models to explain objectively observed interactions. He moves to Vygotsky's "preconcept level" of thinking: using the correct words as adults use them to describe phenomena, but still relying on the concrete image as his frame of reference. This is Piaget's stage of *concrete operations.*

Most of the usual elementary school science programs become available to children during these years. The children can hold two variables in mind at once: the liquid in the thermometer lengthens as it gets hot; cold air falls and pushes hot air up; water and carbon dioxide go round and round in cycles. Complete reversibility allows the child at the level of concrete operations to think of a stone as composed of tiny particles (later he will call them molecules) and to realize that if the stone, in imagination, can be broken into tiny particles, it can also be built up again and "seen" as a collection of molecules which makes a whole. Note that concrete operations include the imaginative—that is, concreteness is incorporated into the thinking, internalized, and projected in the imagination—but it is always related to a concrete image or a concrete experience. The child at this stage can construct models to explain the interaction of the phenomena he describes: "There must be tiny particles of onion coming through the air to my nose."

That matter is conserved becomes clear to him and this understanding helps him to explain chemical change through rearrangements of the atoms. He understands that weight is conserved when he explores an equal arm balance, and that volume is conserved when he pours liquids from one-shaped jar to another. In these cases, the child achieved complete reversibility. The relation of weight to volume as density is not yet clear to him because it involves two abstractions related to each other, but the child

can manage long series and interpolate the "in betweens" so that he can make good use of graphs.

All of these activities are possible as children move through experiences at the level of thinking called "concrete operations." But many children do not think this way. Here we come up against the fact that education could easily embellish this stage, but often does not. Education expects younger children to have an understanding of conservation and reversibility when they cannot, yet it fails, in turn, to enrich the thinking of which nine and ten year olds are capable. The emphasis of our curriculum building might perhaps be on helping children develop Vygotsky's preconceptual thought via model building, of which they are quite capable. How is this to be done?

Just as a rich preparation of contact with real objects through many sense perceptions prepares a child so that he can recognize objects as having many attributes, just as contact with peers in a safe, socializing situation shortens the period of egocentric thinking, and just as the juxtaposition of phenomena which belong together moves a child from syncretic to complex interpretation, so properly structured experiences can engender in a child the ability to make models to account for the interactions he can observe and test in the world around him. The foregoing chapters of this book have largely been devoted to indicating how this may be done. The principle begins with structured materials—structured to lead along the conceptual arrow to a cluster of related concepts. The colloquium requires that the child find words for his thoughts and this speaking engenders new thoughts. By sharing verbal expression with his peers, the child perceives other viewpoints and new facts and hears new ways of describing observations. Through the teacher's juxtaposition of relevant data, the child begins to find the real nexus between interacting objects. The teacher supplies the correct word at the opportune time and a new term in turn leads toward expanded understanding; use of the word *energy*, for example, eventually links all forms of energy into the electromagnetic spectrum. Testing ideas and statements made as predictions or models draws on the concepts of conservation and reversibility and makes sure that the models are viable.

Above all, the fact that the initiative is the child's,

both in recognizing discrepant events and in developing models to explain them, ensures that the learning is ingested and becomes integrated with his own emotional, ideational, and social experiences.

Level of formal operations

The stage of thought which Piaget names *formal operations* can begin with the approach of adolescence at about 11 or 12 years of age. At this time, children become more and more independent of the concrete world. They can have imaginative foresight not based on past experience; they can construct theories and play with axiom-postulate systems; and they can reconstruct their past experience on a new plane, that of reflective intelligence.

The ability to construct a series of thoughts without reference to the concrete is one of the new abilities. A problem such as "Jack is older than Jimmy, but Jack is younger than Jane. Who is the youngest?" can be solved by a child at the level of formal operations, but not by a child who is still at the concrete operations level. At the age of formal operations, mathematical formulas become meaningful and new relationships can be evolved through the manipulation of symbols. The child can set up conditions and figure out possible outcomes (such as those in axiom-postulate systems). In short, the child can enter into the joys of mathematical and scientific creativity on an abstract level.

A paradigm may help to summarize the essence of this chapter thus far:

PIAGET	VYGOTSKY	SCIENCE BEHAVIOR
Egocentric level	Syncretic thought	Personal perceptions juxtaposed.
Intuitive level	Complex thought	Grouping by external likenesses.
Concrete operations	Preconceptual thought	Analogy by hidden likenesses; model making.
Formal operations	Conceptual thought	Structural similarities; abstract models.

Cogwheel 3: Sociological background

We have seen that the conceptual schemes of science and their cogs of subconcepts mesh with the cogs of the genetic growth of the thinking of the child. But this is not all. A third cogwheel is intermeshed with the other two: the social background of the child.

Earlier, in Chapter 3, we followed some of the investigations which showed that the ability to categorize is more limited in children from peasant backgrounds than in children who are subjected to school or urban environments. Senegalese bush children showed more similarity in this ability to Mexican peasant children and to igloo-dwelling Eskimos than they did to their blood cousins who had been to school. Granted that the ability measured (width of categorization) is not the level of thought discussed in this chapter, but we might attempt an analogy through the model which the study offers.

The city child or the child in school must process many, many more stimuli than the child in the fields or bush. The need to dispose of a constant barrage of stimuli forces categorization in even rather dictatorial school systems.

The kind of relational thinking we have been exploring—relating phenomena produced by interacting objects—is more sophisticated than the categorizing mode of thought. Yet both are based on stimuli; both are based on concrete experiences with materials—on sensory experiences. In our type of thinking, there is motivation by the learner, not imposed tasks. The child is encouraged to convert sensory experiences into thought through verbal expression. Without the experiences, there is nothing to think about and slender experiences provide less to think about than rich experiences do. With no encouragement to process the experiences into thought, they remain at the preverbal level. In terms of Piaget's genetic levels of progress in thinking, there may be some doubt about the possibility of speeding the process, although it does seem that certain types of educational experience deepen and enrich the nature of thinking at each level. But let us consider social background in terms of Vygotsky's categories.

Progress beyond each level of thinking—syncretic, complex, or preconceptual—may not be possible at a lower age limit, but *progress toward* the higher levels of thought at the ages where these become possible can be aided through education. In fact, a child may not reach the final conceptual level at all without the appropriate stimuli or experiences. Again, older people revert temporarily to syncretic thinking when they are faced with a new area of knowledge. Most of us have only recently, if at all, come to grips with the concepts related to computers. As we went through our initiation, did we relate facts which were really not at all related in the field? Did we latch onto one aspect of the process and relate it partially to another in a complex manner? Only our previous experience in progressing through the various stages of thought allowed us to complete our thinking quickly, to reach the conceptual level as we worked, talked, asked, and experienced. Familiarity with the concrete, the verbal interchange, and the maturity to nurture the conceptual level are the necessary factors for attaining a concept.

Although we in the United States do not come into direct contact with children of the bush, the backgrounds of the children in Appalachia and the children of migrant workers are often similar in that they, too, lack intellectual stimulus. In larger measure, however, we are faced with the fact that urban children from the inner city, black children from the poverty area, low socioeconomic white children, and the recent arrivals from the rural areas of Puerto Rico have all been unable to develop the more abstract thought required in our school systems, geared as these are to the middle-class child. Why is this so?

Can we find evidence that children of the inner city do conceptual thinking in any area? Do the adults? We submit that the inner city person does think conceptually, but usually not in the areas touched by the school system. Let us take the concept of black power, for instance. It embraces history and has a world-wide frame of reference;

certainly it goes beyond the concrete, the here and now, the act of tomorrow. It is a high-level abstraction—a concept, we maintain—that proliferates through the lives and thinking of many black people. It is talked about. It has a special vocabulary. The children participate concretely in its actions, confrontations, and sit-ins; they suffer the indignities from which the concept has grown; they hear talk about it in many meaningful situations. Children from the inner city at the elementary school level certainly can engage in preconceptual thinking about black power.

In contrast, what does black power mean to a white suburban child? Often it is only a threat to his security—at best a complex thought! Children of the suburb lack the concrete experience and the verbal exchange which gives meaning to black power. They lack a concept. We have only to note how difficult it is for white social workers to be effective in black power strongholds to realize the conceptual gap that exists.

This digression has the purpose of asserting that while children of the inner city may lack conceptual ability in school, they are usually versed well in areas of thought where they have the appropriate social background. Once the ability to think conceptually has been established, its transfer can be fairly quickly achieved, given the right environment. The obvious curriculum responsibility is to provide very rich concrete experiences involving the phenomena related to science concepts and, above all, to encourage the children to exchange these experiences in their own words—and grammar! And this may be one of the rubs! Perhaps we do too much "correcting," allow only middle-class phraseology, and cut off the natural flow of words and, therefore, thoughts.

There are children from low socioeconomic areas who have not had the benefit of identifying with a black power movement. There are white and black children whose enduring poverty has bred a feeling of hopelessness—that nothing can be done, that the world controls them, rather than that they can control at least a part of the world. We recall a small child from a Head Start program who was introduced to the nursery rhyme "There Was an Old Woman Who Lived in a Shoe." Asked why the old woman "didn't know what to do," the child replied, "Because she is poor."

Science taught in the manner we have described can make a solid contribution to the lives of children whose experiences thus far have told them that they are victimized by their environments. *Sciencing* is people learning to control phenomena which they have observed and described. Aren't they controlling the materials before them? Then aren't they discovering interactions which reveal phenomena? Aren't they themselves finding verbal expressions for the manipulations in experiences? They are, in short, coping with a small part of their environment and bending it to their will.

We have found that children from the inner city talk freely about science discoveries from materials, that they understand each other, and that they have much to communicate. They do begin with syncretic thinking, but move quickly to the complex mode of thought. Around the age of eight they seem to have no difficulty expressing discoveries in preconceptual terms. Since the inner city child has had different experiences from those of the middle-class white child—fewer occasions to read books, fewer "educational" toys—he needs more opportunities to use concrete materials and more of a chance to talk in school. The very opposite is often offered him, and so his ability to think conceptually is never revealed to the school authorities. Instead he is required to "listen," to follow directions; he is punished for talking to a neighbor. To compensate for the school's failure to "teach" him, he is given, through small group teaching and after school tutoring sessions, *more* of what has not been effective before.

There is one more aspect of gearing science teaching to the socioeconomic cog: that of learning style. Many tribes of American Indian children learn in a whole "gestalt," rather than gradually in a sequence of small bits. A Navajo child will learn to saddle a horse by watching his father do it. He will take no part until he feels ready to perform the whole process himself. It is then that the father may correct errors, but only errors of detail; the child, when ready, sees and performs the job as a whole.[5] Navajo children are strictly noncompetitive. They will wait for each other when doing math problems at the board so that all will finish together.

[5] Personal communication from Peter Soto, an American Indian of the Cocopah Tribe.

There are, of course, "slow" children from all economic backgrounds. There are, too, emotionally disturbed children whose psychological problems preempt the energy which could be more profitably employed in learning. Such children progress more slowly; they reach each level at a later than average age. But progress they can, if their teacher is aware of the levels and the characteristics which designate them. We can gear our expectancies to the existing cogs and offer materials structurally related to a subconcept which can be expected to mesh with the child's actual thought development. His success is our reward: the evalution that the cogs are turning the wheels.

The cog of social background may slow the turning of other wheels for a while because there must be a translation to a new field: the school context for the inner city child, a new language for the non-English-speaking arrival. But once the three wheels are turning, the cogs mesh, interrelate, and then turn with increasing speed. If we begin early enough to look, listen, and recognize, the social background cog soon synchronizes with the cogs of conceptual schemes and genetic development.

Curriculum suggestions gearing the intellectual level to the conceptual cogs

We will consider each intellectual level separately and list the learnings to be expected from various activities under each of the three major conceptual schemes.

Science learnings expected at the egocentric level

The child at three years is just emerging from what Piaget calls the stage of *sensori-motor intelligence.* This stage lacks reflection, it is

> ...like a slow-motion film, in which all the pictures are seen in succession without fusion, and so without the continuous vision necessary for understanding the whole.[6]

[6] Jean Piaget, *Psychology of Intelligence,* International Library of Psychology, 1960, 121, pb. New York: Humanities Press, Inc.; London: Routledge and Kegan Paul, Ltd.

A child who meets a classroom pet such as a rabbit in one corner of the room and then sees him again in another spot will say that he saw two rabbits. Such a description is also used for the sun or the school building. At this stage, the child needs much experience with objects he can handle, learn to name, and recognize as invariant or constant. He needs to see objects from various perceptual angles and to learn that each object may have a variety of attributes. This is necessary whether the object moves or whether the child moves and sees the same object from a new viewpoint. The child's experiences in science are directed toward giving him the opportunity to fuse various percepts, locales, and attributes so that he can see an object as one whole.

Mass-energy: For the nursery school child at the egocentric level the recognition of objects as entities in their own right—as entities separate from him—has to be developed through naming, handling, and examining. He needs such things as toys, magnets, dry cells, and blocks of all sizes, shapes, colors, and textures. He needs to experience the fluidity of finger paints and water—objects that do change in color, shape, form, and extent. He needs to make applesauce and vegetable soup, to cook muffins, and to pop corn, in addition to his work with Play Dough and clay. Experience with all his senses helps a child to learn about the attributes of objects in his world.

Universe: The child at the egocentric level has a rather limited view of our universe. To have him realize that there is only one sun and only one moon and that they do not follow him as he moves—that he cannot make them move—are aims of learning at this stage. Learning is enhanced by talk with adults; it cannot occur through observation alone. A child has many kinesthetic experiences on swings, jungle gyms, and the like, where he experiences the sensations of up and down. As he feels the wind on him, he may think he makes the wind. Sometimes he does make it with his own movements. But he should also observe the effects of wind on leaves and trees outside a window when he is inside and realize that there are winds he cannot control. It is hard for him to learn that there are phenomena not only beyond his control, but also beyond the control

of adults—that a fine day cannot be ordered for a picnic!

Living organisms: There should be many pets in the classroom for the children to handle—gently, because animals can feel. Pets have babies, small creatures like themselves. Pets have to be fed; they grow. Plants, when watered, grow too; they grow bigger, but still look like the same plant. And the child grows, too. He has feelings; he needs food and rest. When he grows, he is still the same person, perhaps with a different attribute or two!

Such learning for the three and four year old comes from actual experience, from talking with sensitive adults, from handling and using his other senses, from stories that are read to him, and from the songs he sings.

Science learnings expected at the intuitive level

Activities offered to children who are passing through the intuitive stage of intellectual development must allow for the fact that many of these children:

1. will not consider that the quantity of matter in objects is unchanged when the shape alone is changed.
2. will not think that the volume is conserved when liquids are poured from one vessel into another which differs from the first only in shape.
3. may not realize that the number of objects remains constant when the items are spread further apart or crowded more closely together.

We also know that children at this stage of mental growth cannot be expected to make comparisons by arranging many objects in a long series. They will not have a view of distant time or of the far reaches of space that is adequate for studying geological ages or considering the nature of galaxies. However, during these years (approximately five to seven), some of the above abilities can gradually be achieved. Recognition of constancy of weight in relation to its displacement of a volume of a liquid lags into the ninth year; concepts of density come later still.

On the positive side, children of this age will be avid collectors and arrangers of objects, eager manipulators of materials, and perceptive observers of common attributes (though usually one at a time). It is our intention to suggest activities which will foster the growth of these new abilities, while utilizing existing drives to ally the science curriculum to the subconcepts under each major scheme.

Mass-energy: Subconcepts appropriate to the intuitive level of thought are:

1. Matter has certain properties.
2. The *shape* of matter can be changed through the application of energy.
3. The *state* of matter can be changed through the application of energy.

1. For children at the intuitive level, we refer to matter as "objects." The question of what is and what is not an object needs to be explored. For instance, is air an object? Is love or fear? Many of the properties of matter become apparent through handling, describing, and arranging objects in sets (by color, shape, texture, weight, resistance to blows, etc.). Besides looking at *and* handling objects, the child can learn about some properties through touch, smell, or taste alone. None of these operations can be performed on love or fear! That gases are made of matter—are objects—can be learned at this stage: air in plastic bags has resistance; a burning incense cone smolders visibly and has an odor. Onion can be smelled at a distance: some*thing* must be coming to the child's nose. Three balloons filled with air, Freon-12, and helium react differently when played with: there must be some*thing* different filling each; but each is filled with some*thing* which has resistance—with a kind of matter.

The child from five to seven can talk about his observations, his arrangements. Through learning the words for various attributes and listening to his peers give their own descriptions, he brings the properties of matter into awareness. Then he can apply language to the less obvious states of matter—liquids and gases.

He can play grab-bag games and games with the quadribag, both of which require him to match textures or shapes, and sniffing games which require

him to recognize, name, and match odors. [7]

Such activities naturally lead to comparisons, at first only in pairs: larger-smaller, rougher-smoother, brighter-duller, heavier-lighter, etc. Then, gradually the child may be encouraged to arrange three objects in comparative order; this is the beginning of a series: long-longer-lonest, sticky-stickier-stickiest, dark-darker-darkest. Children achieve the three-part series by comparing in pairs; they do not, at first, have an understanding of the "in between" value.

An activity, which helps to build a basis for the concept that matter is conserved, is to have the children guess what object is behind a shadow screen as the turning object projects a shadow which changes in shape. This activity can be done with two-dimensional shapes: surface or outline.

The permanence of matter begins to dawn upon children when they first have experience with solutions. Sugar dissolved in water can be tasted. You cannot see it, but it is still there. Boiling off the water reveals the sugar again. The children will not be aware of the concept of conservation here, but tracing the existence of the unseen is a valuable experience. With solutions of colored crystals such as copper sulfate, the children can follow another attribute (color) through this partial disappearance; again the crystals can be recovered through evaporation.

2. At first, children do not realize that a piece of wood and the sawdust it produces are both the same wood. They do not think of chalkdust and the piece of chalk that made it as the same substance or of sand rubbed off sandstone as the same material. Experience in using their energy (via rubbing, sawing, crushing with a hammer, etc.) helps convince them to apply the same name to the two forms of matter. These are irreversible reactions, which, in itself, is a point it is worthwhile for the children to note.

3. The permanence of matter through changes of state is another subconcept which is pertinent at the intuitive level of thought. Comparing what happens to ice cubes on hot and cold saucers or ice cubes in

[7] Descriptions of a variety of experiences which focus on the senses may be found in the *Participating Teacher's Guide, New Ways in Elementary Science*, a part of the *Starting Tomorrow Programs*, 720 Fifth Ave., New York, N.Y. 10019, 1968.

different locales and then freezing the water again; comparing a cube of butter and a cube of ice in a warm room; playing with and talking about the properties of silicone (silly) putty—all might lead children to a statement that the new substance is like a solid and also like a liquid, an "in between" relationship.

Children need to think of the factor which brings about these changes of a state and/or form. The general term is energy, of course. The child can learn to distinguish different kinds of energy: his muscle energy turns wood to sawdust; heat energy melts ice.

A good way to think and talk about change, as we have mentioned earlier, is in terms of a system of objects which interact. We need to name the objects and to describe the interactions. All changes can be described as the interactions of objects in a system. But all changes also require energy. Naming the energy is an inference; it is the beginning of model making. For example, a hammer and a rock interact: the rock changes to powder; muscle energy is applied to bring about the change. Or, ice and the child's hand interact: the ice melts and becomes water; heat energy is transferred from the hand to bring about the change. At this age, children cannot understand the electrical (ionic) energy which dissolves salt in water; but if they have a beginning concept that all changes require energy, they will find a name of their own for the effect!

A child watching a candle burn will probably not be struck by the permanence of matter, but he will be able to see that a lot of heat energy is required to turn some solids into the liquid state and that even more energy is required to change the candle solids into a new substance (smoke). He can later form a series of things which change from the solid to the liquid state easily, less easily, and least easily. He may even be able to say that one requires little heat energy, the next more heat energy, and the third most heat energy.

Universe: If children during the years of intuitive thinking cannot handle three variables at once—relate three objects in a series, they will not be able to understand the relative motions of the sun, moon, and observer which give rise to phases of the moon;

they will not be able to appreciate that day and night represent a relationship of the sun to the turning earth upon which they stand. But paired relationships are within their grasp; children can make meaningful observations of the relation of two objects which they can see directly. A child can observe the position of the sun in the sky and measure the length of a shadow, and he can repeat this at different times of the day. He will not be able to encompass the concept that the earth turning produces the same phenomenon as the sun rising, nor will he be able to relate the height of the midday sun in December and June to the angle of the earth's axis to the ecliptic. Finding the relationship of light to the shadow of an object by controlling the source of light (a flashlight) prepares the child for a later understanding of the sun's position which he can observe but not control. Through observation, he can understand the relation of shadows to the direction from which the source of light comes, he can even predict one from the other after considerable experience. But he may not be able to explain his act in words yet; prediction precedes explanation.

Other paired relationships can be observed: clouds become rain (there is no rain when there are no clouds), snow becomes water and water becomes ice, puddles disappear (what do they become?). Water appears out of the air: breath in a plastic bag, drops on the outside of a glass of ice water or on the lid of a terrarium. The child can gradually relate the puddle-into-air process to the water-out-of-air process without knowing at first, that the same water can be involved in both. He will not understand the whole water cycle; since it is a series of events on one hand and a conservation and reversibility concept on the other. But he can observe and record the weather conditions day by day and experience, kinesthetically, the movement of the wind. From his study of air as matter, he can begin to think of the sensation of wind as resistance of matter against the matter of his body—that is, the interaction of *objects* in a system.

The thermometer records changes in the universe around the child. The alcohol or mercury interacts with the air or liquid next to it through the glass in which it is encased. Heat energy moves from one to the other. When an equilibrium is reached, the air and the thermometer have the same temperature. The temperature recorded by the thermometer is the temperature of the other object. For this age level, the thermometer should have a scale of colored areas: blue for cold, green for cool, yellow for warm, red for hot. Seven year olds can transfer these associations to the numerals on a real scale.

In a limited way, children experience changes in the universe due to the interaction of their bodies with gravity. They will describe this interaction as movement up or down; later they extend their view by thinking of up as away from the ground (earth) and down as toward the earth. They will know from television presentations of our space-age exploits that an astronaut can speed around a ball-shaped earth in 90 minutes. From this, children may be able to accept that their feet are approximately directed toward the feet of children in Australia.

Living organisms: The most dramatic changes in living organisms can be seen by a child when he grows his own seeds. Strips of construction paper torn off to represent the height of seedlings at spaced intervals (say, twice a week) help him to record growth. If he pastes his strips in order on a large sheet of paper as he makes them, the growth curve can be visualized. If he does not do this daily, however, a collection of strips of varying length will not be easily placed in order all at once. But, of course, he should make this discovery himself!

Change in color is another attribute of many living organisms. Fall leaves are one obvious example. Using water from boiled red cabbage or melted grape jelly and mixing it with acids (vinegar, lemon) or with bases (sodium bicarbonate, ammonia) is a thought-provoking experience for a child.

Using a dissecting microscope (two eye lenses with low magnification) to focus on insects in a clear petri dish offers a child insight into the movements, feeding habits, and other environmental interactions of many small creatures found in open lots, gardens, and fields. [8]

Classroom pets watched over the year show constant change; the growth of chickens, baby hamsters, gerbils, and the development of frog's eggs can be recorded with a Polaroid camera. They can also be described in words or with the child's own body movements during rhythms.

A beginning of classification is possible during the years of five to seven. Animals can be placed together because of a common attribute. It does not matter if the Linnean scheme is not realized at this age: however, children with sufficient first-hand experience will begin to talk about animals with fur, animals with feathers, and animals with scales, as well as animals without backbones.

Science learnings expected at the level of concrete operations

The eight to ten year old has achieved an understanding of conservation of number and of matter. He can mentally reverse the processes when size and shape are changed by pouring, bending, or rearranging. At this stage, too, he can arrange many objects in a long series and interpolate an item "in between." He can understand cycles and realizes that there are many routes by which a starting point can be reached again. He has learned these changes through the manipulation of objects and he can *think* of the changes he has already watched occur. For him reversibility and conservation are internalized in the sense that he can recall the process through thought if it is about a concrete experience he has had.

The child may still be slightly confused about the invariance of weight and volume. Piaget gives two interesting illustrations of this:

> Thus when a child says that a boat floats because it is heavy, he does so because, in his mind, the weight of the boat has not been compared with the volume of the water, but has been evaluated as a function of the subject's own point of view, taken as absolute. [9]

> . . . a boy tells us that large-sized or "big" bodies are heavier than small ones; yet a

---

[8] A small, hollow box of clear plastic with a removable cover which contains a lens that magnifies an insect or crystals in the box 4½X is distributed by Selective Educational Equipment, Inc. (S.E.E.), 3 Bridge Street, Newton, Mass. 02195. (Two boxes stacked together will give a 9X magnification.)

[9] Jean Piaget, *The Child's Conception of Physical Causality*, International Library of Psychology, 1960, 293, pb. New York: Humanities Press, Inc.; London: Routledge and Kegan Paul, Ltd.

moment later he declares that a small pebble is heavier than a large cork. But he does not, for that matter, give up his first affirmation, he only declares that the stone is heavier than the cork "because some stones are bigger than corks." Thus the character "big" has not at all the same meaning as for us. [10]

The child of eight or nine may remain in the intuitive stage with regard to weight and volume. He will not be able to think of them both together—as a relation, as density, as weight per unit volume. We have seen that he begins to say at this stage "heavy for its size." This may be because the size, shape, and number of objects can be seen. Weight and volume are not directly perceivable; each is somewhat of an abstraction. Their relationship as density requires an abstraction related to an abstraction—an ability of thought which belongs to the stage of formal operations (at adolescence), rather than to the level of concrete operations. The child will have similar difficulty with the problem of a pendulum. Here the concept of gravity is related to the period of swing; again an abstraction related to an abstraction. As the child approaches his tenth year, he can predict that two cylinders of equal volume but different weights will raise the level of water into which they are dropped to the same mark. Until this age, children are sure that the heavier of the two equal-volume weights will raise the level more than the lighter weight will. The ability to predict precedes the ability to explain. Allowing the child to relate the volume–weight conflict to a concrete mark on a cylinder helps him build a bridge to a formal-operation statement while using a concrete base for his thinking.

The intellectual stage of concrete operations means that separate concepts of invariance of number, of matter, of weight, and of volume are known concretely and have also been internalized. The child can think about them if he has a concrete frame of reference in his experience. We notice marked growth in conceptual abilities from eight to ten years.

Mass–energy: The acceptance of the concept that objects have permanence enables the child at this stage of development to recognize three-dimensional

[10] *Ibid.,* p. 294.

solids turned about various axes while their shadows project on a screen. This exercise helps the child visualize three-dimensional silhouettes or projections on the plane surfaces of two-dimensional solids. It can lead up to important applications: the shapes seen as phases of the moon and the planets. These, however, are projections on a sphere.

During this stage of concrete operations, the mental act of reversibility allows us to introduce the child to the model that a solid has small parts called molecules and that molecules together form the matter we know. Once he begins to move along the conceptual arrow of molecules, he is in a position to understand the rearrangement of molecules which takes place during a chemical reaction with no loss of the parts. It becomes profitable as well as intriguing for these eight to ten year olds to examine "mystery powders," to test for starch and carbonates and sugar, for acids and bases, and to write equations, at least word equations, to record their observations.

Grappling with the model of matter called molecules means that children can begin to talk about molecular energy to explain the change of state from solid to liquid to gas in terms of the increased energy and therefore the increased motion of the molecules. It is less certain that these same children will be able to *think* of the expansion of gases when heated as the reason for convection currents since this requires a concept of density. They may be able to discover such currents concretely with a "detector" (see page 205).

When children explore electric circuits at this age, they soon discover hot wires, which can be explained according to the model of electrical energy changing to heat energy. As the electric current lights the bulbs, it becomes clear to the children that electrical energy is being changed to light energy. The sun's energy is absorbed by plants during photosynthesis. Children can discover for themselves the relation of greenness and starch to sunlight. When they read about the rearrangements of the atoms of carbon dioxide and water to form the sugar molecule, the energy necessary to bring about this change is easily traced to the sun. Mechanical energy produces electrical energy in the dynamo, and heat energy produces mechanical energy when a candle or steam turns a pieplate wheel. Where friction occurs, mechanical energy produces heat. The realization that one type of energy can be converted to other kinds is achieved by the teacher helping the children to attach the word "energy" to light, heat, electricity, and mechanical phenomena of which they are aware sensewise. The teacher uses the word himself in the appropriate contexts and the children develop their preconcept thinking through the application of the correct terms to their physical experiences. Toward the end of this stage, the children can link electrical and magnetic energy through studying the effects of an electric current on magnetism.

As children put words to their discoveries of chemical exchanges, the need arises to distinguish between atoms and molecules. At this time, it may not be best to present pictorial sketches of the structure of the atom. That an atom is the smallest part of an element is the important aspect. Hence, the meanings of the words *element* and *compound* need to be introduced at the same time as the differences between atoms and molecules are clarified, or at least defined.

Categorizing can become more complicated during the period of concrete operations. Since the child can hold several variables in his head at once, rather extensive keys can be constructed and the data can be transferred to a punch card system for the purpose of retrieving information. Similarly, information can be spotted through the use of the 20 question technique, described in Chapter 1 as the game of *Info*.

This seems to be the level where understanding the nature of sound becomes appropriate. Sound is an ordered sequence of molecular motion (the frequency of waves of air, other gases, solids) detected by the ear. The nature of wave motion as analogous to the ripples in a pond in which a stone is dropped forms a prelude to a more abstract type of wave—the electromagnetic wave.

Universe: Three or more variables held in mind concurrently make it possible for the child at the level of concrete operations to think about the relative positions of bodies in the solar system. He may also discover the reason for phases of the moon and be able to predict what Venus would look like from the moon, or the way the moons would appear to move to the man on Mars.[11] The child can cope with a three-dimensional coordinate system and understand and construct contour maps and play a game of three-dimensional tic-tac-toe.

His ability to encompass the sweep of time gives meaning to a study of geological sequences and formations. Reversibility, along with the sense of extended time span, brings the woodland mineral cycles within his grasp.

Climate and weather become profitable studies at this stage. So do patterns engendered through interaction with gravity. A ball is bounced. The energy of compressed molecules pushes the ball away from the gravitational vector; the ball comes down again and up once more, but with less energy. What is the pattern of the heights of the bounces? A ball rolls down a slope. The distance it moves in each second also forms a pattern related to gravity. This pattern is modified if a cylinder is rolled down a slope—by its different shape as well as by whether it is solid or hollow.

Through the device of Mr. "O" (an entirely objective observer, represented by a cutout) it has been shown that it is easy to introduce a child at the concrete operations level of thought to some of the ideas of relativity.[12] In a similar manner, the child can measure the passage of time and see this measure related to various universal phenomena: an egg timer to gravity, a burning candle to the rate of combustion, a sundial to the earth's rotation, the year to a planet's period of revolution around the sun.

Living organisms: Because the concrete operations level of thought includes holding several variables in mind at once, eight to ten year olds are able to design investigations which control all but one variable at a time. They can therefore observe and discover the basic factors involved in making molds (or micro gardens) grow, seeds germinate, and green leaves photosynthesize. Ecological cycles may be studied in

[11] An exercise in predicting the apparent motions of the two moons of Mars appears in Herman and Nina Schneider and Brenda Lansdown, *Now Try This* 6, D. C. Heath, Lexington, Mass., 1964, pp. 108-109.

[12] Mr. "O" is in the booklet *Relativity,* available from the Science Curriculum Improvement Study (S.C.I.S.), Lawrence Hall of Science, University of California at Berkeley, 1968.

aquaria, desert or woodland terraria, or in nature itself.

Toward the end of this level, the cell is appreciated as a unit of life. The study of the human body—its absorption and disposition of energy via its various organs—becomes fruitful.

Because there is growing understanding of the sweep of time, the extinction of past species such as dinosaurs takes its place along the conceptual arrow. The sequences of evolutionary species can be studied along with certain ecological interactions. A modern theory of evolution can only be sensed; it is better delayed until the level of formal operations.

It is well to recall that each of the foregoing levels of thought imply a passage *through* a lower level to a higher level. The achievements we have described are possible at some time during the ages quoted for most children. This does not mean that a child can promptly accomplish all we have suggested at a specific age. Nor does it mean that every child will reach the full level of thought indicated within the probable age range. Some may have flights into the next level of thought on occasion which are way beyond their age expectancies. One learns where each child is, of course, by listening to what he says and how he explains his perceptions during the colloquia.

Science learnings expected at the level of formal operations

At this stage, the child can begin to relate abstraction to abstraction. He can, for instance, encompass the relationship that if weight remains constant and volume increases, there will be a decrease in density. This is the first moment when the concept of flotation, the Archimedes principle, can actually be developed. The child can now appreciate theories on the origin of the universe—on the birth and death of stars. It is the first time he can understand the many factors which may have been operative as new species appeared, waxed, and waned—as the sequence of amoeba to man was achieved through an endless series of interactions between genes and their environment. Model making becomes more abstract and the consequences may be predicted and tested.

The eleven- to twelve-year-old child is approaching adolescence. He is approaching the ability of full conceptual thought—the stage which grows and flourishes throughout the high school years, provided a sound base for it has been fostered.

Mass–energy: The dawn of the thought level called formal operation most often occurs during the sixth grade. The child can then join the concept of electromagnetism to that of electromagnetic waves in general. He can begin to think of the electromagnetic spectrum which goes all the way from long radio waves of low frequency through television waves to the ultra high frequency (UHF) band on into infrared and then visible light, to ultraviolet light and X-rays, and finally to gamma rays with their incredibly high frequencies and minute wavelengths. A study of how television, radio, and other electronic devices work is appropriate.

The structure of the atom with its electromagnetic

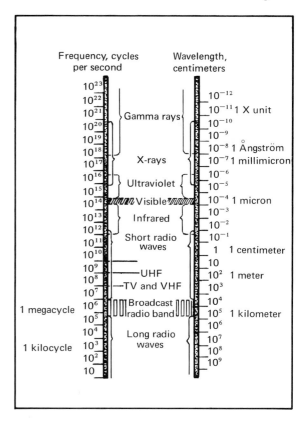

interactions can be understood at this stage, and this leads naturally to a rational explanation or model of the phenomenon of electricity.

That radioactivity transforms atoms from one kind to another by the transformation of matter into energy is an important culmination of the various aspects of the mass-energy concept which has been studied through the grades. The electrolysis of matter in solution ties together many of the above concepts.

On the molecular level, studies of viscosity and surface tension can be undertaken.

Airplane flight involves the concept of density, as does the nature of rocket flight; both are profitably studied at this age.

Universe: Rocket flight, introduced under the mass-energy rubric, continues into a study of space flight with its interesting sum of vectors representing gravity and space capsule velocity. Weightlessness may be understood in the manner described on page 176.

The magnetic fields surrounding the earth and other planets, the van Allen belts, and the Aurora effects all belong to this stage. So, one may say, does the concept of gravity in galactic systems. Notation to describe the very large in light years and the very small in high-frequency wavelengths forms a bridge to a study of new mathematical symbols.

At this stage the various phenomena connected with light may be understood: absorption, reflection, refraction, the use of lenses, and the structure of the telescope and other optical instruments. The wave-particle theory is intriguing to some advanced sixth graders.

Living organisms: Perhaps the most important biological concept at this stage is the relationship of common form to common ancestry in both plants and animals: that fin, wing, and arm are structural cognates; that a Brussels sprout is a bud, a cucumber is a fruit, and the part of celery we eat is a leaf base. This calls for a study of genes, DNA and RNA molecules, and the manner in which characteristics are passed on. It calls for an understanding of mutations by which there are changes in the inherited template. The relation of variants and mutants to survival is the dynamics of evolution: a change in

environment can benefit (select) random changes in the genes. The study of life cycles again emphasizes morphological processes, for we all begin as a single fused cell which divides.

A recent development in the science curriculum, and one which we feel should be kept and amplified, is the introduction of psychology in the "organism" conceptual scheme. Here children can learn something of the nature of learning, forgetting, and habit formation, and something about the paths of insightful thinking.

Many studies of recent experimental researches are possible, and there is a wide list to choose from: hydroponics, nerve reactions, osmotic pressures, the chemistry of photosynthesis, the relation of diet, drugs, and smoking to health and disease, man's responsibility for the ecological effects of pollution.

Curriculum suggestions gearing the intellectual and conceputal to the social cogs

This is much less difficult than it would seem from the fact that it has been so lightly considered. Most curricula are geared to the middle-class background and watered down or taught more slowly for children from inner city environments. And, in general, the curriculum via its units and lessons is imposed upon children, all children, in a preconceived manner. But where science lessons begin with children manipulating materials in a free discovery manner, observation by the teacher reveals whether the activity is profitable, whether it has drive and interest. Most materials do this anyway. The problem is more likely to be conjoined during the colloquium. Here again, the teacher who listens learns what the children think. Their phraseology and their explanations of phenomena clearly reveal the level of thought and the stage in concept level attainment which each child has reached. The levels described by Piaget are very closely age-linked and the leap into the next level often comes quite suddenly—at least the overt expression seems sudden. We have considered that reaching the next level of thought may be slightly hastened by good teaching. A recent study indicated that maturity is coming to children at an earlier and earlier age as the decades role by and that children are growing taller.[13] This may account in part for the Piaget levels of thought being evinced sooner now than when they were first revealed.

The Vygotsky levels are tied far more closely to experience and less closely to maturity. Once a person has reached the level of concrete operations in the Piaget scheme (and this may be reached by people independently of formal education), there is little chance that egocentric thought or doubt about the conservation of matter will intrude anew. But, as we mentioned, the Vygotsky hierarchy is likely to be climbed again each time a new area is approached, albeit the heights are more quickly scaled after having once been trodden. Hence, whatever the social experience of children, it is likely that intuitive thinking will pass into concrete operational thought somewhere between the seventh and ninth years. In making explanations—finding external likenesses in a colloquium, children will naturally draw on their own experiential background. By listening, the teacher learns what this background is. Fluency in language and vocabulary may be limited; still children do manage to convey what they mean to a listening audience.

There is some choice on the teacher's part as to the kinds of materials to be used; these may be even more carefully chosen if a child's background is taken into consideration. We have seen that low socio-economic second graders had had no experience with sieves and funnels, so water play with these preceded the investigation of solutions. We know of a farm boy of nine who could not read, but when he saw a picture of a block and tackle he immediately pointed out that one rope was missing! Suburban children would need to have a pulley in the classroom to find out what the ropes did, let alone the role of each. Children living in the streets between high tenements cannot see the sun rise or set, but they can do some ecological studies of the weeds and insects in an open lot. Country children may not know of the sensation of near "weightlessness" which occurs as an elevator comes to rest near an upper floor.

Children of migrant workers surely know the meaning of sunup and sundown; they have a basis for studying the varying times and locations of sunrise and sunset and thinking about the scientific implications. Mexican-American children can derive a basic understanding of food values from testing tortillas and taco fillings. Navajo Indian children might be more intrigued by the ecological interactions of desert flora and fauna than by the camouflages of arctic animals. Cultural relevancy can play a vital role in some areas of science. In other areas, the phenomena may be universal (such as gravity or flotation) or intrinsically intriguing (such as magnetism or plant growth). Beginning with relevant interests leads easily to extended cultural learnings. For example, we all eat beans: Italian fava, Chinese mung sprouts, Indian succotash, Puerto Rican rice and beans, Boston baked beans, Russian string beans with mushrooms.[14] One might further extend such a study by introducing the complete protein value of the soy seed.

The discovery-colloquium method of fostering science learning minimizes the need to allow for the social background cog (see pages 266-68), but it does not eliminate it. Materials do speak to all—to each in his own meaning, and the colloquium speaks to the teachers as well as to the peers. However, if the discovery period shows lack of initiative and the colloquium lags, it may well be that the type of materials are irrelevant to the child's background and/or his stage of conceptual development. Looking and listening are safety valves which supply clues to irrelevance; they help to avoid the disaster of long-winded explanations!

It is, of course, of paramount importance that the contributions of scientists of various ethnic minorities be made known to all children. Children belonging to these minorities need this knowledge to achieve ego development and a sense of identification. We previously outlined a few such contributions which are not commonly available (see Chapter 1, pages 31-32).

Who chooses the curriculum?

Textbooks on curriculum are full of sets of hierarchies. But whoever has selected the area, the

---

[13] J.M. Tanner, *Scientific American,* "Earlier Maturation in Man," Vol. 218, No. 1 (January 1968) 21-27.

[14] For creative learning suggestions from a study of beans, see Brenda Lansdown, *The Grade Teacher,* "We All Eat Beans," (May 1957), 29.

concept, the unit, or the process, the classroom teacher actually selects the lesson and the materials that go with it. But often the teacher can choose the unit and even the concept to be emphasized as well. The main reason for having an outside body select the sequence and scope of the curriculum is so that children will not find themselves "doing" magnets every year or repeating explorations of what makes seeds grow, just because several successive teachers enjoy doing these units.

We would favor units in each of the areas of the three conceptual schemes each year, but the number of units and the length of each depends much more on the interests of a particular group than on prescribed activities. In every class, there are children who have met some of the materials before; there are some children who find more ingenious ways of manipulating materials than others do; there are children with wider knowledge and more practice in relating facts to patterns or models. This is true whether the unit is carefully selected to be new or whether it is selected because the teacher feels it fits the program and interlocks with other areas of study.

One can avoid materials which are known to have been used by a majority of the children and a previous teacher. If a fourth grade spent six weeks with mealworms, certainly the fifth-grade teacher can find other classroom pets! If a second grade kept an aquarium, the third grade could try a desert terrarium. If a third grade played with electric cells and light bulbs, the fourth grade could use electro-

magnets. So many new suggestions are coming out all the time, both in new editions of textbooks and in new issues of experimental programs.

A guide to the hierarchy of choice might be:

1. The conceptual scheme to be emphasized.
2. The subconcept for unit concentration (probably a cluster of subconcepts).
3. The concept level of the children: intuitive, concrete operation, formal operation.
4. Readily available materials whose science use is novel to most of the children.
5. A matrix which offers a variety of activities and subconcepts to cater to individual differences.
6. A starting lesson which raises a number of problems because the materials interact in many allied ways or provoke questions.
7. Follow-up lessons from observing what the children do with the materials and listening to what they say in the colloquium, as well as collecting the unsolved problems from the Investigators' Log. This last item includes cues the children give the teacher about their socio-economically bound interests, although one must assume that the primary choice of materials and the placement of the concept level of thought required the teacher to know something about the children initially. Where the teacher and the children are completely new to each other, we suggest one of the *Starting Tomorrow* lessons which have very wide appeal.

7

The how and when of books and other learning aids

Books in addition to discovery and colloquium

The role of books in relation to discovery was discussed in Chapter 1 (*What Is Discovery?,* pages 28-33). The points made were that:

1. Books and other learning aids (films, filmloops, and filmstrips) are essential to extend and develop the motivation and learnings provided by the initial discovery–colloquium sessions.
2. Books, films, etc. provide for rich learning when a child brings an appropriate apperceptive base to them.
3. Children who choose to consult these learning aids when they feel the need are liable to discover in them many pertinent facts and explanations which are meaningful.

Apart from this preliminary introduction to the role of books and other learning aids, the preceding chapters have explored the many ramifications, both in theory and in practice, of a full understanding of the implications of the discovery–colloquium approach to science learning. It is once again time to return to the role of books.

Two models may help in clarifying the role of books: one of the learning interactions of the initial discovery–colloquium sessions and a second in which books and other learning aids are added.

The main thrust of our view of sciencing is that the natural phenomena of the universe may be discovered by children through the free manipulation of materials which have been selected to reveal patterns of interaction and which themselves have been related to the concepts constructed by man about the phenomena. The child himself moves along conceptual arrows through interacting with his peers

279

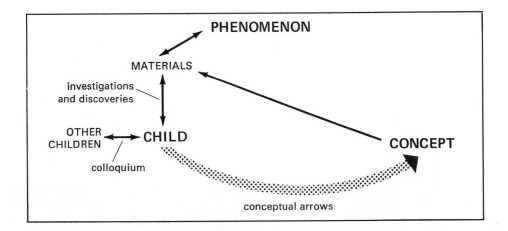

in colloquia. During these activities, he develops skills of *in*dependence as he uses initiative in manipulating the materials and in thinking about what he observes. He engages in skills of *inter*dependence with his peers during the colloquium and, in some measure, as he works in a small group around the same materials. Then, as a child seeks meanings in these various experiences, he begins to move along the conceptual arrows appropriate to his maturity level in relation to the concept behind the materials—again, a skill of *in*dependence.

Now, as we introduce books and other learning aids, a new dimension is added. We tap the sources of our scientific heritage. We extend the framework and meaning of the phenomena and, because concepts are built from multiphasic encounters with the phenomena, we widen enormously the road along the conceptual arrows. We have increased the input and deepened the output.

A word about the interactions represented in our two models by two-way arrows:

Phenomenon–Materials: One or more phenomena are embedded, as it were, in the materials due to their very selection. When the materials are manipulated, the phenomena are revealed.

Child–Materials: The child learns from the materials, but the materials also change what the child does.

Child–Other children: Interaction during colloquia has been extensively documented in previous chapters.

The one-way *Concept-Materials* arrow indicates that the concept is the basis for the materials, but that the materials do not change the concept.

In the extended second model below:

Phenomenon–Scientific heritage: Throughout his-

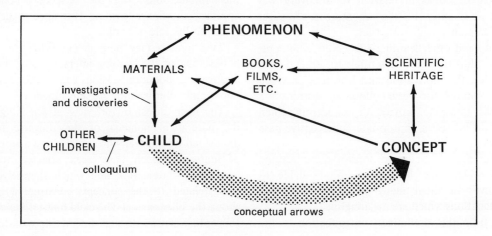

tory man has observed phenomena and changed his way of thinking about them. But these phenomena have also acted on man, as they revealed more or different patterns.

Scientific heritage-Concept: As scientific knowledge accumulates, concepts change. Changed concepts help scientists add to our scientific heritage.

Scientific heritage-Books, films, etc.: Books, films, etc. contain the record of our heritage. They do not change the heritage itself. This is therefore a one-way arrow.

Child-Books, films, etc.: The child brings an apperceptive base to the books which, in part, determines what he learns from them. The books, however, open up new avenues of knowledge and thought to the child as well.

The teacher is omitted from the models because his influence requires too many arrows which would render the chart confusing. He selects the concept and the related phenomena, chooses the materials, conducts the colloquium, provides the books and films, and is, himself, a transmitter of scientific heritage!

We now turn to ways in which books can be used in classrooms where discovery-colloquium sciencing is in progress. We will try to suggest many ways to fit a variety of limitations and realities of the day-to-day problems of organizing time and learning situations.

The time-bind and the textbook

The reader who has reached this chapter may very well be thinking, "Some fine ideas if I had nothing else to teach but science," or maybe, "This is all very well, but I have a textbook to cover," or perhaps, "It seems that each of the lessons suggested will take at least an hour and a half. I have *exactly* 40 minutes for science per week, and it's scheduled for 2:00 on Friday afternoon."

Some good ideas, but who can use them?

In this chapter we will offer some practical as well as some theoretical suggestions on ways to introduce discovery-colloquium lessons within the unit organization of the textbook and the time-bind of the schedule.

The most restricting problem a teacher has to face in a school where there are only 40 minutes (or a similar short time limit) for science is that a discovery-colloquium lesson almost always lasts at least an hour, and the drive and interest it produces usually lasts considerably longer. Moreover, a colloquium loses much of its vitality if other important events of a child's life separate preverbal discovery through the manipulation of materials stage from the talking-together phase which clarifies, develops, and codifies in speech the concepts germane to the structure of the materials. We have to admit that there is curtailment of learning whenever an ardent drive is broken off too soon for a certain satisfaction to have been achieved. This is not to say that a lesson must terminate with all of the ends neatly tied up; we recall that our prototype of the creative teacher is somewhat of a lysiphile! But if the groans of the class when it is time to clean up are too loud, then too much learning will be lost. Usually, if the discoveries have not been translated into symbols of some sort and developed through peer interaction, there is a serious truncation of learning.

The time allowed for science in the elementary schools of the nation varies greatly. A recent national study[1] showed that in almost every kindergarten through sixth grade there were schools that gave science less than 20 minutes a week and others that allowed over 260 minutes a week. It is astonishing that there is such a wide divergence of time devoted to science. The average is about 55 minutes per week.

There are ways to overcome the difficulties of short periods, assigned coverage, and textbook organization.

The unit organization of a textbook, while somewhat different from our matrix organization, can, nevertheless, be well used. We must admit that most of the modern textbooks contribute a great deal to the extended meanings of science, after a child has developed meaning in the area through the manipulation of materials. The textbook adds organized and correct explanations, extends learning beyond the experiential, suggests avenues for further search,

---

[1]*Science Teaching in the Elementary Schools: A Survey of Practices,* U.S. Office of Education (OE-29059), Department of Health, Education, and Welfare, U.S. Government Printing Office, Washington, D.C., 1965, 104 pp., 65¢.

consolidates meaning. For us, books *follow* some experience with the field under study, some personal discoveries with materials, some questions and problems raised through colloquia. Books, whether they are text or trade, are most valuable when they are brought to an apperceptive base—a learner with experience and questions, a learner for whom some meaning in the field has already been evoked. We utilize textbooks and trade books for reference in every science unit, but books are among the stepping stones of the discovery-colloquium matrix.

If you are a teacher who wishes to "cover" a textbook (or even "uncover" it), or one who is expected to expose his children to a major number of units in a specific text during the year, perhaps these suggestions will be helpful.

If there are five units to be covered in a year, two months may be allowed for each. But if there is only one science session a week, that may add up at most to eight times 40 minutes or a little over five hours, plus whatever is assigned for homework. The problem is twofold:

1. Where does one find materials for discovery which can substitute for the teacher-guide suggestion of starting a unit by having the children turn to the picture on page so-and-so and reply to teacher questions?

2. How much of value can be accomplished during 40 minutes using the discovery-colloquium approach?

Fortunately, many textbooks are full of excellent suggestions for materials appropriate to the concepts in each unit. Instead of having the children wait until these are reached in the text, they can be offered to the children as "See what you can find out" experiences to start off the unit. The materials may be used also to further the progress of the unit, to introduce a new stepping stone in the same manner. When the children eventually turn to the pages on which the investigation involving the materials is described (often, alas, with the outcome indicated as well), they are highly stimulated to compare their results and their models with those in the text.

Suggestions for discovery lessons may be drawn from many sources: various textbook investigations, trade book suggestions, one's own experiences, science teaching journals. Sometimes it is a good idea to have a few copies of several texts and books on more than one grade level instead of one similar book for each child. In this chapter, we will offer a number of unit matrices with many sets of materials to present to children.

As to starting a unit by looking at the first page, we feel that a textbook may be approached in various sequences. A unit which offers many practical investigations with materials may be considered a matrix through which the children can wander from stepping stone to stepping stone. They may spend more time on some stones, and even avoid others altogether. May we suggest that the residue of learning is no less valuable through this approach than it would be through "covering," vocally, the whole chapter?

The time-bind

The 40 minute time-bind is the most troublesome restriction. We have never found a science interest that elapsed in so short a period of time. There are several ways in which teachers can maneuver to overcome this obstacle. A teacher convinced of the value of an approach to learning is one of the most ingenious of humans!

One way is to give a science lesson once every two weeks, taking a double period for the session. In this way discovery and colloquium can be encompassed. If the children are full of questions and ideas for further investigations at the end of the period, what better motivation for a homework assignment? If they are at a stage or age where interest may lag during a two-week wait for the next double session, then it may be possible to feature two double periods in consecutive weeks and wait four weeks before beginning a new interest. Some teachers have found that assigning reading in the text after a double period, with a suggestion for writing or investigating at home, carries the children over very well to the next double period. There are many variants of blocking time this way. For instance, over a three-week period there can be one double session for discovery and colloquium and then a single period for discussion based on home investigations and text reading. Or a unit can be pursued with a double period each week for a month and the next month the time may be devoted to another subject area.

Another way to overcome the time-bind is in a classroom organization described variously as "free choice," "open classroom," or "the integrated day."[2] This organization may be employed one period a week, an hour or more each day, or, best of all, most of the time. Free choice is based on the principle that children learn most when they are self-motivated. This is the motivation we have advocated during the discovery periods. Each child has "free choice" about what he will do with the materials, to find which interactions among the materials have meaning for him. There may be free choice about what to do with the materials; there may be free choice also of which subject area to study. Or there may be free choice for a few children working in a science area while the rest of the class does assigned work in another field. In such an arrangement, it would be important for the teacher to make sure that each child has a chance to choose work with science once during, say, each week. Where the children are offered a number of choices at the same time, each offering must be attractive to the children and each child must understand what he has to do in the area. For instance, there are now filmloops which allow children to show themselves silent or sound movies of various duration in any number of areas. Children can look at filmstrips by themselves or in small groups. And there are many ways to prepare optional work which the children can master on their own: a series of tasks written on cards, teaching machines, free use of art materials, committee work in social studies, and many more.

Let us say that the rather common setup called the "Science Table" is reformed to have structured sets of materials relating to a unit of study. A group of children works there, either because it is their turn or their choice. For the colloquium, the teacher moves over to the science area to listen to what the group of investigators has to say. Of course, he can wait until everyone in the class has had his turn at the table and then hold a colloquium with the whole class, but we have seen that this does not produce the best results.

[2] See a series of articles by Joseph Featherstone, *The New Republic,* "The Primary School Revolution in Britain" (August 10, September 2, and September 9, 1967) and Lillian Weber, *The English Infant School: A Model for Informal Education,* Agathon Press, New York, 1969.

With older children, it is sometimes possible to delay the discussion by giving homework in the interim which keeps the experiences firmly in mind. But with younger children, it is essential that the teacher at least listen to their discoveries or, if possible, find time to conduct a colloquium at the science table immediately after the investigation. Where the class has a number of areas of study (mathematics, spelling, reading) available at the same time, then the teacher circulates so that he is with each group for a period of five to fifteen minutes, using the longer time period for the colloquium.

Another way to consolidate science learning after the investigation and while waiting for the colloquium is to have **Suggestion Cards** at the science table. In addition to problems for investigation, suggestions may include recording activities by writing the results or making a graph, planning a presentation, or reading further in a trade or textbook. Books, of course, need to be housed near the science area, or at least on a special shelf in the classroom library.

Other audio-visual materials which add to the richness of learning in science and which are adaptable to individual or small group use can be consulted, either during the regular science period or during spare moments when the children are free to select their activities: filmloops, filmstrips, and charts.

The textbook

With some scheduling of time such as has been suggested above, the next problem is how to find or select materials for introductory and follow-up sessions which are related to the unit in the textbook. To answer this question in various ways, it may be best to present examples giving principles and practice at the same time. We have chosen three subject areas which appear in almost all textbook series on several levels and which were not explored in Chapter 5, "The Matrix of a Unit"—ecology, light, and geology, and present different samplings of textbook usage in the several matrices which follow.

Matrices on ecology: Both Matrices 9 and 10 emphasize the ecological interactions of animals; each matrix is related to a specific unit in one textbook. Matrices 11–14 emphasize the ecological interactions of plants; a variety of trade and textbooks, films, filmloops, and filmstrips is available to the children for free exploration.

Matrix on light: The major focus of introductory materials in Matrix 15 is from a filmloop. Thereafter, individual investigations relate the matrix to two units in one textbook. Finally, three more textbooks are consulted. Audio-visual aids are available.

Matrix on geology: In Matrix 16, a field trip provides the initial emphasis. The study of the mineral cycle can be introduced with materials for discovery. Thereafter, readings in three textbooks to probe into problems provide data for the colloquia. We provide the theoretical framework for the studies.

We would like to be as helpful as possible to teachers who have the most rigid requirements for their science programs, as well as to those who have considerable leeway. Let us say that a situation exists where a teacher has to "cover" a unit in an assigned text and that he has only 40 minutes a week to devote to science. We have already explored several patterns which give leeway to the time-bind. Now let us address ourselves to working with one source, whether it is a book, a set of activity cards, or a workbook.

Discovery–colloquium related to one or more textbooks

We still believe that the presentation of structured materials is the best beginning for a unit as well as the wisest way to boost interest at various stages during that unit. There are creative and thought-producing ways to assign textbook readings and to guide children's activities as an outcome of their reading. We suggest a number of these. The principles involved in formulating questions which raise problems and initiate open-ended search are given on pages 285-86; these may be applied to any unit which requires **Suggestion Cards** at some point. Suggested "experiments" whose materials can be presented for dis-

covery can always be found from reading a textbook unit. There are many sequences by which the content of a unit can be approached or "covered." Materials and activities can be chosen so that children move along the required stepping stones, but follow the order of their interests.

After the first period of discovery from whatever materials the teacher chooses to present (and these may come from the textbook or other sources) and after the follow-up colloquium, the teacher can assign appropriate pages to be read from the textbook for homework or he might suggest that each child read those pages which interest him within the unit chapter. An added requirement to foster self-motivation and growth along conceptual arrows might be:

> Write a statement which tells:
> a. which pages you read,
> b. *what* you would like to investigate next,
> c. *the way* in which you might conduct your investigation.

Reading these papers gives the teacher a guideline for planning the next materials; it gives him, also, an insight into the interests of each child. The teacher might discover that all of the children's needs could be grouped into a few categories or he might find that they have mostly individual needs. In either case, it is possible that one or two sets of materials would satisfy, since a wide range of related concepts may be tapped through use of all structured materials. The papers the children hand in help to pinpoint the subconcepts developed by the text toward which the children are moving. A good procedure at this juncture is for the teacher to write down thought provoking questions of the type he might use during the colloquium or provide as **Suggestion Cards** with the materials. The next lesson, after the children have reacted in writing to the text, might well feature a discussion on the *what* and the *ways* of the children's suggestions.

The children can help each other think of the materials needed and whether these are available in school or must be brought from home. Here the teacher has an opportunity to help the children think of the design of their proposed investigations and whether there are adequate controls.[3] Ways to record observations can be planned at such a time. Because several different investigations might be occurring concurrently in the class, the children become informed about each other's investigations and they are likely to absorb all of the reported data into their understanding of the whole unit. Children often wish to repeat each other's investigations. Even where they do not, they are likely to be motivated to read further and with more comprehension in the text where projects, data, and models have been shared in class.

Another helpful procedure where the teacher has received individual suggestions from each child is to write a note on each child's paper giving procedural clues. For example a teacher might refer a child to an investigation described on a certain page in the textbook or he might name a relevant trade book title or inform the child that a filmloop or a filmstrip exists on his topic. These personal messages can be very effective in many ways, both psychologically and scientifically.

A third manner of responding to the children's papers is to select another set of materials and just leave them for the children to work with freely. The materials would, of course, be relevant to the inquiries suggested by the papers. In this case the children bring an apperceptive base to the materials; their direction of investigations reflects established interests. But they may move off on a new track altogether!

A fourth way is to bring to the children the same, additional, or new materials (chosen from the matrix or the investigation in the text), and to have **Suggestion Cards** which encompass ways for the children to pursue their particular interests. Some guiding principles both for questions to be asked or problems to be posed at appropriate points in the colloquia and for **Suggestion Cards** are:

[3] Many useful suggestions on how to help children to focus on the various procedures of scientists are found for all levels of conceptual development in the A.A.A.S. series of books *Science: A Process Approach*, American Association for the Advancement of Science, 1515 Massachusetts Ave., N.W., Washington D.C. 20005. Kits of materials are available from the Xerox Corporation, Education Division, 600 Madison Avenue, New York, N.Y. 10022.

1. Comparisons:
   "In what way(s) is a goldfish like a snail?"
   "In what way(s) is a dandelion plant like a mushroom?"
   "In what way(s) do red and blue lights act differently?"
   "In what way(s) is slate like shale (or slate like marble)?"

2. Things to do to change something in the environment:
   "Put goldfish in boiled water that has cooled to the temperature of the aquarium. What is the interaction?"
   "Will soaked lima bean seeds germinate in the refrigerator?"
   "Shine a red light on pieces of paper of different colors."
   "Suppose the moon had a layer of air around it; what differences would it make?"

3. Guides to increase perceptiveness of observation:
   "Before you try the goldfish investigation (above), predict what you think will happen. Write it down. Write what did happen after you changed the environment."
   "Find all the things that are alike on these two twigs."
   [The series of four **Suggestion Cards** in stepping stones **T** and **U** (Matrix 15, Part III, pages 626-27) are designed to improve observation.]
   "Try to recognize pieces of sandstone, limestone, and shale by holding them in your hands behind your back."

4. Guides for collecting and recording data:
   "Keep a dated diary of what the frog's eggs look like each day."
   "Tear off a strip of paper to equal the height of your bean plant each day. Paste these strips on a sheet of brown paper."
   "Draw the colors of the spectrum you see when light from a prism falls on papers of various colors."
   "Mark on a globe all the places where you have read that earthquakes occur. What relationships do you see?"

5. Child-child interaction to sharpen thought and language:

"Discuss with your partner whether you think crystals are alive or not." (After children have viewed them forming from a saturated solution.)

"With a few of your friends, figure out what would happen if the sun ceased to shine."

In order not to gear children to the authority of being *told* what to do, it is best to have either a number of **Suggestion Cards** for any one set of materials or to give very open suggestions. Children must feel that they are free to take one, several, or none.

Matrices on ecology

The subject matter of ecology is presented in textbooks under such headings as: "Living things and their surroundings," [4] "Life in the Desert," [5] and "In Water and on Land." [6] These topics emphasize the animal world in its natural habitats. But animals cannot live without plants. Hence, the chapters which deal with seed dispersal, forms of plant life, the water cycle, pollination, and, finally, energy from the sun used in photosynthesis may all be included under the meaning of ecology. Ecology is really one way of interpreting the major concept "Living organisms interact with their environment and their heredity." The increasing emphasis, both in childhood education and through civic concern, on the pollution of our natural heritage is basically an ecological problem tempered through human good or bad will—a part of the concept of conservation. Ecology is a broadly encompassing topic. It is presented to second graders through a study of the growth of plants and the dispersal of seeds. In textbooks, the bulk of ecology topics are directed toward third and fourth graders, while the problem of why we have such a wide variety of plants and animals, each individually adapted to its environment, is usually studied by fifth and sixth graders who can delve into heredity,

[4] Abraham S. Fischler *et al.*, *Science: A Modern Approach 4*, Holt, Rinehart & Winston, New York, 1966. pp. 148-201.
[5] Herman and Nina Schneider, *Science Far and Near*, D. C. Heath, Lexington, Mass., 1965, pp. 20-33.
[6] Paul F. Brandwein *et al.*, *Concepts in Science 3*, Harcourt Brace Jovanovich, Inc., New York, 1966, pp. 244-65.

mutations and, therefore, into the dynamics of evolution.

There are some aspects of study in biology which call for a modification of the free discovery approach because, as we have seen, the materials have to be observed and thought about rather than manipulated. We collect data in order to find patterns, rather than observe patterns and construct models as we do in the physical sciences. Sometimes it is impossible to provide materials; consider the question "In what ways are elephants and whales adapted to their environments?" or "Why couldn't an elephant and a whale exchange environments?" Sometimes a study of biology calls for particularly perceptive observation; we saw this in the study of cells in Chapter 5 (pages 242-57).

We solve the problem of unavailable materials by providing other suitable living organisms which the children can handle and observe. Interaction with the environment is the important theme. There are many good types of classroom ecological systems (ecosystems). A couple of pet animals could also be provided for the children to observe in a free choice classroom situation. The questions asked about the whale and the elephant could be answered with a gerbil and a canary. Later, the results of observing and discussing the relationships of the gerbil and canary to their environments may be extended through pictures, filmstrips, filmloops, and reading to encompass the less experiential problems presented by the whale and the elephant.

Of course, the whole topic of ecology falls under Conceptual Scheme C: **"Living organisms are in constant change."** However, the meaning of ecology is not so much that organisms change, but that they *have changed* and are at present adapted to the environment in which they live. We might, therefore, take as our guiding concept this very statement: "Organisms are adapted to the environment in which they live." Note that we say "are adapted" rather than "adapt." Organisms other than man do not consciously adapt; the various processes of evolution, variations in mutations, natural selection, and change in climate have *fostered* the survival of the better adapted. It is fruitful to consider what is happening now as we live in an environment which is becoming increasingly polluted. Will we adapt to conditions which are basically noxious to life? Will we succumb? Or will we change the climate?

The ecology matrices are organized under the following headings which seem to be convenient for locating the topics usually found in textbooks, although some book units draw topics from more than one of the matrices.

The various matrices on ecology have been separated for convenience of reference. From the conceptual point of view, there is really only one embracing scheme: *ecosystems* in general. The conceptual scheme and the concepts pertinent to ecosystems are given here and apply to each of the above matrices. (See also the Chart of Conceptual Schemes, page 166.)

CONCEPTUAL SCHEME C

CHART FOR ECOSYSTEMS

Living organisms are in constant change.
A living organism is the product of its heredity (genetic code) and its environment.

	EMPHASIS ON HEREDITY	EMPHASIS ON ENVIRONMENT
PRECONCEPT		The capture of radiant energy from the sun is basic to the growth and maintenance of living organisms. Living organisms interchange matter and energy with their environment. There are characteristic environments, each with its characteristic life.
COMPLEX	Living organisms which have a common structure are related. All living organisms go through a birth, growth, death, decay cycle. Related living organisms reproduce in similar ways. There are different forms of living organisms.	Living organisms live and grow in different environments.

Ecological interactions—emphasis on animals

To use these matrices with any particular textbook unit or set of textbooks by different publishers, the teacher will need to make a blend of the concepts implicit in the text units with those from the above chart which seem appropriate. The next step is to select the materials for the initial lesson. These may come from any of the matrices or from investigations suggested by the textbooks. The stepping stones which lead the children along their conceptual arrows may also be drawn from text investigations and/or from the matrices. It is sometimes helpful if the teacher makes a list of possible materials before the unit begins. In this way the book material covered can be embellished from materials suggested by the matrices. The children may then follow their own drives as usual from the near bank to the far bank,

CHART OF CONTENT AND ORGANIZATION OF ECOLOGICAL MATRICES

MATRIX TITLE	SUBSECTIONS	TEACHING METHOD EMPHASIZED	SAMPLE UNIT(S) DERIVED FROM MATRIX
ECOLOGICAL INTERACTIONS— EMPHASIS ON ANIMALS 9. Ecology of Water Animals	a. Conceptual Scheme Chart for Ecosystems (see page 000). b. Vygotsky level of thought. c. Near bank—prior understandings. d. Far bank—points along conceptual arrows. e. Stepping stones: Materials and teacher preparation. f. Children's data and questions expected from the colloquia. g. Teacher's questions during the colloquia or on **Suggestion Cards.** h. Patterns which might emerge and be fostered.	Related to the content of ONE TEXTBOOK, but adapted to the FREE DISCOVERY–COLLOQUIUM APPROACH.	Related to "Travels of a Salmon" in *Concepts in Science 4.* [7]
10. Ecology of Land Animals			Related to "Living Things and Their Surroundings" in *Science: A Modern Approach 4.* [8]
ECOLOGICAL INTERACTIONS— EMPHASIS ON PLANTS 11. Interactions of Plants and Water 12. Interactions of Plants and Sunlight 13. Interactions of Plants and Minerals 14. Adaptations of Plants to Adverse Circumstances	Materials and teacher preparation.	Related to a variety of TRADE and TEXTBOOKS, FILMLOOPS, FILMS, FILMSTRIPS, and TRIPS. (For necessary aids, consult Children's Bibliography, Matrices 11-14.)	

[7] Brandwein et al., *Concepts in Science 4,* Harcourt Brace Jovanovich, Inc., New York, 1966, pp. 175-96.
[8] Fischler et al., *op. cit.,* pp. 148-201.

while the colloquia bring together their various viewpoints about the central topics.

Materials for ecosystems cannot, of course, be selected from a closet. Homes for animals have to be carefully prepared, with due attention to the variables of light, heat, food, and an arrangement which allows the animals whatever privacy they need but provides opportunities for the children to interact with them as well. Thought has to be given to caring for the animals over weekends and holidays, for maintaining the proper temperature if the school's heating system is lowered at night, and, if necessary, finding homes for the animals (or killing them painlessly) after the unit is over. Preparation of ecosystems takes time and requires much thought and considerable knowhow. Hence, beside "Materials" in the stepping stones of the ecology matrices, a second column, "Teacher Preparation," replaces the "Expected Child Activity" column which appeared in previous matrices. It is assumed by this time that the teacher can imagine what the children's interaction with the materials will be.

The reader will recall that the concepts in biology have a genesis different from those in the physical sciences. Whereas the physical sciences perceive obvious patterns and construct models to explain them, in the biological sciences one must first collect much data before the patterns can be perceived. Following the format of the Chart of Conceptual Schemes (page 166), the sections following the materials listings and preparations in the ecology matrices center on:

    f. Children's data and questions expected from the colloquia.

    g. Teacher's questions during the colloquia or on **Suggestion Cards.**

    h. Patterns which might emerge and be fostered.

Ecosystems with the emphasis on animals (Matrices 9 and 10) go into considerable detail about the data, questions, and patterns for each stepping stone. It should not be difficult for the teacher to supply these sections, as well as the Vygotsky levels of thought and the near bank and far bank understandings, for the ecosystems which center on plants. Matrices 11-14, Ecological Interactions—Emphasis on Plants, are, therefore, given in abbreviated form which simply contains the materials and their preparation.

Since the ecology matrices were selected to illustrate ways in which textbooks may be used with the discovery-colloquium approach, Matrices 9 and 10 both end with a sample way of tying the matrix to a specific unit in one textbook. Matrices 11-14 are intended to be illustrative of the use of a variety of books and audio-visual aids combined with discovery and colloquium. The trade and textbooks have been specifically geared to each other and to the matrices. Books which combine well with the discovery-colloquium approach are listed in detail in the Children's Bibliography under Matrices 11-14.

MATRIX 9: ECOLOGY OF WATER ANIMALS

For children at the complex and preconcept levels of thinking.

The near bank—prior understandings.

    Children must know that mammals, as examples of living organisms, eat, breathe, excrete, move, feel, and reproduce creatures like themselves and that some animals reproduce by laying eggs.

The far bank—points along conceptual arrows toward an understanding that:

1. Fish and many other multicellular animals are adapted to life in the water through their shapes, which facilitate locomotion, through gills or membranes which extract oxygen from solution in water, and through the production of a great many eggs.

2. Fish are eaten by larger animals and feed on smaller animals. Smaller animals at the end of the food chain feed on plants. Some large animals such as whales feed directly on plants. The food that animals eat must be adapted to the same environment.

3. Conditions in the environment affect the rate of reproduction and survival of both the plants and animals that live in water. (Life cycles are illustrated by Daphnia, brine shrimp, and water snails.)

Stepping stones:

MATERIALS

A[1]   For every two to four children: a half-gallon aquarium with two male and two female guppies, two snails, and plants. A thermometer and two long straws.

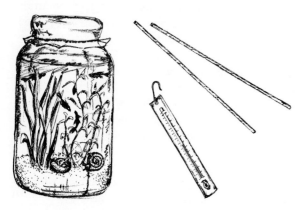

A[2]   For general classroom observation: Four jars from **A**[1] without animals; leave two near the window and two in a dark part of room. Make magnifying glasses available.

A[3]   For every two to four children: a babyfood jar of algae-rich aquarium water (from those jars in **A**[2] which have been near a window for a week) and a small, capped vial of Daphnia culture. A magnifying glass, a microscope slide with a depression (or a small Pyrex dish), and a medicine dropper for each child.

A[4]   For every four children: the jars from **A**[1], a small, capped vial of Daphnia culture, and four magnifying glasses.

TEACHER PREPARATION

Pour an inch of coarse white garden sand into a wide-mouth, half-gallon jar. Fill with water to the level where the shoulders of the jar begin to narrow. The sand and the jars should be thoroughly rinsed with very hot water. (Do not use soap or detergent.) Pond water is best for filling the jars; if tap water is used, it must be left in the jars for one to two days so the chlorine will evaporate. Next, tie some pond plants to a small weight. Sink this into the sand and wait 24 hours. Then introduce the guppies, using a small net, and the snails. Cover openings with cheesecloth held in place with rubber bands.[9] Put a large label on each jar for the names of the children ("owners").

Daphnia

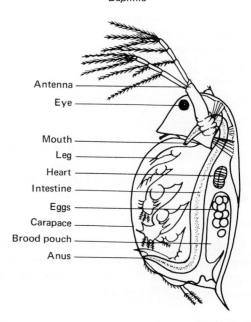

Antenna
Eye
Mouth
Leg
Heart
Intestine
Eggs
Carapace
Brood pouch
Anus

---

[9] Many details for constructing and maintaining, as well as using, aquaria are found in *Organisms* (Teacher's Guide), S.C.I.S., Rand McNally, Chicago, 1968.

MATERIALS

B¹ For general classroom observation: a five-gallon aquarium tank with two or three small goldfish and six large snails. (Tank should be placed in medium light, not directly in the sun's rays. Plants are not essential.)

B² For every six children: a large codfish head, a basin of water, and a thin plastic spread over newspapers to cover tables.

B³ For each pair of children: a large snail, temporarily removed from the aquarium in **B¹** and placed in aquarium water in a large babyfood jar with lettuce or waterweed. A magnifying glass.

B⁴ **Demonstration:** Gently heat some water; then let it cool to the temperature of the aquarium water. Place goldfish in this water. (Remove the fish to the tank in **B¹** as soon as the children have made their observations.)

C¹ For every four children: two tablespoons of Instant Ocean Salts in a souffle cup, a pint of water that has stood for two days, a few pinches of brine shrimp eggs in a second souffle cup, four small glass or plastic containers (Pyrex custard cups), four plastic spoons, and four magnifying glasses.

TEACHER PREPARATION

Prepare the tank in the same way you did the guppy jars. One gallon of water is needed for every inch of goldfish. (Measure from mouth to tail, excluding tail fin.) Make commercial dried and live fish food available, but use it sparingly.[10]

Instant Ocean Salts and brine shrimp eggs may be purchased from commercial biological supply houses. Follow directions on the package for dissolving the salts. The water in some localities contains products harmful to brine shrimps. Distilled water may have to be used for both the fish and the yeast. Brine shrimps (*Artemia*), like Daphnia, are crustaceans. They can be fed on yeast.

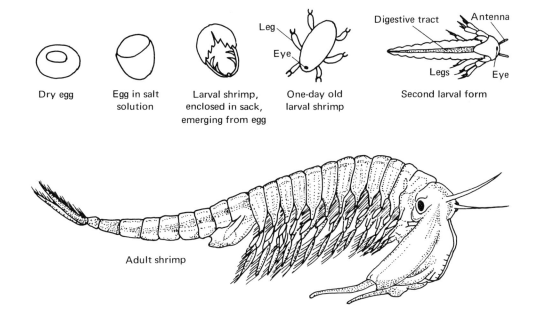

| Dry egg | Egg in salt solution | Larval shrimp, enclosed in sack, emerging from egg | One-day old larval shrimp | Second larval form |

Adult shrimp

---

[10] Useful information on aquaria, fish, and foods is found in Evelyn Morholt *et al., A Sourcebook for the Biological Sciences,* 2nd ed., Harcourt Brace Jovanovich, Inc., New York, 1966, pp. 605-10. (See also Teacher's Bibliography.)

MATERIALS

C2   For every six children: a flat glass or plastic dish holding a quart of ocean salt water containing brine shrimps at various stages in their life cycle. A glass slide with a depression, a medicine dropper, and a magnifying glass for each child. Two or three penlights.

C3   For each pair of children: a plastic container with 6-12 divisions (ice cube tray, etc.), 5 cc of Instant Ocean Salts in a medicine cup, two short straws cut slantwise to form scoops, 2-3 cc of brine shrimp eggs in another medicine cup, a pint jar of water which has stood for two days, and a china marking pencil.

Suggestion Card:
"In what concentrations of salt water do brine shrimps hatch best?"

C4   For each pair of children: a half-dozen adult brine shrimps in a small flat glass container with about 1½ in. of ocean salt water, a penlight, aluminum foil, a few grains of dried yeast, a flat-ended toothpick, a medicine dropper, two magnifying glasses, and a medicine cup. On a supply table: spare medicine cups and droppers, straw scoops, vinegar, sodium bicarbonate, and sugar.

TEACHER PREPARATION

Prepare the materials in **C2** two weeks in advance: Sprinkle some eggs over the surface of the water in a wide, flat dish thirteen, eight, and three days before the lesson. Every second day for each quart, add two or three grains of yeast dissolved in 10 cc of water which has been standing a couple of days (to lose its chlorine). To collect swimming brine shrimps, shine a point of light on the water. The shrimps will move toward the light and can be picked up with a medicine dropper. Select a variety of stages for each dish.[11]

---

[11] Materials for stepping stones **C1–C4** is adapted from four sources, each of which contains many interesting suggestions for study: *Science: A Process Approach*, Part 6, American Association for the Advancement of Science (A.A.A.S.), 1515 Massachusetts Ave., N.W., Washington D.C. 20005, 1966, pp. 221-28; *Environments* (Teacher's Guide), S.C.I.S., University of California at Berkeley, 1968, pp. 92-96; *The Brine Shrimp*, E.S.S. of the Education Development Center, Inc., Newton, Mass. 02160, 1968 (for primary children, grades 1-3); and Evelyn Morholt *et al., A Sourcebook for the Biological Sciences,* Harcourt Brace Jovanovich, Inc., New York, 1966, pp. 598-99.

Children's data and questions expected from the colloquia—Children will give many more facts than those recorded here. Children can find ways to answer their own questions, but technical words may be supplied by the teacher. Facts the teacher might need to know are in parentheses. Many more facts can be found in the references cited in footnote 11 and in the Teacher's Bibliography. Answers to questions and data on other water animals may also be sought in books, filmstrips, and filmloops (see the Children's Bibliography for Matrix 9).

A   *Guppies:* There is a small and colorful guppy and a large grey one. Are they male or female, young or old? The large one gets a swollen belly and (three weeks after mating) gives birth to live fish. Some baby fish disappear (adults eat them, so the parents should be removed to other aquaria). Courting ritual is sometimes observed. Fish swim by moving the tail end of their body; they move up and down by using their fins. Fish open and close their mouths all the time. Are they eating or breathing?

Snails cling to the glass or the waterweeds. There

may be eggs in jelly on some leaves. Baby snails will hatch from these. Aquaria in the light get very green (algae grows in the light). The green disappears (in two weeks) from the aquaria with Daphnia. More small Daphnia appear, they become larger. (Most Daphnia are female; they do not need a male for reproduction except when the environment becomes unfavorable.) Daphnia disappear from the aquarium if guppies are present.

The snail eats by moving his mouth sideways (a rasping tongue scrapes algae off the leaves or glass). How does the snail breathe? (Gases are exchanged through the membrane of a snail's mantle—an extension of the body wall which lines the shells of molluscs.)

B *Goldfish*: Goldfish move like guppies. They eat by gulping food from the surface of the water. Flaps at the side of the head move up and down as the goldfish gulps water (breathes). (The operculum covers the gills.) The gills of the cod's head float featherlike in water and stick together in air. There is a passage from the mouth through the gill opening under the operculum. Gently heated water gives off bubbles (air) and in this airless water the goldfish gasps and comes to the surface.

C *Brine shrimps:* What is the "brown stuff?" Coffee? Seeds? Eggs? Will they grow (or hatch)? They look round in water through the magnifying glass. The "white stuff" is salt (sea salt). Will the eggs hatch in salt water? (Brine shrimps—brine means salt—are found in salt lakes. The biological name of brine shrimps is *Artemia*.) After a few days, something moves; it has six legs and only one eye! There are empty shells (carapaces) on the bottom of the dish. Where do these come from? (Larva molts.) What do we feed the brine shrimp culture? (A grain or two of yeast every second day.) Wherever possible, and it is almost always possible, answer the children by saying, "What do you think?" or "How could you find out?" If a drop of food coloring is added to a few grains of dried yeast, the food can be seen in the shrimp's digestive tract. The brine shrimp moves toward light. It lays eggs (it is ready to mate after each molt as an adult). Will the eggs hatch? (They have to be dried

first.) It has lots of legs that move very fast. The legs are inside the carapace. It can swim with its ventral surface up.

Teacher's questions during the colloquia or on Suggestion Cards:

In what ways are snails like guppies?

In what ways are goldfish like us?

What does a fish do to move up, down, left, and right?

What interactions do you observe in the ecosystem?

Which of the fish's fins act most like the legs of a frog?

In what ways is a Daphnia different from a brine shrimp?

Patterns which might emerge and be fostered:

1. Living organisms go through a birth, growth, death, decay cycle.
2. Eating–digesting–excreting is a common pattern among animals.
3. Algae–daphnia–guppy form a food chain.
4. Plants which capture the energy from the sun are the basis for all food chains.
5. An aquarium is an ecosystem with constant interactions among its objects. An outside change in the system (temperature, acid, food, another animal, etc.) changes the patterns of the interactions.

Application of Matrix 9 to a sample textbook unit

We have chosen the sixth unit in the book *Concepts in Science 4* [12] as an illustration. The title of the unit is "The journeys of a salmon and a duck." The first part, devoted to the salmon, is sufficient for our purposes.

This textbook series, as its name implies, is strictly concept-oriented. We shall not delve into the Teacher's Guide, but approach the children's textbook as we would any book, whether it professed to be concept-oriented or not. The points taken up in the above unit are:

[12] Paul F. Brandwein *et al.,* Harcourt Brace Jovanovich, Inc., New York, 1966, pp. 175-96.

1. A description of the salmon's eggs hatching in the spring.
2. An investigation of what happens to pond (or aquarium) water to which a bit of egg yolk or rice has been added. (Microscopic animals multiply.)
3. A description of the tiny animals in a stream on which the salmon feeds.
4. A food chain listing:
   Bacteria eat decaying plants.
   Paramecium eat bacteria.
   Fish eat paramecium.
   Fish → Paramecium → Bacteria.
5. The journeys and life cycle of the salmon.
6. An investigation of snails' eggs hatching.
7. An investigation of the equipment of a goldfish which makes it well adapted in relation to life in the water.
8. The application of the general structure of a fish to the salmon's survival during its life cycle.

The first problem, of course, is to seek the relevant concepts. The life cycle items obviously relate to heredity, as do the common structures of the goldfish and salmon. From our chart (page 166) we find two subconcepts related to heredity on the complex level under Conceptual Scheme C:

Living organisms which have a common structure are related.

All living organisms go through a birth, growth, death, decay cycle.

What the fish eats and where and how it lives relate to the environment. From the environment column of Conceptual Scheme C, we select two subconcepts on the preconcept level:

Living organisms interchange matter and energy with the environment.

There are characteristic environments, each with its characteristic life.

The major concept which embraces all the subconcepts is:

A living organism is the product of its heredity (genetic code) and its environment.

For help in building a unit around the items in this chapter on the salmon, we can look at Matrix 9 on the *ecology of water animals*.

Since the goldfish is featured in the text, we might select as our first experience stepping stone B^1. Then at different times during one or two school days following the experience, the children can be asked to write down as many observations of facts and interactions as they can from observing the goldfish and other objects in the tank; this keeps the observations fresh for the colloquium. Or the teacher might have groups of six children watch and discuss and then hold their own group colloquium.

Questions from the colloquium might suggest reading the pages on the goldfish (190-93) and then introducing the cod's head at the next science lesson (stepping stone B^2). A colloquium centering on how a fish breathes would suggest the demonstration in stepping stone B^4 as a follow-up.

The relationship of breathing to eating is always brought up when fish are discussed. What and how do fish eat? The series of algae–daphnia–guppy investigations (stepping stones A^1 through A^4) followed by colloquia might be offered in any order the interests of the children indicated, along with reading the text pages on the salmon's food chain (178-81). The investigation in the text on producing bacteria by letting egg yolk or rice (page 177) decay in pond water is also indicated here.

If the children show interest in snails, some or all of them should try the investigation on snails in the book (page 187).

By this time the guppies may have produced their live young. If so, reading about the different development of the salmon could produce some lively colloquia. The journey of the salmon and the rest of its life cycle could be read and then compared with the life cycles of the guppy and the snail.

The questions at the end of the unit on "Using what you know" compare the various habitats of different animals and the way a salmon is not adapted to land. They could be the basis for an evaluation of what the children have gained during the unit.

MATRIX 10: ECOLOGY OF LAND ANIMALS

For children at the complex and preconcept levels of thinking.

The near bank—prior understandings.

It is possible to introduce very young children to some animals (gerbils, toads, insects) and let these inititate their first understandings of living organisms (outside themselves and their acquaintances). For an ecological study, the complexity of the learning including interaction with the environment will have to parallel a more mature intellectual development in the child.

The far bank—points along conceptual arrows toward an understanding that:

1. Some animals undergo metamorphosis during their development (a change in which the young are very different in form from the adult).
2. Different animals are adapted to widely different habitats. There are mutually beneficial interactions between animals and plants and among minerals, plants, and animals.
3. Animals have different forms of life cycles.
4. All animals, plants, and soil can be part of food chains.
5. Multicellular animals perform the functions of ingestion, digestion, and excretion with analogous organs.
6. Insects are the most numerous species on earth; they are adapted to every environment.
7. Insects have many relationships to our economy: they control (and can be) pests, pollinate flowers, remove debris, etc. Earthworms play a role in conveying agricultural poisons (insecticides) to birdlife; one effect—thin or no egg shells and therefore no young—has already affected the Peregrine Falcon and the Bald Eagle. They contribute to the extinction of carnivorous species in whose food the poison becomes concentrated.

Stepping stones:

Ecosystems for the study of land animals can be established in the classroom in a variety of terraria. The population of terraria are best collected on field trips. Hence what any one classroom has for study depends largely on the success of foraging. Almost any type of terrarium allows children to study life cycles, biological functions, and adaptations to and interactions with the environment. Their learnings can then be extended by textbook readings to whatever animals are chosen for that unit. Of course, to obtain an ecosystem from a very different climate, the terrarium population would have to be purchased (desert animals for schools in the temperate zone, woodland animals for schools in the desert areas, etc.) Urban children can find insect life in open city lots.

One large terrarium can suffice for small-group observations over a one- or two-day period or at different times on the same day. One animal can usually be taken from the larger home and observed by individual children either in a small jar or, in some cases, when held in the hand. Individual projects—observing a spider, a cricket, a caterpillar, etc.—may all occur concurrently. Whatever individual children are observing, their data should be shared in small or large group colloquia where their patterns of thought can be developed and built toward concepts. At many points during the observation period as the animals develop (and this will probably be over several weeks or even months), knowledge should be extended through reading. The number of children related to each set of materials in this matrix is therefore omitted. The teacher in each classroom will appraise the needs, the materials, and the time allowance.

MATERIALS

A[1] A tank terrarium of woodland gatherings: plants, perhaps a toad and a salamander, a rotting log, frogs' eggs, a snake, and a small dry branch. A dish, holding 4-6 in. of pond

TEACHER PREPARATION

Line an aquarium tank (one that is not quite watertight can be utilized) with 2 in. of fine gravel and charcoal. Add 3 in. of soil from the woods or good garden loam. Then add some

MATERIALS

water (sink this in one corner), a supply of mealworms for the toad, and forceps.

Suggestion Cards:
1. "Feed the toad by holding a mealworm (or a small earthworm) near him with the forceps."
2. "Keep a record of the changes you see in the frogs' eggs."
3. "In what ways is a salamander like a toad?"
4. "Describe the changes you see in the log. What comes out of it?"

A² A jar terrarium and one or two animals from the rotting log in the main terrarium.

Suggestion Card:
"Observe one animal and keep a record of what it does from day to day. Note the interactions that you see."

A³ A half-gallon terrarium with a lens held in place between two layers of Saran wrap or thin plastic covering the jar mouth.

TEACHER PREPARATION

small plants, moss, a few rocks, and some branching twigs. (Snakes rub against the rocks and branches to shed their skin; insects climb on them.) Water the area with a bulb sprinkler and cover the terrarium with a piece of fine mesh or glass which has been taped around the edges to prevent roughness.

According to the size of the tank and with a few modifications, a variety of animals may be housed in this setup. With the addition of a small dish, sunk in the soil to the level of its lip and filled with water, the tank can provide a home for a small snake, a frog, a salamander, or about 20 frogs' eggs in a jelly cluster (cut the number you need from the larger cluster with scissors). Without water, the tank can house a chameleon, a praying mantis, caterpillars, and earthworms. Four to six in. of soil and good humus should be provided for the earthworms (see the following stepping stones on earthworms, **B¹–B⁵**).

Frogs need to eat live insects. These can be collected by sweeping a net through grass and weeds or by shaking a bush above a white sheet on the ground.

Snakes can be held by circling the fingers gently behind its head.

A rotting log supplies unexpected fauna.

A small terrarium can be made from a half-gallon jar, rested on wooden supports on its side. Fill it proportionately with the materials suggested in **A¹**. If the makings of a terrarium are available in the room, children can make individual terraria from smaller jars for small animals or for temporary observation of larger animals.

MATERIALS

TEACHER PREPARATION

A[4] A magnifying box in the form of a one-inch clear plastic cube. The box holds small insects for viewing. The lid is shaped into a lens whose focal length is such that the insect on the cube bottom is magnified clearly 4½X. Two cubes stacked give a 9X magnification. (These boxes are valuable to take along on a field trip.) [13]

B[1] A glass dish 6 in. deep and with a wide mouth, filled with good loam or woodland soil. An earthworm or two in a small dish.[14]

Earthworms should be collected on a class trip. Worms may be found in rich, leafy soil, although they seem to relish oak leaves and pine needles *less* than other types of humus. To bring the worms to the surface, set off the alarm on a clock and press the clock face to the surface of the soil. (If children see or do this collecting, they can be told that worms do not "hear"; what does bring them up?)

The collected worms may be carried in any vessel that has a few airholes. Some soil from the worms' environment should, of course, be included. If castings can be seen, these might be added, too; they sometimes contain egg sacs. Samples of various soils should be collected in individual plastic bags: gravel, sand, loam, decayed leaves of different species, maybe even clayey soil. To make sure that the classroom "wormeries" duplicate as nearly as possible the worms' natural environment, the temperature of the soil in the burrow from which the worms came should be recorded.

Fill the gallon jar in **B**[2] with one- or two-in. layers of various soils. Hold a newspaper in place over the jar with rubber bands or string. Punch a few holes in the newspaper covering.

B[2] Several plastic bags holding different kinds of soil, a saucer with damp litmus paper placed around it, a gallon jar, a dozen worms, a China pencil, and a clock.

Suggestion Cards:

1. "Find out what you can about the soils."

2. "Arrange the soil in two-inch layers in the jar and mark their levels on the outside of the jar. Pour a cup of water over the layers. How long does it take to trickle down to the bottom? Place the worms on the top layer."

3. [a week later] "Pour a cup of water on the layers. How long does it take to trickle to the bottom?"

4. "Cover one half of the jar from top to bottom with dark construction paper."

5. "Keep a dated record of what you do and see."

B[3] A flat glass "earthwormery" or the gallon jar full of soil and earthworms. Bits of lettuce, carrot scrapings, and hamburger.

A good observation "wormery" may be constructed as in the diagram on page 298. The tape is removed to feed the worms (**B**[3]) or to replenish the water supply.

---

[13] Available from S.E.E. (Selective Educational Equipment, Inc.), 3 Bridge St., Newton, Mass. 02195.

[14] Some of the activities in the stepping stones **B**[1] through **B**[5] are adapted from *Nature and Science*, Vol. 4, No. 14 (April 10, 1967), 10-12.

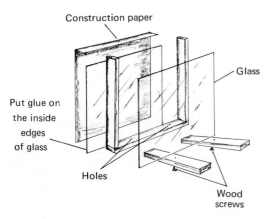

Construction paper

Glass

Put glue on
the inside
edges
of glass

Holes

Wood
screws

MATERIALS

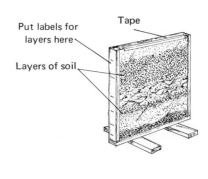

Put labels for
layers here

Tape

Layers of soil

TEACHER PREPARATION

Suggestion Cards:

1. "Place one or more pieces of food in one spot on the surface of the soil. Time how long it takes the worms to find the food. Which of the foods do they eat?"

2. "After two weeks, place the food in a different spot. How long does it take the worms to find it."

B⁴ Three jars with soil and an earthworm in each. Place one jar in sunlight, one in the shade, and one in the refrigerator. Allow three hours to elapse. Provide a thermometer and label the jars to indicate where they were kept.

Suggestion Card:
"Tip the contents of each jar onto separate pieces of wax paper. Compare what the worms do. Watch their heartbeats."

B⁵ Two plants in two pots: one pot with earthworm, one without. A week should elapse after the preparations.

Suggestion Card:
"What makes the difference?"

C¹ A large desert terrarium with a 100 watt gooseneck lamp. Loam and sand at either ends of the tank should reach about one-third to one-half the way up the glass. A pocket mouse, two small sand lizards, an iguana (or chuckwalla or gila monster), large rocks, a thick branch, lettuce, carrot pieces, and a pile of various seeds.

Desert animals need a large space; their terrarium should be at least 3 ft long. Coarse sand and loam should not be mixed. (The pocket mouse will "homogenize" it with his digging overnight!) Large rocks are necessary for hiding places, the thick branch for climbing. The tank covering should be wire mesh, weighed down. (The mouse can build up the soil and will climb out otherwise.) Place the gooseneck lamp so that it shines into the terrarium, but thick newspaper should cover part of the tank top to provide shade. The 100 watt bulb in the lamp will provide continuous warmth. For weekends when the temperature drops, the animals must go to a warmer building—the home of a teacher or child.[15]

C² Everything in **C¹** plus a thermometer.

C³ Everything in **C¹** plus a small dish of water.

[15] We are indebted to the Elementary Science Study of the Education Development Center, Inc., Newton, Mass. 02160 for suggestions on housing desert animals.

MATERIALS

D¹ A cricket in a cage. Grass growing in a flowerpot which forms the base of the cage (see right).

D² A cricket in a glass jar with cheesecloth tied over the top. A thermometer, a stop watch, and a dish of ice cubes.

Suggestion Card:
"Count the number of times the cricket chirps in 14 seconds. Add 40. Read the temperature."

D³ If small crickets can be found, put them in a cage like **D¹**.

Suggestion Card:
"Watch the changes from day to day."

E A Monarch caterpillar on milkweed (or any other caterpillar on the plant it eats) in a caterpillar cage. A magnifying glass.

Suggestion Card:
"Record in words or pictures the changes you see from day to day."

F¹ A spider in a spider frame.[16]

---

[16] Some of the activities in stepping stones **F¹** through **F³** are adapted from *Nature and Science* (Teacher's Edition), Vol. 4, No. 2 (October 3, 1966), 2T, 7T, 8T.

TEACHER PREPARATION

A cricket home can be made from a flowerpot of grass by placing a stiff tube of screening in the soil just inside the pot. Tie a clear plastic cover over the top of the screen tube. Provide dry twig. Keep the grass watered and place the cage in a sunny window. Bits of apple and lettuce serve as food. A small sponge in a dish of water for drink. Bread crumbs, raisins, and lettuce are suitable foods for smaller crickets (see **D³**).

A tube of double cheesecloth or a nylon net is the basic ingredient for a butterfly home. Sew the net tube around a wire coat hanger which has been pulled into a circle. Cover the circle with more cheesecloth. Hang the coat hanger with its cloth tube from a ceiling pipe or wall bracket by the hanger hook. Thumb tack the bottom of the tube to a wooden base which rests on a table or the floor (see diagram at left). Add a jar to hold the branch of milkweed in water or a potted plant on which the caterpillar feeds.

A spider frame has to fit the size of web a particular spider usually spins. After choosing the spider and measuring the diameter of its web, make a square frame of wood to hold it (see diagrams on page 300). Put feet to support the frame on a table (1) or use a screw eye to suspend it (2). Cover both sides of the frame with glass or clear, stiff plastic held in place with tape or rubber bands. Drill a food hole in the side of the frame and plug it with a cork when it is not in use. In an upper corner inside the frame, carve a hole partly through the wood to serve as a hiding place for the spider.

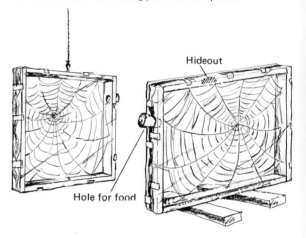

Hideout

Hole for food

Suggestion Cards:

1. "Watch the spider spin its web. Talk about the way it does it."
2. "Remove the web once a day. What happens?"
3. "Introduce an insect into the food hole. Try to remember all the details of what happens."

F² A different species of spider from the one in **F¹** in a spider frame.

Suggestion Card:

"In what way do the two spiders act differently?"

F³ A spider in its frame with an insect it has wrapped in thread. A little caffein smeared on the insect.

Suggestion Card:

"When this spider spins a new web, compare it with the usual web."

G¹ Two to six small turtles in a five-gallon tank. (Turtle species may be: Red-eared, Florida Cooter, Painted, or Mississippi Map. Two of each kind allow for feeding experiments.) A balance and a thermometer.[17]

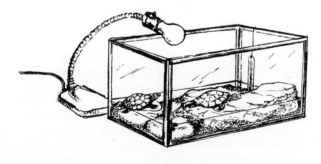

If the lamp is left on, shade should be provided by covering part of the tank top with newspaper.

Suggestion Cards:

1. "Weigh each turtle. Record the date and weight."
2. "What can you learn about the turtle by just looking at it?"
3. "Measure the length and width of the carapace. Record this with the date."
4. "What does a turtle do to swim forward, up, down, or in any other direction?"
5. "How does a turtle feed? Put a little hamburger, chopped fish, or chopped earthworm with some lettuce or fruit on the flat rock."

Turtles seem to be a favorite classroom animal. However, many thousands die each year from neglect, which usually includes starvation. To keep them interacting favorably with an environment, make the following provisions:

A five-gallon tank will serve half a dozen young turtles. There should be at least an inch of water, some *smooth* flat rocks which slop into and out of the water, and a gooseneck lamp to act as a "sun." Keep the temperature at 75-80°F. Water from a pond (or faucet water which has stood two days to evaporate the chlorine) and some mud from the bottom are good materials for a turtle home.

Three or four times a week feed the turtles fresh hamburger, raw chopped fish, or chopped earthworms. Also, offer them a variety of plants such as lettuce and fruit. A piece of decaying log will provide a variety of small creatures for additional food. A little powdered calcium (from a drugstore) should be mixed with their food occasionally; it strengthens their shells.

When the water becomes smelly, it should be replaced, but always with water at the same temperature. Of course remove all uneaten food.

---

[17] Stepping stones **G¹** through **G⁴** have been adapted from "How to Keep and Study Young Turtles," included in *Nature* *and Science Magazine*, Vol. 2, No. 8 (January 18, 1965), 6-7. Copyright © 1964 by The American Museum of Natural History.

MATERIALS	TEACHER PREPARATION

MATERIALS

G2 A jar of water 75-80° F, shallow enough so that the turtle can put his nose above the water level as he stands on the bottom. A thermometer and some ice cubes.

Suggestion Cards:
1. "Count the number of times a turtle comes to the surface in half an hour."
2. "Remove half the water and add ice water. When the temperature is 50°F, repeat **Suggestion Card 1**."

G3 A pair of similar turtles, one with a small mark filed on his carapace to identify him. A balance.

Suggestion Card:
"Feed one of the pair commercial "turtle food" and the other as advised in **Suggestion Card 5** in **G1**. Record the weights of both turtles each week. After four weeks, feed both turtles whichever is the better diet.

G4 Turtles and tank as in **G1**. Raw hamburger and food coloring.

Suggestion Card:
"Color bits of hamburger with vegetable dyes of different colors. Offer the colored bits to the turtles."

Children's data and questions expected from the colloquia:

A *Toad, frog, snake, etc.:* What the children observe depends on who inhabits the habitat! Children will give details of structure, the number and use of parts, and, with a little encouragement, will describe the interactions between specific animals and other objects in the environment. As colloquia continue with the day to day or week to week observations, the changes in and growth of the animals will be stated.

Children can discover more about the larger animals if they hold them in their hands. The children will need to be shown that animals can be held lightly in the hand with the fingers curled to form a cage. From holding the animals, such data as a snake is not slimy, but firm and strong (its muscles press against the fingers) and a frog is slimy, but a toad feels dry will be given.

B *Earthworms:* Children will note the obvious physical features of the worm: its head end is rounded; its tail end is pointed, it can stretch and contract (some children will measure); and it has "rings" (actually from 100–200 segments). Some children notice the *setae*, bristly hairs on the ventral surface which help a worm resist the pull of a robin who tries to tug it from its burrow. Nearer the head end than the tail, the children will see a flat ring without segments. (This ring swells up when eggs develop inside and is shed as a sac full of eggs.)

The litmus paper will tell the children whether different soils are acid or alkaline. From the layers in the jars the children can see where the worms prefer to stay.

In a new situation (such as being put on top of the jar of soil) the worm will curl up in a knot.

As the worms burrow through the soil, chewing their way and forming passages, the soil layers become mixed up and refined into smaller particles. (Air is introduced to the soil, aiding the growth of plants.)

Worms slow down in the cold and move faster in warmth. A change in the rate of a worm's heartbeat can be seen as the blood pulses through the head end.

C *Desert animals:* "Why is he called a pocket mouse?" children always want to know, and they

Matrices on ecology   **301**

offer various hypotheses. It takes many days of watching before the children discover that the pocket mouse carries seeds in his cheek pockets, just as a hamster does. The pocket mouse mixes up the soil with his vigorous hind-leg digging, mostly at night.

The sand lizards move slowly and bury themselves in the sandy soil. They have scales like the iguana, chuckwalla, and gila monster. All are reptiles.

Lizards sometimes drink water when it is available, but they can do without it. The pocket mouse gets enough water from the seeds. Which type of seeds the pocket mouse prefers can be inferred from those he selects first.

Children will report on the preferred temperatures of each animal and whether they hide in the shade or under the soil where the thermometer reading is lower than at the surface.

D *Cricket:* The cricket is an insect. It molts. (The young, called nymphs, resemble the adults.) It has six legs. A strong pair of back legs allows the cricket to jump far. Sometimes children measure how far.

A cricket chirps faster when the temperature is high than when it is low. The number of chirps in 14 seconds plus 40 equals the temperature of the air in degrees Fahrenheit. What does the cricket do to chirp? (He [only the male chirps] rubs the upper part of his wings together where a rasp and file make the noise. A grasshopper rubs a leg against a wing to make its noise.)

One cricket has a spike on its tail (the female's ovipositor).

E *Caterpillar:* The caterpillar has six jointed legs and several pairs of false legs. It has large eyes, antennae, and a mouth. The caterpillar of the monarch butterfly has two whip-like structures at each end of the body. What are these for? (They frighten away parasites.)

The caterpillar eats an enormous quantity of milkweed leaves. It never seems to stop.

It molts. After eleven days it forms a chrysalis (pupa) which hangs. The chrysalis is green and gold, flecked with black. The butterfly emerges after another twelve days.

Butterflies mate and lay eggs.

F *Spider:* A spider has two segments. (An insect has three.) A spider has four pairs of legs. (An insect has three pairs.)

The thread for the web comes from the hind end of the spider. It is a sticky ooze that hardens. The spiral threads of the web are sticky; the radial threads are not. A spider picks its way along the radial threads. The spider wraps its prey in silken threads after killing it with a poisonous sting.

After taking caffein (or any other drug), the pattern of the web is different. (The change in the design of the web can be a test for specific drugs.)

G *Turtle:* A turtle has an arch-shaped upper shell (carapace) and a flat under shell (plastron). Some plastrons are slightly concave (in males). There are rings on the scales of the shell (one ring per year).

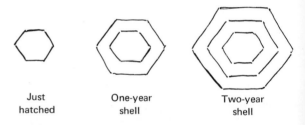

| Just hatched | One-year shell | Two-year shell |

A turtle can draw its limbs, head, and tail into its shell. It can hiss.

It eats by dragging the food from the flat stones above the water to below the water. (Remove all uneaten food!) A well-fed turtle gains in weight (doubles its weight in a year). (Some commercial "turtle food" is the dried exoskeletons of insects. This provides no nourishment!)

A turtle breathes by sticking his nose out of the water and into the air. When his nose is out of the water, his eyes are also. (A turtle has sharp vision, but is deaf. A turtle's body processes slow down in the cold. During winter, he hibernates in the mud at the bottom of the pond.) A turtle comes up for air less frequently in cold water than in warm water.

Teacher's questions during colloquia or on Suggestion Cards—The details of these questions depend on which stepping stones have been selected and with which animals the children are familiar. There are principles of questioning, however, which may furnish useful guides. We are trying to get the children to think of ecological interactions—of ways in which the stimuli in the environment interact with the animals and produce certain responses. We do this by encouraging the children to think about the adaptations of animals in relation to their environment. We are trying to get the children to understand life cycles—the heredity component of ecological interactions.

There are adaptations in relation to:

1. Locomotion:
   on land
   in water
   in air
2. Temperature. Coping with excessive heat or excessive cold:
   with skin coverings
   with fat layers
   through hibernation or estivation[18]
   through migration
3. Obtaining food:
   by hunting techniques
   by camouflage
   with prehensile equipment
   by lethal measures
4. Escape predation (being used as another animal's food):
   by mimicry
   by camouflage
   by moving quickly
   through noxious excretions
   through protective coverings
   by overproductivity
   through parental care
5. Consuming food:
   with special mouth parts
   with specialized internal organs

We can highlight the above adaptations by making comparisons between animals whose similarities or differences are not immediately apparent. For example:

In what ways are two apparently dissimilar animals really alike? For instance, we might do

[18] Estivate: going into a torpid condition to avoid the summer heat.

some thinking about a snail and a guppy or a child and a frog! In what ways are two closely related, but structurally disssimilar, animals adapted to their environments? A turtle and a sand lizard offer such an example. In what ways are two animals from widely diiffering species with somewhat similar general appearances adapted to their environments? We think of a snake and an earthworm.

The adaptations listed above may also be highlighted by putting an animal in an inappropriate environment (through our imagination) (numbers refer to preceding categories of adaptation):

1. If a fish could breathe on land, how do you think it could move?
2. Why does a frog need a dish of water in its terrarium?
3. A spider hunts by hiding inconspicuously near its web. The monarch butterfly larva eats milkweed leaves continuously. Suppose they changed places.
4. The pocket mouse has a few babies; the guppy lays thousands of eggs. What would be the result if the pocket mouse had thousands of babies and the guppy laid only a few eggs?
5. A Daphnia eats algae and an earthworm eats fresh or decayed plants. Why couldn't they exchange diets?

Patterns which might emerge and be fostered:

1. Adult insects mate and lay eggs. The life cycles of some insects have four stages: egg, larva, pupa, adult. Some insects have a life cycle of three stages: egg, nymph, adult.
2. The amphibian life cycle has an aquatic phase (which includes the egg and tadpole stages) and a land phase (the adult). Adult amphibians mate and lay eggs. Some salamanders (the Red Eft is one) become sexually mature and can mate and produce eggs during the water phase.
3. A worm eats its way through soil, digesting the plant matter and excreting the soil in fine grains as castings. If the plants have been sprayed with poisonous insecticides, the poisons remain in the body of the worm. As part of a food chain, worms are eaten by small

birds; small birds, in turn, are eaten by larger birds or mammals and finally huge birds of prey eat the larger birds or mammals. In this way, a great deal of poison is concentrated in the bodies of eagles and peregrine falcons, for example. The poison affects the life functions of these birds who then lay eggs with no shells or thin shells from which the young fail to hatch. This food chain ends with the eventual extinction of the largest animal.

4. The reaction of some animals to a new environment is very different from their reaction to a habitat to which they have become accustomed: worms curl up in knots; the pocket mouse digs so vigorously that he changes the topography of a large terrarium; spiders spin new webs.

5. Animals with hard skins and no backbones molt as they grow bigger.

6. Temperature changes an animal's interaction with its environment. The life processes of some slow down when the temperature drops (hibernation) or rises (estivation). A cricket changes its rate of chirping.

7. A new stimulus evokes a new response: worms react to a change in the acid-alkaline composition of soil; turtles react to color in food; a frog shoots out a long sticky tongue (fixed at the front of his mouth) when he sees food wiggling; a spider changes the pattern of its web after consuming a drug; a mealworm's rate of reaction is slowed just before or after molting.

Application of Matrix 10 to a sample textbook unit

An appropriate textbook unit for use with Matrix 10 is "Living things and their surroundings," in the Grade 4 text of the series *Science: A Modern Approach.* [19] This is a long unit; there are only four for the year, this one being the third. The topics introduced touch upon plants as well as animals, but we will concern ourselves with only the latter here. (Matrices 11-14, directly following, deal with plants.) The unit includes water as well as land animals; hence we may draw from both Matrices 9 and 10.

[19] Abraham S. Fischler *et al., Science: A Modern Approach* No. 4, Holt, Rinehart & Winston, Inc., New York, 1966, pp. 148-201.

The items taken up in this unit are:

1. Description of what a habitat is
2. Activity observing animals in their natural habitats
3. Investigation of a toad feeding in a terrarium
4. Descriptions of mountain, arctic, and desert habitats with adaptation of animals emphasized
5. Underground homes
6. Setting up and observing an ant home
7. Freshwater habitat (frog and guppy mentioned)
8. Seawater habitat
9. Seasonal and temperature changes
10. Investigation of the effects of heat and cold on the cricket and frog
11. Migration of birds and salmon (and seed dispersal)
12. Form, structure, color, and habits related to habitats (spider illustration)
13. Food chains; man's role in domesticating animals
14. Thought provoking questions

The concept underlying this unit is clearly that "there are characteristic environments, each with its characteristic life" (Conceptual Scheme C, preconcept, emphasis on environment, page 166).

The following is one way to provide the experiential background for this unit so that first-hand experiences plus colloquia can provide the apperceptive base to absorb the many factual extensions the unit provides.

Let us begin with the freshwater aquarium (the guppy materials provided by stepping stone **A** in Matrix 9). If we include the algae-daphnia sequence, we will have a base for developing an understanding of the food chain later. The reading assigned could be on items 7 and 8 (pages 162-67) and the food chain development in item 13 (pages 192-99). Man's role in domesticating animals and conserving his environment are taken up in the latter as well.

Next we could set up the woodland terrarium from Matrix 10, stepping stone **A** and populate the habitat with a toad, a frog, and crickets. The children themselves could prepare the smaller jar terraria in **A**[2] to examine the cricket and frog individually. For this experience, ice cubes would be needed. Colloquia would lead well into the reading of pages 150-61 and items 1 through 6. Item 6 suggests that the children set up their own ant homes. Investigations with the terrarium materials would allow for items 9 and 10 on temperature changes (pages 169-72).

Further investigations of land animal habitats is suggested by item 12, which includes some work with a spider. Therefore, we would provide the materials in stepping stone **F** and develop, through colloquia, the relation of form, structure, color, and habits before assigning the reading on pages 180-91.

Reading about the migration of birds and salmon (and the dispersal of seeds) in item 11 becomes optional.

If children reacted in writing to some of the questions at the end of the unit ("Find out why many unusual and rare animals are found only on islands," for example), the teacher could appraise their learnings about adaptation. If the colloquia had emphasized interactions and changes in animals, the children might do well with another of the suggestions: "Select one animal . . . and imagine what would happen to it if it never changed, but everything else did."

Ecological interactions—emphasis on plants

For Matrices 11-14 on plants, we will illustrate another classroom organization—one we might even think of as "the ecology of the classroom" itself!

We will assume that no one textbook is followed, but that several series are available. In this illustration, the children will have access also to a variety of trade books. There will be both a filmloop and a filmstrip projector in the room. The children will operate these film devices themselves, much in the manner that they borrow a book from the classroom library, when they want to. The teacher will project films on occasion.

The materials from any one topic (stepping stones on roots in relation to water or plants in relation to sunlight, for example) will be available at various "stations" around the room along with **Suggestion Cards**. The textbooks will be in a "library corner" and each appropriate text will have appended to its cover a list of pages pertinent to the topic with the added suggestion, "Read what interests you. You will

find pages _____ related to our present study." Trade books will be in the same location.

The ecosystem of the classroom will interact somewhat as follows. The topic of study will be announced to the children, either in writing (a sign on the board or wall) or orally, as the teacher sees fit. The children will select which station they wish to work at during any science lesson. Or if it is a "free choice" classroom, each child will choose both the station and the time at which he wishes to work. If rules about how many children can work at each station at one time are necessary, the children themselves will, no doubt, make these. During the course of a week or two, each child will have worked with several sets of materials, have treated himself to viewing the filmloops and/or filmstrips, and will have read, following his particular interest, in some of the books. After each science lesson, or after a period when a number of children have worked at the science stations, the teacher will hold a colloquium. Since all the materials (including the various audio-visual aids) are centered around one topic, but the content which each child may have gained about the topic will vary, the colloquia serve not only to develop concepts from various viewpoints, but also to alert children to activities they have not yet engaged in and might like to try. Colloquia can be held with small groups to develop some preliminary thinking while the children are at work. **Suggestion Cards** help focus observations for whole group colloquia. This series of activities should continue until the children are making models about the interactions or at least finding patterns among the materials. Children will begin to follow individual bents from suggestions they read in books.

The teacher will probably find it easy to pinpoint the relevant ecological concepts from these matrices as well as the intellectual level for which each set of materials is suitable. Therefore, we will omit discussion of concepts and levels as well as the conceptual arrows the children might follow and concentrate on the materials of the stepping stones, the teacher preparation necessary, and samples of trade and textbooks, filmloops, filmstrips, and films which can be used in conjunction with the materials. A teacher developing units from these matrices will, no doubt, be able to locate additional visual aids.

MATRIX 11: INTERACTIONS OF PLANTS AND WATER

I. Roots in Relation to Water

MATERIALS

A Dandelion, chickweed, ground ivy, plantain, carrot, and radish plants with roots attached, each in a plastic bag with a sprinkling of water.

Suggestion Card:
"What can roots do? Find out all you can."

B[1] Some quick growing seeds (mung beans, radish, grass), germinating on separate sponges in a dish of water or on pieces of damp blotting paper.

B[2] A germinating seed pinned to the underside of a cork which is placed in a small vial.

Suggestion Card (for **B**[1] and **B**[2]):
"What can roots do?"

C One inch of carrot top sprouting in a saucer of wet sand. A supply of other root tops in a plastic bag (turnip, parsnip, radish, and more carrot).

Suggestion Card:
"In what ways do roots interact with water? Suggest some predictions. Write these down on a piece of paper with your name and the date. Set up your own investigations to test your predictions."

D A seed flat whose bottom has been replaced with one-half in. wire screening. Flat is filled with sphagnum or peat moss and quick growing seeds are planted in it. Flat is suspended across two supports (bricks) so that roots are exposed to the air.

TEACHER PREPARATION

The plants suggested in **A** are easily obtainable from weedy places or the grocer. The exact species listed here are not essential. The principle of selection is plants with one tap root or spreading [adventitious] roots or plants with stems which run along the ground and root at intervals. Some roots should be swollen to store food.

After the plants have been pulled up, allow some of the soil adhering to the roots to remain. Then sprinkle each plant with water in a separate plastic bag. Close the bags and place them in the refrigerator until time for class.

If the seeds for **B**[1] are soaked in water for 24 hours, they will start germinating and, in one or two days, will show abundant root hairs. They may twist and turn a bit as they interact with gravity.

One of the radish seeds may be used in **B**[2]. Sprinkle a drop of water in the vial before closing it.

The carrot for **C** should be given a week to sprout leaves before being presented to the children.

MATERIALS	TEACHER PREPARATION

TEACHER PREPARATION

Seed flats come in many materials: fibre, wood, plastic. Any material that can be cut will do. Cut out the bottom, leaving an inch all around on which to rest the screening. Cut the screening the full size of the flat bottom. Allow seeds at least a week to grow so that their roots reach the screening and, instead of continuing downwards have time to curl up again toward the water. Keep the peat moss moist. It needs a lot of water.

Suggestion Card:
"Look under the seed flat. What would you expect? What do you see? Try to offer a model to describe the interaction."

E Milk carton with one side removed and a glass or clear plastic panel in an adjacent side. Plants in soil at one end, but close to the clear panel; water away from roots.[20]

Use a half-gallon milk carton. Remove two adjacent sides and replace one with glass or a clear plastic. Line the bottom of the carton with a little coarse sand or gravel and add good garden soil until the carton is three-quarters full. Punch a few holes in the bottom for drainage. The seeds should be planted at one end, near the panel. Water sparingly. Cover the panel with dark paper. As soon as the roots appear, water only at the end of the carton away from the seeds. Remove the dark paper when presenting the materials to the children. Position the clear panel away from the light.

Suggestion Card:
"Try to think of a model to describe the interactions."

Books and Other Media

Books [21]

Schneider 3 (95-99).
Brandwein 2 (82-87); and 4 (85-86).
Fischler 3 (16-24); and 5 (225).

Gene Darby, *What Is a Plant?* Benefic Press, Chicago, 1960. Simple descriptions of the life functions of plants. Various types of plants from flowers to bacteria. *(primary)*

Carroll Lane Fenton and Hermine B. Kitchen, *Plants That Feed Us*, John Day, New York, 1956. Food from roots and other plant parts.

Filmloops

"Bean Sprouts," E.S.S. (Ealing catalog: 81-424), color. Time-lapse photography shows motion of roots.

"Desert Plants," Walt Disney Nature Library (Ealing catalog: 81-856), color, 4 min. Animals and desert plants. Latter burst into bloom after a rain.

---

[20] Adapted from Elizabeth B. Hone *et al., A Sourcebook for Elementary Science,* 2nd ed., Harcourt Brace Jovanovich, Inc., New York, 1971, p. 60.

[21] The major textbooks emphasized repeatedly in this section in Matrices 11-14 will be referred to simply by the name of the principal author, the grade number of the book in each series, and the appropriate page numbers. The complete bibliographic details for the three series involved are: Herman and Nina Schneider, *Science,* D. C. Heath, Lexington, Mass., 1965; Paul F. Brandwein, Elizabeth Cooper, Paul E. Blackwood, and Elizabeth B. Hone, *Concepts in Science,* Harcourt Brace Jovanovich, Inc., New York, 1966; and Abraham S. Fischler, Lawrence F. Lowery, and Sam S. Blanc, *Science: A Modern Approach,* Holt, Rinehart & Winston, Inc., New York, 1966.

"Structure of Plants," Encyclopaedia Britannica Films, 1962, 44 frames. Roots and stems grow; use water and minerals from the soil to make food.

A Trip

The best introduction to plant adaptation and to ecology in general is an outdoor trip, even to an open lot in the city. Children can be assigned to find two plants of each kind: one dug up from a shady place and one from a sunny location (or one from a dry area and one from a wet area).

Children work in teams. Each team has several plastic bags, tie-on labels, a pen, and a trowel. Each plant is dug up with as much of the roots as possible and placed with some soil in a plastic bag. Each plant is labeled with the name of the team and a description of the growing conditions. (In a weedy area, this expedition of children is of great benefit!)

To help identify the weeds, the library corner might contain a copy or two of *The First Book of Weeds*, Barbara L. Beck, Franklin Watts, Inc., New York, 1963.

II. Leaves and Stems in Relation to Water

MATERIALS

F Celery stalk split into two or three parts, but still attached at leaf end. Each piece of stalk is in a glass of differently colored water (tinted with food coloring). Replacements available in case children cut off parts of the stalks or pull out the stringy fibers which conduct the liquid.

G A geranium (or coleus or other soft leafy plant) and a cactus, both growing in pots; some water plant (such as elodea or duckweed) floating in a dish or pond water.

Suggestion Cards:
1. "In what ways are these plants alike?"
2. "In what ways are these plants different?"
3. "In what ways do their differences relate to their interactions with water?"

H A growing leafy plant in a pot of soil. The soil is covered with aluminum foil which is wrapped tightly around the stem. The whole plant and the pot are covered with a large glass jar or a large, clear plastic bag secured to prevent the exchange of air from inside to outside the bag.

Control: A second pot of soil watered and covered with aluminum foil and a jar or plastic bag. Both sets of material are placed in sunlight.

TEACHER PREPARATION

The materials in this section are easy to set up from the details in the "Materials" column. We could suggest another type of preparation which might be helpful: read about other background materials in children's texts, teacher's guides, and trade books; then write down a few questions phrased to provoke thought during the colloquia and perhaps a list of patterns which might evolve to move children's thinking along conceptual arrows.

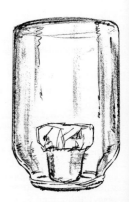

I   Four large leaves hanging by their petioles (stalks) from a coat hanger:
1. one as it came from the plant,
2. one vaselined on top surface,
3. one vaselined on bottom surface,
4. one vaselined on both surfaces and over cut stalk.[22]

Suggestion Card:
"Try to think of a model to describe what is happening to the leaves."

J   A microscope and two prepared slides; one of the top epidermis of a leaf, the other of the bottom epidermis of the same leaf. Also, a lettuce leaf, tweezers, a medicine dropper, a clean slide, a cover slip, and water for each child.

Suggestion Card:
"Make your own slides from the 'skin' of the lettuce leaf. Discuss with a partner what you see. (Come for help in making slides if you need to.)"

Books and Other Media

Books
   Schneider 3 (102-110).
   Brandwein 2 (88-89).
   Fischler 3 (25-41); and 5 (226-27).

   Ross E. Hutchins, *This Is a Leaf,* Dodd, Mead & Co., New York, 1962. Functions and structure of different kinds of leaves. Clear photos.

Film
   "Adaptations of Plants and Animals," narrated by Glenn O. Blough, Coronet Films, [23] 1957, black and white, sound, 16 mm. Adaptations to the environment for protection and to obtain food. Beaver, water plants, time-lapse corn growing, migrating birds, leaf shedding, etc. (May be shown to the whole class.)

Filmloop Series
   Phyllis Busch, "Ecology of the City," produced by Ealing. Ten loops presenting the habitat concept. For this matrix we suggest: "Dandelion," "Plants," and "Trees."

---

[22] For other suggestions for activities with leaves in relation to water see Morholt *et al., A Sourcebook for the Biological Sciences,* Harcourt Brace Jovanovich, Inc., New York, 1958, pp. 46-47.

[23] Consult the latest edition of the *Index to 16mm Educational Films,* R.R. Bowker Co., New York, for the distributor nearest you.

MATRIX 12: INTERACTIONS OF PLANTS AND SUNLIGHT

MATERIALS

A Two dandelion plants pulled or dug out of the earth with some root attached. Each is placed in a plastic bag. One plant has a flat rosette of leaves; the other a bunch of upright leaves.

Suggestion Card:
"What made the difference?"

B Three sets of radish seeds grown inside three plastic tumblers by being pressed against the inside wall of the tumbler with damp blotting paper which reaches down to an inch of water at the bottom of the tumbler. One set is grown in a dark closet (1), one under an electric lamp (2), and one in sunlight (3). [24]

Suggestion Card:
(Directs children to find the three sets of growing seeds.)
"Keep dated records of what you observe in each plant."

C Seeds grown in several pots in cylinders of colored plastic filters. All placed in a sunny window. Once the seedlings have turned green, the color filters have a marked effect. Since an object which appears green is reflecting green light, green plants must be absorbing the other colors. Photosynthesis, and therefore growth, will take place least well within the green cylinder. [25]

D Five small milk cartons, each with seeds germinated and grown to one inch in height. (Seeds may be mung, grass, wheat, bean, etc. Germinated mung beans are the "bean sprouts" eaten in Chinese restaurants.) Three of the cartons of seeds are covered by half-gallon milk cartons; each milk

TEACHER PREPARATION

The plants in **A** might come from a class trip.

For **B**, soak seeds overnight; then place them in tumblers and locate as suggested. Let children observe the growth as long as they are interested.

---

[24] Adapted from Brandwein *et al., Concepts in Science 4,* Harcourt Brace Jovanovich, Inc., New York, 1970, p. 150.

[25] Adapted from *Science: A Process Approach,* Part 7, A.A.A.S., 1966, p. 145-57. The preparations are rather demanding, so we suggest that a teacher interested in the project read the details from the original source. Many activities can be evolved from the basic materials. The A.A.A.S. lessons are teacher-directed, but we suggest beginning with the materials in **C** then seeing which problems and interests arise from a colloquium on the state of each pot of plants. These activities assume the children have a knowledge of the nature of colored light (see Matrix 15).

MATERIALS

carton has a one and a half inch square hole cut in one side (three different positions). One carton of seeds is covered by a half-gallon carton wrapped in black paper and one is left open. All are placed in a sunny window.

E¹ Two covered flat plastic dishes, one containing nasturtium leaves which have been picked in the morning and one containing those picked in the evening after a sunny day. Leaves have been boiled in water to break the cell walls and then warmed in alcohol to remove the chlorophyll. Each dish bears a label explaining the preparation procedures. Squares of wax paper, Lugol's iodine solution, and medicine droppers are provided.

Suggestion Card:
"Find out which leaves have starch in them. Make a model to describe the interaction which produced or did not produce the starch. (It may take up to 15 minutes for the iodine to color all the starch. Hold the rinsed leaf up to the light.)"

E² Variegated leaves, picked in the evening and prepared like the nasturtium leaves in **E¹**. Lugol's iodine solution, medicine droppers, and wax paper.

F Small pieces of soda crackers on a plate, squares of wax paper, Lugol's iodine solution, and medicine droppers.

Suggestion Card:
"Test a piece of soda cracker for starch. Take another piece of cracker. Chew it and chew it and chew it. Then test it for starch. In what way might this experience be related to your model in **E¹**?"

G Elodea under a funnel whose stem and cone are all under water. A test tube full of water is inverted over the stem. The materials are in bright sunlight.

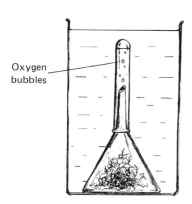

Oxygen bubbles

Suggestion Card:
"Try to make a model to describe what is happening. Devise a test for a hypothesis developed from your model."

TEACHER PREPARATION

For **E**, boil a sufficient number of leaves in water so that there is at least one from the morning picking and one from the evening picking for each child. Set a beaker of alcohol in a bath or pan of hot water; place the boiled leaves in the alcohol and heat. The water breaks the cell walls and the alcohol dissolves out the chlorophyll. Press the leaves between dry towels or blotting paper and keep them in covered plastic dishes, one labeled "Picked in the morning" (or give exact time) and the other "Picked in the evening after a sunny day."

The variegated leaves should be picked in the evening. (During the day, a green plant makes starch in sunlight. Chlorophyll captures the energy from the sun.) At night, the starch is converted to soluble sugar and stored in other parts of the plant. The variegated patches are visible (although not green) after the water and alcohol treatment.

To prepare the materials in **G**, place elodea in deep water. Fill the test tube with water. Place the funnel over the elodea and carefully slip the inverted test tube of water over the funnel stem. To test for the oxygen which bubbles into the test tube from the green plant in sunlight (oxygen is a by-product of starch making), slip a thumb over the gas filled tube after removing it from the funnel stem (but without taking the opening of the test tube above the water level). A glowing splint may be brought to the mouth of the test tube as you remove your thumb.

Books and Other Media

Books

Schneider 6 (42-64).

Brandwein 3 (215-17); and 4 (123-28, 146-51); and 5 (196-98, 227-47).

Fischler 5 (228-30).

Herbert S. Zim, *The Sun,* William Morrow & Co., New York, 1953. The structure of the sun and the effects of its energy on earth. *(upper grades)*

Film

"Plants Make Food," *Heath Science Film Series*, color, 15 min. The processes and organs which contribute to food making. (May be shown to whole class.)

Filmstrip

"Plant Factories," McGraw-Hill, Inc., 1953, 48 frames. Detailed explanation of green plants making food. Interrelationship of green plants and animals.

MATRIX 13: INTERACTIONS OF PLANTS AND MINERALS

MATERIALS	TEACHER PREPARATION
A A rotting log in a clear plastic box with a cover.	If the children become especially interested in molds, the teacher can find many suggestions and materials for activities in *Microgardening*, an Elementary Science Study Unit.[26]
Suggestion Card: "What living things can you find in this log?"	
B Moldy bread and moldy orange, each in a plastic container.	
Suggestion Card: "What happens when bread and an orange rot? Record what you observe over several days."	
C A funnel lined with filter paper, supported by a plastic tumbler. Soil in the funnel. A small pitcher of water, an eye-dropper, squares of wax paper, and a lens (magnifying glass).	It would be wise to test the visibility of the minerals in the soil sample in **C**. Pour half a pint of water through the soil in the funnel. Let it drip into the tumbler. Take a sample of the filtrate with a medicine dropper and put a drop on wax paper. Let it evaporate. Is there a residue? You might have several different soils available for testing.
Suggestion Card: "Try to find out if there are any soluble minerals in the soil."	
D A Venus's flytrap or a sundew plant in a pot, a covered jar of insects, and a pair of forceps.	[26]Several booklets are available from McGraw-Hill, Inc., 1968.

MATERIALS

E Place the following on a supply table so that the children may see and think and discuss. (Maybe a group could plan and investigate, and present it to the class before trying it out.) Seeds (mung, radish, wheat) on a separate piece of damp blotting paper in a container. Containers of sand, soil, humus, lime, vinegar, and water. Paper cups or milk container bottoms.

Suggestion Card:

"Plan an investigation to find out what conditions are necessary for the healthy growth of seeds."

TEACHER PREPARATION

You might want to decide ahead of time if your class is at a level of sophistication where they can plan the investigation in stepping stone **E**. Can they figure out controls so that there is only one variable? Will you let them try and flounder first? (This is often the best initial contact with an experience; it points up the need for careful planning, forethought, and analysis.) Should you warn them to measure the unit of water they use so that each pot receives the same? Will you help them try different amounts of water (in unit measures) in pots containing the same seeds, but under other growing conditions?

There are enough variations possible in the investigation of these materials for every pair or every three or four children to set up a different variant.

Books and Other Media

Books

Schneider 2 (186-99); and 5 (242-53); and 6 (65-69).
Brandwein 3 (218-27); and 4 (152-63); and 5 (252-56).
Fischler 5 (230-32); and 6 (188-96).

Augusta Goldin, *Where Does Your Garden Grow?,* Crowell, New York, 1967. Emphasis on the role of humus. *(preschool/elementary)*

Lucy Kavaler, *The Wonders of Algae,* John Day, New York, 1964. Chlorella as a food for space travel and as a solution to the hunger on earth today. *(elementary)*

Lucy Kavaler, *The Wonders of Fungi*, John Day, New York, 1964. Molds that conquer disease and supply protein; their use in space travel. *(upper grades)*

Bernice Kohn, *Our Tiny Servants: Molds and Yeasts*, Prentice-Hall, Englewood Cliffs, N.J., 1962. Interesting historical notes on a variety of molds. A recipe for making bread. *(elementary)*

Lorus and Margery Milne, *Because of a Tree,* Atheneum, New York, 1963. Ecological interdependence centering around eight different trees, including palm, maple, and saguaro. *(elementary)*

Lynn and Gray Poole, *Insect-Eating Plants*, Crowell, New York, 1963. Detailed information on the functioning of various insect-eating plants. How to prepare a terrarium for insect-eating plants. *(elementary)*

Milicent Selsam, *Birth of a Forest*, Harper & Row, New York, 1964. Photos and line drawings of the ecological changes from a Michigan pond to marsh to swamp to forest. *(elementary)*

Dorothy Sterling, *The Story of Mosses, Ferns and Mushrooms*, Doubleday, Garden City, N. Y., 1955. Life histories of various species. *(elementary)*

Filmloops
"Carnivorous Plants," Walt Disney Nature Library (Ealing catalog: 81-9706/1), color, 2 min. Venus's flytrap, sundew, and pitcher plant all shown catching insects.

"Rotting Pear," E.S.S. (Ealing catalog: 81-449), color, 4 min. Time-lapse photography showing the destruction of a pear through the spread of brown rot fungus.

MATRIX 14: ADAPTATIONS OF PLANTS IN RELATION TO ADVERSE CIRCUMSTANCES

Plants survive a great variety of adverse circumstances through a great variety of adaptations. These, of course, have been developed throughout the history of each genus or species, probably through mutations which happened to be fitted to the particular environmental circumstances of each. As ecological interactions change, a previously successful adaptation might prove to be a liability in the changed system. An epiphyte, for example, which perches on another taller plant in a crowded tropical forest and absorbs moisture from the air through its roots, would fail to survive if the forest became less humid. But a new variant, which might die in one ecosystem can flourish and produce progeny in a changed system. Plants with food potential for man have flourished under cultivation since the farmer became part of the plants' ecological system.

One adverse circumstance common to all living organisms is degeneration. Living organisms eventually die if they are not consumed by other organisms in the environment. Hence, species of plants which have survived have done so because they have a means of regeneration. We can therefore find in all plants some means by which regeneration overcomes degeneration. In this sense, the species survives the death of its individuals. The most common means for survival of a plant species are seeds, spores, food storage organs, and vegetative reproduction.

Individual plants also have various means of surviving adverse circumstances during their lives, ensuring that the plant has more chance to live out its natural life span and reproduce the species. Spines and thorns discourage consumption by animals; toxic substances prevent nibbling by some insects; a small surface to volume ratio (as in cactuses) conserves water, guarding against drought and excessive heat; a period of dormancy allows long-lived plants such as trees to survive the annual onslaught of winter cold.

This matrix addresses itself to many plant adaptions in relation to adverse circumstances. We have grouped the materials into two subsections: adaptations which favor survival of the species and adaptations which favor survival of the individual. For brevity, we will title these sections *Species' Survival* and *Individual Survival.*

Stepping stones:

I. Species' Survival: Seeds

MATERIALS

A Paper baking cups containing both seeds and "not-seeds," some of which look alike: bits of charcoal and beet or caraway seeds; morning glory seeds and fine gravel; vermiculite and radish seeds. A magnifying glass and spare baking cups.

TEACHER PREPARATION

All the materials in the seed section are obviously not available during the same season. The teacher can select those most suitable to his class from those available.

MATERIALS	TEACHER PREPARATION

B Soaked and dry fava beans; some beginning to sprout. A pin (for teasing the parts) and a magnifying glass.

Fava beans are larger than lima beans and, therefore, more easily handled and inspected. They can be purchased in (Armenian, Greek, Italian) stores which sell beans and grains in burlap bags. Otherwise, lima beans will do. If possible, obtain some beans in their pods.

C Various types of seeds, soil, milk carton bottoms, and water.

D Daffodils with fat ovaries and faded petals, maple fruits, peas in a pod, a pin, magnifying glass.

The term *fruit* is applied to the developed ovary which contains one or more *seeds.*

E A fresh daffodil flower.

F Various types of fruits: with burrs or winged (maple, elm, ash, ailanthus); fleshy (berry); feathery (dandelion).

Suggestion Card:
"These can travel. How?"

II. Species' Survival: Spores

G Fern leaf with sporangia, mold with spore heads, a ripe mushroom, and a magnifying glass.

To obtain mold with spore heads, keep wet bread in a damp, dark place for a week. The white mold will produce upright black heads which burst and scatter spores.

Suggestion Card:
"These plants do not produce seeds. Where do new plants come from?"

III. Species' Survival: Food Storage

H An onion, an iris rhizome, a potato, a crocus corm, a daffodil bulb, a sweet potato, a knife, and a magnifying glass.

Suggestion Card:
"These structures survive the winter. Where do new plants come from?"

IV. Species' Survival: Vegetative Reproduction

I Ground ivy or strawberry runners, an onion bulb which has produced two new bulbs, a potato with eyes sprouting, a Piggyback Plant (sometimes called Mother of Millions), soil, water, and milk cartons.

The sets of materials in stepping stones **G, H, I** might be offered for free choice at one time under the topic "New Plants Without Seeds," or several stations with the same materials could be set up, or one of the plant parts in **H** or **I** could be given to each child. There are many other possible organizations as well.

It would be well for the teacher to list the patterns expected during the colloquium, as well as the ecological concepts he sought in the choice of his materials.

Suggestion Card:
"Choose a *part* of one of these plants and try to make it grow."

V. Individual Survival: Dormancy

MATERIALS

J¹ Various winter twigs; maybe one for each child.

Suggestion Card:
"Find the tree your twig came from. Describe some other part of the tree. Find the name of the tree in a book."

J² A twig for each child, a jar, and water.

Suggestion Card:
"Put your twig in water. Keep a record of the changes you see. Write the date of each observation."

J³ A twig for each child and a magnifying glass.

Suggestion Card:
"There are many different parts to a twig. How many can you find? Compare your twig with one which someone else has."

J⁴ Pictures of different types of trees: ponsiana, pine, poplar, etc.

Suggestion Card:
"These trees grow in different ecological systems. Try to think of a model to describe the interaction and growth patterns of tropical trees, evergreens, and deciduous trees."

TEACHER PREPARATION

The materials in **J** may be secured on a class trip to an area where breaking off twigs from trees is permitted.

Choose some twigs with clearly marked leaf scars (showing where each leaf joined the stem with dots where the veins went into the leaf). In the axil, between the leaf scar and the stem, there should be buds for next year's growth.

Choose some twigs that have large lenticels (openings for the exchange of gases). These look like raised dots.[27]

---

[27] Helpful suggestions are found in the E.S.S. working paper on *Budding Twigs*, available from the Education Development Center, Inc., 55 Chapel St., Newton, Mass. 02160.

Books and Other Media

Books

Schneider 1 (83-100); and 3 (92-100); and 4 (31-49).
Brandwein 2 (90-96); 3 (247-77); and 4 (163).
Fischler 3 (39-59); and 5 (236-46).

Matilda Rogers, *A First Book of Tree Identification,* Random House, New York, 1951. *(elementary)*

Irma E. Webber, *Travelers All,* William R. Scott, New York, 1944. Very simple statements on seed dispersal. *(primary)*

Filmloops

"Bean Sprouts," E.S.S. (Ealing catalog: 81-424), color, 4 min. Shows variation in growth of the bean during the first two weeks.

"Plant Growth Graphing," E.S.S. (Ealing catalog: 81-423), color, 14 min. A growing plant makes its own graph.

The matrices on ecology are very useful, even essential bases for helping children relate to our current environmental crisis. More and more we feel that an understanding of man's role in polluting or preserving his natural resources and in taking some responsibility for conservation must begin in the elementary school years. The world has become alerted to the dangers in which we find ourselves; scientists, sociologists, and the mass media deluge us with warnings, facts, and advice about making the world an ecosystem in which life can have its maximum expectancy. Many educational organizations are now developing units and courses of study for people of all ages which, it is hoped, will evoke a more responsible attitude toward the environment. Some of these offerings could, no doubt, extend the matrices developed in this chapter. Some filmloops pointing in this direction can be found in the bibliography.

Matrix on light

Except for a study of shadows, investigation of the phenomena of light belongs mostly to the upper elementary grades. Indeed, although we experience light (and its absence) from the day we are born, its nature is still not fully understood by scientists. Nevertheless many of the manifestations of light may be partly comprehended by ten or eleven year olds through investigations with materials, colloquia, and reading. The only portion of this matrix suitable for children in the primary grades is Part IV, *Relation of Light to Shadow*. This section has been placed at the end of the matrix because its approach is different from the one used to introduce the others.

Light is a form of energy. The colloquia should help the children to think in terms of energy and to apply this concept to the phenomena they are trying to describe through models. Light is the visual manifestation of a small portion of the electromagnetic spectrum; light waves fall between the longer wavelengths of the short radio waves (which abut on the infrared invisible light) and X-rays (which are much shorter and follow the also invisible ultraviolet rays).

Textbooks have many different ways of organizing experiences which children can have with light; each book selects those aspects its authors consider most valuable. All the modern textbooks emphasize energy as the base; all have ways to help children think about the rather complicated models a scientist uses to describe the phenomena.

If you will indulge us as we follow in the footsteps of Madeline (a young lady whom, as you've no doubt noticed, we rather favor!), we will present you with a matrix format which again is somewhat different from those used previously, but which, we feel, will be of the greatest help to you. The phenomena to be observed from the children's interaction with the materials are of particular interest; we will put a description of these "Phenomena to be Observed" in the column which parallels the stepping stone "Materials." The follow-up sections after each group of stepping stones will be devoted to "Ways the teacher may help the children think and talk about the phenomena observed." These ways lead into extended models, explanations, and further investigations offered by textbooks (for which we give the textbook pages).

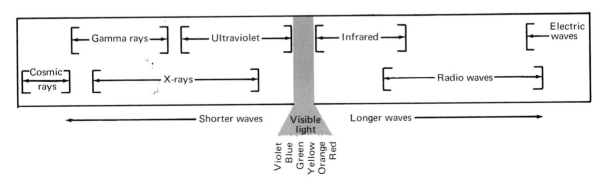

CHART OF CONTENT AND ORGANIZATION OF LIGHT MATRIX

MATRIX TITLE	SECTIONS	TEACHING METHOD EMPHASIZED
15. Light	a. Conceptual scheme charts. b. Vygotsky level of thought. c. Stepping stones: Materials and phenomena to be observed. d. Ways the teacher may help the children think and talk about the phenomena observed. e. Textbook pages for additional information.	Introduce with a FILMLOOP which suggests MATERIALS FOR DISCOVERY. After COLLOQUIUM, pages in several TEXTBOOKS are suggested.

The stepping stones are grouped under the following subtopics:

  I. The bending of light: reflection, refraction, and color.

 II. Energy and absorption: another way to think about reflection, refraction, and color.

III. Light as waves.

IV. Relation of light to shadow.

The concepts underlying the first three subtopics require the upper level of preconcept thinking and full concept ability; in short, the topics are for children in the fifth and sixth grades. We excerpt the following statements from the Chart of Conceptual Schemes (page 166):

CONCEPTUAL SCHEME B

The sum total of mass and energy in the universe remains constant.

EMPHASIS ON ENERGY

PRECONCEPT	CONCEPT
	Energy manifests itself along an electromagnetic spectrum. When energy changes from one form to another, the total amount of energy remains constant.
	The sun is the chief source of radiant energy in our solar system. Energy can change from one form to another.

The fourth subtopic, relation of light to shadow, can be made suitable for primary level children both for early preconcept and for those still at the complex levels of thought. The conceptual arrows here will bridge Conceptual Schemes **A** and **B**, respectively:

The universe is in constant change.

COMPLEX	PRECONCEPT
	There are daily, seasonal, and annual changes within the solar system.
	There are regular movements of the earth and moon.

The sum total of mass and energy in the universe remains constant.

EMPHASIS ON ENERGY

COMPLEX	PRECONCEPT
	Energy can change from one form to another.
	There are many forms of energy.

Discovery–colloquium related to filmloops and textbooks

The major portions of the light matrix, specifically sections I and II, may be introduced through the suggestions presented in a filmloop, "Light," part of a series of filmloops [28] in science designed to help children think. The materials suggested could either be made by the teacher, given to the children for free exploration, and then be followed in subsequent lessons by viewing the filmloop for other suggestions, or the children could view the filmloop to start off their activities and, where appropriate, could then make the materials themselves. At some point during this series of explorations, the children will probably break up into smaller groups designated by different interests; if so, they will need different follow-up materials from the matrix. And because each interest has a consolidating effect, the groups will need to delve more deeply into an understanding of the phenomena, to find models other than those they have been able to construct during their colloquia. The children will want to read. For subtopics I and II of this matrix we are using *Science for Today and Tomorrow.* [29] Many additional investigations on each subtopic of light are suggested in these textbook pages. We will cite page numbers which might be appropriate for each of our subtopics. However, as you know, we prefer to suggest to the children, "Read those parts which interest you. You will find material on our unit in the chapters on 'Light Waves' and 'Optical Instruments.'"

Some of the phenomena of light can best be explained by accepting the model of light as particles. Actually, scientists consider light as bundles of energy called photons. Children at the Piaget level of concrete operations will picture photons as particles and will probably construct models for the phenomena in subtopics I and II as light particles bouncing, much as balls do. The mature concept requires thinking in mathematical relationships, but the children's conceptual arrow will suffice for them. At other times, the phenomenon of light manifests itself in a manner best explained through a wave model. Scientists think of a photon both as a wave and a particle at one time: children will treat the wave-particle duality alternatively.

Subtopic III explores the wave phenomena of light. Here another filmloop in the *Explorations in Science* series, "Springs," will serve as a stimulus to further investigations. The reading material suggested to amplify the wave concept of light comes from three textbooks: Fischler, Mallinson, and Brandwein. [30]

Several activities are suggested for a discovery-colloquium session with light and shadows, subtopic IV, and the reading is geared chiefly to the complex level of thought. References are given to two textbooks, Schneider and Brandwein, both on the first-grade level.

[28] *Explorations in Science*, authored by Harry Milgrom of the New York City Board of Education and produced by the skill and ingenuity of Art Bardige and his coworkers at the Ealing Corporation, 2225 Massachusetts Ave., Cambridge, Mass. 02140.

[29] Herman and Nina Schneider, *Science for Today and Tomorrow 6*, D.C. Heath, Lexington, Mass., 1968, the units on "Light Waves," 159-91, and "Optical Instruments," 192-215.

[30] Abraham S. Fischler *et al., Science: A Modern Approach*, Holt, Rinehart & Winston, Inc., New York, 1966; George G. Mallinson *et al., Science*, Silver Burdett, Morristown, N. J., 1965; Paul F. Brandwein *et al., Concepts in Science*, Harcourt Brace Jovanovich, Inc., New York, 1966.

MATRIX 15: LIGHT

Stepping stones:

MATERIALS	PHENOMENA TO BE OBSERVED
Introduction—filmloop [31] suggestion: Shoe box with one end removed and replaced with coffee stirrers, making slits	Beams of light bend at various angles, making crisscross patterns. Colored bottles throw colored beams which blend. Tumbler brings beams into focus. The spatula acts as a parabolic mirror. More than one mirror create various

[31] "Light," Ealing, see footnote 28.

MATERIALS	PHENOMENA TO BE OBSERVED
between slats. Strong light inside box throws parallel beams of light onto sheet of white paper. Mirrors, various bottles with colored water, a plastic tumbler of water, a shiny cake spatula, and prisms.	complicated patterns. The prism produces a rainbow (spectrum).

Teacher preparation

How to construct a "lightbox": Cut one end out of a shoe box, leaving a rim of 1 in. all around. Tape coffee stirrers or popsicle sticks over the opening, leaving spaces of ¼ in. between the slats. Inside the box and parallel with the end wall, fix a partition after cutting a 1½ in. hole in it. Place the 150 watt uncoated bulb in a socket in the side of the box so that the spiral part of the filament faces the hole in the partition. When in use, it is best to keep the lid slightly ajar or the box will become too hot.

Small rectangular mirrors (such as those used in women's handbags) serve for reflecting the light beams. Any transparent bottle can be filled with water and food coloring or ink and used to transmit colored light. The plastic tumbler should be cylindrical, or nearly so; its interaction with the light beams, bending them similar to the way a lens does, can be clearly seen. A shiny cake spatula can be bent into various curves including a parabola; it then acts as a curved mirror in focusing the light beams.

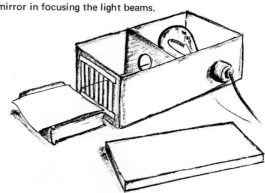

If spiral wire inside bulb is horizontal (when bulb is held upright), place bulb at *end* of box.

I. The Bending of Light: Reflection or Equal Angle Bending.

MATERIALS	PHENOMENA TO BE OBSERVED
A A small pocketbook or metal mirror, a flashlight, and a large, unruled, white index card.	The mirror bends light back to where it came from. A person can see the flashlight (in the mirror) when he is looking away from the light. The mirror can bend the light into a person's eye.
Suggestion Card: "What can you find out about the way a mirror bends light?"	
B The glass of a flashlight is covered with aluminum foil in which a narrow slit has been cut with a sharp knife. A mirror and an index card.	The angles of the light beam and the reflection must be the same.
Suggestion Card: "Work with a partner. Put the mirror on the floor. Try to predict where the bent light will hit the card when your partner holds the flashlight. Test your prediction."	
C The lightbox (from the **Introduction**) with all the slits except one covered by black construction paper, dowels, a mirror, and white paper.	The angle between the mirror and the light beams is the same before and after the beams are bent.

MATERIALS

Suggestion Card:
"Try to use the dowels to mark the positions of the light beams to and from the mirror. Make a record of the position of the mirror and the path of the beams."

D Two mirrors hinged together with masking tape. A coin.

Suggestion Card:
"How many coins can you see?"

E Two mirrors hinged together with masking tape. Colored scraps of paper or cloth.

F A flashlight, a six-inch square of shiny aluminum foil, some crumpled foil, squares of shiny red, blue, and green paper and squares of red, blue, green, and black construction paper. An 8 × 11 in. sheet of white construction paper.

Suggestion Card:
"Shine the light on the various pieces of paper and foil and catch the reflection on the white paper."

PHENOMENA TO BE OBSERVED

The smaller the angle between the mirrors, the greater the number of coin reflections.

Kaleidoscope designs.

Aluminum is like a mirror, but less bright. Crumpled aluminum gives a zigzag pattern of light. Shiny paper shows its color on the white construction paper; dull paper shows a weaker color; black paper shows a dark shadow.

Ways the teacher may help the children think and talk about the phenomena observed—The children soon discover that the angle at which a light beam strikes a mirror (and, later, any smooth surface) is the same as the angle at which the light beam is reflected. However, the children usually think of the angle between the beam and the mirror. In reality, the reflection takes place from any small plane on a surface and the rest of the surface may be any shape. We need to give the children the terms *angle of incidence* and *angle of reflection*, but we have to explain that these angles are measured from the perpendicular to the plane at the point of contact.

It is quite likely that children will offer the

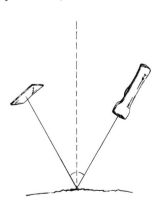

analogy of balls bouncing off the ground or of handballs bouncing off walls or even of billiard balls bouncing off table cushions. But these are very concrete balls bouncing. We can then pose the question, "What do you think light might be made of if it acts as you have seen?" The model that light is composed of very tiny particles will usually be suggested.

Some child will notice that when he reflects light from one or more mirrors, especially while using the lightbox, the beam is weaker than that coming from the light source. "Would it help you to explain this if I reminded you that light energy is one of the forms of energy we have encountered in our studies?" is a good leading question at this point. Children know that a ball bouncing along the ground rises to a lower height at each bounce and that their handball hits the wall harder than it hits their opponent's hand. Energy is therefore lost *en route*. "What kind of energy?" Mechanical energy from friction is the most common thought at this stage. Children who have completed a unit on electricity may recall that light and heat energy are often converted into one another and may suggest that heat may be produced when light bounces. They sometimes recall that it is hot under an electric light.

The concepts that light travels in straight lines,

that it is bent by solid surfaces making equal angles with the perpendicular, and that it loses energy in the process form the bases for understanding what occurs to produce the phenomenon found in investigation **F**. Aluminum is less shiny than a mirror; therefore, less light is reflected and some energy must be found elsewhere. The crumpled aluminum with its pretty pattern of light leads children to say that the surfaces are "every-which-way" and so the reflection is "every-which-way." We can offer the phrase *scattered light* or *diffuse reflection* at this point.

This phenomenon then accounts for the fact that when light is reflected off paper the reflection is a surface of color or light, not an image of the flashlight. The rougher the paper, the more the scattering.

But something is reflected. You see color! The light spot reflected by the mirror is now a diffuse reflection of the paper. What happened to the light beam? The darker the paper, the less light of any kind is reflected. Obviously, part of the light is bent in these cases. What happened to the rest of the light energy?

Stepping stone **D** might lead the children to draw a record of the positions of the mirrors for each number of coin images seen. If this were done and the angles between the mirrors were then measured with a protractor, the following relationship might be seen:

3 images for 120°
4 images for 90°
6 images for 60°

The children can then find the pattern.

Textbook pages which would be helpful during the development of the conceptual arrows outlined above might be Schneider 6, 167-74. These pages take up the following problems: how light travels; that it keeps on going; that when it meets objects, some energy is transferred as heat; the reflection of light from mirrors and opaque surfaces.

Stepping stones:

The Bending of Light: Refraction or Bending Due to a Change in Media.

MATERIALS

G   Three children work together. A cylindrical, plastic vial about 3-in. high, filled with water and covered. A second vial filled with marbles and half filled with water. (Olive jars or instant tea jars can be used instead of vials.) Three pieces of white paper with a few words in small print on each. Sunlight, a flashlight, or the "lightbox." A magnifying glass or lens.

Suggestion Card:
"Find out what you can. In what ways are the three transparent objects alike? In what ways are they different?"

H   A magnifying glass, a piece of white paper, and sunlight.

Suggestion Card:
"Hold the lens to a window and, try to obtain the image on the paper of something outside."

I   A glass half full of water with a pencil leaning in it.

Suggestion Card:
"In what way is this object like the objects in **G**?"

PHENOMENA TO BE OBSERVED

All the objects magnify. The cylinder magnifies in the direction of its sides. Marbles look larger and "broken" by the surface of the water. Light comes to a point through the lens and makes a line through the cylinder.

The image is upside down. In some positions of the lens, the image is fuzzy.

The pencil looks bent or broken.

MATERIALS	PHENOMENA TO BE OBSERVED

J Water in an aquarium with a drop of milk to make it cloudy. A mirror at the bottom under water. A flashlight.

Suggestion Card:
"Shine the flashlight onto the mirror through the water. In what way is what you see like what you saw in I?"

The light beam and the pencil both look bent.

K A penny in a saucer of water.

The penny comes "up" into view.

Suggestion Card:
"Put your eye at a level so that you just cannot see the penny. Pour water slowly into the saucer. Do not move your head. What do you see?"

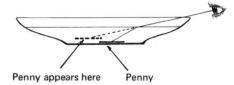

Penny appears here   Penny

Ways the teacher may help the children think and talk about the phenomena observed—We know that light travels at 186,000 miles a second in a vacuum. When light reaches our atmosphere, its speed is slightly reduced because more energy is required to travel through a denser medium. If the angle at which the light meets the surface of the new medium is not a right angle, there is a change in the direction of travel. The light is "bent." The same interaction occurs whenever light travels from one medium to another. If the interface between the two media is curved, the light beams will be bent toward each other or away from each other. It is this double bending which focuses the light beams in a lens or through a cylinder.

Children can be helped to understand this through a series of diagrams or, better yet, by rolling toy wheels over two adjoining surfaces.

These diagrams are clearly paralleled by the path of the light beams from the lightbox.

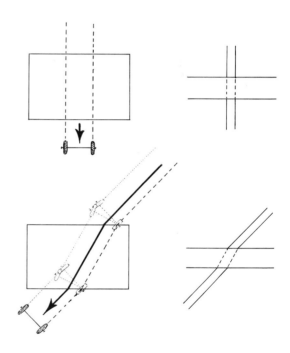

Stepping stones:

The Bending of Light: Color or Different Energies Bent at Different Angles.

MATERIALS	PHENOMENA TO BE OBSERVED

L A prism for each child. Sunlight or beams of light from the lightbox, and pieces of red, white, green, blue, and black construction paper.

The white paper shows all the spectrum colors; red, blue, and green paper show only their own colored part of the spectrum; black paper shows no color.

MATERIALS	PHENOMENA TO BE OBSERVED

M   Prism and sunlight or light beams from the lightbox.

Rainbow colors (spectrum).

Suggestion Card:
"Record the order of the colors you see."

N   Two prisms, a sheet of white paper, and sunlight or light beams from the lightbox.

The second prism can reverse the process of the first prism.

Suggestion Card:
"Try to put the spectrum colors from one prism back together again."

O   Four thermometers under four pieces of cloth of similar weave, but different colors: black, yellow, red, white. All are placed in positions to receive equal light from a 100 watt bulb in a gooseneck lamp (or in sunlight).

The thermometers register different temperatures: the one covered with white cloth, the lowest; with black cloth, the highest.

Ways the teacher may help the children think and talk about the phenomena observed—Where children have a clear understanding of the model of light bouncing off opaque objects and being bent according to the angle formula, it may still be necessary to help them clarify their thinking about the fact that no object can be seen unless light is bent by it to reach the eye. We can start children thinking about this by raising some questions such as "Is a red object red in the dark?" or "We saw that light is bent by objects so that its path makes equal angles with the perpendicular. We can all see this blue paper. Using a piece of string, could you show where the light comes from, how it is bent, and how it reaches each of our eyes?" It may take quite a long interchange of thoughts during the colloquium and many attempts to trace the light paths three dimensionally before the children can give their own versions of light being all around the room, light beams being bent by objects in all directions, and some of these beams reaching the eyes of everyone who sees the paper. Suggested reading which might help children apply the principle of the light in the mirror: Schneider 6, 177-84.

With this much established, children will say that it is the red beam in the spectrum of white light which is bent back by the piece of red paper and hits the eye. "What happens to the other colors?" is the next question raised. Again, it may be appropriate to remind the group that light is a form of energy and that energy can be neither created nor destroyed. The energy represented by the missing colors must therefore be accounted for. The thermometers and colored cloths in stepping stone **O** reveal that light energy is transferred to heat energy. Where all the colors are bent back (by the white cloth), the least heat energy is in the cloth. Where none of the light is bent (the black cloth), most light energy is transferred to heat energy. The other colors bend back part of the spectrum's energy and absorb the rest.

An exploration of why prisms separate the different colors in white light remains. If the children have become familiar with the concept of frequencies (through reading or working with other stepping stones in this matrix), they may realize that different frequencies represent different energies. The colors with the highest frequencies or greatest energies are bent the most. An analogy can be worked out by pushing the pair of toy wheels over a piece of blotting paper (see page 323) at sharp angles and with varying amounts of push (or energy!).

Textbook pages which would be helpful in extending the conceptual arrows: Schneider 6, 159-84. The topics presented are: light as energy, frequency, prisms, invisible light (infrared and ultraviolet), the speed of light, light from the past, opaque colors, and energy transfer.

Stepping stones:

II. Energy and Absorption: Another Way to Think about Reflection, Refraction, and Color.

MATERIALS	PHENOMENA TO BE OBSERVED
P For every two children five squares each of red, blue, and green cellophane, white construction paper, rubber bands, and two flashlights.	Light passing through each filter makes a light spot its own color. Various combinations and effects.
Q A green shape pasted on a red background (both made of construction paper) plus all the items in **P**.	The green and red both look black or dark blue unless a green light shines on the green paper and a red light shines on the red paper.

Teacher Preparation

If the room is not dark enough, the red and green "picture" may be pasted inside one end of a shoe box. Make two holes in the opposite end: one for the flashlight and one for a peephole. Put the lid in place.

R For every two children: same materials as in **P**. *Alternatively*, red and green filters can be pasted over the slits in the lightbox so that half the slits are covered with red and the other half with green. Two mirrors.	A red filtered light and a green filtered light shining on the same spot on white paper make a yellow patch. Yellow changes from greenish to orangish, according to the angles the beams of light make with the paper. Red, blue, and green filtered lights shone on the same spot on white paper make white light.
S Light from the lightbox (or a slide projector). In its path are two glass jars of water, one colored with ink. Each jar contains a thermometer. Various colors may be tried.	Colored water heats up faster than colorless water does.

Suggestion Card:
"Read the two thermometers at equal time intervals. Record your results as a graph."

Ways the teacher may help the children think and talk about the phenomena observed—From these experiences, plus those resulting from stepping stone **O**, children easily offer the model that the heating effect is due to the light energy of the "missing" colors. Hence the heat and color are due to some light being absorbed and some being reflected or bent back. In each case the colloquium can try to account for which colors are bent back and which are absorbed. The children can generalize that opaque colors reflect or bend back the light seen, while transparencies (filters) transmit the color seen. In both cases all the colors which are not seen must be absorbed. The more light energy is absorbed, the warmer the object becomes from the transfer of light energy into heat energy.

That the "primary" colors of filters are red, blue, and green always produces astonishment in children who have mixed paints and found red, blue, and yellow to be primary. To understand this, we must go back to the spectrum and first accept that none of the colors we have used is pure. Referring to the spectrum below, we can explain which colors are absorbed and which are transmitted. The red cellophane allows all the red and some orange and yellow to pass through, but absorbs the green and blue. The green cellophane allows the green, blue, and yellow through and absorbs all the red and orange. The green and red filters combined absorb the green, blue, red, and orange. Yellow is allowed through by both filters.

Filters are used for color printing; red, blue, and green filters produce all the colors needed. In the

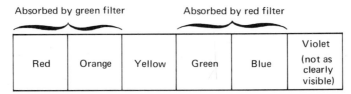

			Absorbed by green filter			Absorbed by red filter		
Red	Orange	Yellow	Green	Blue	Violet (not as clearly visible)

same combinations, filters are used for theater lighting.

From the experiences in this matrix children can figure out under which light green plants could be expected to grow best. Since the leaves reflect green light, it must be the energy of the absorbed colors which the chlorophyll uses to manufacture starch (see stepping stone **C** on page 310).

An extension of this series of investigations helps children understand some of the effects of weather and climate. Black earth heats up faster than snow; this affects the air above and thus is related to winds. The angle at which the sun falls relates to the amount of energy absorbed by a designated area. (Sloping rays cover more ground, hence deliver less energy per unit area.) White clothes in summer are cooler than dark clothes because they absorb the least light energy; black absorbs the most.

A final extension of this subsection would be to leave a radiometer and a flashlight for the children to investigate. The brighter the light (the nearer to the radiometer) on the black vanes, the faster the vanes turn. In dim light, they do not move. So carefully is the spinner poised that energy from the light absorbed by the black vanes gives a push which keeps the wheel spinning.

Textbook reference to extend the learnings in these sections: Fischler 6, 311-31.

Stepping stones:

III. Light As Waves

INTRODUCTION: Up to this point, we have encouraged children to think of light as particles. We might start this section with a demonstration, while we adhere to the particle model, and ask for a prediction. Focus two slide projectors on two screens so that their light beams cross. Turn on one projector: the picture appears clearly. Turn it off. Turn on the other projector: a picture is seen clearly on the second screen. On the basis that light is made of particles, the children can now predict what will happen to the two pictures when both projectors are turned on simultaneously: they will blur due to "bumping" of particles. But both pictures are perfectly clear! Some child has usually read or heard that light is waves or both waves and particles. Could the wave model explain the phenomenon of the crossed beams? Asked to tell what they know about waves, the children will probably reveal hazy concepts. The filmloop "Springs" in the *Explorations in Science* [32] series has illustrations using a Slinky Junior to transmit standing longitudinal waves (the model for electromagnetic waves) and transverse waves (the model for transmission of sound).

An investigation of the nature of waves might include some of the following:

MATERIALS	PHENOMENA TO BE OBSERVED
T An oblong pan with half an inch of water in it.	Waves circle out from the impact of the finger.

Suggestion Cards:
1. "Dip your finger gently into the water. What do you see?"
2. "Dip your finger quickly and forcefully into the water. What is the difference between 1 and 2?" | The waves are higher. |

---

[32] "Springs," Ealing, see footnote 28. Also contains an ingenious way to construct a spring balance.

MATERIALS	PHENOMENA TO BE OBSERVED

U Same as for **T** plus a crumb of cork.

Suggestion Cards:

1. "With the crumb of cork on the water, repeat 1 and 2 above.

2. "Dip a finger into the opposite ends of the water at the same time. What do you see?"

The cork bobs, but does not change its location.

Waves circle out and cross each other; they continue unchanged.

V A rope and a chair.

Wave travels along the rope.

Suggestion Cards:

1. "Tie a rope end to a chair or a door handle. Flick the loose end. Describe what you see."

2. "Try to find a place on the rope where you can balance a narrow strip of paper folded in half so that it does not fall off when you flick the rope."

There is a part of each wave which does not bob up and down.

W Two polarizing grids.[33]

When grids are placed on top of each other and turned, light passing through changes from light to darkness.

[33] Supplied in some science kits. If unobtainable, consult a high school science teacher.

Ways the teacher may help the children to think and talk about the phenomena observed—Children who have been using the *energy* vocabulary throughout the various units and who have now investigated some of the properties of waves, can begin to put the two concepts together: energy is transferred as waves. The material of the flicked rope was not transferred; energy was. Each bit of the rope remained and oscillated in one place. The rings of the Slinky Junior did not move along the spiral; the energy did. Each ring oscillated in place. Electromagnetic energy—the waves which compose the energy spectrum from long radio waves to gamma waves—has no *thing* that moves and a full concept of the model may not be possible without some advanced mathematics. However, the children's experience with physical waves and their investigations of the phenomena of electricity and light allow them to develop a valuable preconcept. An additional experience would be playing with a Slinky Junior and measuring the amplitude, frequency, and wavelength of physical waves, partly to give meaning to these terms and partly to build an understanding of them as variables.

Some helpful activities are suggested in Fischler 6,[34] pages 260-71. Reading about electromagnetic

energy from a new angle may also enrich the concept or at least move children further along their conceptual arrows. We suggest they read what interests them in a book whose chapters are organized around the various manifestations of energy: the sixth grade science book by George Mallinson.[35] For the purpose of the matrix on light, we recommend particularly Chapters 18-21, entitled "Control of Radiant Energy."

Through reading, colloquia, films, and measurement, alongside the experiences with materials, children are able to understand the principal attributes of waves: energy, not the object, moves; waves have frequency, amplitude, and wavelengths; waves of the same type pass through each other undisturbed; waves can be stopped by grids at right angles to one another. An activity to illustrate polarized light is suggested in Brandwein 6,[36] pages 50-51.

Children probably notice that waves "bounce" back off the sides of a basin and come back intact. This may suggest that waves in some way act as particles. That light is thought of as waves *and* particles may best be understood from wide reading.

[34] Abraham S. Fischler *et al., Science: A Modern Approach 6*, Holt, Rinehart & Winston, Inc., New York, 1966.

[35] George G. Mallinson *et al., Science 6*, Silver Burdett, Morristown, N.J., 1965.

[36] Paul F. Brandwein *et al., Concepts in Science 4*, Harcourt Brace Jovanovich, Inc., New York, 1966. "The Bounce of Light," pp. 29-59, offers simpler reading for Matrix 15.

The concept is built gradually as it is approached from many different angles. Some scientists coined the word "wavicles"! Some phenomena are more easily understood by the wave model and some by the particle model. Light is both—at the same time.

Two facts connected with this study which sixth graders can understand are:

1. Light waves, electromagnetic waves of all frequencies, travel at the rate of 186,000 miles a second in a vacuum or the near vacuum of space.

2. The source of the sun's energy is the combining of hydrogen atoms to form helium.

The textbook reference (Schneider 6) describing the nature of light waves is the beginning of the chapter from which we have been selecting references. Pages 159-68 give a historical account of the two theories of light (waves and particles) and describe the properties of light.[37]

[37] The teacher will find further activities on light in a unit on "Optics" by E.S.S., obtainable from the Education Development Center Inc., 55 Chapel St., Newton, Mass. 02160.

Stepping stones:

IV. Relation of Light to Shadow

INTRODUCTION: For younger children, one of the best introductions to a study of light and shadows is to play "Shadow Tag" on a sunny day in the school yard at two or three different times of day: 9 a.m., noon, and 3 p.m. The children can think about whether it is easier to be IT in the morning, noon, or afternoon.

For another outdoor activity, spread brown wrapping paper on the school yard and have the children work in pairs and draw around each other's shadows at the three different times of day. They can then cut around their shadows and hang them on the classroom walls. Can the children tell at which time of day each shadow was made?

One can do the above activities in midwinter and then again in summer.

Where there is a record (as with the cutout shadows), legitimate comparisons can be made. "Shadow Tag" results may have to rely on memory!

MATERIALS	PHENOMENA TO BE OBSERVED
X For each child: a flashlight, an upright object, white paper, and a crayon.	Top of object, top of shadow, and flashlight must be in a straight line.
Suggestion Cards: 1. "Find out what you have to do to make the object's shadow long or short." 2. "Draw around the base of your object and around the shadow. Exchange your drawings and object with a partner. Can you make the same shadow your partner drew?"	Light must be anywhere on the line that joins the object to the shadow, but on the other side of the object.
Y The beam of a slide projector in a darkened room shining on a sheet suspended from a bar higher than the children's heads. One or two children shadow play for the others. Where must the actors be? Where must the viewers be?	Actors must be between the light and the sheet.
Z Use the setup in **Y**. Suspend two-dimensional objects (a disc, hollow circle, geometric cutouts) behind the sheet. Children try to guess each object.	There is always a thin line as the object turns.
This can be done also with three-dimensional objects.	There is never a thin line. The three-dimensional shapes are seen as two-dimensional projections.

Ways the teacher may help the children think and talk about the observed phenomena—Basic to all these activities is the concept that light falls in straight lines and that an opaque object interrupts the light, forming a shadow. Children can look through a soda straw at an object outside the window, and then bend their straws and see only darkness.

Older children can relate this principle to the phenomena of day and night and the seasons. They can also tackle the problem of the nature of the light source in relation to the shadow. A point source of light fans out and makes a shadow larger than the object; a parallel beam (such as that reaching the earth from the sun) casts shadows the same size as the object.

One can, of course, tell time from the angle and position of the sun and the shadow it makes. Sundials use this principle. A practical sundial for school use has been designed by the Hayden Planetarium.[38]

Textbooks which offer some reading material on light and shadows for primary children are:

Schneider 1, "The Sun" and "Colors," pages 1-20;

Brandwein 1, "Light and Dark," pages 49-60;

Brandwein 2, "Darkness and Light," pages 57-76.

Matrix on geology

The major part of the study of geology must be from readings, even if the school is so situated that field trips are both pertinent and possible. Moreover, a teacher needs to be knowledgeable in the subject area as well as familiar with the features of the local environment to be a stimulating guide on field trips.

A field trip under a knowledgeable leader is, of course, the best introduction to a study of geology. The children's interests could then be primed by certain assigned tasks, broad in scope, but specific in action. If a quarry were to be visited, children could be asked to collect rocks in bags and to attach a label to each locating the rock's place on a given map and measuring how far from the top of the quarry it was found. Polaroid cameras can provide pictures of the

quarry face. Rock locations could be marked on a photograph. For an area where there is evidence of an Ice Age, children might obtain pencil and paper rubbings of glacial scratches. The particular area would determine the activity, but purposeful looking and acting sharpen perception and raise certain problems which can be solved later. The *materials* from such a trip become the stepping stones for a matrix.

The rest of the study must be carried on through books and available audio-visual aids. Some of these will initiate interest; others will act as research sources for problems raised during colloquia. From their reading, the children will find suggestions for the construction of concrete models which provide analogies that sharpen thinking. Here we suggest some ways to provide frameworks for the study of geology, organizations which could direct the thinking along conceptual arrows and provide problems for oral interchange during colloquia. The colloquia then build mental models, supported by facts acquired secondhand.

The conceptual scheme germane to geology is that the apparently stable and solid earth is neither stable nor solid, but in constant change. Since many of these changes are slow, they can become apparent only through prolonged study and reading records that others have made. Distant time is an essential concept for understanding the slow geological changes; hence the nine year old is about the youngest child who can profitably begin such a study. Geology units are usually placed in fifth grade textbooks.

Concepts of constant change may center on different features of the earth. We might think of them as:

1. The mineral cycle.
2. The nature of the earth as a whole.
3. The movements of the earth's crust.

The mineral cycle is the only one of these which lends itself to discovery from materials and, therefore, presents a good basic introduction to the whole field of study. The approach has been found to be of interest to children of nine years and up from a variety of backgrounds.

[38] Sundial Template, available from The American Museum, Hayden Planetarium, 81st St. and Central Park West, New York, N. Y. 10024.

MATRIX 16: GEOLOGY

Stepping stones:

I. The Mineral Cycle

MATERIALS	PHENOMENA TO BE OBSERVED

A Up to six children may work around a table, each child having access to at least one rock. Small pieces of shale, limestone, and sandstone, nails, two jars of water, small dishes of vinegar, a scratchplate (optional), and a spread of newspaper are on the table.

Limestone is white and crumbly, leaves a white mark when scratched on something, and gives off small bubbles in vinegar. Sometimes bubbles of air are given off when limestone is put in water. Sandstone glistens, is often brown, and leaves a brown streak which can be rubbed off as sand. Shale is flat and smooth; it feels muddy in water.

Suggestion Cards:
1. "What can you find out?"
2. "Try to guess which rocks are which by touch alone. Play a game."
3. "Try rubbing two similar rocks together. How long does it take to make a teaspoon of powder?"

It takes *ages* to make a teaspoon of powder.

B Same grouping of children as in **A**. Small pieces of slate, marble, and gneiss, nails, water, vinegar, and a magnifying glass.

Marble is hard, usually white, and has crystals in it which are not always visible. Slate is flat and flakes off. Gneiss has crystals of several colors. All are harder than the rocks in **A**.

Suggestion Cards:
(same as for **A**.)

C Small pieces of shale, slate, sandstone, gneiss, limestone, and marble.

Shale is like slate; sandstone is like gneiss; and limestone is like marble.

D One kind of sedimentary rock in a burlap bag and a hammer. (Use school yard or basement for this investigation!)

Rocks can be broken into powders with the use of a lot of energy. Different rocks break into different kinds of pieces.

E Two or three children can work together. Different samples of soil for each group, a pitcher of water, jars, funnels, paper towels, and plastic spoons.

The soil settles in layers with the coarser sand on the bottom, the finer sand next, the mud next, and, perhaps, the lime on top. Various bits of humus will be floating on the top layer of water.

Suggestion card:
"Mix a tablespoonful of soil with half a pint of water. Stir and let it settle. Try to separate the layers you can see."

The layers in the jar look like the rock layers seen on trips or in books. The layers look like the powdered rocks when dry.

Note to the teacher: Children will find some ways to separate the layers. They may approximate the following procedure. If the top layer of water is poured through a paper towel filter into a funnel, the water will drip through and the towel will reveal minerals (see stepping stone **C**, page 312). Open the paper towel and place it in a warm place to dry. (Label it 1.) Add more water to the jar and swish it around to bring the next layer of soil into suspension. Pour this through a new filter into the funnel. Dry the residue on the paper as before. (Label it 2.) Repeat the process until all the layers have been · separated.

The powdered rocks can be mixed; with humus added, this constitutes soil! Will plants grow in separate rock powders and water? Will they grow in a mix? With humus? A whole investigation of seed growth can evolve from stepping stone **E**.

Ways the teacher may help the children think and talk about the phenomena observed—Textbooks usually give a clear account of the erosion of rocks, their transportation to the ocean, and their consequent layering as sediments. The formation of fertile soil en route to the ocean is often described in chapters on conservation.

Since all motion is initiated through energy, it is interesting to have children pinpoint the energy involved in the breakup of rocks into soil and later in their transportation and sedimentation. [**Colloquium Question:** Where does the energy come from which converts soil to sedimentary rocks?] Wind and water are the chief agents. Air is set in motion (winds) through uneven heating by the sun (shining on different topographical features, shining at different angles on the earth, etc.). Water from rivers or rain frozen in cracks in hilly areas breaks up the rocks. Again, it is the sun which raises the water as vapor, while interaction with gravity lets it run down to the ocean.

Children can figure out much of the dynamics of erosion from rock investigation and some reading. They examine the rocks, examine the parts of the soil, and convert rocks to soil. Children gain an immense respect for the powers of wind and rain after they have exerted so much of their own energy converting rocks to soil. Invisible air and soft water can do so much! Children also suggest names for the sedimentary rocks without being told the real names. They usually come up with "sandstone," "chalkstone," and "mudstone." The real names may then be substituted. On their own, children also pair the sedimentary rocks with their metamorphic cognates.

A comparison with the rocks and powders on the moon would be challenging. On the moon there is energy from the sun, but no air to form wind and no water to transport particles. [**Colloquium Question:** What breaks up the rocks on the moon? Is there a mineral cycle?]

We can think of the mineral cycle from the point of view of matter as well as of energy. The metal elements in minerals can enter living organisms during their cycles. Living organisms have evolved and adapted to these natural minerals. But what of man's pollutants? Mercury, for instance. Or the long-lasting pesticides which are cycled in and out of living organisms, destroying the latter on the way? Questions on modern ecological problems belong here. Matter can neither be created nor destroyed!

II. The Nature of the Earth as a Whole

The earth's mineral cycle cannot be completed without including the movements of the earth's crust, but these, in turn, owe most of their dynamics to the nature of the earth as a whole.

The most dramatic entry into the study of the earth as a whole is, of course, through earthquakes. Whenever a violent eruption hits the headlines, new interest is aroused.[39] The enormous destruction and loss of human life raises *why* questions. [**Colloquium Question:** Why are there certain areas of the earth where earthquakes are much more common than in

[39] A filmloop made from editing the actual film of a volcanic eruption could be made available to the children. "A Volcano in Action" from the Ealing Corporation shows the molten rock within the earth's mantle (magma) flowing out as lava.

other areas?] This is a good moment to divide children into groups for reading and other research, or just to make a number of different books available and let the children find their own answers to bring to a subsequent colloquium.[40]

Some of the essential points which should be made:

1. The earth is made of concentric spheres of matter which differ in content, density, and state.
2. There is an outer crust of rock which is about 25 miles thick on land, but only two to three miles thick under the oceans.
3. Next is a denser layer of rock some 1800 miles thick called the *mantle*. It is important for the children to think of the "solid" mantle more in the nature of "silly putty": it can flow very slowly; it can be brittle; it can rebound. From time to time, parts of it get heated up enough to melt. A decrease in pressure, even without heating, can trigger melting (just as a decrease in atmospheric pressure up a mountain allows water to boil at lower than $212°$ F). There is a constant shifting of the material of the mantle; this sets up strains which, in turn, affect the stability of the crust.
4. The innermost sphere of the earth, and the densest, is the *core*. This is thought to be a double layer: an outer core, probably molten iron and nickel, and an inner core of solid metal. (If children wonder why a molten or fluid layer can be denser than a solid crust, ask them to recall their work on flotation. Relative weight of molecules has a relation to density. Mercury is denser than ice because the mercury molecule is much heavier than a water molecule.)

Since the earth is in constant change, the children could consider the source of the energy which sets the rocks in motion. [**Colloquium Question:** What is the source of energy that moves the rocks in the earth?] Once this question is raised, the children may have to return to their books. Again, we suggest the reading of many sources, for there will then be many viewpoints and ways of looking at the phenomena presented and, therefore, better building of concepts. Some of the theories the children are likely to find:

1. Radioactive elements break down in their unique "half-life" manner, releasing an order of energy used in atom-smashing devices and also, in bombs. The accumulation of this energy in the form of heat melts the rocks nearby. The molten rocks expand, produce pressure, and eventually break through weaker places in the surrounding rocks.
2. A theory has recently been advanced by Dr. George Rouse of the Colorado School of Mines.[41] Dr. Rouse notes that all of space is pervaded by electromagnetic fields from the stars and galaxies. He suggests that the interaction of these fields with the iron core of the earth differs from their interaction with the mantle. The tendency would be for the core to shift separately from the mantle and so strains would be set up, particularly at their common boundary.
3. Children will know from reading and trips that there are faults in the earth's crust. Most faults lie several hundred miles down in the mantle. Some of them coincide with places where the strength of the earth's magnetism changes. There is increased stress as these areas interact with the magnetic fields of the planets and stars. Volcanoes and earthquakes occur above these faults.
4. Any shift in the earth's material sets off balancing movements in other portions, for the earth itself is moving as an entity through space (from the energy of its original motion of formation). These balancing-of-equilibrium motions extend the area of shifting matter. [**Colloquium Question:** The earth has motions as a whole: rotation and revolution. What source of energy originated these? (Read theories on the origin of the earth.)]

[40] As good sources for this matrix we suggest: Schneider 5, last three chapters: "Geology: Earth's Forces," "Conservation: Soil and Water," and "Geology: Earth's Minerals"; Brandwein 5, Chapter 1: "The Earth—Inside and Out" and last chapter: "Probing the Earth's Crust"; Mallinson 5, Unit 2: "The Earth"; and Fischler 4, Unit 2: "The Earth's Changing Surface." Other references can be found in the Bibliography.

[41] Dr. Rouse's own work and some of his collaborations with Dr. Ramon Bisque are described in "The Faults of Earthquakes," *Nature and Science* (Children's Edition), Vol. 6, No. 4 (October 28, 1968), 2-4. Other relevant material is cited in the Teacher's Edition of the same issue on pages 1T-3T.

III. The Movements of the Earth's Crust

The piling up of sediments in the ocean presses down on one part of the ocean floor. This in turn forces other parts of sediments up. The strains from all these pressures and shiftings produce cracks in the weaker places. Mountains are pushed up from under the sea to above it. The building of mountains in their various formations is well described in school textbooks.

The extent of movements of the earth's crust is wider and more continuous than one is apt to imagine. For instance, there are as many as 150,000 earthquakes every year, although most of these can be registered only by sensitive instruments. [**Colloquium Question**: Find a pattern that links the earthquake areas together. What models describe the pattern?]

Earthquakes occur mostly in certain definite regions of the earth and the children can discover the way these regions are related. This might be an interesting activity since the concrete work connected with the study of geology is relegated mostly to model making in the sense that the children simulate phenomena which they can only read about, not experience. This activity was developed by Dr. George Rouse who worked with Ramon Bisque in Colorado:

One needs a globe and a piece of cardboard whose sides are longer than the globe's diameter.

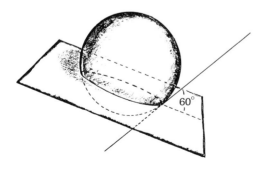

Cut a hole in the cardboard whose diameter is 0.87 times the diameter of the globe. This hole will fit over the globe making an angle of 60° with the surface.

When this hole is fitted over the globe so that the circumference runs through two places where earthquakes occur (such as Mexico City and Costa Rica), the rest of the circumference will lie on other places of high earthquake potentiality (such as Iran).[42]

Dr. Rouse drew some 16 circles on his globe in this manner and found that all the places where earthquakes occur most often were on the circumferences, now named "Rouse belts."

Another set of places which are connected by a Rouse belt and which share earthquake tremors and eruptions is the Red Sea, the Pyrennees, and Chile.

To account for these zones of earthquake, an old explanation which had fallen into disrepute has recently received new life. New data have been found to support the theory of the "continental drift." This theory holds that at one time, perhaps 200 million years ago all the continents on the earth were joined. Their possible "fit" is obvious from the maps on page 334, where one can imagine Brazil fitting south of the hump of West Africa. If one uses the continental shelves which jut gently under the ocean as the outline instead of the sea level coastline, the fit is even better.

If the continents have drifted away from each other, there should probably be weak places where the land masses have pulled apart. Such places have been found under the Atlantic and Pacific oceans. Under the Atlantic Ocean, a high mountain ridge runs north to south. Alongside this range, there is a rift or crack which seems to open and pour hot rock into the gap periodically. The sea floor is pushed outward from the crack as the hot lava comes up in the center. Recently, new islands were formed near Iceland from the activity of this rift by the under-ocean mountain. The thought is now that such cracks and volcanic activity are related to the pushing apart of the continents. Most of the earth's quakes occur on land in the neighborhood of the ocean mountain ridges and their accompanying rifts.

[42] *Ibid.*

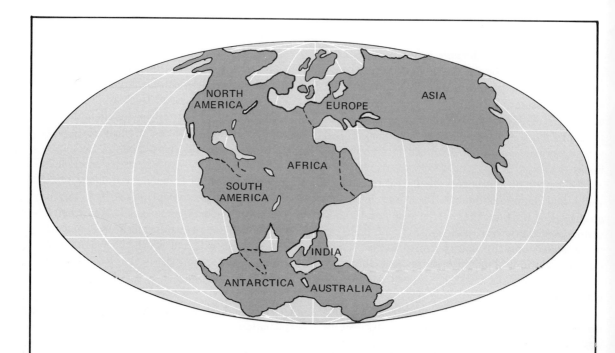

There is evidence that the earth's land masses were once joined (see above). Peaks on map below indicate undersea mountain ranges. The black lines show cracks through which lava may be flowing.

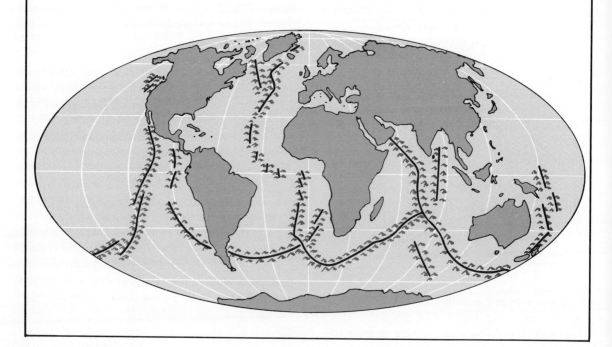

Back to the mineral cycle

Because the mineral cycle of geological activity not only ties together the various phases of study of the earth, but proliferates over into other science areas, it might be well to sum up what we know about this continuous process.

Children can be helped to think through the process by asking them to follow, in their imaginations, the voyages of one mineral. They should be encouraged to include the sources of energy responsible for the changes. For example, we could begin with some radioactive, energy-producing magma within which is a silicate. This might have been belched out of a mountain or intruded among sedimentary rocks; it appears in granite. Through wind, ice, and rain, the sun's energy can weather the granite into grains of sand which might be washed down a stream into the sea. In a soluble form, it could be absorbed into the skeleton of a small sea creature which, when it died, sank to the bottom and later was crushed with pressure from new layers and heated by molten rock until it became sandstone. The shifting of the earth's crust due to settling sediment could eventually raise the sandstone to a mountain.

Suggestions to help you develop a matrix on astronomy

If you would like to try your hand at making a matrix useful for your class, why not try one on astronomy? Two units by the Elementary Science Study,[43] *Where Is the Moon?* and *Daytime Astronomy,* suggest many helpful activities. You might select appropriate chapters from your own textbook, read these E.S.S. units, select the concepts for your grade level, and then pattern a matrix after one of those in this book which you feel is appropriate.

A major problem in learning astronomy is shifting from explaining the perceived phenomena when one is part of the system to constructing a model which requires one to be an observer (mentally) outside the system. Historically, man made this shift in viewpoint or frame of reference as he changed from holding a geocentric to holding a heliocentric concept of the solar system. In essence, each child's education requires him to tread the same path, but first there must be careful observation of the phenomena! Some very helpful filmloops are now available which you might like to incorporate in your astronomy matrix, together with the naked eye observational activities suggested by the E.S.S. booklets.

The series of filmloops are grouped together under the title *The Changing Heavens*[44] which, of course, suggests one of our major conceptual schemes. Here is a brief description of each loop:

The Moving Sky: Time-lapse photography shows the sun, moon, and stars changing positions over a 24-hour period as one watches the sky facing east. Animation shows the sun's day motion across the sky from east to west at different times of the year. Finally, time-lapse photography centers on the stars circling around the North Star. These are the phenomena as a child could view them.

Night and Day: Photography of the earth as seen from a synchronous satellite (one which revolves around the earth in 24 hours so that it remains above the same spot—in this case, Brazil) shows the night shadow moving across the earth's surface. Next we see a globe model, oriented so that the cognate of the place on the earth where the model stands (in this case, Cambridge, Mass.) is on top. The north direction of the globe corresponds to the north direction of the earth. Using the sun as the light source, we see the same night shadow we saw from the satellite move across the globe in twelve hours of time-lapse photography. Finally, a paper cutout of a man on a revolving globe and a beam of light to represent the sun show the night shadow phenomenon from the man's and the satellite's frame of reference (the phenomenon is the same except for the distance) and a long shot of the studio in which the photography is being done. In the latter case, the observer is outside

---

[43] Units by the E.S.S. of the Education Development Center, Inc., Newton, Mass. 02160: *Where Is the Moon?* (Teacher's Guide) and *Where Was the Moon?* (Student Booklet) are both available from the Webster Division, McGraw-Hill, Inc., Manchester, Mo. 63011, 1968; *Daytime Astonomy* is a trial edition available from E.D.C.

[44] *The Changing Heavens,* six super-8 cartridge filmloops in color: The Ealing Corporation (No. 89-4202/1), 2225 Massachusetts Ave., Cambridge, Mass. 02140. Written by Dr. Lloyd Motz of Columbia University, and produced by the technical artistry of Art Bardidge and Pat Sorrentino.

the solar system model and the night shadow is stationary.

The Moving Earth: A model of the earth's rotation and revolution is shown from a frame of reference outside the solar system. The function of the earth's tilt in relation to the seasons is indicated.

The Moon: The moon's phases are explained visually. The phenomena are shown from a frame of reference of an observer on earth, as well as from a model of the earth–moon relationship seen from space using a split screen technique.

The Sun: The theme is the sun as a vibrant, changing body. Solar eclipse, sun spots, prominences, and solar flares are illustrated from actual movie photography.

The Seasons: Because of the angle the earth's axis makes with the plane of the ecliptic, varying amounts of sunlight fall on parts of the earth during winter and summer, producing variations in temperature. A model shows slanting light falling north and south of the equator (blue light indicates where a cooler temperature is produced because the sun's energy is spread over a wide surface; orange light indicates where the light energy is concentrated over a smaller area). A long shot of the model shows what would occur if the earth's axis were perpendicular to the plane of the ecliptic (there would be no change in seasons). A close-up repeats this sequence with the earth's axis tipped at 23½°.

All the filmloops could generate good discussions; the class could replicate some of the activities.

Evaluation

8

How do we learn what they know?

How do we learn what they know? We stop, look, and listen!

Our looking and listening are guided by the criteria we set up; the criteria are related to the overall aims of the program. Our goal, as we have frequently stated, is the building of concepts, the provision of an atmosphere in which conceptual arrows flourish. But this is the big "umbrella" purpose; subsumed under the concepts which the children eventually acquire are the subconcepts pertinent to each unit or to each lesson drawn from the unit matrix. In turn, the manifestations of subconcepts have a hierarchy of levels geared to each child's current development. It is the child's level of development which interests us—the growth he has made since our previous appraisal.

Because no one can know directly either what

takes place inside the person or the thinking he does in his head, we must derive our data from some behavioral evidence—that which we see or hear. Thus, we must stop, look, and listen with special spectacles and earphones which have been attuned to our purposes. Attuning what we see and hear to the goals of our teaching requires that we relate the behavioral evidence each child exhibits to the thinking which he does. The child's thinking is revealed to us mainly through his speech and, to a smaller extent, through his physical acts. We have given many illustrations of children's speech in colloquia and of their acts during free exploration with materials.

Since evaluation of the concept development of children is based on their oral remarks during either exploration with materials or the colloquium, a word on how these records may be obtained is necessary at this point. The obvious answer is "use a tape recorder." Where a small group of children is interacting with the materials and chatting about their findings, the listening teacher can record every word, as Miss Bradford's and Mr. Wilbur's records illustrated (see pages 73 and 162-63, respectively).

With a whole class colloqium and amateur equipment, however, we have found that it is often very difficult to decipher such a record. Instead, a student teacher or an aide can make a verbatim record using some form of speed writing or just rapid note taking. But, strange as it may seem, the teacher conducting a whole class colloquium can best record the flow of remarks! There are at least two methods both requiring determination and a high level of concentration. One is to make key notes as the children speak in order to record accurately specially phrased remarks and the order of topics. Then, as soon as possible after the colloquium, the teacher can fill in the rest of the colloquium while his memory is still fresh and his effort is concentrated. This may sound impossible to do accurately and, obviously, some of the "ums" and "ahs" will be lost, but the flow of remarks and characteristic speech patterns can be recalled because a teacher is usually sensitive to the speech patterns of his children. We have never been able to give a teacher more detailed instructions on how to record colloquia from immediate memory, but we have never found anyone who could not do it! Maybe soon the process will be facilitated by the development of simply operated tape recorders which will pick up individual speeches from a large group of children.

We will now try to organize these data into formats which help a teacher search for, perceive, and record the stages of growth in each child from several angles. We will group the main data we seek under three headings:

1. Concept-seeking skills.
2. Levels of concept attainment.
3. Attitude scales.

Concept-seeking skills are subdivided into: communicating, thinking, and quantifying. Evidence of these skills is provided by the colloquia and the format is a checklist or chart.

Concept-seeking skills blend naturally into concept attainment. There is no sharp division. Obviously, one

must have facts upon which to build concepts and we have seen that observations and thoughts about relationships of facts must be expressed in the child's own words if he is to move along the conceptual arrow. Hence we note (1) the manner and content of the child's *communication* and check these for perceptual accuracy and verbal clarity and then we note (2) the quality of his communication in terms of *thinking*—the manner in which he uses the facts to challenge or question.

Because *quantified* data are a helpful form for recording and arranging accurate observations and because opportunities for quantifying do not always present themselves in science lessons unless specifically provided for, we have added this third category under "Concept-Seeking Skills." Together, communication, thinking, and quantifying comprise concept-seeking skills. Finally we list the criteria which tell us that concept-seeking has reached various levels of *concept attainment*.

Level of concept attainment has to be judged by what a child says and how he says it, not only in the colloquium but also whenever the teacher overhears him express his thoughts freely to a co-worker while investigating materials. The format for recording the levels of concept attainment is a chart that incorporates an anecdotal or verbatim record of each conceptual statement, the exact words the child uses being essential for later analysis. After the statement has been recorded, it may be analyzed to determine its place on the Vygotsky hierarchy and/or for whether the type of thinking comes under perceiving external or hidden likenesses.

Attitudes relate to what the child does and to the way he does it while investigating materials. We separate these into three independent relationships: relations of child to others, relations of child to materials, and work pattern drive.

Attitudes are recorded on a five point scale, each point of which designates a specific behavior. It is possible that a child exhibits behavior which may be scored on more than one point on a scale during one lesson or among several lessons; attitudes may vary widely with circumstances. While attitudes are only indirectly related to the type of concept achieved, they are relevant to the way in which children learn and, therefore, are of great importance to our understanding of and future planning for the intellectual and emotional growth of each child.

We might want to know what facts the child has acquired. We feel that facts used in the context of concept development are vastly more significant to learning than isolated facts. We must assume that none of the thinking our charts probe can be accomplished without the acquisition of a considerable number of facts. However, we think that perhaps the most important facts are those the learner himself freely recalls, for these are the more readily accessible and therefore more meaningful to him.

We indicated one way of learning which new facts were important to each child after Miss Yonika's unit (page 383). Another way would be to note the facts the children *use* toward their concept development during the colloquia. Of course, there are standardized tests also, but these are well known and it is not necessary to describe them here.

Many intangibles occur during a lesson, many learnings not pinpointed by charts, anecdotes, scales, or standardized tests. These, too, may be valuable for a teacher to know. Probably the best way to gain access to these intangibles (such as feeling tone or learning frustration levels or idiosyncratic approaches) is to take an occasional videotape recording of the children during their discovery period or colloquium and then to view the tape at one's leisure. (Tape recordings of lessons and minilessons usually focus on the teacher. We wish to emphasize the learner and would focus on the children.) Such a tape recording may also be used to score the Attitude Scales and other evidences of growth and learning patterns. It is quite possible, however, to score the scales without videotaping the lesson.

We shall now list, describe, illustrate, and apply each of the items under each of the evaluative headings.

CONCEPT-SEEKING SKILLS		
Communicating	**Thinking**	**Quantifying**

Observations:
  Stated clearly
  Accurately perceived
  Relevant to the concept
Interaction described
  operationally
New vocabulary used
Responded to another
  child's remark
	Noticed discrepant event
	Said "I think" or "Is it
	  right?"
	Asked a when, why, how,
	  or where question
	Changed statement in light
	  of new data
	Challenged a statement
	Gave reasons for challenge
		Collected data
		Arranged data
		Made use of data

LEVELS OF CONCEPT ATTAINMENT [1]	
Finding External Likenesses	**Finding Hidden Likenesses**
Generalized Compared Classified	Generalized Made an analogy Suggested a model Hypothesized Suggested a test or investigation Inferred Predicted

[1] We will also examine the level of concept attainment under the Vygotsky categories of syncretic, complex, preconcept, and concept thinking.

ATTITUDE SCALES		
Relations of Child to Others	**Relations of Child to Materials**	**Work Pattern Drive**
Operates alone or independently	Hesitates to use materials	Finishes soon or fails to start
Follows another's lead	Explores materials in a limited manner	Alternates work with materials with other activities
Works cooperatively	Does what is expected	Maintains a steady pace
Suggests activities which others follow	Finds original ways to elicit interactions	Uses materials with concentration and eagerness
Dominates or tells others what to do	Seeks materials not present	Suggests activities for next lesson

These three tables represent a fairly comprehensive roster of behavioral evidences. In practice, no teacher could possibly teach and collect all these data at the same time! Therefore, for each lesson it is suggested the teacher either seek one or two items for all the children in the class or most of the items for just one child. As a semester progresses, the items can be put together; from an examination of a full chart many interesting patterns can be perceived. If a student teacher or an aide is present to record the colloquium or if a clear audiotape recording can be made, the teacher can make the analysis after class. But this deciphering takes a lot of time. After a teacher has sought an item or two per lesson for a while, he gains perception and skill in recognizing the items and can record them directly on the check lists, rather than having to write down the remarks and score them later. A few precious remarks should, however, be recorded for each child to reflect the flavor of his thinking.

Evaluation is a growing technique for the evaluator and a growing picture of the evaluated.

Concept-seeking skills

For the Chart of Concept-Seeking Skills (see page 356), we place a dot beside the name of the child under the appropriate heading to show that the child contributed that particular item. By positioning the dots in each cell (intersection of child's name with a column heading) we can record in which of a series of lessons the child made the remark scored. A visual scanning in the horizontal direction of a completed chart will show where each child's major contributions lie and in which categories he contributed little or nothing. Scanning in a vertical direction tells which categories were not elicited by the series of lessons. Both sets of information are helpful to a teacher for future planning.

A description of each item and how to recognize it follows. Some of the items received preliminary discussion in Chapter 2 (pages 121-22). We give the complete explanations here to make reference easier, even at the risk of some repetition.

Communicating

Observations: Any remark made by a child during the colloquium describing what he has done, discovered, or thought is scored here. We interpret the word *observation* in the sense of "an utterance by way of remark or comment." No score is given for interjections such as "me, too" or "I dunno."

Example: Ivan entered the third colloquium on the microscopic study of cells by saying, "The dye tastes terrible!" Sometimes a child agrees with a previous statement by saying, "Mine did, too."

Stated clearly: This implies, in general, the use of names instead of general words like "things" or "they." It implies definitive statements rather than "Sort of" or "It's like what we did before."

Example: "My ping-pong ball sank."

"Mine didn't."

"Mine didn't" is scored as a remark and as both stated clearly and relevant to the concept. It is not ambiguous.

Accurately perceived: Many discrepant events stem from inaccurately perceived data. Growth in accurate sense perception, which includes knowing what to look for, is worth fostering and noting.

Examples: "The Wiffle ball half sank and half floated."

"My stomach comes up when I go down on the swing."

"The moon was to the left of the chimney before supper."

The above examples are all descriptions of what the children have carefully observed.

Relevant to the concept (meaning the concepts likely to be evoked through interaction with the materials): This involves judgment, but the same person doing the evaluation over a period of time is likely to be consistent in applying his criteria. We have noticed during analyses of colloquia that usually the first remarks are either emotive or straight facts. Emotive remarks are judged *not* relevant and are therefore not recorded here. Comments like "it tastes good," "sounds ugly," or "looks pretty" would not be considered relevant to a concept, but adjectives such as "loud," "bitter," or "sparkling" might.

Examples: "The water tastes sweet" (in an investigation of solutions).

"The sound is deep."

"The plant has grown a (pretty) leaf."

Interaction described operationally: We encourage children to select objects in systems and to describe the interaction of the objects which produce the phenomena. To bolster this attitude,

we keep track of the children's statements which are in this vein. The *negative* of this item—a nonoperational description—is one which implies anthropomorphism ("The balloon *tries* to fly up" or "The magnet *attracts* the iron."[2])

Examples: "The magnet moves toward the iron."

"The magnet and iron interact by coming together."

"When I hit the bar with a spoon, it makes a loud sound."

New vocabulary used: One's listening and reading vocabularies exceed the number of words one uses orally. Part of science education is learning to use the right word at the right time. We have seen ways in which words like "electrical energy" lead toward a more embracing and accurate conceptual scheme than an expression like "juice" does. We will note at which point each child uses, in his natural speech, the new words to which a unit has introduced him.

Responded to another child's remark: A colloquium means "speaking together." At first the remarks are personal, seemingly unrelated to what others have said. But gradually, during the course of discussion, the children more and more begin to think together as they speak together. It may not always be possible to discern whether a child's remark is closely related in his mind to what went before or whether it is a new line of thought generated by his reaction to the general trend of thinking. We will record all remarks following the statement of another child under "responded to another child's remark." We will not score a remark following a teacher's statement.

This item is useful in establishing whether the colloquium is a "chrysanthemum" or a flow chart: whether the teacher-child verbal ratio is one-to-one or the number of verbal interchanges among the children is greater than the number of responses to a teacher.

[2] *Attract* and *repel* are terms often introduced by teachers who do not realize the anthropomorphism they imply. Fortunately, children beyond the nursery school years tend to be more operational in their descriptions!

Example: The following excerpt from the colloquium quoted on page 91 is composed of items which would be scored "responded to another child's remark" (except for the first statement, which followed an interjection by the teacher):

> "Magnets can make iron or steel into magnets."
>
> "Oh, I remember; they will only be magnets for a while. Part of the magnetic power is sent to the other paper clip."
>
> "I can't make the rods stick to the sides of the donuts; they always roll off and stick to the ends. The ends seem stronger."
>
> "The donuts are stronger. They have bigger ends."

All of these remarks would also be scored: observations, stated clearly, accurately perceived, and relevant to the concept. The third one is also an interaction described operationally.

Thinking

Noticed discrepant event: The introduction of a variable which can not be accounted for sometimes comes as a challenge; a child, instead of the teacher may juxtapose two apparently opposing remarks. One child can bring in a fact he has read which seems to contradict an observed phenomenon as stated; the sense perception of an event may have been inaccurate.

Example: In the first grade, Billy offered this piece of wisdom: "Water finds its own level." Terry replied: "When my father empties the fish tank, he fills a rubber tube and the water comes out by coming *up* over the edge."

This is a discrepant event rather than a challenge, because each statement is correct within its own system.

Said "I think" or "Is it right?": We encourage these remarks because they contribute to psychological safety. Children will engage in adventurous thinking more often if they feel there is a way to back down should the words not sound as correct as the thoughts seemed to be. (Illustrates Vygotsky's thesis that thoughts create words and words change thoughts.)

Asked a when, why, how, or where question: This type of attitude is common with scientists as well as with children who are sciencing. Questions prefaced with these adverbs are really questions put to nature; they form part of the wonderment and inquiry which lead to a need for hypotheses and designs for further search for deeper meaning.

Examples: "I wonder why the stars shine."

> "Where do mosquitoes come from each summer?"
>
> "How do birds know when to fly south?"

Changed statement in light of new data: A child can make a statement relating facts which indeed have no nexus in reality (a kind of syncretic thinking). If someone else then points out an inconsistency (a discrepant event) by bringing in new data, the first child may acquiesce in some manner.

Example: Some first graders had grown a crop of carrots in the school yard. Looking at the feathery leaves and the succulent carrot, one child remarked:

> "Roots grow down because they are heavy."
>
> Another child pointed to some strawberry plants which had been pulled up to thin the row and remarked that strawberry *roots* look feathery like the carrot leaves.
>
> "There must be another reason," said the first child thoughtfully.

A statement is sometimes made in a colloquium which attempts to explain a phenomenon without regard for uncontrolled variables. A second child may suggest another variable as the critical factor.

Example: Contemplating several circuits the class had constructed, a sixth grader said that his lights were the brightest because he had used two dry cells.

> "But I used three cells and mine are less bright than yours."
>
> Both boys looked more carefully.
>
> "We joined them differently," the first boy conceded.

One probably had a parallel and the other a series hook up.

Challenged a statement: This does not denote cantankerous objections, but a genuine introduction of discrepancies.

Example: Third graders had been rubbing combs with silk and then picking up pieces of paper with the combs. Another child rubbed a balloon with wool and the balloon stuck on the classroom wall.

> "It's magnetism," said one.
>
> "I don't think it is," said another. "I tried a magnet on the balloon and they didn't come together."

Gave reasons for challenge: This often forms part of the challenge statement as it did in the example above. However, sometimes one child thinks the statement of another is incorrect, but cannot give a reason. Still another child may offer a reason for the challenge.

Quantifying

Whether any quantification takes place at all depends on the materials the teacher selects. Where this activity is possible, the teacher usually sets up problems so that some sort of measurement takes place. Children are not likely to "discover" quantification spontaneously. They may make comparisons or mention that objects are tiny or heavy, but by quantification, we mean some attempt at precision such as repeatable measurements using the same units. Quantification seldom comes during the early lessons or colloquia of units, especially where both the children and the teacher are new to discovery-colloquium procedures. Some units themselves are not appropriate for quantifying; sometimes children do not "take" to the suggestion to quantify, especially when they are busy with self-initiated activities. We saw this in Miss Yonika's series of lessons. When she suggested that the children use their hairwidth as a unit for comparing the size of cells (see page 249), only Charles followed through with:

> "The onion has larger cells; the scallion smaller ones. I measured the length of a cell with my hair. It was six or seven hairwidths."

When the column headed "Quantification" is unmarked, it serves as an elegant reminder that a new lesson might well be oriented toward developing this skill.

Collected data: This may be in the form of tearing strips of construction paper to represent the growth lengths of seedlings, the lengths columns of dropping water reach before beading, etc. Or numerals may be used to represent different temperatures, beans to cover an area, or units of washers, the distances of certain numbers of washers from the fulcrum of a balance, or the lengths of a stretch of spring to measure the weights of objects. Quantifying data implies units of measurements, but these units need not be orthodox.

Evidence that the child has collected data in this category of quantification may come from the colloquium; it may also come from the teacher's observation of the child's activities during an investigation period. If data are being collected, this item should be marked without judging the value of the data or the way they are being used.

Examples: A child records the number of unit weights on each side of a balanced scale (with or without noting the distances from the fulcrum).

In order to compare the area of two leaves, a child covers each leaf with similar sized beans and then counts the number of beans on each leaf.

Arranged data: We try to avoid value judgments of the manner of arranging data as well. A child who pastes growth strips on a large sheet of paper in no apparent pattern is nevertheless arranging them. We have learned that he may even be able to make use of such an unorthodox arrangement. The same is true of an older child who may jot down numerals on odd scraps of paper; he, too, may find patterns from these notes. It is only when one needs to communicate one's findings that a more conventional arrangement becomes necessary or, at least, helpful.

Made use of data: If the child tries to interpolate, extrapolate, predict, generalize, discern patterns, or make models from the arranged data, these activities constitute an attempt to find meaning—to seek concepts—and therefore belongs in this category.

It is to be assumed that more use can be made of data when these are arranged in an organized manner and, therefore, the number of dots a child has under "Made use of data" might be an indication of the clarity with which his data are arranged.

Examples: A child drew the paths of several light beams going to and being reflected from a mirror. He superimposed these paths on each other so that the point of contact with the mirror coincided. (Thus far, he has *collected* and *arranged data*.) Then he said, "Look, the light can go from being nearly parallel with the mirror to being at right angles with it, and every possible angle is covered."

A class of children had graphed the relationship between the length of pendula and the number of round trips taken in a minute. (The graph is a parabola.) "I can find the number of round trips a pendulum of any length will make in a minute from this graph," said one child. (He might have added, or discovered later, that the graph did not cover all possible lengths!)

Levels of concept attainment

In this category, we record what a child is able to do rather than what he is trying to do. Concept attainment, rather than concept seeking, is the emphasis.

Vygotsky levels of thought

We have described these levels in some detail in Chapter 3, pages 150–55. Briefly, each level may be recognized as follows:

Syncretic: Placing objects or events together which are perceived together but otherwise have no intrinsic nexus.

Examples: "If I don't have my teddy bear with me when I go to bed, there's a thunderstorm."

"When I sneeze, the seltzer fizzes."

"The electricity can't get through when the wire is heavy."

Complex: Linking objects or events together through one or more common attributes.

Examples: "All the red flowers belong together."

"It was so hot that the thermometer went up." *(It has to be hotter, not just hot. And the alcohol expands; nothing goes up!)*

Preconcept: Statements which seem similar to an adult's conceptual thought, but which nevertheless have a concrete base.

Examples: "A falling ball interacts with gravity by falling faster and faster as it comes down."

"Fossils are older, the deeper down you have to dig for them." *(Not a fully correct statement because the sediments can be folded which reverses the order.)*

"A carbonate fizzes in an acid."

Concept: An abstraction related to an abstraction without reference to the concrete.

> *Examples:* "Interaction with gravity produces an accelerated motion."
>
> "Sedimentary strata hold fossils which are related to the era of sedimentation."
>
> "A carbonate interacting with an acid gives off carbon dioxide."

External likenesses

Generalized: Extending similarities to a wider domain.

> *Examples:* "You have five fingers and I have five fingers. All men have five fingers."
>
> "Many animals that spend their lives underground are blind."
>
> "Our sun has planets that revolve around it. Do other suns have planets also?"

Compared: Relating one object to another through some sense-perceived feature.

> *Examples:* "The flowerpots reminded me of the xylophone because they went from little to big."
>
> "The boy gerbil is smaller than the girl gerbil."
>
> "The higher up the mountain we go, the scrubbier the vegetation is."
>
> "Things sink faster in air than they do in water."
>
> "The moons around Mars travel at different rates."

Classified: Relating an object to a more inclusive category. Any grouping which implies a class membership or a hierarchy of groups or cognate groups. Classification is based either on sense-perceived features or on data which are elicited by

making the objects do something which is perceivable by the senses.

> *Examples:* "Metals with iron or nickel in them interact with magnets by coming together with the magnet." *(This implies that other metals do not so interact, thus classifying into two subgroups.)*
>
> "Our terrarium has plants, animals, and dirt in it."
>
> "A penguin is a bird. It's got feathers and wings but it doesn't know how to fly."
>
> "This circuit is a form of parallel wiring but that one is mixed: parallel lights and series batteries."

Hidden likenesses

Generalized: Implying an element of inference or a similarity based on investigations which go beyond direct sense perception.

> *Examples:* "Green plants produce starch through photosynthesis."
>
> "Electromagnetic waves travel with the speed of light."
>
> "Intestines change food into simpler substances."
>
> "Inland waters in hot countries with no outlet get saltier and saltier as the sun evaporates the water." *(Of course, this process occurs only up to a certain point, but this is a generalization based on hidden likeness.)*

Made an analogy: A form of comparing which we have seen even quite young children employ. It represents an attempt at elegant thinking, intellectually perceiving a likeness, making a comparison through some kind of imaginative leap. It groups two or more things or events with no tangible nexus together through a similarity which is either created by the speaker or thinker or which the speaker does not *know* is a real nexus.

Examples: "I think it [flour paste] look like what my mother make when she bake a cake."

(Holding strong alnico magnets apart.) "Gee, I can feel it; it's like the wind."

"The flowerpots are like people." [Big people and big pots make deep sounds.]

Suggested a model: In Chapter 2 (page 122), we saw that a model is an elegantly constructed explanation of some natural phenomenon, that it goes beyond the facts and provides a new way of looking at observed relationships. A model is always a mental image which helps to explain rather than reflect reality. Scientists' descriptions of the structure of an atom or a galaxy reflect the models in their minds. A model usually encompasses many relationships; its function is to open the way for a number of hypotheses, inferences, and predictions connected with the observed phenomena.

Children who are sciencing construct models, but naturally these are less grandiose than those of a scientist. Whenever a child offers an explanation of phenomena which goes beyond the facts and has an element of construct or which shows an imaginative leap, we consider it a model.

Examples: "There must be tiny bits of onion coming to my nose [for me to smell the onion]."

"The electrical energy gets used up as it goes through each light—at least partly."

"Since 20 ml of alcohol and 20 ml of water do not add up to 40 ml of mixture, the alcohol must slip in between the water drops."

"There's some kind of power going between the ends of my magnet [or, in more general terms, between the ends of all magnets]."

"Things float better in salt water because it's heavier [than plain water]."

Each of these statements contains a nonobservable construct, an imaginative leap which offers an explanation of an observed phenomenon: particles coming off an onion and moving away, lights using up energy, spaces between drops of an apparently continuous liquid, a power in the space between magnet poles, heavier water related to flotation. Each statement is general enough to suggest many more specific statements which could take the forms of hypotheses, inferences, or predictions.

Hypothesized: A statement in a form which implies a test; often a tentative answer to "Why?" sometimes phrased in the illative (If . . . then . . . .) form. A hypothesis is perhaps the least certain outcome of a model.

Examples: "A large battery is stronger than a small battery."

"I think if you cut the rod into two pieces it will still be magnets."

Suggested a test or investigation: Children offer a variety of ways to test their statements, often without careful controls. Learning to set up a valid experiment is one of the aims of science. However, we count as *testing* any suggestion for trying out the validity of statements which can be classified as *hypothesis, inference,* or *prediction.*

Example: A second grader discovers that the way to make a paper cup telephone work is to have the string taut. He *hypothesized* that: "This is because the sound goes through stiff things better than through soft things." He suggested a test: "Join the cups to the ends of a yardstick and compare the sound with the string telephone—which is softer."

Inferred: An inference, like a model, attempts to explain phenomena, but addresses itself to a subset of the relationships which a model explains. A model remains a mental construct and cannot, itself, be subjected to a test, but an inference can be established as right or wrong. Inferences often masquerade as facts (especially in social conversations!), but they always contain an element beyond sense perception. A statement which is an inference often contains the words *must* or *because*. However, not all statements with these words are inferences. Inferring is a more certain activity than hypothesizing.

Examples: One can hear a symphony played over the radio and infer, if musically educated, that a certain conductor must be holding the baton. By waiting for the announced credits or checking with the newspaper, this inference can be tested.

> *(Seeing that sugar is needed for yeast to multiply.)* "Sugar gets into the yeast and it gets bigger." [This could be stated, "Because sugar gets into the yeast, it gets bigger."]

> "Something must have been burned in this bottle and not in the other."

> "The bell didn't ring because there was no air left."

Predicted: Expressing the belief that the world is not capricious, that it contains discernible patterns or uniformities; forecasting that something will happen given certain conditions. In this sense, a prediction, like a hypothesis, can be phrased with the illative (If . . . then . . . .). In these circumstances, the two may not be distinguishable, but sometimes a prediction follows from a hypothesis. A prediction is likely to have a high percentage of probability.

Examples: From the hypothesis that a large battery is stronger than a small one, a child predicts that, in two comparable circuits, the one with the large battery will give the brighter light. (Of course, it does not! Another hypothesis is in order, such as: a large battery lasts longer than a smaller battery.)

Data arranged on a graph encourage prediction through extension or interpolation: "The bean will be so high next week."

"If I put enough marbles in this paper cup, it will sink even in salt water."

Again, we would like to emphasize that the preceding categories are not watertight compartments, nor need they be. A teacher using them to evaluate the growth of his pupils will be likely to make the same judgment in borderline cases each time and so measure of growth will be consistent. Key words to look for, such as *must, like, because, will*, do occur in statements which are models, as well as in the subcategories of hypothesis, inference, and prediction or in analogy. A model is generally distinguishable from subsets by its larger inclusiveness, by the fact that it cannot be directly tested, and by the opportunities it offers for a variety of outcomes in the form of hypothesis, inference, and/or prediction. An example may help to clarify these distinctions:

Model: "There must be tiny bits of onion coming to my nose."

Hypothesis A: "If particles of onion come off it and reach my nose, then the person nearest the onion will smell it before one who is further away."

Test for A: Place people at different distances from an onion without revealing that an onion is near and note the order in which people say they smell an onion.

Inference: "The particles must have some kind of motion to travel from the onion to my nose."

Hypothesis B: "The motion is natural, residing in the nature of the particles [like the molecules of an onion]."

Test for B: The practical details of a test for this hypothesis might be difficult, but it is still possible to work out the principle. This would entail conducting the particles through a duct into a vessel where the odor could be detected and from there into an adjoining vessel.

Hypothesis C: "The motion is faster in warm air than in cold air."

Test for C: Repeat test for *A* in a cold room and in a hot room.

Predictions: The onion will eventually lose its smell when all the particles have gone.

The people nearer the onion will detect the odor before those further away do.

The people in the hot room will smell the onion before those in the cold room do.

Attitude scales

Although attitudes often seem to be geared to a child's personality, an interesting fact is that they can change. They can change from lesson to lesson or even within a lesson. They can change according to various circumstances—atmospheres for learning, if you will. Hence there may be marks at more than one position on our scales. Over the semester, there may be changes which show a trend, a vectorial growth. Or a child may display one pattern with one attitude or set of attitudes in one set of circumstances and another pattern in another set. It is important to find out what these sets are and then to provide the circumstances which will foster their greatest growth. Growth is behavior which gives the child more personal serenity or happier relationships with others.

Relations of child to others

The scale in this category runs from independence or isolation through cooperation to domination. We do not intend to make a value judgment or to change what a child does unless his type of relationships produces some unhappiness or hurt to him or to others. The important aspect of this scale is that it establishes patterns related to a child's way of learning. It may suggest that we look further, relate the scale findings to some other data, and then formulate a model or a hypothesis about the child's behavior.

The scale to record a child's work relationship with others selects the following behaviors:
1. Operates alone or independently.

2. Follows another's lead.
3. Works cooperatively.
4. Suggests activities which others follow.
5. Dominates or tells others what to do.

Examples: We once tried letting children take tests cooperatively in small groups to help them overcome the tense "testitis" which inhibited their thinking. Most of the children improved markedly the next time they took a test individually; the experience of cooperative success did something for their ability to cope. But Dwayne, who always worked alone (1), did worse on the individual test after his cooperative experience. Evidently, something in an interaction with his peers disturbed Dwayne's thinking. He had had no friends in the class and the group experience did not give him any.

Lee always let others lead her (2), but how did she decide which other child to follow? Is there a group dynamics in which Lee is either afraid or dependent? Would another combination give Lee a chance to experience taking the lead? It's worth a try!

Relations of child to materials

We have found that some children tend to move along this scale; if they begin by being unfamiliar with the experience of self-motivated discovery, they may sit and wait or ask permission to start. After a while, they become heady about initiating explorations and often begin to think up new operations and then to demand more materials. However, some begin by needing more of everything and others remain rigidly at the level of average expectancy. A few might strike an observer as "trouble makers," but the interesting thing about many of these children is that they often actively seek to use the materials with considerable originality. Sometimes such children are not really exploring; they may be feeling dissatisfied with what the teacher gave or they may not be able to share the items which the teacher thought were sufficient for the group. Or these children may be beyond the others in knowledge and investigating experience; they may really need to go beyond the set limits. Again, there can be interpretation of the position of the marks on the scale. A teacher usually learns the learning styles of the children in his class, but to watch change in patterns and growth may require some objective criteria such as the changing position of the marks on the scales. Otherwise, prejudging might obliterate perception of progress.

The scale to record a child's work relationship materials selects the following behaviors:

1. Hesitates to use materials.
2. Explores materials in a limited manner.
3. Does what is expected.
4. Finds original ways to elicit interactions.
5. Seeks materials not present.

Example: A classroom teacher warned the visiting science specialist that Barry always took things from the other children. The implication was that perhaps the science teacher should keep track of the materials he brought! During the first science session when the children were asked to share magnifying glasses, Barry was in constant fights about possession of the lenses. Next time, the science specialist provided exactly one flashlight per child for each of the children at Barry's table. Barry no longer took nor grabbed. His reason for not being able to share was related, probably, less to his science learnings than to some of his personal life experiences. Thus, learning styles can be changed by interaction with a new environment. Barry moved along the scale from (2) to (3).

Work pattern drive

Of course we all like children who concentrate for long periods of time. Or do we? If we have to change activities, clear up for lunch, or get ready to go home, the child who will not relinquish his work may be considered disobedient. It might be fairer to judge him as the concentrated, oblivious, scientific type who will forget to eat lunch or to tell his wife when he cannot be home for supper! "Disobedient" and "scientific type" are both value judgments, however; perhaps we should arrange that such children begin their science investigations earlier in the day so their projects will have more time to unfold. Maybe on another day, they will work equally long in another area. A good argument for the free-choice classroom!

The scale to record a child's work pattern drive selects the following behaviors:

1. Finishes soon or fails to start.
2. Alternates work with materials with other activities.
3. Maintains a steady pace.
4. Uses materials with concentration and eagerness.
5. Suggests activities for the next lesson.

Charting concept seeking and concept attainment

We will now apply our rating scales to the two colloquia quoted in Chapter 2, *Sound Statements by Seven Year Olds* (pages 109–15). Beside each child's statement, we will write in code the categories which seem scorable and also explain those which might appear controversial or difficult to place. We will then transfer all the scores to a composite chart from which we can attempt a pattern analysis. We reiterate that no teacher can do all this unless he has a complete colloquium recorded at the time, as well as the leisure to analyze it later. However, a teacher could record a few items or the acts of a few children in any one lesson. Over the weeks, a chart similar to the ones on pages 356–58 could be expected to develop.

Code for marginal notes:

Concept-seeking skills

Communicating
ob:	Observation stated
cl:	Stated clearly
ac:	Accurately perceived
re:	Relevant to the concept
int:	Interaction described operationally
voc:	New vocabulary used
res:	Responded to another child's remark

Thinking
d.e.:	Noticed discrepant event
th:	Said "I think" or "Is it right?"
?:	Asked a when, why, how, or where question
cha:	Changed statement in light of new data
chl:	Challenged a statement
rea:	Gave reasons for challenge

Quantifying
col:	Collected data
ar:	Arranged data
use:	Made use of data

Levels of concept attainment

Finding external likenesses
gen ex:	Generalized
com:	Compared
clas:	Classified

Finding hidden likenesses
(gen hid):	Generalized
(ana):	Made an analogy
(mod)	Suggested a model
(hyp):	Hypothesized
(tes):	Suggested a test or investigation
(inf):	Inferred
(pre):	Predicted

To differentiate optically between external and hidden likenesses in scoring levels of concept attainment in the following colloquia, external likenesses will be underscored and hidden likenesses will appear in parentheses, except for (mod) which will be circled to indicate an attempt at high-level explanation.

Each child's remarks in each of the following colloquia are numbered sequentially to aid in subsequent charting of the data.

The first colloquium on sound (Chapter 2, pages 111-13)

	CONCEPT SEEKING	CONCEPT ATTAIN- MENT
Mrs. S.: Who would like to tell us what he has discovered after working with the objects?		
1. *Don:* The things made different noises.	ob, ac, re,	
1. *Daisy:* Some noises were nice and some weren't.	ob, res	
Mrs. S.: Could you explain that a little better?		
2. *Daisy:* The xylophone was pretty to hear, but the bottles just made sound. [This doesn't add much. She is still on the subjective level. A comparison is beginning (pretty vs. sound), but it is not sense-oriented.]	ob, cl	
1. *Chris:* The flowerpots were fun. They were kind of like xylophones.	ob, cl, re, res	com
3. *Daisy:* They didn't sound like the xylophone; the xylophone makes music. [This is now a comparison: Pots "made sound"; "xylophone makes music."]	ob, cl, re, res, chl, rea	com
2. *Chris:* The flowerpots reminded me of the xylophone 'cause they went from little to big, just like the bars on the xylophone.	ob, cl, ac, re, res	com
1. *Sophie:* The pots look like the musical bells my little sister has at home.	ob, ci, ac, re, res	com
1. *Albee:* I hit the flowerpots with the stick and some of them sounded nice. [Relevant because impact elicits sound.]	ob, cl, ac, re, int, res	
1. *Matthew:* But they didn't sound the same. The little ones sounded sweet and the bigger ones sounded . . . deeper.	ob, cl, ac, re, res	com
1. *Ellen:* You could hear the deep sound better on the drum. That's why they use them in the band. The little drum sounded prettier.	ob, cl, ac, re, res	
Mrs. S.: When you tapped the flowerpots and the bars on the xylophone, did you hear anything different?		
1. *Patricia:* Some sounded high and some sounded low.	ob, cl, ac, re	com
1. *Marguerita:* We have a piano and the same thing happens.	ob, cl, ac, re, res	com
Mrs. S.: Could you explain that a little better?		
2. *Marguerita:* On one end of the piano the sound is high, and the other end the music is low.	ob, cl, ac, re	com
4. *Daisy:* I heard that on the xylophone, too.	ob, cl, ac, re, res	com
2. *Albee:* The pots sounded high and low, too, on different ends.	ob, cl, ac, re, res	com
1. *Renée:* I heard different noises, but I couldn't tell they were high or low.	ob, re, res	
3. *Marguerita:* See, the little pots make high sounds and the big pots make low sounds.	ob, cl, ac, re, res	com
Mrs. S.: Did anyone hear high and low sounds on anything else?		
1. *Rose:* The two bells made different sounds.	ob, cl, re	
1. *Virian:* The big bell sounded high and the little bell sounded low.	ob, cl, re, res	com
1. *Sarah:* No, that's not right. You got mixed up. The big bell sounded low and the little bell sounded high.	ob, cl, ac, re, res, chl, rea	com
1. *Phil:* The jars did that, too.	ob, cl, ac, re, res	com
2. *Matthew:* These things are like people. Big people voices sound lower than little children voices.	ob, cl, re, res	(gen hid), (ana)
Mrs. S.: Can anyone put what we have said into a good sentence so that our recorder can write it on the board?		
2. *Phil:* Big things make low sounds and little things make higher sounds. Is that right?	ob, cl, re, th	gen ex, com

CONCEPT SEEKING	CONCEPT ATTAINMENT
ob, cl, re	(mod)
ob, cl, ac, re, res, chl, rea	
ob, re	
ob, cl, ac, re, res	com
ob, cl, re, res	com
ob, cl, ac, re	com
ob, cl, ac, re, res	com
ob, re, res	
ob, cl, ac, re	com, gen ex
ob, cl, ac, res	
ob, cl, ac, re, res	com
ob, cl, ac, re	
ob, ac, re	
ob, cl, re, res, th	com, gen ex
ob, cl, ac, re	com
ob, re	
ob, cl, re, res	(hyp)
ob, cl, re, res	(hyp), com
ob, cl, re	gen ex

Mrs. S.: Does anyone have an idea why this happens?

3. *Matthew:* Could it be 'cause bigger things have more space to make more noise? Like the big flowerpot has more air inside, so the sound has to go through more air? [ac is omitted because the remark does not deal with perception. As far as Matthew is concerned, this is a leap beyond the facts that he knows; it is a mental construct.]

3. *Chris:* The xylophone doesn't have any air in the bars. I don't think that's the reason.

Mrs. S.: Maybe the rubber bands could help us. No one has mentioned them yet.

1. *Rod:* I didn't hear any difference and they didn't even sound nice.

1. *Rita:* Some of the rubber bands were thin and some were thick.

1. *Zina:* Oh, they were supposed to be like the xylophone!

Mrs. S.: What do you mean?

2. *Zina:* They were put on in a special way. The skinny one was first, then fatter and fatter.

4. *Chris:* Yeah, they went from skinny to fat, like the pots from little to big.

1. *Gray:* And they made different sounds.

Mrs. S.: Could you describe the difference in sounds?

2. *Gray:* The skinny one was high and the fat one was low, just like we said about the other things.

1. *Perry:* Gray took out the pencil and then the rubber band just snapped.

3. *Gray:* I put it back and when I put the pencil under the different parts we heard different sounds. The shorter the rubber band got, the higher the sound got.

Mrs. S.: Did anyone notice how the rubber band moved?

2. *Perry:* The thin rubber band moved a lot.

Mrs. S.: And what did that sound like?

3. *Perry:* High.

5. *Daisy (Responding to a previous remark by Perry):* The big things don't move as much as the little things when you tap them. Is that right?

Mrs. S.: Why don't we try?

6. *Daisy (Tapping the drums):* The top of the little drum looks like it moves more than the big one.

2. *Sophie:* I can't see them move at all.

4. *Marguerita:* Let's see the little bar on the xylophone. You can't see it move so good. But I know little things move fast 'cause they have less to move.

4. *Gray:* The top of the drum has to move more 'cause it's so big, and it makes a deep sound. Like a big drum in a parade. That really makes a deep sound.

Mrs. S.: Who can say that very clearly for us? Remember what moving has to do with it.

4. *Matthew:* Things that have to move a lot make low sounds.

2. *Ellen:* And things that don't have to move so much make high sounds.
5. *Marguerita:* On my piano all the keys are the same, so I don't understand why some are high and some are low.
4. *Perry:* The piano has wires inside it. Some must be long and some must be short. The short move faster than the long ones. Isn't that right?

	CONCEPT SEEKING	CONCEPT ATTAINMENT
	ob, cl, re, res	<u>gen ex</u>
	ob, cl, ac, re,	
	res, ?	
	ob, cl, ac, re,	(inf)
	res, th	(inf)

Analysis of the first colloquium on sound

From the dots on the concept-seeking chart for this colloquium (page 356), we notice at once that five children did not speak at all: Frank, Hannah, Lionel, Simone, and Ulrick. Our records are deficient in that we do not know whether these children were present or absent. Next we notice the children who have the largest cluster of dots, those who spoke the most: Chris, Daisy, Gray, Marguerita, Matthew, and Perry.

Most of the contributions in this colloquium were in the communicating skills; a scattering of remarks were scored under thinking. Lessons tend to elicit certain types of skills; this may sometimes be because one child starts off on a certain track and the others follow, but there is reason to think that the materials themselves tend to lead thinking into certain channels. For instance, this lesson on sound had nothing in it to encourage measurement and, indeed, no remark is scored under the quantifying skills. This very fact might suggest to the teacher that a subsequent lesson be arranged to encourage just this activity. No new vocabulary was introduced, and only one child described what he saw in terms of interaction. At this particular time, this particular teacher had not been introduced to the "interaction among objects in a system" way of viewing phenomena; it is not surprising that the children do not think this way either.

A few finer points may be noticed. One is the children whose remarks were never in response to another child: Don, Patricia, and Rose. They must therefore have spoken only after the teacher asked a question. Half of the remarks by Daisy, Matthew, and Perry were in response to teacher questioning and half were in response to other children.

From the concept attainment chart for this collo- quium (pages 357–58), we see that most of the concepts elicited by the materials fell in the category of "comparing." The structure of the materials did indicate little to big, high to low, or various object sequences. A few children offered generalizations; one child, Matthew, offered an analogy and a model; Perry made two inferences. The level of conceptual thought is solidly complex here in the Vygotsky sense, and this is not surprising for seven year olds. Matthew made one excursion into the preconcept. Throughout the scoring, Matthew was a lively, contributing, rather advanced thinker.

It is interesting that, although we, as readers of a colloquium, have never seen these children in action, we can begin to build, from the scoring and analysis, a fairly precise picture of the emphases and deficiencies of the lesson and see several of the children's thinking patterns begin to emerge.

You might like to forecast for one or two children what is likely to develop from the next lesson in which the materials were jars with bells and little air, rubber tubes, and string and cup telephones. Which children might be the likely to challenge statements? Who might offer hypotheses? Will there be a greater number of contributions to the analogy column? Will more children infer or predict? If so, which children are the most likely candidates? On the basis of the evidence gathered thus far we cannot be sure, but it is sometimes interesting to make a model of the thought functioning of children and then to formulate hypotheses on what each one might achieve.

The second colloquium on sound (Chapter 2, pages 113–15)

We now repeat the record of the second collo- quium on sound, leaving the margin empty so that

CONCEPT-SEEKING SKILLS

		Communicating							Thinking					Quantifying		
Observations	Stated clearly	Accurately perceived	Relevant to the concept	Interaction described operationally	New vocabulary used	Responded to another child's remark	Child's Name	Noticed discrepant event	Said "I think" or "Is is right?"	Asked a when, why, how, or where question	Changed statement in light of new data	Challenged a statement	Gave reason for challenge	Collected data	Arranged data	Made use of data
●●○○	●●○○	●●○○	●●○○	●○○○		●●○○	Albee									
●●●●	●●●●	○●●●	●●●●			●●●●	Chris					○○●○	○○●○			
●●●●/●●●●	○●●●/●●●○	○○○●/○●○○	○●○●/●●○○			●○●●/●○○○	Daisy		●○○○			○○●○	○○●○			
●○○○		●○○○	●○○○				Don									
●●○○	●●○○	●○○○	●●○○			●●○○	Ellen									
							Frank									
●●●●	○●●●	○●●○	●●●●			●○●●	Gray									
							Hannah									
							Lionel									
●●●●/●○○○	●●●●/●○○○	●●●○/●○○○	●●●●/●○○○			●○●●/●○○○	Marguerita			○○○○/●○○○						
●●●●	●●●●	●○○○	●●●			●●○○	Matthew									
●●○○	●●○○	●●○○	●○○○				Patricia									
●●●●	●●○●	●●●●	○●●●			●○○●	Perry		○○○●							
●●○○	●●○○	●○○○	●●○○			●○○○	Phil		○●○○							
●○○○		●○○○				●○○○	Renée									
●○○○	●○○○	●○○○	●○○○			●○○○	Rita									
●○○○		●○○○					Rod									
●○○○	●○○○		●○○○				Rose									
●○○○	●○○○	●○○○	●○○○			●○○○	Sarah					●○○○	●○○○			
							Simone									
●●○○	●○○○	●○○○	●●○○			●○○○	Sophie	○●○○								
							Ulrick									
●○○○	●○○○		●○○○			●○○○	Virian									
●●○○	●●○○	○●○○	●●○○			●○○○	Zina									

Legend for Concept-Seeking Skills Charts (here and on page 364):

● = child contributed

○ = child did not contribute

Placement of dots in each cell corresponds with the order in which the child made the particular remark. For example, Gray's first and fourth remarks here were not scored "accurately perceived," but both his second and third remarks were. Therefore, Gray's "ac" cell looks like this: ○●●○ .

Each cell can contain up to eight possible entries (two rows of four entries apiece). However, to avoid unnecessary marking, since most of the children charted here (like Gray above) spoke four or less times, the entire eight entries will be marked only if a child spoke more than four times. Daisy, for example, made six observations in a row. Her "ob" cell is therefore: ●●●●/●●○○ .

Only four entries will be made in most of the cells (again, see Gray's above). In these cases, the second row of four entries is understood to be blank. Of course, if a cell is completely blank, none of the child's remarks (if, indeed, he made any) could be classified in that particular category.

LEVELS OF CONCEPT ATTAINMENT

Date of lesson: Lesson topic: Sound (first)

Child's Name	Statements Revealing Concept Development	Vygotsky Level	Finding External Likenesses			Finding Hidden Likenesses						
			Generalized	Compared	Classified	Generalized	Made an analogy	Suggested a model	Hypothesized	Suggested a test or investigation	Inferred	Predicted
Albee	The pots sounded high and low, too, on different ends.	complex		•								
Chris	The flowerpots were fun. They were kind of like xylophones.	complex		•								
	The flowerpots remind me of the xylophone 'cause they went from little to big, just like the bars on the xylophone.	complex		•								
	Yeah, they went from skinny to fat, like the pots from little to big.	complex		•								
Daisy	They didn't sound like the xylophones; the xylophones make music.	complex		•								
	I heard that on the xylophone, too [high and low sounds].	complex	•	•								
	The big things don't move as much as the little things. . .	complex		•								
	The top of the little drum looks like it moves more than the big one.	complex		•								
Don												
Ellen	And things that don't have to move so much make high sounds.	complex	•									
Frank												
Gray	The skinny one was high and the fat one low, just like we said about the other things.	complex	•	•								
	The shorter the rubber band got, the higher the sound got.	complex		•								
	The top of the drum has to move more 'cause it's so big, and it makes a deep sound. Like the big drum in the parade.	complex		•								
Hannah												
Lionel												
Marguerita	We have a piano and the same thing happens [high and low sounds].	complex		•								
	On one end of the piano the sound is high; on the other end the music is low.	complex		•								
	See, the little pots make high sounds and the big pots make low sounds.	complex		•								

LEVELS OF CONCEPT ATTAINMENT

Date of lesson: Lesson topic: Sound (first)

Child's Name	Statements Revealing Concept Development	Vygotsky Level	Finding External Likenesses			Finding Hidden Likenesses						
			Generalized	Compared	Classified	Generalized	Made an analogy	Suggested a model	Hypothesized	Suggested a test or investigation	Inferred	Predicted
Matthew	The little ones sounded sweet and the bigger ones sounded like . . . deeper.	complex		●								
	These things are like people. Big people voices sound lower than little children voices.	complex										
	Bigger things have more space to make more noise? Like the flowerpot has more air inside so the sound goes through more air.	preconcept										
	Things that have to move a lot make low sounds.	complex	●									
Patricia	Some sounded high and some sounded low.	complex		●								
Perry	Some [piano wires] must be long and some must be short. The short move faster than the long ones.	complex									● ●	
Phil	The jars did that, too [big ones sounded high; little ones low].	complex		●								
	Big things make low sounds and little things make higher sounds.	complex	●	●								
Renée												
Rita	Some of the rubber bands were thin and some were thick.	complex		●								
Rod												
Rose												
Sarah	(To Virian) No, that's not right. . . . The big bell sounded low and the little bell sounded high.	complex		●								
Simone												
Sophie	The pots look like the musical bells my little sister has at home.	complex		●								
Ulrick												
Virian	The big bell sounded high and the little bell sounded low.	complex		●								
Zina	Oh, they're supposed to be like the xylophone!	complex		●								
	They were put on in a special way. The skinny one was first, then fatter and fatter.	complex		●								

you may try your hand at the scoring. We offer an alternative arrangement for marking the scores: headed columns under *Communicating* (Concept-Seeking Skills) instead of providing lines for code initials. A dot in the appropriate column indicates that the child's statement represents that particular item. This method facilitates the transference of the scores to the summative chart (page 364). To save space, we have left the columns under *Thinking* (Concept-Seeking Skills) and Concept Attainment blank; here the code initials may be written as they occur. As you saw in our scoring of the first colloquium on sound (pages 353–55), we found it useful when checking the summative chart or when following the statements of any one child to indicate the numerical order of each child's remarks. Hence, the numerals 1., 2., 3., etc. by each child's name record the child's first, second, third, etc. contribution to the colloquium. The key to our scores, should you wish to check them against your own, can be found on pages 377–79. In borderline cases, your consistency is more important.

	CONCEPT SEEKING							CONCEPT ATTAINMENT
Thinking	Communicating							
	ob	cl	ac	re	int	voc	res	

Mrs. S.: Now that you have handled the equipment for a while, who can tell us something he has discovered?

1. *Perry:* The two milk bottles are the same.
1. *Phil:* Yeah, they look alike to me.
1. *Matthew:* They both have corks in them.
1. *Ellen:* They both had bells in them, too.
   Mrs. S.: Then do we all agree that the bottles are exactly the same?
1. *Rod:* Well, I'm not sure. They look the same, but they didn't do the same things.
1. *Sophie:* Mine didn't do the same thing either. 'Cause when I shook one bottle I heard the bell ring, but the bell in the other bottle didn't ring.
2. *Rod:* Yeah, that's what I mean. One bell rang. The other bell you couldn't hear.
1. *Hannah:* Maybe the bell is broken.
2. *Sophie:* No, I looked. I held the bottle up and looked under. I could see the nail in the bell go to the side, but I couldn't hear it.
   Mrs. S.: Sophie would you demonstrate for us? *(Sophie does.)*
3. *Sophie:* See, you don't hear it.
   Mrs. S.: Does anyone have an idea why this bell won't work?
1. *Gray:* I tried both bottles and I could hear the bells. One was very quiet, though.
1. *Daisy:* No. I couldn't hear the bell in one of the bottles when I tried. But I saw black burned stuff in one of the bottles—ashes.
3. *Rod:* I didn't see that.

Charting concept seeking and concept attainment   359

CONCEPT SEEKING								CONCEPT ATTAINMENT
Thinking	Communicating							
	ob	cl	ac	re	int	voc	res	

2. *Hannah:* Sure, look! There's black stuff in the bottle we had, too.

1. *Chris:* Mrs. Schur, is that why we can't hear the bell?

   Mrs. S.: Maybe someone can help us find out.

2. *Ellen:* Which bottle had the black stuff in it?

2. *Perry:* That's a good idea. Can I try the bottles? [Yes.] The bell in the bottle without the ashes rings. The other with the ashes do not ring.

1. *Sarah:* I'll try my bottles. Yeah, the same thing happens.

1. *Ulrick:* I don't see what that means. The ashes aren't stopping the bell.

   Mrs. S.: Are you sure they are ashes?

1. *Renée:* They look like ashes. I could even see a piece of a match.

2. *Chris:* Something must have been burned in this bottle and not in the other.

   Mrs. S.: Why do you think something was burned in this bottle?

1. *Don:* To put ashes in the bottle.

   Mrs. S.: Who remembers what happened to the candle when we put the top of the pumpkin back on?

2. *Daisy:* The candle went out.

3. *Chris:* Yes, because there was no air left to let it burn.

3. *Ellen:* The candle went out, too, when we put the glass over it.

   Mrs. S.: Can anyone tell us how these experiences can help us now?

2. *Matthew:* The burning stuff used up the air. There's no air in the bottle. That's why the cork is in so tight—to keep the air out. [We recall that this is incorrect reasoning.]

3. *Perry:* There's a cork in both bottles, so there's no air in both of them.

3. *Matthew:* But there's only ashes in one bottle, and that's the bell that doesn't ring.

3. *Daisy:* The bell won't ring 'cause there's no air. The fire used up the air and now you can't hear the bell.

	CONCEPT SEEKING							CONCEPT ATTAINMENT
Thinking	Communicating							
	ob	cl	ac	re	int	voc	res	

Mrs. S.: How could you prove what Daisy says is true?

1. *Marguerita:* We could pull out the cork and let the air in. Then we could burn something and put the cork in.

   Mrs. S.: All right, let's do this. *(She uncorks and recorks the bottle.)*

1. *Zina:* Now you can hear the bell.

   Mrs. S.: I'll put some papers in the bottle and light them. Now I'll replace the cork.

2. *Sarah:* I hear the bell just a little now.

2. *Gray:* Yeah. You need air to hear the bell good. If there's no air, you can't hear. Right?

   Mrs. S.: What did you learn about the other materials?

1. *Rose:* I talked to Rita with the telephone.

1. *Frank:* It looks like a telephone. If you talk in one cup, you can hear in the other. I got one of those at home.

1. *Rita:* I even went in the closet and I could hear Rose.

2. *Phil:* My real telephone doesn't have cups and strings. But it's got a ear place and a mouth place.

1. *Albee:* It's got wire, not string.

4. *Matthew:* This is like a telephone. The string is like the wire. It's not as good as a telephone.

   Mrs. S.: You must have to yell very loud to hear with this telephone.

3. *Phil:* No, you could talk very quiet and still hear.

4. *Chris:* If the string's not pulled good you can't hear.

4. *Daisy:* That's what happened to us. Hannah wasn't pulling the string and I couldn't hear what she said.

   Mrs. S.: Are you saying that tightening and loosening the string makes a difference?

5. *Matthew:* It must. They couldn't hear when the string was loose.

2. *Rita:* I felt something funny in my ear when Rose talked.

   Mrs. S.: What do you mean, something funny?

3. *Rita:* It felt like a buzz.

CONCEPT SEEKING								CONCEPT ATTAINMENT
Thinking	Communicating							
	ob	cl	ac	re	int	voc	res	

2. *Ulrick:* I didn't feel that.

4. *Rita:* I'll try it with you. *(She does.)* Do you feel it?

3. *Ulrick:* Yeah. It's like . . . I don't know.

   Mrs. S.: That's called vibration. That's how we hear sounds, by vibrations. Perhaps we could do some experiments next time with sound vibrations.

4. *Rod:* I didn't talk with the telephone, but I talked with Lionel through the hose. That worked swell.

1. *Lionel:* I heard it from over there (*indicating opposite corner*).

1. *Simone:* I could hear through it, too, when Sophie talked to me.

4. *Sophie:* But Gray kept stepping on it on purpose.

2. *Simone:* Then I couldn't hear what she said.

   Mrs. S.: Why not?

3. *Simone:* It stopped her voice from getting out.

6. *Matthew:* I know! It's like the bottle with no air. He stopped the air in the hose, and you can't hear without air.

4. *Ulrick:* There's no air in the string and you could hear through it.

7. *Matthew:* There's air in the string and all around it.

   Mrs. S.: Of all the materials we worked with today, which do you think helped sound become loudest?

3. *Gray:* Not the bottle. You could hear, but not good.

5. *Chris:* The string worked pretty good, but the hose was best.

4. *Perry:* I think so, too.

   Mrs. S.: Why do you think that is true?

5. *Perry:* I don't know.

2. *Frank:* 'Cause everything you say goes right in the hose and out the other side. It don't get mixed up in the air outside.

2. *Don:* I saw a picture about a boat, and the captain whistled in the hose to call somebody in the bottom of the boat.

Analysis of the second colloquium on sound and comparison with the first

A quick survey of the general appearance of both the concept-seeking and concept attainment charts (see pages 364 and 365-66) shows that there were more contributions (more dots) during the second colloquium. Of the children who spoke most during the first colloquium, Marguerita now spoke a fewer number of times. However, all of the noncontributors to the first colloquium spoke in the second. Neither Patricia nor Virian scored on either the concept-seeking or concept attainment charts for the second colloquium; it is possible that they were absent.

Rod is still speaking mostly in reply to the teacher, rather than interacting with the contributions of his peers. He, Sophie, and Ulrick join the children who have made four or more contributions.

It is interesting that there is an increase in the number of dots in the "Interaction" column of the second concept-seeking chart. This type of thinking may have been fostered by new materials or it may represent just the indigenous growth on the part of the children concerned.

No new vocabulary was picked up; we saw before that the word *vibration* seemed inappropriate to the main trend of the children's interest. There are still no quantifying data.

The level of concept attainment shows an increase in model making and an accompanying sortie beyond the complex level toward the preconceptual. This judgment is made because a model, even on the child's level, must include a jump beyond the facts, inventing the possible action of a nonperceptual entity, hence an abstraction. In the cases seen during this second colloquium, the children posit a role for the air which cannot be perceived; the role of the air is an abstraction, a jump beyond the facts, a part of the construct which helps explain the phenomena. In this way we see that the construction of a model implies a step toward preconceptual thought.

Comparing is still the most frequently marked concept level category in the second colloquium. Indeed, the materials were expected to induce this. A number of hypotheses were suggested this time, as well as ways to test them. However, only Matthew suggested a test for his own hypothesis. Three discrepant events were noticed by the children.

All in all, there is growth of individual as well as overall thinking. This is typical of the progress expected as units grow from experience to experience, as thinking and speaking together mature.

Application of attitude scales

We have no data on individual manipulation of materials for the investigations on sound. We do have, however, one anecdotal record of Carl as he worked with the electrical circuits (recorded by Miss Provost, page 52). We will select the statements appropriate to each scale. The first of these is:

Relations of Child to Others

Operates alone or independently

Follows another's lead

✗ Works cooperatively

✗ Suggests activities which others follow

Dominates or tells other what to do

The statements which might fall in the above categories are:

"Do it again," urges Carl. "Here, you don't need no two wires on de top; one's gotta be on de bottom."

"But I didn't have any on the bottom and I saw a light."

Carl drops his equipment, replaces Monte's wires, one on top and one on the bottom of the battery and holds one wire end to the screw on the bulb. Now both hands and most of his fingers are in use.

"Try de udder end somewhere," he tells Monte. Monte probes with the wire and suddenly there's a glitter.

CONCEPT-SEEKING SKILLS

Lesson topic: Sound (second)

Date of lesson: _____

Communicating							Child's Name	Thinking						Quantifying		
Observations	Stated clearly	Accurately perceived	Relevant to the concept	Interaction described operationally	New vocabulary used	Responded to another child's remark		Noticed discrepant event	Said "I think" or "Is is right?"	Asked a when, why, how, or where question	Changed statement in light of new data	Challenged a statement	Gave reason for challenge	Collected data	Arranged data	Made use of data
●○○○	●○○○	●○○○	●○○○			●○○○	Albee									
●●●● ●○○○	○●●●	○●○●	●●●● ●○○○	○●○●		●●●● ●○○○	Chris		●○○○	●○○○						
●●●●	●●●●	●●○●	●●●●	○○○●		●○●●	Daisy									
●●○○	●●○○	○●○○	●●○○			○●○○	Don									
●●●○	●●●○	●○●○	●●●○			●○●○	Ellen									
●●○○	●●○○	●○○○	●●○○	●○○○		●●○○	Frank									
●●●○	●●●○	●●○○	●●●○			○●○○	Gray		○●○○							
●●○○	●●○○	○●○○	●●○○			●●○○	Hannah									
●○○○	●○○○	●○○○	●○○○			●○○○	Lionel									
●○○○	●○○○			○○○●	●○○○		Marguerita									
●●●● ●●●○	●●●● ●●●○	●●●● ●○○○	●●●● ●●○○			●○●● ○●●○	Matthew	○○●○				○○○○ ○○●○	○○○○ ○○●●			
							Patricia									
●●●● ●○○○	●●●○	○●○●	●●●●	○●○○		●○○●	Perry					○○●○	○○●○			
●●●○	○●●○	○●●○	●●●○			●●○○	Phil									
●○○○	●○○○	●○○○	●○○○				Renée									
●●●●	●○●○	●○●○	●●●●			●●○●	Rita									
●●●●	○●●●	●●○●	●●●●	●○○○		○●●○	Rod	●○○○	●○○○							
●○○○	●○○○		●○○○				Rose									
●●○○	○●○○	●●○○	●●○○			●○○○	Sarah									
●●●○	●●●○	●●●○	●●○○			●●○○	Simone									
●●●●	●●●○	●●●○	●●●○	●●○○		●●○●	Sophie					○●○○	○●○○			
●●●●	●○○●	●○○●	●●●●			●●●●	Ulrick	○○○●		●○○○						
							Virian									
●○○○	●○○○	●○○○	●○○○				Zina									

● = child contributed   ○ = child did not contribute

LEVELS OF CONCEPT ATTAINMENT

Date of lesson: Lesson topic: Sound (second)

Child's Name	Statements Revealing Concept Development	Vygotsky Level	Finding External Likenesses			Finding Hidden Likenesses						
			Generalized	Compared	Classified	Generalized	Made an analogy	Suggested a model	Hypothesized	Suggested a test or investigation	Inferred	Predicted
Albee	It's [the telephone's] got wire, not string.	complex		●								
Chris	. . . is that why we can't hear the bell?	complex							●			
	Something must have been burned in this bottle and not in the other.	complex		●					●			
	Yes, because there was no air left to let it burn.	preconcept						●	●			
	The string worked pretty good, but the hose was best.	complex		●								
Daisy	No, I couldn't hear the bell in one of the bottles when I tried. But I saw black stuff in one of the bottles—ashes.	complex		●								
	The bell won't ring 'cause there's no air. The fire used up the air and now you can't hear the bell.	preconcept						●	●			
Jon	I saw a picture about a boat, and the captain whistled in the hose to call somebody in the bottom of the boat.	complex	●									
Ellen	They both have bells in them, too.	complex		●								
	Which bottle had the black stuff in it?	complex		●								
	The candle went out, too, when we put the glass over it.	complex		●								
Frank	It looks like a telephone. If you talk in one cup, you can hear from the other.	complex		●								
	'Cause everything you say goes right in the hose and out the other side. It don't get mixed up in the air outside.	preconcept						●				
Gray	I tried both bottles and I could hear the bells. One was very quiet though.	complex		●								
	Yeah, you need air to hear the bell good. If there's no air, you can't hear.	preconcept		●					●	●		
Hannah	Maybe the bell is broken.	complex								●		
	There's black stuff in the bottle we had, too.	complex		●								
Lionel												
Marguerita	We could pull out the cork and let the air in. Then we could burn something and put the cork in.	complex									●	
Matthew	They both have corks in them.	complex		●								

LEVELS OF CONCEPT ATTAINMENT Date of lesson: Lesson topic: Sound (second)			Finding External Likenesses			Finding Hidden Likenesses						
Child's Name	Statements Revealing Concept Development	Vygotsky Level	Generalized	Compared	Classified	Generalized	Made an analogy	Suggested a model	Hypothesized	Suggested a test or investigation	Inferred	Predicted
	The burning stuff used up the air. There's no air in the bottle. That's why the cork is in so tight. To keep the air out.	preconcept						●	●			
	But there's only ashes in one bottle, and that's the bell that doesn't ring.	complex		●								
	This is like a telephone. The string is like the wire.	complex		●								
	It must. They couldn't hear when the string was loose.	preconcept									●	
	It's like the bottle with no air. He stopped the air in the hose. . .	preconcept					●		●			
Patricia												
Perry	The two milk bottles are the same.	complex		●								
	Can I try the bottles? The bell in the bottle without the ashes rings. The other with the ashes don't ring.	complex		●						●		
	There's a cork in both bottles, so there's no air in both of them.	complex		●								
Phil	Yeah, they do look alike to me.	complex		●								
	My real telephone doesn't have cups and strings, but it's got a ear place and a mouth place.	complex		●								
Renée												
Rita												
Rod	They look the same, but they didn't do the same things.	complex		●								
	One bell rang. The other bell you couldn't hear.	complex		●								
Rose												
Sarah	I'll try my bottles. Yeah, the same thing happens.	complex		●							●	
Simone												
Sophie	Mine didn't do the same thing either. 'Cause when I shook one bottle I heard the bell ring, but the bell in the other bottle didn't ring.	complex		●								
Ulrick												
Virian												
Zina												

"Yippee! We did it!" yells Carl.

In this incident Carl is seen both cooperating with another boy and making helpful suggestions. Carl and Monte succeed jointly in their enterprise ("We did it!"), so we would place crosses on both *works cooperatively* and *suggests activities which others follow.*[3]

The pattern is replicated when Carl announces: "We're de best scientists.... We're great. Here Monte, let's me and you put our stuff togedder—de whole lot."

According to Miss Provost's records, "Carl goes to work right away." He does not hesitate. His first act is described this way: "He takes a piece of wire, pushes the cloth down from the end, places the protruding bare tip in his teeth, and strips off the cloth covering with the thumb and index finger of his left hand. He's holding a battery in his free hand." He then makes a short circuit and cries, "Ouch!" when the wire burns. Probably not the first time he has done this, but still not exactly the behavior expected for the class as a whole. Carl shows originality in these preliminary acts, as well as in the elaborate circuits he and Monte invent.

Relations of Child to Materials

Hesitates to use materials

Explores materials in a limited manner

Does what is expected

✗ Finds original ways to elicit interactions

✗ Seeks materials not present

After one of the circuits has used up all the materials available to the two boys, "Carl shoots up

---

[3] There is a certain element of interpretation here: whether to classify Carl's intervention as dominating or suggesting. Since Monte was not being forced against his own judgment and the activities were cooperative throughout, we consider it suggesting. Other evaluators might disagree. A video tape would be helpful in such a case.

like a cricket, leans across the table, and snatches Bud's battery. Bud grabs it back; they tussle and argue."

On this scale we can mark both *finds original ways to elicit interactions* and *seeks materials not present.*

The whole picture is one of concentrated eagerness, from "goes to work right away" to testing batteries with his tongue when the light doesn't light ("Yow! Dere's juice, all right"). He was in the middle of a new circuit (with Monte's battery) when Mr. McIver called for the colloquium. During the colloquium, Carl expresses a desire to see how many lights he can make go on with two batteries where "two were as bright as one."

Carl's work drive scores on *uses materials with concentration and eagerness* as well as *suggests activities for next lesson.*

Work Pattern Drive

Finishes soon or fails to start

Alternates work with materials with other activities

Maintains a steady pace

✗ Uses materials with concentration and eagerness

✗ Suggests activities for next lesson

From a science learning viewpoint these scales give a highly satisfactory picture of Carl, indicating that materials are stimulating to his ingenuity and that he can work well with at least one other boy. The battery snatching incident is characteristic of his personality development rather than his science development. It might be avoided by giving him access to plenty of materials, since he uses them so creatively.

The Carls do present a problem to a teacher, in spite of the rosy picture revealed by the scales. He is perhaps too active, too often involved in an argument with another child; he tends to disrupt the serenity of the classroom. Without the scales, and the stop, look, and listen which they require of the observer, none of Carl's behavior but the disruptive moments might intrude upon even a well-meaning teacher. One is often grateful when the Carls are not attracting attention; a teacher may fail to recognize these as constructive moments.

Eileen Provost's statement supports this. It was the reason she chose Carl for her anecdotal record. Her prior perception had been: "He's so jittery and all over the place that it's hard to preserve calm in the room. And he doesn't seem to have any respect for authority unless you clamp down on him like a sergeant major. . . . He seeks attention, mine or the children's—a lion's share of it—all the time."

But Miss Provost was not prejudiced against Carl; she followed up her description of his disruptive behavior by saying: "There's something appealing about him. He's frail, has quick coordination, makes jokes; he's a jack-in-the-box who shatters the sober moment. I'm sure he's one of those underachievers."

Yet we saw Carl in moments of extremely constructive concentration. There are obviously two Carls, or one with two ways of reacting according to circumstances. Such records as we have made and analyzed go a long way toward helping a teacher plan for a child to learn deeply in *his* own manner.

Appraising the learning from a discovery–colloquium unit

For this analysis we will refer to the unit described in Chapter 5, where Miss Yonika introduced her fourth graders to a study of cells.

We have entered all the concept-seeking statements from the five recorded colloquia on one chart (pages 370–71). We have similarly written and analyzed the level of concept attainment for all five lessons on another chart (pages 372–74). The reader might like to make his own interpretation of the cluster of dots on the concept-seeking chart. For instance, these questions might be explored:

Which children contributed most? Which contributed least?

Which children responded chiefly to the teacher's questions rather than reacted to a peer?

Which skills were least emphasized? Were these related to the nature of the materials? If so, in what ways?

You might find it interesting to compare the levels of concept attainment of these fourth graders with the cognate charts of the second graders who explored sound (pages 357–58 and 365–66). In what ways are the differences related to the maturity levels of the two groups of children? In what ways are the differences related to the differences in the nature of interaction of the materials or, in other words, to the structures of the materials selected?

Miss Yonika wanted to find out what *facts* the children had learned in addition to the conceptual growth which her charts evidenced. She was interested chiefly in those facts which seemed important to the children themselves, the ones they were likely to recall. These would be only a sampling, of course, for if one probed and questioned each child individually, many other facts would undoubtedly be revealed. She obtained the readily recalled facts by asking the children to write out what they remembered from the unit—to write the facts they felt they had learned. She motivated the children and, at the same time, assuaged the fear that this might be a test by saying, "Did you enjoy this kind of unit?" When they asserted, "Yes!" with a loud chorus, she added, "Many people believe that children do not learn anything when they work on their own initiative, when they are not told just what to do. I would like to have some evidence that a good deal is learned this way. If you feel you've learned some facts or had some new thoughts, will you write these down?" A copy of each child's paper may be read in Appendix I, pages 383–88. We have selected the salient information given by both the evaluative charts and the children's written fact sheets and summarized them in one table (pages 375–76).

Each chart, as might be expected, draws on different learnings. Some children seem to find it easier to write what they know; others to speak it. Many of the pieces of free writing dealt with how to use a microscope. The techniques discovered figured little in the colloquia and yet seemed to be important to the children; perhaps they rejoiced in a newly learned competence. The revelations of written factual knowledge seem less meaningful than the oral contributions from the point of view of sciencing, but of course they do tell us what is especially important to each child. A point has to be made about the written documents in Miss Yonika's unit; coming at the end, they are a kind of summary of residual learnings.

The Nuffield science and mathematics project in England encourages children to make free written records of the work they accomplish after most of their activities. The Nuffield Foundation has explored many new ways to make learning meaningful to children; many experimental classrooms are organized on this "free choice" principle. Each child, after accomplishing what he wishes to do in any one area, writes a paragraph or so about what he did. Even quite young children do this and seem to grow in ability to express themselves in written form much faster than children whose written work is motivated only by assigned compositions.

This practice of self-initiated records has obvious advantages for the teacher. For the child, the practice in expressing his thoughts has partially the same effect as a colloquium in that the discipline of putting thoughts into words helps develop the thought. The child who writes his own thoughts about materials clarifies his thinking individually. If he writes his records after one or more colloquia, he may incorporate the benefit of group interaction and so reach higher levels of clarification.

Most adult thinkers employ some such technique as this to sharpen their thoughts. The surprising thing is that children trained in the Nuffield projects manage to do this, too. Although we have no records of this practice of asking children to write a record of their free choice activities among the lessons quoted in this book, we suggest it is potentially valuable. The practice would serve well where one or a few children at a time work with science materials, so that a day or so might pass before there was a group large enough to engage in a colloquium. As an example of the kind of information children record, we quote from one of the Nuffield mathematics projects, which, like so many of the projects guided by this Foundation, proliferate into several academic areas.

A combined fifth-sixth grade of children from a housing project in London decided to build a duck pond. (The quadrangle among the houses had been turned into a farm and there were a dozen ducklings.) From the introduction to the booklet which was finally published,[4] we quote part of one child's untouched statement which illustrates several of the points just made:

> Most of us knew how to use a spirit level, but we discussed it for a long time before we realised that the bubble moved as the level tilted because the bubble of air was lighter than the liquid and tried to rise to the surface.

Discussion of chart summaries of Miss Yonika's unit

Perhaps the most interesting patterns evident from the chart on pages 375-76 are the learning styles of individual children. One can pick any child, run one's eye across the items by his name, and derive some picture of the productivity of his work. Let us begin with one of the least interesting sets of data—those by Jud's name: three oral remarks, two written facts, no evidence of conceptual development. But now refer back to the more detailed charts. From the concept-seeking skills chart on page 370 we see that Jud spoke only during the third lesson, the first for which we recorded a colloquium. He spoke three times, however. We might now want to know what he said, and how his oral remarks compared with what he wrote at the end of the unit. Jud's three remarks (page 247) were:

> I had too much dye so I didn't see much.
> All parts of the onion [as as a summary of the various analogies for cells].
> Cells [as the name for the parts].

Jud began with some understanding of the cell as the unit of plant structure. In his written record, we find these statements:

> From the cells I looked at none of them are the same.
> When you look at a slide make sure your taurat is clean or you might be looking at his dirt.

Jud gained some understanding of the variety of

[4] *How to Build a Pond,* Nuffield Mathematics Project, published for the Nuffield Foundation by W. and R. Chambers and John Murray, John Wiley and Sons, Inc., New York, 1967.

CONCEPT-SEEKING SKILLS

Note: Alternating symbols ● and ○ are only for perceptual clarity.
(● represents lessons 3, 5, and 7; ○ represents lessons 4 and 6.)

Lesson topic: Cells

Lesson nos: 3,4,5,6,7

#	Observations	Stated clearly	Accurately perceived	Relevant to the concept	Interaction described operationally	New vocabulary used	Responded to another child's remark	Child's Name
1	3●	5●	5●	5●				Adelaide
1	3●4○	3●4○	3●	3●			3●4○	Alice
2	4○							
1	3●4○5●6○	3●4○5●	5●6○7●					Charles
2	4○5●6○7●	4○5●6○7●	5●6○					
3	5●6○7●	5●6○7●	6○7●					
4	5●6○7●	5●6○7●						
1	4○	4○			5○		7○	Don
2	4○				5○		7○	
1	3●4○	5●	5●	5●6●	5●		5○	Doris
2	5●	5●			5●			
3	5●	5●	6●		5●			
4	5●	5●	6●		5●		7●	
5	5●	5●			5●		7●	
1	3●	5○	5●	5●	5○	3●		Dottie
2	5○				5○			
1	3●	5○	5●	5●	5○		3● 5○	Faith
2	3●			5●			3●	
1	4○5●6○	4○5●6○	7●	6○7●	5●6○7●		6○7●	Fred
2	4○5●	5●	6●		5●6○	5●	6○	
3	4○5●	5●	6●					
4	4○5●	5●	6●					
1	3●	5●6○7●	6●7●	6●7●	6●7○		7●	Ivan
2	3●	5●6○7●	6●7●	6●7●	6●7●		6○7●	
3	5●6○	5●	6●7●	6●7●	6●		6○	
4	5●	5●			6●		6○	
1	4○5●6○	5●6○7●	5●6○7●	5●6○7●			7●	Jacqueline
2	4●	5●	5●	6●		6○		
1	3●	5○	5●	5○	5●		5● 7○	Jennie
1	3●	5●		5●			5●	Jud
2	3●	5●		5●				
3	3●	5●		5●				
1	3●4○5●6○	3●4○5●6○	3●4○5●6○	5●6○7●		6○	5●	7○	Keith
2	4●	4●	5●	6●			5● 6●	
1	3●4○5●6○	3●	5●6○	6●			5●6○	Larry
1	5●		5●				5●	Mannie
1	3●4○	3●4○	5●6○	5●6○			5●6○	Mary
1	3●	5○	5●		6○			Natalie
2	3●							
1	4○ 6○	4○	5●	6○				Ole
1	3●4○5●6○	3●4○5●6○	3●4○5●6○	5●6○7●	3●4○5○		3●	Penny
2	3●	5●6○7●	6●7○	5●6○7●	3●	4○		
3	3●	5●6○7●	6○	5●	5●6○7●			
4	5●	5●						
5	5●	5●						
1	3●4○	3●4○	5○	6●	5○		3●4○	7●	Pierre
2	4○	5○		5○			5○	
1	3●4○5●6○	3●4○5●6○	5●6○	5●6○7●		6○	5●6○7●	Ronnie
2	3●4○5●	5●6○	5●6○	5●6○		5●	5●6○	
3	3●	5●	6●	6●			5●	
1	3●4○5●6○7●	3●4○5●6○7●	6○	6●7●	5●6○7●	6○	3●4○5●6○7●	Shaughan
2	3●4○5●6○7●	3●4○5●6○7●	6●		5●6○		5●6○7●	
3	4○	5○		5○				
1	3●4○	5●6○	5●	5●6○7●	5○7●		5●	7●	Shelia
1	3●4○5●	5○	5●6○	5●6○7●			5●6○	Stanley
2	4○5●	5○				6○		
1	3●4○	5●6○	5●6○	5●6○7●	3●4○	5●6○	6○	7○	Thelma
2	5●6○	5●6○	6○7●		5●6○		7●	
3	5●6○		5●6○		5●6○		6○7●	
1	3●4○	5●	5○	5●			5● 7○	Wendy
								Yvonne

370

	Thinking						Quantifying			Child's Name
	Noticed discrepant event	Said "I think" or "Is it right?"	Asked a when, why, how, or where question	Changed statement in light of new data	Challenged a statement	Gave reason for challenge	Collected data	Arranged data	Made use of data	
	3 4 5 6 7	3 4 5 6 7	3 4 5 6 7	3 4 5 6 7	3 4 5 6 7	3 4 5 6 7	3 4 5 6 7	3 4 5 6 7	3 4 5 6 7	

Child's Name
Adelaide
Alice
Charles
Don
Doris
Dottie
Faith
Fred
Ivan
Jacqueline
Jennie
Jud
Keith
Larry
Mannie
Mary
Natalie
Ole
Penny
Pierre
Ronnie
Shaughan
Shelia
Stanley
Thelma
Wendy
Yvonne

LEVELS OF CONCEPT ATTAINMENT

Lesson numbers: 3,4,5,6,7   Lesson topic: Cells
(appear before each statement)

Child's Name	Statements Revealing Concept Development	Vygotsky Level	Finding External Likenesses			Finding Hidden Likenesses						
			Generalized	Compared	Classified	Generalized	Made an analogy	Suggested a model	Hypothesized	Suggested a test or investigation	Inferred	Predicted
Adelaide	3. They [onion cells] looked like bricks. They looked the same dyed or undyed.	complex					•					
Alice												
Charles	3. Mine looked like brick walls or cells.	complex					•					
	4. I saw blue bubbles—like dots inside one layer.	complex					•					
	5. The onion has larger cells; the scallion smaller ones.	complex		•								
	6. Starch made it . . . starch made . . .	preconcept				•						
	6. Carbon dioxide and hydrogen [in a carbonate].	preconcept									•	
	6. Like two water drops run together.	complex					•					
	6. Sugar gets into the yeast and it gets bigger.	preconcept									•	
	7. It stays together and when there's enough for a layer then it makes more layers.	preconcept						•				
Don	6. More starch . . . more energy.	preconcept									•	
Doris	3. All things put together make the onion skin.	preconcept						•				
	4. Your slide wasn't clean.	complex							•			
Dottie	6. Energy . . . the sun gives energy.	preconcept				•						
	6. Energy . . . from hot water.	preconcept						•				
Faith	3. All things make the onion skin.	preconcept						•				
	6. Each one turns into two; each of these two to two more. They divide.	preconcept	•									
Fred	7. Inside the nucleus, it was moving around—like a person blowing on coal and something comes out.	complex					•					
Ivan	3. The onion skin with red dye on it looked like a honeycomb.	complex					•					
	6. Plants make sugar when they're growing. When it [the new yeast cell] gets away from the plant, it still needs the same kind of food.	preconcept				•						
	6. When sugar gets into them, they have the same formula.	preconcept									• •	
Jacqueline	6. Dough has starch in it. The cells of yeast get energy from starch.	preconcept						•				
	7. The tadpole is all the cells together. Then it separates from the jelly.	preconcept						•				

LEVELS OF CONCEPT ATTAINMENT

Lesson numbers: 3,4,5,6,7   Lesson topic: Cells
(appear before each statement)

Child's Name	Statements Revealing Concept Development	Vygotsky Level	Finding External Likenesses			Finding Hidden Likenesses						
			Generalized	Compared	Classified	Generalized	Made an analogy	Suggested a model	Hypothesized	Suggested a test or investigation	Inferred	Predicted
Jennie												
Jud												
Keith	3. I put dye on my hair. It looked like beads—lots of colors.	complex					•					
	5. Different microscopes have different powers. You see more details with some.	complex		•								
	5. We all began as two cells.	preconcept				•						
	6. If you cut up paper, the population of the paper is larger but not the size. In cells, both get larger.	preconcept					•					
Larry	4. It branches. Red, blue, green—like in a wrist.	complex					•					
	5. Onion roots are different from the leaf.	complex		•								
	6. It's like the fresh milk straight from the cow.	complex					•					
Mannie												
Mary	3. Mine looked like brown bricks.	complex					•					
Natalie	6. It's like they're cut up into two. Makes more, but there's less [material].	preconcept						•				
Ole	6. The atom explodes.	preconcept						•				
Penny	3. Nuclei are found in all cells except there are none in blood cells.	preconcept	•									
	3. Different live plants or creatures put together to make a larger thing.	preconcept						•				
	5. (Drew onion cell with scallion inside.)	complex		•								
	6. Just the opposite [two water drops separate].	complex					•					
	6. [Yeast gets bigger] then divides.	preconcept						•				
	7. We're made up of cells and we're alive. Why shouldn't they be.	preconcept				•						
Pierre	3. There were cracks on my slide. Looked like lightning.	complex					•					
	4. I saw bubbles. Maybe they were molecules.	preconcept						•				
	4. It's veins, like in a body.	complex					•					
	7. It squeezes out—like a baby born from its mother.	preconcept					•					
Ronnie	4. . . . it looked like a fence.	complex					•					

LEVELS OF CONCEPT ATTAINMENT — Lesson numbers: 3,4,5,6,7 (appear before each statement) — Lesson topic: Cells			Finding External Likenesses			Finding Hidden Likenesses						
Child's Name	Statements Revealing Concept Development	Vygotsky Level	Generalized	Compared	Classified	Generalized	Made an analogy	Suggested a model	Hypothesized	Suggested a test or investigation	Inferred	Predicted
Shaughan	3. It was the dirty lens.	complex									•	
	4. I saw bricks and nuclei.	complex					•					
	5. If one microscope was 60 power and the other something else, you could—subtract to compare sizes?	complex		•								
	7. One cell makes one cell and keeps on going.	preconcept	•									
Sheila	4. Mine was like a cave with writing on the wall.	complex					•					
	7. Little bugs . . . walking around [yeast dividing].	complex					•					
Stanley	4. Mine was like Ronnie's, but darker.	complex		•								
Thelma	6. Sugar is made in plants and plants get energy from the sun.	preconcept				•						
Wendy	6. Like a baby?	preconcept					•					
Yvonne												

cell structure, a potential concept, perhaps. His experience that extraneous matter might cloud one's view stayed with him throughout the lesson; he mentioned this both first and last.

The summary for Jud, indicating slender achievement, can direct us quickly to the details of that achievement. It remains slender on the evidence, but, minimally, his achievement is in the direction of the structure of the unit.

By contrast we select Charles with his frequent oral contributions, several thinking skills, and growth in Vygotsky levels of thought. But Charles has poor techniques for expressing himself in writing! Only the colloquia records do justice to his sciencing.

The growth in concept attainment for the class as a whole is evident from the summary in the third column as well as from the relative development of each child in this area. The conceptual attainment is about that which might be expected from a mature fourth grade by the end of the school year: a shift from complex thinking toward preconceptual thought. Seven children (Adelaide, Fred, Larry, Mary, Ronnie, Sheila, and Stanley) did not shift from remarks which must be classified as complex thinking, although Sheila, in her written work, made a generalization from a hidden likeness which borders on the conceptual: "I learned every living [thing] has at least one cell." Five children, as it happened, all boys (Charles, Ivan, Keith, Pierre, Shaughan), moved from complex to preconceptual thought during the unit. Nine children were already at the preconcept level. There is no evidence of conceptual level or growth for five. However, if we examine what the "no evidence children" write, each one mentioned in some way or another the variety to be found among cells—in itself a potential concept.

From the summary of oral skills, we see that some children talked much of the time, enabling us to learn what they think. Charles, Ivan, Penny, and Shaughan all had much to contribute and each reached the preconcept stage. This is a fair illustration of Vygotsky's statement that speech engenders thought.

Child's Name	No. of Oral Contributions	No. and Quality of Written Contributions	Concept Attainment Shown in Colloquium
Adelaide	1	8 (All factual.)	Complex; made an analogy.
Alice	2	2 (Showing sharp perception.)	No evidence.
Charles	15 (Measured with hair-widths; challenged; offered hypothesis.)	4 (All on microscope techniques; badly spelled.)	Grew from complex to preconcept. Offered one model; made two inferences.
Don	2 (In response to teacher. Absent until the sixth lesson.)	Missing.	Preconcept, inference.
Doris	7 (Mostly on filmloops.)	8 (Four on cells; four on microscope techniques.)	Preconcept; suggested a model. (Complex statement and inference were asides.)
Dottie	3	5 (All on microscope techniques.)	Preconcept; suggested a model.
Faith	3	4 (One generalization: "Food is made up of cells.")	Preconcept; offered one model.
Fred	8 (All during last two lessons; three were one word answers to the teacher.)	2. (Vague preceptions.)	Complex, but made an elegant analogy: "like a person blowing on coal and something comes out."
Ivan	11	4 (All on microscope techniques.)	Grew from complex to preconcept. Made to analogies, one generalization (hidden likeness), and two inferences.)
Jacqueline	4 (All during last three lessons.)	4 (One on "how one cell of yeast multiplies.)	Preconcept; offered two models.
Jennie	2	2 (Used word *nuclei*.)	No evidence.
Jud	3	2	No evidence.
Keith	6	3 (Two on cell concepts; used term *time lapse*.)	Grew from complex to preconcept. Made an elegant analogy: "If you cut up paper, the population of the paper is larger, but not the size. In cells, both get larger." and a generalization: "We all began as two cells."
Larry	4	6 (Four on paramecia; two on what one "might see.")	Complex.
Mannie	1	4 (Two were conceptual.)	No evidence.
Mary	2	Missing.	Complex.
Natalie	3	4 (Two were conceptual.)	Preconcept.
Ole	2 (In response to teacher.)	Missing.	Preconcept; offered one model, based on an incorrect concept.

Child's Name	No. of Oral Contributions	No. and Quality of Written Contributions	Concept Attainment Shown in Colloquium
Penny	15	3 (Her own investigations with paramecia.)	Mostly preconcept: a challenge, two generalizations, and two models.
Pierre	4	6 (Important learnings.)	Grew from complex to preconcept; offered a model and a beautiful analogy: "It squeezes out like a baby born from its mother."
Ronnie	8	3 (One full statement on onion skin structure; one on microscope powers.)	Complex.
Shaughan	11	1 (Weak statement.)	Grew from complex to preconcept; test, a good generalization, and an inference.
Sheila	4 (Three were in response to teacher.)	3 (Two good generalizations; one on microscope technique.)	Complex.
Stanley	5 (Three in response to teacher.)	3 (Perceptual, rather than conceptual.)	Complex.
Thelma	8	5 (Poetic listing.)	Preconcept; offered a generalization (hidden likeness).
Wendy	3	5 (All perceptual.)	Preconcept.
Yvonne	0	3 (All microscope perceptions.)	No evidence.

Charles and Shaughan had great difficulty in expressing in writing what they knew. If that had been all that was required of them, how little it would have told us about what they really learned! Jacqueline remained quiet until the last two lessons. Hers must have been a technique of inner speech about what the other children said, for, when she spoke, she came out with preconceptual statements: "The cells of yeast get energy from starch," and "The tadpole is all the cells together. Then it separates from the jelly." Mannie was another child who said little during the colloquia, but he wrote that "I found out the two cells can become one and one can become two." He also generalized that "every living thing has cells in it."

A few children's learning styles seem much simpler than the others; Jennie, Mary, Sheila, and Yvonne might need special attention or encouragement next time.

We mentioned before that this unit offered little opportunity for quantitative records, although the suggestion had been given to use the hairwidth as a measure. While only one child (Charles) performed such a measurement, two other children mentioned it in their writing:

Adelaide: "I learned how to measure cells by hair width."

Jacqueline: "Also I learned that you tell the width or length of a cell by hairwidths."

Other children, who did not see fit to mention this bit of information may, nevertheless, have stored it in their memories. But the unit did not foster quantification; another unit, if there had been time for one more that year, might well have offered more opportunity for this skill. We see from the charts that inferring, formulating hypotheses, and challenging statements also need more emphasis or opportunity to develop; the thinking skills *per se* are sparsely represented. The communicating skills were well represented, with the exception of the way of looking at phenomena as interaction. There was little interaction among the materials themselves, however.

No observations were made on the attitudes of the children. The attitude scales, therefore, cannot be marked.

The variety of behavioral observations described and organized into scales, charts, and summaries in this chapter provide a pool of evaluative techniques from which a teacher may choose. He may choose to observe one type of activity for each child in his class, such as who takes the lead and who follows when materials are explored in small cooperative groups (Attitude Scale: Relations of Child to Others). He may wish to jot down the remarks of one particular child during a colloquium in order to collect evidence of the conceptual level he has attained. Then again the teacher may be interested in who tends to see hidden likenesses and which ones, or in what facts the children choose to record if they write comments after a discovery period.

We feel that some evaluation should be planned for each lesson and that, cumulatively, these will reveal patterns of growth for each child. After a little practice, one perceives and can record evaluative evidences with little effort. It all becomes part of the stop, look, and listen technique! Regular, planned evaluation is an essential guide to choosing materials for follow-up lessons.

We have seen that self-selected records of what a child had done or learned from his own explorations sometimes taps learnings not revealed during a colloquium; self-selected records after several colloquia sometimes reveal conceptual levels not expressed orally by the less verbose children. In these ways, children's free writings have value. However, for most elementary school children, such records are a hampering chore and, for primary school youngsters, often impossible. We learn what these children know almost entirely from observing the way they work and listening to what they contribute to the colloquia. The same is true for older children whose general literacy is below that expected for their maturity.

Scoring of the Second Colloquium on Sound (pages 359-62):

Child's Name	Thinking	CONCEPT-SEEKING Communicating							CONCEPT ATTAINMENT
		ob	cl	ac	re	int	voc	res	
1. Perry		•	•		•				com
1. Phil		•			•			•	com
1. Matthew		•	•	•	•			•	com
1. Ellen		•	•	•	•			•	com
1. Rod	th, d.e.	•		•	•	•			com
1. Sophie		•	•	•	•	•		•	com
2. Rod		•	•	•	•			•	com
1. Hannah		•	•		•			•	(hyp)
2. Sophie	chl, rea	•	•	•	•	•		•	
1. Gray		•	•	•	•				com
3. Sophie		•	•	•	•				
1. Daisy		•	•	•	•			•	com

Child's Name	Thinking	ob	cl	ac	re	int	voc	res	CONCEPT ATTAINMENT
					CONCEPT SEEKING — Communicating				
3. Rod		•	•		•			•	
2. Hannah		•	•	•	•			•	com
1. Chris	?, th	•			•			•	(hyp)
2. Ellen		•	•		•				com
2. Perry		•	•	•	•	•		•	(tes), com
1. Sarah		•		•	•			•	(tes), com
1. Ulrick	?	•	•	•	•			•	
1. Renée		•	•	•	•				
2. Chris		•	•	•	•	•		•	(hyp), com
1. Don		•	•		•				(hyp)
2. Daisy		•	•	•	•				
3. Chris		•	•		•			•	(mod), (hyp)
3. Ellen		•	•	•	•			•	com
2. Matthew		•	•	•	•				(mod), (hyp)
3. Perry	chl, rea	•	•	•	•			•	com
3. Matthew	d.e.	•	•	•	•			•	com
3. Daisy		•	•		•			•	(mod), (mod)
1. Marguerita		•	•		•	•			(tes)
1. Zina		•	•	•	•				
2. Sarah		•	•	•	•				
2. Gray	th	•	•	•	•			•	(mod), com, (hyp)
1. Rose		•	•		•				
1. Frank		•	•	•	•	•		•	com
1. Rita		•	•	•	•			•	
2. Phil		•	•	•	•			•	com
1. Albee		•	•	•	•			•	com
4. Matthew		•	•	•	•			•	com
3. Phil		•	•	•	•				
4. Chris		•	•	•	•	•		•	
4. Daisy		•	•	•	•	•		•	
5. Matthew		•	•	•	•				(inf)

Child's Name	CONCEPT SEEKING								CONCEPT ATTAINMENT
	Thinking	Communicating							
		ob	cl	ac	re	int	voc	res	
2. Rita		●			●			●	
3. Rita		●	●	●	●				
2. Ulrick		●			●			●	
4. Rita		●			●			●	
3. Ulrick		●			●			●	
4. Rod		●	●	●	●				
1. Lionel		●		●	●			●	
1. Simone		●	●	●	●			●	
4. Sophie		●						●	
2. Simone		●	●	●	●			●	
3. Simone		●	●	●	●				(hyp)
6. Matthew		●	●		●			●	(ana), (hyp)
4. Ulrick	d.e.	●	●	●	●			●	
7. Matthew	chl, rea	●	●		●			●	
3. Gray		●		●	●				
5. Chris		●			●			●	com
4. Perry		●			●			●	
5. Perry		●							
2. Frank		●	●		●			●	(mod)
2. Don		●	●	●	●			●	gen ex

Adieu Madeline

We have reached the far bank of one river crossing.

We have accepted the near bank of current science teaching where it is—or even when it isn't. We have accepted schools which have a range of freedom from almost none to the cutting edge of experimentation, placing our faith that teachers, given a choice of stepping stones, will find their way across the river to the bank where science teaching can begin an exciting adventure. We have addressed ourselves to teachers whose previous wanderings along the banks of educa-tion left them still seeking better ways to bring children and science learnings together. Teachers, we assert, are the key to all school learning, for they create the atmosphere where change in behavior can take place, fan the flames of growing intellectual desire, convey compassion for each child, and nurture in him the competence which gives him the courage to grow. Whatever aids are offered to teachers—an understanding administration, closed and open circuit television, electronic gadgets, materials, books, flex-ible classroom walls—may be adjuncts to learning, but without the teacher who offers affection and support, who feels *with* the children, who himself has a zest for discovery and intellectual challenge, the aids become mere trappings, even millstones.

Our discovery-colloquium principle of introducing children to sciencing has been explained, illustrated, and justified with theoretical rationale as *a* widely tried, easily successful way to create an atmosphere for science learning. Recognizing the fears attendant upon radical departures in classroom procedures, we have documented the manner in which various teachers with different teaching styles may put a toe on the first stepping stone. The saying that, "Ce n'est que le premier pas qui coûte" guided us to devote a large portion of this book to the ways, means, and reasons which would launch teachers on that first step *Starting Tomorrow*—the step which offers children working in small groups, free exploration of structured materials.

The supreme gift of man which sets him apart from the animals is his ability to symbolize his experiences using the fluid symbolism of speech. We devoted many pages to exploring the interaction of children's speech with their thoughts and among groups of children engaged in colloquia. We illustrated and analyzed the amazingly rich learning which takes place during the process of speaking together among peers.

We considered the content of science—its facts, theories, and ways of looking at phenomena—as potential stepping stones, only to find them inundated with the onrushing river of the explosion of knowledge. We, therefore, chose concepts as our more enduring footholds. Concepts are adult concerns, somewhat mountainous rocks towering above the tumult. Children climb these rocks, meshing the best of their maturity with the opportunities we offer. Vygotsky and Piaget have posted behavioral signs which indicate to an aware teacher the ability of each child to stretch toward the next of these toeholds. We then paired the children's expected abilities with the conceptual schemes of science and with the subconcepts along whose arrows the children move.

We built lessons into a unit, units into a curriculum. We thought of the latter as three intermeshing cogwheels: the conceptual schemes of science, the conceptual development of the child, and the child's socioeconomic background and needs.

It was not our intention to exhaust all areas of science nor to provide an encyclopedia of lessons on every concept. We tried, rather, to touch upon all common areas of science among our total illustrations; we tried to introduce the contributions of many of the new science programs and new textbook series.

Our principles are clear and firm to offer sure footing across the river. The many smaller stepping stones—sources and matrices of materials, ways to organize classrooms, various uses for books and audio-visual aids, and a roster of evaluative techniques—we indicated, but left open for choice. Are there not many Madelines among the nation's teachers, even as there are many warmhearted Miss Clavels? There are teachers who prefer a set order and those who prefer to make order out of chaos; there are lysiphobes and lysiphiles. Both can have compassion. Both can engender competence. Both can create an atmosphere for learning. We hope our book offers arrows with choices.

Appendices
and
Bibliographies

Appendix I

Papers showing what fourth graders learned from a unit on cells

Adelaide

What I learned About <u>Cells</u>

I learned that onion cells are sometimes different.
I also learned that yeast cells multiply.
I learned that cells are different shapes.
I learned that an onion is made up of several different kinds of cells.
I learned how to measure cells by hair width.
An onion cell is sometimes are shaped like brick walls, bobwired fences, and many other shapes.
I learned that a yeast cell is very small.
I learned that dye helps to see cells much better.

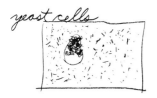

Alice

1   Cells are all different shapes.

2   When you look at onion skin with blue and red die, it looks like cells with two lines bordering the cells all around, with both lines a different color.

Charles

1. To have a peace of hair as a ruler to measure the sells.
2. Make sure your slide or microscope is clean.
3. To us[e] a lower power for it to be smaller and less detale and a larger power to make it bigger with more detale
4   Sells are all diffrent sizes and shapes
5

Doris

1 Cells can proudce more cells by one cell spliting up into two cells
2 Cells have neculars in them. Some times you can see them under a microscope. They look like black dots. Some cells have more than others.
3 Cells are in different shape.
4 When you're looking under a microscope, be sure to get only one layer thick of things like onions, skin, and other things.
5 If you can't foucos anything try to do it with the shortest turet [objective] first and them work to the longest.
6 Onion cells like like bricks.

7 Don't put the truet down to far or you might break the glass.
8 Use stain or idoane to see things more cleary.

Dottie

1 You can see more of the object you are looking at if you move the slide.
2 If you keep turning the adjusting knob turn to another objective because the one you were using might be broken.

On Cells

1 Get a small piece of something. Then pull one layer off and put in on a slide to see it better put food coloring on it. Put the cover slip on and put it under the microscope objective. If you are lucky you will see a black dot in the middle of the cell it is a nucleus.

Faith

Cells are all diffrent sizes.
Cells are all diffrent shapes.
Food is made up of cells.
There are neclei in cells.

Fred

1. When I focused my microscope I saw molaclues down there.
2. When I looked at a nucleus I saw something that looked like a thumbprint.

Ivan

Facts on Cells

1 Well I noticed that the cells of an onion are always differ in shape.
2. And that the dye put on makes the outline of the cell the colore of the dye
3. Hair looks like tube
4 The lower power like 5-S gives you more detail but not as big a picture

Jacqueline

What I Learned

I learned that onion cells look like bricks or honeycone. I also learned that sugar, water and yeast mixed together, the cells looked like dots. Also I learned that you tell the width or length of a cell by hairwidths. I learned how one cell of yest multiplyses

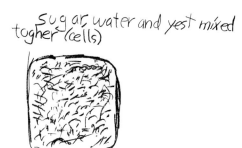

Jennie

One day the onion skin looked like a bobbed wired fence and another day it looked like bricks.
When I looked at some kind of plant, I saw some nuclei.

Jud

1) From the cells I looked at none of them are the same.
2) When you look at a slide make sure your taurat [objective] is clean or you might be looking at his dirt.

Keith

1. I learned that many onion cell make up an onion
2. There are one cell, living creatures.
3. I leared that time lapse is the opposite of slow motion

Larry

1. Parameciam is a animal
2. These animals are small
3. You use microscopes to see them
4. They eat off balls of algae
5. You might see a cell inside an onion skin
6. There are sometimes nuclei that you can see.

Mannie

The Microscopic
World
1. I found out the two cell can become one and one can become two
2. Cells are honey combed shapes. Every living thing has cells in it
3. I also found out that cells have nuclei in them
The End

Natalie

1 Cells are so tiny that it is hard to see even if you magnify them 60 times.
2 Cells alone produce other cell, and there cells produce other cells.
3 When you have one lay of onion and put dye on it. Then put in your microscope, you might be able to see the nucleus. The nucleus is usually black.

Penny

1. You can see paramiciam without a microscope, but you can not identify them without a microscope
2. Many cells have nuclei, but some cells do not have nuclei.

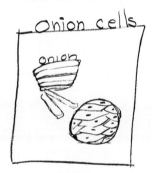

3. Paramiciam are fast little one celled pond creatures.
4.

Pierre

1. Onion cells are like a brick wall.
2. Cells of diffrent things are diffrent shapes.
3. Having one layer of what your looking at helps you see the cells.
4. The outside of the cell is called the cell wall.
5. Sometimes the cell wall is "broken." ⟋see back. [See diagram below.]
6. The cell of an onion are always connected.

broken cell

Ronnie

1 When you look at an onion skin you'll find that if you get one layer of skin (or close to one) you will find some nuclei inside one a sell. If you are lucky you might eaven see a nuclei in every cell.
2 I found out how to use a microscope and which power you shoud use. The powers you can use if you have a three power microscope are 8 power 20 power and 40 power.

Shaughan

1. A nucleus is a cell with small dots. Illustration
2.

Sheila

1. I learned that cells are many diffrent shapes and sizes.
2. I learned every living has at least one cell.

Slides

1. I learned that in order to be able to see any thing that you must have clean slides and very clean cover slipes and clean lends.

Stanley

I learned that cells can be in diffrent shapes like some are bratted [braided?] and some aren't there are alot more shapes that cells can be in. Inside cells threre are diffrent shapes like circles and some other shapes like lines these diffrent shapes are call nucleus if there's many you call the word nuclie. I saw nucleus that means one it was black.

Thelma

Sells

A bunch of eyes starring.
Brick walls.
Honey comb.
funny shapes.

These are discriptions of sells. I've never noticed the pattern in in onion skin, or the things shooting across the clean water, except under a micriscope.

Wendy

1 I learned that cells are all diffrent shapes

2 I also learned that the yeast cells look like to little circules. Like this

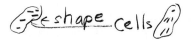

3 The onion cells were in a shape.

4 The onion skin looked like fish scales with little dots.

5 Hair under a mirscope looks like a big brown rod

Yvonne

Onion skins can be diffrent in many ways such as they can be thin and when you look across you see thick ones.

In order to see what you want to you need a clean slide and cover.

Cells can be diffent colors depending on the dye you use.

Appendix II

Mathematics concepts for sciencing

Scientists, throughout history, have needed the shorthand and symbolization of mathematics to express observed phenomena and relationships. Once events are coded into a concise symbolic form, a rearrangement of the symbols often suggests new phenomena. The suggested new phenomena form the basis for prediction and search.

In 1934, the Italian Nobel Laureate Enrico Fermi predicted the existence of a subatomic particle which he named the *neutrino*. He described its properties some 30 years before it was finally discovered. The prediction stemmed from an unbalanced equation which was to account for the loss of mass–energy occurring when an electron escapes from a nucleus. Radioactive elements shoot out particles from their nuclei. One such particle, a beta ray or electron, escapes from time to time from a bismuth atom (the isotope Bi^{214}). In such reactions, mass is often converted into energy (according to the Einsteinian formula $E = mc^2$). It is the sum total of mass–energy which has to be conserved. This is one of science's main conceptual schemes, as we have seen.

But the mass–energy of the electron escaping from radioactive bismuth proved to be *less* than the mass–energy lost by the atom. Since there was no other track left in the cloud chamber where positive and negative particles are pulled in opposite directions by an electromagnetic field, Fermi predicted that the extra particle of mass–energy was neutral. Its mass-energy was also very, very tiny, but sufficient to throw out the conservation of mass-energy concept. Hence Fermi named the extra particle *neutrino*, the Italian word for "little neutral one."

A mathematical relationship had revealed a discrepant event; a prediction was made to account for the imbalance and a long search eventually revealed the predicted particle.

Scientists often have to invent a mathematical formulation to represent the phenomena they observe and wish to record. Newton invented the calculus to keep track of the forces he posited existed between celestial bodies. Sometimes scientists seek a new mathematical formulation from existing endeavors of the "pure" mathematicians. Einstein found that Riemann's (non Euclidean) geometry served his relativity theory.

The habit of recording observations through equations, graphs, diagrams, and in columns of variables—of measuring as accurately as need be in some appropriate unit—is one all scientists possess. Children who are sciencing can adopt the same procedures. They too can predict through interpolating in graphs, through extending patterns, through finding ratios or other relationships.

Scientists never use science as an excuse for *practicing* mathematics. We do not believe that children should either: planting beans is not a good excuse for practice in counting; weighing a hamster is not a good excuse for learning about grams; and recording the heights of the children in the class is not a good excuse for using graph paper. Yet all these and other activities can have scientific and mathematical implications. Let us follow a few of them.

In general, mathematics is a discipline based on conceptual schemes in its own right. Sometimes the mathematics schemes have science cognates. These natural linkages illuminate both disciplines and enrich the child's conceptual growth in both areas.

In Chapter 1 (pages 61-67), we described some of the activities which intrigue children while they experience the meaning of sets. Grouping discrete objects or ideas into sets is a way of classifying the items. Robert Karplus, the physicist who initiated the Science Curriculum Improvement Study (SCIS), uses this same idea when he talks of systems. His systems

are sets. He isolates objects from the rest of their environment in order to study them. He uses the concept of system and subsystem as mathematicians use the concept of sets and subsets.

To apply the set idea to science, we might describe a set as containing all the furry animals who suckle their young. Many possible members of that set come to mind. Now take the set of all the animals who lay eggs. A great number of these come to mind. But what about the Duck-billed Platypus? Remember him, or rather her, from Australia? She lays eggs, is covered with fur, and suckles her young. Into which set shall we place her? We could diagram the sets of furry and egg laying animals. We could overlap them. Then we say the two sets *intersect* (see diagram). If, on the other hand, we think of the set of people who are in Australia at this moment, and then of the set of people who are in Canada at this same moment, we shall have two *disjoint* sets. No member straddles the two (see diagram). Whether sets are intersecting or disjoint is a concept that is important to the activity of classifying. Classifying in disjoint sets is the better way to feed data into a computer: the item does or does not belong in a punched hole; it does or does not make electrical contact for computation purposes.

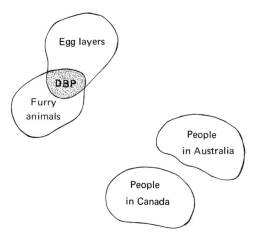

These concepts were introduced through the choice of materials suggested in Chapter 1 (again, see pages 61-67). The child who chose a set of small things and the child who chose a set of red things are asked to place the red marble. Children sometimes say that it belongs in both sets. But there's only one

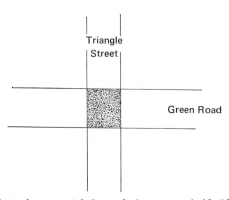

Triangle Street

Green Road

marble; who gets it? It can't be cut in half. If the children are then given loops of colored cord to define their sets physically, sooner or later they place the loops in an overlap. The words "intersection of the sets" can be introduced to designate the location of the item belonging to both sets. The intersection concept is very clearly objectified in the Attribute Block game when children find a place for the green triangle at the crossroads of Triangle Street and Green Road (see diagram). To build a concept of set intersection one needs to present many different experiences and to represent them in a variety of symbols. As well as the overlapping loops and crossroads, such devices as overlapping figures of many shapes and committees of children where one or more children are on both committees can be used.

The concept of subsets (Karplus' subsystems) is another link between math and science. Mammals are a subset of the vertebrates; the halogens are a subset of all the elements. The Duck-billed Platypus is a subset of both the set of mammals and the set of egg layers. Subsets can be diagrammed by a loop within a loop (see below).[1]

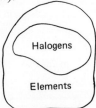

Halogens

Elements

Arranging objects in a rank order according to an attribute is another form of classification, another activity which belongs both to science and to mathematics. As early as the kindergarten years, children enjoy arranging square section rods such as the Minnebars[2] and the Cuisenaire materials. These rods have the property of being in regular increments so that ordering them according to size produces an arrangement of steps which seems to fascinate children. A little more challenging is the activity of ordering sticks or strips of paper whose lengths are not multiples of simple units. The need for this might come about in recording the growth of plants or measuring the unbroken columns of liquids before they break into drops.[3]

The forerunner of the need to measure growth would be an investigation of seeds. Place four small cupcake papers on a paper plate. In each cake paper, place a dozen or so seeds and not-seeds. Choose items which can produce confusion or lead to ambiguity or to a discrepant event. For instance: morning glory seeds and bits of charcoal, radish seeds, mung bean seeds, beet seeds, zinnia seeds, and a fragment of vermiculite. Four children seated around a table, each with a cup, examine the contents, and discuss what the objects might be. First and second graders are

Seeds

Not-seeds

?

[1] *Science: A Process Approach*, Part Five, American Association for the Advancement of Science (A.A.A.S.), 1964, pp. 692-98, describes a punch-card system of classifying minerals. McBee cards employ knitting needles to pull out cards having a combination of attributes, each of which is recorded by a notch in a certain position on the edge of the card.

[2] Produced by the Minnemast Project, Minnemath Center, University of Minnesota, 720 Washington Ave., S.E., Minneapolis, Minn. 55414.

[3] Both of these activities are described in the E.S.S. (Elementary Science Study) units *Growing Seeds* and *Kitchen Physics,* respectively. Now available from the Webster Division of McGraw-Hill, Inc., Manchester, Mo. 63011.

usually sure that some are seeds and some are not; their selection of what belongs in each category is usually erroneous. (So, often, are the selections of nongardening adults!) At this point each table can be offered three paper cups: one for seeds, one for not-seeds, and one for "not sures." How can the children find out if their predictions are correct? The children will say, "Plant them." Transparent plastic containers (the view inside is interesting) or empty half-pint milk containers or paper cups, filled with sand, dirt, or perhaps vermiculite and small pitchers for water will be needed. Or seeds may be stuck with Elmer's Glue-All on the inside of a small plastic bag which is taped on a window. Water or a nutrient solution in the bottom of the bag will provide a moist atmosphere for germination.

Whether a choice of planting media or only one medium is offered depends on your judgment of the maturity of the children. Whether the children make their own labels or simply stick on prepared ones depends on their writing ability. Sometimes the children may need the experience of dumping all of the chosen seeds and not-seeds into two planting cups. Before this step is taken, the children may be asked how they will know which seed has grown if there are several different kinds in each cup. Trying out one idea and then finding it does not yield clear results is a good experience for most children. Then, on their own, they formulate the need for "controls," although the word may have to be given to them. Very often, however, the children say, "We'll count how many there are," and they think of labeling each

cup with a seed of the kind planted, but stuck on the outside with plastic tape!

While the seeds and not-seeds wait to reveal the category to which each belongs, the children can be given ears of corn (the hybrid variety which has red and yellow kernels on the same ear). Children know these are seeds and they will plant them. As these begin to sprout, the children may be given strips of colored construction paper (say, 1 x 12 in.) to use to measure the heights of the plants day by day. The children tear off the measured lengths. Each child keeps his own lengths in an envelope or notebook. He may write his name on each strip.

One Monday there will be some comments about how much the corn has grown! Now is the time to begin organizing the strips. Each child will have an easy time finding his most recent Monday strip. Could each child find the first day's strip? The second day's? Suggest each child paste his strips on a sheet of construction or brown paper. *But, give no instructions!* The results can then be exhibited around the classroom walls. This moment is a good time for a colloquium.

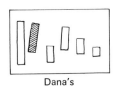

Dana's

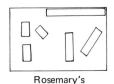

Rosemary's

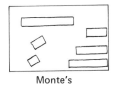

Monte's

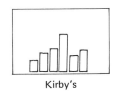

Kirby's

One set of results from an extension of parts of Matrix 14 (page 314) looked like the drawings above. The children sat in a semicircle facing the exhibits and began to talk about their products. It is surprising how meaningful unorthodox arrangements are to children, so do not be discouraged if the strips are not ordered in a conventional way. You, too, can find answers through careful inspection. Remarks usually come freely. If they do not, discussion can be initiated by questions such as: "Can you tell which strip is the one made today?" Children identify the strips by their positions on the paper or by their colors.

"How much did each person's corn grow between Friday and Monday?"

"We can tell on Dana's."

"How?" [Which day's height does the hatched strip on Dana's represent?]

The children will tell, but someone may suggest ordering the strips according to size or adding a new strip to the row each morning. Both are excellent discoveries about record keeping.

Should the strips be ordered from left to right, right to left, top to bottom? Does it really make any difference?

"Mine are in the right order," asserts Kirby.

"They are?"

"Yes, the last strip I made this morning." Kirby has tongue in cheek, enjoying his challenging joke.

"So how come today's strip is shorter than Thursday's, and Friday's is shorter, too?"

"Want to know?" asks Kirby, mischievously. [Of course everyone wants to know by this time.]

"We-e-ll, I took my plant home for the weekend and my rabbit ate a bit!"

It was fortunate that the teacher had not told Kirby to make a different ordering assuming that size ranking would be day ranking!

Some children may want to rechart their data by tearing off and pasting matching strips. (This is fine. Others may want to continue recording data on their original charts.)

Once the children begin to make their graphs in day and growth sequence, they can consider questions like: "Between which two days did Rosemary's corn grow most?" If everyone agrees the biggest growth occurs between Friday and Monday, "Is that *a* day's growth?" So the plan of leaving spaces on the graph for Saturday and Sunday occurs. Then the children can guess how much the plant grew in each of these weekend days. The tops of the strips can be joined by a smoothed out pencil line to make a kind of roller coaster curve. From this line, a child can predict how tall his plant will be tomorrow. A pencil mark can be made on the chart; tomorrow's strip tests the prediction.

With older children, the slope of the line joining the tops of the strips becomes evidence of the *rate of growth*. Could this give a slight sense of the calculus?

Fifth and sixth graders working with pendula have another chance to symbolize and order their findings and to rearrange data for prediction.

To begin the pendulum investigation (see pages 86-87 and 177), each pair of children is given two pendula. These can be made of string (nylon fishing cord is very good) attached to iron washers. One bob may be made from a fisherman's sinker. Attach the strings to the edge of the table with masking tape (lengths can thus be easily adjusted) and place a few spare washers of different sizes on the table.

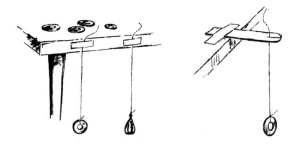

During the first two or three periods of free investigation and colloquium, the children usually find that the weight of the bob makes no difference in the number of round trips the pendulum makes in a given period of time. They discover this because the structure of the materials usually suggests that the two pendula with different bobs can be set to swing together when they are "about the same length." Adding another weight to one of the pendula does not alter this phenomenon.

At the end of a colloquium, the teacher can ask, "How do you measure the length of a pendulum—from where to where?" The answers always vary: from the point where the string is attached to the support to the top of the washer to its bottom part, but, rarely, to its center. The teacher then hangs a yardstick from a very short string and asks, "How long would your washer pendulum have to be to swing with this one?" It takes at least another period to discover that the length of a pendulum is measured from the point of attachment to the center of gravity of the system.

At some point in these investigations, the children become interested in counting the number of round trips a pendulum makes in a certain period of time. This activity can be helped by having a metronome ticking away in the room. Or a tin can with a hole in it can be suspended, filled with water, and allowed to drip onto an inverted aluminum pie plate placed in a bucket. The resounding drip, drip, drip makes an excellent metronome. Once we suggested this to a teacher and she replied, "We won't need the can; our roof's leaking!"

In order to compare the results in a way which leads to discovery of their structure, the teacher

should suggest that each pair of children count the number of round trips their pendula make for every 30 ticks, or some other convenient number. Each child tears off strips of construction paper to measure the length of his pendulum and then writes on the strip his name and the number of round trips this length made in the prescribed time. The teacher tapes a roll of brown paper along the wall. On the bottom he spaces a scale of "Number of Round Trips per 30 Ticks." The ordinate axis is marked with a scale of "Length of Pendulum." Each child finds the place to paste his graph of the pendulum length strip. The results will look something like the diagram below.

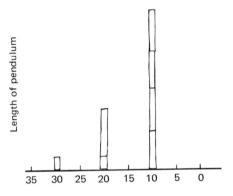

Number of Round Trips per 30 Ticks

Fifth and sixth graders sitting in colloquium before their jointly made graph, begin to think and to talk about it. Because of their previous experiences with graphs, they are likely to suggest joining the tops of the strips. The curve produced is an exciting new datum derived from an ordering of the lengths. What kind of predictions can be made? How long must the pendulum be for there to be 30 round trips in 30 ticks? To make the pendulum swing twice as fast (make twice as many round trips in the same time), should the length be halved? Try this for the graph of the pendulum that makes 16 round trips in 30 ticks. What length makes 32 round trips in the same time? What is the relationship of these two lengths? Have you a hunch about the pattern? Test out your hypothesis by taking the length of the pendulum that makes 40 trips in 30 ticks. How long is the pendulum that makes 20 trips?

The shape of this graph is a parabola, which expresses a relationship with a square in it: $y = x^2$ or $x = \sqrt{y}$. For the pendulum, the time of the period T has this relationship to the length: $T = 2\pi \sqrt{\frac{l}{g}}$, where l is the length of the pendulum and g the constant for gravity.

Some children can figure out from the graph, much as you did, that double the time requires four times the length, treble the time nine times the length, and so on. Where children are conversant with ratios, they can find the times and lengths from experiment and then record them as ratios:

Times	Lengths
2:1	4:1
3:1	9:1
4:1	16:1

Their results will not come out this clearly, but a combination of the graph and measured ratios will help the more mature children make this discovery.[4]

The interaction of falling bodies with gravity produces the same kind of parabolic curve. Allowing a ball to roll down a gently sloping groove and having the children mark with their fingers where the ball has traveled at each second, can produce such a graph. The lengths the ball has traveled in 1, 2, 3 . . . seconds can be placed similarly on a graph.[5] The same shaped graph can be obtained by plotting the length of the side of a square against its areas. These are all linear to square ratios; their hidden likeness is generalized by the equation $y = x^2$.

The principle behind measuring a length is to take a little length as the unit. The principle behind measuring an area is to take a little area as the unit. What science activities might motivate a need to measure or compare areas?

One reason for comparing areas occurs in the study of ecology. Leaves in the shade often grow larger than leaves in the sun. But in some plants, such as the cut-leaved philodendron, the sunny leaves become indented. Is this area less than that of the entire leaf or does it just look that way? Another study might compare the area of the footprints to the body weight of animals that live in snowy climates.[6] Given the tracings of two footprints, can you find the larger? Given several, can you order them according to area?

Four children and four different footprints can be placed on a table with paper plates holding large and small beans in the center. The children readily come upon the device of covering each area with beans, counting the number, and then ordering the footprints according to the number of units covering each surface. Do they use only one kind of bean for comparison? Here is a chance for them to discover that units of the same size must be used in comparisons.

The next stage is to give each child a transparent grid (Xerox Education Series, 600 Madison Ave., New York, N.Y. supplies a ruled acetate sheet) so that the number of squares covering each irregularly shaped area can be counted. A group decision disposes of what to do with the part-squares around the edges.

If lengths are measured by little lengths and areas by little areas, volumes are measured by little volumes. Science often calls for using graduated cylinders to measure volumes. Cylinders are not usually found in elementary school classrooms, however. True, kitchen measuring cups may be used, but these, too, cost money. It is useful and interesting to graduate one's own "cylinder." Any shaped vessel will do: the greater variety of jars, bottles, cups, and cans there are in a classroom, the better. With a set of vessels in front of each group of children and a shoebox of marbles (or beans, rice, pastina, lentils, macaroni shells, etc.), each child is asked to mark his vessel in halves, fourths, thirds, or any other desired fraction. One way the children determine the various volumes is to fill each vessel with the small objects, count them, and then find the number of units in the fraction required. This number is then put in the vessel and the level marked with plastic tape or a ceramics pencil.

[4] See *Pendulums,* an Elementary Science Study booklet available from the Webster Division of McGraw-Hill, Inc., Manchester, Mo. 63011.

[5] See Brenda Lansdown, "Exploring Rate Graphs with Gifted Ten Year Olds," *The Arithmetic Teacher* (March 1964), 146-49.

[6] Outlines of the footprints of various animals are traced in American Association for the Advancement of Science (A.A.A.S.), *Science: A Process Approach*, Part Two, 1965, pp. 114-18.

"Is it more accurate to use marbles or rice for a quart jar?"

"Marbles, because you lose count with rice," was one child's opinion.

"No, rice," said another, "Because I weighed the rice on a balance, half in each pan until the pans were even."

If the children are offered small plastic bags and rubber bands, they soon think of putting a certain number of units in each bag and counting the bags.

Let us suppose that the objective of having graduated volumes available was to measure a certain amount of water for a plant growth experiment. Will these assorted vessels and fractions serve as a group comparison? Obviously not. Can the measures be standardized? There are simple ways to do this; during a colloquium the children find them.

Such an approach to volume often leads to an interest in counting large numbers, as well as in estimating the number of units which will fill each bottle. Keeping track of successive estimations and checking counts greatly improves everyone's ability to estimate accurately. "How many stars in a part of the sky?" "How many blood cells on a slide?" "How many birds in a migrating flock?" There are many science reasons for being able to estimate large numbers. It leads to ways to record large numbers and ways to understand number systems with different bases.

First, think of the divisions of a fertilized egg cell.

Divisions	Cells	Record
0	1	?
1	2	2^1
2	4	2^2
3	8	2^3
etc.		

Children easily extrapolate that the starting point, the one-cell stage, should be written 2^0.

How would the number of cells in the twentieth division be written? The pattern of recording shows us. "How many is this *really*?" It is really 2^{20}, of course! What the questioner probably wants to know is how many that would be recorded in the decimal system.

Here we can tell the old story of the beggar who pleased a bored king by teaching him chess and then asked for his reward, which had been offered as "anything he wanted." The beggar used the chess board: "One grain of rice on the first square; double the number on the second; double that on the third; and so on." "Oh, ask something better than that," urged the king.

How much rice did the beggar receive? Was he well or poorly paid? The children can set out the grains for themselves on a large chess board chalked on the floor. Others could calculate by multiplying. Those who assemble the number of rice grains can then dump them in their graduated vessels (graduated for rice, of course!) and estimate the number of grains.[7]

As a final point of measuring a dimension by using little bits of the same dimension, we remind ourselves that time is measured by small instances of time (as we found in using the intervals of dripping water to measure the time period of the pendulum swing). The unit space-time, c in the formula $E = mc^2$, is a measure of length or distance. One c is the *distance* traveled by light in one second: 180,000 miles.

Another form of ordering which is done more kinesthetically than through ratiocination and is more appropriate for nursery school and kindergarten children is using bins of rice, beans, and shell macaroni with sieves. The sieves are made from wire mesh or hardware cloth with different sized squares so that each sieve stops and lets through different units. The lid or bottom of a small cardboard box with a rectangular hole cut in the surface may be used; tape a slightly larger rectangle of hardware cloth over the hole.

A sectioned bin is a good way to make the materials available for young children, assuming that the classroom is one in which children can choose their activities freely. The bin should be in a large tray or on a table with slightly raised edges (to slow the scattering of units on the floor). Make small paper plates, plastic scoops, and paper cups available. Through play with the materials children discover that some of the units go through the sieves, but

[7] This and other activities for estimating large numbers are described in *Peas and Particles*, an Elementary Science Study booklet available from the Webster Division of McGraw-Hill, Inc., Manchester, Mo. 63011.

others do not. Shortly, all the units are in a gloriously homogenized state! Can they be separated? Of course. The mesh sizes actually order the particles by letting through the smaller and retaining the larger.

To establish what meshes retain what units is a matter of trial and error. Sometimes a bean which looks as though it will not go through a mesh, will if the sieve is shaken enough so that the bean slips through endwise. One set of relationships of mesh to units is given in the diagram below.

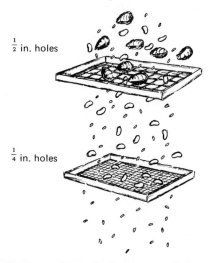

$\frac{1}{2}$ in. holes

$\frac{1}{4}$ in. holes

In a number of chapters we have shown how finding likenesses and differences is a common science activity. A time comes when differences among or within likenesses can be emphasized. This concept emerged from the first grade lesson on inheritance when the children talked about their special Tootsie Roll (see page 180). When children in any one class are measured for height and weight by the school nurse, a good science activity is to have each child measure his cubit (the length from his elbow to his finger tip). The units can be in centimeters or inches. The teacher prepares a large chart of dots (see diagram below) which will become the histogram of the children's variations in cubit

```
.  .  .  .  .  .  .
.  .  .  .  .  .  .
.  .  .  .  .  .  .
.  .  .  .  .  .  .
.  .  .  .  .  .  .
.  .  .  .  .  .  .
.  .  .  .  .  .  .
```

lengths. (The same kind of histogram can be constructed from the class's height and weight measurements.) An estimation has to be made ahead of time of the probable shortest and probable longest measurements. Let us say the numbers range from x to $x + 6$ units; the numerals are written in seven equally spaced positions along the bottom of the dot chart. Each child then puts an X on a new dot in the column which represents his cubit measurement. The final result always comes out in a rough bell curve.

However, the most important outcome is the thinking which the children can do in this way of ordering data. The children will readily perceive that most of the cubits cluster around a center position. They can learn to use the word *mode* for the most common length and the word *mean* for the average. (The latter is for older children.)

The teacher can announce or pretend that a new boy is coming into the class soon whose cubit is___ and that she will choose some number in the $x - p$ range or in the $x + 6 + p$ range for him.

"He must be a midget."

"Or a giant!"

"You're kidding, aren't you?"

Then the teacher knows the children have derived a meaning from their histogram as a range of *possible* data. Could the class predict from the histogram what length cubit he is *most likely* to have? Could the class predict, on a chart where the dots extend in both directions along the abscissa, how the histogram might look for the cubits of children two years old? Would their predictions be more accurate if they were told what the mode length was? Children can be shown histograms where the number of items are much larger and hence the bell curve is considerably more bell-like. Many thinking activities may result from this type of graph.

Of course, the children should make several graphs of their own. Then each child is given the dotted columns to work with and asked to find the number of black stripes on sunflower seeds, each child having several to increase the total number of items. Peas in a pod, or the thermometer readings the class makes of the temperatures of ice in snow slush[8]

---

[8] See *Temperature* (Revised Trial Edition), Science Curriculum Improvement Study, 1966, University of California, Berkeley, p. 29.

may also be used. The modes of such curves are easily spotted and the children can find reasons (hypotheses) why there are only one or two readings at the extremes and why there is any variation at all.

Vectors, we recall, are quantities with direction. Children who have marked shadows of the sun for each hour on several school days and have discussed the meaning of the different sundial lengths may be presented with a set of sun shadows (see diagram). These can be drawings or sticks. The children are asked to place these on a chart in a probable relationship to a marked compass direction

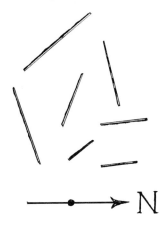

After the children have come to an agreement by discussing their various results in a colloquium, a consensus chart should be exhibited. Then the teacher can say, "I forgot to tell you that these sticks were measured in Chile!" "What difference does that make?" What indeed? Or he could say that they were taken in midsummer or midwinter and give the height of the stick which cast the shadows. Under these circumstances, where would the likely places on earth be for these shadows to have been produced? Children can then produce their own set of shadows, carefully measured from the sun-shadow triangle and the angle of the noonday sun from specific places on earth. An exchange of these among the children in the class is a stimulating activity.

Vectors can be used to represent motion and equilibrium, as we saw in Chapter 4 following Bob Fotheringay's search for a concept (page 175).

At the end of Chapter 4 we asked you to explore some pendulum problems and to use vectors to clarify some of the data you obtained. The problem set was one originally written by Galileo, who was reported to have passed a church service wondering why the chandelier swung in time to his pulse whatever the size of the arc.

A pendulum bob is raised to position A (see figure (1)). It falls through B and rises again to C. The height from level A to level B and the mechanical energy acquired as the bob falls through this distance (as it interacts with gravity) is represented by vector **s**. The same quantity of energy is expended as the bob swings up again to C. Vector **t** thus cancels out vector **s**. The input energy equals the output energy—nearly. In a practical situation, the resistance of air and the friction at the point of suspension always use up some of the acquired energy.

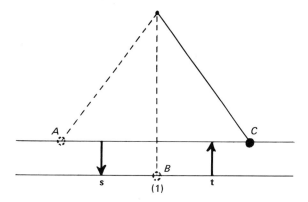

(1)

When the pendulum swing is interrupted by pin P (see figure (2)), the bob still has the same acquired energy, only partially expended. It therefore swings to the same height as before. Vector **t** again cancels out vector **s** (nearly).

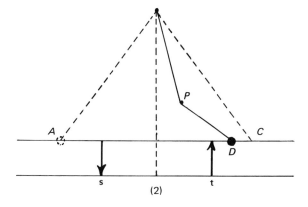

(2)

Suppose now the pin Q is placed so that the string is not sufficiently long to allow the bob to reach level C (see figure (3)). As the bob rises to the maximum height allowed by the string, vector **v** represents the energy used up. There is still a quantity represented by vector **w** in the system (**w** = **t** − **v**). The bob continues moving. The only direction it can go is in a circle. It curls around the pin until the total energy is expended.

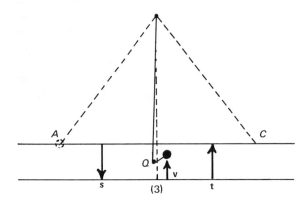

(3)

There is a game which helps children (even as young as second graders) to discover the balance or final outcome of several vectors. This game applies only to vectors operating in multiples of right angles with relation to each other.

A grid of numerals is written on the blackboard. It can be multiples of any number: the basic row constitutes the base of the number system (in our case, base five, although we have written it in the decimal numerals). But this is more of a mathematics activity. The teacher then writes a series of vectors such as: $8 \downarrow \downarrow$. He asks, "Where will I land?" Whatever answers the children give are all accepted without sign or comment. The teacher may then write: $2 \rightarrow \rightarrow \rightarrow$, again asking, "Where do I land?" After a while, the children seem to agree that each arrow represents a jump of one in the direction indicated starting from the numeral. Then what about $17 \leftarrow \rightarrow$ or $9 \uparrow \downarrow$? The children sense that these pairs cancel each other out. They may answer, "You don't move." Is "not moving" the same as "moving out and back again?" In a long series, such as $4 \downarrow \downarrow \rightarrow \uparrow \downarrow \rightarrow \leftarrow \downarrow$, it does not take much time before the children discover the economy of ignoring

1	2	3	4	5
6	7	8	9	10
11	12	13	14	15
16	17	18	19	20
21	.	.	.	.

opposite vectors and concentrating on the unpaired ones. The game aspect is enhanced if, after the initial trials, the teacher as a player does not utter one word and the children argue over discrepant interpretations until they chorus a consensus. There are many extensions of the game, such as indicating numbers of the grid and having children name them or write them in (for example, $18 \downarrow \downarrow$.) Children mentally combine some vectors such as $\rightarrow \uparrow$ and think of the diagonal $\nearrow$. What is the pattern on the chart of $16 (\uparrow \rightarrow)$ $(\uparrow \rightarrow)(\uparrow \rightarrow)\ldots$?

Angles can be further explored by recording the number of reflections seen in two mirrors taped together along one edge. Suppose one holds the mirror at a right angle (see diagram 1). How many images of a penny can be seen? (In this case, four.) If one opens the angle to $120°$ (one third of a whole circle; see diagram 2) or closes the angle until it is only half of a right angle (one eighth of a circle; see diagram 3), how many images can then be seen? By this time, a pattern should become evident. But for children who do not know about the number of degrees, this pattern must be learned through the experience of seeing fewer or more numerous images.

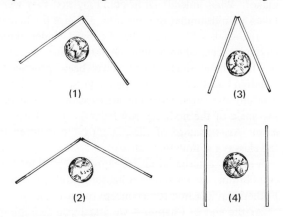

(1)

(3)

(2)

(4)

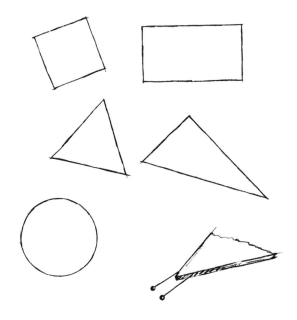

Two pins pushed into a corner through the thickness of the cardboard can be pinched together. This gives a hold which manipulates the positions easily and keeps the fingers out of the shadows.

How many images can be seen with the parallel mirrors in diagram 4?

The principle of angled mirrors is the principle of the kaleidoscope. The images become very attractive esthetically if one uses confetti or small colored bits of cloth in place of the penny. The different kinds of symmetry seen reflect various symmetries in nature: six points in a snowflake, three in some lilies, five in other flowers, and so on.

We will illustrate one final activity with a mathematics–science concept: showing the kinds of shadows an object can throw on various surfaces. The mathematical concept resides partly in projective geometry and partly in the concept of invariance under transformation.

After various experiences with shadow play or shadow tag, the children can be introduced to this topic by working in groups. Each child is given a flashlight, and a variety of geometry shapes cut out of thin cardboard are distributed among the group members. Each child has a light surface on which to throw shadows of the shapes. The room should be as dark as convenient. After a period of free investigation, the children can be asked to work in pairs and to draw the shapes of the shadows they have made. The shapes which are best to begin with are the circle, square, rectangle, and triangle. During the colloquium, one child at a time holds up his drawing and others guess which shape he used to project the shadow.

Here the children discover that some shadows can be thrown from more than one of the shapes and that other shadows have only one object which can project them. However, although each shadow in all but one position looks different from the shape that threw it, there is always something common about the shape and shadow. Some features are invariant under the transformation of projecting them at an angle onto another surface. Can a triangle ever throw a four-cornered shadow? Can a rectangle have fewer than four sides?

All the two-dimensional shapes can throw a shadow which is just a straight line if the light is at right angles to the plane surface. This contrasts dramatically with the shadows thrown by three-dimensional shapes. Good solids to use for exploring the shape of shadows thrown by three-dimensional objects are cubes and rectangular blocks (such as those used in children's block building), a ball, a cone-shaped drinking cup, and a frozen juice can. (A nail driven in one corner of a

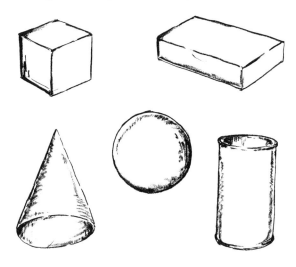

block, a thumbtack pushed through the paper cone and then into a pencil eraser on the outside, and a short length of coat hanger wire taped to the side of the can are all devices for holding and manipulating the objects while keeping the fingers out of the shadow.) The children now discover that hexagon shadows can be made by both cubic and rectangular blocks and that, as the shapes change, a thin line is never produced. The cone, ball, and cylinder can each throw a circular shadow, but only the ball never changes its shadow shape.

An activity in which the whole class can engage is described in *Science: A Process Approach*, Part Two, A.A.A.S., 1965, 84-86. Two shadows of a single object are thrown simultaneously using two translucent screens and two beamed lights from projectors. The problem is to reason about the nature of the solid hidden behind the screens and revealed only by the two shadows. One screen may be used if the object is rotated.

At a later date, or as a follow-up experience, the children can use the same two- and three-dimensional objects to throw their shadows on a large ball or cylinder. Here straight lines of the flat shapes can become curved, but the number of lines and angles still remain invariant.

Bibliography for the Teacher

Teachers need different types of written materials according to (1) the level of knowledge in their own subject area and (2) the requirements of specific units. We will indicate the ways in which each of the recommended items may serve.

A teacher about to launch a unit on which his factual or conceptual knowledge is weak may find it helpful to begin by reading children's trade books on the topic. Recommendations are grouped in the children's bibliography under the matrix to which they pertain. A next step might be to read explanations of the topic in textbooks, but several grades above the one for which the unit is planned. This assumes a more sophisticated viewpoint than the one necessary for the unit and yet the explanations and examples are kept simple. Further information can be acquired by reading current science journals and science teaching journals; here the most modern concepts are likely to be presented along with the latest facts. We recommend also a study of the matrix sections in this book: "Models for the teacher—ways to think and talk about the phenomena encountered in this matrix." By browsing in several sources a teacher is presented with a variety of facts, relationships, and abstractions from which he can enrich his own concepts.

Organization of the Teacher's Bibliography:

SECTION I: *Background Information.*
A. Books on a high-school level or for the nonspecialist adult, page 401.
B. Textbooks on a junior-high or elementary-school level, page 403.
C. Journals, page 403.

SECTION II: *Sources of materials and their use.*
D. Sourcebooks and sources of materials, page 402.
E. Mimeographed publications, page 404.
F. The major new science curriculum programs, page 404.
G. Bibliographies, page 407.
H. Newsletters, page 408.

SECTION III: *Psychology,* page 408.

SECTION IV: *Philosophy,* page 408.

SECTION I: *Background information.*
A. Books on a high-school level or for the nonspecialist adult.

PHYSICS:

Baker, Adolf. *Modern Physics and Antiphysics.* Reading, Mass.: Addison-Wesley, 1970. A very human and readable account of modern concepts in physics, including relativity, mass-energy, waves and particles, quantum. Amusingly and pertinently illustrated by the author.

The Project Physics Course. New York: Holt, Rinehart & Winston, Inc., 1970. This is the concept-oriented textbook which has been much tested in tryouts of the Harvard Project Physics Course. Chapter titles: "Concepts of Motion," "Motion in the Heavens," "The Triumph of Mechanics," "Light and Electromagnetism," "Models of the Atom," "The Nucleus." Interesting and pertinent historical information is included.

CHEMISTRY:

Choppin, Gregory R., and Jaffe, Bernard. *Chemistry: Science of Matter and Change.* Morristown, N. J.: Silver Burdett, 1971. A popular text with clear explanations, useful diagrams, and full coverage of the usual high school syllabus. Much interesting historical and biographical material.

BIOLOGY:

High School Biology, BSCS Green Version. Chicago: Rand McNally, 1968. This is one of the books developed by the Biological Science Curriculum Study; it emphasizes the "World of Life"—the "Biosphere." Content explores the ideas and facts in these and other areas: "The Web of Life," "Communities and Ecosystems," "Diversity Among Living Organisms," "Patterns in the Biosphere," "Man and the Biosphere."

Simpson, George Gaylord. *The Meaning of Evolution.* New Haven: Yale University Press, 1960, pb. Modern theory of the course and mechanisms of evolution and its meaning for man's future.

GEOLOGY:

Heller, Robert L., and the American Geological Institute. *Geology and Earth Science Sourcebook for Elementary and Secondary Schools.* New York: Holt, Rinehart & Winston, Inc., 1962. Basic information listed as "Facts and Ideas" paralleling a column on "Methods and Activities." A good coverage from minerals, rock formation, earthquakes, the atmosphere, astronomy, the earth's origin, fossils, geologic maps, and the relation of geology to other sciences. Presentation of unsolved problems is thought provoking.

OCEANOGRAPHY:

Some of the subsections of oceanography overlap with the subsections of geology: there are earthquakes under the sea (such as the one which produced Surtsey) and the atmosphere is affected by both the land and the ocean under it. The following trade books seem more helpful in providing background information than any one particular adult text.

Bascom, Willard. *Waves and Beaches,* Science Study Series. Garden City: Doubleday, 1964. pb. A lot of information about waves and their effects on shorelines. Accounts of tsunamis are included.

Battan, Louis J. *The Nature of Violent Storms,* Science Study Series. Garden City: Doubleday, 1961. pb. A readable explanation of what is and is not known about tornadoes, hurricanes, cyclones, etc.

Behrman, Daniel. *The New World of the Oceans.* Boston: Little Brown, 1969. Written for the layman under a grant from UNESCO. About the men who explore the resources of the ocean, how they do it, and the implication of their discoveries for man. Continental drift and pollution receive a share of the discussion.

Carson, Rachel. *The Sea Around Us.* New York: Oxford University Press, 1961. A research-based study of the sea, its origins, the life it harbors, the tides, the mineral content.

Cousteau, Captain Jacques-Yves. *The Living Sea.* New York: Harper & Row, 1963. An account of the many wonders under many seas by a man who was there as diver both in an aqualung and in his oceanographic ship, the *Calypso.* Exciting undersea photography.

B. Textbooks on a junior-high level.

Matter: Its Forms and Changes
Life: Its Forms and Changes
Energy: Its Forms and Changes

All by Brandwein, Paul F., Stollberg, Robert, and Burnett, R. Will. New York: Harcourt Brace Jovan-

ovich, Inc., 1968. Concept-oriented texts and investigations.

Textbooks on an elementary-school level.

Textbook series which we have used and quoted at various points in our matrix development and which we feel will give helpful background material to a teacher are the following:

Brandwein, Paul F., Cooper, Elizabeth K., Blackwood, Paul E., Hone, Elizabeth B. *Concepts in Science* (Grades 1-6). New York: Harcourt Brace Jovanovich, Inc., 1966.

Fischler, Abraham S., Lowery, Lawrence F., Blanc, Sam S. *Science: A Modern Approach.* New York: Holt, Rinehart & Winston, Inc., 1966.

Fischler, Blanc, Farley, Lowery, Smith. *Modern Elementary Science.* New York: Holt, Rinehart & Winston, Inc., 1971. A later edition of the above.

Mallinson, George G., Mallinson, Jacqueline B., Brown, Douglas G. *Science* (Grades 1-6), Teachers edition. Morristown, N. J.: Silver Burdett, 1965.

Schneider, Herman and Nina. *Science* (Grades 1-6). Lexington, Mass.: D. C. Heath, 1965. Each grade level has a separate subtitle.

C. Journals.

Scientific American, 415 Madison Avenue, New York, N. Y. 10017. Monthly. Keeps one abreast of modern developments in all areas of science. Many articles are available as offprints.

Science and Children, a publication of the National Science Teachers Association, 1201 Sixteenth Street, N. W., Washington, D. C. 20036. Monthly during the school year. Contains science information and new ideas for elementary-school teachers. Reviews books and lists sources of materials.

Nature and Science, published by Doubleday for the American Museum of Natural History, New York, N. Y. This publication is now out of print, but it would be worth looking up back copies if any are available. It was issued fortnightly during the school year. It contains fascinating and thought provoking articles on a number of forefront science topics addressed to children. A Teacher's Edition provides a cover sheet of helpful suggestions for using the materials in the classroom.

SECTION II: *Sources of materials and their use.*

Where a teacher is fairly sure of the facts and feels competent in the concept area, he may still need help in finding suitable materials to offer the children. These have been discussed and listed at some length throughout the book. However, Section II covers some additional sources.

D. Sourcebooks and sources of materials.

Cornell Science Leaflet, Building 7, Cornell University Research Park, Ithaca, N. Y. 14850. A large series of pamphlets concerned with all manner of science topics. Each gives information, suggested investigations, and bibliographies. Send for listings.

Geology and Earth Science Sourcebook for Elementary and Secondary Schools (see Section I A., page 401).

Hone, Elizabeth B., Joseph, Alexander, Victor, Edward, Brandwein, Paul F. *A Sourcebook for Elementary Science,* 2nd ed. New York: Harcourt Brace Jovanovich, Inc., 1971. Many practical suggestions in every field usually explored in elementary science textbooks. Not much on astronomy, although space travel has good coverage.

Morholt, Evelyn, Brandwein, Paul F., Joseph, Alexander. *A Sourcebook for the Biological Sciences,* 2nd ed. New York: Harcourt Brace Jovanovich, Inc., 1966. Oriented largely toward high-school students, but still some very valuable suggestions—a number of which would enhance discovery learning in the elementary school.

Nuffield Junior Science has several books on materials and their uses, including:
Animals and Plants (How to care for and use.)
Apparatus (Lots of ideas for homemade equipment.)
Teacher's Guides 1 and 2 (Records of classes with children.)
All London: Collins, 1967.

UNESCO Sourcebook for Science Teaching. UNESCO Publications Center, 650 First Avenue, New York, N. Y. (Ask for the latest edition.) Investigations of science phenomena through use of easily obtainable materials. Appendices list useful data on weights and measures, stars and planets, latitudes and dates when the sun is directly overhead at noon, relative hardness of various types of rocks.

KITS for textbook units and the new programs are available from the publishers who produce the books. *Individual items* (should you not wish to purchase a whole kit as listed) are sometimes available from these same publishers. However, several firms now specialize in making individual items for the new programs available. It would be wise to send for catalogs to see just which items are currently supplied. It will take experience to learn who supplies the equipment fastest and most reliably to your particular area. There are undoubtedly other local firms which your high school science teachers have used.

Here are some sources for many of the items required by the new program:

American Science and Engineering, Inc., 20 Overland Street, Boston, Mass. 02125. (617) 262-6500.

Oregon Museum of Science and Industry (OMSI/Kit, Inc.), 10655 S. W. Greenburg Road, Portland, Oregon 97223. (503) 639-6112.

Selective Educational Equipment (SEE), 3 Bridge Street, Newton, Mass. 02195. (617) 969-3330.

Webster Division, McGraw-Hill, Inc., Manchester Road, Manchester, Missouri 63011. (314) 227-1600. (Also has several locations in other states.)

Xerox Education Sciences, 600 Madison Avenue, New York, N. Y. 10022. (212) 758-7100. Supplies kits and individual items for the AAAS booklets *Science: A Process Approach.*

ORGANISMS such as Daphnia, algae, etc. will be delivered quickly and in good condition from Connecticut Valley Biology Company, Valley Road, Southampton, Mass. 01073. (413) 527-4030.

The Haledon Hatchery and Breeding Farm, 1048 Hamburg Turnpike, Wayne, N. J. 07470. (201) 742-3824. Supplies fertile eggs.

Preparing aquaria: In addition to the teacher preparations described in Matrix 9 (pages 290–92), we record here some other helpful procedures which have been supplied by the kindness of Arthur Greenberg, the biologist to SEE. The information came too late to be printed with the matrix, but the reader was referred to this part of the bibliography.

One of the main problems in preparing a culture of organisms such as Daphnia is that water considered fit for human consumption often kills a culture of delicate organisms. Here is a way to *condition faucet water for a small organism culture.* First, the water must not come from copper pipes. Draw it from a standpipe, use distilled or natural spring water, or boil water from a pond (to kill unwanted organisms). If city water is used, it should stand 48 hours for the chlorine to escape. Water selected and treated in this manner is referred to as *conditioned water.*

The vessel: To clean a glass or other large vessel to hold conditioned water, wash thoroughly with soap and rinse, preferably in a dishwashing machine (without the detergent cycle, of course!) Rinse with sea salt water (see the section on Brine Shrimps, this page) or diluted vinegar. Soap tends to decrease the surface tension of the water so that air is not held in solution very long. The rinse restores this capacity.

Fill the vessel with conditioned water. Then add one-quarter teaspoon of *sheep* manure to each gallon of water. Leave another 48 hours; then strain. This produces a clear seasoned liquid with microscopic organisms (seasoned water) which will help the larger organisms in the culture (the Daphnia) survive.

Small aquaria for individual children can be made from strong 18 x 19 in. plastic bags supported by a wire trash bag holder or by a frame made from coat hangers. (Use strong pliers to bend the two hangers into circles over which the edges of the plastic bag may be held in place by spring clothespins. The two hooks on the hangers can be bent to make leg supports; the weight of the bag of water should rest on the surface of a table.)

Algae: In an aquarium, algae will multiply well if one drop of fishmeal plant food is added to half a gallon of conditioned water.

Gravel: In an aquarium do *not* use extra fine white silica sand. This has sharp corners which tear the alimentary canals of tender organisms. Buy what is called "white sand" from a gravel supply store (the sand is actually slightly yellow in appearance). It is sold in 100 lb. bags.

Temperature: Guppies, goldfish, and Daphnia survive best in water which does not rise above 65°F. Keep the vessel in a dark part of the room and light it with a 100 watt bulb positioned 8 in. above the surface of the water for six hours a day.

Daphnia: "Daphnia fish food" is dried, but contains both species: small *Daphnia pulex* and large *Daphnia magna.* As the culture grows, dip the *Daphnia magna* out with an eye-dropper and place them in a separate culture. Daphnia should be kept at no more than

65°F. The culture can be placed outdoors overnight without harm even if the water freezes nightly.

If the water is allowed to warm above 65°F, the rounded head of the *Daphnia magna* become more and more pointed until the temperature reaches 72°F. Strangely, the young produced by Daphnia with pointed heads have pointed heads themselves, even if they always live in cool water. Above 72°F, the Daphnia react as they do to any adverse circumstance: some of the young produced are males who fertilize the females; each female then develops two capsules (called an ephippium) and these release eggs which can withstand the adverse condition.

Daphnia can be fed yeast which is prepared by adding one package of dried yeast (sold in grocery stores for baking) to 8 oz. of conditioned water. Feed one eye-dropper full of this cloudy liquid daily to a batch of Daphnia culture supplied for 25 students.

Snails: Snails have different habits, so a variety in an aquarium will enliven interest as well as help the ecosystem. *Pond Snails* eat algae which grow on the walls of the aquarium. *Ramshorn Snails* eat water plants and lay eggs on the leaves. *Small Mystery Snails* are carnivorous and dispose of dead fish and snails.

Brine shrimps and salt water aquaria: Instant Ocean Salts can be made cheaply from Kosher salt and Epsom Salts. Dissolve 5 tablespoons of Kosher salt in water which has stood for 48 hours; add one teaspoon of Epsom Salts.

A brine shrimp aquarium can be made by placing an airstone (made from pumice) in the bottom of a V-shaped plastic bag (called a brine shrimp stocking). Attach the airstone to an aerating pump by a plastic tube. (A good, inexpensive pump is the Hush-I Meta Frame; it can aerate several stockings of shrimp at once through separate plastic tubes.)

E. Mimeographed publications.

The following may be obtained by writing to Dr. Mitchell E. Batoff, Department of Science Education, Jersey City State College, Jersey City, N. J. 07305:

From Egg to Egg to Egg. Incubation and embryology of chicks in the elementary-school classroom. How to construct an incubator, where to buy the eggs, how to study the incubating chicks.

How to Prepare Children, Organize, and Conduct a Successful Star Party in the Elementary School. 1970. Just what the title says, plus an extensive multimedia bibliography and a star chart of the northern skies.

The Use of Black Box Investigations to Introduce Elements of the Philosophy of Science to Elementary-School Children. 1969. How to construct sealed boxes which contain objects whose presence can be inferred through sound, odor, kinesthetic sense, or which can be made to interact with magnets, probes, and other test objects. The experience in some measure parallels that of scientists who must formulate models of the unseeable or unreachable.

F. The major new science curriculum programs.
Each of the new government- and foundation-supported science curricula has devised, tested, and made available a fine collection of materials with which children can work. The programs advise a wide range of pedagogical techniques from free discovery to teacher-directed activities. Each program offers many sets of materials that could be used in the manner suggested in this book. It is useful to browse through the printed materials when seeking new ideas or new materials.

In the process of devising, testing, and revising the units and materials, the programs often move from local (university) publishing to one or more commercial firms. You may find that a booklet we have listed as obtainable from one source has been taken over by a new publisher or distributor by the time you request it. We therefore ask your indulgence while assuring you that whether you write to the original source or to the final production firm you will be given help to find the item you need.

AAAS
The American Association for the Advancement of Science
1515 Massachusetts Avenue, N. W.
Washington, D. C. 20005

Science: A Process Approach, Parts I-VII. 1967. Emphasis is on the processes of science: observing, communicating, making hypotheses, predicting, etc. The method is teacher-directed and the organizing theme is the procedures that scientists use. The materials used to illustrate the theme could be useful in matrices designed for self-motivated activities.

> *Materials* are marketed by Xerox Education Sciences, 600 Madison Avenue, New York, N.Y. 10022.

Science: A Process Approach, Commentary for Teachers. 1965. A chance for the teacher to experience the processes he will teach to the children. Thought-provoking questions and ways to evaluate your own progress.

Science: A Process Approach, Guide for Inservice Instruction. 1967.

Science: A Process Approach has a coordinated testing program for each grade.

COPES
Conceptually Oriented Program in Elementary Science
New York University
New York, N. Y. 10003

Conservation of Energy Sequence, Teacher's Guide. 1967. Many suggested activities and materials which could be adapted to free discovery for grades K–6. Explanations of phenomena in terms of system and energy, although the old terms "force" and "cause" are also used.

EIS (Experiences in Science): See page 406.

ESCP
Earth Science Curriculum Project
Houghton Mifflin Co.
2 Park Street
Boston, Mass. 02107

Investigating the Earth, Teacher's Guide. 1967. Although directed at the high-school level, many of the activities could be adapted to upper elementary grades. The information from behavioral, conceptual, and historical viewpoints is clearly stated. Included are observations relating to the solar system and physical geography, the moon, the atmosphere, the sea, erosion, evolution, and the interior of the earth.

ESS
Elementary Science Study
of the Education Development Center, Inc.
55 Chapel Street
Newton, Mass. 02160

The ESS Reader. 1970. A collection of articles on the ESS program by its developers.

ESS units are available under the following titles:

Animal activity*	Making maps
Animals and the class-	Mapping
room	Match and measure
Attribute games and	Microgardening (2 vols.)*
problems*	Mirror cards*
Balloons	Mobiles*
Batteries and bulbs (4	Mosquitoes
vols.)*	Mystery powders*
Behavior of mealworms*	Optics
Bones*	Outdoor mapping
Brine shrimp*	Pattern blocks*
Budding twigs	Peas and particles*
Butterflies*	Pendulums*
Changes*	Pond water*
Children printing	Primary balancing*
Clay boats*	Rocks and charts*
Colored solutions*	Sand
Crayfish*	Senior balancing
Daytime astronomy	Sink and float
Drops, steams, and con-	Slips and slides
tainers	Small things*
Earthworms	Spinning tables
Eggs and tadpoles*	Starting from seeds
Euglena	Structures
Gases and "airs"*	Tangrams*
Geo blocks*	Tracks
Growing seeds*	Waterflow
Heating and cooling	Where is the moon?*
Ice cubes*	[with "Reminders"–
Kids, cameras, and com-	(Suggestion Cards) on
munities	what to look for in the
Kitchen physics*	sky on specific calen-
Life of beans and peas*	dar dates]
Light and shadow	Whistles and strings

*Not available from ESS. Contact the Webster Division of McGraw-Hill, Inc., Manchester Road, Manchester, Missouri 63011.

No attempt is made to present a curriculum; each unit is complete and is designed to be used separately.

A detailed description of each unit has been excerpted from the ESS material and published in mimeograph by Dr. Mitchell E. Batoff, (Department of Science Education, Jersey City State College, Jersey City, N. J. 17305) as Part II of *The Testate Series of Student Teaching Monographs.* Similar excerpts from the other new programs are planned.

ES
Environmental Studies
Box 1559
Boulder, Colorado 80302

An outgrowth of the Earth Science Educational Program and the Earth Science Teacher Preparation Project. Is developing sensitive materials to help children orient themselves to their total environment. An interactional approach which centers on change, mapping, counting, and judging. (Also ask for the ES *Newsletter.*)

EIS
Experiences in Science
Webster Division
McGraw-Hill, Inc.
Manchester Road
Manchester, Missouri 63011

Tannenbaum, Harold E., Tannenbaum, Beulah, Stillman, Nathan, and Stillman, Myra. *Experiences in Science.* 1967. Thirty-six units, each consisting of a child's Recortext (a guide with spaces for recording observations), Teacher's Guide, and Equipment Kit. The unit titles follow, in approximate order of difficulty:

Hot and cold	Solids, liquids, and gases
Young animals	Adaptations
Light and shadow	Atmosphere and weather
Earth and sun	Chemical change
Weather	Geologic processes
Plants in spring	Ecology
Magnets	Microscopic life
Batteries	Molds
Groups	Unbalanced forces
Balances	Balanced forces
Air	Mapping
Living things	Time
Motion	Electricity
Earth, sun, and seasons	Life processes of plants
Heat	Continuity of life
Sound	Light
Life histories	Color
Plant and animal	The universe
responses	

Tannenbaum, Stillman, and Piltz. *Science Education for Elementary School Teachers.* Rockleigh, N. J.: Allyn and Bacon, 1965. Teacher's Handbook for *Experiences in Science* series. Each unit is described in Batoff, *The Testate Series of Student Teaching Monographs,* Part I.

MINNEMAST
Minnesota Math And Science Teaching Project
Minnemath Center
University of Minnesota
720 Washington Avenue, S. E.
Minneapolis, Minnesota 55414

The Minnemast project is basically a mathematics project initiated and developed by Dr. Paul Rosenbloom. The science was added later and coordinated with the mathematics curriculum. Some of the concepts are introduced by stories which can be read to the children. The lessons are teacher-directed. At present there are 29 units in booklet form for grades K-3, published between 1967-1970.

Overview of the Minnemast Project (booklet). 1960.

Questions and Answers About Minnemast (booklet). 1968.

SCIS
Science Curriculum Improvement Study
Lawrence Hall of Science
University of California
Berkeley, California 94720

Initiated and developed by Robert Karplus, this is a total science curriculum worked out on six levels (roughly grades 1-6). Each level has an extended unit from the physical sciences and one from the life sciences. There is a clear philosophy guiding the choice and development of the units (very much that described by Stephen Toulmin. *The Philosophy of Science.* London: Hutchinson and Co., 1953. (New York: Harper & Row publishes a 1960 paperback edition.)

The teaching pattern begins with guided use of materials, then an Invention Lesson where the teacher helps the children develop the appropriate concept, followed by application of the concept in what is called a Discovery Lesson.

The materials and booklets (both children's and teacher's) are *marketed,* as they become finalized, by Rand McNally, P. O. Box 7600, Chicago, Illinois 60680. Prior editions as well as final editions also may be obtained from the Berkeley address. The units, in approximate order of difficulty, are:

Biology:	*Physics:*
Organisms	Material objects
Life cycles	Interaction and system
Populations	Subsystems and variables
Environments	Relative position and motion
Communities	Energy sources
Ecosystems	Models: electric and magnetic interaction

Jacobson, Willard, and Kondo, Allan. *SCIS Elementary Science Sourcebook.* Berkeley: University of California, 1968. The necessary science background and down-to-earth ways to teach the SCIS program.

Karplus, Robert, and Thier, Herbert D. *A New Look at Elementary School Science.* Chicago: Rand McNally, 1969. [Part of the *New Trends in Curriculum Series,* John U. Michaelis (ed.).] History, theory, and practices of the SCIS program.

Thier, Herbert D. *SCIS and the Disadvantaged: A Report from the Field.* Berkeley: University of California, 1970. Brief reports on the way SCIS units worked in a variety of low socioeconomic areas from Hawaii to Harlem.

Thier, Herbert D. *Teaching Elementary Science: A Laboratory Approach.* Lexington, Mass.: D. C. Heath, 1970. (Based on the SCIS program.)

Books and media about the new curricula:
de Hart Hurd, Paul, and Gallagher, James J. *New Directions in Elementary Science Teaching.* Belmont, Calif.: Wadsworth Publishing Co., 1968. A critical appraisal of the new curricula.

Integrated Information Unit. Far West Regional Laboratory for Educational Research and Development. A multimedia presentation of the essence of the new programs by filmstrips, audiotapes, and booklets.

G. Bibliographies.
To keep up with the many new developments in science teaching as well as with new children's books and new audiovisual aids, there are several bibliographic sources and newsletters.

Appraisal, children's science books reviewed three times a year by a committee based at the Graduate School of Education, Harvard University, Longfellow Hall, Cambridge, Mass. 02138. Chairman: Frances Doughty. Subscription: $3.00 a year. Reviews are by librarians and by scientists. Often their appraisals disagree. Books chosen to be reviewed are carefully selected.

Environmental Education Bibliography ranges from preschool through grade 9 and supplies background reading for the teacher. Prepared by the Massachusetts Audubon Society, Lincoln, Mass. 01773 for the U. S. Office of Education. Presently in mimeographed form. A comprehensive (but not exhaustive) annotated list of books, films, filmstrips, recordings, activity guides, curriculum materials on ecology, conservation, pollution, and outdoor interests.

I Wonder Why Readers, a series published by Holt, Rinehart & Winston, Inc., under the consultantship of Abraham S. Fischler. Send for the *Teacher's Guide* by Lawrence F. Lowery and Evelyn Moore. The guide describes all the books in the series and suggests ways to use them in language arts and science lessons.

Science Books: A Quarterly Review, published by the American Association for the Advancement of Science, 1515 Massachusetts Avenue, N. W., Washington, D. C. 20005. Subscription: $4.50 a year. Reviews science books in 24 categories, giving age-level interest and appraisal on a four point scale from *highly recommended* to *not recommended.*

Information on the contributions of scientists from the ethnic minorities is still hard to locate. A few science works can be culled from the following general sources:

Books, Films, Recordings by and about the American Negro, selected by young-adult librarians, the New York Public Library. Available from the Countee Cullen Library, Regional Branch, 104 West 136th St., New York, N. Y.

Koblitz, Minnie W. *The Negro in Schoolroom Literature.* The Center for Urban Education, 105 Madison Avenue, New York, N. Y. 10016. 1967. Resource materials for the kindergarten-sixth grade teacher. A few mention scientists.

The Negro in the United States: A List of Significant Books, compiled by the New York Public Library. Available from the Office of Adult Services, 8 East 40th St., New York, N. Y. ($1.00) Books about and by black Americans.

Standard audiovisual catalogs of educational media (New York: R. R. Bowker) are:
  Index to 16mm Educational Films
  Index to Educational Overhead Transparencies
  Index to Educational Filmstrips
  Index to Educational 8mm Cartridges (Filmloops)

H. Newsletters.
There is usually no charge to have your name placed on the mailing list to receive these *newsletters:*

Environmental Studies, ES Newsletter (see Section II F, page 404).

ESS Newsletter, published several times a year by the Elementary Science Study, Education Development Center, 55 Chapel Street, Newton, Mass. 02160.

SCIS Newsletter, published on occasion by the Science Curriculum Improvement Study, Lawrence Hall of Science, University of California, Berkeley, Calif. 94720.

WIMSA Newsletter, published on occasion by the Webster Institute of Mathematics, Science, and Arts, Webster College, St. Louis, Missouri 63119. Interesting, creative developments in many curricular areas. Chief science contributions have been "The Shell Game" and "Even Flies Remember." Both are multimedia approaches.

SECTION III: *Psychology.*

A teacher who feels in need of more detailed information on the cognitive development of children or on creating the kind of atmosphere where self-motivated learning can take place, may enjoy some of these works on psychology:

Bartlett, Sir Frederic. *Thinking: An Experimental Study.* London: George, Allen, and Unwin, 1958. An interesting presentation of creative and adventurous thinking.

Baruch, Dorothy. *New Ways in Discipline.* New York: McGraw-Hill, Inc., 1949. Simple descriptions of the principle and the effects of accepting children's feelings.

Piaget, Jean. *Six Psychological Studies.* New York: Random House, 1967. Perhaps the most readable account of Piaget's contribution to an understanding of the thought development of the child.

Vygotsky, L. S. (translated by Eugenia Hanfmann and Gertrude Vakar). *Thought and Language.* Cambridge: M.I.T. Press, 1962, pb. Although most people find this book an effort to read, a further elaboration of the concept levels we have used for our analyses may be valuable to some teachers.

SECTION IV: *Philosophy.*

Toulmin, Stephen. *The Philosophy of Science.* London: Hutchinson and Co., 1953. (New York: Harper & Row publishes a 1960 paperback edition.) A modern philosophy of science which is applicable to science curricula in the elementary school. The SCIS program most nearly approaches this philosophical outlook.

Bibliography for the Children

This bibliography is arranged by matrix. A possibility of five categories then exists within each matrix:

Textbooks
Trade Books
Film(s)
Filmloop(s)
Filmstrip(s)

In each of these five categories, books are alphabetized by author and films by title under three subcategories designating level of difficulty:

P. (primary)
I. (upper elementary)
E. (for use in all levels of the elementary school)

Code for other abbreviations:

b/w: black and white
c: color
s: silent

Film producers and distributors:

CF: Churchill Films*
CORF: Coronet Films*
EBF: Encyclopedia Britannica Films, Inc.
FA: Film Associates

AIR (GAS) IS MATTER (MATRIX 1, PAGE 192)
TEXTBOOKS

The concept of molecules is a difficult one for young children to develop. However, by thinking of very tiny particles in motion, children in the second and third grades can begin to build the concept. Investigations and explanations for these levels are found clearly presented in:

Brandwein, Paul F. *et al. Concepts in Science 2*. New York: Harcourt Brace Jovanovich, Inc., 1966. Unit 1, "The Very Small."

Brandwein. *Concepts in Science 3*. Unit 4, "The Forms of Things."

Schneider, Herman and Nina. *Science in Your Life 4*. Lexington, Mass.: D. C. Heath, 1965. Chapter 3, "Molecules of Matter." Emphasis on states of matter and molecular motion.

TRADE BOOKS

P.   Bendick, Jeanne. *Space and Time* (Science Experiences). New York: Franklin Watts, 1968. Illustrated by the author. Space and time linked in

Note: These are film producers. Consult the latest edition of the *Index to 16 mm Educational Films* (New York: R. R. Bowker Co.) for the *distributor* nearest you.

a manner suitable to the understanding of young children ("Can you think of a question that asks 'Where?' without asking 'When?' "). Many open-ended questions and investigations. Running through the book are the concepts that matter in any form occupies space and that matter is conserved. The book would be useful to provoke thought in older children.

I.   Stone, A. Harris. and Siegel, Bertram M. *Take a Balloon*. Englewood Cliffs, N. J.: Prentice-Hall, 1967. Illustrated by Peter P. Plasencia. Many open-ended investigations with balloons which would serve to help children understand airplane and rocket flight, expansion, permeability, and sound, among other topics.

FILM

I.   "The World of Molecules," CF, 1958 b/w, 11 min. Animation and clear, simple demonstrations are combined to illustrate the different energies of molecule activity in gases, liquids, and solids. Examples include: the smell of a freshly broken donut, ink diffusing through water (filling up the spaces between the water molecules), water changing to ice or steam, atmospheric moisture condensing on the outside of a cold bottle of milk.

FILMSTRIP

"Molecules," Heath Science Films, Set 4 A, No. 3. The molecule is presented as the smallest portion of a substance (different substances are made up of different molecules). The smell of a pickle is explained in terms of molecular activity. Temperature and motion of molecules are related.

GASES AND HEAT ENERGY (MATRIX 2, PAGE 200)
TEXTBOOKS

As for Matrix 1, and:
E.   Schneider. *Science in Your Life 4*. Chapter 4, "Causes of Weather." Motion of molecules applied to some phenomena of weather.

TRADE BOOKS

P.   Lowery, Lawrence F. *Clouds, Rain and Clouds Again. I Wonder Why Readers* (Consultant, Abraham S. Fischler). New York: Holt, Rinehart & Winston, Inc., 1969. Illustrated by Jan Pfloog. Raises questions without answering all of them.

I. Ruchlis, Hy. *The Wonder of Heat Energy*. New York: Harper & Row, 1961. Illustrated by Alice Hirsh. Many manifestations of heat explained in modern, scientific language: in geology, life, weather, radiation, refrigeration. Interesting photographs which pose problems. For example: icicles hang from the white strips of an awning and not from the dark colored stripes. Why? (Solutions are in an appendix!)

I. Stone. *Take a Balloon* (see Matrix 1).

E. Stone, A. Harris and Siegel, Bertram M. *The Heat's On!* Englewood Cliffs, N. J.: Prentice-Hall, 1970. Illustrated by Peter P. Plasencia. Many simple, open-ended investigations on heat, including its effects and measurement, described in few words. Each investigation is followed by thought-provoking questions extending the principles.

Winchester, James H. *Hurricanes, Storms, Tornadoes*. New York: Putnam, 1968. Illustrated with b/w photos. A fascinating account of dramatic weather phenomena. A first-hand and graphic description of the effects of violent weather on people who have survived tornadoes and hurricanes. Safety rules are given.

FILMS

I. "Explaining Matter: Molecules in Motion," EBF, 1958, b/w, 11 min. The film concentrates mainly on water in its various forms. Animated sequences show the effect of changes in molecular energy from the solid state (ice) to liquid (water) to gas (steam). A further example extends the concept by showing that carbon dioxide from ginger ale bubbles can be frozen to dry ice at low temperatures.

I. "Things Expand When Heated," McGraw-Hill, Inc., 1962, b/w, 10 min. Animation superimposed on the investigations of a child in the family kitchen explains expansion as increased molecular activity: a balloon on top of a teakettle, then in cold water; a glass coffee maker; a thermometer cooled and heated; a pickle jar in hot water pops its lid. Metal expansion is illustrated by showing a steel rod fitting into a metal plate at room temperature and not fitting when heated. The film ends with three thought-provoking problems.

FILMLOOP

I. "Convection in Liquids," Gene Gray, Newton Public Schools, Newton, Mass. Produced by the Ealing Corp. (super 8: 82-0050/1), c., 3 min. 40 sec. Very clear demonstrations of the interaction of hot and cold liquids (really liquids and heat energy). Many of the activities children could repeat for themselves. Questions are posed at points during the loop.

FILMSTRIP

"Molecules" (see Matrix 1, page 409).

GASES AND MECHANICAL ENERGY (MATRIX 3, PAGE 206)

TEXTBOOKS

Schneider. *Science in Your Life 4*. 1965. End of Chapter 7 on "Moving Through Air."
Schneider, Herman and Nina and Lansdown, Brenda. *Now Try This 4*. 1966. Open-ended workbook investigations, pp. 87-96.

TRADE BOOKS

I. Bendick, Jeanne. *Space Travel*. New York: Franklin Watts, 1969. Illustrated by the author. Much interesting factual information about gravity in the solar system and its relation to space travel. Clear explanations and pertinent illustrations. The historical approach includes a transition from Newtonian thinking to modern thinking.

I. Herbert, Don and Ruchlish Hy. *Flying: Beginning Science with Mr. Wizard*. Garden City, N. Y.: Doubleday, 1960. Illustrated by Mel Hunter. Experimental approach; clear, attractive, and meaningful illustrations. Good explanation of why an airplane lifts. However, the book uses the Newtonian concept of "action and reaction" to explain rocket flight instead of the more modern interaction concept.

I. Posin, Daniel Q. *Exploring and Understanding Rockets and Satellites*. Chicago: Benfic Press, 1967. Rocket thrust and why a satellite stays in orbit are well explained. Questions and thought problems conclude each chapter.

E. Pacilio, James V. *Discovering Aerospace*. Chicago: Children's Press, 1965. Illustrated by George Rohrer. Many suggested activities illustrating the principles of plane and rocket flight.

FILM

I. "Airplanes: Principles of Flight," CF, 1960, c., 11 min. The film begins with some early Leonardo da Vinci models and moves on to show how the "aerial screw" was a forerunner of the helicopter. Clear explanations and animation present the interaction of the angle of a kite or an airplane wing to pressure exerted by moving air and the relation of the shape of a wing to lift. The mechanics of manoeuvering a plane with rudder and ailerons are introduced.

FILMSTRIP

"Rocket Propulsion," Heath Science Series, Set 7A, No. 1. Illustration using steam in a can shows balanced pressure on all sides; this is unbalanced when a small hole emits the steam and unbalanced pressure pushes in a direction opposite to the hole. The principle is elaborated with a model using clay, marbles, and sticks. The message of equilibrium and non-equilibrium in relation to rocket propulsion is well communicated.

LIQUID-SOLID INTERACTIONS (MATRIX 4, PAGE 212)

TEXTBOOKS

Brandwein. *Concepts in Science 3*. Unit 4, "The Forms of Things." The role of molecules in evaporation, in solutions, as combinations of atoms. Many investigations. Emphasis on conservation of matter.

Schneider, Herman and Nina. *Science for Today and Tomorrow 6*. Chapter 1, "Basic Chemistry." A considerable extension of the matrix activities.

TRADE BOOK

P. David, Eugene. *Crystal Magic*. Englewood Cliffs, N. J.: Prentice-Hall, 1965. Illustrated by Abner Graboff. Very simple (but informative) suggested activities for growing crystals of salt and sugar.

FILM

I. "States of Matter," McGraw-Hill, Inc., 1957, b/w, 13 min. Rather dated and a bit too talkative, but the examples, when they come, are clear and well related. That gases have weight (are a form of matter) is shown with air and carbon tetrachloride. Salt in a glass of water does not make it overflow; an analogy is made by "filling" a glass of marbles with sand. Conservation of matter is shown by burning a match; it does not tip the scales if the products are kept together.

FILMSTRIPS

"Atoms and Chemistry," Heath Science Series, Set 6A, No. 3. Good explanations of physical and chemical changes and mixtures. Examples: salt, fire, water, roast corn, iron rust.

"What Things Are Made Of," S.V.E. Row Peterson Text-Film. Describes solids, liquids, and gases; gives some examples of compounds: copper, mercury, oxygen, salt, sodium sulphite, baking soda, sugar, water.

CHEMICAL INTERACTIONS (MATRIX 5, PAGE 219)

TEXTBOOKS

Brandwein. *Concepts in Science 4*. Unit 4, "The Travels of Some Molecules."

Brandwein. *Concepts in Science 5*. Unit 2, "About 100 Building Blocks."

Fischler, Abraham S. *et al. Science: A Modern Approach 6*. Unit 1.

Schneider. *Science for Today and Tomorrow 6*. Chapter 1, "Basic Chemistry."

All four books offer a wide variety of related topics, suggest many investigations, and give clear explanations. The Brandwein books emphasize conservation of matter; the Schneider unit centers on bonding; and the Fischler variant makes chemistry part of the major study of atoms, molecules, and radioactivity. All three recount historical contributions.

TRADE BOOKS

P. Carona, Philip. *The True Book of Chemistry: What Things Are Made Of*. Chicago: Children's Press, 1962. Illustrated by George Wilde. Elements, symbols, atoms and molecules, formulas. Very simply written, large print and clear illustrations.

I. Stone, A. Harris. *Chemistry of a Lemon*. Englewood Cliffs, N. J.: Prentice-Hall, 1966. Illustrated by Peter P. Plasencia. The lemon reacts to indicators made from red cabbage or cherries; it releases carbon dioxide from baking soda, powers an aluminum foil boat, and dissolves the oxidation from a tarnished copper penny. Very amusing illustrations. Raises questions to be explained by the reader.

FILM

I. "Speed of Chemical Changes," FA, 1968, c., 12 min. Although this film is intended for the high-school level, we recommend it here because the visual material is explicit and clearly illustrates the principles involved. It shows the roles of atoms and molecules and their relative energies and concentrations in relation to chemical change. Children *would* need help in understanding the vocabulary.

FILMLOOPS

I. "Conservation of Mass," Don Herbert, Prism Productions (Science adviser: Dr. M. H. Shamos), c., 3 min. 45 sec. Candle is burned in a sealed bottle on a scale so that the products of combustion are collected. Scale maintains its balance.

I. "The Mouse and the Candle," Education Development Center, Inc. Produced by the Ealing Corp. (super 8: 80-0839/1), c., 3 min. 30 sec. Two white mice occupy a closed glass jar in which a candle burns. After the candle goes out, the mice continue their lively antics—for a while.

FILMSTRIP

"Chemical Changes," S.V.E. Row Peterson Text-Film. The concept of change is introduced by breaking a stick and then burning it; adding sugar to lemonade; adding vinegar to baking soda. Physical changes introduced are: water heated to steam; egg whites beaten fluffy; carbon dioxide frozen to dry ice. Chemical changes are shown through burning magnesium, leaves changing color in the fall, iron and water producing rust, color fading, milk souring, etc.

PHYSICAL INTERACTIONS (MATRIX 6, PAGE 229)

We suggested on page 229 that the reader might like to try his hand at constructing a matrix for a series of lessons to follow the "white powder" experiences. On an upper elementary level, the concept of *schlieren* is a valuable one to introduce. Suggestions for materials and activities in this area may be culled from two booklets, available from the Science Curriculum Improvement Study (SCIS):

Systems and Subsystems, Teacher's Guide, SCIS, Lexington, Mass.: Raytheon Education Company, part 3, "Solutions." Preliminary edition available from SCIS, University of California at Berkeley, California 94720.

Phases of Matter, Teacher's Guide, SCIS, University of California at Berkeley, California 94720. (Available as above).

ELECTRICAL INTERACTIONS (MATRIX 7, PAGE 230)

TEXTBOOKS

Brandwein. *Concepts in Science 6.* Unit 6, "Electrons in Action." Electricity and electromagnetism related to motion of electrons. Explanations of the way the telephone, radio, television, and relay satellites work. Open-ended investigations.

Schneider. *Science Far and Near 3.* Chapter 9, "Electricity at Work."

Schneider. *Science for Today and Tomorrow 6.* Chapter 5, "Sound and Communication" (on the working of electrical machines) and Chapter 8, "Radio and Television." Clear explanations.

TRADE BOOKS

I. Morgan, Alfred P. *The Boy Electrician.* New York: Less, Lothrop and Shephard, 1957. Illustrated by the author. A mine of information; many projects in electricity and magnets for the advanced student.

I. Neal, Charles D. *Safe and Simple Projects with Electricity.* Chicago: Children's Press, 1965. Illustrated by Robert Borja. A great many fascinating constructions described with easy-to-follow directions. Stunning and meaningful illustrations. Having made each construction, the child should be encouraged to design his own investigations.

I. Seeman, Bernard. *The Story of Electricity and Magnetism.* Irvington-on-the-Hudson, N. Y.: Harvey House, 1967. Illustrated by James Barry. Clear illustrations and theory; easy to obtain materials for child investigations. Part I covers electricity and Part II magnetism, but the interrelationships are well shown.

E. Neurath, Marie. *Around the World in a Flash.* New York: Lee, Lothrop and Shepard, 1959. Tells how messages are sent via telephone, telegraph, radio, and TV. A description of what happens physically more than the scientific why.

FILM

"Sources of Electricity," Cenco, 1964, c., 11 min. Demonstrates how mechanical energy of motion is used to produce an electric current: a magnetic field cut with a moving coil of wire records alternating current on a meter. The way in which chemical energy is used to generate direct current is shown with wet and dry cells and their components.

FILMSTRIPS

EBF puts out a series of seven filmstrips under the general title *Electricity*. We find the first five pertinent to this matrix; their titles are self-descriptive: "Experimenting with Static Electricity," "Electricity by Chemical Reaction," "Electricity in Circuits," "Electricity and Heat," "Electricity and Magnetism."

FILMLOOP

I.   "Bulbs and Batteries," Ealing Corp. (super 8: 82-0084/1), c., 4 min. (Part of the thought-challenging series, "Explorations in Science.") Bare copper wires are attached to bulbs in sockets and to dry cells. By placing the bulbs and batteries in various series and parallel arrangements, the demonstrator intrigues the viewers, motivating them to try the same (or other) effects.

MEALWORMS (MATRIX 8, PAGE 238)

TEXTBOOKS

Most modern textbooks are rich in illustrations of ecological interdependence. For the purposes of this matrix on mealworms, the life cycles of insects would provide appropriate reading matter. The first unit in Schneider, *Science in Your Life 4*, "The Insect World," is devoted to a study of the structure, metamorphosis, and social significance of insects.

TRADE BOOKS

P.   Adrian, Mary. *Honeybee Tells Honeybee*. New York: Holiday House, 1960. Illustrated by Barbara Latham. The life of a worker honeybee. Simply told, easy to read, good illustrations.

P.   Hutchins, Ross E. *The Travels of Monarch X*. Chicago: Rand McNally, 1966. Illustrated by Jerome P. Connelly. The 2,000 mile journey of a Monarch butterfly tagged by a scientist. Illustrations convey the feeling of adventure.

P.   Lowery, Lawrence F. *Animals 2 by 2. I Wonder Why Readers* (Consultant, Abraham S. Fischler). New York: Holt, Rinehart & Winston, Inc., 1969. Pairs of similar animals are compared and differentiated: butterfly and moth, insect and spider, etc. Helps perception of likenesses and differences.

P.   Lubell, Winifred and Cecil. *The Tall Grass Zoo*. Chicago: Rand McNally, 1960. Illustrated by Winifred Lubell. Poetic writing and delightful illustrations of fauna to be found in grasses and weeds. Information about some of the habits of each.

P.   Schoenknecht, Charles A. *Ants*. Chicago: Follett, 1961. Illustrated by Dimitri Alexandroff. Simple description of the life history and habits of ants. Skips over what happens on the nuptial flight!

I.   Hopf, Alice. *Monarch Butterflies*. New York: Crowell, 1965. Chapters 2 and 3 covering housing and collecting Monarchs should be useful.

I.   Kohn, Bernice. *Fireflies*. Englewood Cliffs, N. J.: Prentice-Hall, 1966. Illustrated by Erwin Schachner. The science of bioluminescence.

I.   Poole, Lynn and Gray. *Fireflies*. New York: Crowell, 1965. Description of the research on the nature of luminescence.

I.   Sterling, Dorothy. *Caterpillars*. Garden City, N. Y.: Doubleday, 1961. Illustrated by Winifred Lubell. Delightfully written; beautiful and informative illustrations. An ecological approach.

I.   Sterling, Dorothy. *Creatures of the Night*. Garden City, N. Y.: Doubleday, 1960. Illustrated by Winifred Lubell. Catching and studying a great variety of insects that are attracted to light at night.

I.   von Frisch, Karl. *Ten Little Housemates*. Oxford, England: Pergamon Press, 1960. The life histories and habits of household pests such as flies, fleas, roaches, lice, bedbugs. However, control is suggested by using such poisons as DDT. Contains some charming, if extraneous, information, such as training fleas for a circus!

I.   Zim, Herbert and Bleecker, Sonia. *Life and Death*. New York: William Morrow & Co., 1970. Illustrated by Rene Martin. Discussion of the chemical elements of which life is composed; life cycles and population explosion; the physiology of death. Helping children develop an acceptance of death as a part of life is this passage from page 163:

> Since death always comes, people have learned to expect it and accept it. Day by day they try to add joy in living for themselves and for their relatives and friends. People who are loved and have useful, happy lives come to accept all of life, including the end.

The illustrations are clear but unattractive.

E.   Hussey, Lois Jackson and Pessino, Catherine. *Collecting Cocoons*. New York: Crowell, 1953. Illustrated by Isabel Sherwin Harris. Finding, identifying, caring for, and hatching various cocoons.

E. Selsam, Millicent E. *Questions and Answers About Ants.* New York: Four Winds Press 1967. Illustrated by Arabelle Wheatly. How to observe ants and their habits, both in their natural habitats and in a home made "antery."

E. Shuttleworth, Dorothy Edwards. *The Story of Ants.* Garden City, N. Y.: Doubleday, 1964. Beautiful illustrations by Su Zan N. Swain. The habitats of various ants from all over the world.

FILMLOOPS

"Black Swallowtail Butterfly," a series of six loops produced by the Elementary Science Study (ESS) of the Education Development Center, Inc., Newton, Mass. and marketed by the Ealing Corp. Beautiful time-lapse photography. Descriptions of each loop follow:

"Egg-Laying, Hatching, and Larvae," (super 8: 81-4566/1), c., 3 min. 50 sec. An adult butterfly lays eggs which then darken and hatch. The larvae are shown moving about and feeding on parsley.

"Larval Molt," (super 8: 81-4574/1), c., 3 min. 5 sec. A caterpillar wriggles out of its old skin which is then consumed.

"Preparing to Pupate, I," (super 8: 81-4582/1, c., 3 min. 40 sec. Larva empties its gut, finds a suitable spot, and attaches itself with a thread.

"Preparing to Pupate, II," (super 8: 81-4590/1), c., 3 min. 25 sec. Larva attaches itself with a sling of silk to a twig.

"Pupal Molt," (super 8: 81-4608/1), c., 3 min. 35 sec. Skin splits along the back; pupa emerges as skin is dropped. The insect's proportions have changed radically.

"Emergence," (super 8: 81-4616/1), c., 3 min. 45 sec. Pupa splits its skin and the adult emerges quickly. Wings dry, proboscis parts join, butterfly flies.

Viewing this series is an unforgettable experience.

ECOLOGY OF WATER ANIMALS (MATRIX 9, PAGE 289)

TEXTBOOKS

Whatever water animals your textbook includes, the information is likely to be helpful. The better descriptions relate structure to function and indicate the way inherited characteristics may be modified by changes in the environment.

The essential interactions of aquatic animals with plants, water, and sunlight suggest that some references in Matrices 9, 11, and 12 may be interchangeable.

TRADE BOOKS

P. Goudey, Alice E. *Here Come the Whales.* New York: Charles Scribner's Sons, 1956. Illustrated by Carry MacKenzie. Interesting information about the the habits of the Blue Whales and others. A group of whales is called a *pod* (synonym for "set"!)

P. Wong, Herbert H. and Vessel, Matthew F. *Pond Life: Watching Animals Find Food.* Boston: Addison-Wesley, 1970. Illustrated by Tony Chen. The book is oriented toward the SCIS booklets *Organisms* and *Food Chains.*

P. Zim, Herbert S. *Goldfish.* New York: William Morrow & Co., 1947, Illustrated by Joy Buba. Do not be put off by the ancient date. This book has never been superseded. It describes the different kinds of goldfish and gives wise rules for their care. Simple text, large print, clear illustrations. A *must* if you keep goldfish in your classroom.

I. Ripper, Charles L. *Trout.* New York: William Morrow & Co., 1966. Illustrated by the author. A general description of the trout's characteristics, habits, and habitats. Clear illustrations.

I. Waters, Barbara and John. *Salt Water Aquariums.* New York: Holiday House, 1967. Illustrated by Robert Candy. A complete guide to setting up and maintaining salt water aquaria, both from natural and manmade sea water. Excellent section on marine animals. Emphasis is on nontropical marine ecology.

E. Fichter, George S. *Fishes and How They Live.* New York: Golden Press, 1960. Illustrated by Rene Martin and James Gordon Irving. A great deal of information about many fishes.

E. Lauber, Patricia. *The Friendly Dolphins.* New York: Random House, 1963. Illustrated, with photographs and drawings, by Jean Simpson; with diagrams, by Charles Gottlieb. Very interesting information about the life and habits of dolphins. Clear and exciting photographs, including one of a baby dolphin being born—tail first.

E.   Leavitt, Jerome and Huntsberger, John. *Funtime Terrariums and Aquariums*. Chicago: Children's Press, 1961. Illustrated by Bill Armstrong. How to set up and stock a variety of homes for land and water animals, including marine creatures.

FILMS

I.   "Life Story of a Snail," EBF, 1963, c., s., 11 min. How a water snail moves, eats algae, builds its shell from the mantel, produces eggs, hibernates. Fish and duck eat snails and slugs, their shell-less relatives. Other relatives are squid, octopus, oyster. Film is valuable for study of external parts of the snail.

I.   "Life Story of a Water Flea" (*Daphnia*), EBF, 1965, c., s., 10 min. Daphnia shown as a part of the web of life; its relation to other crustaceans and its basis for the fish economy. Close-up microscopic views of heart, eye, food digesting, eggs. Young daphnia seen in brood pouch and then being born. Females appear without fertilization. Males appear (film does not show from where) and fertilize the eggs which survive the winter.

E.   "Animals Breathe in Many Ways," Norman Bean (producer), FA (distributor), c., s., 11 min. Animals shown are dog, amoeba, porpoise, flatworm, earthworm, salamander, crayfish, goldfish, grasshopper, and underwater beetle. Extreme close-ups show gills forcing fresh supplies of water and oxygen into the bloodstream of the salamander, the airholes of the grasshopper opening and closing, the water beetle's silvery air bubbles, and the porpoise surfacing to breathe through the hole in the top of its head. Animated diagrams show how the oxygen is passed into the body of the amoeba, flatworm, and earthworm (diagrams are superimposed over the films of these animals as they breathe). A simple but beautiful film, cleverly shot.

FILMLOOPS

E.   "Brine Shrimp, I," Elementary Science Study (ESS) of the Education Development Center (EDC), Inc. Produced by the Ealing Corp. (super 8: 81-4624/1), c., 3 min. 15 sec. Eggs hatch; larvae molt and grow to adulthood.

E.   "Brine Shrimp, II," ESS of the EDC. Ealing Corp. (super 8: 81-4632/1), c., 3 min. 15 sec. Differences between male and female, action of appendages, mating, egg laying, and live birth are shown.

I.   "Frogs: Pairing and Egg laying," ESS of the EDC. Ealing Corp. (super 8: 81-4392/1), c., 3 min. 35 sec. A male and a female frog shown in mating position in an aquarium. Male squeezes the female; she lays eggs on which the male ejects his sperm.

I.   "Frog Egg: First Cell Division to Neural Fold, I," ESS of the EDC. Ealing Corp. (super 8: 81-4368/1), c., 3 min. 30 sec. Time-lapse photography of egg development during the first five days. Ends at the gastrula stage.

I.   "Frog Egg: Development of the Body Regions, II," ESS of the EDC. Ealing Corp. (super 8: 81-4376/1), c., 3 min. 30 sec. From the gastrula stage to the tadpole shape in time-lapse photography.

I.   "Frog Egg: Continued Development to Hatching, III," ESS of the EDC. Ealing Corp. (super 8: 81-4384/1), c., 3 min. The eye buds, mouth, and tail develop. The tadpole begins to use its muscles; twitches, then breaks through the jelly and hatches.

I.   "Tadpoles I: Hatching Through Initial Leg Growth," ESS of the EDC. Ealing Corp. (super 8: 81-7023/1), c., 4 min. 10 sec. Tadpole hatches, close-up of gills showing blood flowing within and water circulating around. Mouth, heart, eyes, and hind legs develop. Tadpole is seen eating.

I.   "Tadpoles II: Metamorphosis," ESS of the EDC. Ealing Corp. (super 8: 81-703/1), c., 3 min. 50 sec. Tadpole develops into a frog: front legs push through the skin, tail is absorbed, eyelids become froglike, throat pumps air into lungs.

ECOLOGY OF LAND ANIMALS (MATRIX 10, PAGE 295)

TEXTBOOKS

Again, the many variants of land animals described in textbooks provide good reading. If there is a choice of topics, look for structure related to function, heredity modified by changes in the environment, and ecological interdependence.

TRADE BOOKS

P.   Bronson, Wildrid S. *Turtles*. New York: Harcourt Brace Jovanovich, Inc., 1943. Illustrated by the author. Don't let the date throw you. This is still one of the most valuable books on turtles, their species, habits, care, and cognate anatomy to a baby crawling. Large type.

P.   Busch, Phyllis S. *Once There Was a Tree*. Cleveland: World, 1968. Photographs by Arline Strong. Ecological interdependence of a tree, both alive and dead, with other plants and animals. Written in a manner designed to motivate young children to explore and discover. Excellent appropriate photographs.

P.   Conklin, Gladys. *I Caught a Lizard*. New York: Holiday House, 1967. Illustrated by Artur Marokvia. Temporary keeping of such pets as the lizard, salamander, horned toad, praying mantis, and toads. Sensitively written and illustrated.

P.   Lowery, Lawrence. *Tommy's Turtle*. *I Wonder Why Readers* (Consultant Abraham S. Fischler). New York: Holt, Rinehart & Winston, Inc., 1969. Illustrated by Eleanor Mill. What is it that makes a turtle alive; how is it different from a rock?

I.   Barker, Will. *Winter-Sleeping Wild Life*. New York: Harper & Row, 1958. Illustrated by Carl Burger. General habits as well as hibernation of many animals from mammals to molluscs.

I.   Fenton, Carroll Lane and Pallas, Dorothy Constance. *Reptiles and Their World*. New York: John Day, 1961. Illustrated by Carroll Lane Fenton. Stories of various reptiles, detailing their structure in relation to habitat.

I.   Fisher, Aileen. *Valley of the Smallest*. New York: Crowell, 1966. Illustrated by Jean Zallinger. Fictional story of the life of a shrew. A good book to read to children in the primary grades.

I.   George, Jean Craighead. *The Moon of the Wild Pigs*. New York: Crowell, 1968. Illustrated by Peter Parnall. Without any trace of anthropomorphism, vivid description lets the reader contact the lives of many desert animals (rattlesnake, roadrunner, elf owl, etc.) as encountered by a baby peccary pig. Excellent illustrations.

I.   Hess, Lilo. *The Remarkable Chameleon*. New York: Charles Scribner's Sons, 1968. Mostly superb photographs accompanied by a text which describes the chameleon's eating habits and its strange reaction to light.

I.   Hoke, John. *Turtles and Their Care*. New York: Franklin Watts, 1970. Illustrated by Barbara Wolff. Many kinds of turtles described in their habitats. Detailed, knowledgeable directives are given for their care in captivity. Many good photographs and drawings.

I.   Milne, Lorus J. and Milne, Margery J. *Gift from the Sky*. New York: Atheneum, 1967. A delightful story book of the way a swan, alighting on a local pond in New Hampshire, affected the lives of the townspeople. Few, but exquisite, black and white photos.

I.   Selsam, Millicent E. *How Animals Tell Time*. New York: William Morrow & Co., 1967. Illustrated by John Kaufman. Recent experiments on the way animals respond to their biological clocks, presented to capture children's interest. Various theories are described. Animals discussed include fruit flies, cockroaches, bees, fish, squirrels.

E.   David, Eugene. *Spiders and How They Live*. Englewood Cliffs, N. J.: Prentice-Hall, 1964. Illustrated by Delos Blackmar. The structure and habits of many different kinds of spiders described in a clear and interesting manner.

E.   Gans, Roma. *Birds at Night*. New York: Crowell, 1968. Illustrated by Aliki. The various ways different birds spend the night. Function of feathers in relation to body heat and energy use. Book is packed full of interesting facts. Imaginative drawings aid learning and memory.

E.   Hutchins, Ross E. *The Last Trumpeters*. Chicago: Rand McNally, 1967. Illustrated by Jerome P. Connolly. The story of the life and habits of Trumpeter Swans since before Columbus; their near extinction until they came under Federal protection in 1935. Interesting facts with an ecological message.

FILMS

I.   "Adaptations in Animals," McGraw-Hill, Inc., 1963, c., 16 min. Emphasis is that those who survive live to reproduce. Stags are shown battling over a mate, plants are not washed away after a heavy rain, bacteria adapt to streptomycin. Protection of the embryo increases from frogs to puppy; brain increases in power and function from bird to man. Protective coloring blends with the environment of the deer, chameleon, jaguar, leopard, etc.

I.   "Adaptations of Plants and Animals," CORF, 1957, b/w, s., 16 min. Narrated by Glenn O. Blough, who makes the point that nonadaptive animals face destruction. Adaptations to special environments are illustrated by the beaver, water plants, cactus, migrating birds, and leaf shedding. Time-lapse photography of corn growing. Special protection illustrated by kangaroo, snowshoe rabbit, whippoorwill, measuring worm, and turtle.

I. "Animals of the Desert," Justin and Byers, 1964, c., s., 12 min. Emphasis is on adapting to conservation of water by the coyote, kangaroo rat, roadrunner, horned lizard, owl (in a hole in the ground), fox, skunk, peccary, raccoon, ant. Flowers and saguaro shown, too.

I. "Reptiles Are Interesting," FA, 1955, c., s., 10 min. The alligator, turtle, Galapagos tortoise, lizard, horned lizard, chameleon, and Gila Monster are shown at the San Diego Zoo. If children cannot see any of these animals live, the film would be helpful.

E. "Animals: Ways They Move," EBF, 1956, b/w, s., 11 min. Each of the following is shown in its natural environment: porpoise, turtle, starfish, hermit crab, blue crab, snail, jellyfish, elephant seal, millipede, sidewinder rattlesnake, inchworm, grasshopper, toad, kangaroo, elephant, mountain-sheep, mackaw, squirrel monkey, ostrich, emu! In slow motion: flamingo, flying squirrel, pelican. Film would have to be shown more than once and children alerted to look for adaptations.

FILMLOOPS

"Chameleon," Walt Disney Nature Library, Ealing Corp. (81-8237), c. Excellent close-up of tongue action as the chameleon catches its prey.

"Giant Anteater," Walt Disney Nature Library, Ealing Corp. (81-9086/1), c. A giant anteater scoops up ants with its long tongue, escapes from a jaguar by crossing the river, then curls up and sleeps.

E. "How Spiders Capture Prey (With Webs)," Thompson and Skinner, Oxford University, Ealing Corp. (super 8: 81-3451/1), c., 4 min. 10 sec. Shows different types of webs and the way they function to catch insects. Spider subdues prey by wrapping it in silk thread before consuming it.

E. "How Spiders Capture Prey (Without Webs)," Thompson and Skinner, Oxford University, Ealing Corp. (super 8: 81-3469/1), c., 3 min. 50 sec. Notes on the film container help viewer see details of the way this type of spider captures prey. Enzymes in its saliva digest prey into liquid form before spider sucks up the food.

E. "Praying Mantid," Ken Middleton Production, Ealing Corp. (81-3485/1), c., 4 min. A praying mantid captures prey, eats, grooms itself, lays eggs, and molts.

INTERACTIONS OF PLANTS AND WATER (MATRIX 11, PAGE 306)

The interaction of plants with water, sunlight, and minerals forms an organic whole, although it is often valuable for children to concentrate on one sub-division at a time. Books and films tend to include more than one aspect. Hence these additional listings for Matrices 11-14 (see also the Books and Other Media Sections in each matrix) are in some measure interchangeable. We have selected, where possible, a major emphasis under each single matrix in this bibliography.

TEXTBOOKS

Brandwein. *Concepts in Science 3*. Unit 8, parts of "In Water and on Land." Includes desert and pond life.

Schneider. *Science Far and Near 3*. Chapter 2, "Life in the Desert," and "Making a Water Community." Discusses animals as well as plants.

Schneider. *Science in Your Life 4*. Chapter 6, "Water and Living Things."

TRADE BOOKS

P. Goldin, Augusta. *The Sunlit Sea*. New York: Crowell, 1968. Illustrated by Paul Goldone. A simple, but clear, presentation of the food chains, in the upper (sunlit) layers of the ocean. The book raises questions which provoke thought.

P. Jordan, Helene Jamieson. *How a Seed Grows*. New York: Crowell, 1960. Illustrated by Joseph Low. Simple directions for growing ten seeds in eggshells and pulling them up at intervals to watch details of growth. Large print.

P. Lowery, Lawrence F. *How Does a Plant Grow? I Wonder Why Readers* (Consultant: Abraham S. Fischler). New York: Holt, Rinehart & Winston, Inc., 1969. Illustrated by Richard Amundsen. Emphasis is on the variety of plant life.

P. Zim, Herbert S. *What's Inside of Plants?* New York: William Morrow & Co., 1952. Illustrated by Herschel Wartik. Functions of all parts of the plant are described. Large print for the children, smaller print with information for the adult.

I. Miner, Frances F. *Growing Plants*. New York: Golden Press, 1959. Illustrated by Aubrey Combs. Many practical investigations related to water in plants. Other interesting information on growing plants and vegetables.

I.   Silverberg, Robert. *The World of the Rain Forest*. Des Moines: Meredith, 1967. Illustrated with photographs. Fascinating information told so that the reader sees and feels as though he were in the rain forest. Strong ecological emphasis.

E.   Kavaler, Lucy. *The Wonders of Algae*. New York: John Day, 1961. Illustrated with photographs and drawings by Barbara Amlick and Richard Ott. Past, present and future uses of algae. Chlorella as food for space travel and as a solution to the hunger on earth today.

FILM

E.   "Life of Plants," Duart, b/w, s., 13 min. Shows clearly and simply how a seed progresses from germination underground to break through the earth's surface. Root hairs are shown absorbing nutrients from the soil. Time-lapse photography throughout. Vocabulary on printed slides is a bit advanced, but the film is self-explanatory.

INTERACTIONS OF PLANTS AND SUNLIGHT (MATRIX 12, PAGE 310)

TEXTBOOKS

Brandwein. *Concepts in Science 3*. Unit 1, "Energy from the Sun."

Brandwein. *Concepts in Science 5*. Unit 6, "Green Cells as Building Blocks."

Schneider. *Science for Today and Tomorrow 6*. Chapter 2, "Sunlight and Life."

TRADE BOOKS

P.   Blough, Glenn Orlando. *Wait for the Sunshine*. New York: Whittlesey House, 1961. Illustrated by Jeanne Bendick. Discusses how plants manufacture food by the aid of the sun, although there is no mention of energy.

P.   Darby, Gene. *What Is a Plant?* Chicago: Benefic Press, 1960. Illustrated by Lucy and John Howkinson. Simple descriptions of essential life processes of plants. Varieties range from flowers to bacteria.

I.   Silverberg, Robert. *The World of the Rain Forest* (see Matrix 11).

E.   Baker, Laura Nelson. *A Tree Called Moses*. New York: Atheneum, 1966. Illustrated by Pene-lope Naylor. The life story of an actual giant Sequoia tree, 2,500 years old, told in terms of its struggle for existence through various vicissitudes. The ecology of the animals and plants related to the Sequoia's environment is described interestingly.

E.   Milne, Lorus J. and Margery. *Because of a Tree*. New York: Atheneum, 1963. Illustrated by Kenneth Gosner. Ecological interdependence centering around eight different trees, including palm, maple, saguaro.

E.   Selsam, Millicent. *Birth of a Forest*. New York: Harper & Row, 1964. Illustrated by Barbara Wolff and with photographs. From a Michigan pond, to marsh, to swamp, to forest.

E.   Zim, Herbert S. *The Sun*. New York: William Morrow & Co., 1953. Illustrated by Larry Kettel-kamp. Discusses how plants manufacture food by the aid of the sun. No mention of energy.

FILMS

I.   "A Plant Through the Seasons: Apple Tree," EBF, 1966, c., 11 min. A combination of animation and time-lapse photography illustrates the life processes of the apple tree through the changing seasons: blossoms open, bees pollinate them, fruit pushes through dead flower, apples ripen and are picked, seeds are given a rest and then planted, shoots grow from them. Water travels from roots to leaves; carbon dioxide enters the underside of a leaf and, in the presence of sunlight and water, sugar is formed. Leaves change during fall. Leaf scar is shown and explained. Spring returns; bud opens. A splendid presentation.

I.   "Learning About Leaves," EBF, 1957, c., 11 min. An excellent presentation in time-lapse photography of leaves budding and growing. The investigations suggested in Matrix 12 (stepping stone E, page 311) on boiling leaves to extract chlorophyll and test for starch are shown. An animated sequence shows how a leaf absorbs the sun's energy and uses carbon dioxide and water to make sugar. Sugar, first stored in the leaf, passes down the stem. Potatoes are shown as storages for starch which is then used as the potatoes sprout.

FILMLOOPS

E.   "Climbing Vines," Walt Disney Nature Library, 1959, c., 2 min. Plants climbing by tendrils and leaf stalks are shown in time-lapse photography.

E. "Exploring Urban Environments," (In preparation by Ealing Corp. Send for information.) A series of twelve loops directing attention to the ecological development in open city lots: in a tree, in a park, up a wall, in a crack, along a street, etc.

INTERACTIONS OF PLANTS AND MINERALS (MATRIX 13, PAGE 312)

TEXTBOOKS

Brandwein. *Concepts in Science 3*. Unit 5, "Treasures in the Earth."

Brandwein. *Concepts in Science 4*. Unit 5, "The Fall of a Tree."

Mallinson, George G. and Jaqueline B., and Feravolo, Rocco. *Science 3*. Morristown, N. J.: Silver Burdett, 1965. Chapter 6, "Living Communities" discusses a variety of habitats and food chains.

Schneider. *Science in Our World 5*. Chapter 9, "Plants on Our Planet."

Thurber, Walter A. and Durkee, Mary C. *Exploring Science 6*. Boston: Allyn & Bacon, 1966. Chapter 2, "Plants That Are Not Green."

TRADE BOOKS

I. Kavaler, Lucy. *The Wonders of Fungi*. New York: John Day, 1964. Illustrated with photographs and drawings by Richard Ott. Discusses molds that conquer disease and those that supply protein; their use in space travel.

I. Selsam, Millicent. *Microbes at Work*. New York: William Morrow & Co., 1953. Illustrated by Helen Ludwig. Cultivation and elimination of bacteria.

I. Sterling, Dorothy. *The Story of Mosses, Ferns and Mushrooms*. Garden City, N. Y.: Doubleday, 1955. Photographs by Myron Ehrenberg. Life histories of various species.

E. Poole, Lynn and Poole, Gray. *Insect-Eating Plants*. New York: Crowell, 1963. Illustrated by Christine Sapieha. Detailed information on the functioning of various insect-eating plants. Tells how to prepare a terrarium for such plants.

E. Simon, Seymour. *A Handful of Soil*. New York: Hawthorn Books, 1970. Illustrated by Valli. Many aspects of soil are investigated: its formation from rocks; its various contents and acidity; its relation to plants and small organisms and to water. Open-ended investigations are suggested.

FILM

I. "Life in a Cubic Foot of Soil," CORF, 1963, b/w, 11 min. The film emphasizes the fact that dead animal and plant life decay into humus which is then broken down, absorbed by the roots, and then used to feed growing plants. Told more than shown. A teacher and two children dig up a cubic foot of soil and its plant cover and transfer all of this to a tank. They observe the changes in the tank, test the soil for nitrates, examine mold under the microscope. They find larvae, pupae, grasshopper eggs, and an earthworm cocoon.

ADAPTATIONS OF PLANTS IN RELATION TO ADVERSE CIRCUMSTANCES (MATRIX 14, PAGE 314)

TEXTBOOKS

Brandwein. *Concepts in Science 1*. Unit 7, "Plants and More Plants."

Brandwein. *Concepts in Science 6*. Unit 8, "Code of Heredity." Mechanism of change through hybridization and mutation.

Schneider. *Science Far and Near 3*. Chapter 2, "Life in the Desert" and Chapter 5, "Plants and More Plants."

Schneider. *Science for Work and Play 1*. Chapter 5, "Seeds to Plants."

Schneider. *Science in Your Life 4*. Chapter 5, "Climate and Living Things."

Schneider. *Science in Our World 5*. Chapter 9, "Plants on Our Planet."

TRADE BOOKS

P. Jordan. *How a Seed Grows* (see Matrix 11).

I. Larsen, Peggy. *Life in the Desert*. Chicago: Children's Press, 1960. Illustrated by Robert Borja. "The true magic of the desert is that life not only survives here but actually flourishes" is the announced theme. A page per animal or plant, with picture and basic information.

I. Stefferud, Alfred. *The Wonders of Seeds*. New York: Harcourt Brace Jovanovich, Inc., 1956. Illustrated by Shirley Briggs. Seeds that "slept" 1,000 years; formation, growth, and use of seeds; how to grow them and buy them. The value of hybrids.

E. Fenton, Carroll L. and Kitchen, Herminie B. *Plants That Feed Us.* New York: John Day, 1956. Illustrated by Carroll L. Fenton. The story of grain and vegetables since earliest known farmers began to grow crops in western Asia (about 7,000 years ago). Three maps show how important plants have travelled. Richly illustrated with excellent black and white drawings.

E. Hammond, Winifred G. *The Riddle of Seeds.* New York: Coward McCann, 1965. Illustrated by black and white photographs from various sources. A variety of interesting information about different kinds of seeds, their structure, growth, and formation. Many valuable projects suggested with clear directions. Simple text.

E. Selsam, Millicent E. *Maple Tree.* New York: William Morrow & Co., 1968. Illustrated with photographs by Jerome Wexler. Really a "photographic essay" in which black and white and color close-ups show development of tree from seed to reproduction. Clear explanations, plus diagrams.

FILMS

P. "Learning About Flowers," EBF, 1957, b/w, 11 min. Time-lapse photography showing shoots growing, seeds sending out roots, flowers blooming, fruit developing from dead flower, and seeds dispersing. Lovely photography, sharp close-ups.

I. "A Plant Through the Seasons" (see Matrix 12, page 418).

FILMLOOPS

"Carnivorous Plants," Walt Disney Nature Library, Ealing Corp. (81-9706/1), c., 2 min. Venus's flytrap, sundew, and pitcher plant all shown catching insects.

E. "Desert Plants," Walt Disney Nature Library, Ealing Corp. (81-8567/1), c., 4 min. Shows birds living in and around a variety of desert plants; rain followed by the blooming of many beautiful flowers.

E. "Exploring Urban Environments" (see Matrix 12, page 419).

E. "Seeds Sprouting," Walt Disney Nature Library, Ealing Corp. (81-9656), 1959, c., 2 min. Time-lapse photography shows motion of roots and shoots of various seeds.

E. "Self-Planting Seeds," Walt Disney Nature Library, Ealing Corp. (81-9649/1), 3 min. 30 sec. Time-lapse photography of wheat and cranesbill seeds freeing themselves from their parent plants and burying themselves in soil.

LIGHT (MATRIX 15, PAGE 319)

TEXTBOOKS

Brandwein. *Concepts in Science 4.* Unit 2, "The Bounce of Light."

Brandwein. *Concepts in Science 5.* Unit 7, "The Building Blocks of the Stars."

Fischler. *Science: A Modern Approach 6.* Unit 4, "Waves, Sound and Light."

Mallinson. *Science 4.* Chapter 15, "Characteristics of Light."

Mallinson. *Science 6.* Chapters 18-21, "Characteristics of Radiant Energy."

Schneider. *Science for Today and Tomorrow 6.* Chapter 6, "Light Waves."

TRADE BOOKS

P. *Seeing Red*
Hello Yellow
Feeling Blue

Three books for kindergarten and early-grade children by Robert Jay Wolff, New York: Charles Scribner's and Sons, 1968. Illustrated by the author. Striking drawings and one-line text portraying perception and the use and interaction of colors and giving names to various hues.

I. Freeman, Mae and Freeman, Ira. *Fun and Experiments with Light.* New York: Random House, 1963. Every page has a picture of an investigation on one side and a description and explanation of it on the other.

I. Paschel, Herbert P. *The First Book of Color.* New York: Franklin Watts, 1959. Drawings by Caru Studios. Clear explanations aided by well-planned and executed illustrations.

I. Ruchlis, Hyman. *The Wonder of Light and Color.* New York: Harper & Row, 1960. A thought-provoking exposition of modern theories.

E. Zim, Herbert S. *Waves*. New York: William Morrow & Co., 1967. Illustrated by Rene Martin. The nature and the origin and effects of waves in the ocean. A basic understanding of these more tangible waves is an essential preliminary to understanding electromagnetic waves which describe the motion of light, etc.

FILM

I. "Nature of Color," CORF, 1956, c., 11 min. An excellent film which relates the rainbow colors to the way light is bent. The film shows and explains that a color an object appears to be is due to the rays of reflected light, all others being absorbed. The effect of color filters, which subtract rays of certain wavelengths, explains how white minus blue makes yellow, white minus green makes magenta, and white minus red makes blue-green. The four-color printing process is a practical application of these phenomena.

FILMLOOPS

I. "Light," one of the *Explorations in Science* series by Harry Milgrom. Designed and produced by Art Bardige, the Ealing Corp., 1969, c., 3 min. 35 sec. There are five thought-provoking investigations using a special "lightbox" whose construction is shown (see also page 320 of this book):
   1. *Shadows*: Various objects, including the earth, block light and leave shadows. Light travels in straight lines.
   2. *Reflection*: The lightbox enables children to draw or follow the bending of light by mirrors.
   3. *Refraction*: Light bends as it passes from one medium to another. Various curved containers of colored liquids bend light to a focal point.
   4. *Dispersion-Prisms*: Blue light bends more than red light. White light is dispersed into prism colors which are reunited to form white light again. Prisms can act as mirrors.
   5. *Single beam*: A single beam from the light-box enables a precise investigation of the way light behaves.

This filmloop is exciting and well-organized. Black film between each investigation permits the loop to be turned off so that viewers can conduct their own investigations.

"Springs," *Explorations in Science* series, c., 3 min. 40 sec. A Slinky Junior is used to demonstrate wave motion, to build scales, and to illustrate the effects of linking springs together in series and in parallel. The three kinds of wave motion (long-ways, sideways, and twisting) are presented to suggest further investigation by the viewers.

GEOLOGY (MATRIX 16, PAGE 330)

TEXTBOOKS

Brandwein. *Concepts in Science 3*. Unit 5, "Treasures in the Earth." Mostly about soil and the way it supports and feeds plants.

Brandwein. *Concepts in Science 4*. Unit 7, "The Travels of a Handful of Soil." The mineral cycle from rocks to soil to rocks. Emphasis is on water erosion.

Brandwein. *Concepts in Science 5*. Unit 8, "Stories in the Earth." Fossils and evolution; various types of rocks.

Fischler. *Science: A Modern Approach 4*. "The Earth's Changing Surface." Discusses erosion, mountain building, volcanoes.

Schneider. *Science Far and Near 3*. Chapter 11, "The Earth's Surface." Rocks to soil through weathering. Chapter 12, "Learning About Rocks" (origin and characteristics of various kinds of rocks). Chapter 13, "The Water Cycle." Chapter 14, "Cycle of a Mineral" (calcium).

Schneider. *Science in Our World 5*. Chapter 10, "Geology: Earth's Forces" (mountain making and breaking; volcanoes). Chapter 12, "Geology: Mineral Treasures" (coal, oil, and iron). Well explained and illustrated.

Schneider. *Science for Today and Tomorrow 6*. Chapter 3, "Prehistoric Life." Finding, describing, and interpreting fossil evidence of evolution. Weak on the reasons for changes in forms of animal life.

TRADE BOOKS

P. Gans, Roma. *The Wonder of Stones*. New York: Crowell, 1963. Illustrated by Joan Berg. Simple descriptions of the origin of stones, with an emphasis on wonder. Delicate illustrations.

I. Ames, Gerald and Wyler, Rose. *Planet Earth*. New York: Golden Press, 1963. Illustrated by Cornelius De Witt. A reference book on the earth in space, on what is inside the earth, on the oceans and the atmosphere.

I. Bendick, Jeanne. *The Shape of the Earth.* Chicago: Rand McNally, 1965. Illustrated by the author. The origin and structure of the earth, both old and new concepts.

I. Lauber, Patricia. *All About Planet Earth.* New York: Random House, 1962. Illustrated by Lee J. Ames. Discusses the theory of the drifting continents, volcanoes, our ocean of air, the aurora borealis.

I. Lauber, Patricia. *This Restless Earth.* New York: Random House, 1970. Illustrated by John Polgreen. Begins with a description of the birth of the island of Surtsey and ends with theories of the continental drift whose residues generated Surtsey. In between, the earth is represented as moving in space, shaken by earthquakes and volcanoes. Interestingly written; pertinent photographs, clear drawings, and well-conceived diagrams illustrate the concepts in the text.

I. Matthews, William H. III. *The Story of the Earth.* Irving-on-Hudson, N. Y.: Harvey House, 1968. Illustrated by John E. Alexander. A simple, but clear, account of the major earth sciences. Ideas are sophisticated, but are aided by the illustrations. The message is well delivered.

I. Thorarinsson, Sigurdur. *Surtsey.* New York: Viking Press, 1967. Translated from the Icelandic by Solvi Eysteinsson. Colored and black and white photographs and diagrams by many different artists in Iceland. Staggering photography, both colored and black and white, records the stages of appearance and development of the island which began to emerge from the ocean at the end of 1963. The descriptive and explanatory text is adult-level reading, but the photographs can be enjoyed by children of almost any age.

E. Cosgrove, Margaret. *Plants in Time: Their History and Mystery.* New York: Dodd, Mead & Co., 1967. Illustrated by author. From primordial cell to angiosperms. Good full-page chart. Ecological interdependence of animals on angiosperms.

E. Fenton, Carroll Lane and Fenton, Mildred Adams. *Riches from the Earth.* New York: John Day, 1953. Illustrated by Mildred Fenton. Reference book on the minerals of the earth—their appearance and uses.

E. Pringle, Lawrence. *Dinosaurs and Their World.* New York: Harcourt Brace Jovanovich, Inc., 1968. Illustrated with photographs of paintings of fossils, field sites, etc. The morphology and evolutionary history of dinosaurs; methods for restoration of museum exhibits. Probably an essential book for a school library.

E. Ravielli, Anthony. *From Fins to Hands: An Adventure in Evolution.* New York: Viking Press, 1968. Illustrated by the author. A Junior Literary Guild selection. Beautiful illustrations and well-written text trace the story of evolution through the development of paired limbs. Structure and use are linked from lobe-fins to man, whose added brainpower enlarges his manual skill.

E. Ruchlis, Hy. *Your Changing Earth.* Irving-on-Hudson, N. Y.: Harvey House, 1963. Illustrated by Alex D'Amato. The how and why of changes.

E. Simon. *A Handful of Soil* (see Matrix 13).

FILM

E. "Prehistoric Animals," FA, 1957, c., 14 min. A lively film presented in animation. Shows the development of life on earth from the earliest organisms through the rise and fall of the great reptiles. Included are: changes in earth's surface, volcanoes, forests, and mountains forming, and the adaptation of early animals to land, sea, and air. The story of fossils gives a clue to our knowledge about these animals.

FILMLOOPS

I. "Sedimentation" (M. Schwartz, Brooklyn College), Ealing Corp. (super 8: 85-0149/1), c., 3 min. 15 sec. Particles of various size and density are seen settling in a tank. Coloring makes layers clear.

I. "Structural Processes: Faults" (M. Schwartz, Brooklyn College), Ealing Corp. (super 8: 85-0180/1), c., 3 min. Real examples of faults are followed by moving models.

E. "A Volcano in Action" (Hawaii Natural History Association), Ealing Corp. (super 8: 85-0198/1), c., 3 min. 40 sec. The volcano at the summit of Kilouea is shown erupting with lava flowing slowly to the sea.

Index

for "Liquid-Solid Interactions" matrix, 215–16
  methods of building, 167–73
  for "Simple Machines" lesson, 169–73
  for universe, 165, 166
  value of, 165, 167
Conceptual thinking, 153–55
  and age, 149–50
  cross-cultural study of, 155
  of inner-city residents, 267
  matrix for, 230–36
Concrete operations level, 265–66
  science learning expected at, 272–75
Conditioned response, compared with thought, 102
Conditions of Learning, The, 29n
Confidence, development of, 262
Conservation language, 263
"Continental drift," theory of, 333
Controlled variables, 127
Controls, 114
Core of earth, 332
Corrections, by teacher, 90, 142
Creativity
  and classroom atmosphere, 139
  and discovery, 44
  and inner speech, 105
  and language, 105
  personality factors related to, 80–81
  and playfulness, 4
  potential for, 82
  and self-initiated behavior, 188
  and uncertainty, 80
Cronbach, Lee J., 28, 28n
Crust of earth, and earthquakes, 331–32
  See also "Movements of Earth's Crust" matrix
Cuisenaire materials, 390
Curriculum
  components of, 278
  at concrete operations level, 272–75
  cultural relevancy of, 277
  at egocentric level of development, 261, 268–69
  at formal operations level, 275–77
  geared toward intellectual, conceptual, and social cogs, 276–77
  and genetic development of concepts, 259–60
  for grades five, six, and seven, 259
  for intuitive level, 269–72
  responsibility for choice of, 277–78
  structure, 258–59
  and unit organization of textbooks, 281–82
  See also Matrices; Study units

D

Data
  in biological science matrices, 237
  blocked, 75

collecting and recording, 75–76, 285
learning, 76
of "Mealworms" matrix, 241, 242
new, response to, 344–45
organizing, 82–88
quantification, 345–46
See also Categorization ability; Data and questions expected; Object grouping; Phenomena
Data and questions expected
  from "Ecology of Land Animals" colloquium, 301–302
  from "Ecology of Water Animals" matrix, 292–93
Davisson, Clinton, 67
Daylight Astronomy, 335, 335n
Decentralization, conceptual development and, 265
Deductive logic, 17
Demonstrations
  responsibility for, 57
  by teacher, 74
Device of Mr. "O," 274
Dienes, Dr. Z.P., 26n, 63, 84–85, 85n
Differences, perception of, 61
Digressions, 27–28
Directives, 13, 22
  for intuitive level, 263
  and self-initiated behavior, 188
  versus Suggestion Cards, 252
Discipline, 36–37, 51, 161
  in discovery-colloquium lesson, 16
  and disrupters, 94–96
  and sustained adaptation, 186
Discovery
  and discrepant events, 66
  errors in, 56–59
  and "hands-off" policy, 59
  in "Mealworm" lesson, 43
  meaning of, 28–33
  nature of, 32–33
  of neutrino, 388–89
  role of colloquium in, 60
  role of teacher in, 59–61
  as sciencing, 45–47
  substitute approaches to, 28–29
  unrelated, 27–28
  See also Discovery–colloquium method; Free discovery
Discovery–colloquium method
  advantages of, 4–5
  description of classroom using, 129–32
  educational view behind, 107–109
  and loose ends, 61
  review of, 377, 380
  role of books in, 279–81, 284–86
  structure of, 121
  and textbook and TV experiments, 189
  See also Colloquium; Discovery; Science lessons

Discrepant events, 47, 60, 64, 127, 137
  in colloquium scoring, 121, 122
  disclosure of, 137–38
  and evaluation of thinking skills, 344
  and juxtaposition of statements, 14, 140–41
  resolution of, 61
  and serendipity, 66–67
Discussion, compared with colloquium, 119
Disrupters, 94–96
Diverting activities, 19
Dolphins, 101–103, 104, 106
"Doughnut Is a Squished Rod" lesson, 88–93
Dreaming, by animals, 102
Duck-billed Platypus, 389, 390
Duckworth, Eleanor, 108, 108n

E

Earth, composition of, 332
  See also Geology matrices
Earthquakes, 331–34
  See also "Movements of Earth's Crust" matrix
Ecology matrices
  "Adaptations of Plants in Relation to Adverse Circumstances," 314–16
  conceptual schemes for, 286–89
  content and organization of, 288
  "Ecology of Land Animals," 295–305
  "Ecology of Water Animals," 289–94
  emphasizing animals, 287, 289
  emphasizing plants, 305
  "Interactions of Plants and Minerals," 312–14
  "Interactions of Plants and Sunlight," 310–12
  "Interactions of Plants and Water," 306–309
  materials for, 286
  textbooks relating to, 283–84
  "Ecology of Land Animals" matrix, 295–305
  "Ecology of Water Animals" matrix, 289–94
Ecosystems, 287
  of ecology matrices, 305
  for study of land animals, 295
Education
  and coalescense of thought and language, 105–106
  and cross-cultural study of conceptual thinking, 155
  and growth during egocentric period, 260–62
  See also Discovery–colloquium method; Learning; Science learning; Science lessons
Egocentric level, 260–62
  science learning expected at, 268–69

evaluation of. *See* Concept attainment evaluation
and freedom of choice, 44
and manipulation of materials, 17
meaning of, 31
problem solving, method of, 29
by rote. *See* Rote learning
self-initiated, 107–108, 188
and talking, 115–17
without meaning, 5
See also Cognitive learning; Science learning
Learning by Discovery, 28
Learning aids. *See* Books; Filmloops; Films; Filmstrips
Learning styles, 268, 377
"Leaves and Stems in Relation to Water" matrix, 308–309
Lehrman, Dr. Daniel, 179, 179*n*
Level. *See* Concept-attainment level evaluation; Conceptual development; Piaget schema; Vygotsky schema
Light matrices
"Bending of Light," 320–24
books related to, 284
conceptual schemes for, 317–18
content and organization of, 318
"Energy and Absorption," 325–26
filmloops and textbooks related to, 319
"Light," 319–20
"Light and Shadow," 328–29
"Light Waves," 326–27
organization of, 317
Likenesses. *See* External likenesses; Hidden likenesses
Linnean scheme, 272
"Liquid-Solid Interactions" matrix, 212–19
Liquids, properties of, 211–12
Living organisms, in conceptual scheme of universe, 165
Living organisms units, 269, 272, 274–76
Logic, patterns of, 17

M

Machines lesson, conceptual schemes for, 169–73
Mackworth, Norman, H., 81, 81*n*
Madeline books, 186, 188, 188*n*
Magnets, 90–94, 132–34
conceptual scheme for lessons on, 18
See also "Doughnut Is a Squished Rod" lesson
Mantle of earth, 332
Maslow, Abraham H., 139, 139*n*
Mass, concept of, 165, 165*n*
Mass-energy concept, 388–89
conceptual scheme for, 18
at concrete operations level, 273–74
at egocentric level, 269

at formal operations level, 275–76
at intuitive level, 270–71
Material(s)
for "Air (Gas) Is Matter" matrix, 192–94
for "Bending of Light" matrices, 320–21, 322–23, 323–24
for biological science matrices, 237, 244, 245
for "Chemical Interactions" matrix, 219–23
children's explanations for teacher's choice of, 142
children's suggestions for use of, 188
criteria for selection of, 19–20, 26–27
discovery through manipulation of, 43
for distinguishing patterns, 86–87
for "Ecology of Land Animals" matrix, 295–301
for "Ecology of Water Animals" matrix, 290–92
for "Electrical Interactions" matrix, 230
for "Energy and Absorption" matrix, 325
for "Eureka!" lesson, 18–19, 20–21
and experience, 6–14
for "Gases and Heat Energy" matrix, 200–202
for "Gases and Mechanical Energy" matrix, 206–209
for "Individual Survival" matrices, 316
for inner-city children, 277
interactions among, 119
for "Interactions of Plants and Minerals" matrix, 312–13
for "Interactions of Plants and Sunlight" matrix, 210–11
for "Leaves and Stems in Relation to Water" matrix, 308–309
levels of meaning derived from, 24–25
for "Light" matrix, 319–20
for "Light and Shadow" matrix, 328–29
for "Light Wave" matrix, 326–27
for "Liquid-Solid Interactions" matrix, 213, 214
loss of interest in, 142
and matrices for science units, 188–89
for "Mealworms" matrix, 238–39
meaning of structure in, 16–25, 93
methods of offering, 12, 59, 60
for "Mineral Cycle" matrix, 330
patterns of relatedness in, 16–17
relations of child to, 280, 350–51, 367
role of, 28
for "Roots in Relation to Water" matrix, 306–307
and search for meaning, 14–16
for "Species' Survival" matrices, 314–15

with Suggestion Cards, 189
teacher's role in relation to, 25–26
and thinking, 120
and underachievers, 51
See also Books; Filmloops; Films; Filmstrips; Stepping stones; Suggestion Cards
Mathematical concepts, 388–400
and cell studies, 395
and classification activities, 389–91
and finding likenesses or differences, 396
and pendulum investigations, 392–94
and planting activities, 391–92
and seed study, 390–91
and shadows, 399–400
and vectors, 397–98
Mathematics
grouping in, 62
patterns in, 83
See also Mathematical concepts
Matrices
on astronomy, 335–36
books and learning aids related to, 281–86
content and organization of, 191
and materials, 188–89
organization of, 190–92
structure of, 189–90
See also Biological science matrices; Ecology matrices; Geology matrices; Light matrices; Physical science matrices; Science lessons
Matter, concept of, 165, 165*n*, 215, 223
at intuitive level, 270
and preconcepts, 194
Maturation. *See* Conceptual development
"Mayhem minus five," 26*n*
"Mealworm" lesson
behavior patterns during, 99–100
colloquium, 120
discovery in, 43
See also "Mealworms" matrix; "*Tenebrio Monitor*" lesson
"Mealworms" matrix, 238–42
Meaning
and experience, 5–6
and structure in materials, 16–25
and use of materials, 14–16
Measurement
of lengths, 393–94
of volumes, 394–95
Memorization. *See* Rote learning
Mental growth. *See* Concept building; Conceptual arrows; Conceptual development
Mental images. *See* Images
Microscopes, 242–57, 272
Mill, John Stuart, 81–82
"Mineral Cycle" matrix, 330–31, 335
Minnebars, 390, 390*n*

Potential
environmental influences on, 30
for scientific creativity, 82
Potential models for children
in "Air (Gas) Is Matter" matrix,
196–97
in biological science matrices, 190
in "Chemical Interactions" matrix,
225, 226, 227, 228
in "Electrical Interactions" matrix,
231–36
in "Gases and Heat Energy" matrix,
203–205
in "Gases and Mechanical Energy" matrix, 210–11
in "Liquid-Solid Interactions" matrix,
216, 217, 218
in physical science matrices, 190
Potential patterns and problems for children, 190
Potential procedural learnings, 216, 217
Power, concept of, 90
Pratt, Caroline, 4
Preconceptual level, 153–55, 219,
238–42
and decentralization, 265
ecology matrices for, 289–94,
295–305
evaluation of, 346–47
matrices for, 206–211, 230–36
Preconcepts
for "Air (Gas) Is Matter" matrix, 194
for "Chemical Interactions" matrix,
223
for "Electrical Interactions" matrix,
231
for "Gases and Heat Energy" matrix,
202
for "Gases and Mechanical Energy"
matrix, 209
for "Light" matrix, 318
for "Liquid-Solid Interactions" matrix, 215
for "Mealworms" matrix, 239
Predictions, 61, 113
and evaluation of concept attainment
level, 349–50
of measurements, 396
of plant growth, 392
of scientific discoveries, 388–89
Preverbal behavior, 103, 104
Preverbal level, stagnation at, 266–67
Preverbal thought, 105, 127
description of, 102–103
and sciencing, 106
Problem solving
as learning method, 29
and thinking, 102–103
Problems
for follow-up activities in "Mealworms" matrix, 240, 241, 242
unforeseen, 254

"whole and its part," 262–63
See also Potential patterns and problems for children; Problem solving
Psychological safety, 139, 139n, 141–42
Psychology, introduction of, 276

Q

Quadribag games, 270
Quantifying, and evaluation of concept-seeking skills, 341, 345–46
Questions
and evaluation of thinking skills, 344
in rote learning, 6
stimulation of, 138
by teachers, 114
Quizzes, 6

R

Radioactive elements, 388–89
breakdown of, 332
Radioactivity, 276
Random events, linking. See Syncretic thinking
Rats, response to patterns, 103
Reading level
and motivation, 31
and science ability, 35
"Rearview-mirror" syndrome, 29n
Recall, compared with conceptual thinking, 149
Recognition of right answer, compared with conceptual thinking, 149
Rediscoveries, 30, 46
Reflection of light, 320–21
Relationships between children, 350
Relativity theory, 389
Relevance
of colloquium comments, 343
in colloquium scoring, 122
Repetition
of child's remark, 142
in colloquia, 116
of data, 75
See also Rote learning
Rephrasing children's remarks, 142
Repulsion, concept of, 343, 343n
Research. See Inventions; Sciencing
Reversibility, 265, 273
Rocks. See Geology matrices
Role-playing, 101–102
Rotational symmetries, 86
Rote learning, 5–6, 30, 115
compared with concept building, 149
of data, 75
and sustained adaptation, 186
Rouse, Dr. George, 332, 332n, 333
Routines, 9, 186
Rutherford, Ernest, 119

S

School teachers. See Teachers
Science behavior, and conceptual level,
266
Science ability, 35
Science Curriculum Improvement Study,
229, 389
Science history, 31–32
guidelines for selecting, 32
and science teaching, 280
and scientists' role, 45–47
Science learning
and books, 30–31, 189
in early grades, 6
and experiments in books or on TV,
189
and mathematics, 84, 388–400
response of children to, 188
and scientific procedures, 28–29
and serendipity, 67
steps involved in, 186
See also Discovery–colloquium method; Science lessons; Science teaching
Science lessons
building conceptual schemes for,
167–73
"Doughnut Is a Squished Rod,"
88–93
"Eureka!," 20–25
follow-up matrices for. See Matrices
"Heredity," 180–82
"Hook Up a Circuit," 48–56
and loose ends, 80
on molecules, 159
"Pond Model," 16
for preverbal level, 106
syncretic thinking in, 150–51
tape recording, 341
Tenebrio Molitor," 33–42
textbooks as sources for, 281–82
"They Learn as They Speak Together," 129–35
and time-bind problems, 282–83
traditional, 106, 380
"What's Inside?" 7–14
"Yeast Model," 15–16
See also Discovery–colloquium method; Matrices
Science: A Modern Approach, 304, 304n
Science: A Process Approach, 390n,
394, 400
"Science Table," 283
Science teachers. See Teachers
Science teaching
attitudes toward, 3–4
creativity fostered in, 80–82
curriculum selection for, 76–82
data selection for, 76–82
in depth, 29
and digressions, 27–28
discovery methods in, 28–33

in future, 164–65
and heterogeneous grouping, 7–8
and materials in, 16–17
and rediscovery, 29–30
and science history, 31–32
structure related to concepts in, 17–25
and time-bind, 89
traditional, 15
in units. *See* Matrices; Study units
Science units, year-long, 259
See also Matrices; Science lessons
Science vocabulary. *See* Vocabulary
Science in Your Life, 4, 199
Sciencing
at Cavendish Laboratories, 119
colloquium as, 119–20
compared with scientists' work, 45–47
definition of, 45, 120
discovery in, 45–47
discovery–colloquium view of. *See* Discovery–colloquium method
and finding hidden likenesses, 64
in "Hook Up a Circuit" lesson, 56–59
mathematical concepts for use in. *See* Mathematical concepts
and object grouping, 62–63
and serendipity, 67
Scientific procedures, 28–29, 47, 114
Scientists
of Babylonia, 46
colloquium of, 119
and computers, 81
function of, 45–47
of future, 81
and mathematics, 383–84
medieval, 46
and pattern finding, 82
thinking methods, 17
Seasons, The, 336
Seating arrangements, 36–37, 52, 139, 144
"Seeds" matrix, 314–15
and mathematical concepts, 390–91
Self-initiated behavior, 188, 246, 265–66, 373–74
Self-selected records, 377
Sensori-motor intelligence stage, 268–69.
Serendipity
and discrepant events, 66–67
from water play. *See* "Water Play" lesson
"Sets," 62
applied to science, 389
Shadows, and mathematical concepts, 399–400
See also "Light and Shadow" matrix, 328–29
Similarity. *See* Categorization ability; External likenesses; Hidden likenesses

"Sink and Float" lesson
erroneous statements in, 144
factual relationships in, 43
See also "Eureka!" lesson
"Slow" children, 268
Small Things, 243, 243*n*
Snails, 33
data and questions expected on, 292–93
Social experience, and learning 101–102
Sociological background, conceptual development and, 266–68
Solar system, 87
Solids, properties of, 211–12
See also "Liquid-Solid Interactions" matrix
"Sound Statements of Seven Year Olds" colloquium, 109–115
evaluation of concept attainment in, 351–68, 377–79
Speaking. *See* Language; Talking
"Species' Survival" matrices, 314–15
Spider frame, 299–300
"Spores" matrix, 315
"Starting Tomorrow" lessons. *See* Discovery–colloquium method; Matrices; Science lessons
Statements during colloquium, 121
challenged, 345
changed in light of new data, 344–45
concept seeking, 368
correction by other children, 116
correction by teacher, 25
emotional and factual, 109–115
juxtaposition of, 60, 140–41
repeating or rephrasing of, 115, 142
unclear, 140
Status, and participation in colloquium, 141–42
Stepping stones, 190
for biological science matrices, 243–44
books as, 282
of "Chemical Interactions" matrix, 219–23
of "Ecology of Land Animals" matrix, 295
of "Electrical Interactions" matrix, 230–31
for "Liquid-Solid Interactions" matrix, 212–13
for "Mealworms" matrix, 238–39
meaning of, 186
Stimulus, blocked, 75
Strategies, for problem solving, 29
Structure of materials, 93–94, 127
definition of, 16
levels of meaning through, 24–25
relationship to concepts, 17–25
relationship of patterns, 83–86
Study units, 185–88, 335
See also Curriculum; Matrices; Science lessons

Subconcepts, 18
formation of, 188
for "Mass-Energy" unit, 270
of "What's Inside?" lesson, 18
Subsets, concept of, 390
Suggestion Cards
for "Air (Gas) Is Matter" matrix, 193, 194
for "Bending of Light" matrices, 322, 323, 324
for biological science matrices, 237, 244
for "Chemical Interactions" matrix, 221, 222, 223
for ecology matrices, 289, 293, 296-301
for "Electrical Interactions" matrix, 230
for "Gases and Heat Energy" matrix, 206
guiding principles for, 285–86
for "Individual Survival" matrices, 316
for "Interactions of Plants and Minerals" matrix, 313
for "Interactions of Plants and Sunlight" matrix, 310–11
for "Leaves and Stems in Relation to Water" matrix, 308, 309
for "Light and Shadow" matrix, 328
for "Light Wave" matrix, 326, 327
for "Mineral Cycle" matrix, 330
for "Roots in Relation to Water" matrix, 306, 307
for "Species' Survival" matrices, 315
uses for, 189, 283
versus directives, 252
Suggestions
by children, 188
by teacher, 189
voiced versus written, 189
See also Suggestion Cards
Sun, The, 336
Symmetries
three-dimensional, 86-87
two-dimensional, 83-86
Syncretic thinking, 150–51, 259
evaluation of, 346
object grouping in, 153

T

Talking
earliest stages of, 106
fostered by colloquia, 139
and learning, 28, 115–17
and thought, 102
See also Language
Tape recording of science lessons, 341
Tasting, 74, 270
Taxonomy, for set of objects, 17
Tea Room concept, 119

Teacher(s)
and analysis of levels of concept development, 160–63
as authoritarian figure, 186
choice of subject area, 3
and conceptual schemes, 167–73, 174–82
and correction of faulty statements, 25, 90
and directives. *See* Directives
and discrepant events, 61
and disrupters, 94–96
errors of, 144
and evaluation of learning. *See* Concept attainment evaluation
impact of change on, 164–65
limited freedom for, 44–45
and material selection, 26–27
method of greeting class, 21
models for. *See* Teacher models
and perception of emerging behavior and thought patterns, 94–100
preparation of. *See* Teacher preparation
rating, 41
role. *See* Teacher's role
suggestions by, 189
use of children's phraseology, 74
and use of matrices, 197–99, 205–206, 218–19, 228–29, 242
Teacher models
for "Air (Gas) Is Matter" matrix, 194–96
for biological science matrices, 190
for "Chemical Interactions" matrix, 223–25
for "Electrical Interactions" matrix, 231–36
for "Gases and Heat Energy" matrix, 202–203
for "Gases and Mechanical Energy" matrix, 209
for "Mealworms" matrix, 239–42
for physical science matrices, 190
Teacher preparation
for "Air (Gas) Is Matter matrix, 193–94
for "Chemical Interactions" matrix, 220, 221, 222
for "Ecology of Land Animals" matrix, 295–301
for "Ecology of Water Animals" matrix, 290–92
for "Individual Survival" matrices, 316
for "Interactions of Plants and Minerals" matrix, 312–13
for "Interactions of Plants and Sunlight" matrix, 310–11
for "Leaves and Stems in Relation to Water" matrix, 308–309
for "Light" matrix, 320

for "Liquid-Solid Interactions" matrix, 213, 214
for "Roots in Relation to Water" matrix, 306–307
for "Species' Survival" matrices, 314–15
Teacher's questions
for "Ecology of Land Animals" matrix, 302–303
for "Ecology of Water Animals" matrix, 293
Teacher's role, 6, 377, 380
in "Bending of Light" matrices, 321–22, 323, 324
in colloquia, 139–45
in conceptual development, 260
in discovery, 7–14, 43–45, 59–61
in "Energy and Absorption" matrix, 325–26
in learning, 28
in "Light and Shadow" matrix, 327
in "Light Wave" matrix, 327–28
in "Mineral Cycle" matrix, 331
in relation to materials, 25–26
in using patterns, 98–100
Teachers' Guide to Pendulums, A, 87
Teaching
definition of, 4, 44
by dolphins, 102
inductive, 28
See also Science teaching; Teacher's role
Teaching models, 15–16
interactions in, 280–81
See also Teacher models
Television, science demonstrations on, 127, 189
Temperature, 396n
"Tenebrio Molitor" lesson, 33–42
Termination of colloquium, 26
Terminology. *See* Vocabulary
Terrarium, 298
Testing, 114, 348
Textbooks. *See* Books
Thermometer, 159, 271–72
"They Learn as They Speak Together" lesson, 129–35
Thinking
and abstraction of principles, 103–104
adventurous, 141, 253
behavioral manifestations of, 101–103
in colloquium, 106–107, 109–115, 118, 135–38
communication and, 104–105
conceptual, 104
definitions of, 102, 104
and evaluation of concept attainment, 378–79
and evaluation of concept-seeking skills, 341, 344–45, 359–62
and generalization ability, 103
and images, 104

independent of language, 105–106
and intelligent behavior, 104
and learning, 28
and ordering, 396
patterns of, 88
perception of patterns in, 94–100
preverbal. *See* Preverbal thought
in scoring colloquium, 121, 122
and sets of strategies, 29
and TV education, 127
without language, 105
See also Chain complex thinking; Conceptual thinking; Inner speech; Syncretic thinking
Thomson, J.J., 119
Thought. *See* Thinking
Tic-Tac-Toe, three-dimensional, 274
Time-bind
solutions for, 282–83
and use of books, 281–82
Time concept, at egocentric level, 261
Time-lapse photography, in astronomy filmloops, 335
Time restrictions. *See* Time-bind
Tools, thinking and, 102–103
Toulmin, Stephen, 236–37, 237n
Tulloch, Dr. George, 179

U

Uncertainty, 79–80
Underachievers, 51
Understandings, prior. *See* Near bank
Universe units
at concrete operations level, 274
at egocentric level, 269
at formal operations level, 276
at intuitive level, 271–72
overall conceptual scheme for, 165–66

V

Vectors, concept of, 175–77
and development of mathematical concepts, 397–98
and pendulum problems, 397–98
"Vegetative Reproduction" matrix, 315
Visitors to classroom, 39
reactions of, 129–32
Visual cortex, and generalization, 103
Visual stimuli, generalization of, 103
Vitamins, discovery of, 32
Vocabulary, 71
for "Air (Gas) Is Matter" matrix, 192
for biological science matrices, 247, 248
of black power concept, 267
chemical names, 224
in colloquia, 140
in concrete operations stage, 265

of dolphins, 106
and evaluation of concept-seeking skills, 343
for "Gases and Heat Energy" matrix, 205
for rock study, 331
used by teacher, 74, 99, 115
See also Language; Talking
"Voice off" policy, 188
"Volcano in Action, A," 331*n*
Volume, concept of, 272–73
Vygotsky, Lev Semenovitch, 105, 105*n*, 106, 121, 149
See also Vygotsky schema
Vygotsky schema, 150–55, 190, 254
compared with Piaget schema, 259–60
and complex thinking, 151–53
and conceptual schemes, 165, 167
and evaluation of concept attainment, 346–50

and experience and maturity, 277
and preconceptual and conceptual thinking, 153–55
and science behavior, 266
social background in terms of, 267
and syncretic thinking, 150–51

W

Water. *See* "Interactions of Plants and Water" matrix; "Water Play" lesson
"Water Play" lesson, 67–75
matrices to follow, 211–29
Weather. *See* Climate and weather studies
Weight, concept of, 272–73
"What's Inside?" lesson, 71–74
discrepant facts in, 61
diversion from, 27

matrices to follow, 192–99
and object grouping, 63–64
structure of materials used for, 18
use of language in, 106
Where Is the Moon?, 335, 335*n*
Where Was the Moon?, 335, 335*n*
White suburban children, and black power concept, 267
"Whole and its part" problem, 262–63
Wiener, Norbert, 81–82
Wind, and rock break-up, 331
Work pattern drive, 351, 367–68
Writing, and growth of thinking, 117
Written contributions, and evaluation of concept attainment, 375–77

Y

"Yeast Model" lesson, 15–16

A 1
B 2
C 3
D 4
E 5
F 6
G 7
H 8
I 9
J 0